AF321491

About **Bridget Riley** Selected Writings 1999–2016

About Bridget Riley

Selected Writings 1999–2016

Ridinghouse

About Bridget Riley

Selected Writings 1999–2016

Ridinghouse

Contents

Foreword
Doro Globus | Karsten Schubert

The present volume includes the vast majority of significant essays on Bridget Riley written since 1999. This was a particularly fruitful period in the reception of her work, as the discourse broadened and her reputation as one of the most important painters of her generation was established.

The essays range from biographical overviews to detailed analysis of specific aspects or themes that occur throughout Riley's working life. The selection reflects a rich body of work, which sustains the interest of important authors, as evidenced by multiple pieces by Éric de Chassey, Lynne Cooke, Robert Kudielka, Paul Moorhouse and Richard Shiff. Together, this volume of essays tells the story of an artist whose art has continuously evolved over nearly six decades.

Most of the critical texts have been written in close consultation with the artist, the result of long conversations, sudio visits and archive access. Largely commissioned on the occasion of particular exhibitions, these essays track and trace Riley's focus and influences at different moments in time. Each essay builds upon the next, with more recent authors clearly responding and referencing earlier discourse. The result is a collection of great breadth and cohesion.

The selection opens with a group of general texts that help to situate Riley within a wider artistic and cultural context. John Elderfield's essay for the Dia Art Foundation analyses the theoretical discourse that surrounds the artist (pp.91–128); Paul Moorhouse's overview for Tate charts Riley's own life and career, from tentative beginnings to recent curve paintings (pp.169–207); and in her essay for the Serpentine Gallery, Frances Spalding introduces the impact of art history on Riley's thinking and practice as she looks at artists including Jackson Pollock and Piet Mondrian (pp.13–37). Dave Hickey takes an altogether more radical approach in his 2000 essay, 'Bridget Riley for Americans' (pp.63–70).

Later writings are primarily concerned with specific moments in Riley's career, or analyse recurring themes and preoccupations. Starting with her formative work from the 1950s, Robert Kudielka offers insight to a period of artistic self-discovery (pp.373–82); Paul Moorhouse meanwhile charts Riley's ongoing engagement with stripes as she addresses this pictorial device at various moments between 1961 and 2015 (pp.507–16). Marla Prather looks at the genesis of the large curve paintings (pp.333–47), whilst Nadia Chabli explores Riley's radical jump from canvas to wall work (pp.419–26). Finally, Éric de Chassey takes on Riley's newest body of work, revealing its origins in her 1962 black-and-white painting *Tremor* (pp.561–67).

The range of voices represented in this volume highlights the universality of Riley's appeal. In 'How Seeing Feels', Richard Shiff analyses the experience of looking at Riley's work as a personal exploration of perception (pp.569–90); Michael Bracewell too focuses on a close visual reading, but also adds a cultural perspective with different sets of reference points (pp.427–37). The most recent text, Karen Serres and Barnaby Wright's expansive essay, takes a close look at Riley's ongoing engagement with the art of Georges Seurat (pp.545–59).

An important resource, *About Bridget Riley* represents a monumental body of research and analysis by some of the most important art historians of today. It also offers the opportunity for the reader and the viewer to approach Riley from a plethora of perspectives to form their own view, much reflecting Riley's own particular approach to art history. As John Elderfield puts it: 'Effectively, Riley makes a pact with the viewer, through the medium of the painting, that they will collaborate in eliciting from a particular painting a particular sort of mobile visual array. And, when the viewer stops looking at the painting, it will therefore be as if leaving something that continues to go on.'

Essays

Bridget Riley and the Poetics of Instability
Frances Spalding

> 'Nature is on the inside', says Cézanne. Quality, light,
> colour, depth, which are there before us, are there
> only because they awaken an echo in our body and
> because the body welcomes them.
>
> — Maurice Merleau-Ponty, *The Primacy of Perception*, 1964

One of the most radical moves in the history of post-1945 British art was Bridget Riley's decision to destabilise the image. When she first began working with the energies inherent in purely pictorial relations in her black-and-white paintings of the 1960s, she shifted the arena for dramatic confrontation from the surface of the canvas into the space between the spectator and the work of art, as Bryan Robertson has observed.[1] Brought into dialectical process with the eye, the surfaces of her canvases appeared to shimmer, buckle, jitter, heave and twist. Later, as she moved through coloured greys into colour, making her chosen unit the stripe, she saw that 'the basis of colour is its instability'.[2] The realisation that she could exploit the way in which colours resonate, interact and spread, each stripe affecting and modifying its neighbour, again reaffirmed the necessary dialogue between eye and image, the content of the work only fully existing when activated by the dynamics of looking.

This new exhibition invites reassessment of Riley's work of the 1960s and 70s. It is, therefore, an apt moment to explore some of the intellectual roots that fed into her creative process; to investigate those tracings and promptings that spurred her imagination and which led, directly or indirectly, to the manifestation of movement in her art, fleeting presence and the visual dialectic of action and counteraction, all of which contribute to an unsettling discrepancy between pictorial fact and aesthetic effect.

The denial of fixity in her art has proved richly rewarding. As the artist herself has observed, a loss of certainty or focus can open up a new range of experience, so that we become 'open to things that were previously less accessible'.[3] In the course of this century, advances in science, such as quantum mechanics and Heisenberg's uncertainty principle, have exposed the unpredictability within nature and have dissolved the separation between a deterministic world and the impartial human observer. This classic dichotomy became no longer tenable once the act of observation was seen to affect the thing observed. And although there is an enormous distance between particle physics and the world of art, the repercussions have been undeniable – Cubism, for instance, playing in part on the recognition that the perceiver's situation had to be taken into account. This acknowledgement of an inherent uncertainty may be one reason why Riley's work, far from receding into history as a period style, continues to zing with challenging authority. Its relevance to a younger generation of artists has been actively demonstrated in a variety of ways. In the mid-1980s Philip Taaffe appropriated Op art images by Riley, which he found 'emotionally and psychologically compelling', in the course of his postmodernist investigation into the achievements of late modernism.[4] More recently, Damien Hirst has acknowledged Riley as the starting point for his 'spot' paintings; and Peter Davies, listing idols and mentors in one of his text paintings, included the accolade, 'Bridget Riley so complicated but such eloquent funky results'. More generally, Riley's committed stance has helped sustain and renew an interest in abstract painting. Her work also has relevance in the present climate in which, chiefly owing to critical theories which have followed a similar path to scientific thinking, categories have become unfixed and meaning is often seen to be ambiguous, elusive and unstable. The opposition posited by the 1960s imperative 'Make Love Not War' rings hollow today, not least because such violent hierarchies can be undone, reversed, as Jacques Derrida has shown. Likewise, the abstract/figurative debate, which was so vital at the time when Riley began her career, still identifies two diametrically opposed ways of making art but has altered its tenor with the growing recognition that abstract art can be rooted in bodily sensations and can act as a compelling vehicle for human experience.

Intense looking is a condition of Bridget Riley's art. Her career began in traditional fashion with an interrogation of appearances. John Rothenstein claimed that she gained admission to Goldsmiths in 1949 on the strength of her 1947 copy of Van Eyck's *Portrait of a Man in a Red Turban* (1433), whose sharp, astute gaze has encouraged the theory that the painting may be a self-portrait.[5] At Goldsmiths she worked compulsively at life drawing, under the tutelage of Sam Rabin, and developed an interest in the drawings of Ingres, which, with their incisive accuracy, uniquely blend the particular with the universal. Riley has acknowledged her debt to Rabin, who not only took her to the British Museum print room to study drawings by Ingres, Rembrandt and Raphael, but also taught her to work methodically, to strip down visual imagery in order to uncover its structure and to develop a sense of pictorial organisation.[6] 'He stressed the importance of the relationship between things', she recollects; 'how everything matters… how to make an advance and consolidate… how to raise the level of work slowly. That was gold – and something I have kept with me.'[7]

Rabin's contribution to Riley's career has often been acknowledged. Much less attention has been given to the fact that another key figure at Goldsmiths at that time was Kenneth Martin. He was then moving away from the Camden Town and Euston Road School method, so prevalent at English art schools during this period, into an abstract language, in which field he was to be closely allied with Victor Pasmore and the Constructionists. Following Pasmore's example, Martin made his first non-figurative painting in 1948 and his first abstract mobile in 1951. Though Riley at this time did not conceive of herself as anything other than a figurative artist, and was aware that Martin despised life drawing, she noted his presence and was familiar with his work.[8] This knowledge she added to what she already knew about abstract art, for, having spent the war years in Cornwall, she had heard of Ben Nicholson's and Barbara Hepworth's association with St Ives and had gained some understanding of their work. Nicholson had featured in one of the Penguin Modern Art series and this small but influential book had been brought to her attention by her mother. But if she was already intrigued by what lay beneath when subject matter in art is stripped away, she found no clear directional signposts at the Royal College of Art in London, to which she transferred in 1952. Her three years there were followed by an unhappy period in which she nursed her father, following a serious car accident, and was herself hospitalised owing to a nervous breakdown. She worked as a shop assistant while regaining health, then taught art for a period in a convent school in Harrow. Following this she did the first of two stints in the offices of the advertising agency, J Walter Thompson, where she was assigned to the making of preparatory drawings as the basis for subsequent work by photographers.

During this ragged period of intense artistic and personal crisis, she encountered Abstract Expressionism. Like many other artists of her generation, she first experienced its impact at the 1956 Tate Gallery exhibition *Modern Art in the United States*, which contained in its final room work by Arshile Gorky, Franz Kline, Willem de Kooning, Robert Motherwell, Jackson Pollock and Mark Rothko. Riley has put on record her response to this show as bearing witness to modern art as 'a living, ongoing reality *now*'.[9] Pollock especially impressed her, and she felt 'inordinately moved by the extreme measures' that he had adopted in his art.[10] Two years later a major Pollock exhibition at the Whitechapel Art Gallery in London reinforced the impression she had gained of his enormous vitality and artistic courage. At first glance it is hard to see what relevance his freely rhythmic, open linear compositions had to her later development of a precise and measured visual language. But in the work of both artists can be found a desire to explore the architectonic potential of the picture plane, also a stress on an evenness of expressive emphasis to give the work plastic coherence. Pollock's work also showed the use of an open, shallow, multifocal space, with which Riley feels more sympathy than 'the focally centred situation of the European tradition'.[11] And it is possible that at some level the vibrant energy of Pollock's drip paintings, and the absolute stillness that sometimes emerges from within their surging network of lines, encouraged Riley's own search for a dynamic equilibrium in which painting, no longer a self-contained activity, is always in a state of becoming, and all emotion, no matter how fleeting or extravagant, is translated into pictorial sensation, to be caught on the wing by the creative attention of the spectator.

Even in the late 1950s, Riley recognised the tragedy in Pollock's art — that the tremendous liberation he had achieved, through his reliance on instinct, led to a cul-de-sac, the conditions of its success being also those of its failure.[12] In 1959, the year after the showing of his art at the Whitechapel, she not only saw at the Tate Gallery the *New American Painting* exhibition, devoted entirely to Abstract Expressionism, which made an indelible mark on her, but she also visited *The Developing Process: New Possibilities in Art Teaching* exhibition at the Institute of Contemporary Arts, London. The show consisted of work produced in the Fine Art Departments of Leeds College of Art and King's College, Newcastle, around the 'Basic Design' principles promoted by Harry Thubron, Maurice de Sausmarez, Victor Pasmore and Richard Hamilton. This method of art education had its origins in the Bauhaus, and in particular the pedagogic work of Paul Klee, and it endeavoured to give the student information on the nature of materials, colours and the operation of formal and spatial relationships. Thubron worked, for instance, with families of form, showing how shapes could evolve and change in character. By making reference not only to the study of nature but also to mathematical, geometrical and scientific forms, he hoped to widen the field of comparative study. Riley was extremely interested and took part later that year in a summer school in Suffolk, led by Thubron, with assistance from, among others, De Sausmarez, the art historian Norbert Lynton and Anton Ehrenzweig. Ehrenzweig was to write a major essay on Riley's art and analysed 'art's deep substructure' in his book, *The Hidden Order of Art: A Study in the Psychology of Artistic Imagination* (1967), which drew, in part, on his conversations with Riley and knowledge of her art.[13]

Thubron's summer school proved the turning point, an important aspect of the course being a survey, part practice, part theory, of the major art movements of the twentieth century. Although Riley had read fairly widely as a child, she now developed a more specialist appetite for books that had direct relevance to her painting.[14] She was partly helped to do so by her association with De Sausmarez, whose book on Basic Design had a wide-reaching influence on art education. He became an intimate friend, the two travelling in Spain and Portugal in the summer of 1959 and touring Italy in the summer of 1960. At that time little had been published in English on Italian Futurism, which, like Dada, had become a

largely forgotten aspect of modern art history. De Sausmarez was the
first person to lecture on this subject in London, giving three talks at
the Royal College of Art on the occasion of the fiftieth anniversary of the
Futurist Manifesto. He not only developed his ideas for these lectures in
conversation with Riley but with her made an abortive attempt in the
summer of 1960 to visit one of the original founders of the Futurist
movement, Gino Severini, who was too ill to see them. But one of the
memorable aspects of this trip for Riley was the exhibition of Futurist art
which formed a part of the XXX Venice Biennale.

If Futurism, both formally and conceptually, is overshadowed by
Cubism, it has nevertheless come to be recognised as one of the most
important progressive movements in twentieth-century art. Though
initially concerned with literary reform, it quickly expanded to embrace
painting and sculpture, architecture, music, theatre and film. A series of
provocative, anarchical manifestos, full of rhetorical flourish and
nationalistic sentiment, urged readers to immerse themselves in the
dynamism of modern life. In Severini's view, the modern sensibility was
particularly adept at grasping the idea of speed. When confronting the
paradox of how to represent movement within the static confines of a
two-dimensional canvas, the Futurist painters drew on their awareness of
the chronophotography which the pioneer in time-motion studies,
Étienne-Jules Marey, had developed in the 1880s. He had succeeded in
making visible the invisible, through photographic inventions which
enabled him to capture successive spatial movements, both the figure or
animal and its trace, by means of a single camera. Fascinated also with
the greater pace of life made possible by technological advances, the
Futurist painters promoted in their manifestos the idea of 'universal
dynamism' and 'dynamic sensation' and, generally, an overriding desire
to register, and thereby render eternal, both the sensation of speed and
its emotional character.

In Venice Riley had an opportunity to study at first hand the pictorial
solutions arrived at by the Futurists. These became noticeably more
complex after they assimilated aspects of Cubism in 1911. As the moving
figure or object, multiplied or fragmented, passes through, and
interpenetrates, space, the material consistency of the perceived world is

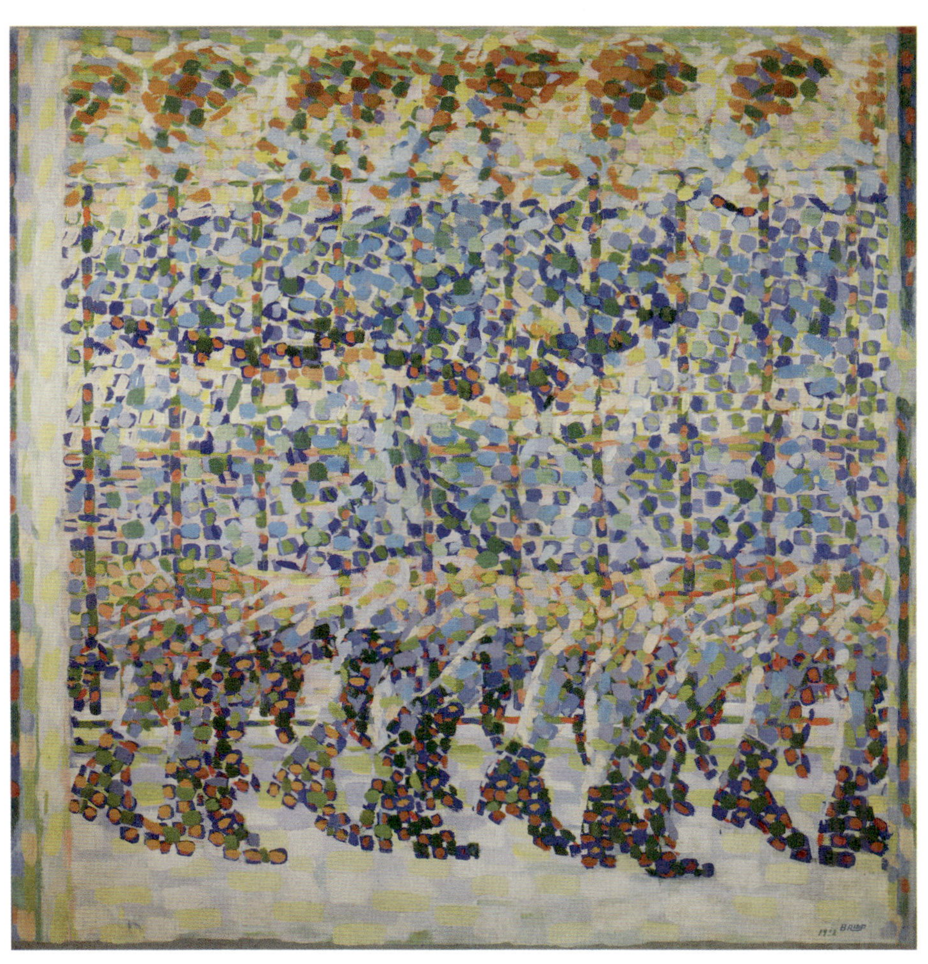

Giacomo Balla
Girl Running on a Balcony 1912
Oil on canvas
125 × 125 cm | 49¼ × 49¼ in
Private Collection

destroyed. What instead becomes pronounced is a fresh sense of sequence and rhythm, a visual pulse working often across the entire field. This search for a pictorial equivalent to the dynamism of modern life led the Futurists to talk of 'lines of force', which, they argued, not only conveyed the character of an object but also how it might unfold and develop in space as it tended towards infinity. Giacomo Balla's attempt to uncover the inner life, energy or 'emotion' of lines and colours led him into the field of non-figurative art.[15] For Riley, this search for equivalence was more important than the concern with movement, which she was to discover in her own way when she began subjecting forms to a method that she had yet to evolve. But the Futurist desire to draw the spectator into the work of art set a useful precedent for Riley's work. As the Futurists wrote: 'He [the spectator] will no longer simply observe but will participate in the action… The lines of force must envelope the spectator and draw him on so that in a way he is compelled to fight along with the figures in the picture'.[16]

One painting which particularly impressed Riley in the Venice exhibition was Balla's *Girl Running on a Balcony* (1912), which, employing a divisionist approach, renders movement through a mosaic of colour. This method of dividing up compound colour in nature into separate touches in order to register light, shadow, local colour, reflected colour and the overall ambience, was already familiar to Riley through her study of Impressionism and neo-Impressionism. The previous year, 1959, she had copied Georges Seurat's *The Bridge at Courbevoie* (1886–87), working not from the original in the Courtauld Institute Galleries, London (now The Courtauld Gallery), but from a reproduction. As this suggests, there was no attempt to imitate Seurat's pointillist touch or the beautiful surface texture created by his tiny dots of colour. Riley's decision to copy Seurat was fired by her desire to know what colours he had used and to find out what he had put where and why. And as the painting proceeded, she discovered that the blues and yellows, in their alteration of pitch, kept pace with each other, working together through a network of balanced contrasts.

Riley's appreciation of the divisionist method was heightened by her awareness that it had formed the basis of many artists' colourism and structural thinking. Important to Paul Gauguin, Vincent van Gogh and Henri Matisse, as well as the Futurists, it therefore had a validity not confined to any one period or style. She connected this realisation with the possibility of an abstract art that was universal and could transcend cultural barriers. Debates on the universality of art were current at that time, as she was aware through her reading of art magazines and growing familiarity with the contemporary art scene at home and abroad. At the same time Clement Greenberg was promoting a greater degree of 'singleness and clarity' in abstract art, encouraging a development away from the subjective excesses of Abstract Expressionism towards a cooler 'post-painterly' or 'hard edge' abstraction. In Greenberg's view, an abstract painting should insist on its own material attributes, on paint, the shape of the canvas and its own ineluctable flatness; the whole of the picture should be taken in at a glance and its unity should be immediately evident, its 'at-onceness' affecting the viewer like a sudden revelation.[17]

Riley had met Greenberg in New York and saw him a couple of times in London at Anthony Caro's house. However, although attracted to a cooler, more objective approach, she was less in tune with New York formalism, feeling more at ease with the openness of European attitudes to abstract art which were rooted in Cubism and aimed at transcending the personal approach. Riley, herself, removed her own hands from the process of making around 1961, handing over the fabrication of her work to studio assistants, thereby marking out a clear distinction between creative work and the craft necessary for its execution. But she did not, as certain geometrical abstractionists and Constructivists did, turn to industrial methods and materials, nor did she patronise the notion of group work, anonymous authorship and the making of 'multiples'. These and other notions were fostered by certain European collectives, such as Gruppo N, an association of artists founded in Padua in 1959, and Equipo 57, formed by five Cordoban artists in 1957, the latter exhibiting at Denise René's gallery in Paris, which became a focus point for geometrical abstraction and for 'multiple' art. As Riley did not agree with the latter, she kept away from this gallery, a decision that reflects on her need to stand apart from prevailing ideologies and styles in order to establish her own line of enquiry. Although much geometrical abstraction at this time was directed towards a socialist society, it had no overt political content. The situation was very unlike that which had prevailed in revolutionary Russia where non-figurative art was employed as propaganda, and also in the 1930s when abstract art had again been aligned with political idealism and associated with a 'free' international style. By the 1960s abstract forms were no longer burdened with iconic and symbolic associations or political overtones. 'They were simply forms without pretensions', Riley recollects, 'in a condition for working with. Just "to hand".'[18]

Riley was certainly not alone in her gradual move towards an abstract language based on optical effects. An interest in the aesthetic manipulation of light and movement, for instance, was central to the Groupe de Recherche d'Art Visuel (GRAV), founded in Paris in 1960. Here we find a Constructivist leaning towards a depersonalised approach, machine-like precision, a desire for a greater degree of collaboration with the spectator, for a more scientific attitude towards art and a belief in its potential universality. This last was firmly upheld by one of GRAV's most energetic supporters, Victor Vasarely, the Hungarian painter who had settled in Paris in 1930. He first adopted geometrical abstraction in 1947 and in the mid-1950s began writing a series of manifestos on the use of optical phenomena for artistic purposes. He became associated with the Galerie Denise René, and, owing to the visual ambiguities explored in his paintings and prints, he was soon recognised as one of the main originators of Optical art, or Op art, as it came to be called. Riley knew of Vasarely but did not meet him until she herself was well established as an artist. They argued over universality in art, Vasarely believing that this would be achieved through the multiplication of imagery made possible by mass reproduction. Riley disagreed: if an artist is fortunate enough to touch the universal, she said in a conversation with Vasarely, the test would lie in the quality of the work itself rather than in the quantity of the images produced. Instancing works that achieved universality, she quoted Van Gogh's Sunflowers series (1888).

Throughout these early years, Riley, through her connections with other artists, thinkers and writers, through her reading and growing familiarity with past art, was steadily building a raft of ideas and sensations on which to float her own pictorial language. One transfiguring experience in the summer of 1960 had been caused by a sudden squall in Venice. Riley watched as rain drove its way over black-and-white paving in a piazza. Her attention was seized by the way in which the veil of water dissolved the pattern of the stones. The downpour did not last long and, as the weather was hot, the stones steamed and dried and the clarity of the pattern soon returned. But this consciousness that the equilibrium within a rigid structure could be disturbed and then restored stayed with her, and within a year or two had begun to appear in her work.

In the autumn of 1960 came a fresh personal crisis. Riley's close association with De Sausmarez ended, and, although they remained friends, the difficult feelings associated with this change in relations momentarily led her to conceive of abandoning art. She had been toying, like other of her contemporaries, with hard-edge abstraction and decided to paint one final, entirely black picture. She did so and was disappointed to find that it did not express all the emotional energy she had invested in it. The question – what is wrong with it? – brought the realisation that it contained no contrast, that it was not in itself divided or had any opposition within it to give it life.[19] She therefore decided to paint one more picture in which she not only offset a straight line with an off-centre curve but also introduced the contrast of white against black. Where the descending black curved shape, as it approaches the black rectangle filling the lower half of the canvas, exerts the most pressure on the intervening area of white, squeezing it into a thin line, a sudden flash of light occurs. This not only gave rise to the title – *Kiss* (1961) – but was the small, startling optical dynamic that proved to be the origin of Riley's pictorial identity.

The question – why has this happened? – was to be a recurrent one as she began to explore optical relationships within a formal geometrical framework. From *Kiss* she moved on to the first of two paintings called *Movement in Squares* (1961) in which the chequerboard squares gradually diminish in width, thereby heightening the frequency at which the eye has to register the black-and-white contrast. At the point of climax, where the units are most tightly clenched, the picture surface appears to buckle inwards, while the agitation created in the eye's retina causes this part of the image to vibrate, the painting as a whole offering contrasting states of tension and release. With these two paintings she established a principle that was to act as a staple ingredient in her work over many years: constancy against inconstancy, one aspect of the structure, such as the horizontal divisions in *Movement in Squares*, remaining fixed, while another changed. She began to look for this principle in other art, finding it, for instance, in Piet Mondrian's *Composition with Grid 3: Lozenge Composition* (1918) where the grid remains constant while the lines thicken and thin and planes emerge and recede. This principle, of something simultaneously constant and varied, was essential to the portrayal of movement, for the suggestion of shift or progress required an underlying stasis. From here onwards, it was a journey of increasing sophistication in her handling of black-and-white relationships, as she alternated fast with slow movement, leading the eye along a definite path or setting up crosscurrents, and at other moments, as in *Shiver* (1964) and *Tremor* (1962), causing movement to happen all over the picture surface. In *Fall* (1963) and *Crest* (1964) an intense point is reached where the falling curves, initially slack and full of lassitude, are suddenly compressed, the switches in direction creating a horizontal visual disturbance that challenges the downward movement of the curves. In other paintings, such as *Pause* (1964) and *Burn* (1964), the addition of a tonal contrast, as the elements move from darkest black to palest grey, enabled Riley to combine sweeping movement with dazzling effects of light.

Riley's steady increase in recognition, as her work appeared in exhibitions and became the subject of critical appreciation in the art press, is not part of this essay. But mention must be made of the *Responsive Eye* exhibition held at the Museum of Modern Art, New York, in 1965, as this broad survey of a contemporary interest in perceptual abstraction included enough instances of art that shocked or disrupted vision through the use of optical devices or perceptual ambiguities to give rise to the term Op art. It also marked the onset of Riley's international reputation, for it coincided with her solo exhibition at

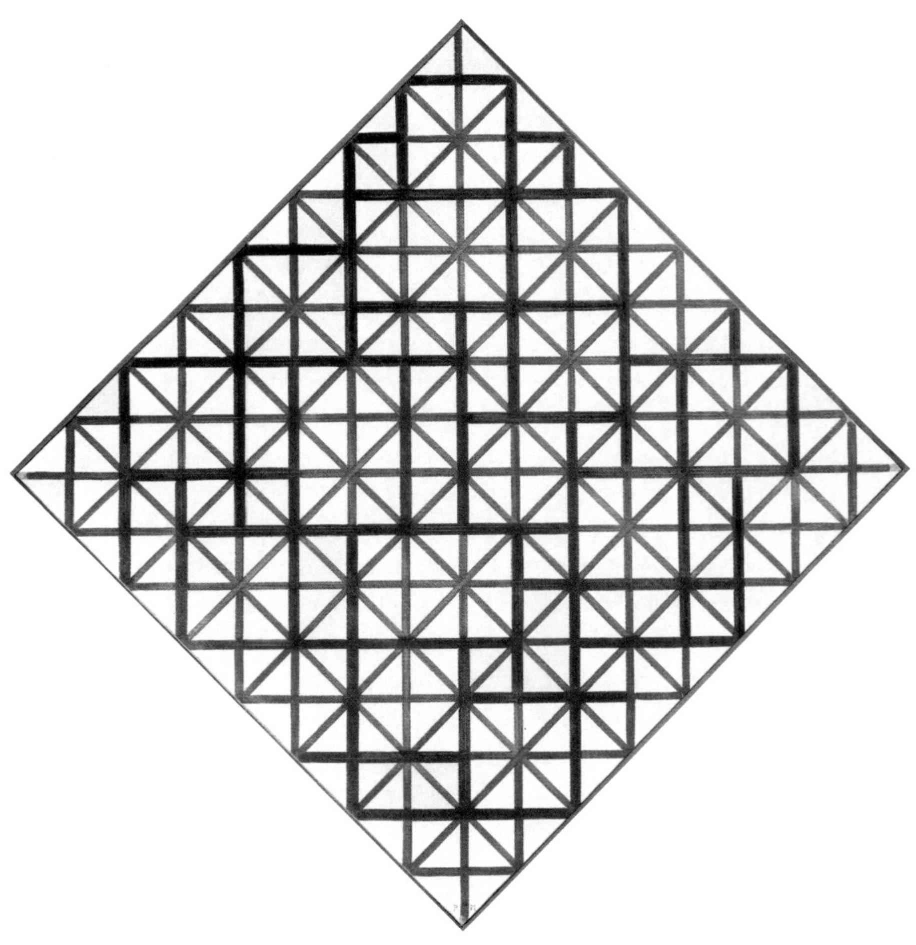

Piet Mondrian
Composition with Grid 3: Lozenge Composition 1918
Oil on canvas
84.5 × 84.5 cm | 33¼ × 33¼ in
Gemeentemuseum Den Haag, The Hague

Richard Feigen Gallery, which – unusually for an English artist exhibiting in New York – sold out before the opening. With her painting *Current* (1964) on the cover of the *Responsive Eye* catalogue, Riley was swiftly identified as a key figure within the new development which the curator William C Seitz saw as the intent 'to dramatize the power of static forms and colours to stimulate psychological responses'.[20]

The idea behind the *Responsive Eye* exhibition had initially been announced in November 1962. At that time Seitz had the idea of showing the development of perceptual art from Impressionism to the most recent optical painting. But in the intervening period the proliferation of painting and construction employing perceptual effects was so rapid that the demands on gallery space did not leave room for a retrospective view. Seitz did not confine his attention to any single tendency, group or country, but included work by groups and individuals representing tendencies in 15 countries. Thus Riley's work was positioned within a very mixed representation of recent art, including, for instance, reliefs and line constructions by Jesús Rafael Soto and Gerald Oster, optical paintings by Vasarely and Benjamin Frazier Cunningham, and large heraldic canvases by Morris Louis and Kenneth Noland. In the catalogue Seitz argued that 'the perceptualism of the present… is more concentrated than that of Impressionism because the establishment of abstract painting has made it possible for colour, tone, line and shape to operate autonomously'. His analysis of certain effects of movement and illumination concluded with the remark: 'the impression of brightness and pulsation can reach a startling intensity. The eyes seem to be bombarded with pure energy, as they are by Bridget Riley's *Current*.'

With hindsight, we can see that this interest in optical effects had a wider context, for perceptualism played a key role in postwar debates about philosophy, psychology and art in the United Kingdom, the United States and France. In an address, summarising and defending his *Phenomenology of Perception*, shortly after its publication in 1945, Maurice Merleau-Ponty insisted that 'the perceived world is the always presupposed foundation of all rationality, all value and all existence'.[21] He was to identify the perceiver not as a pure thinker but as a 'body-subject', implying that some pre-logical form of knowledge or consciousness is

incarnate in the body and inheres in the world.[22] Likewise, the
existentialists focused on the actual human situation as the starting point
for any authentic philosophy, emphasising the fact that we are situated
participants in a continuous, open-ended, socio-historical drama, and
that it is necessary for us to have a keen awareness of our freedom and
responsibility in shaping the situation in which we are already involved.
Awareness of these theories led De Sausmarez to write of Bridget Riley
in 1970: 'In all that she does she declares herself a true descendant of
the phenomenologists, rejecting pre-suppositions (theoretical or
habitual) and looking for the extension of her knowledge through the
direct engaging of her senses and her total consciousness.'[23]

It was not, however, Merleau-Ponty's key work, *Phenomenology of
Perception*, that had direct relevance to Riley's thinking, but his essay
'L'Œil et l'Esprit', which, in translation as 'Eye and Mind', was included in
his *Primacy of Perception*, published in 1964. An entire thesis could be
constructed on the relevance of this essay to Riley's art. Suffice it to say
here that in questioning the enigma of vision, Merleau-Ponty stressed
how phenomena derived from our perception of space – such as
orientation, polarity, envelopment – are always linked to our being or
presence. It is not enough to think in order to see, he argued: 'Vision is a
conditioned thought; it is born "as occasioned" by what happens in the
body; it is "incited" to think by the body'.[24] His insistence that we look
out from the inside has relevance not only to the painter but also the
viewer. 'Things have an internal equivalent in me', he writes, 'they arouse
in me a carnal formula of their presence.'[25] And because of this two-way
relationship, between the see-er and the seen, within a body which
opens itself to the world, it makes little difference if the artist does not
paint from nature, for 'he paints, in any case, because he has seen,
because the world has at least once emblazoned in him the ciphers of
the visible.'[26] In this and other ways, Merleau-Ponty may have reinforced
the corporeality of Riley's art and licensed its relation, not to an idealised,
disembodied spectator, but to a viewer, immersed in the world, in whose
body is an intertwining of vision and movement. Equally significant is
Merleau-Ponty's metaphysical notion that the painter does not impose
her or his view on the outside world:

The world no longer stands before him through representation;
rather, it is the painter to whom the things of the world give birth by
a sort of concentration or coming-to-itself of the visible.' The painter
goes beyond representation, breaks through the 'skin of things' to
show how the things become things, how the world becomes
world.[27]

Among art theorists and historians, the study of perception helped
change ways of looking. Perceptual analysis richly informs the early art
historical writings of EH Gombrich; found a vital outlet in Anton
Ehrenzweig's *The Hidden Order of Art: A Study in the Psychology of
Artistic Imagination* (1967), which introduced a psychoanalytical
approach to the study of aural and visual perception; and fired Rudolf
Arnheim to write his seminal book, *Art and Visual Perception: A
Psychology of the Creative Eye* (1954), at headlong pace over 15 months.
Like others, Arnheim was greatly indebted to Gestalt psychology which
derived scientific principles from sensory information and stressed the
importance of the integrated structure of the whole: only within the
overall pattern was it possible to determine the place and function of
each element. The same principles had been shown to apply to various
mental capacities, so that, it was argued, seeing, far from being a
mechanical function, involved a creative apprehension of reality. Thus
looking at the world required, as Arnheim pointed out, 'an interplay
between properties supplied by the object and the nature of the
observing subject'.[28] Since then neurologists have evolved increasingly
complex theories of vision in an attempt to explain what happens when
the eye and mind are engaged in looking, proving incontrovertibly 'the
awe-inspiring complexity of vision'.[29]

The issue of perceptualism gained urgency with the revival of interest
in abstraction, for without the mask of representation artists needed to
find some other framework for their art. 'The artist of today', Paul Klee
had written, 'is more than an improved camera; he is more complex,
richer and wider.' When Klee's *Notebooks: Volume I, The Thinking Eye*
appeared in translation in 1961, it rapidly became a cult book, and was
read by Riley soon after it was published. Made persuasive by the fact

that Klee's theoretical discussions and analyses were accompanied by illustrations of his own work, which further elucidated his ideas, the book showed the logic of plastic thinking that can underpin an artist's distillation of pure formal relations. Klee not only taught painters how to 'take a line for a walk', but made movement a central aspect of his thinking about form. For Riley, Klee was crucially important as a thinker, builder and maker of art. 'Seurat, Paul Klee and the Futurists were my roots', she has put on record. 'Particularly Klee. In the 1960s I had the opportunity to explore what those forms and lines and colours could do when they no longer had to describe anything. I wanted to discover their own character.'[30]

The notion that art is in essence constructive is implied in everything Klee wrote and was openly stated by Stravinsky in his *Poetics of Music in the Form of Six Lessons* (1947).[31] This series of lectures, which Stravinsky delivered at Harvard University, Cambridge, forms another of the books indicated by Riley to have had particular importance for her.[32] In this instance she may have read Stravinsky less for direction than for confirmation of the stance she herself had already adopted. Stravinsky firmly upholds the necessity of order and discipline. 'The more art is controlled, limited, worked over, the more it is free', he argues.[33] And elsewhere:

> Let me have something finite, definite – matter that can lend itself to my operation only insofar as it is commensurate with my possibilities. And such matter presents itself to me together with its limitations. I must in turn impose mine upon it. So here we are, whether we like it or not, in the realm of necessity… in art as in everything else, one can build only upon a resisting foundation… My freedom thus consists in my moving about within the narrow frame that I have assigned myself for each of my undertakings. I shall go further: my freedom will be so much the greater and more meaningful the more narrowly I limit my field of action and the more I surround myself with obstacles. Whatever diminishes constraint, diminishes strength. The more constraints one imposes, the more one frees one's self of the chains that shackle the spirit.[34]

When Bridget Riley began using colour the most obvious constraint
was the limitation in hue. The magisterial effect of *Late Morning*
(1967–68) is achieved through vertical paired stripes of red, green and
blue, where the combination of colour interaction with the high
frequency of the small white interval between the coloured bands sets
up a terrific energy and beat. The realisation that purely visual
relationships can bring about powerful sensations led on to *Rise 1* (1968),
where the horizontal emphasis set up by the tripartite stripes (composed
of green, lilac and red in varying order) is counterpoised with alternating
warm/cool effects created by the oranges, yellows and greys which
bloom from the canvas like a rising mist. Here, as Bryan Robertson has
written, we encounter 'an art of perception, made concrete by conceptual
speculation', in which, as he goes on to argue, 'the imaginative qualities
of the painting radiate beyond that optical encounter and pass through
to another dimension.'[35] That other dimension is never illustrational.
Though Riley's titles, such as *Deny 1* (1966) and *Arrest 1* (1965), often link
her pictures with psychic or physiological sensations and in some
instances suggest analogies with music or dance, these associations are
echoes rather than intrinsic. *Tremor*, for instance, with its delicate overall
suggestion of movement, has a quivering quality similar to that which the
wind stirs in the leaves of a tree. In her choice of title, Riley acknowledges
that potential link, but the sensation created by the painting goes beyond
any specific or fixed allusion. And when making her early black-and-white
paintings, Riley was too involved with perceptual discoveries to look for
such resonances. 'For quite a long time', she has recalled, 'I was
embarrassed by using the word "I"… in relation to my work – I much
preferred to say "one", because I felt this thing, the medium, was so
strong and rich that I was just an agent who caught the various
inflections and allowed them to play their own thing freely.'[36]

But if for Riley the meaning of a work of art remains immanent, she
recognises that it is also a structure through which we can reach past
echoes and experiences. Her reading of Merleau-Ponty may have alerted
her to the need to re-examine the relationship between past and
present, for in his definition of the past, not as a conglomeration of
sensations and memories, but as a 'horizon' or 'atmosphere' or 'field'

that 'envelopes' the present, he was asserting that an inherently
meaningful present experience at every moment has access to a past.
Whether or not this recognition came from Merleau-Ponty, it was
abundantly proven by her reading of Proust. Riley's introduction to this
author came through Samuel Beckett's writing. As his short monograph
on Proust reveals, Beckett had only qualified admiration for *À la
recherche du temps perdu* (In Search of Lost Time) (1913–27), but he
was abundantly interested in Proust's use of involuntary memory, in the
negation of time and in Proust's pessimism.[37] Beckett's brilliant analysis
of what makes involuntary memory so powerful leads him to the
following conclusion:

> The identification of immediate with past experience, the recurrence
> of past action or reaction in the present, amounts to participation
> between the ideal and the real, imagination and direct apprehension,
> symbol and substance. Such participation frees the essential reality
> that is denied to the contemplative as to the active.[38]

Riley began reading Proust in 1974, after Robertson gave her the first
four volumes of CK Scott Moncrieff's translation. She also began making
regular visits to Cornwall, owing to her mother's final illness. The long
train journeys, to a part of England where she had spent a significant
part of her childhood, not only carried her back in time but also echoed
Proust's imaginary world. The fascination of the book can be so intense
that it is difficult, on first reading, to see the relationship of the parts to
the whole, to appreciate the thematic links and connecting episodes and
to separate the underpinning philosophy from the narrative. Riley, on
reaching the end of the novel, began reading it again, making, for her
own purposes, a summary of the text, with the notion of extracting from
this a lexicon in which would be listed all the various insights out of
which Proust wove his creative vision. Though this project was abandoned
when she reached the end of *Swann's Way*, both summary and lexicon
attest to her desire to assimilate Proust at a deep level.[39]

For Riley, one of the fascinations offered by Proust may have been
the constantly shifting nature of his imagery: the places he describes, the

characters, situations, small epiphanies, obsessive emotions and patterns
of behaviour are never presented in fixed and definite form, but reveal
new aspects and invite different interpretations as the story unfolds and
the revelations accumulate or the point of view of the observer changes.
As Edmund Wilson has written: 'The conviction that it is impossible to
know, impossible to master, the external world permeates his whole
book.'[40] Like Pollock's paradoxical achievement of stillness within a
concentrated network of flung lines, Proust's novel contains change
within apparent immobility. Impressed by the power of Proust's
imagination, Riley has observed that the book seems to chart 'the entire
process of creativity', and that a possible key to the power of Proust's
imagination lies in the remark made by the painter Elstir in the final
volume – that we must renounce what we love in order to recreate it.[41]
But on first reading Proust, the encounter with his imaginative journey
back in time to his childhood may have fostered in Riley a similar
retrospective mood, enabling her to rediscover the extent to which she
had internalised the Cornish coastline. First taught the pleasures of
looking while walking along the cliffs with her mother, she now
recognised that many of these experiences had formed the basis of her
visual life. In 1984 she wrote about them at some length in the catalogue
for the Arts Council of Great Britain exhibition *Working with Colour:
Recent Paintings and Studies*.[42] Lyrical and intense, the experiences
listed include violent contrasts, unexpected colour relations, sudden
switches in the direction and layering of landscape and the glittering,
ever-changing surface of the sea – 'the entire, elusive, unstable, flicking
complex – subject to the changes of the light itself'. The revelatory
content of this essay invites the conclusion that Riley's paintings, not only
those included in this show but also those made in the last 20 years,
reach through, consciously or unconsciously, to echoes and allusions that
accrued in her childhood.

At one point in *À la recherche du temps perdu* Proust holds up, as a
token of artistic integrity, the little patch of yellow wall in Vermeer's *View
of Delft* (c.1660–61), which the writer Bergotte, overcoming his reclusive
instincts brought on by ill health, goes to see. Though made giddy by the
effort, he fixes his eye on this little patch of yellow. '"That is how I ought

to have written", he said. "My last books are too dry, I ought to have gone over them with several coats of paint, made my language exquisite in itself, like this little patch of yellow wall.'"[43] A little further on, Proust unfolds thoughts on the possibility of immortality and asks what 'burden of obligations' caused Bergotte and Vermeer to create. 'All these obligations', he concludes, 'which have not their sanction in our present life seem to belong to a different world, founded upon kindness, scrupulosity, self-sacrifice, a world entirely different from this…'.[44]

Riley herself has often gained encouragement by looking at other artists. Her involvement with the Old Masters found a fruitful outlet in 1989 when the National Gallery, London, asked her to select one of the *Artist's Eye* exhibitions. All the paintings that she chose were large, complex compositions, which brought together a number of figures, most in motion, in a dynamic shifting pattern that led the eye in a variety of directions. The link with her own work was revealed in the catalogue where, in conversation with Robert Kudielka, she related the organisation of colour to the compositional movement. But in all the various aspects of her career, including her involvement with the 1997 Mondrian exhibition, *Nature to Abstraction*, at the Tate Gallery, her lectures on colour and painting, her contributions to television documentaries on art, her dialogues originally produced for radio, and in the steady unfolding of her own work, she has promoted a better understanding and appreciation of creativity in all its complexities and difficulties, as well as its pleasures. 'The first merit of a painting is to be a feast for the eye.' So wrote Eugène Delacroix in his journal, which remains another of Riley's key texts.

She has shown how, in Merleau-Ponty's words, 'the uncertain murmur of colours can present us with things, forests, storms – in short the world.'[45] When she rings to alter the time of an appointment owing to 'a colour problem', one subsequently discovers that it was the fractional alteration of tone in a cream or blue that was of such burning urgency. Not surprisingly she reads Jack Flam's collection of Matisse's writings with enjoyment, glimpsing the spirit of this great colourist through his words as well as his art. She also delights in Baudelaire's swingeing attacks on sloppiness and vulgarity in his Salon reviews,[46] and quotes with pleasure Rilke's mention of 'the good conscience of these reds, these greens' in Cézanne's paintings.[47] It is, Rilke comments, faced with the colossal reality of Cézanne's art, 'as if these colours could heal one of indecision'.[48] Something similar can be felt in front of Riley's art, for a rare certainty underlies her willingness to take extreme measures; to look for the shifting, the unexpected and evanescent, and to find a stringent plenitude.

Lisa G Corrin (ed), *Bridget Riley: Paintings from the 1960s and 70s*, exhibition catalogue, Serpentine Gallery and Koenig Books, London, 1999, pp.11–22.

FRANCES SPALDING

1   Bryan Robertson, 'Introduction and Biographical Note', in *Bridget Riley: Paintings and Drawings 1951–1971*, Hayward Gallery, London, 1971, pp.5–6.

2   Bridget Riley, 'Practising Abstraction: Talking to Michael Craig-Martin' (1992), in Robert Kudielka (ed), *Bridget Riley: Dialogues on Art*, Zwemmer, London, 1995, p.56.

3   Bridget Riley, 'The Experience of Painting: Talking to Mel Gooding' (1988), in Robert Kudielka (ed), *The Eye's Mind: Bridget Riley, Collected Writings 1965–1999*, Thames & Hudson, London, 1999, p.91.

4   For Taaffe's discussion of his use of Riley's work, see 'Philip Taaffe', *Flash Art*, no.124, October/November 1985, pp.72–73.

5   See John Rothenstein, *Modern English Painters: Wood to Hockney*, Macdonald and Jane's, London, 1974, p.213.

6   Bridget Riley, 'In Conversation with Maurice de Sausmarez' (1967), in Kudielka (ed), *The Eye's Mind*, op.cit., p.214.

7   Bridget Riley, 'Personal Interview: By Nikki Henriques' (1988), *ibid.*, p.15.

8   Riley remembers him as a 'Corridor Meister'.

9   Quoted in John Gruen, *The Artist Observed: 28 Interviews with Contemporary Artists*, Chicago Review Press, Chicago, IL, 1991, p.151. See also her comments quoted in Jeremy Lewison, *Interpreting Pollock*, exhibition catalogue, Tate Publishing, London, 1999, p.9.

10 See her comment in *The Artist Observed*, *ibid.*, p.151: 'I remember looking at my first Jackson Pollock, I know it seems ridiculous but I wept all night over the colossal [emotional] price involved… Pollock and Rothko were enormous revelations to me.'

11 Bridget Riley, 'In Conversation with Bridget Riley', in Maurice de Sausmarez, *Bridget Riley*, exhibition catalogue, Studio Vista, London, 1970, p.62. In the same passage Riley also acknowledges a debt to Mondrian: 'I tend to work with open area space – and when I refer to this as American space we must not forget that it had its origins in Mondrian. It demands a shallow push-pull situation and a fluctuating surface.' Reprinted in Kudielka (ed), *The Eye's Mind*, op.cit., p.62.

12 Conversation with the author, 3 March 1999. See also *Interpreting Pollock*, op.cit., p.9.

13 Anton Ehrenzweig, 'The Pictorial Space of Bridget Riley', *Art International*, vol.9, no.1, February 1965, pp.20–24.

14 Riley has listed those books which had especial importance to her, in the order in which she encountered them, in conversation with Isabel Carlisle. See *Bridget Riley: Works 1961–1998*, Abbot Hall Art Gallery, Kendal, 1998, p.10.

15 An achievement that has led to him being recognised as an important precursor for Italian Minimalism. See Achille Bonito Oliva (ed), *Minimalia: da Giacomo Balla a…*, exhibition catalogue, Palazzo Querini Dubois, Venice, 1997.

16 Catalogue introduction to the 1912 Futurist Exhibition, shown in Paris, London, Berlin and ten other European cities.

17 Clement Greenberg, 'The Case for Abstract Art', in *Clement Greenberg: The Collected Essays and Criticism: Volume 4: Modernism with a Vengeance 1957–1969*, University of Chicago Press, Chicago, IL, 1993, p.81.

18 'Bridget Riley in conversation with Robert Kudielka', in *Bridget Riley: Paintings and Drawings 1961–1973*, Arts Council of Great Britain, London, 1973. Reprinted in Kudielka (ed), *The Eye's Mind*, op.cit., p.82.

19 This passage paraphrases Riley's own words as used in a lecture on her work given at Abbot Hall Art Gallery, Kendal, 19 January 1999.

20 William C Seitz, *The Responsive Eye*, exhibition catalogue, Museum of Modern Art, New York, 1965, p.41.

21   Merleau-Ponty, 'Eye and Mind', in *The Primacy of Perception*, Carleton Dallery (trans), Northwestern University Press, Evanston, IL, 1964, pp.160–61.

22   'My act of perception, in its unsophisticated form… takes advantage of work already done, of a general synthesis constituted once and for all, and this is what I mean when I say that I perceive with my body or my senses, since my body and my senses are precisely that familiarity with the world born of habit, that implicit or sedimentary body of knowledge.' Maurice Merleau-Ponty, 'Sense Experience', in *Phenomenology of Perception*, Colin Smith (trans), Routledge & Kegan Paul, London, 1981, p.238.

23   De Sausmarez, *op.cit.*, pp.87–88.

24   Merleau-Ponty, 'Eye and Mind', *op.cit.*, p.175.

25   *Ibid.*, p.164.

26   *Ibid.*, p.166.

27   *Ibid.*, p.181.

28   Rudolf Arnheim, *Art and Visual Perception: A Psychology of the Creative Eye*, University of California Press, Berkeley, CA, 1974, p.6. Originally published in 1954.

29   This quotation comes from a conversation between Riley and EH Gombrich in which Gombrich alludes to the discoveries of certain neurologists as to how various parts of the brain react to colour, to shape and to movement and how these systems interact in surprising and bewildering ways, 'so that what another student of vision, JJ Gibson at Cornell, called "the awe-inspiring complexity of vision" has by now become a scientific fact.' See Bridget Riley, 'Perception and the Use of Colour: Talking to EH Gombrich', in Kudielka (ed), *Dialogues on Art*, *op.cit.*, p.43.

30   Bridget Riley, 'Self-Portrait', *The Independent*, 30 August 1994. Riley also acknowledges the importance of Klee's *The Thinking Eye*, in Kudielka (ed), *Dialogues on Art*, *op.cit.*, p.34.

31   Igor Stravinsky, *Poetics of Music in the Form of Six Lessons*, Arthur Knodel and Ingolf Dahl (trans) University of Oxford, London, 1947, p.11.

32   See Ehrenzweig, *op.cit.*

33   Stravinsky, *op.cit.*, p.63.

34   *Ibid.*, pp.63, 64–65.

35   Robertston, *op.cit.*, p.8.

36   *Ibid.*, p.11.

37   Beckett's interest in Proust also lay in the fact that he was one of the authors who encouraged his search for 'an intellectual justification of unhappiness'. See Beckett's letter to Tom MacGreevy as quoted in James Knowlson, *Damned to Fame: The Life of Samuel Beckett*, Bloomsbury, London, 1997, p.118.

38   Samuel Beckett, *Proust*, Grove Press, New York, NY, 1931, pp.55–56.

39   Both summary and lexicon remain in the artist's possession.

40   Edmund Wilson, *Axel's Castle: A Study in the Imaginative Literature of 1870–1930*, Penguin, London, 1993, p.156.

41   See Riley's remarks in conversation with Bryan Robertson, in Kudielka (ed), *Dialogues on Art*, *op.cit.*, p.87, 89.

42   Bridget Riley, 'The Pleasures of Sight' (1984), in Kudielka (ed), *The Eye's Mind*, *op.cit.*, p.30.

43   Marcel Proust, *The Captive: Remembrance of Things Past*, vol.9, CK Scott Moncrieff (trans), Chatto & Windus, London, 1968, p.2.

44   *Ibid.*, p.250.

45   Galen A Johnson *et al.*, *The Merleau-Ponty Aesthetics Reader: Philosophy and Painting*, Northwestern University Press, Evanston, IL, 1993, p.133.

                                                                     FRANCES SPALDING

46   Collected in Charles Baudelaire, *Art in Paris 1845–1862: Salons and Other Exhibitions*, Jonathan Mayne (ed), Phaidon, London, 1965.

47   Rainer Maria Rilke, *Letters on Cézanne*, Clara Rilke (ed), Jonathan Cape, London, 1988, p.50.

48   *Ibid*.

Building Sensations: The Early Work of Bridget Riley

Robert Kudielka

> We find certain things about seeing puzzling, because
> we do not find the whole business of seeing puzzling
> enough.
>
> — Ludwig Wittgenstein, *Philosophical Investigations*, 1953

During the winter of 1998–99, Abbot Hall Art Gallery in Kendal mounted
a small retrospective of Bridget Riley's work. In the first room many of
her celebrated black-and-white paintings of the early 1960s, such as
Movement in Squares (1961), *Blaze 4* (1964) and *Pause* (1964), were
brought together. It was interesting to see the curiosity and
circumspection with which the public approached these works. People
spent a considerable length of time looking and comparing, reading the
catalogue and pointing things out to each other, returning to certain
paintings and changing their place of viewing. Young people seemed
impressed and some of the elderly visitors went up close, lifting their
spectacles to see more clearly what they were looking at. No one in this
gathering behaved as though they were in any way threatened or in
imminent danger.

Some 30 years ago the general attitude to Riley's work was quite
different. Even those who were open-minded and prepared to encounter
a new experience could not help being affected by the fashionable view
of what they were going to see. In 1965, at the height of the excitement
surrounding the *Responsive Eye* exhibition at the Museum of Modern Art
in New York, which launched Riley's reputation, the contemporary art
world seems to have been engaged – partly innocently, partly
deliberately – in generating a peculiar sort of myth. Riley's work became
the centre of a critical tale of violence and aggression inflicted on the
spectator by so-called Optical or Op art, and this view persisted right
through the seventies. Even supporters called her paintings dazzling or
blinding, relating the experience to states of hallucination and 'feeling
high'; the majority, however, denounced them as mindless, nauseating

and detrimental not only to the standards of art, but almost physically harmful. Erich Sokol, the cartoonist, put his finger on this hysteria when he drew a woman desperately trying to save her husband from being sucked into the centre of Riley's painting *Fission* (1963).

It could be said that the composure of today's spectators merely demonstrates that the novelty of the work has worn off. But this would mean that the effect was never merely physical, and makes it even more interesting that people who now see the paintings for the first time seem to be quite at ease with them. It is also beside the point to claim that the artist herself has paved the way towards a more balanced response by refraining in later paintings from the violence of her early pieces. Although the element of instability in Riley's work has undergone several transformations since she moved from her black-and-white paintings to her present preoccupation with colour, the tension between structural firmness and shifting perceptions, so particular to her, has remained remarkably constant. Both these rationalisations are inadequate because they overlook the beginning of Riley's public career. Following her first solo exhibition at Gallery One in London in 1962 she rapidly gained a certain measure of international recognition without which she would never have been invited to participate in the *Responsive Eye* exhibition; and during these three years there was no review complaining of 'eye-bashing', although the disturbing factor built into her work was observed right from the beginning. In his review of the show at Gallery One, David Sylvester clearly saw this quality and recognised its balance within the work:

> The disturbing element is not only imaginative in conception but has the sort of rightness in its placing that a good actor has in his timing – it seems at once unexpected and inevitable. This proposing and disposing of order seems no mere game with optical effects, it seems to symbolise, dramatically, an interplay between feelings of composure and anxiety.[1]

In drama and the other arts, the sensation of unstable situations and identities shifting between disruption and restitution is well established and accepted as a viable 'imaginative' equivalent to life. So why was this recognition denied in painting? With hindsight it is clear that the exhibition *The Responsive Eye* coincided with the start of the controversy between Minimalism and modernism in American art.[2] Visual complexity did not suit either camp. Riley's paintings were aesthetically too energetic and demanding to fulfil the need for 'disinterested contemplation' which Clement Greenberg had put forward as the historical role of abstraction in his essay 'The Case for Abstract Art' (1959).[3] Conversely, the intricacy of her structures must have looked to the partisans of 'holism' and 'non-composition' like the epitome of that 'fussiness' (Frank Stella) and 'juggling' (Donald Judd) which they associated with European art.[4] It was the current taste for blandness and vacancy – post-painterly or Conceptual – which could not help but feel challenged and confused by Riley's work.

Thirty years later the situation has certainly changed, although it has not necessarily led to a more appropriate understanding. Ironically Bridget Riley now figures, for many of her new admirers, as the 'last modernist' in painting as though her work had never been condemned as a deviation from the Road to High Art. It is time to lay aside these various clichés and try to see Riley's work in its own terms. The exaggerated attention paid to its 'effect' has obscured its true character for far too long. There is an astonishing lack of plain observation in the reviews and appreciations of the past 20 years. Talking about the 'blinding' quality of the work has become a licence not to bother with it any further and prevented a long overdue rediscovery. None of Riley's paintings have been created to bring about an optical effect as such; they are built, with a unique inventiveness and ingenuity, to house that particular sensibility for disruption and instability which is all her own.

An equilibrium at risk

There was no such thing as Op art when Bridget Riley first showed her paintings. The opening sentence of Sylvester's review states: 'Bridget Riley is a hard-edge abstractionist.' The big, flat, sharply delineated areas of *Kiss* (1961), fully justify this classification. Of course, the elusive optical flash at the point where the curvilinear shape almost touches the straight form beneath seems to herald further developments. But this harbinger can easily divert attention from a more important aspect. Being based on a square format the unequal division of forms and masses in *Kiss* lays out the ground plan of Riley's earliest pictorial order. Traditionally painters have tended to avoid working within equal dimensions because it does not give a bias from which to start. But for this very reason Riley seems to have chosen the square as the basic format for most of her paintings right up to 1967. It provided a static equilibrium which could be upset by asymmetrical divisions. In *Kiss* the total field is divided twice, horizontally as well as vertically, each time in a ratio of approximately two to one. The edge of the straight form delineates the horizontal division whereas the near touching point of the large curved shape above indicates the hidden vertical.

The recurrence of such bisections in later paintings shows that there is no mathematical system behind it. Although some of the measurements may come close to the golden section, they are not established by that proportional device. Nevertheless there is a certain range within which these divisions are positioned whether they are horizontal or vertical. Either the proportions are clearly irregular as in *Kiss* and *Cataract 3* (1967), in *Movement in Squares* and *Pause*; or these divisions are just off centre, narrowly avoiding symmetry, as in *Serif* (1964), *Crest* (1964) and *Current* (1964). Furthermore, there is another option which refines the use of this destabilising factor. Instead of being apparent the asymmetrical disposition can be hidden, as in *Black to White Discs* (1962), *Breathe* (1966), *Arrest 2* (1965) or *Cantus Firmus* (1972–73). Such latency heightens the sensation of a given equilibrium at risk.

As Riley developed her means, an important extension to this structural device emerged that is still effective in her recent work. In circular compositions such as *Uneasy Centre* (1963) and the Blaze paintings the axial asymmetry has been turned into a displacement of the centre. But as the few remaining preparatory drawings for these works show, this displacement can take on a wider role. In the *Study for*

Broken Circle (1963), for instance, the coherent form of the circle is dismembered and reassembled in a new way. This treatment can also be found in *Fission*, where two different formal progressions, one long and one short, are displaced cross-wise so that a tension arises which gives the painting its name. From about 1963 onwards dislocation becomes a basic building practice in Riley's work, independent of formal changes and even of the move into colour. For instance, in *Where* (1964) the tonal movements are dislocated in such a way as to form a regular tripartite structure which recurs in different forms in later paintings. Eventually this principle of breaking up a given unity and reassembling it encompasses both ends, as it were, of the building process. In the paintings which Riley began in 1986 the continuity of the vertical bands is broken up by a diagonal, and this upheaval is counteracted and rebalanced by the dislocation of the rhomboid colour forms it produces.

This later development emphasises that destabilisation and disruption in Riley's work is never an end in itself but a crucial step in transforming astatic equilibrium into a dynamic one. A stable position is turned into a balance between stability and instability. It is obvious, however, that on the basis of *Kiss* alone it would not have been possible to push ahead with considerations of such extreme abstraction. *Kiss* shows only the ground plan of Riley's pictorial world, the means and methods to construct it still had to be found.

Progressions – formal and tonal

There were only a few early paintings done in a similarly intuitive manner, among them *Horizontal Vibration* (1961) and *Serif*. Both are characterised by areas of compression and expansion achieved through the varying widths and intervals of the black-and-white bands, and it is clear that *Serif* is a kind of reprise prompted by the curve painting *Crest*. In 1961 Riley had already begun to look for a structure that would allow her to articulate and develop her interests more satisfactorily. The discovery took her by surprise. While working on a sequence of black-

and-white squares she suddenly found that by steadily diminishing their widths she could generate a movement, and in one long working session, as she remembers, she completed *Movement in Squares*, the only painting done in such bravura manner.

The progressive structure of this painting could look like an abstract version of a futurist depiction of movement, and Riley's earlier interest in Futurism – particularly in Giacomo Balla – seems to confirm this connection. But there is an essential difference. *Movement in Squares*, and all subsequent paintings using progressive sequences of form and tone, does not represent movement in its successive phases, but enacts it autonomously in the picture plane. That is to say, we perceive these sequences as movement, rather than reading them as chains of incident, because they are pitched against a constant. With *Movement in Squares*, Riley discovered for herself the plastic principle that in order to define an experience she had to bring in its opposite. The squares 'move' because, while their widths decrease, their heights remain the same.

However, this progressive reading precipitates yet another kind of movement, a sudden dissolution which periodically engulfs the entire pictorial field. It is as though the accumulation of tension in the compressed zone leads to a momentary flash or disturbance. But this disruption is never final, it is held in check by the overall structure. Stability is regained, only to be challenged again, in what seems to be a cyclic process. In 1965 Riley herself described this momentum:

> The basis of my paintings is this: in each of them a particular situation is stated. Certain elements within that situation remain constant, others precipitate the destruction of themselves by themselves. Recurrently, as a result of the cyclic movement of repose, disturbance and repose, the original situation is restated.[5]

This perceptual phasing, which EH Gombrich related to the periodical momentum of Western music,[6] reappears in many variations and guises throughout her work. But it is particular to the early black-and-white paintings that one can read the score, so to speak, before the performance starts. The spectator can survey the structure, distinguish

                                                ROBERT KUDIELKA

and perceive the progressive sequences, and yet is still drawn into the cadence with which the cycle begins again.

In *Fission* the character of the performance is changed according to the different structural potential of the chosen element. The progression of a circle to an oval is read in reverse as an expansion towards the full form, and because the units do not touch, as the squares did, the whole field behaves differently. The distress caused by the rupture of the vertical axis is 'healed' by long looping arcs which curve diagonally across the canvas. Because of this greater flexibility the sequence of circles to ovals proved to be one of the most fertile themes in Riley's repertoire. As *Where* and *Pause* show, the formal progression can be combined with tonal sequences from light to dark, to create more subtle and complex sensations.

Tonal progression was first introduced as a theme on its own in *Black to White Discs*, Riley's largest canvas to date. The painting accommodates a centrally placed diamond of evenly spaced identical discs which advance and recede according to a successive modulation of tone. Although the fullest sequence from the palest grey on the left to the black is longer and slower than its reverse on the right, the suggestion of symmetry is so strong that the eye tends to cling to the vertical centre of the diamond until one discovers that the true tonal centre of the image, the line of absolutely black discs, is just a little to the right. Such veiled, subliminal moves play an important part in the fabric of Riley's paintings right through to the present day. But in her early studio practice this tonal structure also lent itself to a kind of crossbreeding with formal progressions, resulting in a method of differentiating visual time.

Where and *Pause* are both about the modification of a basic formal movement through the different visual tempi provided by tonal sequences. In *Where*, two different gradations to and from a central grey – one quick, the other slow – are imposed on a regular structure of increasing and decreasing forms, with the result that the shifting paces completely change the character of the space. The underlying compression becomes almost explosive, and only the dislocation of the tonal sequences relieves the tension. *Pause* is a much more mysterious painting. Here the shift of tempi veils the structure altogether. As so often in Riley's work, a clue is given at the top and the bottom of the painting, because even in contriving the most elusive and enigmatic sensations she remains a builder, erecting a painting rather than inscribing it on a flat surface. Along both edges one can see that the two tonal movements from black to the palest grey – one in 13 and the other in seven stages – do not converge with the formal structure which clearly echoes that of *Movement in Squares*. By turning these sequences inside out as they travel down and across the painting, the absolute black circle in the top left corner becomes the slimmest oval in the compressed area at the bottom. In reverse, the palest grey circle at the bottom right moves up through the compression turning into an oval just off centre at the top. And yet, however rigorously these concerted movements may be fashioned, they eventually combine to form a light and serene divertimento.

With such complex organisations the stable starting point of the original scenario was slowly eroded giving way to an instant sensation of flux and motion. This development is most apparent in a group of paintings employing a device which in Riley's studio parlance is called 'point movement'. Their archetype is *Shift* (1963). The scale study reveals how the triangles are brought about. A regular vertical and horizontal register provides a constant proportion of width and height while the moving points of the triangles are established by a crossing diagonal. It may be noted that this is already a step from the progressive phrasing of single units towards the organisation of a total field. But in the actual painting the literal scenario of the 'cyclic movement of repose, disturbance and repose' can still be recognised. The points of the black triangles in the vertical compartments move progressively in one direction, then turn, and finally return back into the original direction. The key units for this organisation are the rectangular triangles. They can be seen along the top and the bottom of the painting, and they mark the turning points within the structure. While the first change of movement drops steadily through the addition of one triangle each time, the return back into the original direction is increased by a ratio of two units. As a result the centre passage opens out like the segment of a fan until it

                                                                ROBERT KUDIELKA

spans almost half the height of the painting. Conversely the long return movement is gradually reduced to a succinct clause in the bottom right corner, one right angle against another.

The two subsequent paintings however, *Shiver* and *Burn* (both 1964), can no longer be seen in this way. It takes close analysis to discover that the highly energetic field of shifting directions in *Shiver* is controlled through firm structural divisions also marked by rectangular triangles. The total structure is divided by a pair of V-shapes which together form a hidden chevron. In the enclosed area at the top all the diagonals of the point movement 'lean forward' and straighten up towards the middle, before swinging back to their original position. The central chevron area is made up of repeated parallel movements, all the same length and all 'tilting backwards'. The return in the lower part repeats the upper movement, but in reverse sequence, the diagonals 'tip downwards' from an almost upright position and straighten up again. But this description of the formal means of the painting conveys little of its sensation. *Shiver* is the pure visual equivalent for certain states of being. They may be identified with the actual title of the painting, but Riley remembers that at the time she was also thinking of the beaded skirts and rapid little movements of the shimmy – a dance popular in the twenties.

It is the advantage of such rigorous formalism that it can structurally encompass a variety of meanings. Paradoxically this requires that the artist lays aside any direct interest in content, as Riley has shown in her recent writing on Bruce Nauman's formalism.[7] She was surprised that an artist of such different persuasion should in some of his best pieces employ literally the same formal procedures as she herself has done: repetition, reversal, dislocation, asynchronism and accumulation of density. The only criterion for the successful articulation of an experience seems to be the unadulterated response to the specific plastic conditions in hand. In *Burn* she has given a fine example of this secret of formalist expression. By turning the structure of *Shiver* on its head she upset the equilibrium, and in trying to counteract the dislocation of weight she introduced the two tonal movements diffusing the gravitational pull downwards. But in adding this further complexity it became apparent that the scale had to be changed to a coarser grain to withstand the intense dissolution of the field. The result is not only a different sensation, an expressive paradox like 'cold heat', but a painting that exposes a critical contradiction that had emerged in Riley's pictorial world.

Images and fields

As early as 1963, Norbert Lynton noted a divergence between two distinctly different groups of paintings in Riley's work: 'image paintings' and 'field paintings'.[8] The first group contains all the images using dislocated circles, like *Uneasy Centre* for example, and is epitomised in the Blaze paintings. They are among the most explosive structures that Riley invented, because they carry the principle of dislocation directly into the 'quintessential and most dramatic space of all', as Bryan Robertson remarked: 'the distance between the spectator and the canvas.'[9] Far from being merely a geometric form amongst others, the circle is seen as the mirror image of our focus in looking; and by dislocating this relationship Riley touches the core of our vision.

This is undoubtedly an iconoclastic act and it is not by chance that Anton Ehrenzweig, the great theoretician of iconoclasm in twentieth-century art, wrote one of the best analyses of Riley's early work.[10] But it should also be seen that there is a steady, consistent move after 1963 to open up the all too immediate confrontation between the eye and its mirror. Although the surprising smallness of many of Riley's early works is due to the fact that they can only function and display their potential when they are encompassed by our view, the development of the work in general, and in particular the theme of point movement, shows that Riley began to undermine this confinement. The concern with images gave way to a more open field organisation which she attributed at the time to the example of American painting: 'open space, shallow space, a multifocal space as in Jackson Pollock.'[11]

By 1965 the conflict of orientation seems to have been resolved. The zigzag theme which had been instrumental in the powerful impact of the Blaze paintings was finally concluded in *Descending* (1965), a classic

   ROBERT KUDIELKA

'field' painting. In an even vertical register every other division is a curve which progressively traverses the painting in a slow, dropping movement; and the dislocation in the zigzag fabric brought about by this irregular gradient is no longer tense and spasmodic, but a sharp and angular ripple across an open field.

It is interesting to see that this shift had already begun in 1963 with a theme that bypassed the main preoccupation with structural progressions. In *Fall, Current* and *Crest*, Riley articulated the sensation of a whole field simply by reiterating and amassing a particular curve. The only other structural devices are the irregular proportions governing the areas of contract on and expansion. Even more than the complex edifices of *Pause* or *Shiver* these repetitive structures, despite their graphic firmness, generate an immediate sensation of flux. Particularly in *Current* one can see the new structural problem posed by this 'virtual movement', as Riley calls it. Although there could be no 'return', as in the original scenario, because there is no stable starting point, the visual frequency unleashed had nevertheless to be contained. Only before the actual painting can one properly appreciate the master stroke: the horizontal zones of parallel arcs in the areas of compression do not break loose but are firmly held within the tension of the curvilinear field. The change of scale in reproductions usually falsifies this sensation by producing a moiré effect instead.

The increasing involvement with this immediacy of perception brought about new forms of field organisation which were essential in preparing the ground for the move into colour. In *White Discs 2* (1964) Riley created a powerfully elusive sensation by deleting parts of the regular structure spanning the field. Once the 'white discs' have started to emerge under one's eyes it is not difficult to intimate the complete field of black discs. In a similar way, although with entirely different means, *Breathe* calls directly on sensation. This phalanx of elongated triangles is clearly built with an off-centre organisation consisting of a short and speedy movement on the left and a long, slow one to the right. But the grand, voluminous pulse, the 'breath' of the painting, is nevertheless puzzling, and it is with a mixture of surprise and delight that one realises that it is through an ingenious distraction of our attention that this sensation is achieved. The pace of the progressions is dilated by moving in steps of two instead of one by one.

The connection between *Breathe* and the formal organisation of the Orient paintings is so obvious that with hindsight one might think that the transition to colour could have been more direct than it actually was. But for Riley using colour was not simply a problem of finding an adequate form, it required a profound revision of her pictorial approach which had so far mainly been based on the principle of contrast and opposition. With the introduction of grey this reckoning had already begun to change, and another clue seems to have been provided by structures in which the physical presence of form and contrast have been considerably eroded. *Static 1* (1966) is all about virtual movement and perceptual energy. The actual structure of minute ovals turning in different directions and at different speeds is barely discernible in this even, highly charged field. It was this achievement of having turned the picture plane into a field of pure disembodied energy that, together with the infinite range of delicate shades available in grey, allowed Riley to make the transition from her black-and-white work to pure colour painting.

The transition to colour

In his 1970 monograph on Bridget Riley, Maurice de Sausmarez reproduced a study of 1965 which shows that Riley had tried to apply colour within the structure of her earlier black-and-white paintings. But she soon realised that a bigger step was required, a kind of denial of previous practices and attitudes, as she later explained in referring to the Deny paintings: 'I didn't choose the title *Deny* by chance. The whole group of paintings grew out of, and away from, the absolute opposition of black and white. I wanted something which operated on more levels, was capable of more development, had a more grey'd quality, like the indeterminate nature of reality.'[12]

The complexity of *Deny 2* (1967) can be seen as operating on several different levels of 'denial'. Obviously the structural movement of the ovals works against the regular grid which supports them. The basic theme is the slow spin of a slender upright oval – vertical to horizontal, and back to vertical again. At the edges of the canvas one can see the two different forms of progression: along the top and the bottom the return sequence simply reverts, whereas down the sides one long complete turn-over takes place. The regular halfway position of the horizontal ovals draws one's attention to the internal organisation of the movement. The total field is divided into four equal compartments in which the units are moved around in such a way that the uppermost sequence is reversed in the lowest, and vice versa. But what is more, these four quarter field movements are related to one another in a complementary way. In the top half of the painting the horizontal oval in the middle moves successively down and out towards the edges of the canvas, while in the lower part the movement rises from the vertical ovals in the corners to meet in the centre. This results in a sensation simultaneously centrifugal and centripetal. All formal agents seem to be dispersed and drawn together at the same time.

In sheer formal terms this structure is not unlike that of *Static 1*, but in *Deny 2* Riley has 'denied' the simple black-and-white contrast by introducing an opposition between a warm reddish grey for the ground and a cool bluish grey for the ovals within a common tonal harmony. Furthermore, the bluish grey of the units is organised in three different tonal gradations which in turn 'deny' the structural developments. If one once more uses the edges of the canvas as a guide one can see that there is a slow progression from light grey to middle grey, a fast one from light to dark grey, and again a slow one from dark to middle grey. They combine to form a diffused dark area at the bottom, clearly reminiscent of the V-shaped dissolution in *Burn*.

As with the complex point movements, however, the description of the operative means falls short of the actual appearance of the painting itself. The sombre elegance of *Deny 2* springs from an unexpected visual opposition between colour and tone. Where the tone of the ground and the ovals are equal the colour contrast between red and blue emerges. In reverse, where the light–dark opposition is at its maximum, the colour differentiation, in a supreme, perceptual form of 'denial', is virtually suppressed. So at one extreme there is an almost metallic glitter, reminiscent of shining leaves turning in the wind, and at the other, our sense of depth and distance is lost in a soft, shadowy mist.

With the Deny paintings one has the feeling that, if only one could lift a veil, one would stand in the light of *Chant 2* (1967) and *Late Morning* (1967–68). But again, there was no such direct continuation. *Deny 2* was an end rather than a beginning, the culmination of a development that includes *Turn* (1964) as well as *Shiver*, *Burn* and *Static 1*. The real advance was prepared for by a group of paintings on which Riley worked concurrently. She had in fact introduced warm and cold greys for the first time in 1965 when she began to extend the curve theme of *Crest* and *Current*. By enlarging the body of the curve the visual speed was slowed down and the alternation of warm and cold greys provided a subliminal tension. However, the main aspect of this group of paintings – called *Arrest 1* (1965) – was a complex interlocking between the formal structure and sequences of coloured greys. In *Arrest 2* (1965) a steep diagonal fall of curves on the left corresponds to a larger and shallower rise on the right, both movements being slightly bowed. The progression of warm and cold greys obliterates this off-centre organisation in two ways. Firstly, a fast sequence from dark to light grey transgresses beyond the formal division, and then, most importantly, a second, slower tonal movement starts in the actual centre of the square format with a sharp contrast between the palest grey and the deepest saturated black. *Arrest 2* is a magnificent display of the dynamic stillness that can be effected through the interrelationship of opposing thrusts and weights.

However, as a first step beyond mere tonal modulation the *Arrest* paintings did not lead much further. Rather, in working with coloured greys on a large scale Riley seems to have familiarised herself sufficiently with the still remote problem of colour to realise two things: that intricate formal structures would inhibit the presence of colour, and that the greatest forte of the curve was not the weight it could carry but its long supple edge. The solution did not come at once. But when it was achieved in *Cataract 3* it looked both inevitable and quite unexpected.

The formal structure of the painting is quite simple – an even diagonal displacement of one and the same curve. The whole stage belongs to what happens to colour, *with* colour and *through* it. Sharing the same curve, two coloured greys – one red, one turquoise – travel in close proximity the full span from a tonally equal, chromatically neutral grey to the full untempered colour contrast. But as soon as they draw nearer to the area of open brilliance something extraordinary takes place, the colour seeming to break loose from its formal vehicle. This may be due partly to the familiar displacement of the area, partly to the high frequency of the curvilinear field and partly to the granular friction which Riley has unobtrusively built into the gradation. The sequence, instead of proceeding smoothly, advances by always moving on, in a kind of 'roll over' rhythm, from one stage before the last (that is to say 123/234/345 etc.). But whatever the cause may be, the result is visibly there: a cool, fresh, rosy aura envelopes the heart of the contrast, shimmering and sending off sparkles, like dancing reflections, into the greyer areas of the painting. With *Cataract 3* the transformation of the original cyclic scenario, 'repose, disturbance and repose', was almost complete. Colour could obviously be put into action in an analogous way, as a sensation embracing the tension between an actual hue and its dissolution in coloured light.

There was only one more step to be taken, the relinquishing of the grey envelope. In *Chant 2* this is accomplished. The colours are reduced to a pair of red and blue, the strongest chromatic contrast, and the forms are simplified into stripes, the most neutral structural vehicle possible. But from these stark means a painting of great presence and authority is extracted. Red and blue in two different combinations, red surrounding blue, blue surrounding red, alternate as they spread across the canvas. The width of the bands increases towards the centre while the white intervals remain constant. Depending on the spectator's distance, the painting offers two different but interrelated experiences. Up close one can see the radiation of colour energy along the edges of the bands: the blue-red-blue combination gives off a dark blue violet shine, whereas the red-blue-red band appears as a lighter red violet and flickers with a luminous yellow orange. As one steps back these elusive details give way to a powerful collective sensation. In the centre, where the broader bands are amassed, an unplumbable depth opens up, radiating an almost colourless light.

Chant 2 was shown at the Venice Biennale in 1968 together with *Late Morning*, the other great painting that confirmed Riley's breakthrough to pure colour. A wide horizontal canvas of well over three metres, it is based on a continuum of regular periodic units which carry a cumulative momentum. The pace is set by the brilliant red chord consisting of two red stripes facing one another over a white interval. This steady pulse is accentuated on one side by an adjacent blue stripe which acts as an asymmetrical constant beat. On the other side the only progressive movement, a sequence from blue to green, provides a rhythmic flow in response to this driving thrust. It is organised according to the artist's 'roll over' principle, drawing out a mere ten stages to a span of 30 positions. But this movement is not continuous. The whole passage is subdivided into three phases and rearranged in a dislocated manner. Instead of beginning with blue or green the first part on the left starts from a central position of turquoise. This appears like a premature echo anticipating the second part which advances from blue to turquoise and continues through into the third part where it culminates in yellow green. With this sequence being mirrored on the right side, the total organisation describes a circular movement encompassing the instantaneous sensation of a volume of pale yellow light emerging in the centre. In a talk at the Tate Gallery in September 1994 Bridget Riley said that she chose the title *Late Morning* because the sensation reminded her of that hour in the Midi just before noon, 'when the heat is about to reach its zenith and the air is alive with the dry sound of cicadas.'

Extending the range

The breakthrough to colour resulted in a burst of activities which can roughly be divided into three developments. First of all Riley started to explore the new terrain she had found through *Chant 2* and *Late Morning* (*Rise 1, Byzantium, Orient 4*). Then, having discovered certain limitations, she made various attempts at strengthening the intensity of colour and giving more body to the fugitive sensations (*Zing 1, Cantus Firmus*), and finally, she reintroduced the curve element to give her newly acquired experience with colour a more sympathetic form (*Entice, Aurulum, Song of Orpheus 5, Andante 1*).

The first group shows the extent to which colour changed her pictorial practice. Formal complexity was sacrificed for the unassertive character of stripes and bands, and for some time *Chant 2* remained the last square format because the extension and opening up of the scope of vision seemed as essential to the release of colour activities as the confinement had been to her explosive black-and-white images. The big horizontal format entered Riley's repertoire. In retrospect she wrote: 'In the same way that I had to sacrifice distinctive forms in order to release the energy of colour-light, it was necessary to increase the scale of the event in order to prevent focused looking.'[13]

The paintings *Rise 1* (1968), *Byzantium* (1969) and *Orient 4* (1970) are each based on a palette of three colours only without any gradation. After *Late Morning* Riley gave up this kind of colour progression, developing colour's perceptual interaction instead. The relationship of the three chosen colours is therefore crucial. *Rise 1* is made up of orange, violet and green, *Orient 4* operates on the triad of magenta, turquoise and ochre. These are, as David Thompson saw, 'colours which are already biased towards other colours',[14] that is to say composite colours which destabilise each other to form new perceptual identities. However, on close comparison one realises that these colour groups are selected according to a familiar principle because two of them always seem to work more actively together, thus forming a contrast to the third one. The orange and violet in *Rise 1*, for instance, when juxtaposed provide a cool carmine red to which the green then acts as a contrast. Likewise, the blue sensation produced by the green-and-violet pair is counteracted by the orange. In short, the principle of unequal balance reappears in Riley's colour calculations.

But the paintings are not demonstrations of colour theory. The apparent 'phenomena' of Riley's colour paintings are, in fact, sensations which can only happen under precise conditions, within the specific scale, pitch and frequency established by the plastic structure of the particular painting. It is so indispensable to the upward movement that gave *Rise 1* its name that the horizontal structure of the bands is organised, for the first time since *Horizontal Vibration*, in a purely perceptual way. Only in this context can the most powerful colour accent, the carmine of the orange backed up by the violet, exert its visual pull. *Byzantium*, on the other hand, is not only made up of a different group of colours, red, yellow-green and blue, but the even diagonal organisation of two alternating bands, red enclosing either yellow-green or blue, sets up a tension that creates a completely different sort of colour interaction. The extreme displacement of the vertical axis unleashes a vigorous counter-thrust to redress this imbalance. The whole field reverberates with disembodied energies striking a grand, ceremonial colour chord: purple, gold and white.

The powerful tension of *Byzantium* alerts one to a fundamental paradox in the new colour paintings which explains why Riley increasingly preferred the vertical emphasis for her structures. The perceptual activity of colour seems to be at its most intense when it is seen as a horizontal spread against the vertical forms that carry it. But in order to give some pull to this horizontal diffusion she introduced the steep angle of elongated triangles in a group of paintings all titled *Orient*. The result is a tense 'zone-ing' of the field which in *Orient 4* is further differentiated by a new structural element. It may be remembered from *Shift*, *Pause* or *Deny 2* that, when Riley was involved with progressive movements, crossover passages played an important part in her plastic vocabulary. In the colour work this concept seems to have been transformed into a literal 'crossover' device, a band of two colour stripes crossed by a third. *Orient 4* shows the enormous potential of this device. The basic pair of turquoise and ochre is crossed by magenta in a regular stroke. Thanks to the tapering points of this magenta stripe, thinning out at the top and bottom of the canvas, the colour relationships within each band are destabilised, giving rise to an astonishing range of colour sensations. The magenta itself travels from a violet inflection at the top to a pinkish orange at the bottom, the turquoise turns towards blue in the middle before settling in a greenish shade, and most dramatically, the ochre shifts from a yellow variant through a warmer rosy tint to a burnt orange appearance. These may be very faint incidents in themselves, but amplified through repetition they gather considerable

ROBERT KUDIELKA

force. The firmly spanned structure of *Orient 4* opens up into an orange
and reddish zone across the top and a blue and greenish one at the
bottom.

Extension and amplification were initially important means to
accommodate and harvest the profusion of dispersed coloured light. But
with time and experience Riley became increasingly concerned with
stabilising and substantiating this elusive experience. *Zing 1* shows one
direction in which she proceeded. By multiplying and increasing the
crossover device she acquired a new structural element called, in her
own studio parlance, 'colour twist', although the literal association of
twisting ribbons is misleading. It is in fact a form of movement that
allows all three colour stripes in a band to mutually cross one another in
turn. In *Zing 1* there are four diagonal crossings in each band. At the top,
green crosses over red and blue, then red crosses blue and green,
followed by blue crossing green and red, and finally at the bottom, the
sequence returns to its starting position with green again crossing red
and blue. This sets off a multitude of minute colour inflections, in effect
a virtual colour totality, which in the tight repetitive structure of *Zing 1* is
firmly held together in glittering horizontal zones, recalling the
compressed intensity of the curves in *Current*.

Although this was only one direction which Riley pursued, *Zing 1*
shows very clearly the limits of the attempt to enhance the presence of
colour energy as such. Mere intensification would not lend more body
and volume to sensations which by their very nature are fugitive and
immaterial. So it must have seemed an alternative to tackle the problem
from another angle. Between 1970 and 1973 Riley made a whole group
of paintings in which she tried to give more weight and density to the
play of colour by reintroducing black-and-grey sequences. *Cantus Firmus*
(1972–73) is the most successful of these canvases because, despite its
reduced colour presence, it is a masterpiece of pictorial building. The
impression of a powerful spatial movement is so strong that it takes
some time to realise that almost all the component parts of this painting
are identical and constant. *Cantus Firmus* is built on a regular alternation
of black, white and grey bands which are surrounded by bands of three
colours mirroring one another: olive, magenta and blue facing blue,

magenta and olive, etc. Both the periodic repetition of this colour constellation and the width and sequence of the black and grey bands are constant. Only one factor, the grey, moves from a mid-tone pitch at both sides of the painting in two different progressions – slow on the left and quicker on the right – towards a dark grey, virtually indistinguishable from the black bands close to it. This off-centre organisation is buried in a manner comparable to *Black to White Discs*. But the sensation is completely different. However reduced the colour activity may be, the fusion with the greys destroys the notion of a regular metre as well as the perception of any continuity in tone. The width of the bands and their planes in space seem to glide and fluctuate, disclosing a dense and yet curiously permeable space.

Reintroducing and transforming earlier themes and devices is obviously one of the ways in which Riley proceeds. Sometimes this produces an odd unruly painting but it can also open up unexpected territory. At first glance *Entice 2* (1974) seems simply to combine the curve element with greys, rather in the manner of *Cantus Firmus*. A vertical curve is diagonally displaced so that a continuous field of narrowing and widening forms emerges, every third interval carrying a constant grey of the same tonal pitch as the colours that flank it. There also seems to be a repetition of the blues, greens and reds, which mirror each other across the white intervals. But this order is deceptive because the continuity is undermined by rhythmic syncopations attracting and evading our attention. Identical colour pairs are interspersed with contrasting pairings, and the apparent overall organisation harbours a number of hidden accents and shifts, the most notable of which is the emphasis towards warm greens and reds on the right side.

In spite of the power and novelty of this image, Riley did not carry it further. As with the earlier choice of stripes, she never goes for 'imagery' as such, but rather for pictorial function and the sensation conveyed. In this way a structural observation in *Entice 2* seems to have indicated a change of direction. The narrowing of the curves in the pinched parts virtually severs the curvilinear field, and these acute passages seem to have suggested a new role for colour twists used in paintings such as *Zing 1*. In turning three colours around a curvilinear axis, Riley saw the

ROBERT KUDIELKA

possibility of accumulating groups of disembodied colour across the surface, quite independently of the previous confinement to horizontal zones. This became the dominant approach in her work for the next few years.

Aurulum (1977) is already a highly developed painting. One clue to the building up of complexity in Riley's work is her ability to take small and steady steps. First, she let the colours down with grey to facilitate their interactions; then, lightening and clearing them again, she explored the two different structural possibilities inherent in turning colours around a curve: tight twists and open expanding loops. And eventually, with paintings like *Aurulum*, the white intervals gave way to pale tinted greys which act as a conduit for the spread of colours.

The whole field of *Aurulum* is organised in two ways, firstly, by changing the number of curves carrying the same sequence of colours, and secondly, by reversing this sequence within the continuous formal structure. Each colour movement involves seven crossover stages. At the top left corner, for instance, it begins with blue, rose and yellow ochre crossing in turn, continues with a full repeat of this sequence and finishes with blue again at the bottom. Varying the number of curves carrying the same progressions and steadily shifting their positions along the diagonal drop of the field creates vivid clusters and chords of luminous colour. These golden, pink and yellow sprays are supported by a hidden inversion of the initial colour sequence to yellow ochre, rose and blue. Through this a slight inflection is added to the loose glissandi, lending a kind of iridescent bloom to the painting.

It seems almost impossible to go beyond such subtleties. But having trained her vision in this high-keyed colour fluctuation Riley went one decisive step further. In the *Song of Orpheus* paintings she split up the grey intervals which so far had served as receptacles for the colour activity into two more hues. This meant that the whole balance of colours 'already biased towards other colours' had to be readjusted to a shifting constellation of five colours: violet, blue, green, yellow and pink. In *Song of Orpheus 5* (1978) this palette is separated into two different colour twists. A theme of three colours, pink, blue and green, is interlaced with another consisting of two, yellow and violet. Their intricate structural relationships truly defy penetration. But far from being confused the resulting sensation is a clear contrast between rippling green and yellow clusters and hazy rose passages working against one another.

By the time Riley painted the *Song of Orpheus* paintings she had achieved her primary objective, to find a footing in colour, though with an unexpected consequence. In 1992 she said in conversation with Michael Craig-Martin:

> I saw that the basis of colour is its instability. Instead of searching for a firm foundation, I realised that I had one in the very opposite. That was solid ground again, so to speak, and by accepting this paradox I could begin to work with the fleeting, the elusive, with those things which disappear when you actually apply your attention hard and fast.[15]

So successful was this achievement that if one views the *Song of Orpheus* paintings with an open, unfocused gaze they come precariously close to dissolving into coloured light. But this of course provoked Riley's building temperament. However subtle and refined her paintings may become from time to time, the cultivation of sensitivity is not her aim.

In the curve paintings after 1978 this tendency towards evanescence is counteracted by deepening colour and modifying the overall organisation. One of the very last curve paintings, *Andante 1* (1980–81), shows how far this could be carried. Green, turquoise, violet, magenta and dull orange-ochre are the constituent colours which are organised in a new plastic way. Instead of regular or periodically recurring rhythmic patterns, broader structural considerations are brought into play. Vivid accents of green, in conjunction with turquoise and violet, flash across a bed of warm colours which draws upon interactions between magenta, dull orange-ochre and, once again, violet. This free disposition of the curving colour twists includes a shift in the colour emphasis. Whereas in the larger part of the painting reddish interactions prevail, the balance is reversed in the lower right side in favour of a cool blue-green giving weight to the sharp breaks and interjections of these colours elsewhere.

In 1981, when Bridget Riley completed *Andante*, she had already begun to extend and transform this free perceptual organisation. The broad simple colour band reappeared, carrying a palette of unprecedented strong and bright hues. After ten years of intense involvement with chromatic interaction Riley had shifted the basis of her work once again; and this not for the last time in the past two decades. Such changes are neither capricious nor deliberately engineered in pursuit of novelty. She herself scorns any value attached to change as such, because to her sensibility movement is an essential condition of preserving the vitality of life. In this sense the rich and continuous development of her work, now spanning more than 40 years, is a rare and precious achievement in itself.

Lisa G Corrin (ed), *Bridget Riley: Paintings from the 1960s and 70s,* exhibition catalogue, Serpentine Gallery and Koenig Books, London, 1999, pp.23–34.

1   David Sylvester, 'Bridget Riley', *New Statesman*, 25 May 1962.
2   Although from today's point of view Minimal art is subsumed into 'modernism', this was not so at the time. The supporters of Clement Greenberg's view of the evolution of modern art were opposed to the claims of the Minimalists, as one can see from Michael Fried's essay 'Art and Objecthood' (1967). One of the critical points was the notion of 'presence', whether the picture plane was an area in its own aesthetic right or simply a physical fact among the other objects existing in the world. The whole debate is well documented in Gregory Battcock (ed), *Minimal Art: A Critical Anthology*, Studio Vista, London, 1969.
3   Clement Greenberg, *The Collected Essays and Criticism*, John O'Brian (ed), 4 vols., University of Chicago Press, Chicago, IL, 1986–93, vol.4, p.80.
4   Bruce Glaser, 'Questions to Stella and Judd' (1964), in Battcock, *op.cit.*, p.150.
5   Bridget Riley, 'Perception Is the Medium' (1965), in Robert Kudielka (ed), *The Eye's Mind: Bridget Riley: Collected Writings 1965–1999*, Thames & Hudson, London, 1999, p.66.
6   EH Gombrich, 'Perception and the Use of Colour: With EH Gombrich' (1992), in Robert Kudielka (ed), *Bridget Riley: Dialogues on Art*, Zwemmer, London, 1995, p.42.
7   Bridget Riley, 'Nauman's Formalism' (1999), in Kudielka (ed), *The Eye's Mind*, *op.cit.*, pp.212–16.
8   Norbert Lynton, 'London Letter', *Art International*, vol.7, no.8, October 1963, p.84.
9   Bryan Robertson, 'Introduction and Biographical Note', *Bridget Riley: Paintings and Drawings 1951–1971*, Arts Council of Great Britain, London, 1971, p.7.
10 Anton Ehrenzweig, 'The Pictorial Space of Bridget Riley', *Art International*, vol.9, no.1, February 1965, pp.20–24.
11 Bridget Riley, 'In conversation with Maurice de Sausmarez' (1967), in Kudielka (ed), *The Eye's Mind*, *op.cit.*, p.62.
12 Bridget Riley, 'Into Colour' (1978), *ibid.*, p.90.
13 *Ibid.*, p.92.
14 David Thompson, 'Bridget Riley', *Studio International*, vol.182, no.935, July – August 1971, p.21.
15 Bridget Riley, 'Practising Abstraction: Talking to Michael Craig-Martin' (1992), in Kudielka (ed), *Dialogues on Art*, *op.cit.*, p.56.

ROBERT KUDIELKA

Bridget Riley for Americans

Dave Hickey

> Pollock has always been a hero of mine. But if there's any
> similarity whatsoever, I have arrived at it by a very different
> route. The unexpected thing in his free structure is the
> immense control. The unexpected thing in my controlled
> structure is the free play of visual forces… I try to keep
> the constituents of any complexity simple.
>
> — Bridget Riley, 'Into Colour: In Conversation with Robert Kudielka', 1978

> My freedom consists in my moving about within the
> narrow frame that I have assigned myself for each one of
> my undertakings. I shall go even further: my freedom will
> be so much greater and more meaningful, the more
> narrowly I limit my field of action and the more I surround
> myself with obstacles. Whatever diminishes constraint
> diminishes strength. The more constraints one imposes,
> the more one frees oneself from the chains that shackle
> the spirit.
>
> — Igor Stravinsky, *Poetics of Music in the Form of Six Lessons*, 1947

Thirty-five years ago last February, Bridget Riley arrived in New York
for the opening of the *Responsive Eye* exhibition at the Museum of
Modern Art. She immediately embarked on one of the swiftest, most
vertiginous and peculiar trajectories of praise and blame in the history
of Manhattan art celebrity. Riley's paintings in *The Responsive Eye* were
instantaneously the talk of the town and were universally recognised as
the dominant works in the exhibition. Her concurrent solo exhibition at
the Richard Feigen Gallery sold out before the show opened, and not
long thereafter, Josef Albers publicly claimed her as his 'daughter.'
New York's acknowledged master of rigorous abstraction, Ad Reinhardt,
volunteered to squire her around town (to protect her from the
'wolves'), and even Salvador Dalí, who could *smell* buzz, sought

Riley out and paid court to her, with his full retinue and live leopards
in tow.

Then things got crazy. Her paintings were hardly on the walls at
MoMA and Feigen before Op art imitations of her work began to appear
on dresses and scarves in fashionable shop windows along Fifth Avenue.
Fashion spreads proliferated in popular magazines and daily newspapers.
Head shops in the Village began offering straight knock-offs of her
paintings as posters. These soon adorned the walls of crash pads all over
lower Manhattan, providing visual accompaniment to the strains of
Chocolate Watchband and Strawberry Alarm Clock. Shocked and
astonished, Riley accepted the support of Barnett Newman and tried to
take the predators to court, but damage had been done. Local critics,
unnerved by the enthusiastic popular appropriation of their newly
discovered diva, were soon muttering. They began hedging their original
enthusiasm with terms like 'decorative', 'psychedelic' and 'purely retinal'.
Carnaby Street fashion was mentioned. The bane of Warholian celebrity
was bemoaned and the dread spectre of the egregious Peter Max evoked.

For Riley, devotee of Paolo Veronese and Georges Seurat, haunter of
museums, and rigorously adept in the young tradition of abstract
painting, the carnival of celebrity and merchandising must have been hell
on earth, but, as a friend of mine remarked at the time, Riley, at least,
got to go home – unlike poor Jackson Pollock who had to live in the
mess celebrity had made of his life. So home she went, to London, in a
state of stunned dismay, fully convinced that it would be 20 years before
anyone would look at her paintings seriously again. This turned out not
to be the case, but henceforth, Riley would pursue her career in the
United Kingdom and on the Continent, always keeping New York at
arm's length, as one would a foolish and fickle lover. Looking back at that
moment now, with the length and richness of Riley's subsequent career
in evidence, one thing becomes clear: the clamour over her work was
certainly justified and the work itself almost fatally misconstrued.

We always see what's new, of course, and recognise it as such, but
we see it with old eyes – until the new work makes our eyes new again.
It was Riley's fate in the sixties to make works of art that *any* eyes could
see, to make work that *happened at* a moment when artists *let* things

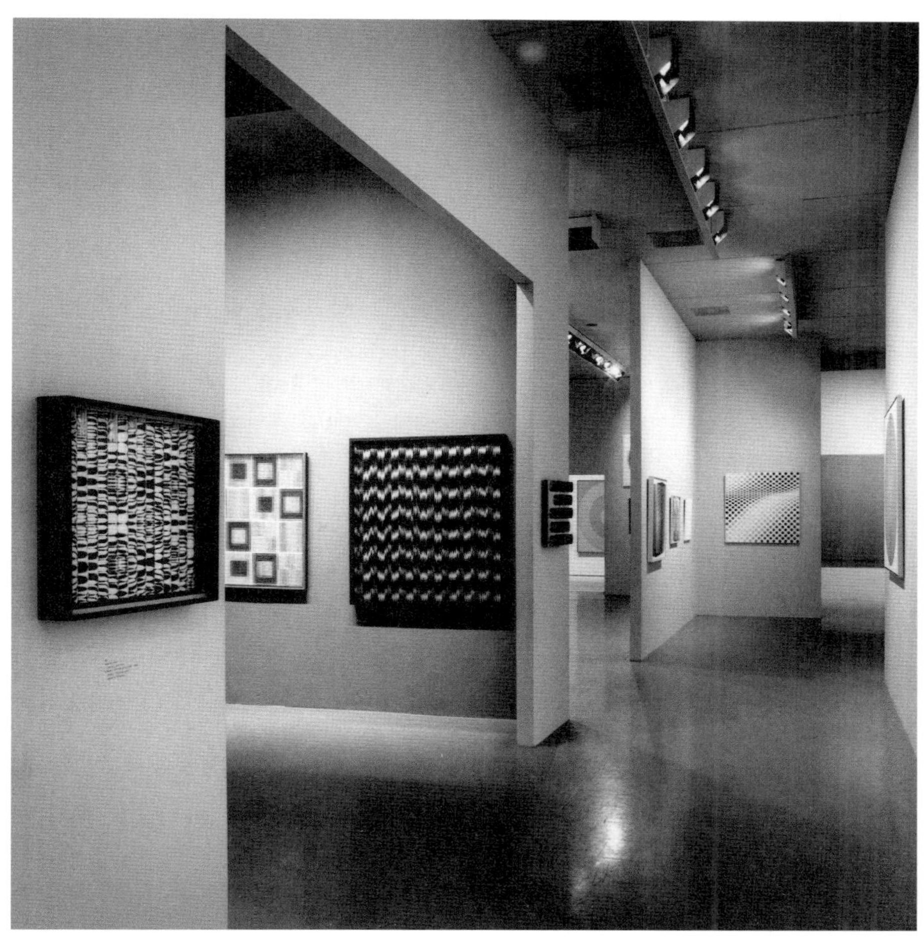

Installation view, *The Responsive Eye*, Museum of Modern Art, New York, 1965

happen, when works of art were things that things *happened* to. Such works existed to be discovered, praised, analysed, selected and historicised by the old eyes of a discriminating elite. In an environment like this, paintings like Riley's that aspired to the rhetorical efficacy of the sixteenth-century Venetians and nineteenth-century Parisians whom she revered – paintings that could not help but be looked at – were simply anathema. In a moment when the painter's innocence, purity and impudence were presumably redeemed by the critic's sensitivity, knowledge and rigour, Riley was clearly more knowledgeable, sensitive, rigorous and radical than any of her critics. What's more, she presumed that it was the artist's responsibility to be so. How else could one make new things happen?

Consequently, when you look at the progress of Riley's subsequent career, you discover the history of an artist perpetually trying to exploit the resources of tradition to keep from repeating it. This untraditional traditionalism is grounded in Stravinsky's edict that 'that which is without tradition is plagiarism', and informed by Riley's own understanding that tradition is not history. 'There are good traditions and bad traditions', she remarks, and to distinguish one from the other Riley is always narrowing her focus, creating rigorous, formal parameters and physical limits within which she can exercise her improvisational empiricism. Accepting Goethe's edict that 'nothing but the law can give us freedom', she seeks out those places where the law releases energy. 'The perceptual medium is so strong,' she says, 'the elements that one is using – that all painters use – have the dynamics of natural forces. They have their own laws, not rules but *laws*, and woe betide you if you upset the boat.'

Riley's practice, then, might be described as a sequence of controlled efforts to rock the boat without upsetting it. Her Op paintings from the sixties, for instance, evolved from her desire to demonstrate that 'there *are* some absolutes: Black is not white.' Even so, something happens at the intersection of black and white. There is a zone of dynamic mystery there that is anything but absolute. So, having observed that 'Titian achieves his unity by building the painting according to those very factors which would seem most likely to tear it apart', Riley sets out to do the same land creates paintings that maintain their cognitive unity while remaining virtually imperceptible. In her subsequent work, Riley will gradually relax the rigorous destabilising controls on her paintings in order to achieve more controlled effects.

In the Op paintings, Riley destabilises the entire zone between the beholder and the work. In her next series, which I call her Flavin paintings (1967–79), she focuses on the ambience of coloured light created by extended edges of juxtaposed pictorial colour. These paintings operate in a more restricted pictorial space than the Op paintings, but, like them, they still flicker and flash almost at random with the dynamics of our retinal accommodation to them, like thunderstorms seen from the air. In her next series of work, which I call her Stravinsky paintings (1979–90), Riley seriously addresses the musical analogy that her paintings evoke as a matter of course. Throughout Riley's career, her studies for paintings have always functioned less as plans to be executed than as scores to be performed. In the Stravinsky paintings, Riley's performance aspires not just to activate space but also to shape it. By intuitively juxtaposing a restricted palette of vertical stripes in musical sequences, she creates a narrow zone of advance and recession within which the space-making dynamics of our perception make the surface roll like the soft Pacific off Newport Beach.

The space created by Riley's more recently completed series of paintings, which I call her Veronese paintings (1990–97), is even narrower – a taut, vibrating veil stretched across the surface of a canvas divided into an irregular pattern of diagonal parallelograms. The high-contrast colour palette of 'these paintings is dispersed in such a way as to create cross-tensions that counter the radical thrust of the diagonals, à la Veronese's *The Adoration of the Kings* (1573). These cross-tensions keep the paintings from 'moving' as Riley's previous painting have, but they clearly *want* to move, and we feel this tension in our visual accommodation to the field. Riley's more recent paintings open up this field into large areas of soft-toned, closely valued colour enclosed by overlapping curves of similar speeds. In their faux-naif clarity, these new paintings evoke Rousseau and Matisse. Speculation about what these new works are *doing*, however, must wait until Riley is done with them. Until then, we can comfort ourselves with Riley's reminder that, if

Mondrian was the Giotto of abstract painting, the High Renaissance is yet to come, and presume that, in one way or another, she is reaching toward that.

Now Bridget Riley is back in New York – not a moment too soon and without excuses. Her work is still in progress. Her paintings still succeed, as they always have, in their cool brightness, as art of the highest order within its deepest tradition. Should they fail in this aspiration, there are no fall back positions. If you care about them, then, you must care about this kind of art and recognise the anxious dazzle of the experience. Beyond that, none of the fashionable excuses, which justify art by identifying it with something other than what it is, are applicable. You can't get a note from your teacher, your therapist, your clergyman or your decorator excusing your frivolous enthusiasm. The best you can expect is a note from a critic who recommends prolonged exposure to Riley's paintings and serious contemplation of their unnerving benison – of pleasure without comfort, mystery without explanation, wisdom without education – but mostly, always, pleasure – what Riley herself describes as stimulating, active pleasure, comparable to 'running… early morning… cold water, fresh things, slightly astringent… certain acid sorts of smells… like wood being cut.'

This is the experience Americans now have the opportunity of rediscovering, which, in fact, is an experience that young American artists have been rediscovering for the last 15 years, coming up to me at odd moments with tattered copies of the *Responsive Eye* catalogue in hand, pointing to a reproduction of Riley's work and demanding to know, 'What's this? Why haven't I been told about this?!' I never have an answer, but I am reassured that young artists are now finding in Riley's work what she found in Seurat, what, in her own recounting, Delacroix found in Rubens. In an essay called 'Painting Now' (1996), Riley reminds us that Delacroix, 'convinced that painting had gone astray and lost sight of its basic principles… went hunting in the Louvre – scrutinising, analysing and searching the paintings he found there. In Rubens and later in Veronese he found what he was looking for: clean, fresh colour used for the building of a painting.'

What young Americans are discovering in Riley's work, of course, is exactly what she brought to New York in 1965 and brings with her now in the year 2000 – clean, fresh colour, to be sure, but also the idea of a clean, fresh, virtually authorless modernism expressed in painting and dependent for its authority on nothing more than what happens when we look at the work. What interests these young artists about Riley's work, however, is something more specific. For them, her work constitutes an articulate precursor to the rhetorical-empirical brand of 'behaviourist modernism' practiced by Bruce Nauman and Richard Serra, for whom, as for Riley, the manipulation of material and formal means is directed toward the evocation of a local, cognitive-kinesthetic experience that is quite distinct from linguistic communication (which presumes that the work of art bears a message) and formal appreciation (which posits the work of art as a dead thing, artfully manipulated and sensitively perceived).

For this generation of artists, Riley's work constitutes the missing link between what they know and what they would know better. By connecting the concerns of Nauman and Serra with those of Seurat and, through Seurat, with a tradition of art-making that leads back to the triumph of Venetian painting, Riley's work infers a direction and a vision that heals the schism created by our recent, obsessive preoccupation with the dead nominality of physical objects and the putative circularity of linguistic expression. Most critically, however, Riley's work liberates young artists from the tyranny of explanation, since the reinstatement of Riley's work has, demonstrably, taken place without it, and contrary to all received opinion. Because *something happens* when we look at Riley's paintings, and that 'something' resides neither in our perception of their objecthood nor in our understanding of them as works of art, but in their 'plasticity', a quality which, according to Riley, 'hangs between the cognitive reading of an image and its perception'.

In his famous study, *Logique du sens* (The Logic of Sense, 1969), Gilles Deleuze calls the attribute of 'plasticity', the 'sense' of an object – an attribute that operates according to its own 'logic' that operates along the border between the proposition and the thing, between *de jure* and *de facto*. Apropos of Riley's method of bounded experimentation, Deleuze remarks that:

the logic of sense is inspired in its entirety by empiricism. Only empiricism knows how to transcend the experiential dimensions of the visible, without falling into Ideas, and how to track down, evoke and perhaps produce a phantom at the limit of a lengthened or unfolded experience.

It is likewise appropriate, then, that Riley would use Deleuze's term in likening the experience of Seurat's *A Sunday Afternoon on La Grande Jatte – 1884* (1884–86) to confronting a phantom in which 'the unfathomable appears in the guise of total visibility'.

In all of her discussions of artists she loves, in fact, Riley focuses on the realm of 'sense', insisting the art occurs when the way we see something and the way we know it impinge upon one another. She identifies 'the vital tension between knowledge and sensation' as the wellspring of Seurat's vision; she quotes Cézanne's remark that colour is 'the place where our brain and the universe meet', and observes that 'Veronese lays bare the web which hangs between perception and cognition more openly than Titian because he doesn't seem to be interested in expression.'

She repudiates Clement Greenberg's materialist reduction of the painter's medium to mere stuff, arguing instead that the means of painting are turned into a 'medium' only by the response of the artist who, through those means, is trying to make something happen in the realm of sense. It is exactly at this level of abstraction that Riley thinks and works, and only at this level of abstraction that a tradition stretching from Titian to Nauman (both of whom Riley greatly admires), can even begin to exist. The fact that such a tradition does exist, however, and that Bridget Riley participates in it, is heartening. It promises that something new will happen.

Bridget Riley: Paintings 1982–2000 and Early Works on Paper, exhibition catalogue, PaceWildenstein, New York, NY, 2000, pp.5–9.

                                                            DAVE HICKEY

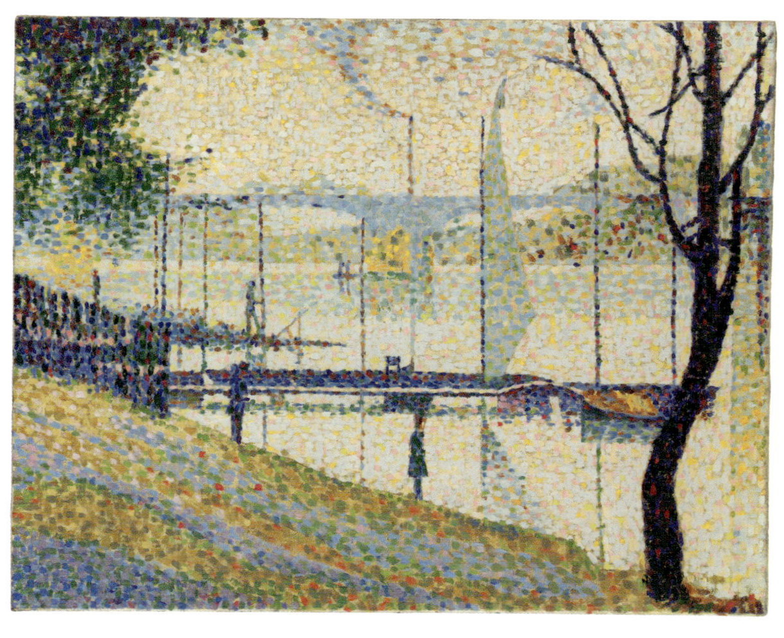

Copy after 'The Bridge at Courbevoie' by Georges Seurat 1959
Oil on canvas
71.1 × 91.1 cm | 28 × 35⅞ in
Private Collection

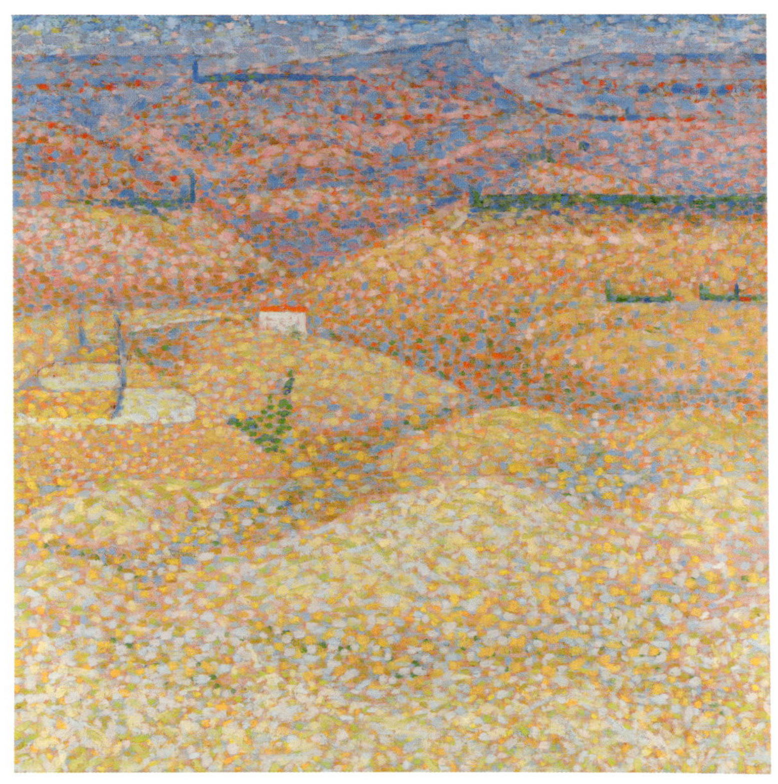

PLATE 2
Pink Landscape 1960
Oil on canvas
101.5 × 101.5 cm | 40 × 40 in
Private Collection

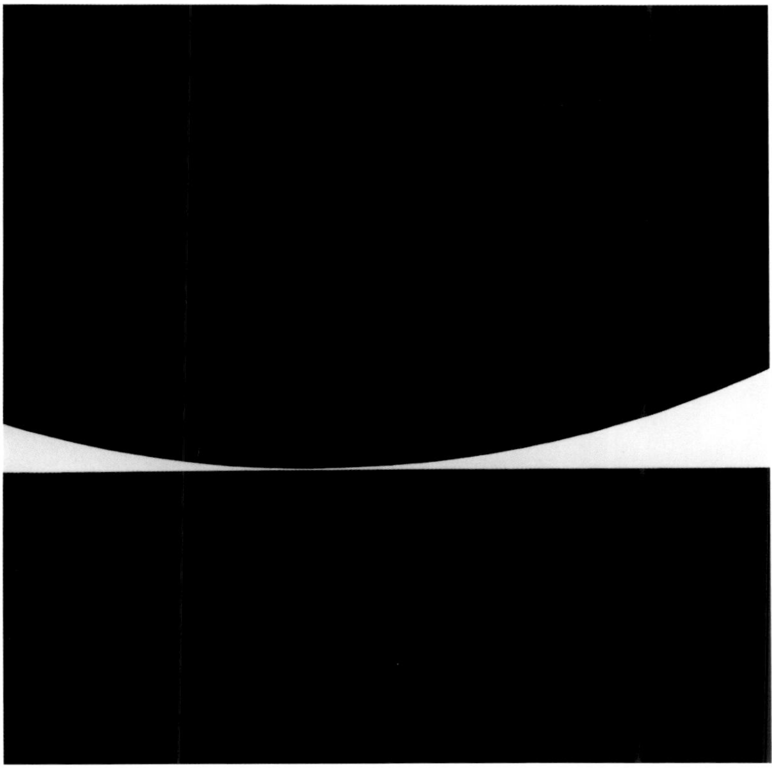

PLATE 3
Kiss 1961
Acrylic on linen
122 × 122 cm | 48⅛ × 48⅛ in
Private Collection

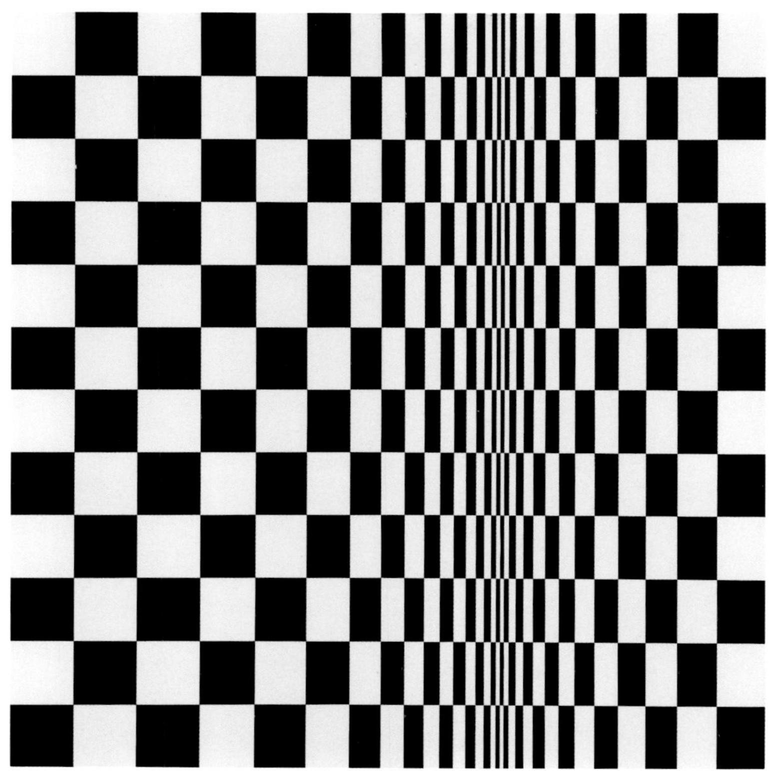

PLATE 4
Movement in Squares 1961
Tempera on board
123.2 × 121.3 cm | 48 1/2 × 47 3/4 in
Arts Council Collection, London

Tremor 1962
Emulsion on board
122 × 122 cm | 48⅛ × 48⅛ in
Lambrecht-Schadeberg Collection, Museum für Gegenwartskunst Siegen

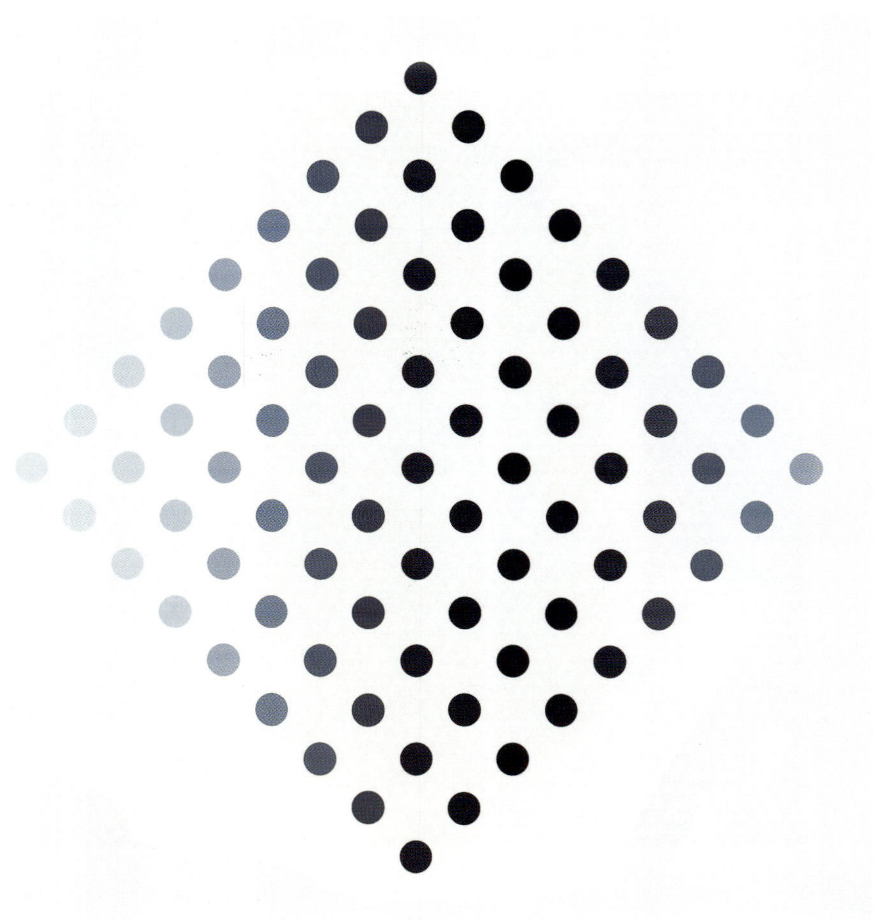

Black to White Discs 1962
Emulsion on canvas
177.8 × 177.8 cm | 70 × 70 in
Private Collection

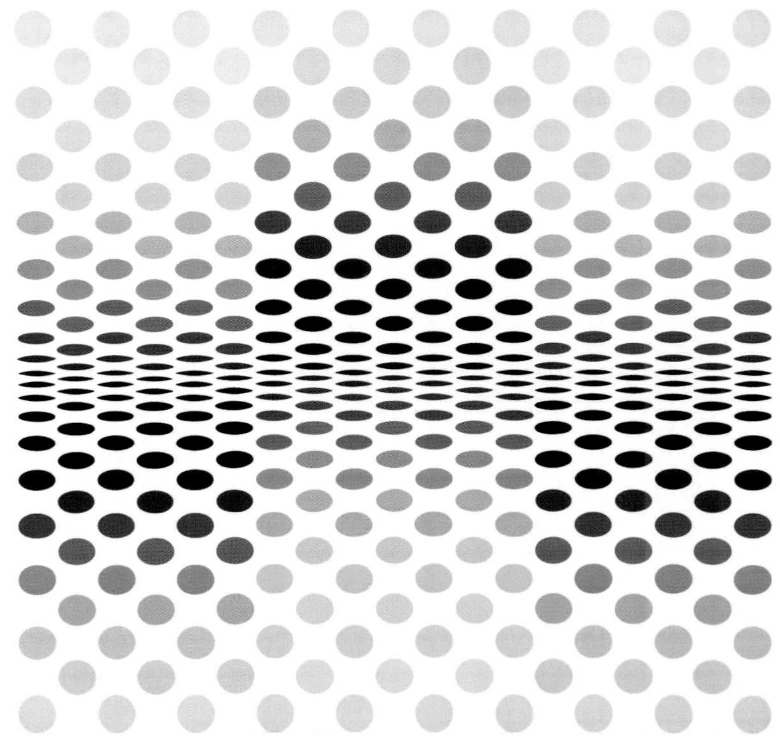

PLATE 7
Where 1964
Emulsion on hardboard
106.7 × 113 cm | 42 × 44½ in
Private Collection

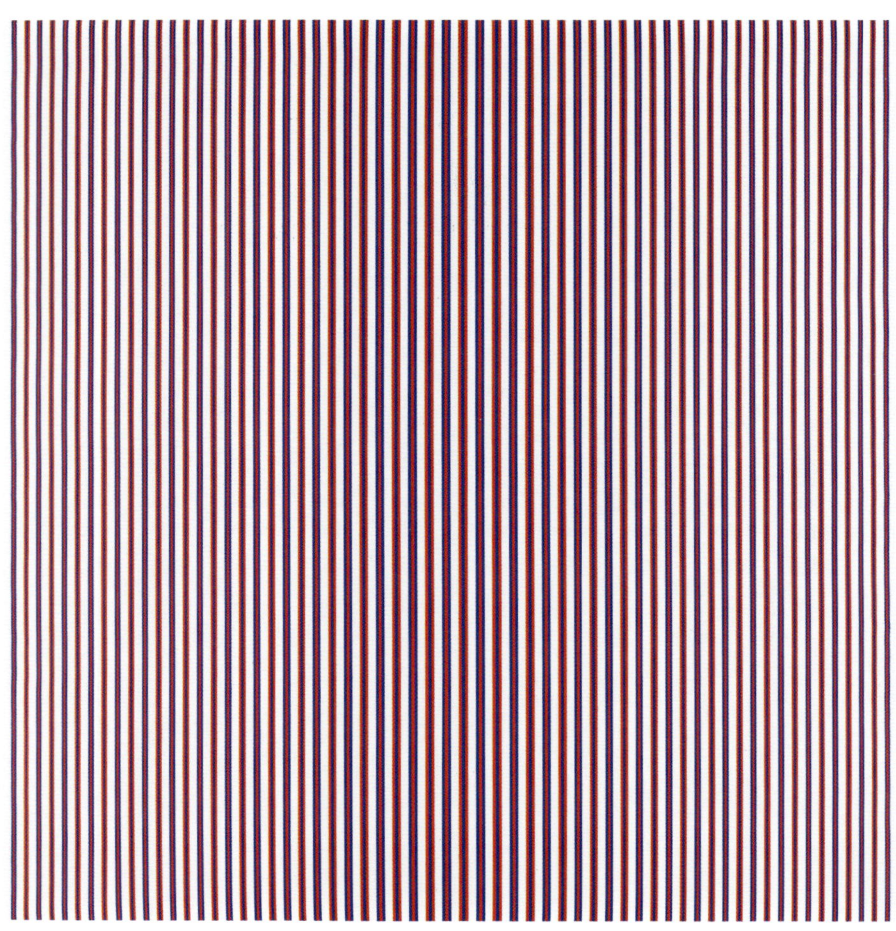

PLATE 8
Chant 2 1967
Emulsion on canvas
231.1 × 228.6 cm | 91 × 90 in
Private Collection

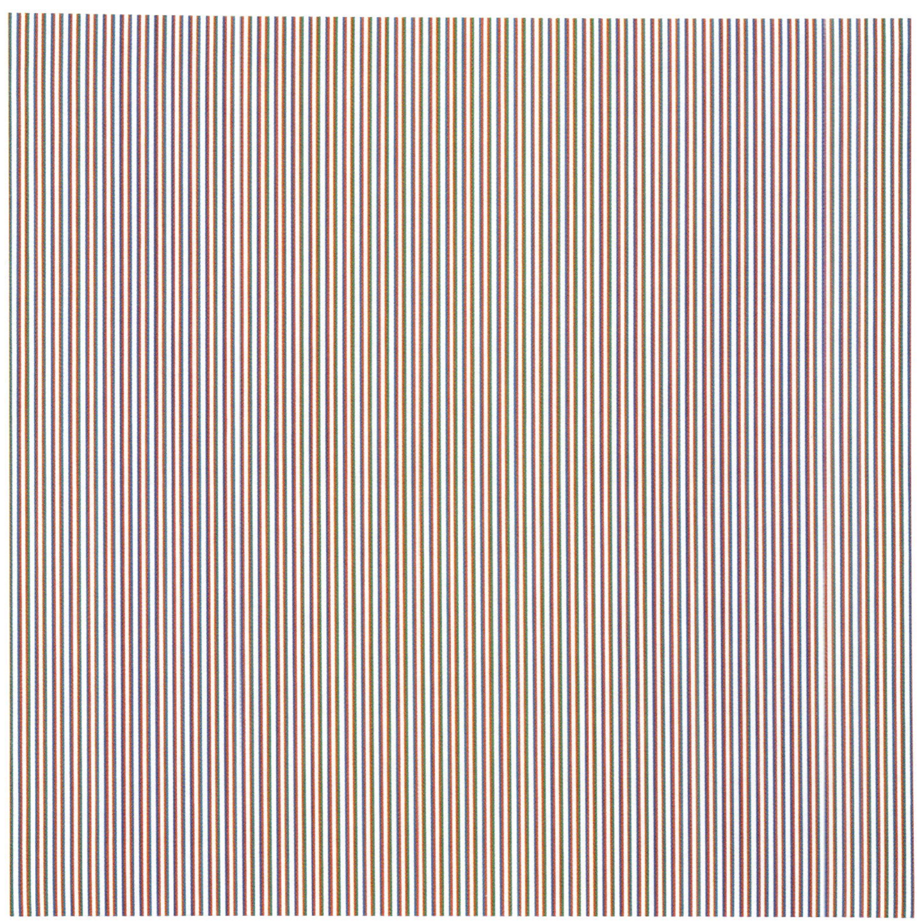

PLATE 9
Late Morning 1 1967
Acrylic on linen
227.3 × 227.3 cm | 89½ × 89½ in
Private Collection

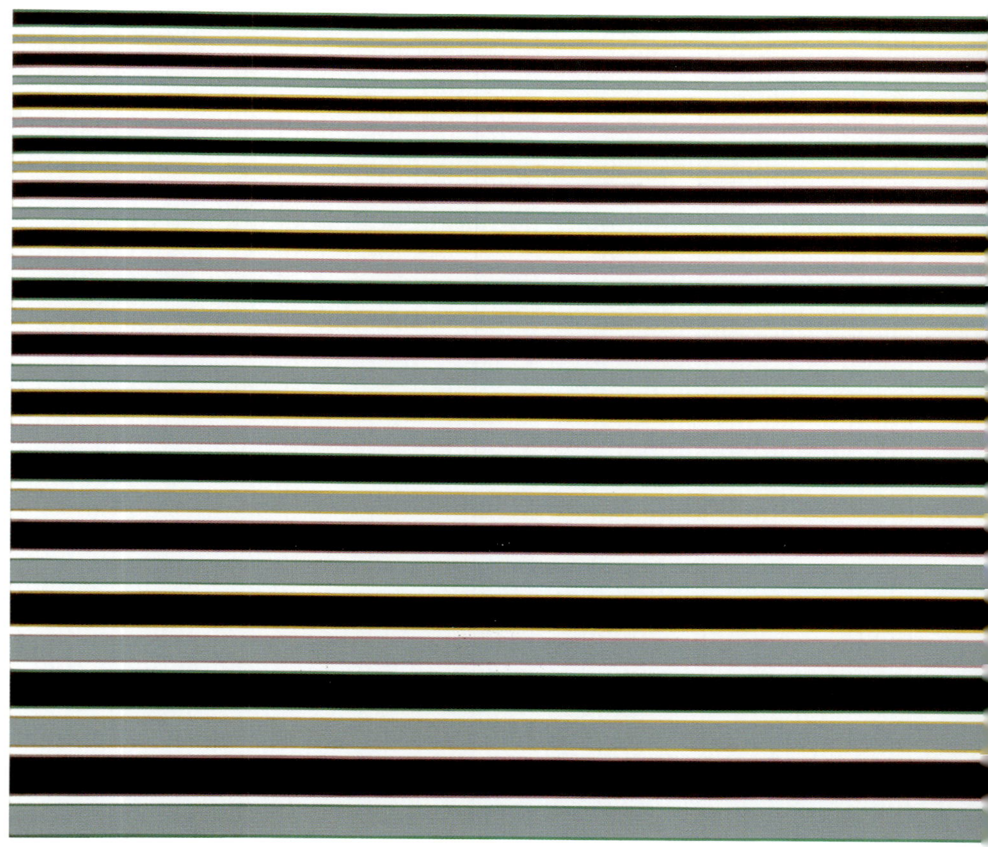

PLATE 10
Apprehend 1970
Acrylic on linen
163 × 405 cm | 64⅛ × 159½ in
Stedelijk Museum, Amsterdam

PLATE 11
Orient 4 1970
Acrylic on canvas
223.5 × 322.6 cm | 88 × 127 in
Berardo Collection, Sintra Museum of Modern Art, Lisbon

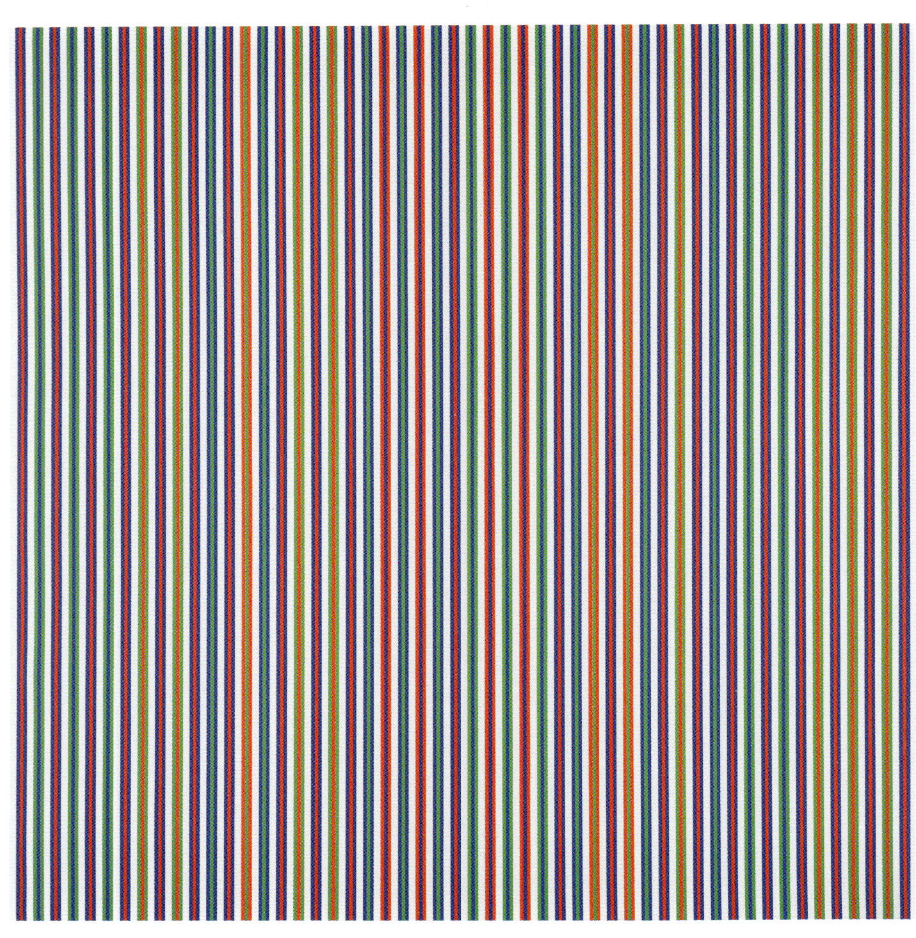

PLATE 12
Pæan 1973
Acrylic on canvas
289.5 × 287.3 cm | 114 × 113⅛ in
National Museum of Modern Art, Tokyo

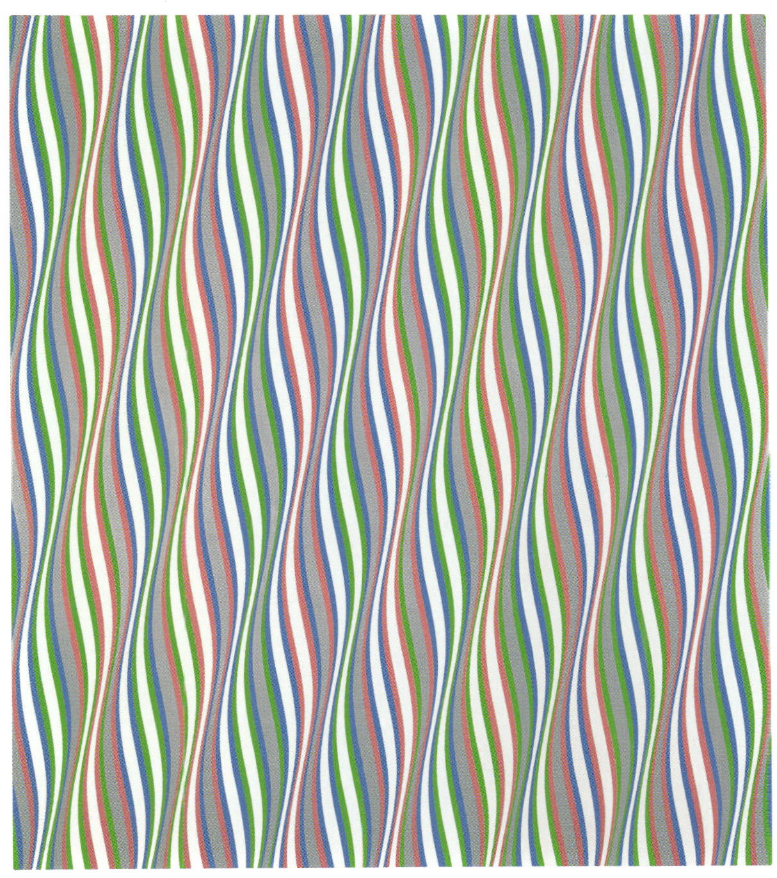

PLATE 13
Entice 2 1974
Acrylic on linen
154.3 × 137.5 cm | 60¾ × 54⅛ in
Private Collection

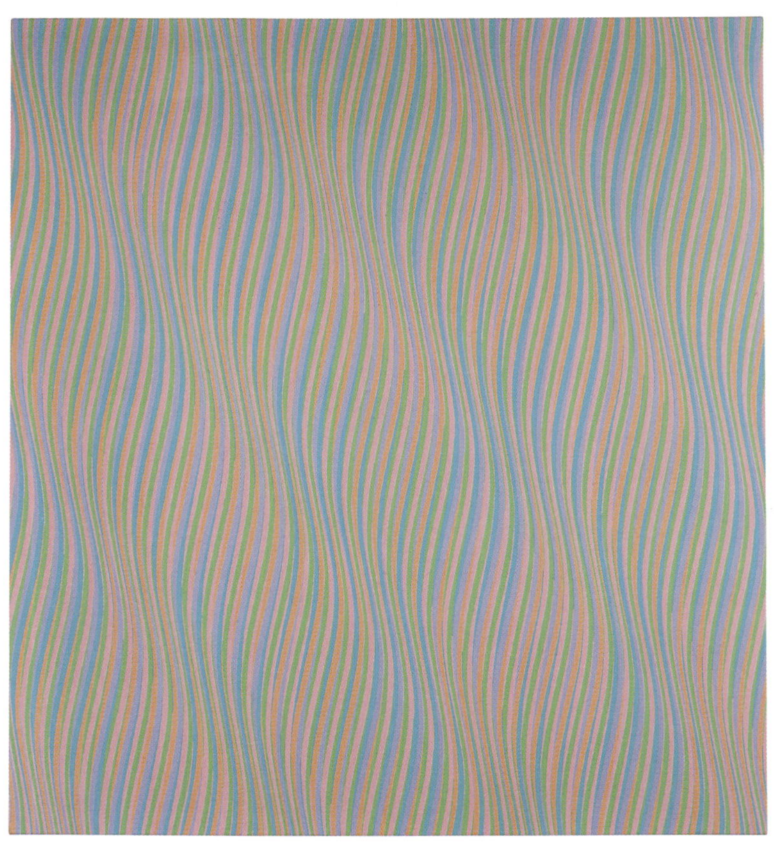

PLATE 14
Orphean Elegy 2 1978
Acrylic on linen
140.3 × 130.2 cm | 55¼ × 51¼ in
Iwaki City Art Museum

The Change of Aspect
John Elderfield

The appearance of a painting will change in the viewing of it; in much the same way that, TS Eliot said, the existing order of a tradition is altered by the appearance of the work that is truly new. It is not just a matter of becoming aware of a previously unnoticed feature; the whole existing order adjusts to accommodate the new perception. This allows 'order to persist after the supervention of novelty', Eliot said of a change in tradition.[1] In a similar vein, Ludwig Wittgenstein writes of a change in visual experience: 'The expression of a change of aspect is the expression of a new perception and at the same time of the perception's being unchanged.'[2]

Echoes in sight

Wittgenstein uses the term 'change of aspect', in the second half of his *Philosophical Investigations* (1953), to discuss the implications of seeing a new entity appear in the field of vision. What he says is an essential attribute of any and all changes of aspect turns out to be what Bridget Riley insists is an essential attribute of any and all pleasures of sight – and is an essential attribute of her own paintings: 'They take you by surprise. They are sudden, swift and unexpected.'[3]

I look at something and am able to report on what I see, but a sudden change in what I am looking at calls forth an exclamation. 'Both things,' Wittgenstein says, 'both the report and the exclamation, are expressions of perception and of visual experience. But the exclamation is so in a different sense from the report: it is forced from us. – It is related to the experience as a cry is to pain.' Furthermore, he says, that 'flashing of an aspect on us seems half visual experience, half thought.' Since the criterion of the visual experience is 'the representation of "what is seen"', the thought will search for possible matches between the representation just delivered and representations previously delivered by visual experience. Thus, when visual experience delivers to me a new aspect of what I am looking at, 'what I perceive in the dawning of an aspect is not a property of the object, but an internal relation between it and other objects… "The echo of a thought in sight."' If this is the effect of the change of aspect, and if it turns out that the change of aspect is integral to Riley's paintings, then it may be said that to produce such echoes is what Riley's paintings are for.

Three shocks await the viewer in quick succession, increasing in sum and substance.[4] The first shock is contextual. Objects, even paintings, being expected to be still and silent,[5] the sudden, surprising experience of a painting by Riley will seem like a silence that has been broken – the approach to the painting almost as if to a living thing. Activated by the viewer, the painting responds, and at that very instant the viewer will sense, with another shock, that he is no longer quite in control. (The painting, under this interpretation, is not simply receiving the viewer's sight but is determining and constraining his sight.)

The viewer may be excused for thinking, for a split second, that this shock of determination and constraint is akin to that of optical diagrams and reversible figures that force single surprising effects. But only for a split second. For the painting quickly will unfold a choreographed programme of effects, whose changes evidently respond to variations both in the patterned surface and in the viewer's visual attention. The viewer will then realise that the qualities of the perceptual experience that he derives from the painting are what comprise its meaning to him. The painting does not *control* the viewer; rather, it draws him at once into symmetry with it, enlisting his collusion with the artist's calculated modulation of the perceptual field. This is the third shock, and the most telling.

Even the experienced viewer, accustomed to paintings that change in aspect under a prolonged inspection, will be little prepared for the surprise of a painting that, co-opting his participation, bursts quickly into movement, immediately to offer a modulated, temporal delivery of a visual display. Riley's black-and-white paintings make a point of the surprise by staging an optical ambush. Their movement launches over

the surface, accelerating fast, and corrugates the surface alarmingly as
it speeds into the glare of an oscillating, disintegrating light. After a
disconcerting minute or two, things become reasonably stable, until the
viewer shifts and the disturbance starts up again. Thus, the black-and-
white paintings appear to change in consecutive movement. The
paintings made (from 1967 onward) with chromatic colours appear to
change in slower, continuous movement, as if without beginning or end.
The build-up of movement in these paintings is experienced as the
gradual adjustment of the eyes to something that is *already* changing,
and there is an engulfing ebb and flow in them, unlike the sharper,
cyclical shifts of their predecessors. In both the coloured and black-and-
white work, though, the surprise of the first encounter with a painting –
with its change of aspect, that is – is that an inanimate object is in
communication with the viewer.

There is something deeply atavistic about this experience, attaching
as it does to myths that keep alive an animistic mode of thinking that
logical thought has surmounted. And the viewer's surprise, the viewer
recognises, is a self-created surprise. The form that it takes is the
painting's, hence the artist's, creation. But it is viewing the painting that
triggers it. To attend to a painting is, therefore, also to attend to our own
attention, for the performance of the painting self-evidently takes place
not in the painting but in our eyes.

An enforced subjectivity would distance and isolate the viewer.[6]
Before a painting by Riley, the viewer is enrolled in a consensual
subjectivity. Through the medium of the painting, viewer and artist make
a pact that they will collaborate in eliciting from this particular painting
this particular mobile visual array. When the viewer stops looking at the
painting, the pact is broken, which makes the viewer unusually conscious
that the painting awaits someone else. Every painting is an agent for
sharing sights that may be fully claimed and held only while we look at
the painting. Riley's paintings tell us that to traffic in the sights is also to
traffic in the means by which we seek to claim and hold them.[7]

Other thoughts echo in sight: thoughts of other sights and their echoes –
earlier aspects of the painting, other visual arrays: other paintings, as well

as sights in the external world. *Movement in Squares* (1961). The change
of aspect that furrows the surface in my perception of it causes me to
think and look back to the squares at the left of the painting; then
forward to how the furrow is created by successive decreases in their
width; then further forward to how the furrow flattens out through
successive increases in width. I see that the increases in width are
insufficient to deliver up squares again, but the rectangles are somehow
imminent with equilaterality, as if waiting to return to squares. It is,
perhaps, at this moment that I start to think of other visual arrays:
possibly a futurist painting that represents movement as a chain of
successive images, or a Quattrocento painting depicting a tiled pavement
disappearing into the distance. Then, in contrast to both, I see myself
looking not onto a surface marked out to carry movement but into a
mobile space that hovers *before* the surface. But is it possible to speak
of a 'surface' if I see only a mobile, tessellated space? Then the shifting
tiles are filaments attracted to a magnet, the sides of a concavity, a
sensation of almost falling then being caught, a vertical stairway, a
horizontal lattice, flashes of intense, coloured light, an image of
reflections on a curved surface, a dawning pinkish tint… And so it goes
on, building and dismantling an architecture before my eyes.

White Disks (1964). Noticing the change of aspect that delivers the
after-images described in the title, I might remember something singular
in the external world: 'Looking directly into the sun over a foreshore of
rocks exposed by the tide – all reduced to a violent black-and-white
contrast, interspersed, here and there, by the glitter of water.'[8] But, more
likely, I will think of something less specific, perhaps the experience of
looking from light into dark.

Song of Orpheus 5 (1978). Noticing the twisting streams of yellows
and pinks and greens, I might point in my mind's eye to a painting by
Rubens where the flesh is infused with these colours as they twine
through the composition.[9] But I will probably continue to summon up
comparisons to works by other artists who have painted fluid, luminous
substances. And I am much more likely first to think of elusive, shiny
effects delivered by the external world: 'the shine of hair, the shine of
skin, of certain fabrics, of leaves, of water, and many other things'.[10] For

                                                                JOHN ELDERFIELD

what will echo in the painting are thoughts of sensations, of remembered sensations, one opening onto the next. 'It's the recognition of the sensation *without* the actual incident which prompted it', Riley says.[11] ('Paint, not the object, but the effect it produces' is how Stéphane Mallarmé put it.)[12] And thus my thoughts of other paintings and my thoughts of the external world will be thoughts that intertwine, layer upon layer, to congeal into one changing representation.

They will also multiply at a rate that has some incalculable relationship to the rate of optical alteration of the painting. And since the optical alteration of the painting, being a subjective function, is itself the echo of a thought, my perception of the painting and my thoughts of, and caused by, the painting will be as one. The thoughts that are stirred up to echo in my sight will voice one over the other, the deeper internal imagery eventually rising to layer over and into the more immediate or the more superficial. Not despite but *because* the surface of the painting is pristine and illusory, a revisional intensity will accrue to it. The accumulated echoes and multiplying changes that roll over it may be used imaginatively to represent the dense, overdetermined layering of visual and therefore of psychic life.

What are thus represented in the painting cannot be said to be associations, precisely; they are, indeed, more properly recognitions, identifications discovered in the experience of the painting, not thoughts that stray. What echo in my sight are thoughts of sights already seen: the supervenient novelty is there, not because it is a surprise, but to stir into consciousness the epiphanies that have burst from ordinary moments and the memorable sights and sensations forgotten. The familiar revelation – 'It came to me' – of the creative process is thus gifted to the viewer. This is the surprise; as Czesław Miłosz explains: 'A thing is brought forth we didn't know we had in us, / so we blink our eyes…'[13]

Perception is the medium

Now that we have a preliminary account of an unprepared experience of Bridget Riley's paintings, and therefore a glimpse of some of the topics that lie ahead – the varied changes of aspect of the black-and-white and the coloured works, the collusions between the surprised viewer and the gently controlling artist, the thoughts echoing in sight – I want to explain the structure of what lies ahead.

This essay commemorates the first extensive presentation of Riley's paintings in a cultural institution in New York City since the notorious exhibition *The Responsive Eye* at the Museum of Modern Art in 1965.[14] This second section of the text therefore addresses her relationship to the New York School through her interpretation of the work of Jackson Pollock, which she has named (along with the work of Piet Mondrian) as critically important to the development of her black-and-white paintings.[15] The third section examines Riley's early black-and-white paintings of 1961 through 1964 as works composed around, and increasingly expressive of, the theme of disturbance, and the change to a more beneficent mood in the later works. The fourth and final section of the essay addresses the theme of substitutive distraction in the unfolding of her work in chromatic colour from 1967 through the Egyptian paintings of the early 1980s – an appropriate end for this exhibition since it is with these paintings that, in a dramatic change of aspect, Pollock finally was laid aside as a principal mentor of Riley.[16]

A popular biography of Pollock bears the subtitle *Energy Made Visible* (1972).[17] The implication is that something immaterial (energy) is made visible by becoming something material (paint). That was one interpretation of Pollock's art. An opposed interpretation would add to the chain that, then, something material (paint) becomes something immaterial (energy) when the painting, not merely the paint, is seen. This is, in a nutshell, the opposition of 'materiality' and 'opticality' in the critical reception of Pollock's paintings.[18]

The 'materiality' interpretation stresses, first, the density and tactility of the marked surface (especially when seen close-up) and, second, how the pictorial performance is thus mapped indexically upon the surface in routes to be followed empathetically by the viewer. In both of its emphases, this interpretation opens either backward, onto an affirmation of Pollock's (albeit unconventional) skill as a draughtsman, or

   JOHN ELDERFIELD

forward, onto the 'crisis of the easel picture' that produced Happenings, Minimalism, installation art and *l'informe* (formless), or in both directions simultaneously. Both emphases open onto an affirmation of process. However, the first emphasis affirms the process of making within an idea of the medium as synonymous with the material support, thus tends to look backward, and is an objective emphasis. In contrast, the second emphasis affirms the process of making within a consciousness of the mobile body in a spatial arena, thus tends to look forward, and is a subjective emphasis.

The historical consequence of a subjective view of Pollock's materiality is the end of easel painting. Yet, the subjective emphasis itself attaches to the 'opticality' interpretation of Pollock, whose main historical consequence is the amplification of easel painting, opening onto perceptual abstraction from colour-field painting to Op art. That interpretation also has two emphases. Its first opposes the first emphasis of the materiality interpretation, to posit an experience of the marked surface as of a suspended materiality (when not seen close up, and especially when seen at distance enough to capture the surface as a whole). Its second emphasis agrees with the second emphasis of the materiality interpretation, in recognising the performative presence of the painter, only it attributes to the performance the function not of creating a bodily record, but, rather, of packing the surface with the visual movement of intertwined, collaborating and competing, energies. In neither emphasis does this interpretation open onto the draughtsmanlike or the environmental understanding of process afforded by the materiality interpretation. In the opticality interpretation of Pollock, process is but the instrument for creating a perceived homogenous visual fabric, uninterrupted by incidents that require separate focus. Process is empathetically acknowledged through its traces, yet that acknowledgment is porous more to the viewer's visual performance, which it sponsors, than to the artist's material performance, which has become invisible because visually untraceable.

Riley says that, in her work, 'the pictorial object doesn't exist factually, in a way, but only in the performance of the painting by the viewer from a certain distance.'[19] In a way, the object of Minimalist and other post-easel art also doesn't exist factually, but has presence only in the varying images delivered up by the object owing to changes in the environment and in the spatial position of the viewer with respect to the object and to its environment. (Thus, Riley's subjective 'opticality' interpretation attaches to Minimalism's subjective version of the 'materiality' interpretation.) Yet, in another way, the object of Minimalism exists not only factually but also persistently so, in order to maintain the performance of the viewer whereas the object disappears in the performance of Riley's work. Of her work of the 1960s, Riley has said: 'I wanted the space between the picture plane and the spectator to be active. It was in that space, paradoxically, that the painting "took place".'[20] Again, this sounds like a Minimalist's statement: a spatial arena between object and viewer where the perceptual performance is enacted. Yet Riley does not say 'object'. She says 'picture plane'.

The picture plane. The rarity with which this term is now heard is a synecdoche of a huge cultural shift in art since Pollock. The term describes not the physical, literal surface of the canvas, or other support, but the elusive, nominally parallel plane, invented in the execution of a painting, which shapes the pictorial space in which the represented visual activity (abstract or figurative) takes place. The function of the picture plane is to disengage the visual activity from the flat, material support so as to spatialise the visual activity. (In the absence of a picture plane, a painting is merely an object on the literal surface of which a visual activity is to be seen.)

Riley, with her 'opticality' interpretation of Pollock (whose paintings she first experienced in a significant number in 1958),[21] noticed a shallower, more continuously, more evenly articulated picture plane than she had previously seen. (Later, she realised that Mondrian's last paintings offered a comparable experience.)[22] The classical modernist painters who, after her powerful but contradictory response to Pollock's paintings, became of particular interest to her – among them, Georges Seurat and the Futurists – would have aided an interpretation of Pollock not as energy made visible but as energy made from the visible. But the 'materiality' of her own early compositions would have resisted it.[23] The breakthrough did not come until 1961, under curious circumstances, but

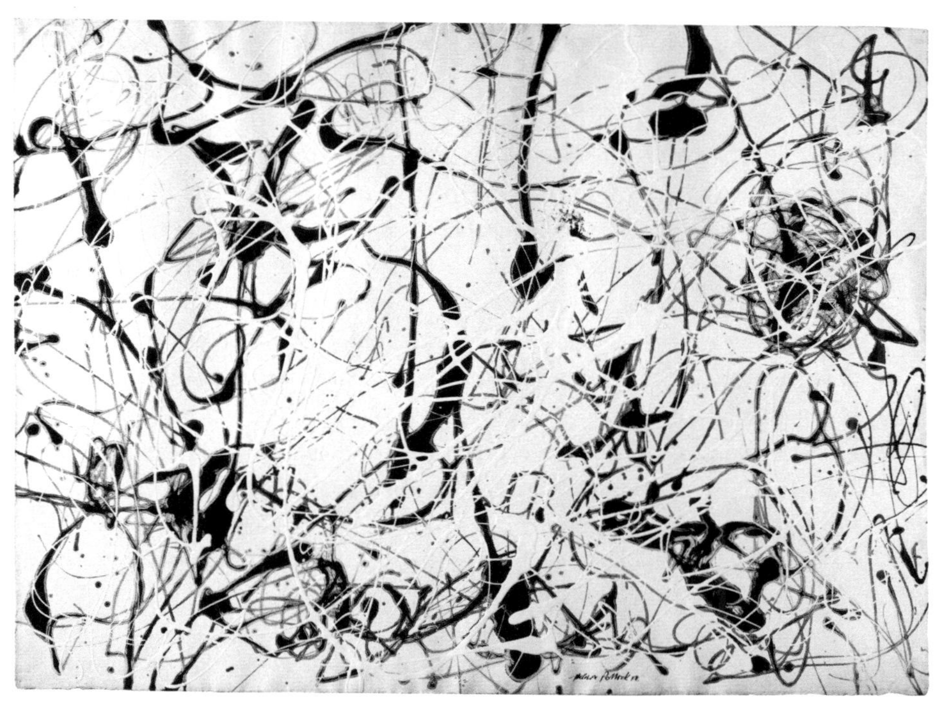

Jackson Pollock
Number 23 1948
Enamel on gesso on paper
57.5 × 78.4 cm | 22⅝ × 30⅞ in
Tate, London
© The Pollock-Krasner Foundation, ARS NY and DACS, London 2016

when it came it brought with it an emphatic rejection of materiality and, with it, of objecthood. A logical consequence of this, taken as a matter of course, was to remove her own physical presence from the creation of her finished paintings, using assistants instead. (As of the time of this writing, Riley herself has not painted one of her finished paintings for 40 years.)[24] This may seem extreme; but now, as she says, 'perception is the medium', not the canvas and the paint.[25]

'Perception is the medium' was a notion that took Riley into areas far from Pollock's. But Riley's use of the medium of visual perception concentrates on those components of it called forth by the following numbered attributes of Pollock's paintings, which became her own. These attributes belong to the work of both artists; their elaboration applies specifically to Riley's – but describes only the visual mechanics of her paintings, not their visual experience nor what the artist had in mind while making them.

I. *The drawn structure*. Drawn lines are particularly vulnerable to the uncertainties of immediate, precategorical perception, as is any drawn structure, one that exhibits contrasts of either value (the black-and-white scale) or hue (the chromatic scale) sufficient to create an effect of 'figure' and 'field'. This is because, in all visual perception, the fine registration of central, foveal vision cannot easily distinguish between occluding edges, inscribed lines, surface cracks and other surface discontinuities; the coarse registration of parafoveal and peripheral vision cannot easily distinguish between sharp and soft edges. Thus, a drawn structure is an excitingly uncertain one, immanent with possibilities to be revealed.[26]

II. *The repetitively drawn structure*. The uncertainties of a drawn structure increase when it is composed of similar, repeated elements that are neither so indistinguishable – because small and compacted – that they optically fuse, nor so easily distinguished – because large and isolated – that they remain separate. The visual tug of war between the fusion and the separation will quickly tire the eye, whose fatigue will manifest itself in a pulsation of the picture plane. The result will be induced movements that skim and flutter across painted boundaries –

lines or edges – as if the painting is forming, dissolving and reforming under our gaze. Technically, this loss to perception of surface materiality caused by units that 'assimilate' but do not blend into a total optical mixture is known as a shift from a 'surface' mode to a 'film' mode. The surface mode refers, obviously, to perception of a visual array attached to experience of the object on which it is represented. Perception in a film mode is detached from experience of the object: it will appear as frontal in a two-dimensional plane but extremely difficult to localise spatially.[27]

III. *The repetitively drawn, luminous structure*. Contours do not belong to visual experience, only to two-dimensional surfaces.[28] Conversely, light does not exist for the painter, Paul Cézanne is reputed to have said, meaning that the painter's pictorial means had to be used to create it.[29] Thus, lines drawn on two-dimensional surfaces have long been used not only, as contours, to create a resemblance of volume but also, as agents of contrast, to create a representation of light. The induced movement that occurs across lines as optical fusion approaches is proportionate in its velocity to the density of the lines. Beyond a certain velocity, the eye will be frustrated in its attempt to count and register the individual contrasts of figure and ground across the multiplied lines, as the flicker of continuous after-images further confuses the visual field. The resultant oscillation can register as transmitted light, even coloured light.[30]

IV. *The non-objective structure*. If the pictorial performance in the picture plane, being cast in the film mode, floats on or above the literal surface, this means that, conversely, the literal surface recedes behind the foreground of perception.[31] Either way, picture and object, the visual envelope and the literal surface, part company. Thus, there will be no objective, factual events, only subjective, perceived ones: not paint but chroma; not line but division; not shape but obstruction; not difference but distinction; not similarity but indistinctness… And there will be no 'as if' situations, only virtual ones: not an illusion of glowing, but a glowing…[32]

V. *The dense, non-objective structure*. The priority placed on density as a correlative of intensity – of so filling and packing the surface with incident that it bursts in a discharge of expansive light – is, perhaps, the most important of the lessons that Riley learned from Pollock. She has, therefore, spoken enthusiastically of Pollock's 'American space as being open space, shallow space, multifocal space', as opposed to 'centralised European space, the focally centred situation of the European tradition'.[33] But, unsurprisingly, in the nearest affinity the greatest diversity is found.

When Riley first saw Pollock's paintings, she found their alliance of pictorial density and emotional intensity 'shattering'; because it was created by means of a pictorial method that was carried by emotional intensity, it tended fatally toward what Dylan Thomas called 'stigmata on paper'. But the alliance, if sustained by a clear head and workmanlike approach, also pointed toward exhilaratingly extreme possibilities.[34]

The extremism of Pollock's paintings was, for Riley, not simply a matter of their radical pictorial features, but also how their multifocal space afforded a radical pictorial illustration, almost, of the 'lack of a centre' that, in the absence of traditional beliefs, had long been an ethical aspect of classical modernist paintings. In a period that was opening at long last to a postwar optimism, an acknowledgment of loss of certainties seemed not pessimistic but enabling. 'In losing this focus,' she said later, 'we find ourselves moving in a new range of experience, open to things that were previously less accessible.'[35] 'Losing this focus' is not merely a metaphor when composed with a multifocal Pollock painting in mind. His renunciation of appearances and pictorial convention surrendered the old view of nature only to broach, with a new method, a previously unreachable alternative. An idealism is attached to a technique, as Riley points out: 'Our bearings still suffer from the concept or suppositions of Renaissance theory, which is "man as the measure of all things". But man is only a part of a bigger whole and this whole is neither centripetal nor centrifugal. It is much more open and egalitarian.'[36] Riley's art, we need hardly remind ourselves, emerged contemporaneously with the democratic libertarianism of the 1960s.

It would, I think, be wrong to read the foregoing statement with the gendered emphasis that it allows. Nevertheless, it is impossible not to be aware of this option, which produces a 'feminine' interpretation, written by a younger female painter, of the work of an older male painter, well known for 'masculine paintings'.[37] But her reference to Renaissance theory surely means that she was thinking of how nature might be represented outside an inherited culture, and Pollock's defiant 'I am nature' surely fostered her own rebellion.[38] Still, she was working not simply against Renaissance Europe and toward Pollock's North America. Her (feminine) 'opticality' interpretation of Pollock may be thought a defence of the modernist Europe of perceptual painting against an increasingly popular (masculine) 'materiality' interpretation that, for all its novelty, attaches to an older valorisation of the presence of the corporeal.

Nonetheless, as observed earlier, the two interpretations share a common subjectivity. Riley has, indeed, recognised that the materiality interpretation of Pollock's art that was manifested in Happenings had an affinity with what she was doing: precipitating a disturbance that was latent in a sociological or psychological situation, whereas her work was precipitating a disturbance in a visual situation. 'I identify with this "event"', she said.[39] Dislocation is truly basic. Her paintings represent breakup making reassembly possible. A disturbance is repaired in a visual evolution staged for the viewer: 'the cyclic movement of repose, disturbance and repose' resulted in the 'original situation', the repose, being restated.

Yet the disturbance itself had to have 'a quality of inevitability', she said. 'There should, that is to say, be something akin to a sense of recognition within the work, so that the spectator experiences at one and the same time something known and something unknown.' It was of this splitting, this coexistence of two attitudes persisting side by side without influencing each other, that she said, 'I identify with this "event"'. In this 'event', something known, a rational periodic structure, is elaborated until it seems to go irrationally out of control, then recovers — providing that the disturbance doesn't 'go too far and actually break the space.'[40] The classical Freudian view of the unconscious as separated off from the field of consciousness by the action of repression was a development of this old idea of splitting (*Spaltung*).[41] Riley's version also presumes discrete known and unknown worlds. The 'disturbance' that brings them together is a performance, constantly replayed in the picture plane, of the imagined incursion, then victorious confinement, of irrational representations that threaten to break the envelope separating known and unknown.

Pollock's lesson that density is a correlative of intensity meant, in Riley's interpretation, that the increase in density of a periodic structure – to the point of almost breaking the spatial envelope – could be used to represent an increase in intensity to the point of almost provoking unpleasure, and, therefore, requiring 'repression' by turning such unpleasure away. In the open, multifocal space, this disturbance of desire will attract focalisation, only to refuse focalisation; this area of optical disturbance will be the most blinding, for the flickering intermittencies are the means of 'losing this focus' and opening onto the unknown.

Disruption: black and white

In 1967, Anton Ehrenzweig, a friend and supporter of the artist, offered a historical account of a work of art that was built around a change of aspect:

> The third (slow) movement of [Beethoven's] *Hammerklavier Sonata* (1817–18) still startles me by a sudden twist that breaks into the broad beautiful cantilena and produces a melodic as well as a harmonic rupture. The notebooks tell us that it was not the broad adagio theme but this abrupt transition which Beethoven first noted down. How strange: a transition between melodies not yet existing! The melodies themselves unfolded later from this rupture between them… Here we have a good example of an inarticulate disruptive idea which guides and unfolds the large-scale structures.[42]

Riley's early black-and-white paintings, from 1961 through 1964, may similarly be thought to be compositions guided by the wish to accommodate a change of aspect, and the artist has been very frank about the biographical source of an 'inarticulate disruptive idea' in the period of personal and artistic crisis from which these paintings emerged.

                                             JOHN ELDERFIELD

Angry and hurt at the end of an affair with an older male mentor, she thought: 'I can't communicate verbally with you… but I'll paint you a message so loud and clear you'll know exactly how I feel.'[43] She wanted to make 'an extreme statement, of something violent, something that definitely did disturb… to say: *that there were absolutes*; that one could not pretend that black was white… to make a deliberate statement, to make a thing that put itself into hazard by some aspect of its own nature'.[44] She continued, 'And that was the beginning of the black-and-white paintings. People at the time thought, and some people still seem to think, that they were paintings having to do with optical experiment… really they were an attempt to say something about stabilities and instabilities, certainties and uncertainties.'[45]

Later, that same mentor tactlessly asked her if her work had any relationship to Futurist art, which they had seen together, where elements evoke 'states of feeling or states of mind'. She replied: 'Yes, it is a question of substitution.'[46]

All of Riley's black-and-white paintings are based on choosing a compositional unit that is a known, primary form; on displaying it in sufficient number for it to read as a stable, unifying element in the picture plane; and on showing its periodic transformation to the point of creating an unstable disturbance in the unity of the plane. She used two sorts of compositional units: *molecular* and *striated*. (In the vocabulary of painting, they are a mark and a stroke; in drawing, a point and a line; in nature, a grain and a filament.)

The earliest molecular structures were tessellated, their units arranged contiguously in grid-like tiles. In 1961–62, they comprised interlocking rectangles with one variable dimension (as in *Movement in Squares*); in 1963–64, triangles in 'point movement' with their bases aligned (as in *Shiver* of 1964), at least one (in 1964) in tonally graduated forms.[47] The compositions of rectangles seem to have been short-lived because they prioritise a monodirectional reading along the axis where the dimensions of the rectangles alter. The compositions of triangles encouraged two readings, afforded by the periodic transformation of two of their sides, and, additionally, proved capable of generating some curving movement as the apexes of the triangles sequentially change direction. A potential of all tessellated structures is that, because their compositional units are contiguous, they readily form continually reversible fields. (What may look, at first, like white ground will reverse to become white figure on black ground, and so on.) For Riley, risking but just pulling back from reversibility was (like risking but just pulling back from optical fusion) a way of precipitating a disturbance almost, but not quite, to the point of breaking the unity of the visual field.

In works like the aptly named *Shiver* – and similar highly, more-or-less evenly packed structures of black-and-white triangular units of more-or-less similar size – this brinkmanship creates an all-over disturbance. The result is a highly, even alarmingly mobile visual field, charged in its entirety and containing individual blurring drifts and tremors according to the density of the packing in any area. This is what Riley had come to want of her black-and-white paintings: more than just the progressive, directional phasing of a single unit, a whole *field* in cyclical movement. The liability, though, is that such a field, thus composed, may be pushed over into reversibility by the will of the viewer. If this happens, it induces the illusion of a pattern of toothed or indented volumes – and illusionism, in the sense of conjuring up a *trompe l'oeil* material presence, was something that Riley did not want.[48] She did want certainties and uncertainties, but she also wanted to say that *there were absolutes…*

Thus, *non-tessellated* molecular structures gained in prominence in the form of paintings with disks: in 1962–67, in tonally graduated forms or transforming into ovals, or both together (as in *Pause*, 1964); in 1964, with induced after-images (*White Disks*) and in the form of open ovals thickened into circles on their peripheries (*Disturbance*); in 1966, with miniaturised ovals (like *Static 2*); in 1966–67, with tonally graduated disks and ovals on a coloured grey ground (as in *Deny 2*, 1967).

Whereas tessellated molecular structures are, potentially, continually reversible, non-tessellated molecular structures are not. The vitality of the former is owing to the continuing optical vibration of figure and ground

　　　　　　　　　　　　　　　　　　　　　　　　JOHN ELDERFIELD

contiguously bonded as a single visual fabric. In the latter, figure and ground are not contiguously bonded; they are mutually reinforcing.

A drama plays out. The negative ground of *Pause* is not a surface because it reads in the film mode. The positive disks are figures on a ground, and read in the surface mode. As the disks periodically change shape or tonality, they mould the surface. The intangible ground has to follow the shape of the mould, and the disks therefore are carried on its film. In other paintings, when the disks are made to induce white after-images, or transform into ovals, or the ovals are miniaturised, they further confuse the distinctions of figure and ground, of surface and film modes, and the means of the medium are enriched. And when disks, the most efficient molecular containers of visual energy, transform into ovals to mould the surface, what they surrender in density they can gain in directionality, curving folds in a visual fabric that moves in the eyes – perhaps in waves like shifting sand, or in the fluttering movement of dotted transparent gauze, or in a sensation that prickles the eyes as by heat or as in awakening.[49]

The disk paintings would later lead to the introduction of colour into Riley's work, as will be discussed in the following section. Before this happened, however, Riley would develop her striated black-and-white paintings to compose her most optically aggressive works. In 1961, Riley adapted the contraction-expansion principle of *Movement in Squares* to compositions of black-and-white bands of varying widths. In 1963, and again in 1966 (as in *Breathe*), she experimented with bands in the form of attenuated triangles. The unquestionable connection of these works to the tessellated compositions with triangles alerts us to the fact that the compositional units of the striated works are likewise contiguous and, therefore, potentially may form continually reversible fields. Only they are not fully tessellated works because the intervals between the units may be adjusted at will. Therefore, these works may combine features of tessellated and non-tessellated compositions. This potential was not yet to be developed. Instead, in 1963, Riley took her striated, banded paintings in two directions. The first began with the shaped, usually circular paintings of concentric bands, varying in width to produce effects of contraction and expansion. In some works, the circumfluence of a set of bands is abruptly shifted off course, then repositioned, as if in a gear change, in a larger or smaller circuit. This approach led into the circular images composed of zigzag bands of 1964–65. (The second direction was into the curved, banded paintings of 1963–67, which I shall discuss in the next section because it moved into colour.)

The zigzag-banded paintings are high-impact works, most especially those comprising concentric circles, such as *Blaze 1* of 1964, for in them the eye meets its own mirror. 'It is idiomatic,' Ehrenzweig wrote, '…to speak of our eyes "devouring" something. Here the reverse happens, our eyes are attacked and "devoured" by the paintings.'[50] He continues to say that a 'voluptuous moment' of warmth and sharpened awareness follows, yet his words still make the paintings sound like Sigmund Freud's famous drawing of the dream of the wolves.[51] This opens them to interpretation as 'replications': events whose status is conferred upon them by *Nachträglichkeit*, or delayed activation, of originally unconsidered historical events whose meanings are retrospectively created in their replication.[52] But what, then, do they replicate?

Four things, I think. First, the powerful experience of the 'real' – long sought by Western painting to the extent that, as Michael Fried puts it, the definitive realist painting would offer so powerful an experience that the viewer could not bear to look at it, but nor could he bear not to see it.[53] The prototype in this image bank is the 'Medusan' shield, of which Riley's blazing tondos are distant replications.[54] The second replication in Riley's paintings is of the aggressiveness of the classical modernist tradition. Since it was said of Edouard Manet that 'his sharp and irritating colour pierces the eye like a steel saw', modernist paintings frequently have been optically disturbing to the extent that they have set out to perform a repudiatory, destructive operation on some aspect of the past.[55] In this respect, they are 'sadistic', as Georges Bataille has it.[56] But Bataille also refers to something slightly different when he speaks (in words that recall Riley's paintings, too) of Joan Miró's disintegration of reality into *poussière ensoleillée* (sun-shot dust) as if ETA Hoffmann's Sandman had cast moving grains of sand into the field of vision. Bataille is also speaking of a destructive operation done on quotidian reality; this is the third replication of an antimaterialist, optical art like Riley's: a destruction that results in an animation and is, for that reason, 'uncanny' – disconcerting, because what is thought to be inanimate appears to be alive. This attaches to the fourth replication, that nature itself will perform such an operation in moments of epiphany: 'People would be very shocked indeed,' Riley observes, 'if the world itself was as dead in its appearance as they seem to expect a painting to be.'[57] Painting should be enlivening.

These intertwined replications twine also with what we have learned about a 'disturbance' in a painting by Riley: how its splitting of known and unknown prevents the splitting of the division between them; a violence that provokes but ultimately prevents unpleasure. A painting juxtaposes the certain and uncertain to uncover a vulnerability: to 'make a thing that put[s] itself into hazard by some aspect of its own nature'.[58]

It was in Riley's paintings of 1964 that 'disruption' was most completely, clearly articulated. That was also the only year in which she used the full compositional range of her black-and-white paintings – tessellations, disks, curves, bands and zigzags, plus shaped formats – as if testing them all for the amount of optical energy that they would produce. Unfortunately, it was the violence that was noticed, in the main, and not the vulnerability, when Riley was suddenly famous in 1965 as a result of her participation in the *Responsive Eye* exhibition and the concurrent plagiarism of her work by fashion designers.[59] Then, in 1966–67, a new sort of disruption occurred.

Deny, the title of Riley's disk paintings of 1966–67, refers to the denial of black and white. They deploy cool bluish ovals on a warm reddish ground or vice versa, and make use of a very simple principle of colour juxtaposition: the more similar the tonal values, the more visible the colours; the more different the tonal values, the less visible the colours. This bare fact tells us nothing about the actual experience of denial in the pattering through the mist of these more enigmatic and more generous paintings than any before them. Nor does even a detailed analysis of the carefully calibrated use of tonal values for the ovals qualify both the sense of dispersal and attraction afforded by their axis-changes and the degree of their mutuality with the ground.[60] But such information does tell us that the artist – having slowly expanded her range from the absolute opposition of black and white to the increasing use of tonal gradations has now infused the tonalities with colour and thus created a new opposition: colour and tone. The pictorial sensation, we see, still occurs in the space between the picture plane and the viewer, only the picture does not so press itself on us; there is a new responsiveness to it. Looking ahead, the Deny paintings seem more an end than a new beginning; no more disk paintings would be made. Yet, there is a breaking free in their buoyant loveliness, and the recognition of that sensation is of movement in the natural world.

Distraction: colour

The change of aspect and the pleasures of sight both take you by surprise. 'They are sudden, swift and unexpected', we have heard the artist say. To this she adds: 'If one tries to prolong them, recapture them, or bring them about wilfully, their purity and freshness [are] lost.'[61] Yet one can learn how to be open to the surprise, and Riley has spoken of how that learning was provided to her. As a child, she lived with her mother, younger sister and aunt in a primitive cottage in Cornwall; her father was a prisoner of war of the Japanese on the infamous Siamese railway, and was heard from only three times in three years. Her mother would take Bridget and her sister on walks in a varied landscape and point to the visual sensations of things – the colours, the illumination, the elusive transitions – encouraging them to notice surprising effects.[62] To do this most efficiently seemed to require a kind of collaboration between the suddenly visible effect and a visual receptivity alert enough to capture it.

This childhood experience was important and determining. In an essay entitled 'The Pleasures of Sight', written in 1984, she was able, amazingly, to recount in detail some dozen specific visual pleasures captured 40 years earlier. In the same text, she spoke of how such experiences led eventually to the realisation that the objects of the visible world were agents of a greater reality of visual sensations that she 'was painting in order to "make visible".'[63] Looking for unusual visual sensations was also a distraction from the anxieties of childhood – in particular, from the absence of her father. And that interpretation of the sudden visual pleasure – as a distraction – is one that remains. Her conception of painting as making visible the sensations remembered as exceptional includes the idea of a distraction from quotidian reality. And it stretches to the further idea that the representation of a distraction is beneficent, a way of restoring to sight what is exceptional.[64]

Distraction is a drawing asunder, a drawing of the sight, mind, or attention to a *different* object. It is not only a looking at something or for something, but also a looking away from something, at something else. In this respect, it is destructive and, as such, has its affect: a drawing asunder, a pulling away, implies strong agitation arising from conflicting emotions or loyalties. Originally, the act of distraction had been a representation of an enforced separation, and that representation had been repeated, with an exaggerated agitation, in the discovery of Riley's artistic identity. The result was an optical art that pulverised materiality for the sake of a destruction that results in an animation. The brilliantly simple proposal was: isn't that precisely what distraction is – a destruction of one object that results in an animation of the object that replaces it? Art is 'a question of substitution', we have heard Riley say. In the mid 1970s, absorbed in reading Marcel Proust, she discovered a fuller motto: 'You can make a new version of what you love only by first renouncing it.'[65] A technique of pictorial (and literary) composition – erasing the favourite part – translates into an ethic of working through attachments.

Distraction often seems to be a movement of attention not from one object to another but from subjectivity to external reality. Thus, its agitation becomes the vehicle of a pulling away from self-absorption, a relief from its excess of feeling that takes one out of oneself. Riley's paintings have, therefore, sometimes been thought cold. But the motto from Proust accompanies, and amplifies, one from Cézanne: 'One has to sacrifice what one feels – you understand, it is enough that one feels – One never loses this, one's feeling…'.[66]

After Riley's valedictory Deny paintings, the new beginning came out of the sequences of paintings of curving bands. Before 1967, these had passed through two principal stages: in 1963–64, equidistantly spaced, black-and-white bands bent into serpentine curves of successive tightness and hence increasing optical frequency and hence oscillation (as in *Crest* of 1964); in 1965–66, undulating bands of warm and cool greys whose sequentially graduated widths both vary the speed of the bands and produce a pattern of 'crests' and 'hollows' at a diagonal angle to the direction of the bands (as in *Arrest 2* of 1965).

As discussed earlier, the band paintings could potentially form continually reversible fields, like the tessellated molecular paintings, if figure and ground (the black-and-white bands) were kept equal in emphasis. Works like *Crest* (1964) play a similar game of brinkmanship with this possibility, just as *Shiver* did. Alternatively, the intervals between the bands could be adjusted to separate figure and ground. If this happened, as it did in *Arrest 2* and similar paintings, the effect approximated that of the non-tessellated molecular paintings, the disks. Thus, the later curve paintings occupied a similar territory to the disks, and were able to pick up from the last disks, the Deny paintings, that, in the separation of figure and ground, colour could shine.

Riley began to develop the Deny principle of colour-tone opposition. The title of the astonishing Cataract series of 1967–68 nicely conflates cause and effect as apprehended in their viewing: an overwhelming liquid flow; a resultant opacity in its perception. In *Cataract 3* of 1967, each curved band is now a pair of greys, one infused with turquoise, one with red. At the top and bottom of the painting, the turquoise and red fuse in a mutual grey; at the centre, they separate. Reading either up or down, the two emerge from tone as colour only to disappear from colour into tone. Meanwhile, a torrent of induced diagonals confuses the scene, as the convention for lashing rain does in a print by Utagawa Hiroshige. And then, the final, most unexpected thing happens: the colour of the colour-tone bands seems to seep out into the white intervals between them, which glow with the irradiated hues like wet pavements.[67]

First, in 1963–64 works like *Crest*, it seemed that the bands were lines clattering against one another like sounding strings. Then, in 1965–66

JOHN ELDERFIELD

works like *Arrest 2*, it seemed that the bands were agents for carrying tone and even colour. But, finally, it became clear in the Cataract series that it was the long edges of the bands that mattered. The most productive of the molecular structures were the disks, but disks gathered and contained visual energy. The long, sharp edges of bands released energy as they cut into and moulded the ambient space. Once this was understood, as it was even in 1967, the grey envelope could be abandoned and paintings of pure colours immediately followed – paintings of the expanded size that the spread of colour seemed to require.

Colour simplified to black and white had required formal complexity. Conversely, the elaboration of colour required formal simplicity, and the most neutral of all vehicles, repeated bands, not only could carry a multiplicity of colours but also provided a doubled multiplicity of edges. Very soon, the pattern was set, for what would be almost a decade of work, using three colours plus white: on a conventional chromatic triangle, two nearly opposite colours and a colour adjacent to one of them – magenta and olive with turquoise in *Orient 4* of 1970; red and green with blue (the most frequently used combination) in *Pæan* of 1973. The two nearly opposite colours vibrate at a high-intensity, simultaneous contrast as they shift mutually in space; the colour adjacent to one of them destabilises their equality to release the colour sensation and let it spread into the white field.[68] Moreover, the inhibition of the colour within the edges of the bands causes it to interact with the colour of adjoining bands and spill into the noncolour of adjoining white space. The simultaneous contrasts of adjoining colours, which under other circumstances would increase their colour differences (enhancing contrast along the edge of each colour toward its complementary), are simply overwhelmed by the flood of induced colour-showing how colour that spreads, or assimilates, can tinge with its hue an area wider than can be affected by interacting colour contrasts. On the one hand, there is the actual, literal colour of the bands; on the other, the actual, visual experience of colour, formed mainly by assimilation. The viewer cannot know the colour of the bands except through the visual experience of the colour, which is an experience, however, not actually of colour but of coloured light.

The cognitive challenge is amplified in *Orient 4*, because the painting immediately engages the viewer in an uncertainty as to whether he is seeing a magenta-olive or magenta-turquoise opposition – before the awareness dawns that the visual sensation was always of the magenta-olive opposition *destabilised* by turquoise to flood a delicately shifting illumination in the field of attenuated zigzags. (The brain always seems to be sluggishly catching up with the eye in Riley's coloured paintings.) The placement of the three-coloured bands in alternating steep diagonals both builds an expanding graphic movement to open the visual field and creates long, tapering points that cannot possibly protect themselves or their white noncolouration from the influence of their chromatic neighbours. But it is the 'crossovers' within each band – the crossing of one coloured line diagonally over the other two – that modulates the tint of the coloured light travelling in horizontal zones across the painting. (Remarkably, it was at this point only four years since the compositionally similar *Breathe* of 1966.)

These 'crossovers' will eventually lead to 'twists' of colour in the latter part of the period of curve paintings of 1974–81, but only after a group of paintings of parallel bands that includes *Pæan*. Before the crossovers, the first pure colour paintings (such as *Late Morning* of 1967–68) had been in a parallel-band format. And, after the curve paintings, Riley was to return to that format, in the Egyptian paintings of 1981–84. Thus, the development of her colour paintings may be said to reveal an alternation between the two formats. It would be misleading, though, to look to the graphic format for the development that takes place in Riley's paintings, especially in her colour paintings. *Pæan*, then, is continuous with *Orient 4* in seeking to shape the light that filters around the colour bands. It is discontinuous not because the bands are now parallel verticals. Rather, they have *become* parallel verticals because, this way, light can be shaped around the bands while the bands can be composed in blocks according to their perceptual presence. A paean, a hymn of joy or praise, was originally addressed (its etymology indicates) to Apollo, as one who *strikes* blows in order to heal. In Riley's painting, the light gains momentum through the visual field by striking against the composed verticals, in an only apparently random way, and the space expands in the centre to contract at the edges, as if a beneficent breath has gone through the painting. This is discontinuous with what preceded it. On the one hand, the colour sensation is more free and 'painterly' than before; on the other, it is ordered by the substance and rigour of the graphic composition.[69]

Discussing the lesson of *Pæan*, the artist has said: 'You can see in Matisse just how essential drawing is if one is going to be involved in colour.'[70] It is not the relationship of vertical and curved graphic formats that shapes the development of these paintings, but the relationship of drawing and colour; the desire actually to draw in (with the sensation of) colour.

The change that next occurred from columns to curves was a change in the drawing of colour from the straight line to the arabesque. Yet Riley develops her arabesque around a fictive vertical that passes through it – determining a direction by its opposite – as Matisse did, and said that Ingres did. Matisse called it composing with 'the draughtsman's compass.'[71]

Thus, while coloured light passes in lateral arabesque waves in the columnar paintings, fictive straight lines pass through the curve paintings. In *Entice 2* of 1974, it is hard to believe that the steep diagonals are fictive, but, indeed, drawing has now been induced as well as colour. The diagonals momentarily form troughs to carry the colour sensations in an oblique direction to that of the bands. In *Cataract 3*, from 1967, the diagonals were bands that turned in concert to pick up a reflected light. Now they are ungraspable edges that draw down the light – draw it away, out of the colour, almost: the light spiralling down the channels; the colour slumbering down the width of the picture plane.

Riley is continuing to use the format of red, green and blue; only she has separated (and joined) with grey instead of white every third pairing selected from these colours. Since grey is more sensitive to colour interaction than any other colour, it absorbs its neighbouring colours like a sponge as together they twist and narrow, then swell and flatten, to create the elusive, lambent enticement. The next step was to enlarge even further the colour activity by surrendering the white to all-grey intervals. The next was to tint the grey with colour – and the next was to replace the grey with two colours. (This reprises the move into colour in the first place: from the tinted grey of the Deny paintings to the turquoise and red that replaced grey in the Cataract paintings.)

Such momentous, complicating changes in colour composition required a response if they were not to get out of control. Therefore, once the pale-tinted greys appeared, the chromatic colours were lightened to balance, and the vividness of contrasting complementary colours was surrendered for the dominance of the midtone into which colours would assimilate, even to the point of dissolving. At the same time, the drawing was adjusted lest the unifying grey become too dominant. The acute, almost severing diagonals in *Entice 2* may perhaps have recalled the crossovers in the diagonals of *Orient 4* and similar works. In any event, Riley began to 'twist' her three colours along the rise and fall of each curving band; their juxtapositions, both within the band and with respect to the grey ground, change continually, to throw off varied sensations that modulate the whole field. When, finally, the grey was replaced, in the Song of Orpheus series of 1978, by a two-colour twist, to accompany the three-colour twist, the result was a five-colour field – violet, blue, green, yellow and pink – of continually twisted curves, so fleeting and elusive that their drawn order is an almost unnoticed vehicle.

This is Pollock territory, as Riley acknowledges, while stipulating: 'It's almost the opposite approach. The unexpected thing in his free structure is the immense control, whereas the unexpected thing in my controlled structure is the free play of visual forces. In effect, my formal scaffolding is buried to such an extent that it becomes subservient to the "action" of the colour.'[72] But it is also earlier territory. It is impossible, in fact, not to wonder whether the idea of 'twists' of colour drifted in from the *peinture optique* of the nineteenth century, from Michel-Eugène Chevreul's discussion of weaving with coloured threads or from musing on the literal meaning of *l'enchaînement*, Delacroix's term for the mutual dependence of all colours, which signifies not only concatenation but also interlacing.[73] A painting such as *Song of Orpheus 5* (1978) makes highly sophisticated use of this and Delacroix's other three cardinal

JOHN ELDERFIELD

principles of colour painting: the importance of the midtone, the complementary structure of colour and the perceptual induction of colour. Most surprising, and part of the reason that colour rolls so freely and profusely in this painting, is Riley's address to the complementary structure of colour. She has forgone the simultaneous contrast of complementary colours and, instead, has miraculously induced the missing complementaries from the visual fusion of the colours actually present. (Hence, the painted blue and green evoke a turquoise complementary to the painted pink; the painted pink and violet evoke a magenta complementary to the painted green, and so on.)[74] Although the actual mechanics are not in the experience of the painting, their breathtaking sophistication surely is.

The year she made this painting, she explained its mechanics to her friend Robert Kudielka, whose own analyses of her art have been its most constant and illuminating critical companion. She said: 'I am getting into an area of such delicacy and refinement that I feel I cannot be right. I adjust and adjust and the whole thing is poised so precisely that I fear it is too vulnerable, too rare an endeavour to be healthy. I need something more robust, something stronger.'[75]

Riley's vertically banded Egyptian paintings of 1981–84 take their generic name from their deployment of five colours – brick red, ochre-yellow, blue, turquoise and yellow-green – which Riley remembered from tomb paintings she saw in Egypt in 1979–80. Her revelation in the tombs at Luxor had been twofold: at their 'painted-in' architecture that produced firm walls, and at their particular palette of colour, forged in the sun, that seemed to embody the brilliant North-African light.[76] Consequently, there was a twofold change brought by the Egyptian paintings: first, a new strength and robustness gained by building them as walls instead of fields; and, second, a new sense of the particularity of the individual colours in the all-over illumination. Flat, upright constructions of groups or blocks of colour bands therefore replaced the ethereal all-over organisation of the twists. Using broader bands than before meant that the local colour of the bands was noticed as never before; it was like putting a magnifying glass on an earlier stripe painting, the artist has said recently. Oil paint used for the first time instead of acrylic added intensity and saturation to the colour. And a highly restricted palette dominated by two pairs of contrasting colours allowed, at one and the same time, continually echoing and rebounding colour interactions, and a continual reminder of the brilliance and separateness of the individual hues.

The temptation should be resisted, though, to think that Riley was leaving Pollock territory for Barnett Newman territory. In the Egyptian paintings, she develops the painterly freedom of her earlier vertical-band paintings, such as *Pæan*, by building from the colour sensations themselves. And she renews, with a greater urgency, the search for space in the interaction of colour, which search takes her into the territory of Cézanne.[77]

Works such as *Pæan* had offered the sensation of a large, single, layered space of varying depth. The aim now was, to use Cézanne's term, the *modulation* of space, the building of space from (narrow) planes of colour. Or, more precisely, it was to modulate the planes of colour so that the viewer could build the space for himself. Instead of the artist proffering a space for the viewer to explore, the viewer is asked to construct a space in his perceptual performance from the planked wall of colours the artist has built.

The early paintings in the series, among them *Après Midi* of 1981 and *Serenissima* of 1982, do not yet include the fifth Egyptian colour, yellow-green. They build from the juxtaposition and separation of the red-turquoise and yellow-blue complementaries a sensation of strands of colour advancing and receding within a pearly light. Only a few years earlier, Riley had spoken of not liking to work only with complementary contrasts, preferring an uneven number of colours, so as to be able to add a neighbouring colour that will break the locking of contrasts and release the colour energy.[78] In the early Egyptian paintings, the unlocking is achieved, instead, by the introduction of air and space (i.e. white) and a rhythmic structure (i.e. black).[79] Neither the black nor the white is intrinsic to the chromatic activity itself. The black verticals space the surface like bar lines to control the rhythmic movement of the colour. The whites are breathing spaces, like those in some of Cézanne's canvases, for the colour planes to have room enough to shift about in

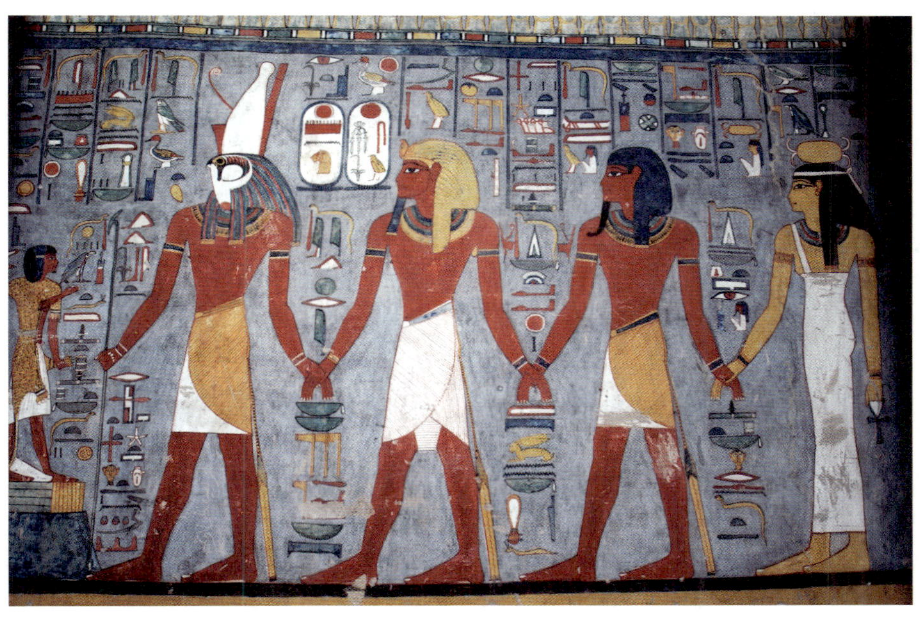

Wall painting, New Kingdom, 19th Dynasty, c.1290 BC
Tomb of Ramesses 1, Valley of the Kings, Thebes

space. In the main, then, the black bands are a function of the surface, therefore of flatness, while the white bands are a function of space, therefore of depth. Only they will switch functions in the time of the viewing, the whites advancing and the blacks falling back. Consequently, when the black bands were eliminated in 1983, in such works as *Bali*, the white bands were unlocked to respond more actively to the chromatic colours. These had lightened so remarkably, because no longer subject to assimilation by black, that the fifth Egyptian colour, yellow-green, was added. A colour outside the pairs of complementaries, like black, but, like them, a chromatic colour, it could act almost like black in orchestrating the chromatic activity while actually participating in that activity. The colours, no longer anchored in shallow space by the black bars floating on the surface, swim at different spatial depths, forward and backward, in the duration of the viewing.

The daring but logical next step was to chromatise the white – although this would open the way to overturning the limits of Riley's Egyptian palette – by replacing it with lilac in 1984, in such works as *Samarra*. This lilac had somehow always been implicit in the series of paintings, induced by them but awaiting its realisation. As a result, the painting solely, dangerously, comprises three pairs of complementaries. Thus, more weight than ever before is placed on the actual chromatic composition. Just as perceptual activity takes place in opposition to the graphic field, so the freedom of the colour composition takes place in opposition to the stability of the complementary contrasts. The relationship of actual and induced colour in Riley's paintings is now matched by that between the actual chromatic quality of colour, on the one hand, and the spatial and other attendant qualities that colour can induce, on the other. In consequence, the perceptual is flooded more deeply with affective sensations than ever before, with a myriad of recognitions of sensations, one breaking over the next. A *peinture optique* is a *peinture optique, sensuelle*.

Wonderfully peculiar colours swim in spatial depths, infused with light to form one pulsing pneumatic envelope. The resultant woozy sensation is a reminder that this surprising interpretation of Cézanne is via Matisse, who claimed that his own drawing was 'like the breathing of the sea.'[80]

JOHN ELDERFIELD

But Cézanne's voice comes insistently through: 'Everything we see is dispersed and disappears. Nature is always the same, but nothing remains of it, nothing of what we see. Our art should give to nature the thrill of continuance with the appearance of all its changes. It should enable us to feel nature as eternal.'[81]

This is not the end. Between *Samarra* and the date of this exhibition, there are 15 years of paintings and, now, wall drawings, most recently the wall drawing in this exhibition, *Composition with Circles 2* (2000). It is new in the slowly unfolded complexity of its transparency; it looks back to the black-and-white work begun almost 40 years earlier; it asks the old questions again:

> The change of aspect. 'But surely you would say that the picture is altogether different now!'
>
> But what is different: my impression? my point of view? – Can I say? I *describe* the alteration like a perception; quite as if the object had altered before my eyes.
>
> 'Now I am seeing *this*', I might say (pointing to another picture, for example). This has the form of a report on a new perception.
>
> The expression of a change of aspect is the expression of a *new* perception and at the same time of the perception's being unchanged.[82]

Lynne Cooke and Karen Kelly (eds), *Bridget Riley: Reconnaissance*, Dia Center for the Arts, New York, NY, 2000, pp.11–43.

Note: This essay benefited from my conversations with Bridget Riley, who also read the penultimate version, offering useful suggestions, as did Jeanne Collins, Lynne Cooke and John Golding.

1   TS Eliot, 'Tradition and the Individual Talent', in *The Sacred Wood* (1920), Methuen, New York, NY, 1960, p.50.

2   Ludwig Wittgenstein, *Philosophical Investigations*, GEM Anscombe (trans), Prentice Hall, Englewood Cliffs, NJ, 1958, pp.196–98, 212, for the quotations that follow. This subject, 'the change of aspect', weaves through part 2, section 11 of the *Investigations*.

3   Bridget Riley, 'The Pleasures of Sight' (1984), in Robert Kudielka (ed), *The Eye's Mind: Bridget Riley, Collected Writings 1965–1999*, Thames & Hudson, London, 1999, p.32.

4   Except in first-person descriptions, 'the viewer' of Riley's paintings is spoken of here as male in order to avoid confusion between the viewer and the artist. In this and subsequent sections, I have drawn opportunistically on the vast literature on the psychology and neurology of visual perception. Since I am not qualified to cite from this material in a way that accurately reflects the authorship of individual discoveries, I have provided individual notes only to add or to direct the reader to necessary supplementary material. Readers interested in pursuing this subject might wish to begin with the chapters on 'optical effects' in Cyril Barrett, *Op Art*, Viking, New York, NY, 1970, pp.38–75; Floyd Ratliff, *Paul Signac and Colour in Neo-Impressionism*. Rockefeller University Press, New York, NY, 1992; the entries for 'eyes', 'illusion', 'perception' and 'vision' indexed in the remarkable Richard L. Gregory (ed), *The Oxford Companion to the Mind*, Oxford University Press, Oxford and New York, NY, 1987; and the sources listed in John Elderfield, 'Seeing Bonnard', in *Bonnard*, Museum of Modern Art, New York, NY, 1998, p.49, 2n. This last essay is itself another study of the change of aspect.

5   This is one of the reasons, colour being another, for the traditional association of painting and femininity: see WJT Mitchell, *Iconology*, University of Chicago Press, Chicago, 1986, pp.109–12; Jacqueline Lichtenstein, *The Eloquence of Color*, University of California Press, Berkeley, 1993, pp.42–43, 189–90. These facts have an obvious relevance to Riley's black-and-white paintings.

6   The issue of potential coercion of the viewer in Op art was raised by Michael Fried, 'New York Letter: Kelly, Poons' (1963–64), in *Art and Objecthood: Essays and Reviews*, University of Chicago Press, Chicago, IL, 1998, pp.310–11. This relates (the issue of coercion not being limited to Op art, of course) to the important critique of theatricality in his 'Art and Objecthood' (1967), *ibid.*, pp.40–47, 148–72. In order to keep the present essay to a manageable shape and length, I have omitted a discussion of Riley's repudiation of 'objecthood', contenting myself with the brief remarks in the second section of this essay. It is worth noting, though, that Riley did flirt with 'theatricality' in the no-longer-extant environmental structure *Continuum* of 1963; the installation is illustrated in Bryan Robertson, John Russell and Lord Snowdon, *Private View*, Nelson, London, 1965, pp.206–07, and is discussed, with illustrations of preparatory studies, in Maurice de Sausmarez, *Bridget Riley*, exhibition catalogue, New York Graphic Society, Greenwich, CT, 1970, pp.29, 32.

7   To look away from a black-and-white painting is to slide one's eyes off a surface that, owing to the packing of incident that occurs in peripheral vision, seems miraculously to have stopped being a source of optical energy and to have become an object, and a complex three-dimensional object, at that. See, for example, Andrew Forge, 'On Looking at Paintings by Bridget Riley', *Art International*, vol.15, no.3, March 20, 1971, pp.16–21. In contrast, to look away from a chromatic painting is to slide one's eyes from a continuing source of optical energy onto an adjacent surface that, owing to the 'adaptation' that occurs after looking at a monodirectional, repetitiously moving array, seems miraculously to have become a source of optical energy itself.

    The phenomenon of 'adaptation' – whereby a specific neural channel (say, one that

                                                                 JOHN ELDERFIELD

registers downward movement, or one that registers red) is adapted (or fatigued) by overstimulation, causing its receptors, until they recuperate, to fire at a lower relative rate than those of its opposite neural channel (say, one that registers upward movement, or one that registers green) – is critical to the mechanics of Riley's art as a whole. 'I had found out quite early', she has said, 'that perceptual activity takes place in opposition to the graphic field.' See Bridget Riley, 'Into Colour' (1978), in Kudielka (ed), *The Eye's Mind*, *op.cit.*, p.95. Only in the coloured paintings, however, does the perceptual activity spread significantly beyond the limits of the field, to persist there momentarily after the field has been surrendered to vision. Momentarily, then, the viewer is conscious of retaining sight of the perceptual activity while surrendering the field of vision to another viewer. A simple, nontechnical account of adaptation may be found in Mark Fineman, *The Nature of Visual Illusion*, Dover, New York, NY, 1996, pp.18–19, 29–34. However, the imagery of Riley's paintings is not easily remembered for the same reason that Bonnard's is not; see Elderfield, *op.cit.*, pp.47–48). But the sensations they evoke are remembered – just as the paintings themselves recall sensations from nature without the imagery that prompted them. The artist has recently referred to her paintings as 'agents' in this respect.

8   Riley, speaking of her memory of a childhood experience, in 'The Pleasures of Sight' (1984), in Kudielka (ed), *The Eye's Mind*, *op.cit.*, p.30.

9   See Riley's description of a Rubens, in Bridget Riley, 'The Colour Connection' (1989), *ibid.*, pp.158–60.

10   Bridget Riley, 'Something to Look At: In Conversation with Alex Farquharson' (1995), in Kudielka (ed), *The Eye's Mind, ibid.*, pp.128, 130.

11   Bridget Riley, 'A Reputation Reviewed' (1992), in Robert Kudielka (ed), *Bridget Riley: Dialogues on Art*, Zwemmer, London, 1995, p.72.

12   Stéphane Mallarmé to Henri Cazalis (autumn 1864?), in Rosemary Lloyd (ed and trans), *Selected Letters of Stéphane Mallarmé*, University of Chicago Press, Chicgao, IL, 1988, p.39.

13   Czesław Miłosz, quoted in Christopher Bollas, *Being a Character: Psychoanalysis and Self Experience*, Hill and Wang, New York, NY, 1994, p.87. This and the preceding paragraph are informed by Bollas's work.

14   See William C Seitz, *The Responsive Eye*, exhibition catalogue, Museum of Modern Art, New York, NY, 1965; Bridget Riley, 'Perception Is the Medium' (1965), in Kudielka (ed), *The Eye's Mind, op.cit.*, p.66; Riley, 'A Reputation Reviewed', in Kudielka (ed), *Dialogues on Art, op.cit.*, pp.69–70; Lisa G Corrin, 'Continuum: Bridget Riley's 60s and 70s: A View from the 90s', in Lisa G Corrin (ed), *Bridget Riley: Paintings from the 1960s and 70s*, exhibition catalogue, Serpentine Gallery and Koenig Books, London, 1999, pp.38–40.

15   See Bridget Riley, 'In Conversation with Maurice de Sausmarez' (1967), in Kudielka (ed), *The Eye's Mind, op.cit.*, p.62; Riley, 'Into Colour', *ibid.*, p.99; Bridget Riley 'According to Sensation', *ibid.*, p.120; and Bridget Riley, 'Mondrian: The "Universal" and the "Particular"' (1995), *ibid.*, p.197. As Robert Kudielka has pointed out, 'the conjunction between Mondrian and Pollock is a staple point of reference in Riley's thinking'; see Riley 'According to Sensation', *ibid.*, p.137, n.4; hence, Mondrian could have fulfilled the role that Pollock occupies in this essay, except that it was Pollock who precipitated the crisis of 'materiality' versus 'opticality' discussed below, and who was an immediate, contemporary conduit for the *peinture optique* of Seurat and Mondrian.

16   Pollock may have made a return appearance in Riley's paintings since the later 1990s, especially in the large horizontal canvases of 1999 and 2000, for which see *Bridget Riley: New Paintings and Gouaches*, exhibition catalogue, Waddington Galleries and Karsten Schubert, London, 2000.

17   BH Friedman, *Jackson Pollock: Energy Made Visible*, McGraw-Hill, New York, NY, 1972.

18   This still highly contentious topic is best approached through Kirk Varnedoe with Pepe
     Karmel, *Jackson Pollock*, exhibition catalogue, Museum of Modern Art, New York, NY,
     1998; and more specifically through two responses to this publication, from which I draw:
     Michael Fried, 'Optical Allusions', *Artforum* 37, no.8, April 1999, pp.97–101, 143, 146;
     Rosalind Krauss, 'The Crisis of the Easel Painting', in Kirk Varnedoe and Pepe Karmel
     (eds), *Jackson Pollock: New Approaches*, exhibition catalogue, Museum of Modern Art,
     New York, NY, 1999, pp.55–179.

19   See Bridget Riley, 'In Conversation with Robert Kudielka' (1972), in Kudielka (ed), *The
     Eye's Mind*, *op.cit.*, p.85.

20   Bridget Riley, 'The Experience of Painting' (1998), *ibid.*, p.122.

21   See Frances Spalding, 'Bridget Riley and the Poetics of Instability', in Lisa G Corrin (ed),
     Bridget Riley: Paintings from the 1960s and 70s, *op.cit.*, p.13.

22   See Riley, 'Mondrian: The "Universal" and the "Particular"', *op.cit.*

23   On these works, see De Sausmarez, *op.cit.*, pp.26–27; and Spalding, *op.cit.*, pp.13–15.

24   See Bridget Riley, 'Practising Abstraction' (1992), in Kudielka (ed), *Dialogues on Art*,
     op.cit., pp.59–60.

25   Riley, 'Perception Is the Medium', in Kudielka (ed), *The Eye's Mind*, *op.cit.*, pp.66–68.

26   For the relevant optical mechanisms making uncertain an earlier painting, see Michael
     Baxandall, 'Fixation and Distraction: The Nail in Braque's *Violin and Pitcher*' (1910), in
     John Onians (ed), *Sight and Insight: Essays on Art and Culture in Honour of EH
     Gombrich at 85*, Phaidon, London, 1994, pp.399–415, especially pp.403–05.

27   For a discussion of the mechanics of adaptation (visual fatigue) in Riley's *Current* (1964),
     see Robert L Solso, *Cognition and the Visual Arts*, MIT Press, Cambridge, MA, 1996,
     pp.58–61. For 'surface' and 'film' colour, see David Katz, *The World of Colour*, Kegan Paul,
     Trench, Trubner, London, 1935; also Sanford Wurmfeld, 'Color in Abstract Painting', in Kurt
     Nassau (ed), *Color for Science, Art, and Technology*, Elsevier, Amsterdam, 1998,
     pp.169–94, for an excellent account of this and related subjects.

28   This subject is discussed in relation to a part of the 'change of aspect' section of
     Wittgenstein's *Investigations* in sections 19–21 of Richard Wollheim, 'On Drawing an
     Object' (1965), in *On Art and the Mind*, Allen Lane, London, 1973.

29   'La lumière n'existe, donc pas pour la peintre' (to Emile Bernard, 23 December 1904), in
     Michael Doran (ed), *Conversations avec Cézanne*, Macula, Paris, 1978, p.44. Riley refers
     to this statement in Riley, 'Colour for the Painter', in Trevor Lamb and Janine Bourriau
     (eds), *Colour: Art and Science*, Cambridge University Press, Cambridge, 1995, p.32.

30   For the relevant optical mechanisms in the work of an earlier artist, see Elderfield, *op.cit.*,
     pp.43–45. See also 'Bentham's Top' in Gregory, *op.cit.*, pp.78–79, for subjective colours.

31   See Robert Kudielka, 'Nothing But Appearance' *op.cit.*, p.14. See also the comments on
     the same phenomenon in the paintings of Jules Olitski in Fried, *Art and Objecthood*,
     op.cit., pp.86–87, where the discussion of pp.247–48, on the importance of the viewer's
     performative role, bears comparison to Riley's art.

32   See Forge, *op.cit.*, p.16.

33   Riley, 'In Conversation with Maurice de Sausmarez' in Kudielka (ed), *The Eye's Mind*,
     op.cit., p.62.

34   See Spalding, *op.cit.*; Robert Kudielka, 'Bridget Riley', in *Bridget Riley: Paintings 1982–1992*,
     exhibition catalogue, Southbank Centre, London, in association with Verlag für moderne
     Kunst, Nuremberg, 1992, p.22; Bridget Riley, 'Statement' (1970), in Kudielka (ed), *The
     Eye's Mind*, *op.cit.*, p.136, n.1, where Kudielka explains how he drew Riley's attention to
     Thomas's statement; Bridget Riley, 'Personal Interview' (1988), *ibid.*, p.25; and Bridget

                                                                    JOHN ELDERFIELD

Riley, 'Painting Now' (1966), *ibid.*, pp.198–211 for emphasis on clarity and the workmanlike.

35   Riley, 'The Experience of Painting', *ibid.*, p.122

36   Bridget Riley, quoted in Bryan Robertson, 'Introduction and Biographical Note', in *Bridget Riley: Paintings and Drawings 1951–71,* exhibition catalogue, Arts Council of Great Britain, London, 1971, p.14.

37   Bridget Riley, 'The Hermaphrodite' (1973), in Kudielka (ed), *op.cit.,* p.39, is appropriately ambiguous in its guidance on such questions.

38   Kudielka, 'Bridget Riley', *op.cit.*

39   Riley, 'Perception Is the Medium', in Kudielka (ed), *The Eye's Mind, op.cit.,* p.68, and for the following quotations.

40   Riley, 'In Conversation with Maurice de Sausmarez', *ibid.,* p.62.

41   For definitions and bibliography, see Jean Laplanche and Jean-Bertrand Pontalis, *The Language of Psycho-Analysis,* Norton, New York, NY, 1973, pp.390–94, 427–29.

42   Anton Ehrenzweig, *The Hidden Order of Art: A Study of the Psychology of Artistic Imagination,* University of California Press, Berkeley, CA, 1967, p.50. This remarkable, although dated publication is an essential source for consideration of the conceptual bases of Riley's black-and-white paintings.

43   Riley, 'Personal Interview' in Kudielka (ed), *The Eye's Mind, op.cit.,* p.25.

44   Riley, 'A Reputation Reviewed', Kudielka (ed), *Dialogues on Art, op.cit.,* p.66.

45   Riley, 'The Experience of Painting', in Kudielka (ed), *The Eye's Mind, op.cit.,* p.125.

46   Riley, 'In Conversation with Maurice de Sausmarez', *ibid.,* pp.53–54. I should make it clear that this interview was not on personal subjects; thus Riley continued: 'As Cézanne said, painting is a parallel to nature…'

47   This account concentrates on the principal forms of the black-and-white paintings. Illustrations of types of paintings mentioned but not reproduced, details of other variants and further information may be found in the following sources, which I have found the most useful. In the historical literature: Anton Ehrenzweig, 'The Pictorial Space of Bridget Riley', *Art International,* vol.9, no.1, February 1965, pp.20–24; De Sausmarez, *op.cit.,* the fullest and most copiously illustrated account; Forge, *op.cit.*; Robertson, *op.cit.* In the recent literature: Kudielka, 'Nothing But Appearance', *op.cit.*; Kudielka, 'Bridget Riley', *op.cit.*; and especially Kudielka, 'Building Sensations: The Early Work of Bridget Riley', in Corrin (ed), *op.cit.,* pp.23–33.

48   Riley, 'In Conversation with Maurice de Sausmarez', in Kudielka (ed), *The Eye's Mind, op.cit.,* p.62. On *trompe l'oeil,* illusion and the problem of falsification, see Wollheim, *op.cit.,* section 22.

49   An account of the genesis of the 'visual prickles' of *Static 1* (1966) appears in Bridget Riley, 'Interview with David Sylvester' (1967), in Kudielka (ed), *The Eye's Mind, op.cit.,* pp.76–78.

50   Ehrenzweig, *op.cit.,* p.21.

51   See Sigmund Freud, 'From the History of an Infantile Neurosis' (1918), in James Strachey (ed), *The Standard Edition of the Complete Psychological Works of Sigmund Freud,* Hogarth, London, 1953–1974, vol.17, pp.3–124; Whitney Davis, *Drawing the Dream of the Wolves: Homosexuality, Interpretation, and Freud's 'Wolf Man',* Indiana University Press, Bloomington, IN, 1995.

52   See Laplanche and Pontalis, *op.cit.,* pp.111–14, 335–36; Whitney Davis, *Replications: Archaeology, Art History, Psychoanalysis,* Pennsylvania State University Press, University Park, PA, 1996.

53   See Michael Fried, *Realism, Writing, Disfiguration: On Thomas Eakins and Stephen*

Crane, University of Chicago Press, Chicago, IL, 1987, pp.64–65; pp.65–69 for the psychoanalytical implications.

54   See Sigmund Freud, 'Medusa's Head' (1922), in Strachey (ed), *The Standard Edition, op.cit.*, vol.18, pp.273–74. See also the gloss on Leo Steinberg's Medusan interpretation of *Les Demoiselles d'Avignon* in Yve-Alain Bois, 'On Matisse: The Blinding', *October*, no.68, spring 1994, pp.103–04. In 1963, the year that saw Riley's first shaped compositions, Norbert Lynton noted presciently that she made 'image paintings' and 'field paintings'; see Norbert Lynton, 'London Letter', *Art International* 7, no.8, October 1963, p.84. Readers willing to accept the Medusan association of the image paintings (as the artist tells me she is) may want to consider the terms 'shields' and 'cups', as explained in WJT Mitchell, *Picture Theory*, University of Chicago Press, Chicago, IL, 1994, pp.151–81, for their expression of the paintings' use-relationship to the viewer.

55   Michael Fried, *Manet's Modernism, or, The Face of Painting in the 1860s*, University of Chicago Press, Chicago, IL, 1996, p.294, for the quotation; pp.354–58 for the broader implications and the terminology of performing an operation, deriving from Georges Bataille. Fried also speaks (pp.294–95) of Manet's suppression of halftones to enforce a rapidity of perception of his paintings.

56   See Briony Fer, '*Poussière/Peinture*: Bataille on Painting', in *On Abstract Art*, Yale University Press, New Haven, CT, 1997, pp.77–91; Sigmund Freud, 'The "Uncanny"' (1919), in Strachey (ed), *The Standard Edition, op.cit.*, vol.17, pp.219–56. The mechanisms that produce Sandman effects in Riley's art have been demonstrated in the so-called Hermann grid (see Solso, *op.cit.*, pp.65–72), and McKay rays (see Richard L Gregory, *Eye and Brain: The Psychology of Seeing*, Princeton University Press, Princeton, NJ, 1990, pp.143–45). It is worth mentioning here that Clement Greenberg is reminiscent of Bataille in speaking of Pollock's 'sprinkled' paintings of 1950 thus: 'value contrasts are pulverized as it were, spread over the canvas like dusty vapor'. See '"American-Type" Painting' (1955), in John O' Brian (ed), *Clement Greenberg: The Collected Essays and Criticism*, vol.3, University of Chicago Press, Chicago, IL,1993, p.233.

57   Bridget Riley, 'In Conversation with Isabel Carlisle', in *Bridget Riley: Works 1961–1998*, exhibition catalogue, Abbot Hall Art Gallery, Kendal, 1998, p.7. (The choice of the word 'dead' affords, of course, an association with the 'uncanny'.)

58   Riley, 'The Experience of Painting', in Kudielka (ed), *The Eye's Mind, op.cit.*, p.125.

59   Riley, 'A Reputation Reviewed', Kudielka (ed), *Dialogues on Art, op.cit.*, p.66.

60   An extended analysis appears in Kudielka, 'Building Sensations', *op.cit.*, pp.28–29. The brief analysis in De Sausmarez, *op.cit.*, p.76, has almost the quality of a description of change-ringing, which adds a welcome association to these works.

61   Riley, 'The Pleasures of Sight' in Kudielka (ed), *The Eye's Mind, op.cit.*, p.32.

62   See Riley, 'Personal Interview', *ibid.*, pp.21–22.

63   See Riley, 'The Pleasures of Sight', *ibid.*, pp.30, 32.

64   The thematisation of painting as a release from blindness goes back at least to the seventeenth century: e.g. to the idea that Poussin's *Christ Healing the Blind Men* (1650) is an allegory of painting, which (in a modern paraphrase) 'causes us to glimpse (to see would be presumptuous) nature, as she is in reality'. René Démoris, 'Chardin and the Far Side of Illusion', in Pierre Rosenberg *et al.*, *Chardin*, exhibition catalogue, Metropolitan Museum of Art, New York, NY, 2000, p.99. 'Bridget Riley believes that true appearance is best revealed through the casual glance – and then only momentarily'; Kudielka, 'Bridget Riley', *op.cit.*, p.8, is an important essay that elaborates the lessons of 'The Pleasures of Sight'. The artist has said: 'I discovered that I was painting in order to "make visible"'; Riley, 'The Pleasures of Sight' (1984), in Kudielka (ed), *The Eye's Mind, op.cit.*, p.33. The

                                                    JOHN ELDERFIELD

axis of blinding-unblinding (and its analogue, unpleasure-pleasure) is critical to Riley's art. Further, her modernist interest in the axis of attention-distraction locates her art in the context of Walter Benjamin's 'The Work of Art in the Age of Mechanical Reproduction' (1936), in Hannah Arendt (ed), *Illuminations*, Collins/Fontana, London, 1973, pp.219–53; see also Jonathan Crary, *Suspension of Perception: Attention, Spectacle, and Modern Culture*, MIT Press, Cambridge, MA, 1999, pp.46–54, and *passim*, for an important study of how, within modernism, attentiveness, rather than securing the world, led to perceptual disintegration.

65 See Kudielka, 'Bridget Riley', *op.cit.*, pp.20–22, 28.

66 *Ibid.*, 22.

67 The most useful accounts of Riley 's transition into colour appear in Kudielka, 'Building Sensations', *op.cit.* and in interviews with and statements by the artist, where its development may be tracked: Bridget Riley, 'Conversation' (1972), in Kudielka (ed), *The Eye's Mind, op.cit.*, pp.80–86, describes the introduction of colour; Riley, 'Into Colour', *ibid.*, pp.89–104, does the same and adds information on the curve paintings; Bridget Riley, 'A Visit to Egypt...' (1984), *ibid.*, pp.106–13, describes the genesis of the Egyptian paintings. Robert Cumming's contributions to *Working with Colour: Recent Paintings and Studies by Bridget Riley*, exhibition catalogue, Arts Council of Great Britain, London, 1984, are exemplary demonstrations of how to make complex works such as the Egyptian paintings broadly accessible without a hint of condescension. I have drawn freely on these sources.

68 Kudielka, 'Building Sensations', *op.cit.*, p.30. In fact, Riley did not choose these colours from a conventional chromatic triangle. Wanting to add a third colour to red and blue, she realised that the obvious choice offered by that triangle, yellow, would not suffice because it could not be brought tonally level with the red and blue without losing its identity of hue. She, therefore, turned to green in the 1967–68 painting *Late Morning*, and found herself astonished by the induced golden-tinted light. A studio assistant mentioned Seurat. This led Riley to a contrast-diagram by Ogden N Rood, which Seurat had copied, and which she copied in turn. It pairs off 22 colours in exact complementary relationship, and in so doing places red, green and blue equidistantly on the colour wheel. Rood's and Seurat's diagrams are illustrated in William Innes Homer, *Seurat and the Science of Painting*, MIT Press, Cambridge, MA, 1964, pp.39–41; the forgoing information comes from Riley, who adds that Seurat, therefore, showed the way to go. Also worth noting is that red, blue and green are, of course, the component colours of our trichromacy of vision; thus every colour (including white) can be matched by a suitable mixture of red, green and blue 'primaries'. See Denis Baylor, 'Colour Mechanisms of the Eye' and John Mollon, 'Seeing Colour', in Lamb and Bourriau, *op.cit.*, pp.103–50.

69 See Riley, 'Into Colour', in Kudielka (ed), *The Eye's Mind, op.cit.*, p.97.

70 *Ibid.* It may be said that, in these coloured paintings, Riley engages what Matisse famously described, in a letter of 1941, as 'L'eternel conflit du dessin et de la couleur dans un même individu.' See Dominique Fourcade, *Henri Matisse: Écrits et propos sur l'art*, Hermann, Paris, 1972, p.188.

71 *Ibid.*, p.237.

72 Riley, 'Into Colour', in Kudielka (ed), *The Eye's Mind, op.cit.*, p.99.

73 See Homer, *op.cit.*, pp.70–74; Riley, 'Painting Now', *ibid.*, p.202, which refers to Delacroix's four cardinal principles.

74 Riley, 'Into Colour', *ibid.*, pp.100–01, with an amazing diagram of the colour organisation.

75 *Ibid.*, p.104.

76 Riley, 'A Visit to Egypt...,' *ibid.*, p.110.

77 Riley's interest in Cézanne (and Monet) in the late 1970s is noted in Robert Kudielka.
'Biographical Notes', *ibid.*, p.225.

78 Riley, 'Into Colour', *ibid.*, pp.93, 95. Since the Egyptian palette is formed with two pairs of
complementaries and ends with three, it is fascinating to plot their positions on the
Rood-Seurat-Riley colour-contrast diagram referred to in 68n, to discover the surprising
symmetry that marks the moment the palette is overturned.

79 See Cumming, *op.cit.*, cat.8 on another work.

80 Matisse, quoted in Fourcade, *op.cit.*, p.284. Matisse also once said, in words relevant to
Riley's work: 'A good drawing should be like a wicker basket… where you can't remove
one of the strands without making a hole in it.' *Ibid.*, p.201 .

81 Cézanne, to Joachim Gasquet, as quoted in Roger Fry, *Cézanne: A Study of His
Development*, Noonday, New York, NY, 1958, p.54, a book that Riley was reading as this
essay was being written [2000].

82 Wittgenstein, *op.cit.*, pp.195–96.

JOHN ELDERFIELD

Around and About *Composition with Circles 2*

Lynne Cooke

> I would be at great pains to say where is the painting I am
> looking at. For I do not look at it as I do at a thing; I do not
> fix it in its place. My gaze wanders in it as in the halos of
> Being. It is more accurate to say that I see according to it,
> or with it, than that I *see it*.
>
> – Maurice Merleau-Ponty, *The Primacy of Perception*, 1964

Reconnaissance

'As Matisse knew, to preserve a freshness in working one sometimes has
to go back to first principles', Bridget Riley stated in an interview
conducted in 1990 for a catalogue accompanying the presentation of a
group of new rhomboid paintings. Expanding further on their genesis,
she added: 'they have been preceded by dispensing with a few notions
such as the exclusivity of an absolute, extreme stance, rigorous control,
even the *new*. In making them I am trying to use a way of working…
which as an abstract painter I might have considered obsolete earlier.'[1]
This is an important explication, for it was made at a time when Riley
was immersed in a series of works that could easily be read as
retrospective, even revisionist, in character. Composed of small integers
of diagonally aligned rhomboids, keyed in an extremely wide-ranging
palette that could encompass up to some 20 or more hues, the first
works in this series – in particular, works such as *Rio* (1989) – were
made by incrementally building or, better, weaving these elements
rhythmically through a linear scaffolding of regularly repeating vertical
ribs. The consistently midsized dimensions of this series effects a
delicate balance between the proliferating units adumbrating dynamic
relations within the field and the encompassing framing entity. The
shifting, plastic depth that results unfolds in a harmonious flow
orchestrated colouristically, by tone as much as hue, by visual weight as
much as luminosity.

References to Paul Cézanne's work and thought abound here, as Riley herself is quick to acknowledge, and may be seen by comparing how, for example, Cézanne wove space by means of regularly applied taches that, as in tapestries, create the foreground foliage in *Turning Road at Montgeroult* (1898); additionally, the same painting's implicit linear scaffolding, intimated in the truncated contours of partially concealed architecture peeping through the trees, functions somewhat analogously to the lattice-like armature – buried but never fully obliterated, increasingly sensed rather than observed – of Riley's later rhomboid paintings, such as *Dark Light* (1991) and *In Attendance* (1993).[2] As a group, these works are far less dependent than are previous series on purely luminous effects based in chromatic interaction, for colour no longer simply activates space dynamically; it also (and more importantly) shapes it. In their dependence on the reintroduction of certain internal hierarchical relations – relations that are established, demolished and revised within the unfolding compass of the whole – these compositions recall certain harmonies found in classical music: they evoke voyages of expressive discovery that, as in music, offer precise sequences of sensations that are specific even as they may remain verbally unidentifiable or indefinable.

The basis for this method of composing emerged in a body of work begun after Riley's return from a visit to the Nile Valley in the winter of 1979–80, known familiarly as the Egyptian series. A significant shift occurred when the artist began to construct a fictile space by putting together groups of coloured stripes that incrementally mould an unstable shallow depth behind the picture surface. In the earliest of these, which include *Après Midi* (1981), white stripes introduce a gentle release from the taut armature produced by their black counterparts, a punctuation that sets up a kind of harmonic pacing in response to the chords of complementary colours sculpting a luminous space. As she explored the potential of this repertoire of elements, Riley, in characteristic fashion, gradually made a number of crucial changes within her deliberately restricted lexicon. Appropriating a palette drawn from memory of those five hues codified in over three thousand years of use by early Egyptian artists – red, blue, turquoise, green and ochre – plus black and white,

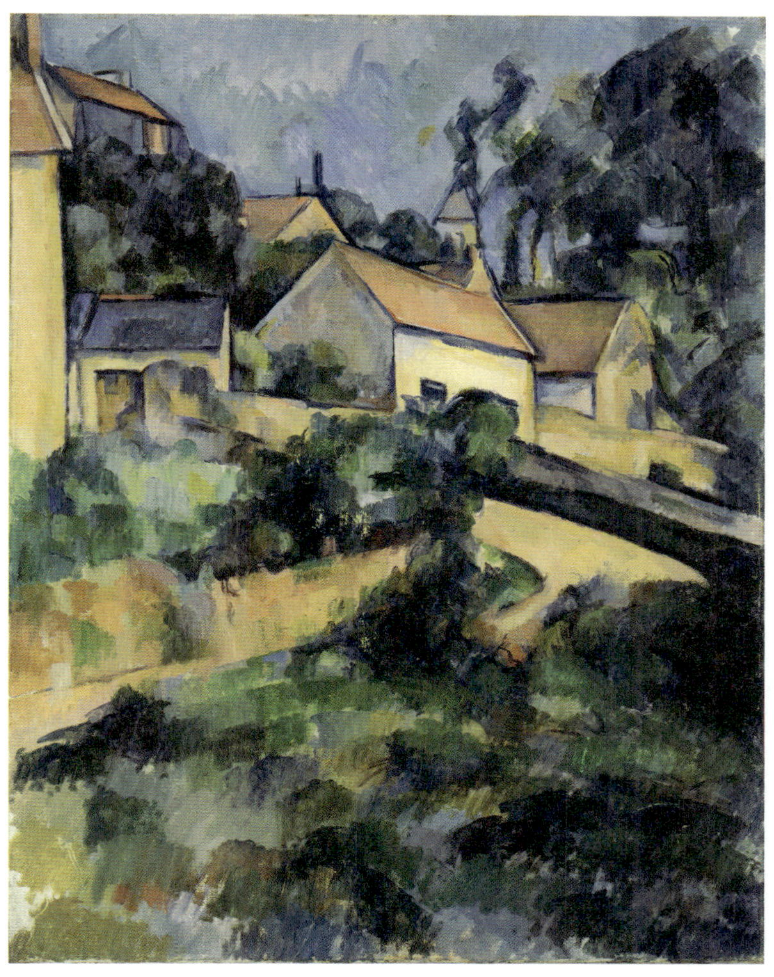

Paul Cézanne
Turning Road at Montgeroult 1898
Oil on canvas
81.3 × 65.7 cm | 32 × 25⅞ in
Museum of Modern Art, New York

this series of works was composed in vertical stripes. To reinforce the effect of maximum chromatic luminosity made possible by this format, Riley confined herself to narrow parallel bands, and switched from acrylic to oil paint. Soon, replacing black with green, and white with lavender, she created works that, like *Samarra* (1984) are memorable for their high-key vibrating chromatic veil. While she could long have continued to mine the possibilities of this seductive palette, she abruptly (but not atypically) veered off course in order to give reign to a need to move the viewer's eye around the canvas in diverse directions and along multiple axes, as well as to prevent herself from becoming unduly engaged with refinements of tone and hue.

When developing the rhomboid series – often known in studio parlance as the zig paintings – over the course of the late 1980s, she felt she was approaching more closely than hitherto what she deems 'the real problems of painting'.[3] Reinforcement and confirmation of this conviction seems to have been provided by the manner in which she responded to an invitation from the National Gallery in London in 1987 to participate in its ongoing exhibition series *The Artist's Eye*, for which artists select works from the museum's collection. Rejecting her initial idea of focusing on the perception of nature, and foiling expectation (or at least expectation premised on knowledge of her early work and influences), Riley did not base her presentation around figures formative to her development, such as Claude Monet and George Seurat. As centrepieces of the show, she chose neither the former's *Water Lilies* (after 1916) nor the latter's *Bathers at Asnières* (1884), and, instead, curated an exhibition in 1989 of hallmark works by some of the greatest Western colourists whom she also reveres: Titian's *Bacchus and Ariadne* (1520–23), Veronese's *The Adoration of the Kings* (1573), Rubens's *Allegory of Peace* ('Peace and War', 1629–30), and Cézanne's *The Bathers* (1900–06), in addition to two works by Poussin – *The Adoration of the Shepherds* (1633–34) and *The Triumph of Pan* (1636) – and El Greco's *Christ Driving the Traders from the Temple* (c.1600). Riley's close formal analysis of several of these paintings in the catalogue reveals how centrally these works embody perennial pictorial concerns – concerns that were to preoccupy her too during the five or so years that span the zig paintings.[4]

Riley's deep engagement with the art of the past, and more particularly her increasing effort to establish her place and practice as part of a long and continuing pictorial tradition, positioned her in the later 1980s at a point of departure quite different from the one she had forged in the early 1960s with such key works as *Movement in Squares* (1961), *Pause* (1964) and *Crest* (1964). Wide-ranging though these paintings are, they frequently share a pictorial structure that may be identified as a cycle of repose-disturbance-repose. Stretched almost to breaking point, the picture plane is finally righted and re-established in a precariously held balance, generating an optical sensation that seems to take place in the space between the painted surface and the spectator. She explained retrospectively:

> In my earlier paintings, I wanted the space between the picture plane and the spectator to be active. It was in that space, paradoxically, that the painting 'took place.' Then, little by little, and to some extent deliberately, I made it go the other way, opening up an interior space, as it were, so that there was a layered shallow depth. It is important that the painting can be inhabited so that the mind's eye, or the eye's mind, can move about in it credibly.[5]

Conceived holistically, each of these paintings presents itself as an entity that impacts vividly and instantaneously on the viewer, since it is not experienced as a composition comprised of the sum of its parts, nor are its parts orchestrated hierarchically, nor do they embody a figure-ground relationship. Detailed scrutiny may reveal how the composition was precisely determined, what and where shifts in tone were introduced in order to construct the desired effect, but a fully resolved reading occurs only when the viewer steps back to take in the work as a whole and to permit the inevitable occurrence of that involuntary visual response to the determining optical sensation. Crucial to Riley's formulations of this starting point – and a fundamental premise of these works beginning in the 1960s and continuing through the 1970s to the Egyptian series – was the example of Jackson Pollock's work, which she first encountered in the late 1950s, soon after graduating from art school.

In Pollock's large field paintings, such as *One* (1950) and *Number 32* (1950), Riley discovered a new kind of pictorial space for which European art provided no precedents – Piet Mondrian excepted.[6] It is a shallow optical space that is apprehended as a single entity, rather than built cumulatively via part-to-part relationships. Boldly paring her palette and vocabulary, she felt empowered to make clarity of purpose and statement henceforth a goal.

Throughout her career, Riley has, when necessary, always been willing to digress, to shift obliquely, only to return refreshed by new possibilities and options. Equally telling, she relishes establishing a carefully calibrated set of limitations, the better to explore, mine, test and refine potential options. Such a 'detour' occurred in the late 1990s in the midst of a difficult period of prolonged transition, as she sought to find a route beyond the zig paintings by experimenting with arcs, inserting narrow slivers of circles into the linear matrix of repeating verticals and diagonals, as found, for example, in *Lagoon 1* (1997).

During this intense stint of research and experimentation, she was invited to make a mural for an exhibition to be held at the Kunsthalle Bern, titled *White Noise*.[7] The result, a site-specific, monumental wall drawing, *Composition with Circles 1* (1998), was at first glance as unexpected as it was remarkable. On a large wall measuring some 204 by 367 inches, Riley created an ebullient work comprised of overlapping transparent circles. Painted with a narrow black outline 9 millimetres in width and 1 metre in diameter, they have sometimes been aligned and sometimes overlapped in a series of parallel registers, which themselves also overlap. Though represented only by their dark contours, these transparent disks nonetheless construct a volatile dynamic space made from planes that emerge and recede, moving forward and back in relation to the picture surface. Simultaneously, as linear trajectories in the guise of interlinking arcs and arabesques, they set up brief but lyrical cadences across and along the expanse of the entire wall. In addition, the visual flickers that erupt whenever two lines intersect or meet, and that create a scintillating field of radiant darting points, constitute a third pictorial element that further contributes to the sense of vital animation and movement in this astonishingly fresh and immediate work.

                                                          LYNNE COOKE

Eschewing symmetry and centralised or systematic compositional structures, Riley fine-tuned dispersed peripheral events to effect a carefully honed equilibrium of gently vying forces, accents and intervals in which a dynamic stillness poised in balance and order ultimately prevails.

Created some two years later, *Composition with Circles 2* (2000), refines and extends Riley's initial foray to a consummate degree. It evolved concurrently with a group of canvases, including *Parade 1* (1999–2000), in what is now a clearly recognisable and discrete series of works, colloquially named the new curve paintings. Comparison of the two suggests that Riley is simultaneously pursuing certain seminal pictorial inquiries through related but distinct vocabularies. For example, in the autonomous works, the curves, composed from segments of a sixth of a circle, produce a curvilinear, not a circular, grid, which is then woven through a series of regularly paced diagonals. The resulting poised cross-tensions are reinforced by the interplay of a restricted palette of three or four soft-toned, close-valued hues that repeat and echo across the surface. Despite crucial differences in colour and composition, which impact on opacity and transparency in the layers of planes and therefore on the types of spatial construction that ensue, certain constants may be identified between the two modes, not least a growing preoccupation with visual speed and pacing, made possible by a proclivity for an increasingly elongated frieze-like format. The prevailing echoes of Matisse in these recent canvases were recognised with hindsight rather than as the product of a conscious engagement with his work.[8] Nonetheless, a dialogue with the older artist seems to have been percolating for some time, at least in the inner reaches of Riley's mind, as may be gauged from a short text she wrote in 1990 on *La Danse* (1910) – a painting she not only venerates but one that has striking affinities with her *Parade 1* and some of its companions, such as *Rêve* (1999). In this brief statement, which today reads as an uncanny foreshadowing of her current preoccupations, Riley argues that:

> even if at first glance it may appear as though it is in the colour that
> the expressive power lies, it is really in the rhythm that its full extent

is unleashed and controlled... [For Matisse] concentrates his efforts
on pulling out the huge curves and diagonals which play with and
against each other around the canvas... The group [of figures], subject
to the overall organisation of colour and rhythm and entranced by
the act of dancing, lose their separate identities and become one
pictorial form, one organic unit... The content as it emerges is the
plastic expression of the spirit of dance, movement represented as a
visual rhythm in which interchange acts as a constant.[9]

While her own work remains rigorously abstract even as the
individual components become more apparently irregular and singular in
shape, the sensations that they evoke bear, as always, upon sensory and
phenomenal experiences, albeit pared and filtered through memory.
Prior to accepting the invitation from Bern, Riley had reabsorbed herself
in the art of Mondrian, exploring and probing his practice and thought in
what proved a more sustained and thorough investigation than any she
had previously undertaken. This intensive study arose in part from
repeated trips (first to The Hague's Gemeentemuseum in 1995 and the
next year to the Museum of Modern Art in New York) to see the
impressive and encompassing retrospective organized jointly by those
two institutions in conjunction with the National Gallery in Washington,
DC. It not only led her to agree to participate in an accompanying
symposium held in Manhattan in 1996 but also gave her the confidence
to co-curate a show of Mondrian's formative works for the Tate Gallery,
London, drawn from the unrivalled holdings of the Gemeentemuseum.
In her essay in the exhibition's catalogue, Riley pays special attention to
the Dutchman's transition to abstraction through his rigorous and
relentless exploration of a few select motifs in which he gradually
discerned the basis of an autonomous pictorial language:

The recurrent subject of sea, sky and dunes provides a theme of
vast, uncentred openness. The lack of differentiation in such motifs
gives a singular prominence to the horizon line and its
reverberations. By stacking and interlocking horizontal divisions of
different weights and distances, Mondrian creates a fluctuating,

impalpable envelope of space… From very early on there seems to have been a special attraction to trees and to the pictorial problem of how branches, sky and foliage or blossom interact and interpenetrate. Being especially a subject that cannot be treated 'realistically', the tree offers a marvellous pretext for the fabrication of a rhythmic structure of shallow recessions and advances that have little or nothing to do with the void and solid of the original motif.[10]

Such powerful insights seem highly pertinent to, and in turn informed by, concurrent concerns in her own work. Thus her evocative summary of the final work in Mondrian's great Pier and Ocean series offers a foretaste of her contribution to *White Noise*, centred as it was in what in that context must have been seen as a radically audacious and unbridled manifestation of an aesthetic rooted in visual pleasure. 'In the final painting an immensity of sensation opens up; one feels oneself surrounded by the sparkling stillness and the rhythmic movement of some boundless continuum.'[11]

Reimmersion in the work of another, or, rather, *the* other artist formative on Riley's early mature work occurred not long after. For, in the spring of 1999, an extensive Pollock retrospective travelled to the Tate Gallery,[12] prompting memories for her of that first retrospective held some 40 years before at the Whitechapel Art Gallery, extraordinary both in its enduring and its initial effect: 'The impact of that exhibition has reverberated down the years and still – with its original insights intact – remains a touchstone for me', she revealed recently.[13] Though that landmark retrospective had been seminal, renewed contact with the great poured paintings of the late forties and early fifties, such as *Number 32*, proved timely, in that a year later Riley journeyed to New York to prepare for her forthcoming exhibition at Dia Center for the Arts. Her principal purpose was to study carefully the site for a proposed wall drawing that was to be the sole new work in her show. 'The particular proportions of the Dia wall, being so extremely long and narrow, emerged as a primary issue. The imperative to organise a rhythm strong enough to carry the composition along the entire length of the wall became urgent', she explained. This pictorial problem was closely congruent with issues that had preoccupied her when reviewing Pollock's signature works, in which free-wheeling, seemingly unfettered linear trajectories, harnessed by a chiselled certainty of control, coalesce momentarily into visual polyphonies of tensile nodal densities that anchor the cursive graphic flights: 'My visit to the Pollock exhibition in 1999 allowed me to reengage with the American artist although this time from a different standpoint', Riley later confirmed. 'In particular, I studied his use of rhythm, noting in which formats this was exercised with the greatest ease and freedom. To this end Hans Namuth's famous film sequences of Pollock at work, both in the studio and in the garden, were very interesting. They showed him building his rhythm (albeit gesturally) by working across and along the canvas. This seemed to me to reveal, perhaps, something of the intrinsic nature of pictorial rhythm. Is it best expressed, or rather, most purely expressed, in movements that cross the picture plane?' she had speculated, leaving to her practice the option of a concrete answer.[14] Throughout the spring and summer of 2000, she concentrated on studies for the wall drawing, which, given the very different dimensions and proportions of the New York gallery from that in Bern, offered a substantially fresh set of challenges.

Larger in total area and more emphatically horizontal in orientation, the surface for *Composition with Circles 2* encouraged a more sequentially orchestrated compositional structure and focus. But, like its predecessor, this wall drawing marries the two unexpectedly compatible, yet fundamentally contrasting, types of spatial experience found in Riley's art to date: the first, based in a participatory engagement that occurs between the picture surface and the spectator, was a hallmark of her work of the 1960s and 70s; the second, emerging within the Egyptian series, was induced by a layered, shallow interior depth. Encountered from across the gallery, from directly opposite, this vast field of interlocking and overlapping circles, which seem to shift both across as well as back and forth within a shallow, elusive space, initially is cursorily scanned. Alighting on a particular arc, segment or intersection, which comes to serve as an entry point, the eye then begins to discern and articulate series of visual connections, rhythms, accents and incidents, counterpointing one another in a dynamic flow, finally structuring a complex and diverse journey around the surface. As these different trajectories are slowly distilled, the spectator comes to apprehend how the whole has been built into a cohesive composition, in a virtuosic performance that depends as much on the exercise of an unprecedented ebullient freedom as on the deployment of control. Later, re-entering the gallery from the side – that is, from the second point of egress – the visitor spies *Composition with Circles 2*, this time from a steep, oblique angle, in close-up. This vantage point reveals a second, quite distinct structure, one that seems composed from rolling groups of ovoids and rippling lines, reminiscent of giant sine-curves dissolving and re-emerging down the length of the wall. But irrespective of whether circular fragments, linear trajectories, or optical flickers – generated by the intersection or overlap of lines – initiate the visual journey, this lexicon with its implicit linear scaffolding offers a point of departure for a work based on movement through spaces – actual and conceptual, as well as pictorial, in character.

In *Composition with Circles 2*, Riley pays homage again to the work of the two primary mentors from the start of her career: Pollock and Mondrian. The lessons she learned then are no longer unmitigated but complicated and refracted in sophisticated and nuanced ways, integrated with more recent interests that previously seemed to contradict or even exclude them; it is, above all, however, the changing status of the role of line in her work, together with a new sense of scale reconciling free-flowing, improvised, open rhythm with deeply grounded tectonic strength, that marks a crucial requestioning. Line here both belongs to the geometric planar form and simultaneously is revealed as a source of harmonious rhythmic motion in itself, curling and unravelling in sinuous arabesques and slow and swift trajectories. In addition, a supporting linear grid – implicit rather than exposed, as in, say, Mondrian's *Composition with Grid 3: Lozenge Composition* (1918) – holds the composition rigorously in place at the same time as it is counterpointed, contradicted, revoked, or even obliterated by a shifting pattern of dispersed oscillating points. Controlled structure is parsed against exuberant freedom, improvisation builds on a sure foundation, in ways that recall precedents in the work of both twentieth-century pioneers.

By readdressing these formative predecessors, Riley reprises their work differently as she revises, permutates and cross-pollinates what she defines as their respective legacies. Restricting herself to a linear vocabulary in black and white allows a different kind of spatial movement to enter her art, as abutting and intersecting transparent planes overlap in a space more ambiguous and fluidly continuous than any she has hitherto devised. Although forms are literally bounded and thereby create residual areas, these interstices do not constitute a field of negative shapes set off against positives, but are entities in themselves, equivalent not subordinate. Mostly, however, the circles are read less as perfect closed forms than as segments, arcs and arabesques – sinuous traces of energy or vibrating waves – or as clusters and densities of fugitive incidents that together breathe like a single enveloping membrane. Revisiting Riley's early works has aptly been compared to the opening of a time capsule and finding inside today's date; conversely, the unexpectedly, insistently contemporary *Composition with Circles 2* carries within itself, like a persistent melodic phrase, echoes of a far-reaching and deep-seated art history.

Legacies of Lascaux

Whether spurred primarily by circumstantial events – that is, by the exceptional retrospectives of these two preeminent twentieth-century modernists, providentially coinciding with challenging curatorial offers – or by a more internally determined need and design, Riley's readiness to re-engage her founding roots seems to have been accompanied (again consciously or subconsciously) by a third and equally momentous act of return, of reconnaissance. In the mid-1960s, the publication of Maurice Merleau-Ponty's seminal essay 'Eye and Mind' (1964) proved deeply important to this young British artist, who numbered it among a small group of select texts central to her aesthetic – together with Samuel Beckett's essay on Marcel Proust, Proust's magnum opus itself, and Paul Klee's pivotal guide, *The Thinking Eye* (1961).[15] 'Eye and Mind' contains much that congealed at the heart of Riley's aesthetic henceforth, beginning with Merleau-Ponty's central thesis: 'In whatever civilisation it is born, from whatever beliefs, motives, or thoughts, no matter what ceremonies surround it – and even when it appears devoted to something else – from Lascaux to our time, pure or impure, figurative or not, painting celebrates no other enigma but that of visibility.'[16]

In the mid-1980s, as she revised her work, reconsidering her relation to formal issues that once she might have considered 'obsolete' and which could best be identified in the art of Cézanne, Riley may have been drawn again to this extraordinary text – given that for Merleau-Ponty, Cézanne explores the central pictorial problem, namely, that of depth, and with it, and in unparalleled ways, the creation of a plastic space by means of colour. If such was to become the cornerstone of Riley's art in the Lozenge series, it continues into her current work, albeit mediated and suffused with echoes and memories of Matisse.

'Eye and Mind' also contains an acute and pertinent passage in which the philosopher speculates about the potential of line for serving similar ends. Line need not function merely as edge or boundary, Merleau-Ponty argues; its role may be more independent and multilayered. As substantiation, he refers to both Henri Bergson and Leonardo da Vinci, quoting at length from the latter's *Treatise on Painting* (c.1452–1519): 'The secret of the art of drawing is to discover in each object the particular way in which a certain flexuous line, which is, so to speak, its generating axis, is directed through its whole extent.' Although Merleau-Ponty contends that the early twentieth-century philosopher only 'rather timidly advanced the idea that the undulating line could be… no more here than there', and yet 'gives the key to the whole', he concedes that Bergson was:

> on the threshold of that gripping discovery, already familiar to the painters, that there are no lines visible in themselves, that neither the contour of the apple nor the border between field and meadow is in this place or that, that they are always on the near or the far side of the point we look at. They are always between or behind whatever we fix our eyes upon; they are indicated, implicated and even very imperiously demanded by the things, but they themselves are not

things… This contestation of the prosaic line is far from ruling out all lines in painting, as the Impressionists may have thought…

It is simply a matter of freeing the line, of revivifying its constituting power; …as Klee said, the line no longer imitates the visible; it 'renders visible'; it is the blueprint of a genesis of things… The beginning of the line's path establishes or installs a certain level or mode of the linear, a certain manner for the line to be and to make itself a line, 'to go line'. Relative to it, every subsequent inflection will have a diacritical value, will be another aspect of the line's relation to itself, will form an adventure, a history, a meaning of the line – all this according as it slants more or less, more or less rapidly, more or less subtly. Making its way in space, it nevertheless corrodes prosaic space and the *partes* extra *partes*; it develops a way of extending itself actively into that space which subtends the spatiality of a thing… Figurative or not, the line is no longer a thing or an imitation of a thing. It is a certain disequilibrium kept up within the indifference of the white paper; it is a certain process of gouging within the in-itself, a certain constitutive emptiness… The line is no longer the apparition of an entity upon a vacant background, as it was in classical geometry. It is, as in modern geometries, the restriction, segregation, or modulation of a pregiven spatiality.[17]

Further refining this brilliantly suggestive analysis, Merleau-Ponty distinguishes two alternatives, exemplified in two drawings, one by Klee and the other by Matisse. In the former's work, he discerns a more purified or single-minded usage, which cleaves 'rigorously to the principal of the genesis of the visible'. In the case of the latter, line assumes in addition a representational role, since Matisse puts

into a single line both the prosaic definition … of the entity and the hidden… operation which composes in it such softness or inertia and such force as are required to constitute it as *nude*, as *face*, as *flower*… It is Matisse who taught us to see their contours not in a 'physical-optical' way but rather as structural filaments, as the axes of a corporeal system of activity and passivity.

Given that, ultimately, Merleau-Ponty acknowledges 'it makes little difference which one is chosen', his comparison of these variants on an abiding pictorial problem throws an acute light on Riley's current practice of pursuing twin lines of inquiry, simultaneously working in modes allied to both.[18] Merleau-Ponty's theory of vision – in which the body is imbricated in the world, in which seeing cannot be divorced or separated from what is seen – is most fully explored in a companion essay, 'The Visible and the Invisible', which has proven widely influential for postwar art in both Europe and the United States of America.[19] Preoccupied more narrowly in this text with the relations among vision, visuality and painting, he makes no fundamental distinction between abstraction and figuration, for his inquiry stops short in order to concentrate on the act of seeing itself. For Riley, however, this distinction is of some importance: for her, abstraction is the appropriate language for the contemporary era since it not only engages these problems more directly, and more incisively, it also embodies a metaphysics that speaks to the present condition.[20] Perhaps nowhere in her oeuvre is this better expressed than in *Composition with Circles 2*, as may be gauged by considering the credo expressed through the following statements made over the past five years:

> In general, my paintings are multifocal. You can't call it unfocused space, but not being fixed to a single focus is very much of our time. It's something that seems to have come about in the last hundred years or so. Focusing isn't just an optical activity, it is also a mental one. I think this lack of a centre has something to do with the loss of certainties that Christianity had to offer. There was a time when meanings were focused and reality could be fixed; when that sort of belief disappeared, things became uncertain and open to interpretation. We can no longer hope as the Renaissance did that 'man is the measure of all things'.[21]
>
> I think that an artist today has to totally accept this lack, has to start from a 'placelessness' virtually as a point of departure.[22]
>
> Painting is, I think, inevitably an archaic activity and one that depends on spiritual values. One of the big crises in painting – at

least a century, or two, or maybe three centuries old – was precipitated by the dropping away of the support of a known spiritual context in which a creative impulse such as painting could find a place. This cannot be replaced by private worlds and reveries. As a painter today you have to work without that essential platform. But if one does not deceive oneself and accepts this lack of certainty, other things may come into play.[23]

Properly treated, formalism is not an empty thing but a potentially very powerful answer to this spiritual challenge of an unavailable truth.[24]

Riley has consistently located in sensation those 'other things [that] may come into play'. The pleasures of sight, and those lingering sensations that imprint themselves indelibly in the eye's mind or in memory – which Paul Valéry resonantly dubs 'the stains of the pure instant' – have remained at the core of her art for the past 40 years. Discovered and pursued, elucidated and pinned down, only during the elaborate preparatory studies crucial to the evolution of any painting, and never in themselves the point of departure, these sensations are enormously wide-ranging in scope, often familiar in character, and generally invigorating – '[like] cold water, fresh things, slightly astringent… certain acid sorts of smells… like wood being cut', or reflections on water, light playing on the ocean at sunset.[25] There is perhaps no better invocation of the ways in which they may be incarnated than the account Merleau-Ponty offers of an analogous experience:

When through the water's thickness I see the tiling at the bottom of a pool, I do not see it despite the water and the reflections there; I see it through them and because of them. If there were no distortions, no ripples of sunlight, if it were without this flesh that I saw the geometry of the tiles, then I would cease to see it as it is and where it is – which is to say, beyond any identical, specific place. I cannot say that the water itself – the aqueous power, the syrupy and shimmering element is in space; all that is not somewhere else either, but it is not in the pool. It inhabits it, it materialises itself there,

yet it is not contained there; and if I raise my eyes toward the screen
of cypresses where the web of reflections is playing, I cannot gainsay
the fact that the water visits it, too, or at least sends into it, upon it,
its active and living essence. This internal animation, this radiation of
the visible is what the painter seeks under the name of depth, of
space, of colour.[26]

The sense of placelessness in what he is looking at, so marvellously
evoked here, is nonetheless a place available not only to the eye's mind
but to the mind's eye; and Merleau-Ponty is as alert to its presence in
the art of the past as in sensations generated in the phenomenal world.
'The animals painted on the walls of Lascaux are not there in the same
way as the fissures and limestone formations', he contends. 'But they are
not elsewhere. Pushed forward here, held back there, held up by the
wall's mass they use so adroitly, they spread around the wall without
ever breaking from their elusive moorings in it.' And he concludes this
passage with a statement that uncannily encapsulates the effect made
by Riley's monumental wall drawing: 'I would be at great pains to say
where is the painting I am looking at. For I do not look at it as I do at a
thing; I do not fix it in its place. My gaze wanders in it as in the halos of
Being. It is more accurate to say that I see according to it, or with it, than
that I see it.'[27]
    Conjuring an existential philosophy of placelessness engendered,
paradoxically, by site-specificity, and embodied in a philosophy of
perception, *Composition with Circles 2* is a work of extraordinary visual
complexity, the cohesion and coherence of whose underlying structure
may be readily apprehended without, however, being either wholly
comprehended, or indeed wholly comprehensible. Although her late
work is akin to music in various respects, and not least in the terms that
Beckett defines it – that is, as 'an art that is perfectly intelligible and yet
perfectly inexplicable' – Riley, unlike the writer, does not find it a
limitation or failing that the viewer, or 'the listener… being an impure
subject, [will] insist on giving a figure to that which is ideal and invisible
[or abstract], on incarnating the Idea in what he conceives to be an
appropriate paradigm.'[28] For irrespective of whether they are considered

sensations or 'paradigms' or 'figures', such imbrications are, for her, inseparable from and intrinsic to the very nature and function of vision. They are, equally, the source of its manifold and enduring pleasures.

Coda

Riley's visit to Egypt in 1979 had momentous consequences in another arena also. In the late 1970s, she had been invited to contribute some form of decoration to the newly renovated and expanded consortium of Liverpool hospitals. Studying the complex, she determined that the principal problem facing most visitors and outpatients was one of orientation. The solution she devised, and realised in 1983, drew again on her experiences while visiting ancient sites in the Nile Valley. It involved creating a mural comprised of bands of bright coloured stripes that run the length of the corridors, emphasising at key points – at waist height, skirting board and frieze – principal zones within the field that both orient the visitor and establish the surface plane. The pattern of contrasting hues interspersed with white bands generates light and visually unifies the wall, imparting a distinctive sense of presence and identity to it.

So successful and effective was her solution that she employed it again, in newly revised form, when invited to work on a project for St Mary's Hospital in London several years later. Far from underestimating the significance of design, Riley stresses its importance and meaningfulness:

[Taken as a whole] a decoration should not demand scrutiny, should have no details to attract attention. It should be passive on exactly those points where a painting [is] active… you should become aware of decoration almost bodily… [Going] way beyond mere visual embellishment [it serves to] extend the architectural bones into a flowing rhythmic space and to establish those points of reference through which human beings relate to their surroundings.'[29]

More recently, she completed a commission from Citibank in London, which resulted in a work that relates closely to the 'zig' paintings. It functions somewhat differently in that it was designed to hang suspended in the interior atrium of a 16-storey Minimalist building, relieving the effect of uniformity and repetition in the identical inner facades and helping occupants orient themselves by responding askance to its shifting patterns and rhythms as they pass by.

For Riley, the role of such architectural embellishment is not only different in kind from painting proper, but it remains distinct from her oeuvre as an artist. In this one area, therefore, she has little in common with Mondrian who, with other members of De Stijl, theorised the eventual dissolution of easel painting into architectonic installation and whose preliminary experiments in this direction may be seen in his treatment of his studio and living quarters, beginning in the 1920s in Paris.

Comparison with the work of Riley's contemporary Sol LeWitt serves to elucidate certain crucial differences often amounting to antitheses underpinning their work and aesthetics. For Riley, wall drawings, which constitute a form of painting by other means, are primarily about visual experiences. Virtually the converse underpins the American's approach, informed and governed as it is by conceptual ideas. LeWitt's wall drawings exist first, and often for years, as a series of instructions to be carried out by assistants; execution is essentially a perfunctory affair, though a certain interest resides in the tension between the way a work may be envisioned in the mind's eye and in an actual installation, or in the differences that occur when that same work is sited in different locations. Riley's works, on the other hand, are not adaptable: the dimensions, scale and execution are highly prescribed; each is essentially site-specific.

When LeWitt began his body of wall drawings in the late sixties, he was prompted in part by the desire to remove what he considered an additional layer separating the graphite and the support, and so to fuse the drawing with its ground. In these early years, he did not specify the dimensions of the work as it should be installed, nor the proportion that the work should take in relation to the total surface of the wall. When he switched medium – to coloured ink washes – in the early 1980s, LeWitt focused primarily on solid forms, on volumes in contradistinction to space per se, and sought to integrate the work into its containing architecture by stretching the composition to the bounding edges, even providing for such interruptions as doors and other apertures.

Riley, by contrast, is solely interested in the surface plane that a monumental wall in a gallery or museum can offer, and carefully defines and establishes the limits to her work, which are not those of the wall itself, and not related inherently or necessarily to the location: in short, this approach presupposes the white cube of the art gallery or museum – not public, commercial, or other kinds of sites. By avoiding any spillover into the perimeters of the architecture, and by retaining a margin that separates the wall drawing from the total area of the surface, her work ensures its self-contained character and, most importantly, its autoreflexivity. Similarly, since its internal scale and the dimensions of the elements have been determined by the pictorial field, and not by volumetric or other external dimensions, it remains securely within its own spatial and temporal parameters, emphatically self-affirming. Unlike LeWitt, who is increasingly preoccupied by such commissions (now constituting an important part of his practice), Riley regards herself as fundamentally a painter of easel paintings, however large they may become, and only rarely, and with great circumspection, undertakes mural commissions.

Lynne Cooke and Karen Kelly (eds), *Bridget Riley: Reconnaissance*, Dia Center for the Arts, New York, NY, 2000, pp.45–65.

1   Bridget Riley, 'According to Sensation', in *Bridget Riley*, exhibition catalogue, Sidney Janis
    Gallery, New York, NY, 1990, n.p.

2   'One of my great heroes is Cézanne', Riley affirmed recently, as quoted in Lynn
    MacRitchie, 'The Intelligence of the Eye', in *Bridget Riley: New Paintings and Gouaches*,
    exhibition catalogue, Waddington Galleries and Karsten Schubert, London, 2000, p.13.
    Riley has long been engaged with his work, and has made numerous study trips to his
    exhibitions. Cézanne's great late painting *The Bathers* (1884), with Titian's *Bacchus and
    Ariadne* (1520–23), formed the cornerstone in the exhibition *The Artist's Eye*, which she
    curated at the National Gallery, London, in 1989.

3   Riley, 'According to Sensation', *op.cit*

4   See Bridget Riley, 'The Colour Connection: In Conversation with Robert Kudielka' (1989),
    in Robert Kudielka (ed), *The Eye's Mind: Bridget Riley, Collected Writings 1965–1999*,
    Thames & Hudson, London, 1999, pp.142–73.

5   Bridget Riley, 'The Experience of Painting: Talking to Mel Gooding' (1988), in Kudielka
    (ed), *op.cit.*, p.122.

6   'I tend to work with open area space – and when I refer to this as "American" space one
    must not forget that it had its origins in Mondrian. It demands a shallow push-pull situation
    and a fluctuating surface.' Bridget Riley, 'In Conversation with Maurice de Sausmarez'
    (1967), *ibid.*, p.62. 'I see little significant difference between the two. *Autumn Rhythm*
    meant as much to me as *Broadway Boogie Woogie*.' Riley, 'According to Sensation', *op.cit.*

7   *White Noise* at Kunsthalle Bern, 1998. Her wall drawing *Composition with Circles 1* (1998)
    was her only contribution to a group show of mostly younger artists from various
    countries (including Gillian Wearing, Christian Marclay and Liza May Post) working in a
    variety of media other than painting. Riley, in fact, was painting's sole representative. It
    was both challenging and exciting for her to see her work in the context of a younger
    generation in this way. The situation presented by the invitation from Dia in New York
    was significantly different. Not only the layout of the galleries but the selection and
    hanging of the works were carefully orchestrated, so that, on first entering the show, the
    spectator would encounter works from the Egyptian series – that is, from the pivotal
    moment of the early eighties. Not until the third gallery did the visitor to the exhibition
    come upon the earliest works – signature paintings, including *Movement in Squares*
    (1961), *Crest* (1964) and *Pause* (1964). Moving on, the viewer then found her or him self
    at the threshold of the largest gallery, the core of the show, confronting, across the broad
    expanse of the room, Riley's latest work, *Composition with Circles 2*. This wall drawing
    was executed by assistants, as has been all Riley's work of the past four decades. The
    three Swiss artists who painted her first wall drawing also carried out *Composition with
    Circles 2*. The size-specificity of each work derives from and depends exclusively on the
    dimensions of the wall (156 by 588 inches in contrast to 204 by 367 inches in Bern; the
    diameters of the circles were 36 inches and 1 metre respectively, and in both cases the
    widths of the lines were 9 millimetres).

8   'I didn't come from Matisse, I arrived at Matisse, which was very surprising for me', Riley
    revealed recently, adding, 'One drew courage from the fact of Matisse, after the event, as
    it were.' Riley, quoted in MacRitchie, *op.cit.*, p.13. Riley's interest in Matisse also led her to
    visit the retrospective of his work held at the Museum of Modern Art, New York, in
    1992–93, which she credits with rekindling contemporary interest in and recognition of
    the artist's achievement.

9   Bridget Riley, 'Henri Matisse, The Dance,' unpublished text, September 1990.

10 Bridget Riley, 'Mondrian Perceived', in *Mondrian: Nature to Abstraction*, exhibition
    catalogue, Tate Gallery, London, 1997, p.10.

11   *Ibid.*, p.12.

12   *Jackson Pollock* at the Museum of Modern Art, New York, 1 November 1998 – 2 February
     1999. The exhibition was shown at the Tate Gallery, London, 11 March – 6 June 1999.

13   Bridget Riley, letter to the author, 12 December 2000.

14   *Ibid.* Once again, precedents not only were at hand from the art of the past but had
     already claimed Riley's attention, as evidenced in an interview from 1992 with Neil
     MacGregor, director of the National Gallery in London, concerning her experiences as one
     of its trustees. When discussing the collection, Riley remarked upon her relatively recent
     interest in Mantegna's grisaille, *The Introduction of the Cult of Cybele at Rome*
     (1505–06), before adding: 'I was amazed to see that Mantegna holds together the narrow
     horizontal format of his frieze in one long, all-embracing rhythm. The verve with which
     the first figure steps in is stopped – cut short by the straight line of the statue – as
     though by an enormous comma: then this movement, introduced by the first figure is
     picked up by the next two, turned around in the supplicating figure and continues in
     reverse until the very last figure where it changes back to echo the first.' Bridget Riley,
     'The Artist of the Past: Talking to Neil MacGregor', in Robert Kudielka (ed), *Bridget Riley:
     Dialogues on Art*, Zwemmer, London, 1995, p.23.

15   Maurice Merleau-Ponty, 'Eye and Mind', in *The Primacy of Perception*, James M Edie
     (ed), Northwestern University Press, Evanston, IL, 1964; Samuel Beckett, *Proust,* Grove
     Press, New York, NY, 1970; Marcel Proust, *À la recherche du temps perdu* (In Search of
     Lost Time), Gallimard, Paris, 1919–27; Paul Klee, Jürg Spiller (ed), *The Thinking Eye*, Ralph
     Manheim (trans), Lund Humphries, London, 1961. Klee's text was of enormous
     importance to Riley, both in encouraging a mode of inquiry, and in its thesis that pictorial
     elements, such as line, tone, colour, space, etc. – 'the basis of vision rather than its
     appearance', as Riley terms it – constitute the necessary point of departure in painting.
     Riley's engagement continues, as she is currently planning to co-curate an exhibition of
     Klee's work for the Hayward Gallery, London, in 2002 [*Paul Klee*, 17 January – 2 April 2014].

16   Merleau-Ponty, *op.cit.*, pp.165–66.

17   *Ibid.*, pp.183–84.

18   *Ibid.*, p.184. Note Merleau-Ponty's important recognition: 'Ultimately the painting relates to
     nothing at all among experienced things unless it is first of all "autofigurative". It is a
     spectacle of something only by being "a spectacle of nothing", by breaking the "skin of
     things" to show how the things become things, how the world becomes world.' *Ibid.*,
     p.182.

19   Maurice Merleau-Ponty, *The Visible and the Invisible*, Northwestern University Press,
     Evanston, IL, 1968. Riley seems momentarily to have experimented with such a course, as
     witnessed by her brief foray into installation-based work. *Continuum* (1963), a large-scale,
     three-dimensional structure whose walls were painted black and white, was ultimately
     destroyed because she felt it to be too literal.

20   Of course, Merleau-Ponty himself recognised that 'any theory of painting is a
     metaphysics… Painting is… a central operation contributing to the definition of our
     access to Being.' Merleau-Ponty, 'Eye and Mind', *op.cit.*, p.171.

21   Riley, 'The Experience of Painting', in Kudielka (ed), *The Eye's Mind, op.cit.*, p.122.

22   Riley, 'The Artist of the Past', in Kudielka (ed), *Dialogues on Art, op.cit.*, p.28.

23   Riley, quoted in Lisa G Corrin (ed), *Bridget Riley: Paintings from the 1960s and 70s,*
     exhibition catalogue, Serpentine Gallery and Koenig Books, London, 1999, n.p.

24   Riley, 'The Artist of the Past', in Kudielka (ed), *Dialogues on Art, op.cit.*, p.28.

25   Riley, quoted in Dave Hickey, 'Bridget Riley for Americans', in *Bridget Riley: Paintings
     1982–2000 and Early Works on Paper*, PaceWildenstein, New York, NY, 2000, p.8.

                                                                    LYNNE COOKE

26   Merleau-Ponty, 'Eye and Mind', *op.cit.*, p.182.
27   *Ibid.*, p.164.
28   Beckett, *op.cit.*, p.71.
29   Bridget Riley, 'A Visit to Egypt and the Decoration for the Royal Liverpool Hospital' (1984), in Kudielka (ed), *The Eye's Mind*, *op.cit.*, pp.112–13.

Bridget Riley and the Performance of Colour
Martin Hentschel

1 In New York City, in London studios

The two-venue exhibition of work by Bridget Riley in the Dia Center for
the Arts and at PaceWildenstein had already been open for a month
before I had the chance to go to New York in October 2000. There was
clearly a commotion amongst the painters there. Whether David Reed
or Fabian Marcaccio, Lydia Dona or Alan Uglow – they had all visited
the exhibitions and were now engaged in wide-ranging discussions.
I remembered that for Bridget Riley the major retrospectives of the work
of Paul Cézanne and Claude Monet, and of Jackson Pollock, had been
something of a touchstone for her own artistic eye; now her work had in
turn become a catalyst for the mid-generation painters in New York.
    Despite the furore that had accompanied Riley's appearance in 1965
at the exhibition *The Responsive Eye* in the Museum of Modern Art, her
work since then had been something of a myth to American artists. But
now, all of a sudden, it had become a tangible fact of life, a gauntlet that
could not be ignored. The challenge lay in the tautly drawn line running
through the two exhibitions, from works produced in the 1960s right up
to the present day, and back again. The immense rigour with which one
group follows on the previous one, and which reveals the compelling
nature of each artistic decision, *post festum*, had rarely been so
powerfully present as now in New York. And the same could be said for
the cyclic nature of her work: breaking off at a given point, taking up
certain issues from the past and embarking on yet another new
beginning. 'Nothing important really gets lost',[1] as Bridget Riley herself
once said – a fact that became stunningly clear to the New York public in
these two exhibitions.
    Barely a year later I was in England ringing the doorbell of the typical
London terrace house, where Bridget Riley was expecting me. As we
walked into the first-floor room to view her most recent works I could not
conceal my surprise, and as picture after picture was carefully unpacked

my excitement grew. Although my visit to New York had left a strong
impression, even this paled in the presence of these paintings. I was
surrounded by a cavalcade of colours, and it seemed as though each
one of these pictures was inviting me to view a dance of sights and
sensations. And although there are many places on this earth where
I have experienced what Riley calls 'the pleasures of sight', nevertheless
I was overcome by what I saw on that morning in London.[2]

Later, as the daylight faded we sat together in her East London
studio, exhausted by looking, but glad in the knowledge that we had
finished the selection process. Suddenly my eye was caught by one of
the gouaches pinned to the wall. The colours seemed noticeably muted,
the studio was silent around us, and only a few pale pinks and peach
tones refused to bow to the approaching twilight, like a distant echo of
the wealth of colour chords that I been aware of all day. When even
these last colours became submerged in the darkness, we called it
a day.

2 The preliminary drawings

Anyone contemplating Riley's large-format paintings could hardly imagine
that these compositions, apparently so light-footed and uncontrived, owe
their existence to a lengthy, meticulously organised working process,
which involves endless hazards, different directions, 'highways and
byways', to quote Paul Klee. First of all there is a drawing: for without a
formal framework, without the self-imposed rigours of an internal order –
which is already indicated by the use of graph paper – the distribution of
colours might take on a certain arbitrariness, which is not what Riley's
work is about. On the other hand, no lineature – however brilliant – can
prevent a false move when it comes to organising the colours. For in
Riley's paintings colour is also by definition form, and when a particular
colour-form has taken up its position in the picture field, it inevitably
already modifies the underlying drawing. All the various modifications
that feed into the final painting are beset with a high level of risk and
have the potential to fail. Even if it sometimes seems as though the

                                                   MARTIN HENTSCHEL

colour compositions were the outcome of a highly developed system, the fact is that – unlike the drawings – they derive entirely from the process of looking and a capacity for simultaneous vision. And although the armature provided by the drawing is never simply abandoned, at the sight of the finished composition it can seem quite distant. One might try in vain to extrapolate the original drawing from the final painting, for the paint has almost entirely absorbed it. So it is all the more fascinating to look specifically at the process leading to the final composition.

Taking as our example the four studies for *Curvilinear Grid* (1998), it is possible to identify various stages in the genesis of forms. The first two drawings, for instance, contain arcs of various sizes, and we can see that the decision went in favour of the shallower of these. Working along the verticals, Riley develops sequences of curves running on one side of the vertical, linked to others that appear alternately on the left and the right. The crucial point here is the distance separating the two different sequences of curves. It is only in the third drawing that the whole becomes a field of resonant curves.

Before that, in the second study there is an experiment with lines running at regular intervals from the verticals to points on the curves. But the fish-bone pattern that results and which is more than a little reminiscent of the early, black-and-white work *Descending* (1965) did not pass muster. In *Descending* the strongest curves occur more or less in the centre of the picture, and it was possible to link them to the intervening straight lines. In the drawing before us here, because of the comparative shallowness of the curves, a similar link would lead to the connecting lines cutting across each other. So the investigation was abandoned.

Nevertheless Riley pursued the sequence with curves to either side of the verticals and in the fourth study we already see these in combination with a new organisation of diagonal bands. In the centre of the drawing the regularity of the diagonals is interrupted by a vertical line, and restarts on the right side of the line, having shifted upwards by a third of its own vertical depth. Ever since Riley started to explore the 'plastic' energy of colour in 1986 she has worked at different times with caesuras and shifts of this kind. They serve primarily to generate particular rhythms in the colour texture, extending right across the picture field, from one edge to the other. In addition to this we can also see in the intersecting arcs and diagonals the characteristic curved wedge-shapes and pointed ovals that are often to be found in the newer paintings.[3] And with that the foundations have been laid for the colour combinations of the final composition.

3 Diversified colour-forms in the gouaches

But that is still a long way off. First there will be experiments with initially one or two colours and the various configurations of forms that they can assume. These are generally followed by a second pair of colours which greatly increases the level of complexity. Particularly at this early stage, where the drawing is still visible under the paint, the relativity of the drawn structural plan becomes evident: looking for instance at *Ground Study for July 24th, Bassacs '98* (1998) or *Ground Study for Revision of August 6th '99* (1999), we can clearly see how here and there the colour does not follow the drawn lines but creates different forms. These may or may not remain but either way this is determined by the needs of the composition as a whole. Their final role is governed by intuition and many long years of seeing.

Intuition and the experience born of years of seeing also direct the subsequent decision-making processes especially at the stage when Riley makes a whole battery of colour-forms, which are then placed temporarily in possible positions on the composition in order to test out the final effect. It is not unlike the process that Matisse used. As an example, *Rough Study for September 17, Bassacs '99* (1999) still has some of these coloured papers; they introduce a light and a dark green as well as a third midtone. Often it turns out that at certain stages in the making of a gouache a number of different solutions present themselves. Then the existing state is meticulously copied so that different highways and byways can be pursued simultaneously. Whether one or the other will prove to be successful can take a considerable time to discover, and at times these interim solutions can in fact lead to finished paintings with distinct characters of their own.

                                                                                      MARTIN HENTSCHEL

On the other hand, one and the same distribution of forms can lead to differently coloured outcomes. If we take, for example, *Ground Study for 28th August '98* (1998), the final combination of colour-forms (which itself contains a number of pentimenti compared to the original drawing) led ultimately to three independent gouaches. All had the same magenta as their base colour (on the sheet Riley refers to the magenta as 'architectural colour') and a different second colour. The results are astounding; depending on whether the second colour is yellow, green or blue, the magenta seems to have such a different level of saturation that one might imagine the same tone had not been used in all three gouaches. It is as though Josef Albers's textbook examples of colour squares interacting are transformed here into a dynamic musical sequence with different resonances and overtones. And so we see that the yellow bends the magenta towards the complementary violet, while the green bends it towards the complementary red. The more harmonious blue affects the architectural colour very differently, not least because the tonal values scarcely differ.

Unlike Albers's squares, the complex structure of these gouaches – and the more or less equal distribution of the two colours in the picture field – means that we also see sudden spatial reversals, especially where the colours come close to creating a complementary contrast. In other words, one's perception of those colours – and forms created by these colours – which are dominant, can change as often as one looks at the paintings. At times it seems impossible to say which colour-form is the ground and which the figure.

As the work proceeds, the addition of two or three further pairs of colours, or single colours, generally does not alter this uncertainty as to which colour-forms are dominant and which are ground. And this very instability in the colour-form combinations – like the shifting diagonals mentioned earlier – also creates rhythm, or rather, it creates the rhythms of a painting, with the result that colour sequences clearly flow across large expanses of the composition. One could even say that the speed of the colour movement in the painting is crucially dependent on the inconstant dominance of individual colours or pairs of colours. Thus in configurations with more than one colour, different speeds can be set,

which in turn connect differently to each other depending on the overall
organisation of the composition, as we will see later. And vice versa: the
more distinctly certain configurations detach themselves from the overall
colour composition, the more static the virtual movement becomes.

4 'Reliefs', optical levels, rhythms and cross-rhythms

Before Riley arrived at her present pictorial form she created a series of
paintings that took the stripes that she had used up until the mid-1980s
and crossed these with diagonal forms. These works, which first appeared
in 1986 and are identifiable by their characteristic rhomboids, are of
particular interest in that the latest of these already herald the new form.

Initially, for instance in *New Day* (1988), the basic structure of
verticals and diagonals was transformed by disturbances in the forms
and colours to such an extent that the painting took on depths one
might associate with a sculptural relief. In places, larger colour-forms can
be identified, both clearly defined and interlocked. Meanwhile the
inclusion of black and white contributes to the fact that overall the 'relief'
is kept fairly shallow.

Throughout these paintings the distribution of colour followed the
underlying structure ever more closely, which decreased the spread of
individual colours. At the same time, the range of chromatic passages
gained dramatically. Moving at different speeds, the colours now drifted
through the pictorial field, forming an imaginary optical level with its own
intangible spatiality which seemed to detach itself from the actual picture
surface. *Set Fair* (1989) and *High Sky 2* (1992) are amongst the most
outstanding examples of this pictorial form. Gradually the caesuras and
disturbances increased and with that, so too did the colour contrasts. As
the colours themselves became ever more plastic, the colour speeds
decreased. *In Attendance* (1993) is one of the works that marks this
change.

The next step – which is about finding a way of combining the three-
dimensional, 'plastic' effect of the colours with stronger rhythms – is
apparent in the gouaches of 1995–96. And here the artist takes up an

interim solution developed during work on the stripe paintings and realised in the painting *Gentle Edge* (1986): vertical stripes separated at irregular intervals by vertical bands of diagonals in two alternating colours. In the gouache *Preliminary Study for July 18th, Bassacs '95* (1995) the vertical bands provide the dominant pictorial rhythm while the extended rhomboids set up a cross-rhythm. Rhythm and cross-rhythm create an unstable colour field with a variety of different depths. By contrast, in the gouache *Preliminary Study for October 6th, Bassacs '96* (1996) the two rhythms are more closely related by virtue of the more similar tonal values. In keeping with this, the sequence of spatial depths seems smoother. The result is a harmonious colour chord with magenta and green as its main colours, interspersed by accents in light and darker blue, orange and cream.

In these works the movement (or 'drive' as Riley calls it) runs exclusively from left to right across the composition, that is to say in the direction one would read a Western book. Perhaps because of this the artist added in 1997 a new element to the existing forms: the curved segment. In *Lagoon 1* (1997) this new possibility is seen in paradigmatic form. And since the 'backwards-facing' curves are also painted in the most radiant colour, orange, there is a clear counter-weight to the diagonal drive. Although the spatial effect of the colour is comparable with *Preliminary Study for October 6th, Bassacs '96*, now the two different drives are so carefully balanced that it seems as one looks at the painting that a halting circular motion ensues – from left to right and back again. This in itself points to the structure of Riley's most recent paintings which operate with segments curved in both directions.

5 Polyphony and simultaneity

Strictly speaking Riley's current compositions also include elements that go back to seeds sown many years ago. Here I am thinking of paintings like *Arrest 2* (1965) or *Drift 1* (1966), where pulsating, garland-like bands curving to left and right set up a vertical movement that has, at the same time, a diagonal impulse derived from the interconnections between the bands as a whole. Yet the configurations in Riley's current works are also more complex in that they coordinate verticals, horizontals and double curves. The painting *Rêve* (1999) is the first large-format instance of this coordination. It is also apparent here that the vertical system is only implied, with curves and diagonals more or less dividing the picture field between themselves. Compared to *Lagoon 1* the colours are considerably reduced, and each covers relatively large areas. This in turn changes the overall impression of the colour chords. While the colours in *Lagoon 1* could be described as orchestral in their effect, in *Rêve* there is just one gently resounding chord.

Riley soon came to the conclusion that these new rhythms needed a horizontal picture format and in the case of *Evoë I* (2000) the width is almost three times that of the height. The result is again musical in the extreme. Constructed using two pairs of colours (pink/magenta and green/blue), the pink sets up a diagonal rhythm that paces out the full length of the painting. A second rhythm is instigated by the green, which partially follows the pink one and partially echoes the different swing of the blue colour-forms. The blue enters with great force at the left edge of the painting and decreases as it moves from left to right. With its directional schema the blue prepares the way for the main subject, performed by the colour magenta which after a halting entrance comes into its own more or less halfway through the painting. Here, magenta flanked by blue and green, resounds in a powerful chord. Towards the end of the run of the painting, and in reverse formation – green and blue flanked by magenta – an echo of the same chord is heard.

The visual experience of *Evoë* is similar to that of the three versions of *Parade* (1999–2000) in that it derives from the simultaneity of multi-layered colour processes. The large format of *Evoë* can only be taken in from a suitable distance and perhaps encourages the viewer into sequential looking. This may be why Riley realised the subsequent series – her most recent – in a somewhat more compact form. On the other hand the level of interaction between the colours also seems to be heightened in these recent works.

A fine example of this is *Two Reds* (2000), where a dark green sets up an underlying diagonal rhythm running the full length of the

    MARTIN HENTSCHEL

composition, only to find a paler neighbouring colour playing around it and in a sense interrupting it. Throughout the interplay of these two tones, the thematic reds stand out, graceful and light-footed. And while the glowing magenta always takes a foreground position, the more muted red moves with greater ease between the green tones. Two different movements in red can be distinguished: the first runs in an arc across two thirds of the composition, before returning in the opposite direction. At the height of the turning point (which Riley usually calls the 'twist') a second movement ensues, which also makes a slight backwards turn towards the end of the painting. The different radiance of the two reds generates a spatial differentiation that encompasses both movements. Arc-like motion and diagonal upward movements seem to be caught in suspended animation, which can largely be attributed to the open blue that also gives the painting its characteristic, indeterminate depth. Since the complementary contrast red/green is only ever implied, but never fully realised, the main colours readily unite, yet without solidifying into one single colour-form. And the repetition of forms in different colours also underpins the rhythmic flow, particularly clearly in the upper third of the painting, where pointed arcs moving across the full length of the composition form a kind of staccato.

Given that in the preceding works one could sense a tendency to accentuate the beginning and the end of a composition, thereby defining the extent of its drive, in *Blues and Greens* (2001) Riley treats these limits in a firm but subtle manner: two curved segments, one each in the upper left and lower right, mark the beginning and end of the painting. Unlike *Lagoon 1*, where the arcs are clearly separate, these are incorporated into the flow of the composition by their neighbouring colour-forms. As indicators these arcs are very helpful, pointing to the tension of the diagonal descending arc of colours which in itself forms the counter-balance to the multicoloured upwards drive of the forms. Compared to *Two Reds*, the overall impression of the painting is one of greater fluidity, for the colour contrasts have been minimised, and the tonal values are much closer.

In comparison to the cool colours of *Blues and Greens*, the painting *Magenta and Peach, Blue and Green* (2001) radiates a light warmth. It has the strongest colours of any in this series, one might even describe it as opulent. As I endeavoured to grasp the colour combinations, Riley pointed out that as it happened, they had perhaps a certain affinity to the flora in Monet's paintings. ('This may be a way into seeing the structure', she remarked.) At the beginning there is a dense chord of four colours, setting in train a downwards movement which restarts – fanned out a little – at the halfway point of the composition. Although the magenta is certainly the most dominant colour – supported by the chromatically close peach tone – it is extremely interesting to see how the green, which one would normally regard as a background colour, moves forward into the closest foreground. With its high level of saturation it is even responsible for the distinct caesuras in the colour-flow.

Although every painting in the series has its own colour character, they are all based on the same structural drawing. This alone links them as a group, and here again the artist refers to the practice of Monet: only by creating a given, immutable order of things in the shape of the garden he himself laid out in Giverny was he in the position to register precisely the subtlest of changes in the colours at any time of the day or year. The same garden, the same trees, the same pond – and a never-ending metamorphosis of colours. While Riley, for her part, does not draw on a model in nature, it is as though the abstract plans of her drawings are her garden in Giverny. And this in turn leads to the many coloured modalities that give each of her paintings its unmistakable character.

6 The visual forces of nature – Delaunay – music as a metaphor

It is clear that any verbal analysis of Riley's painting can never catch up with all there is to be seen; added to which, words are in constant danger of missing the point. This is partly because language is linear while the visual perception of a painting is comparatively 'simultaneous', although one has to work to achieve this simultaneity particularly in the case of Riley's paintings, where the changing and multifocal colour impulses seem to make it almost impossible to take in the work as a whole. But it is also because language is filled with metaphors. In the case of a representational painting, the wealth of verbal metaphors can positively help to establish a connection to the image. By contrast, in the description of a non-representational painting the metaphor can become a hindrance: it creates images where there are none. So how can we talk about pure colour-forms?

In the early days of abstraction writers still had recourse to metaphysics. Wassily Kandinsky's 'cosmic world',[4] Kazimir Malevich's 'non-obiective truth',[5] Piet Mondrian's 'Neue Gestaltung' as 'forming of the universal',[6] Robert Delaunay's 'vital movement of the world'.[7] All these were modes of explanation and legitimation that sought to solve the perplexing question of the perception of pure colour-forms by attributing to these a fundamental connection to the totality of human existence. However, since the dawn of the New Age, metaphysics has few followers, and so once again we have to turn our attention to the paintings themselves.

As far as Riley's work is concerned, some years ago Robert Kudielka notably took as his starting point the relationship between her painting and the sensations we experience in the face of living nature. He showed that her work is not about abstract mimesis but reactivates the 'visual forces'[8] that evoke an image of nature as though seen from the 'interior of a tree'.[9] Seen in this light, natural phenomena do not precede the paintings as such but rather come into their own through the impact of painting. Kudielka cites Riley's own comment: 'Isn't it curious that nature immediately looks so much better once I've got a painting together?'[10]

In the interview with David Sylvester we find a singular occasion where nature leads to a painting.[11] In her account of the conception of *Static 1* (1966) she describes seeing a huge area of shimmering shale at the top of a mountain in France: 'Visually it was total confusion'. This account is enlightening in two respects; in the first place it points to the pre-conceptual nature of her visual perception and in the second it shows that there is an unbridgeable hiatus between the first-hand impression of nature and the final composition. No one, however inventive, would be likely to see an expanse of shale of whatever kind in

Static 1. This alone ought to make one think twice before using metaphors from nature to describe Riley's paintings. But is it possible to control one's perception of her paintings so as to exclude any memories of the colours of the natural world – which are themselves scarcely separable from natural objects?

Yet this is precisely the assumption made by Delaunay when, in response to Michel Eugène Chevreul's harmonies of similarity and contrast, he developed his *peinture abstrait vivante*, which he also called *peinture pure*.[12] In fact it is possible that Delaunay's notion of painting comes closest to that of Riley's. Like Riley, Delaunay was interested in creating different speeds by means of colour contrasts and relationships, hastening or slowing down the movement within the configuration of colours. And when he talks of the combined static and dynamic forces in his paintings as a *simultanéité rythmique*, it is as though he were anticipating a characteristic feature of Riley's paintings.[13]

Of course there are also clear differences between the work of the two artists. In Riley's work there is no place for equating the simultaneous and synchronous movement of colour with the 'universal drama',[14] and one could also question whether Riley's colour sequences lead to a 'consolidated overall view'.[15] Is it not rather the case that the instability of the chromatic movement in Riley's work mean that the viewing process can never be deemed finished? Moreover in the works made after the move towards 'plasticity' there is little or no suggestion of light, whereas the creation of coloured light was central to Delaunay's painting. Despite this, in some of Delaunay's late works, for instance the series Endless Rhythm (1933–35), there does appear to be a rudimentary version of the coloured drive that Riley has taken to new heights in her latest works.

Yet this still does not adequately answer the question as to how one should talk about colour-forms. It seems virtually impossible to find a way to avoid metaphors, although as long as one is aware that they are no more than temporary props, they may be of some use in our contemplation of a painting. As we have seen, the artist herself has referred to the architectural aspect of the use of colour. On one hand a single colour can function as a structural (architectural) element. On the

                                                MARTIN HENTSCHEL

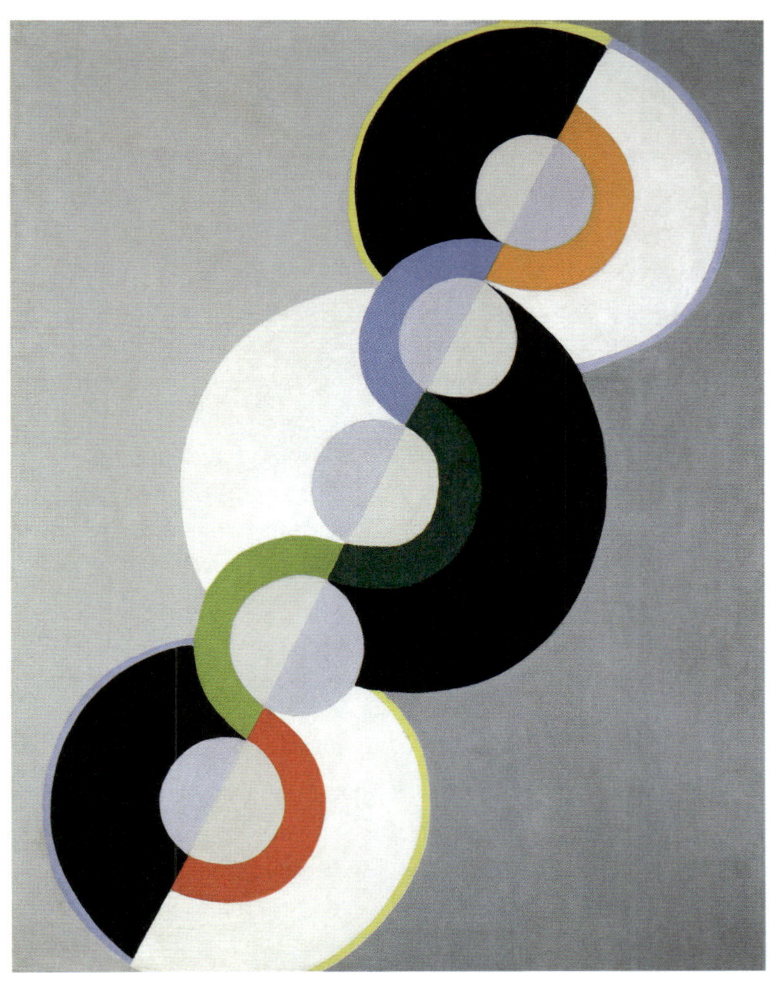

Robert Delaunay
Endless Rhythm 1935
Oil on canvas
161.9 × 130.2 cm | 63¾ × 51¼ in
Tate, London

other hand – and this goes right back to Riley's earliest paintings – the paintings clearly also need a constant architectural schema for the coloured orchestration and the different colour speeds to come into their own.[16] Thus the colours and forms used in a painting are often contrapuntal, although the forms always derive from the distribution of colours.

It seems much more apt to draw on the musical features of the work, which inevitably surface in any description, and which we have turned to more than once here. Even if music is linear and does not have the same simultaneity as painting, it is nevertheless, like Riley's paintings, non-representational.[17] In this connection one cannot help but be struck by the fact that the titles of her most recent works – unlike the earlier works – contain few, if any, poetic metaphors, and predominantly use names of colours. In fact the process by which the final colour distribution is arrived at could also support a musical reading: it is only when the coloured papers, having been shifted from position to position, have found their final configuration that the composition acquires its own particular resonance. Thus the 'score' and the 'performance' are as one. A feature of Riley's current paintings is without doubt the fact that even in the first moment of one's looking each has its own 'key', which is utterly non-conceptual. And ultimately the dual resonance of her most recent works (a term that applies equally to colours and sounds) encourages the viewer to respond to their musicality.

Yet this should certainly not be taken to mean that the outside world is now excluded. For Riley the 'pleasures of sight'– in nature as in everyday human existence – that nourish her imagination are as vital as ever. Perhaps the true individuality of these works comes from their capacity to evoke music, architecture and nature at the same moment. These different elements combine yet hold their own, setting in motion an alchemy of seeing that suddenly allows what is painted to be recognised as itself.

Martin Hentschel (ed), *Bridget Riley: New Work*, exhibition catalogue, Kunstmuseen Krefeld, Krefeld and Hatje Cantz Verlag, Ostfildern, 2002, pp.49–59.

                                        MARTIN HENTSCHEL

1   As cited in Robert Kudielka, 'The Paintings of the Years 1982–1992 in the Context of the Previous Work', in *Bridget Riley. Paintings 1982–1992*, exhibition catalogue, Kunsthalle Nürnberg, Nuremberg, 1992, p.32.

2   See Bridget Riley, 'The Pleasures of Sight' (1984), in Robert Kudielka (ed), *The Eye's Mind: Bridget Riley, Collected Writings 1965–1999*, Thames & Hudson, London, 1999, pp.30.

3   If one were seeking associations one might be tempted to describe these not so much as pointed ovals but as leaf-shapes or even mandorlas. But any such glib identification is entirely at odds with the non-representational character of Riley's work. The difficulties of finding a suitable language to discuss her work are touched on in section 6 of this essay.

4   'Thus, next to the "real" world abstract art puts a new world that in its externals has nothing to do with "reality." Internally, however, it is subject to the general laws of the cosmic world.' Wassily Kandinsky, in Kenneth C Lindsay and Peter Verga (eds), *Kandinsky: Complete Writings on Art*, Faber & Faber, London, 1982, p.832.

5   'Breaking the objective world down into its constituent parts certainly does not mean breaking art down or destroying the spirit of art. On the contrary, it endows the spirit of art with new rights, it raises it into the non-objective truth, into a new reality of being.' Kazimir Malevich, in W Haftmann (ed), *Suprematismus – Die gegenstandslose Welt*, H Riesen (trans), Dumont, Cologne, 1962, p.67.

6   '"Neue Gestaltung" should not be called abstract, not only because it is the direct forming of the universal, but also, because in its forming it excludes the individual (the natural-concrete).' Translated from Piet Mondrian, 'Die Neue Gestaltung in der Malerei', in *De Stijl*, 1917–18.

7   'L'idée du mouvement vital du monde et son mouvement est simultanéité.' Robert Delaunay, *Du cubisme à l'art abstrait*. SEVPEN, Paris, 1957, p.146.

8   'For me nature is not landscape, but the dynamism of visual forces – an event rather than an appearance', Bridget Riley, 'Working with Nature' (1973), in Kudielka (ed), *The Eye's Mind, op.cit.*, p.88.

9   Robert Kudielka, 'Bridget Riley', *op.cit.*, p.9.

10   'Riley's attachment to the great *plein air* colourists strengthened her resolve not to rely on any kind of external reality. If Monet and Cézanne had to retreat to the edge of abstraction *sur le motif*, why should it not be possible to do the reverse, to develop a relationship with nature from working within abstraction itself? Riley's newly built studio in the South of France deliberately has no window overlooking the splendid panorama of the plateau of Vaucluse. And in leaving the house and walking on the hillside in the hour before dusk when the colours are released from the domination of the sun, she is not "hunting for visual sensations", not searching for "material" for her paintings. It is rather like someone returning home after a perfectly normal day at work. Yet it is not quite so normal. When she had completed the full-size cartoon for *Dark Light* last winter she remarked: "Isn't it curious that nature immediately looks so much better once I've got a painting together?"' *Ibid.*, p.12.

11   Bridget Riley, 'Interview with David Sylvester' (1967), in Kudielka (ed), *op.cit.*, p.70.

12   Delaunay, *op.cit.*, p. 61, 95. For a detailed discussion of Delaunay's use of colour see Max Imdahl, *Farbe. Kunsttheoretische Reflexionen in Frankreich*, Wilhelm Fink Verlag, Munich, 1987, p.134.

13   Delaunay, *op.cit.*, p.146.

14   *Ibid.*, p.180.

15   Imdahl, *op.cit.*, p.149

16   I am thinking here, for instance, of the painting *Where* (1964).

17   At one point Delaunay writes: 'I played with the colours, in the same way that one can express oneself in music with the colour and forms of fugal phrases.' Delaunay, *op.cit.*, p.81.

A Dialogue with Sensation: The Art of Bridget Riley

Paul Moorhouse

For over 40 years Bridget Riley has been making paintings in which the
experience of sight is a central, abiding concern. It could of course be
argued that seeing is a necessary condition of all painting – that there is
no other way of approaching a pictorial image. But among contemporary
painters, few have made visual sensation *itself* so integral to their work.
Since 1961, Riley's subject matter has been restricted to a simple
vocabulary of abstract shapes – squares, circles, ovals, lines, stripes and
curves – disposed in increasingly complex and subtle arrangements. In
the absence of any external motif, such elements have been her starting
point. Her paintings are the outcome of the dialogue she establishes
with these agents: a close, empirical and essentially intuitive way of
working which offers, in its final resolution, visual experiences of
astonishing resonance and beauty.

Riley's paintings exist on their own terms. Each work has its own
character and each is self-contained in the sense that, like a piece of
music, its structure arises from purely internal formal or expressive
considerations generated by the relationships between its component
parts. They do not refer to other objects and they do not seek to evoke
specific earlier phenomena. It is perhaps surprising, therefore, to realise
that the source of Riley's engagement with visual experience is nature. In
her compelling essay 'The Pleasures of Sight' (1984) she describes in
detail the inspiration and joy she derived from looking at the landscape
and the effects of light and weather during her childhood in Cornwall.[1]
Significantly, such encounters with her surroundings are Riley's first vivid
memories of enjoying perception for its own sake. Her account of these
revelations strongly conveys a sense of sheer wonder in the act of
looking: in part arising from the splendour of the natural scene, in part
from the fresh, untainted gaze of the observer. A child's eyes are open to
such experiences. That they occur less frequently in later life is lamented
by Riley, and she concludes: 'It seems to me that as an artist one's work
lies here.'[2]

Riley's art is in this sense apparently paradoxical. The pleasures of sight yielded by nature that she knew as a child formed the basis of her visual awareness; and, as an artist, the creation of visual pleasure is her stated purpose. Nature, however, is not Riley's subject. Early on she perceived the futility – indeed, impossibility – of attempting to convey the experience of seeing by depicting an external subject. In the same essay she observed:

> The pleasures of sight have one characteristic in common – they take you by surprise. They are sudden, swift and unexpected. If one tries to prolong them, recapture them or bring them about wilfully their purity and freshness is lost. They are essentially enigmatic and elusive. One can stare at a landscape, for example, which a moment ago seemed vibrant and find it inert and dull – so one cannot say that this lively quality of sight is simply 'out there in nature', or easily available to be commanded as wished. Nor is it a state of mind which, once acquired, can bend the most stubborn and unrewarding aspect of external reality to its own purposes. It is neither one nor the other but a perfect balance between the two, between the inner and the outer.[3]

The depiction of a subject in nature is rooted, in Riley's view, precisely in that which is to be avoided, namely the attempt to recreate an earlier visual experience. Such attempts at depiction are, in her view, forlorn. In reproducing the appearance of an external subject the resulting image would fail completely to convey the special relationship – that state of perfect balance – that existed fleetingly between the subject and the observer and in which the pleasures of sight are to be found.

For Riley, such singular visual experiences are events. They exist in the present and they cannot be relived as memories. In addressing the lively quality of sight that Riley first identified in nature, paradoxically her work withdraws from the depiction of the external world and creates new relationships. These connections exist on a formal level, within the work of art itself in harnessing and liberating visual forces to which the viewer can respond. In addition, they exist in the bridge formed between the

work of art and the observer's inner perceptual and emotional
responses, so that, as in nature, the inner and the outer are drawn into a
dialogue. There is also a new, parallel relationship between Riley's art
and nature – based, not on depiction or resemblance, but on
equivalence, metaphor and recognition. Part of the fascination exercised
by her work lies in the viewer's perception that individual paintings
comprise simple formal units; yet in the act of looking, these units begin
to generate a new level of visual experience – one that seems not
simply specific to each painting but, surprisingly, to recall things seen
previously. The creation of these relationships has underpinned the
development of Riley's art, colouring the way it forms both a celebration
and an exploration of a fundamental human experience: sight.

Early years

Seen as a whole, Riley's work suggests a remarkable degree of internal
cohesion and orderly, even logical, progression. It would, however, be
misleading to suggest that her development as an artist has proceeded
according to pre-determined assumptions or in the pursuit of particular
objectives. This would be inimical to the spirit of enquiry and sense of
discovery which more truly are its guiding lights.

Riley's paintings, it is true, fall into particular phases or groups in
which it is possible to discern a central, underlying idea being worked
through and its possibilities being teased out. However, rather than
following a programme as such, these internal connections more closely
resemble the musical principle of variations on a certain theme in which
a formal motif is subjected to ideas of repetition, inversion, modulation,
transposition and transformation. In this respect Riley's art, rather than
following a simple line of development, may be seen to have advanced
in more complex ways: in terms of statement, contradiction, fusion, echo
and the redevelopment and mutation of earlier ideas.

Riley was born in 1931 in London. Following a year spent in
Lincolnshire, during the war she lived with her mother, younger sister
and aunt in a cottage near Padstow in Cornwall. At this time she had

little contact with her father, who, at the start of the war, had enlisted in the Royal Artillery and subsequently spent three years as a prisoner of the Japanese. For Riley this was a formative period. Her mother loved to walk in the landscape and had a gift for looking – a visual sensitivity to her surroundings – which she conveyed to her children.

To this day, Riley recalls the 'rich and varied' character of these early encounters with nature, subject as ever to the transforming hand of the weather and to the pervading influence of the changing light: 'My mother took us out for walks on the cliff. She was always pointing out colours in the sea; the sparkle of dew; changes of colour when the dew was brushed away.'[4] These fleeting, unstable chromatic effects in nature are echoed in the analogous language of paint after 1967, when Riley's work embraced pure colour. Riley's aunt, who had been an art student at Goldsmiths, London, was also instrumental in forging the artist's early appreciation of the appearance of things, not least when she began making her first drawings and paintings.

Riley's formal art education was a traditional one, being rooted in the principles of observation. It commenced at Cheltenham Ladies' College in 1946 where her art teacher was Colin Hayes, who later became a tutor at the Royal College of Art, London. Hayes impressed on his pupil the importance of tonal relationships, confirming a sensitivity to the play of light that would later be a vital aspect of Riley's work. Under his guidance she also laid the foundations of her art historical knowledge. Significantly, her earliest affinities were with artists who emphasised the role of colour. She formed an enthusiasm for impressionist painting and in 1947 she saw the Vincent van Gogh exhibition at the Tate Gallery. This feeling for colour is manifest in her decision in 1949 to make a copy of Jan van Eyck's painting, *Portrait of a Man in a Red Turban* (1433), prompted, it appears, by her interest in the colour relationship between the intense red of the sitter's headdress and the dark background. Even at this fledgling stage, Riley's tendency to approach a subject in formal terms is apparent.

Riley subsequently submitted her copy of the Van Eyck as part of a successful application to Goldsmiths, where she studied from 1949 to 1952. Here she received intensive training in life drawing, benefiting

PAUL MOORHOUSE

especially from the tutelage of Sam Rabin, whom Riley recalls as 'a marvellous teacher'.[5] A regime of continuous drawing from the model sharpened the students' visual acuity; but Rabin's particular strength as a teacher lay in his ability to develop an awareness of the need to structure the response to a motif. This meant that illustration of the appearance of the subject was insufficient. The image had to be considered in terms of its autonomous pictorial organisation, with all of its constituent elements weighed in relation to the whole. For example, in a life drawing of a nude made around her second or third year, the degree to which Riley has digested this approach may be seen. The figure is turned away from the observer and is treated as no more or less important than the setting. Rather, the focus of attention is on the tonal relationship between the model's back and the wall against which the figure is seen, using the exposed white ground of the paper to define both these elements and to imply mass. With hindsight, Riley later recognised a developing appreciation of 'the abstract nature of what one was doing.'[6]

Towards abstraction

Rabin stressed the value of adopting a methodical approach and of building pictorial relationships carefully. In visits to the Prints and Drawings room at the British Museum, London, this was a discipline he substantiated by reference to drawings by such masters as Raphael, Rembrandt and − of particular importance to Riley − Ingres. When she transferred to the Royal College of Art in 1952, the absence of a structured way of working made itself felt. Notwithstanding contact with a group of talented fellow students − which included Frank Auerbach, John Bratby, Richard Smith and Joe Tilson − and the continued support of Colin Hayes and John Minton, Riley did not prosper. Concentrating now on painting, for a while she adopted the loose, expressive handling of paint being developed by some of her contemporaries but found that this did not suit her. This would not be the last time that Riley found greater freedom inimical to creativity.

On leaving the Royal College of Art in 1955, Riley entered a period of personal unhappiness which lasted for over two years. In addition to illness, it was a time marked by indecision in artistic terms about how to proceed; and although she continued to paint she did so without reaching any clear sense of personal direction or purpose. There were, however, signposts on the way. In early 1956, as for so many artists of her generation, the exhibition at the Tate Gallery *Modern Art in the United States* was a revelation. The final room contained paintings by the leading Abstract Expressionists; and among these, Jackson Pollock, whose solo exhibition at the Whitechapel Art Gallery, London, in 1958 she also saw, made the greatest impression on Riley. Pollock's radical invention of a new kind of shallow, multifocal pictorial space, his intuitive, non-hierarchical organisation of elements within that virtual space, and his absolute renunciation of depiction, all seemed to contain important implications. Even so, the insistent subjectivity of Pollock's expressive approach – manifest in his observation: 'I am nature'– and his emphasis on the paintings' status as objects, gave rise to doubts.[7] Though these were radical developments, at the same time Riley sensed that they were 'an end'.[8]

Her inability to find a path continued to the end of the decade. Maurice de Sausmarez, who later wrote the first monograph on Riley, recalled the impression made by a visit to her studio in 1959, shortly after they met: 'there was proof enough of the desperate struggle she was having to find some firm ground, following an enforced break of three years'. The influences he detected in her work included late Matisse, Bonnard, Ingres and Signac. He concluded: 'None of these influences, explored with a mounting sense of desperation, was to prove wholly irrelevant to her later work, although the way forward was entirely unknown and unpredictable.'[9] Nevertheless, the tide had perhaps begun to turn. Earlier that year, Riley had seen and been greatly stimulated by *The Developing Process: New Possibilities in Art Teaching* exhibition held at the Institute of Contemporary Arts, London. The show was organised by Harry Thubron and Victor Pasmore, both of whom were influential teachers, at Leeds and Newcastle respectively, who had pioneered radical teaching methods based on Bauhaus principles. The exhibition

                                                    PAUL MOORHOUSE

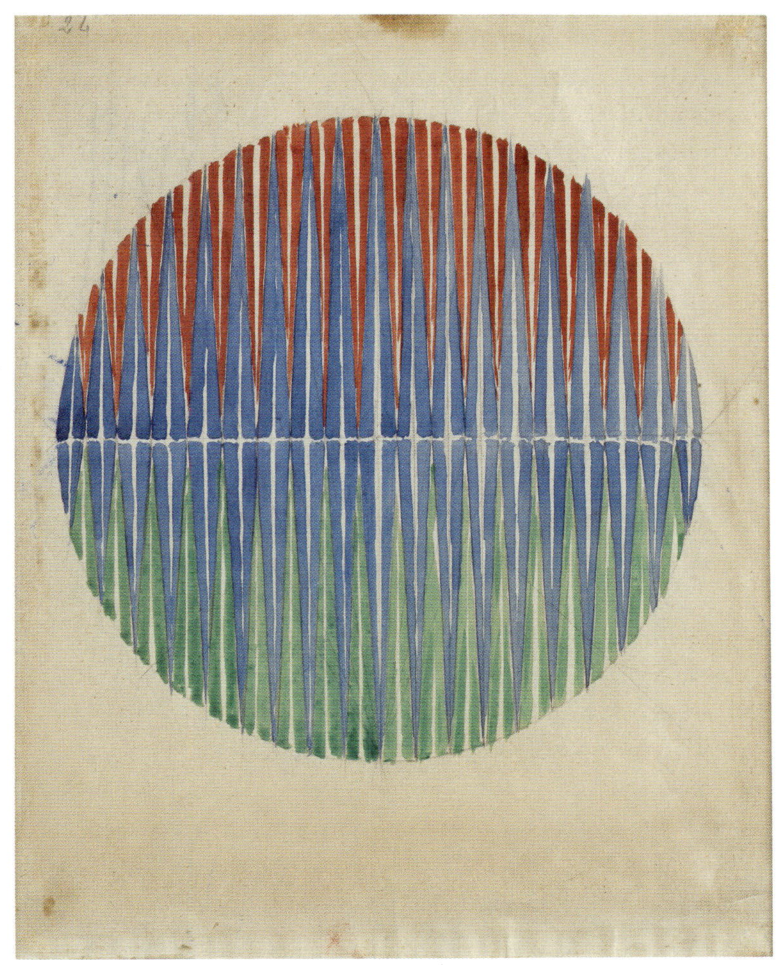

Giacomo Balla
Study for Iridescent Interpenetration No.2 1912
Pencil and watercolour on paper
22 × 17.7 cm | 8½ × 7 in
Galleria Civica d'Arte Moderna, Turin

drew attention to the work being made as a result of their new Basic Form ideas. On the courses they ran, Thubron and Pasmore both emphasised the potential of working directly with relations of form and colour and of liberating these elements from a purely descriptive role. The essence of this approach is contained in the following statement by Joseph Albers, who was director of the Bauhaus course from 1925: 'Our start is not retrospection, nor the ambition to illustrate, to embellish or to express something. We try to learn, i.e. to see, that every visible thing has form...'.[10] Riley had the opportunity to explore these principles further when she attended Thubron's summer school in Suffolk in 1959. Hitherto, Riley had remained convinced that a visual language of abstract form was not for her. However, the notion of pictorial autonomy now began to register, not least given her growing equivocation about the role of literal depiction.

Riley had met Maurice de Sausmarez at Thubron's summer school and immediately afterwards the two travelled to Spain and Portugal. In the following summer, they visited Italy. De Sausmarez was then carrying out research on futurist painting and at the Venice Biennale they were able to absorb the impact of seeing 143 major paintings by such painters as Umberto Boccioni, Gino Severini and Giacomo Balla. The last, in particular, made a deep impression. Riley often speaks of responding to hints about possible lines of development which are contained in her own work. The hint she recognised in Balla was that sensations of movement and light are most effectively evoked, not by illustration, but by *equivalent* pictorial means. In *Girl Running on a Balcony* (1912), the figure in motion is evoked by multiple, repeated images of the girl's body in different positions. In a work such as *Iridescent Compenetration No.2* (1912), Balla uses purely abstract means – the interpenetration of repeated lines – to generate a sensation of iridescent light. This is an idea echoed by Riley in *Breathe* (1966), a work she painted six years after her visit to Italy.

Concurrent with these discoveries, Riley's earlier interest in Impressionism had led to a deeper immersion in nineteenth- and twentieth-century French painting. This culminated in a prolonged and detailed engagement with the work of Seurat. In Seurat, Riley recognised an artist struggling to identify and to apply those underlying natural laws implicit in the Impressionists' representation of light. This realisation led Riley to attempt to analyse Seurat's approach and in 1959, working from a reproduction, she painted an enlarged copy of his *Bridge at Courbevoie* (1886–87). The following year, she applied the insights she had gained in painting *Pink Landscape* (1960) a powerful evocation of heat and blinding light based on studies made in the sun-drenched hills south of Siena.

Pink Landscape is both a beginning and an end. A beginning in that, arguably, it is her first fully realised painting. Turning now from literal depiction, Riley's understanding of the role of equivalent pictorial means is manifest in her use of small discrete dots of colour which mix optically to generate a sensation of heat and light. An end in that, as a response to an external motif, this method had limitations. As Riley later observed of Seurat: 'he was depicting not so much an external reality as his own structure of sight'.[11] Nevertheless, her study of Seurat had yielded valuable insights. In particular, his relaxation of description and liberation of chromatic energy from pictorial elements demonstrated 'an abstract sensibility' whose expressive potential was clear.[12] The problem that remained was how to create an appropriate formal architecture – one capable of generating and containing visual sensation. Riley felt she had come to a better understanding of colour, largely through her investigation of Seurat's technique, and in that respect the option to continue her neo-Impressionist manner existed. At the same time, however, she felt that this way of working had reached some sort of conclusion. Her deliberations about the next move were overtaken in autumn 1960 by a break in her relationship with De Sausmarez, an event which provoked a personal as well as an artistic crisis.

Her initial response was an impulse to abandon painting completely. This was succeeded by a desire to make a new beginning, to put her previous experience behind her and start again. To achieve that she felt she had to be as clear as possible. Whatever she did had to be absolute, unqualifiable. These considerations plunged her in repeated attempts to make a single, all-black painting. Riley saw this as an attempt to send 'a very personal message to a particular person, about the nature of things.

At that point in time I wanted to say *that there were absolutes*, that one could not pretend that black was white.'[13] This was, as she has observed with hindsight, a highly emotive gesture and in artistic terms it proved unsuccessful. Despite the emotional intensity with which it was invested, an all-black painting – to her surprise – said nothing.

In attempting to create a completely unqualifiable structure, Riley saw that she had eliminated any possibility of visual and expressive tension. The lesson she drew from Seurat was that contrast is essential: the relationships created between clearly differentiated elements are an animating force, stimulating the eye, exciting the senses and conveying a sense of life. With these considerations in mind, Riley began a new work, *Kiss* (1961), a painting containing the seeds of the subsequent black-and-white works that would occupy her for the next six years. This is no less a 'personal message' than its all-black predecessor but in terms of its success as a painting it is a world away. Most surprising perhaps is the extreme economy of means responsible for this quantum leap. A skein of white is stretched across a black square, fanning out at the edges and dividing the black into two areas of unequal size. The relationships between these contrasted shapes carry the painting's expressive resonance: generating a sense of unequal opposition in the way the larger shape bears down on its counterpart, and of compression, revealed in the narrowing of the white division. Yet, this feeling of weight is effectively counteracted by an impression of extreme delicacy as the two black shapes almost touch – but not quite. As a result, the narrow gap between the two shapes creates a point of extreme visual tension.

Although she had not intended to make more than one black-and-white painting, the formal and expressive potential of restricting her means in this way intrigued Riley and she decided to explore this further. Building on the principle of contrasted elements, *Movement in Squares* (1961) followed and, though it is not immediately apparent, this is closely connected with *Kiss*. Essentially *Movement in Squares* turns *Kiss* on its side so that the zone of compression now runs vertically and slightly to the right of centre. In order to increase contrast, the large shapes in *Kiss* have been subdivided into smaller black-and-white squares. So as to activate these individual units further, their regular progression across the

   PAUL MOORHOUSE

space is modulated. Looking at the painting from left to right, the units' height remains constant while their width diminishes and then expands – thus creating an impression of asymmetrical compression. This visual disruption is the key to the work's expressive character. Released from a descriptive role, the relationships between the pictorial elements now take on a new significance. Riley's intention was, as she explained later, to make a statement about 'stabilities and instabilities, certainties and uncertainties'.[14] The expression of states of being – of composure and disturbance – is manifest, in formal terms, in the structure that Riley established and explained in the following way: 'The basis of my paintings is this: that in each of them a particular situation is stated. Certain elements within that situation remain constant, others precipitate the destruction of themselves by themselves. Recurrently, as a result of the cyclic movement of repose, disturbance and repose, the original situation is restated.'[15]

This concern with expressing emotional states using the progression and modulation of individual, contrasted visual units, is the dominant theme of Riley's early paintings in black and white. After *Movement in Squares*, the possibility of using other simple units – triangles, lines, circles and curves – configured in a variety of alternative structures, opened up the way forward. At the same time, the now rapid development of her work was galvanised further by a growing awareness of the optical energies latent in the units she was using. In the interaction of contrasted elements, she saw the tendency of the formal structures she was creating to destabilise, dissolving into intense and unsettling perceptual experiences. For example, in those paintings which use periodic structures – the close repetition of similar elements – the eye is overloaded with information, is frustrated in its ability to distinguish between discrete visual sensations and, in effect, is unable to interpret the information with which it is presented. The perceptual crisis thus provoked, in which the eye and mind veer from one contradictory impression to another, results in a range of hallucinatory phenomena from iridescence to violent movement – which appear to take place in the space *between* the viewer and the painting. The title *Movement in Squares* thus refers not only to the painting's formal progression; it alludes to the virtual movement which is also part of the experience of the work.

The implications of this visual dynamism are, as Riley realised, profound. Such experiences are the result of the viewer's visual engagement, or dialogue, with the sensations provoked by the painting. Consequently, the conventional relationship between the work of art and the observer is reversed. The painting is no longer an inert object, passive under the viewer's gaze. Instead, it seems invested with life, this illusion being sustained by an active connection between the painting and the observer. As a result the painting conveys its emotional content through the medium of perception, connecting directly with the viewer's physical and psychological responses.

Uplifted by these realisations, the paintings Riley made in the next four years are extraordinarily diverse and there is a strong sense of her wish both to explore this new visual language and to test its boundaries, pushing it to extremes. At the same time, within their diversity, certain clear lines of exploration are apparent. These include structures comprising triangles and zigzags respectively; open structures containing discrete elements such as ovals; repetitive linear curved structures; and structures containing repeated units in which the creation of after-images and the pace and frequency of formal progression are central concerns. Permeating and inflecting these arrangements certain recurrent preoccupations can be seen, notably: notions of expansion and contraction, static and active, cross-breeding between structures, the opposition of formal and tonal progressions, obliteration as a kind of visual disturbance, reversal, the accumulation and dispersal of density, multilayering and, towards the middle of the 1960s, the opposition of warm and cold greys.

At the source of these different tributaries lies the principle of 'pacing'. This process involves selecting a particular formal unit – a line, a triangle or some other shape – and then putting this unit 'through its paces'.[16] In practice this entails carrying out a methodical trial-and-error investigation, using detailed preparatory drawings, in order to establish certain sequences and also those relationships that will liberate particular optical energies. Significantly, after *Movement in Squares*, Riley began

entrusting the actual execution of paintings to assistants, thus freeing her
to concentrate on this preparatory stage. As she has pointed out, her
paintings 'breed'.[17] In terms of genealogy, the starting points for much of
that which followed were the paintings *Horizontal Vibration* (1961) (to
which successive generations of paintings using lines and then curves
can be traced) and *Black to White Discs* (1962) (which introduced tonal
gradation as a form of modulated progression).

Movement in Squares, in which the notion of a dynamic 'field' was
introduced, can be seen as the progenitor of a group of related paintings
which includes *Tremor* (1962), *Shift* (1963), *Shiver* (1964), *Burn* (1964)
and *Turn* (1964). The structure of each of these paintings comprises a
sequence of connected elements – triangles – and in each painting this
development moves from a state of stability, through disturbance, before
returning to 'repose'. In *Tremor*, for example, this serial transformation is
caused by taking a basic equilateral triangle shape (whose size remains
constant), which at various points is modified by making one of its sides
either convex or concave. Shift develops the idea of serial transformation
by introducing the notion of point movement. Here, the basic triangle
shape is established at the top edge of the painting (the state of
repose). This shape is modified in stages as the apex of each individual
unit moves its position relative to its base. It finally reaches a state of
repose at the base of the painting, having shifted its direction in the
process. The titles of these works suggest the way that such formal
progressions have an expressive resonance – as Riley puts it: 'repetition,
contrast, calculated reversal and counterpoint also parallel the basis of
our emotional structure'.[18] But the affective character of the works'
structure is paralleled, indeed deepened, by the perceptual experiences
that these structures induce. In *Shiver*, for example, the physical
convulsion that passes through the image is an experience in which the
visual and the visceral are inseparable.

The visceral element in Riley's early works – which was linked by
some critics with inducing pain – is at its most potent in the works
produced between 1961 and 1962, reaching its zenith in *Blaze 1* (1962).[19]
In sharp contrast to those images that generate a field of energy, here
the visual dynamism is concentrated into a circular structure. This

contains what appears to be a spiral. Actually it is a series of concentric circles expressed as zigzag lines. Among Riley's paintings, this is one of the fastest as well as the most visually intense. The use of 16 extreme contrasts – in direction and in the opposed character of zigzag and circle – immediately takes possession of the eye, returning its gaze in a display of blazing light, energetic upheaval and dervish motion. Self-evidently, these impressions arise from the structure of the work itself. Yet, it is with a shock of surprise that we realise that they are in no sense synthetic in the sense of having no identity outside the painting. Everything we perceive in *Blaze 1* – light, convulsion, movement – we recognise as such by drawing on a range of wider previous experiences. In this way, the black-and-white paintings do not exist outside nature they return us to nature.

Transition

In April to May 1962, Riley held her first solo exhibition at Victor Musgrave's Gallery One in London in which *Movement in Squares* was shown for the first time. This was followed in September 1963 by a second exhibition, also at Gallery One, which included 16 works, among them *Blaze 1*. The recognition which accrued as a result led to Riley's participation in a number of significant group exhibitions in Britain and abroad. It was, however, the inclusion of two of Riley's paintings in the *Responsive Eye* exhibition, William C Seitz's seminal survey of Op art held at the Museum of Modern Art, New York, in 1965, that announced the arrival of an artist of international importance. This elevation was underlined by a concurrent sell-out show at the Richard Feigen Gallery, also in New York. Despite this success, Riley felt her experience in New York was marred by the appropriation of her work for commercial ends. At the same time, the perceptual – hence virtual – content of her work was, as she now realised, on a collision course with the then dominant ethos of the New York art world, hugely influenced as it was by Clement Greenberg's ideas which placed a premium on art emphasising its purely material nature.

Riley's feelings were qualified, to say the least, as she returned to London. There followed a period, lasting until 1967, which, in the context of her work as a whole, can be seen as transitional. Her response to New York, if anything, appears to have been a desire to deny further the material nature of her paintings, and to seek ways of making their formal and perceptual characteristics more subtle, more complex and more indeterminate. The principal development resulting from this outlook is an increased involvement with the role of tonal gradation and the use of grey.

Tonal gradation is of course an aspect of Riley's work almost from the outset. It is, for example, the subject of *Black to White Discs*. There it is used as a means of modulating a regular progression of circles and, as that painting suggests, its effect is to inform the visual argument with a sense of pace and time. Manifest here is the notion that grey, as an intermediate step between black and white, can be used to introduce stages in the transition between these two opposites. In this painting the eye moves across a field of dots and has to negotiate the graduated tonal differences it encounters en route. In this way tonal gradation functions in Riley's paintings as the basis of 'visual time', an idea analogous to the notion of the number of beats in a passage of music being responsible for its tempo.

Riley has explained this further as follows: 'Grey is midway between black and white and clearly this relation is encompassed in three stages; white, mid-grey and black. But you can make a progression of five beats, seven beats, 24 and so on and all the time you are in fact changing the tempo.'[20] The relation of formal and tonal progression, presented either in harmony or in opposition, is the subject of a group of paintings which includes *Loss* (1964), *Pause* (1964) and *Where* (1964). As these works show, introducing grey deepened the formal argument by introducing further layers of visual significance; at the same time the stark opposition of black and white is qualified, producing visual experiences which are no less compelling, but somehow, in the mind's eye, paler and more slowly burning.

Of these developments Riley later commented: 'I wanted something which operated on more levels, was capable of more development, had a more "grey'd" quality, like the indeterminate nature of reality.'[21] Tonal gradation had, to use a musical analogy, introduced the equivalent of sharps and flats to what essentially had been a diatonic scale of black and white. Between 1965 and 1967, notably in *Arrest 1* (1965), *Deny 2* (1967) and *Cataract 3* (1967), Riley extended this chromatic use of grey in a literal way by introducing a new, wider palette embracing warm and cold greys. *Deny 2*, for example, is a complex, multilayered painting in which formal progression, tonal gradation and the opposition of warm and cold greys are all implicated. A progression of oval forms moves through the familiar pattern of repose, disturbance, repose through a carefully orchestrated spinning movement. In counterpoint to this theme, the painting operates on another level as a result of the relationships drawn between tone and colour. A tonally modulated progression of cool bluish-grey ovals is set against a warm reddish-grey ground. Where the tonal values of the ovals and ground are closest, the colour contrast is most evident. Where the tonal contrast between the ovals and ground is greatest, the colour difference is diminished or – as the title implies – denied.

By adopting a graduated palette of coloured greys Riley had also, in effect, denied black and white. In this respect, Riley's infiltration of grey is a significant broadening of her visual argument, a development from the sense of absolutes advanced by the earlier black-and-white contrasts. It is achieved through an embracing of tonal values which introduce an element of visual qualification. This is a movement, as it were, from an unqualifiable position to one that says 'possibly'. In visual terms, the effect of this subtle interaction of toned and coloured greys in *Deny 2* is to create instead a strange, impalpable light – the opposite perhaps of that generated by *Blaze 1* – a pale, disembodied sheen, softly glinting. As such, the use of grey carries a further, deeper significance. It laid the ground for Riley's adoption of colour, a major development that would extend her work in new and unpredictable ways.

                                                    PAUL MOORHOUSE

Colour and light

In 1968, Riley was the joint British representative (with Phillip King) at the
XXXIV Venice Biennale at which she won the International Prize for
Painting: the first living British painter to achieve this distinction. The
exhibition of her work included a number of black-and-white paintings,
notably early works such *Blaze 1* (1962) as well as several more recent
canvases such as *Static 2* (1966) and *Deny 2* (1967). Comparison of
these early and newer works made plain the distance that Riley had
travelled in what was a relatively short period of time: from the extreme
motive force and iridescence of paintings such as *Blaze 1*, which operate
in terms of a central contained image and a surrounding ground, to such
works as *Static 2*, in which the ground has itself been transformed into a
quiet, imperceptibly moving, disembodied expanse of energy. Implicit
too, in this growing engagement with black-and-white images which
generate a total field of energy, are the foundations for Riley's new use
of colour, exemplified at Venice in *Cataract 3*, *Chant 2* (1967) and *Late
Morning* (1967–68).

Cataract 3 stands at the beginning of Riley's engagement with colour
and, from the outset, the impression of a subtle, dispersing light is
apparent. In formal terms, the argument is relatively straightforward. Two
coloured greys, one vermilion and one turquoise, are bound to each
other as the twin components of a continuous wave. At the top and
bottom edges of the painting, these complementary greys are tonally
and chromatically close. In an echo of Riley's repose, disturbance, repose
principle, as the curves approach the centre of the painting the
pigmentary relationship of the greys is modulated to produce an intense,
complementary contrast between the vermilion and the turquoise. The
effect of this progression is to create an impression of brilliant light,
glittering within a surrounding envelope of greys, the overall field being
traversed by diagonal channels of energy produced by corresponding
undulations in the curves.

Inherent in this situation are those inter-related elements which
underpin the subsequent development of Riley's work, namely: colour,
transformation and light. Of the first of these, she later commented:

I saw that the basis of colour is its instability. Instead of searching for
a firm foundation, I realised I had one in the very opposite. That was
solid ground again, so to speak, and by accepting this paradox
I could begin to work with the fleeting, the elusive, with those things
which disappear when you actually apply your attention hard and
fast – and so a whole new area of activity, of perception opened up
for me.[22]

The extent and significance of these developments can be
appreciated when it is realised that, for more than six years, the entire
basis of Riley's work in black and white had been the principle of
contrast between stability and instability. While certain elements
remained unchanged, others underwent various kinds of modulation and
transformation – these formal progressions being, in turn, the catalysts
for the perceptual experiences which then occurred. Riley's introduction
of colour was thus brought about with not a little trepidation for, as she
had been long aware – not least as a result of her immersion in the
work of Seurat – colour had no such basis in stability. Rather, the
experience of colour is entirely relative: subject to contextual relationships
and, in empirical terms, difficult if not impossible to pin down. In its
intrinsic susceptibility to qualification, colour implied the exact opposite
of the absolutes she had first sought in her black-and-white paintings.
The importance of paintings such as *Cataract 3*, *Chant 2* and *Late
Morning* was in demonstrating that relinquishing absolutes, and working
instead with pictorial elements that are entirely unstable, had enormous
visual and expressive potential.

In common with her earlier black-and-white work, Riley's adoption of
a new visual language of colour was motivated by a desire to investigate
and to liberate the optical energies inherent in certain formal units. And,
in the same way that the structure of the black-and-white paintings was
not an end in itself but was orchestrated to generate dynamic perceptual
experiences, so Riley's engagement with units of colour now also served
ends which were not simply formal but essentially perceptual. In using
colour, perception remains the medium; though now, the perception of
colour serves increasingly to convey the experience of *light*. Riley

summarised this point in the following way: 'I don't paint light. I present a colour situation which releases light as you look at it.'[23]

These ideas are manifest in *Chant 2*, Riley's first essay in pure colour. Here two colours, blue and red, alternate in two different ways: firstly, with vertical stripes of blue enclosing the red; secondly, with the red stripes enclosing the blue. This alternating progression is modulated through broadening the width of the stripes as they approach the centre. Any intimation of visual violence is now completely absent. Previously there may have been a sense of growing visual disorientation in which the structure of the paintings would be seen to shift and in some cases collapse. Here the eye is seduced, as it were, from the start transported into a kind of relaxed gaze which, it is discovered, more readily receives the slow, steady pulse of diffusing light.

In the progressive broadening of the stripes, which has the effect of concentrating visual energy at the centre of the painting, it is possible to see an echo of the repose, disturbance, repose structural principle that operated previously. Now, however, the gap between pacing and perceptual response has closed. The second and third characteristics of these works, alluded to earlier, enter the viewer's dialogue with the painting almost immediately, transforming the sensation of colour into the perception of light. 'Pacing' is still an underlying organisational principle. But whereas previously a formal sequence would be destabilised and then reconstituted, now new dynamics are apparent, ones which serve particular needs to do with the generation of light, its chromatic character and the way it disperses or is made to cluster. These new dynamics include a greater emphasis on the repetition, accumulation and massing of units of colour.

The effects of these new ways of working can be seen in *Late Morning*. Here, the width of the stripes remains constant while the organisation of colour relationships is subject to complex patterns of inflection. The basis of these modulations is the repeated triad of red – white – red. The red stripe on the left of each of these units is juxtaposed with a progression of stripes modulated from blue to turquoise. The red stripe on the right is abutted with a varying progression of green stripes, modulated from turquoise to yellowish green. Riley has always maintained that her engagement with the optical characteristics of her raw materials – shapes and colours – is not based on detailed theoretical knowledge but rather is entirely empirical. Referring to her procedure in the early 1970s, she observed: 'In working on a painting I choose a small group of colours and juxtapose them in different sequences, to provide various colour relationships and to precipitate colour reactions.'[24] Underlying this process are, however, certain optical principles. Consciously deployed or not, these principles inform the artist's dialogue with paintings during their development, and are responsible for the visual experiences which they generate after their completion.

In *Late Morning*, for example, *simultaneous contrast* (the tendency of two adjacent colours to modify the other in the direction of its own complementary), *successive contrast* (the tendency of a colour to produce a complementary after-image when seen against white) and *mixed contrast* (the tendency of a colour to produce a complementary after-image which mixes with the colour of the ground against which it is seen) are all, in varying degrees, contributing factors in the extraordinary visual performance which forms the character of the painting. Suffice it to say, the act of looking becomes an active, ongoing and constantly changing experience in which viewers are entirely complicit, drawn as they are into a spectacle of interacting colour contrasts and fugitive after-images. It is in this close relationship between, on one side, the painting as the source of sensation and, on the other, the viewer's perceptual responses, that the 'balance between inner and outer'– identified by Riley as an essential aspect of the pleasures of sight – can be grasped.

Stripes, crossovers and twists

Evident in these developments is the stirring of a new relationship between Riley's work and nature. This is not to suggest that the black-and-white paintings were divorced from natural phenomena. On the contrary, as seen, the perceptual experiences yielded in those works, by purely pictorial elements, are invested with a keen sense of familiarity. As

   PAUL MOORHOUSE

Riley put it: 'I wanted to bring about some fresh way of seeing again what had almost certainly been experienced, but which had been either dismissed or buried by the passage of time.'[25] Even so, as she also pointed out, there were differences: 'People frequently experience visual events in nature which are far more violent, and even blinding, than anything I have ever done on canvas.'[26]

With the advent of colour, the sense of equivalence between her work and nature is heightened. *Late Morning* is no less abstract, in formal terms, than its black-and-white predecessors; but, arising from an optical fusion of three colours, the impression it creates of a soft golden haze is familiar to anyone who has stood in nature and observed the warm, dissolving effect of sunlight as it reaches its zenith towards midday. Riley explained these changes as follows:

> I had to give visual sensation more rein – my black-and-white paintings had been about states of being, states of composure and disturbance, but when I introduced colour in 1967 this began to change. Colour inevitably leads you to the world outside; in *Late Morning* and the other paintings I made in the late 1960s I was beginning to find my way with a whole host of sensations to do with colour.[27]

Both *Chant 2* and *Late Morning* manifested a number of early discoveries, important to Riley, about the relation of colour and light. She had observed that the basis of colour is its instability and the tendency of colours to affect, and be affected by, their context. Working with this instability entailed finding ways of increasing and encouraging the optical interaction of colours. The formal implications of this realisation for her work became apparent. Riley's adoption of the colour stripe as the dominant characteristic of her work from 1967 to the mid-1970s is not simply a stylistic choice. Rather, it was an expedient that recognised the need for a more neutral, less assertive form, which would maximise the role played by colour. Since chromatic interaction occurs where two colours meet, edges assumed a new importance; clearly, the stripe offered the longest edge and, hence, the greatest propensity for optical fusion.

Changes in scale, too, had to be made to accommodate the behaviour of colour. Riley's adoption of colour coincides with a new, larger and more expansive format than she had used previously, its purpose being to prevent focusing on discrete pictorial elements and, rather, to create an area which the resulting fusion of colours could inhabit. The resulting space echoes precisely those characteristics she first noticed in Pollock's dripped paintings: a shallow, multifocal expanse. Notable, though, is the way that in Riley's paintings this virtual space now appears to advance from the surface of the painting towards the viewer, hanging like a veil of light *between* the viewer and the painting.

One of the most remarkable aspects of Riley's work is its absolute clarity. It withholds nothing. Though her aim is the creation of a perceptual plane, for those willing to look it is always possible to penetrate beneath this, and to return to the paint surface – to the source of sensation. This clarity of purpose and means is manifest in the development of Riley's engagement with colour, in which her thinking can be sensed: the weighing of options, the advances, the trails not followed and, every so often, the sudden recognition of a way forward.

After establishing the vertical stripe format of *Late Morning*, this work was followed by its opposite – a horizontal painting – *Rise 1* (1968). The complexity of graduated colour introduced by *Late Morning* (in the progression of different greens) was not followed up, though this degree of colour complexity would reappear in the paintings from the mid-1980s onwards. Instead, at this early stage *Rise 1* simply adds a third, unmodulated colour to the equation, thus establishing a basis that would be followed – notwithstanding the later addition of black and grey – until the adoption of five colours in 1978. In *Rise 1* the connections with *Late Morning* are apparent, as are the new gambits.

Rise 1 presents orange, violet and green in an irregular sequence of stripes traversing the breadth of the painting. This palette marks a development from the direct opposition of primary colours (red and blue) evident in *Late Morning*. Instead, orange, violet and green are already composite colours whose proximity leads to other complex, optical combinations. These combinations are characterised by the

   PAUL MOORHOUSE

tendency of certain colours to draw into mutually destabilising pairs which then modify, and are modified by, the third, adjacent colour. The overall effect comes as a surprise – a shield of light traversed by linear stresses of colour, not unlike the experience of looking upon movements on the surface of a lake.

The impression made by *Rise 1* is quite different from *Late Morning*. The vertical stripe format of the earlier painting discharges a glowing light that passes across the stripes. In contrast, in *Rise 1* the stresses of light follow the horizontal orientation of the stripes. Through this difference, Riley recognised an important optical principle, namely that perceptual effects appear most intense when they run counter to the underlying formal structure. This realisation would greatly inform her future thinking. Riley went on to make other paintings utilising horizontal stripes (notably *Apprehend*, 1970), as well as number of works in which the stripes run diagonally (for example *Veld*, 1971, and *Rattle*, 1973). Increasingly, however, her preference for the additional visual tension that results from placing the formal organisation of a painting in opposition to its perceptual field is evident.

These considerations provided the genesis for a group of works which employ a device known to Riley as crossovers. Seeking to maximise the friction between directional colour and diffuse areas of light, in the Orient series of works Riley destabilised the vertical stripe configuration by crossing one colour stripe over the other pair. This diagonal disruption is then pushed further by tilting each triad of colour stripes towards its neighbour, so that they join at the top and bottom of the painting in a zigzag formation. The immediate roots of this remarkable invention can be traced to the earlier black-and-white painting *Breathe* itself an echo of Balla's Iridescent Compenetration series of 1912–15. As a result the stripes are pushed into linear, but entirely non-regular, chromatic relationships, underpinned by adjacent areas of white which are drawn into a sawtooth formation. The effect is to generate differentiated, horizontal clusters of light – warm at the top, cool at the bottom. This is a significant step forward, for it represents a painting process in which the manipulation of colour has been fully subsumed into orchestrating the play of light.

The advances exemplified in *Orient 4* (1970) are also important in opening up a new seam of development, one which initially runs parallel to the vertical stripe paintings but which eventually, by the mid-1970s, supplants that other, earlier line of progression. The crossover principle loosened the grip of the regular verticals, leading in paintings such as *Vapour* (1970) and *Zing 1* (1971) to the appearance of 'twists'. Essentially, this is a furthering of the crossover in that, within a vertical triad of colour stripes, all three colours repeatedly cross each other. In *Zing 1* this happens four times within each vertical. In consequence, the viewer experiences the painting as an overall field containing numerous overlapping and shifting zones of differently coloured light. The danger of this approach is that the image collapses into iridescent confusion. That it does not can be attributed to Riley's restricted means. Despite the extreme subtlety and complexity that her paintings had attained by the early 1970s, Riley was still using three colours only. This limited chromatic range is crucial, for it gives each work its overall colour bias, clearly seen for example in the cool, leaf-fresh atmosphere that infuses *Vapour*.

Alongside this investigation of different ways of disrupting the vertical stripe, Riley produced a succession of paintings – including *Gamelan* (1970), *Canticle* (1973) and *Pastorale* (1973) – in which the presence of this linear unit of colour was progressively asserted in ways that are not simply to do with the perception of light. In *Gamelan*, for example, it has a rhythmical role, the repetition of colours functioning like bright percussive beats.

This line of development reaches its climax in two major, related paintings – *Cantus Firmus* (1972–73) and *Pæan* (1973). *Cantus Firmus* was motivated by two connected concerns. The first of these relates to the use of black and grey, and not simply white, as zones in which colour interaction takes place; the second addresses the use of black and grey to restore a sense of substance to those fugitive washes of light that had figured so prominently in Riley's thinking. The painting is a triumph, adding weight, body and formal proportion to chromatic interaction. Surprisingly, extending her palette in this way also had significant plastic and spatial connotations. The blacks and greys now punctuate the envelope of light, advancing and retreating, creating an impression of ambiguous, shifting depth. *Pæan* seeks a similar sense of substance but uses pure colour without tonal gradation. It relies instead on strong chromatic relationships organised – unusually for Riley – in a freer way and according to the sense of spatial depth yielded by particular groupings. Although she would not pursue this way of working for the present, the prospect of building a visual fabric intuitively, in terms of plastic chromatic relations and in dialogue with the spatial sensations yielded by colour, is one to which Riley would return in the early 1980s.

A rhythmic vehicle for colour

That break with the perceptual basis of her work lay, however, in the future. In the interim, Riley's work from the mid-1970s until the end of the decade took her concern with colour interaction and its relationship with light to new levels of complexity. The vehicle for these developments was her adoption, in 1974, of the curve form as the fundamental unit of her paintings.

Riley's use of this shape reveals her tendency to return to earlier, familiar ways of working, and to apply that experience in a new context, when seeking a road through uncharted territory. Riley was interested in the way that her use of twists in such works as *Zing 1* resulted in the effect of clusters of light. This innovation in turn raised the question of how this perception might be developed. To achieve that seemed to require finding a way of dissolving the formal structure further in order to facilitate even greater chromatic interaction. At the same time, Riley remained aware of the danger posed by denying the stripe and allowing colour activity to develop in an uncontrolled way. Her solution was to develop the twist shape itself.

In *Zing 1* this had already become sinuous and winding; as a result it created a number of different colour juxtapositions within the confines of a vertical stripe. Greater interaction between different, adjacent stripes could be achieved by combining the twist shape with a continuous arabesque: a shape that had appeared previously in paintings such as

Fall (1963) and later, *Cataract 3*. *Entice 2* (1974) anticipates these developments but is not a fully formed twisted curve. Instead, each curve cascades downwards in an unbroken continuum. However, in *Clepsydra* (1976), the curve incorporating twists is fully realised through the delicate interlacing of magenta, olive and turquoise within each wave. It is as though elements from *Fall*, *Zing 1* and *Cataract 3* have intermingled. As so often in Riley's work, the gathering and crossbreeding of different forces provide the genesis for unexpected advances.

Underlying her reintroduction of the curve was the realisation that the length of the edge is crucial in facilitating the interaction of colour: a meandering wave form extends that edge. Also, subjecting a field of curves to diagonal stresses so that they are pulled out of regular alignment, and simultaneously varying their width, means that the juxtaposing of different colours is vastly increased. To facilitate this colour fusion further, the first curve paintings, such as *Entice 2*, introduce passages of grey, in addition to the white ground. The reduction of tonal contrast in order to increase the intensity of colour recalls the theme of *Deny 2*, and is a further instance of Riley's recycling of earlier ideas. This tonal device was taken further by introducing grey into the colours themselves, as in *Aubade* (1975). Although the white ground is still at this point retained, the evenly toned colours dissolve into a diffuse field of luminous clusters. The step which then beckoned was that of eliminating white completely and replacing this with a coloured grey ground: a development that reaches something of a climax in the yellow-greyed *Aurulum* (1978). In this ethereal painting the fully realised creation of an envelope of pale, coloured light can be seen – an ambient, translucent atmosphere, lit by glowing, flame-like tints.

A broadening and a deepening of Riley's understanding of the relation of colour and light can be discerned in her curve paintings. The key to this is the role of the curve in creating a more pliable, less assertive structural armature – one which readily recedes behind the light displays – so that occasionally the effect is as delicate as stained glass. This is also a structure in subtle movement. The eye follows the course of a curve and loses the thread as the shapes begin to fuse, dissolving like a rising haze of heat or undulating like ripples on the surface of water. These effects are non-descriptive yet tantalisingly evocative, recalling the patterns and rhythms of nature. They are also deeply expressive. Before commencing the curves, Riley had observed: 'My paintings are, of course, concerned with generating visual sensations, but certainly not to the exclusion of emotion. One of my aims is that these two responses shall be experienced as *one and the same*.'[28] The curve paintings include some of the most serene and emotionally radiant that she has ever painted, an implication that blossoms in the connotations of poetry and music contained in some of their titles.

In the Song of Orpheus series of 1978, Riley divided the coloured grey ground she had been using into a further two colours. With a now expanded palette of five colours – violet, blue, green, yellow and pink – the paintings draw the eye into an intoxicating optical experience. The simultaneous contrast of adjacent colours, and the evocation of fugitive colours resulting from optical mixing, build cumulatively. They take the paintings within a hair's breadth of their overall colour focus being lost. Yet always, within this dissolution, a sense of order remains. Even so the complex and extremely fine-tuned nature of these paintings signalled a growing refinement which she felt, in the longer term, could be inimical to further development. Having taken the dissolution of colour to an extreme, the reinstatement of a firmer sense of structure now seemed necessary, although what form that would take remained to be seen.

From perception to sensation

In the winter of 1979–80 Riley travelled to Egypt. During that trip she visited the Nile Valley and the museum at Cairo, and was able to study, at first hand, the tombs of the later pharaohs in the Valley of the Kings. Riley was astonished by the art she found in these ancient burial sites carved out of rock and located deep in the earth. These sacred places were dedicated to the dead, yet the tomb decoration was a vivid evocation of life and light. Though their creators had used only a limited

number of colours – red, blue, yellow, turquoise, green, black and white –
the walls of the chambers receded behind images in which could be
seen a bustling affirmation of everyday existence. In looking at the art
and craft of Ancient Egypt in the Cairo Museum, Riley recognised that
the same colours had been used in all aspects of the Egyptians' material
lives, from the decorative to the purely functional.

On her return to London, Riley found that these colours continued to
exercise a fascination. Any possibility of using them in her work was,
however, tempered by concern about an implicit act of appropriation.
These misgivings were assuaged during the process of recreating the
colours when she felt it was important to work from memory, rather than
copying the palette from reproductions in books. As she began to
explore this new, so-called Egyptian palette, it was clear that radical
structural changes to her work would be required. Though limited in
number, the admission of a range of intense colours needed a formal
vehicle that was simpler than the curve she had been using for the last
six years. For this reason, she now returned to the more neutral stripe.
Working again with stripes, her first instinct was that the new colours
could be deployed using her usual procedure of building a field of
accumulated visual sensation that leads inexorably to the perception of
light. Almost from the outset, however, Riley found that a freer
arrangement seemed appropriate – an approach which echoed her
earlier experiments with a more intuitive organisation in *Pæan*.

This new structuring principle is immediately apparent in the Ka
series of paintings (1980), which announces the new palette. In *Ka 7*
(1980), for example, the degree of unequal chromatic distribution is
striking. Instead of a steady overall rhythm, the painting works in terms of
particular connections between individual colours that take their place
within the whole. The effect is analogous to phrasing within a passage of
music: the internal relationships articulate the larger structure. The
paintings which followed, notably *Après Midi* and *Silvered*, both 1981,
emphasise this dimension even more strongly through their use of black.
This dominant element now functions almost like a bar line in musical
notation. It exposes, punctuates and connects areas of internal relation.
In visual terms, it beds discrete combinations of colour, and the

                                              PAUL MOORHOUSE

sensations these yield, into the total field that forms the experience of each painting. The white stripes function in a different, though complementary way, providing pauses – areas of visual silence – which absorb the surrounding chromatic activity.

The stripe paintings made between 1980 and 1985 reveal a progressive structural reorganisation and in that sense they are an important watershed in Riley's work. They form a passage from the perceptual – optically mediated – character of her art before 1980, to her work from the early 1980s onwards which addresses pure sensation directly: visual experience as a direct response to its source. Riley made this distinction clear as follows:

> Right up to, and in some ways including, the stripe paintings I used to build up to sensation, accumulating tension until it released a perceptual experience that flooded the whole as it were. Now I try to take sensation as the guiding line and build, with the relationships it demands, a plastic fabric which has no other *raison d'être* except to accommodate the sensations it solicits.[29]

From the early 1980s, there is an increasing sense of the paintings' underlying composition. A work such as *Luxor* (1982), for example, suggests analogies with music in the way that certain formal elements are drawn into relationships which are variously stated, contrasted with other faster and slower passages, transformed and recapitulated. This sequential reading is, however, only one way of looking at the painting. When seen in its entirety, its plastic and spatial character comes into view. The relation of colour stripes produces discrete areas of colour sensation which suggest a range of other qualities: from density and weight to dullness and brilliance; from closed impenetrability to open airy space; from advancing planes to shallow recession. The composition of the works is therefore additive in the musical sense of individual units being drawn into an experience that unfolds in time. But parallel to this, their composition also relates to the moulding and shaping of discrete units of visual sensation so that they simultaneously inhabit and create a virtual space.

This growing engagement with abstract relations of form and colour –
'plastic' issues – would at one time have been seen by Riley as outmoded.
She now addressed these issues with a renewed sense of their
importance, seeing their development as being as relevant to abstract
painting as the treatment of figurative subjects had been to artists a
thousand years previously. This wish to engage more closely with the
'real problems of painting'[30] informs the progress of the Egyptian paintings.
After those works made in 1982 in which black is a dominant element,
during the following year she eliminated this protagonist. In *Bali* (1983),
for example, it is replaced by yellow-green, the fifth Egyptian colour
which now makes its debut. In *Tabriz* (1984), produced the following
year, white, too, was removed, being replaced by lilac. Finally, in 1985,
this movement away from the original palette embraced an influx of new
colours, resulting in the rich, sonorous splendour of *Burnished Sky*. It was
as if an earlier sonata such as *Après Midi* had been orchestrated.

Burnished Sky is in many ways a consummation of the changes
which had been set in motion five years earlier, revealing the full, plastic
potential of the structural principles she had been developing. As before,
however, inherent in the extreme complexity and degree of refinement
that her work had now attained was the sense that taking this further
would present problems. The change in direction she now began to
formulate was therefore motivated, as she later observed, by the
conviction that 'to preserve a freshness in working it is important to get
back sometimes to first principles'.[31]

The recognition of nature

This necessity to return to fundamentals can be understood in two ways.
In a primary sense it refers to Riley's desire to focus on the formal
composition of her paintings – their architecture, as it were – and in this
respect, the relation of shape and colour would be central. At the same
time, these plastic considerations can be seen in the context of a
deepening of the relation between her paintings and nature. In both
instances, the role of sensation is a central issue.

PAUL MOORHOUSE

Prior to the early 1980s, her work's connection with nature was rooted in equiva ence rather than mimesis: 'For me nature is not landscape, but the dynamism of visual forces – an event rather than an appearance. These forces can only be tackled by treating colour and form as ultimate identities.'[32] Yet, arising from the inner, self-contained workings of the paintings, the viewer was drawn into visual experiences in which recognition, surprisingly, was complicit. Riley's progressive movement now towards an art of pure sensation can be understood in plastic terms, as echoing Matisse's observation: 'I want to reach that state of condensation of sensations which constitutes a picture.'[33] She has also provided a clue to her engagement with sensation in the following terms: 'If I am outside in nature, I do not look *for* something or *at* things. I try to absorb sensations without censoring them, without identifying them. I want them to come out through the pores of my eyes, as it were – on a particular level of their own.'[34] Embracing sensation as a first principle situates within the process of making paintings that phenomenon of sight, sometimes encountered in nature, when colour, form and light *precede* interpretation and evaluation and, instead, are experienced directly, in all their purity, immediacy and freshness.

In nature, of course, a particular sensation is never experienced in isolation; but rather as part of a larger, complex, shifting matrix. Relating this to picture making, Riley commented:

> the masses open and closed spaces, the lines, tones and colours can be organised in a parallel way. It as though these relationships are built up in all their complexity to provide a vehicle for those things which cannot be objectively identified but which can nevertheless be expressed in this way.[35]

Significantly, in Riley's work from the mid-1980s to the present, there is an increasing emphasis on the relationships between varying sensations and a corresponding need to find an appropriate fabric for accommodating and articulating the sources of those sensations.

In concentrating on internal relationships, Riley now returned to the principle of contrast that had figured so strongly in her work at the outset. This approach is evident in two paintings – *Gentle Edge* and *Broken Gaze*, both 1986 – that announce the transition to Riley's new way of working. Seeking to activate the visual argument in the strongest way, the vertical register of the Egyptian paintings has been disrupted by the introduction of truncated diagonals. This is a radical departure that, once again, incorporates elements used previously – diagonals were implied in *Deny 2* and they are the subject of *Vela* (1971). Now, however, they are used to offset the strong pull of the verticals and to create opposition in directional terms. Nevertheless, overall the effect is one of evenness, something which Riley was quick to dispel in subsequent works.

Ease (1987) is in many ways a much more developed painting. The domination of the verticals – 14 columns in this work – has now been successfully counteracted by diagonals which break out of the vertical passages and appear to pass across them. To accommodate this development, the diagonal units ('zigs' in studio parlance) have been considerably enlarged, encouraging a much more robust interaction of directional shapes. Most significant of all, the lattice effect, which results from the way the diagonals appear to pass through or in front of the verticals, opens up the space of the painting in new and unexpected ways. Previously, the space in Riley's paintings had appeared to advance towards the spectator. Now the reverse is made to happen. A strange, ambiguous space is sensed in the opposite direction – opening up depth and drawing the gaze inside the virtual space of the painting. However, this is an unstable, elusive arena in which planes of colour alternately advance and recede, suggesting positive shapes and then apertures, depending on the eye's inclination and its response to a particular context.

The way these paintings redefine the relationship with the viewer is one of their most significant developments. Previously, the viewer's optical interaction with a painting led inexorably to an 'event' in the form of apparent movement or light. Now this performance *by* the work has been replaced by a situation in which the viewer and the painting are in a balanced dialogue. The eye inhabits the space of the image and is at liberty to experience the relation of its parts, and their relation to the whole. The musical analogy is still appropriate. For in seeking to develop internal contrasts, the danger posed is that the image disintegrates into confusion and dissonance. As in a piece of music, the composition must have internal momentum but this can only be the case if the rhythms are controlled. The paintings work in terms of *contrasts* in direction, colour, tone and density – yet these opposed elements are *harmonised* by the plastic relationships that form the visual fabric of each image.

The development of the works follows a course towards greater internal variation. The use of black in *New Day* (1988) and *Gaillard* (1989) articulates the surface of the paintings in a non-regular way, providing accents which punctuate a sequence of motifs, echoes, inversions and repeats. Even when black is absent, as in *High Sky 2* (1992), particular juxtapositions of other colours are used to differentiate the surface, producing, in this instance, marked contrasts between left and right. The way an image such as this unfolds, unevenly and as an accretion of contrasted episodes, is light years away from the steady pulse of an earlier painting such as *Late Morning*, although the connection with nature is no less marked. As with that earlier work, looking leads ultimately to a sense of recognition and in both cases, as Riley has pointed out, this state of recognition occurs 'without the actual incident which prompted it'.[36] However, while *Late Morning* works in terms of a build-up of sensation leading to a perceptual event, a work such as *High Sky 2* is configured more as a visual journey which unfolds in time. Even though the following statement prefigures the zigs, Riley's words evoke precisely the analogy between the imaginative space of the painting and the physical arena of nature, and the eye's experience of both:

> the colours are organised on the canvas so that the eye can travel over the surface in a way parallel to the way it moves over nature. It should feel caressed and soothed, experience frictions and ruptures, glide and drift… One moment there will be nothing to look at and the next second the canvas suddenly seems to refill, to be crowded with visual events.[37]

A kind of place

Among first principles, there is one other that, perhaps above all, has guided the progress of Riley's art. 'The first of all principles,' Eugène Delacroix noted, 'is the need to make sacrifices.'[38] This is a sentiment with which Riley would concur. It stands, for example, at the beginning of her work: 'When I gave up painting external reality I realised I was giving up a vast pleasure and from now on it was not going to be just pleasurable.'[39] This refusal to plough the same, familiar furrow, and a restless need to readdress and redefine her working practice is evident throughout her art. Relinquishing a position which has been hard-won is nevertheless one of the greatest challenges to an artist; failure to do so can, however, also prove to be one of the worst obstacles. Riley encapsulates this dilemma in the following way: 'You can't maintain an extreme position by preserving it. To do so would mean turning it into the very opposite.'[40]

By 1997, Riley's engagement with the zig format had reached an extreme position. In *From Here* (1994), subdividing the vertical register into proportions of one third and two thirds had fractured the space of the painting further. The eye inhabits a space which is multifocal – as, for example, in Pollock's paintings – but also syncopated. The gaze does not drift but darts and skips: caught up in the rhythmical inflections of the space. These were important developments, but problematic. Further subdivision would shatter the picture plane completely. This hazard is addressed in one of the last zig paintings, *Harmony in Rose 1* (1997), where stability is restored through drawing certain areas of the image into larger units of colour. Such paintings are fully realised manifestations of what Riley has described as 'a kind of place',[41] a virtual arena defined entirely in terms of the spatial properties of form and colour. The imperative to develop the rhythmic vitality of this space has driven the course of her work from 1997 to the present.

Lagoon 1 (1997), which commences this most recent phase, reveals the sacrifice that had to be made. The large shapes that began to appear in *Harmony in Rose 1* are retained; but now the direct opposition of vertical and diagonal directional forces is qualified by the introduction of

a number of curved elements. Already this is different territory. Although
the curve recalls her earlier use of this shape, previously it was deployed
as a continuous wave form when it functioned as the sole formal unit
within individual paintings. In this new incarnation, the curve is
segmented, its sinuous outline apparently refracted through a contrasting
geometric structure. The effect is to create a new range of amorphous
shapes – neither curve nor lozenge, but the unexpected offspring
resulting from the interaction of those forms. As in the zig paintings they
articulate the space; but, mysteriously, there is now a stronger implication
of a formal presence inhabiting that space. Recognition would be too
strong a word, yet there is a lingering sense of familiarity, recalling the
experience of things half-glimpsed at the peripheries of vision.

Having put down this marker Riley became stuck, uncertain how best
to take forward these ideas. She found confirmation in an unconnected
activity: the invitation to make a wall drawing for a group exhibition titled
White Noise, held at the Kunsthalle Bern in 1998. The work she created,
Composition with Circles 1 (1998), occupied an entire wall, 5 by 9 metres
overall. Its economy of means was, to say the least, surprising, given the
complex nature of her concurrent painting preoccupations. Taking a
complete circle as its starting point, the drawing repeated this shape
across the surface of the wall, creating a web of abutting, nearly touching
and overlapping hoops. Freely composed, the resulting structure is
remarkable, marrying organic asymmetry with an underlying sense of
order, proportion and harmonious relation, stasis with movement, two-
dimensionality with depth. The nearest equivalent in nature would be
formed by droplets falling on the surface of water.

Though the work exists on its own terms, certain analogies with the
paintings are apparent, not least in the drawing's creation of an envelope
of space from discrete units of sensation. The drawing achieves this,
however, through the relation of transparent, overlapping circles that also
connect in other surprising ways. In particular, they generate longer,
linear wave forms which activate the space rhythmically, linking and
easing the transitions between its internally related parts. Afterwards,
Riley resolved to explore further the combined spatial and rhythmical
characteristics of the curve form in the context of the paintings.

As studies for the works that followed reveal, Riley continued to work with an underlying grid structure comprising verticals and diagonals. This provided the framework within which the curve shapes, using a segmented sixth of a circle, could be positioned and then blocked out as large colour shapes. This way of working is an extension of her previous practice using the zigs which Riley had described as follows:

> I don't begin with the appearance of form and colour as such, but with their spatial properties. That is the first step, and through building a coherent spatial order various and diverse sensations emerge. I try to sort these out and to assign them their rightful places… If this 'placing' goes well the actual sensation becomes part of the formative fabric of the painting. But until the whole is brought together, everything is uncertain and subject to change.[42]

The effect of these innovations can be appreciated in *Rêve* (1999), the first fully realised curve painting. Immediately apparent is the break with the vertical register. Instead, the curves move freely and discursively. Most striking is the new, grand scale which Riley now began to employ, a development continued in *Parade 2* (2002) and one which reaches its fullest realisation in *Evoë 3* (2003). In these works there unfolds a new and surprising treatment of pictorial space. The geometric world of the zigs, with its sharply articulated textures, myriad densities and unstable areas of reflected light and shade, has led to another kind of place. This is a world of sinuous, winding movement in which expanded areas of contrasted colour flicker and dance – space, shape and hue joined in a rhythmic celebration of sensation. In this respect, the curve paintings move towards nature, but nature in which there now resonates a living, moving presence.

In part, this implication of life is responsible for the new emphasis on a larger scale. The shapes and their expansive gestures suggest the scale of the human body and this is accommodated by Riley's expanded pictorial field. In this respect, more recent, chromatically charged, curve paintings such as *Magenta and Peach; Blue and Green* (2001), with their closely argued internal rhythms, bring to mind Matisse's great canvases:

PAUL MOORHOUSE

Dance 1 (1909) and *Dance 2* (1910). In Riley's painting, however, it is as if, in the absence of depiction, colour and form have found a new, surprising synthesis and movement itself has been distilled to its pure, disembodied essence.

From the outset Riley's work has challenged and extended the language of painting, maintaining faith in its expressive vitality when its relevance as an art form has been questioned. And in the paintings that Riley is making now, themes which have preoccupied her from the outset – the expression of states of being, movement, colour, light and space – are drawn into fresh and unexpected relationships in which there is an undiminished sense of creative potential. It is significant that these recent works should so vividly convey a sense of life, of *élan*, for at a fundamental level this is the underlying theme of her work. In Riley's own words: 'An artist feels a need "to do something" about the very fact of being alive, rather like a bird feels the need to sing.'[43] Her art constitutes an ongoing dialogue with visual experience, manifesting its pleasures, illuminating its connection with emotion and affirming the capacity of sight to reveal the mysterious connection between the individual and the world.

Paul Moorhouse (ed), *Bridget Riley*, exhibition catalogue, Tate Publishing, London, 2003, pp.11–23.

1 Bridget Riley, 'The Pleasures of Sight' (1984), in Robert Kudielka (ed), *The Eye's Mind: Bridget Riley, Collected Writings 1965–1999*, Thames & Hudson, London, 1999, pp.30–34.

2 *Ibid.*, p.33.

3 *Ibid.*, p.32.

4 Bridget Riley 'Personal Interview by Nikki Henriques' (1988), *ibid.*, p.22.

5 *Ibid.*, p.24.

6 Lecture given by Bridget Riley at Tate Britain, 2 September 2002.

7 Bruce Glaser, 'Jackson Pollock: An Interview with Lee Krasner', *Arts*, vol.42, no.6, April 1967, p.38.

8 Conversation between the author and Bridget Riley, 9 December 2002.

9 Maurice de Sausmarez, *Bridget Riley*, exhibition catalogue, Studio Vista, London, 1970, p.26.

10 Josef Albers quoted in Cyril Barrett, *Op Art*, exhibition catalogue, Studio Vista, London, 1970, p.32.

11 Bridget Riley, 'Practising Abstraction: Talking to Michael Craig-Martin' (1992), in Robert Kudielka (ed), *Bridget Riley: Dialogues on Art*, Zwemmer, London, 1995, p.52.

12 Conversation between the author and Bridget Riley, 12 December 2002.

13 Bridget Riley, 'The Experience of Painting: Talking to Mel Gooding' (1988), in Kudielka (ed), *The Eye's Mind*, *op.cit.*, p.125.

14 *Ibid.*

15 Bridget Riley, 'Perception Is the Medium' (1965), in Kudielka, *The Eye's Mind*, *op.cit.*, pp.66–67.

16 Bridget Riley, 'In Conversation with Isabel Carlisle', in *Bridget Riley: Works 1961–1998*, exhibition catalogue, Abbot Hall Art Gallery, Kendal, 1998, p.9.

17 Bridget Riley, 'Interview with David Sylvester' (1967), in Kudielka (ed), *The Eye's Mind*, *op.cit.*, p.73.

18 Riley, 'Perception Is the Medium', *ibid.*, p.66.

19 See Riley, 'Interview with David Sylvester', *ibid.*, pp.73–76. It is illuminating to consider these early black-and-white paintings in the context of the following passage by Samuel Beckett: 'Before no supreme manifestation of Beauty do we proceed mildly up a staircase of sensation and sit down mildly on the topmost stair to digest our gratification: such is the pleasure of Prettiness. We are taken up bodily and pitched breathless on the peak of a sheer crag: which is the pain of Beauty.' Samuel Beckett, 'Assumption' (1929), in *The Complete Short Prose 1929–1989*, Grove Press, New York, NY, 1995, p.4.

20 Bridget Riley, 'In Conversation with Maurice de Sausmarez' (1967), in Kudielka (ed), *The Eye's Mind*, *op.cit.*, p.64.

21 Bridiget Riley, 'Into Colour: In Conversation with Robert Kudielka' (1978), *ibid.*, p.90.

22 Riley, 'Practising Abstraction: Talking to Michael Craig-Martin', in Kudielka (ed), *Bridget Riley: Dialogues on Art*, *op.cit.*, p.56.

23 Bridget Riley, 'In Conversation with Robert Kudielka' (1972), in Kudielka (ed), *The Eye's Mind*, *op.cit.*, 1999, p.85.

24 Bridget Riley, 'Working with Nature' (1973), *ibid.*, p.88.

25 Bridget Riley, 'The Pleasures of Sight' (1984), *ibid.*, p.33.

26 Riley, 'In Conversation with Isabel Carlisle', *op.cit.*, p.7.

27 Bridget Riley, 'A Repetition Reviewed: Talking to Andrew Graham-Dixon' (1992), in Kudielka (ed), *Bridget Riley: Dialogues on Art*, *op.cit.*, 1995, p.70.

28 Bridget Riley, 'Statement' (1970), in Kudielka (ed), *The Eye's Mind*, *op.cit.*, p.79.

29 Bridget Riley, 'According to Sensation: In Conversation with Robert Kudielka' (1990), *ibid.*, p.116.

                                                           PAUL MOORHOUSE

30   *Ibid.*

31   *Ibid.*, p.114.

32   Riley, 'Working with Nature', *ibid.*, p.88.

33   Henri Matisse, 'Notes of a Painter' (1908), in Herschel B Chipp, *Theories of Modern Art: A Source Book by Artists and Critics*, University of California Press, Berkeley, CA, 1968, p.132.

34   Riley, 'A Repetition Reviewed: Talking to Andrew Graham-Dixon', in Kudielka (ed), *Bridget Riley: Dialogues on Art, op.cit.*, pp.79–80.

35   Bridget Riley, 'Perception and the Use of Colour: Talking to EH Gombrich' (1992), *ibid.*, p.42.

36   Riley, 'A Repetition Reviewed: Talking to Andrew Graham-Dixon', *ibid.*, p.72.

37   Riley, 'The Pleasures of Sight', in Kudielka (ed), *The Eye's Mind, op.cit.*, p.33.

38   Eugène Delacroix, in Hubert Wellington (ed), *The Journal of Eugène Delacroix*, Lucy Norton (trans), Phaidon, London, 1980, p.397.

39   Riley, 'Personal Interview', in Kudielka (ed), *The Eye's Mind, op.cit.*, p.27.

40   *Ibid.*

41   Lecture given by Bridget Riley at Tate Britain, 2 September 2002.

42   Bridget Riley, 'Something to Look At: In Conversation with Alex Farquharson' (1995), in Kudielka (ed), *The Eye's Mind, op.cit.*, p.130.

43   Riley, 'In Conversation with Isabel Carlisle', *op.cit.*, p.8.

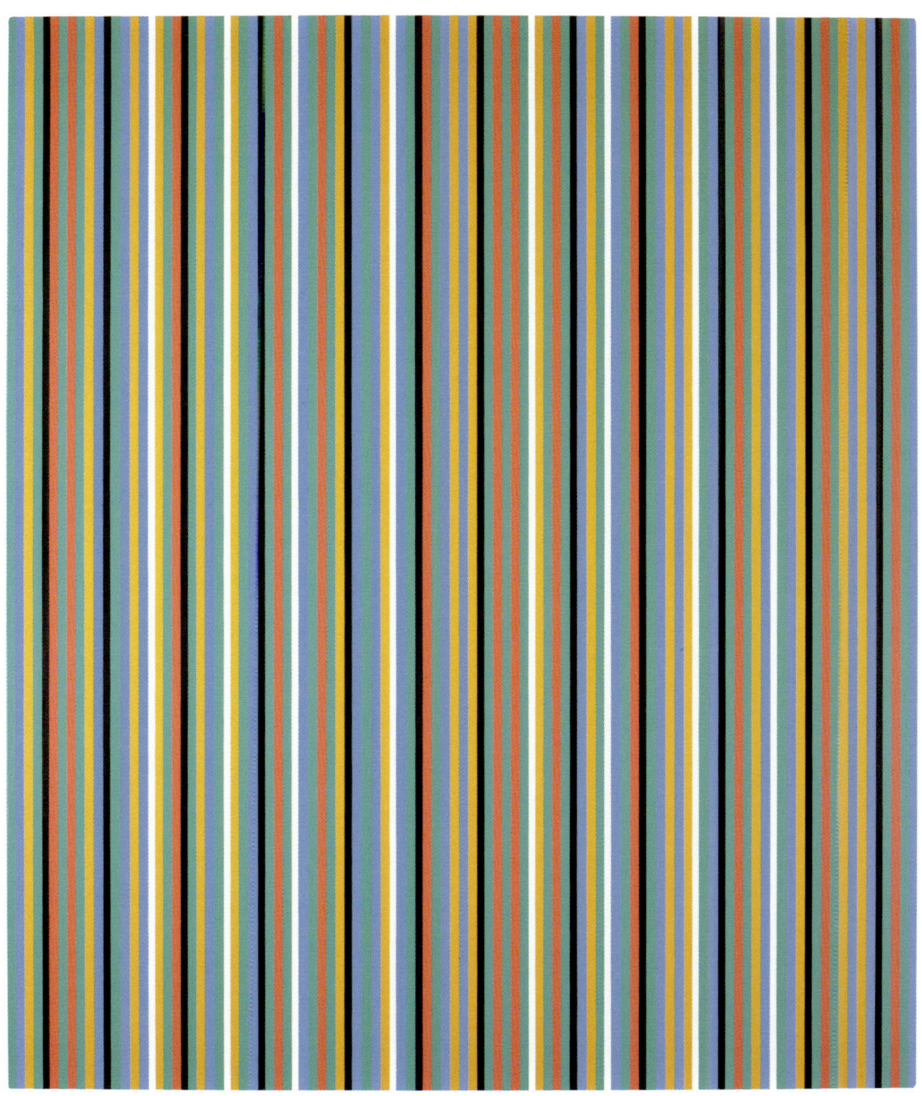

Après Midi 1981
Oil on linen
231 × 197.5 cm | 91 × 77¾ in
Private Collection

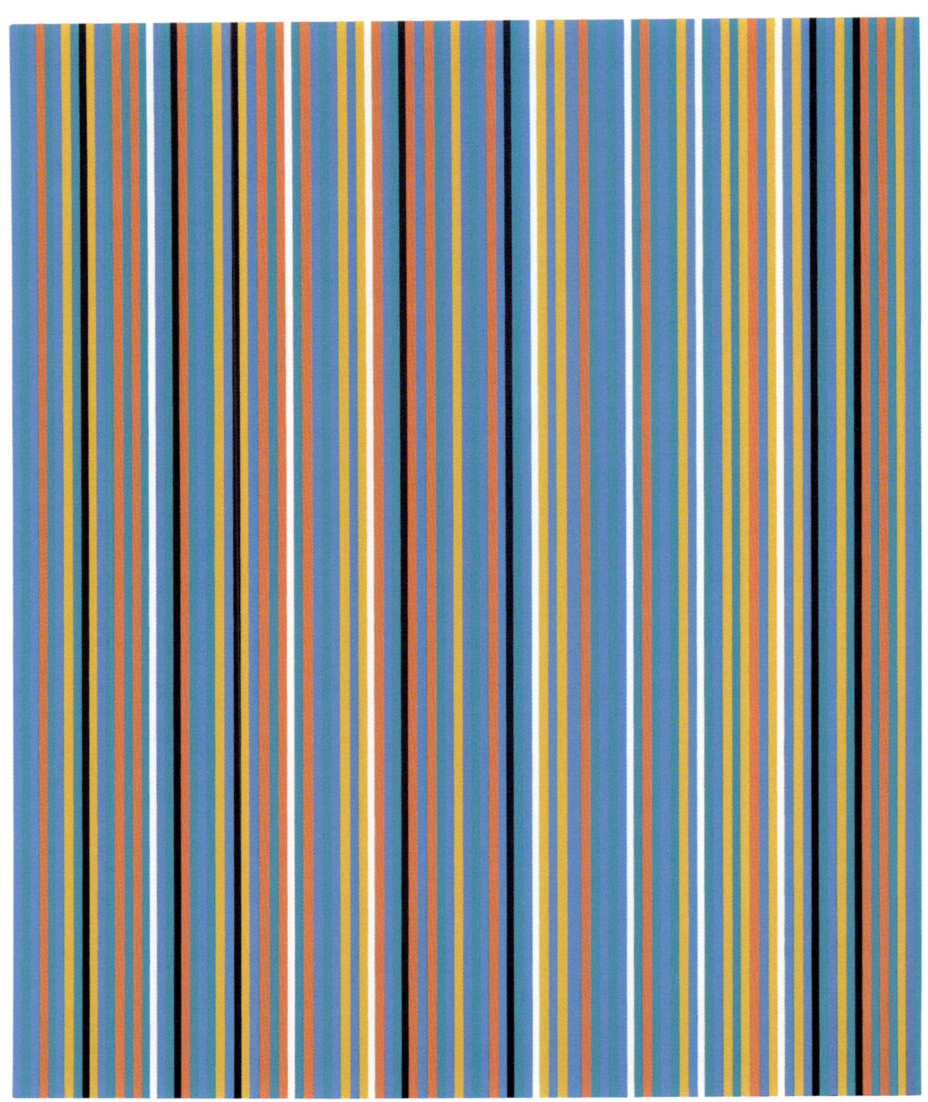

PLATE 16
Big Blue 1981–82
Oil on linen
238.1 × 201.3 cm | 93¾ × 79¼ in
Queensland Art Gallery, Brisbane

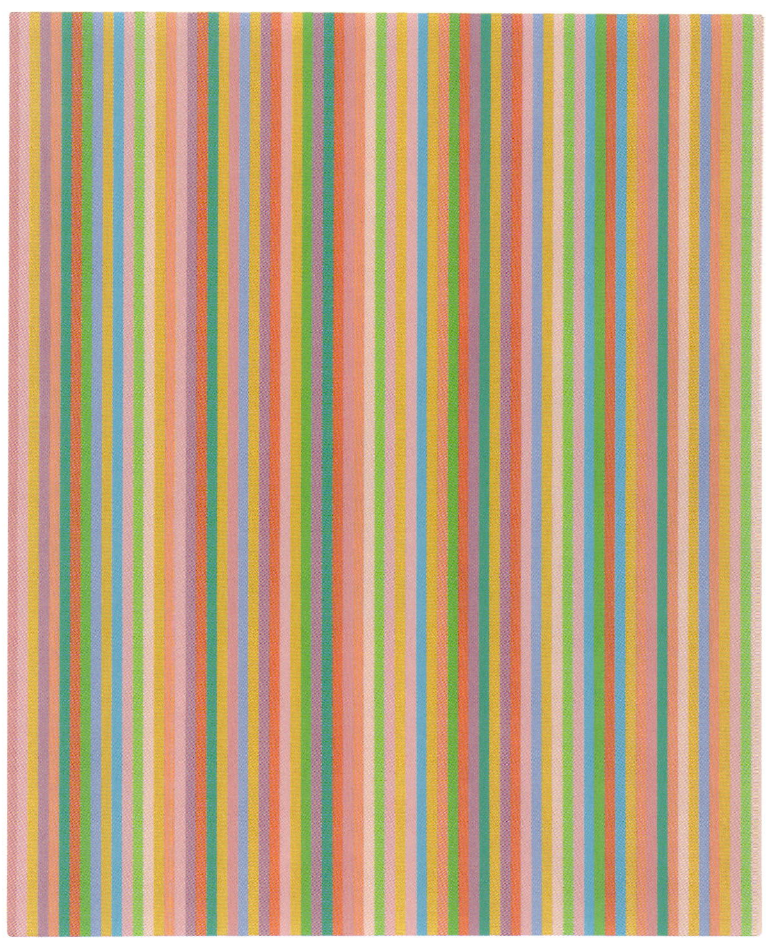

PLATE 17
Saraband 1985
Oil on linen
166.5 × 136.5 cm | 65½ × 53¾ in
Private Collection

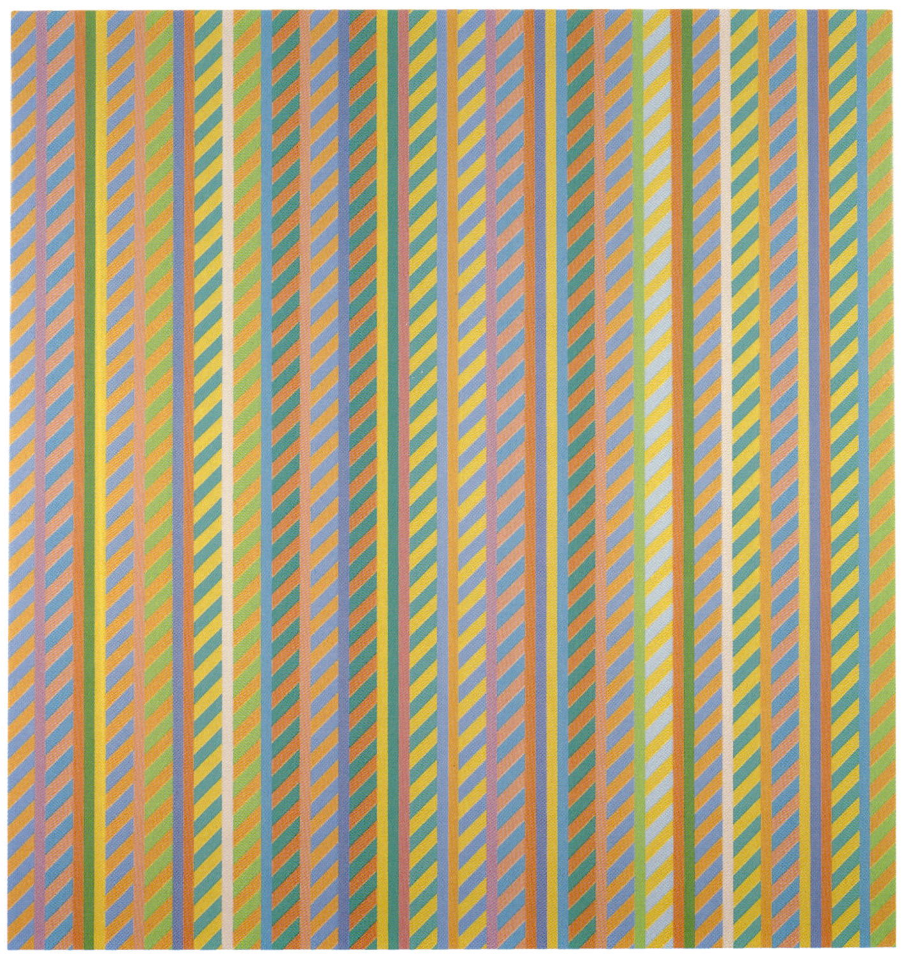

Broken Gaze 1986
Oil on linen
155 × 146 cm | 61 × 57½ in
Private Collection

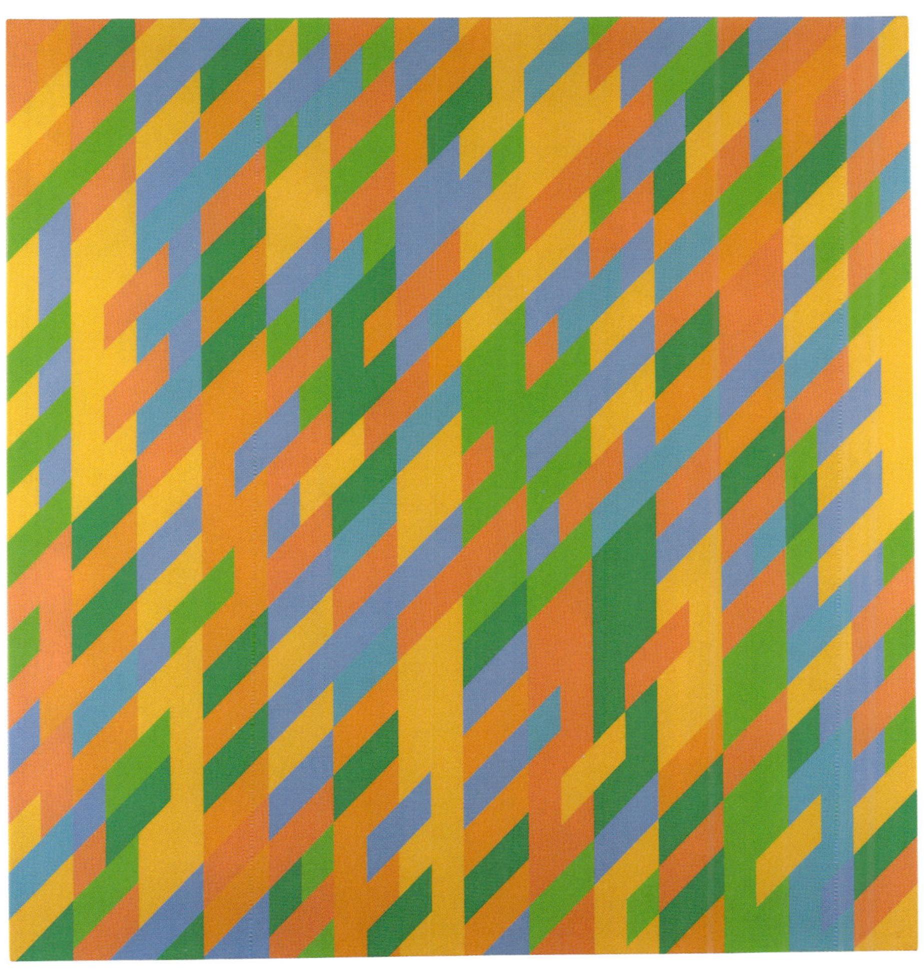

PLATE 19
Ease 1987
Oil on linen
168 × 163 cm | 66⅛ × 64⅛ in
Private Collection

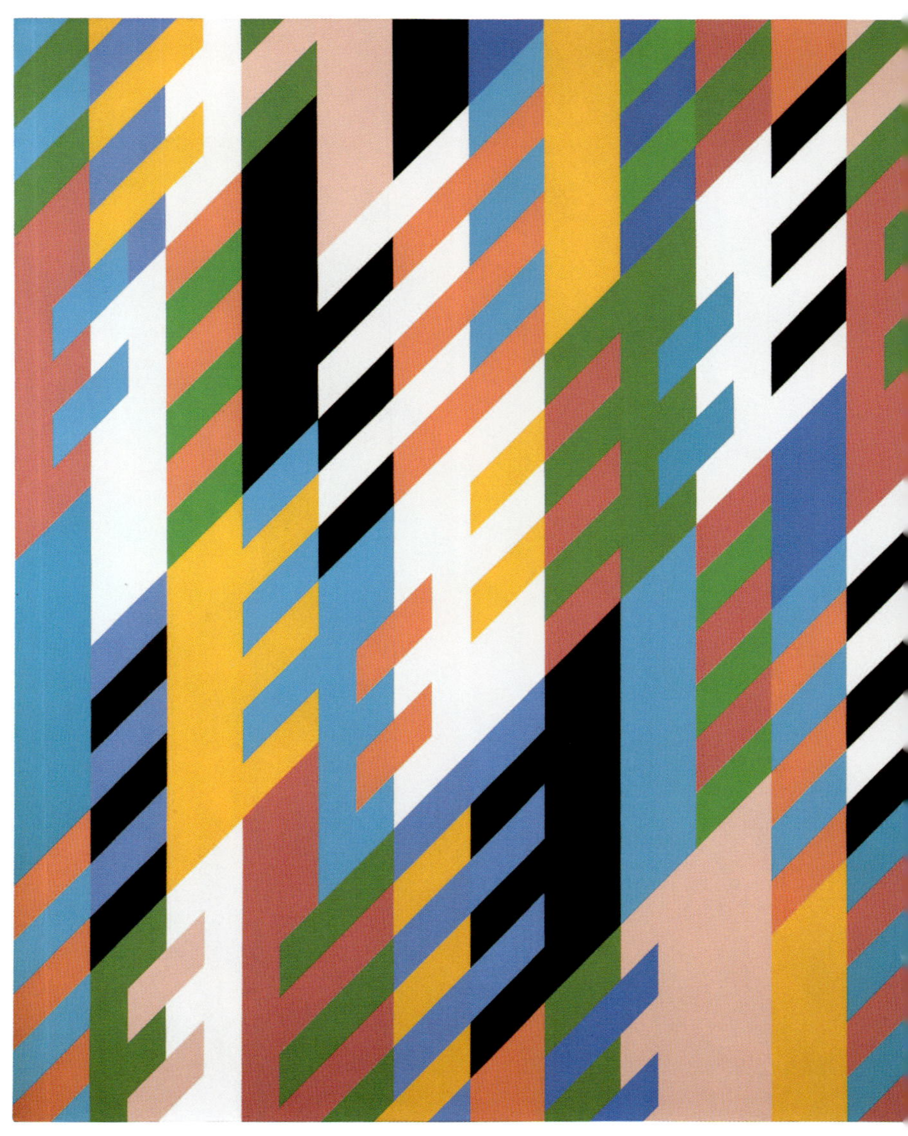

PLATE 20
New Day 1988
Oil on linen
160 × 226 cm | 63 × 89 in
Private Collection

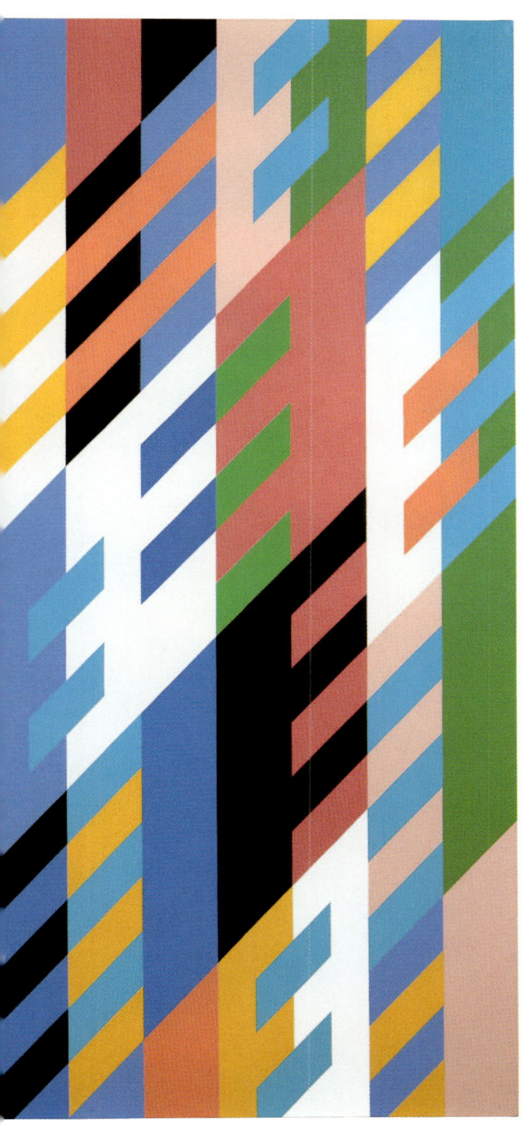

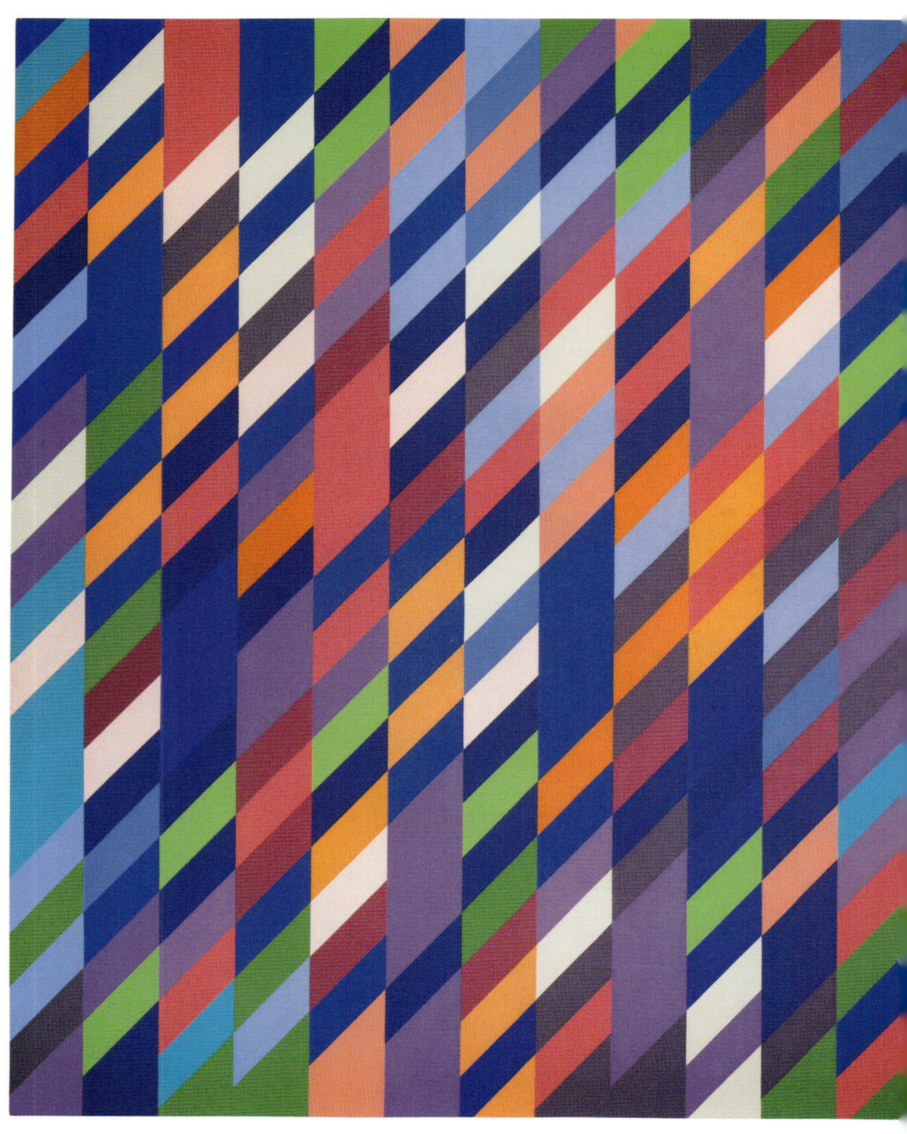

November 1990
Oil on linen
165 × 227.3 cm | 65 × 89⅜ in
Private Collection

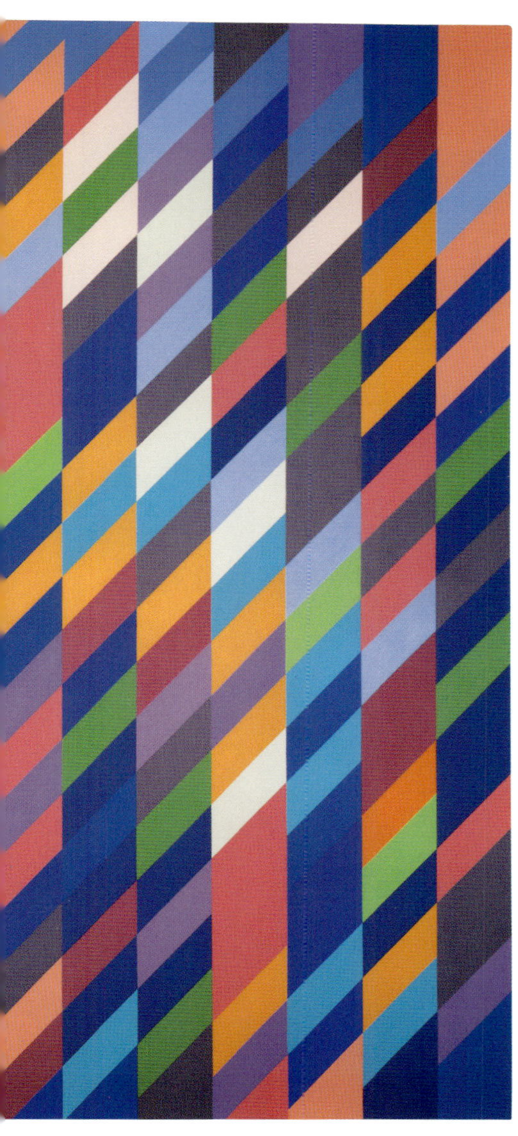

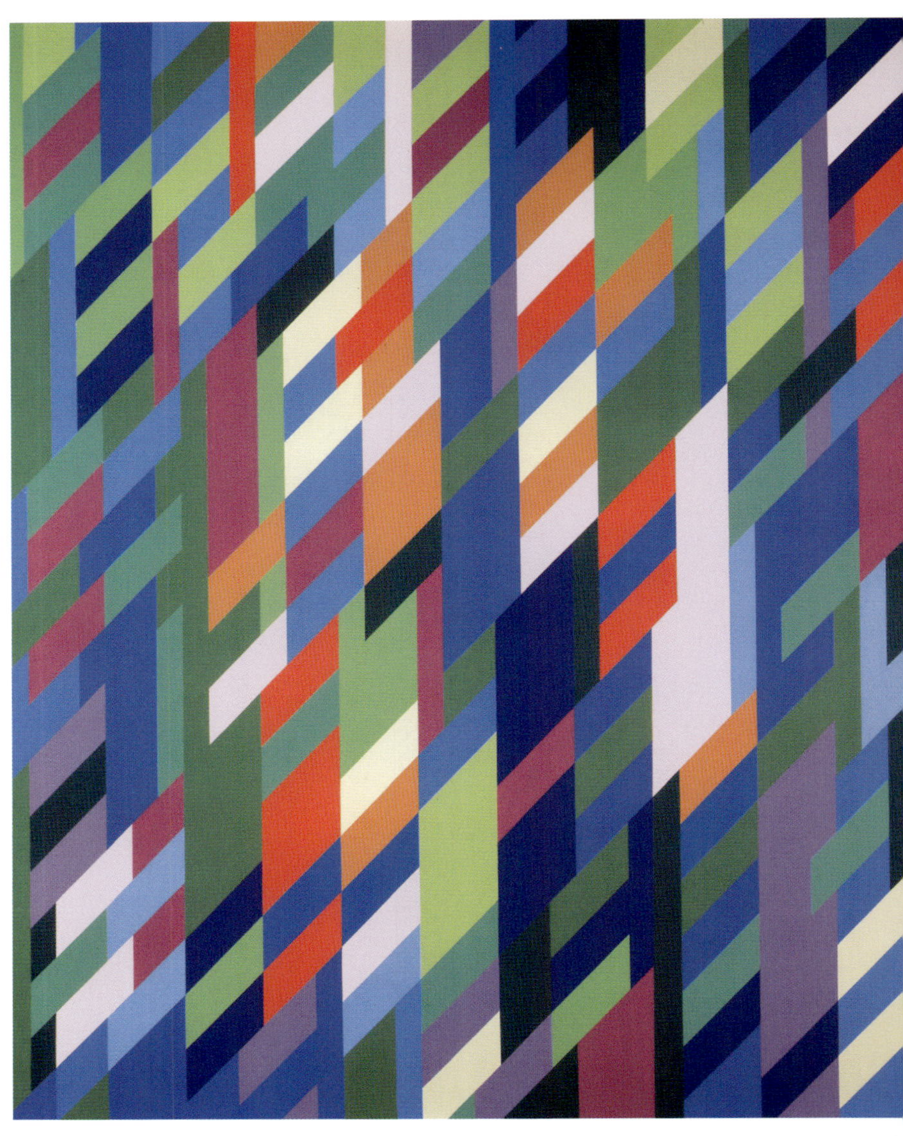

PLATE 22
In Attendance 1994
Oil on linen
165.5 × 227 cm | 65⅛ × 89½ in
Private Collection

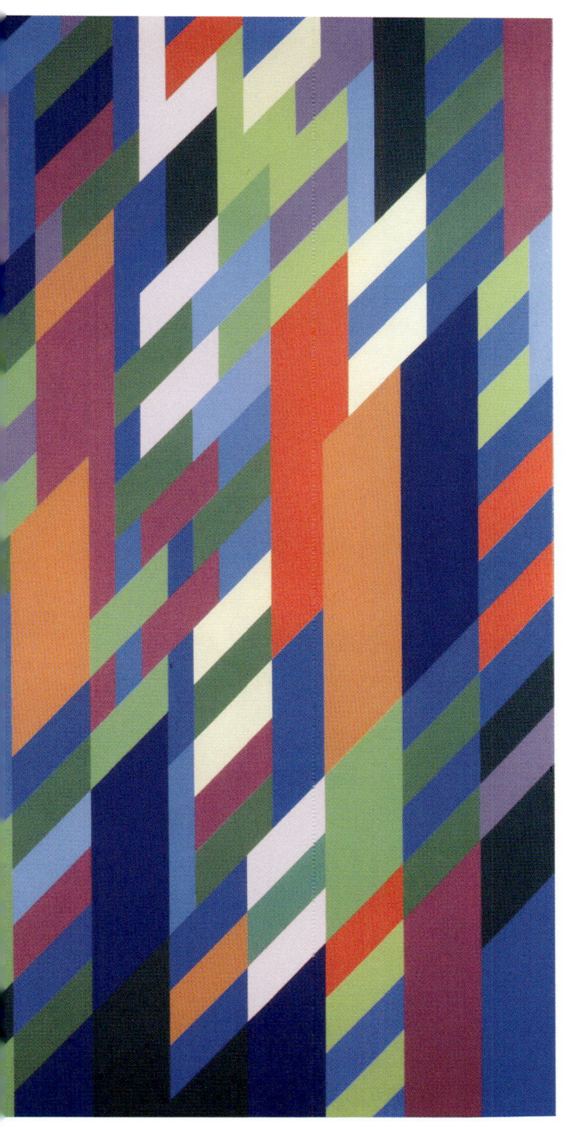

PLATE 23
Lagoon 2 1997
Oil on linen
147.3 × 199.4 cm | 58 × 78½ in
Private Collection

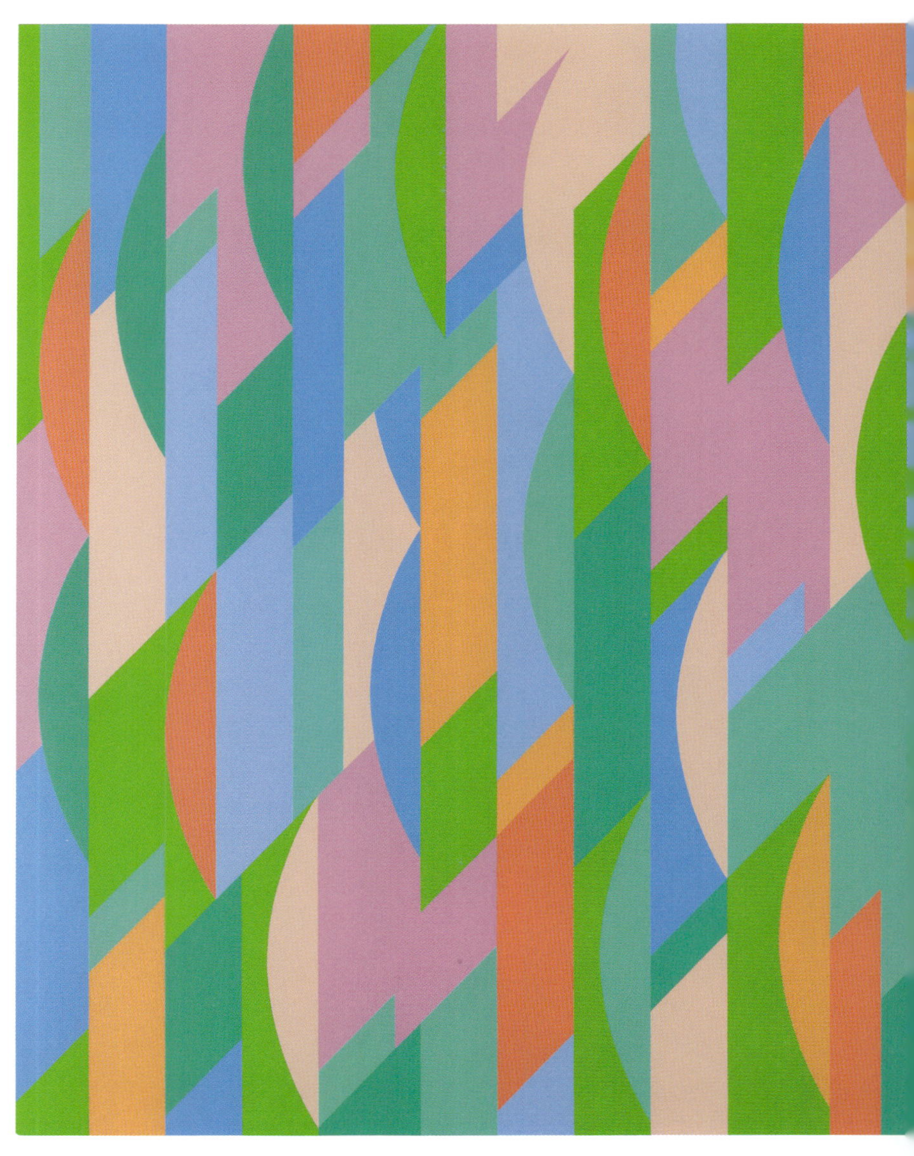

220

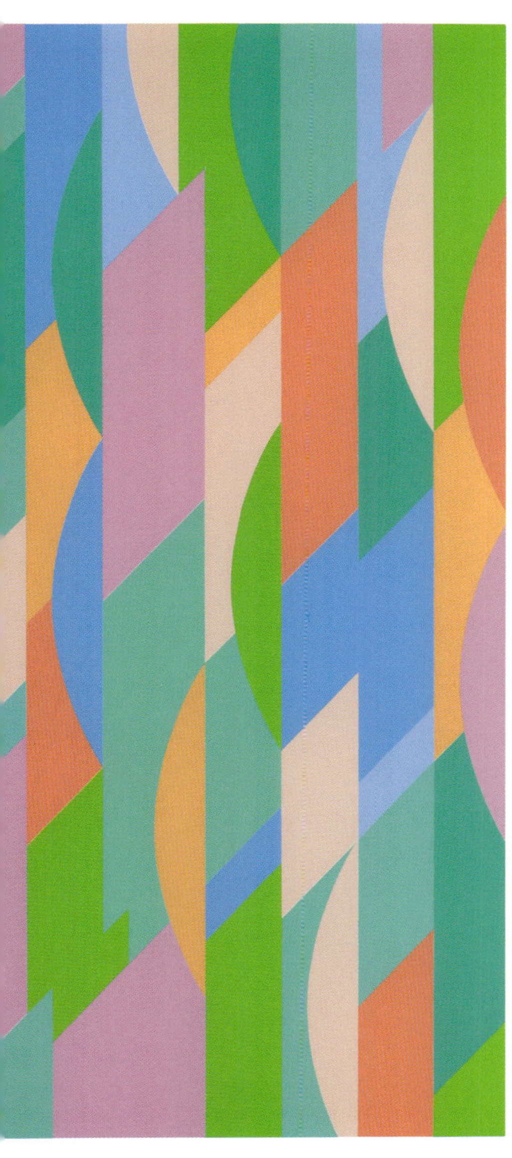

OVERLEAF | PLATE 24
Composition with Circles 1 1998
Graphite, acrylic and permanent marker on plaster wall
5 × 9 m | 16⅓ × 29½ ft
Installation view, Kunsthalle Bern

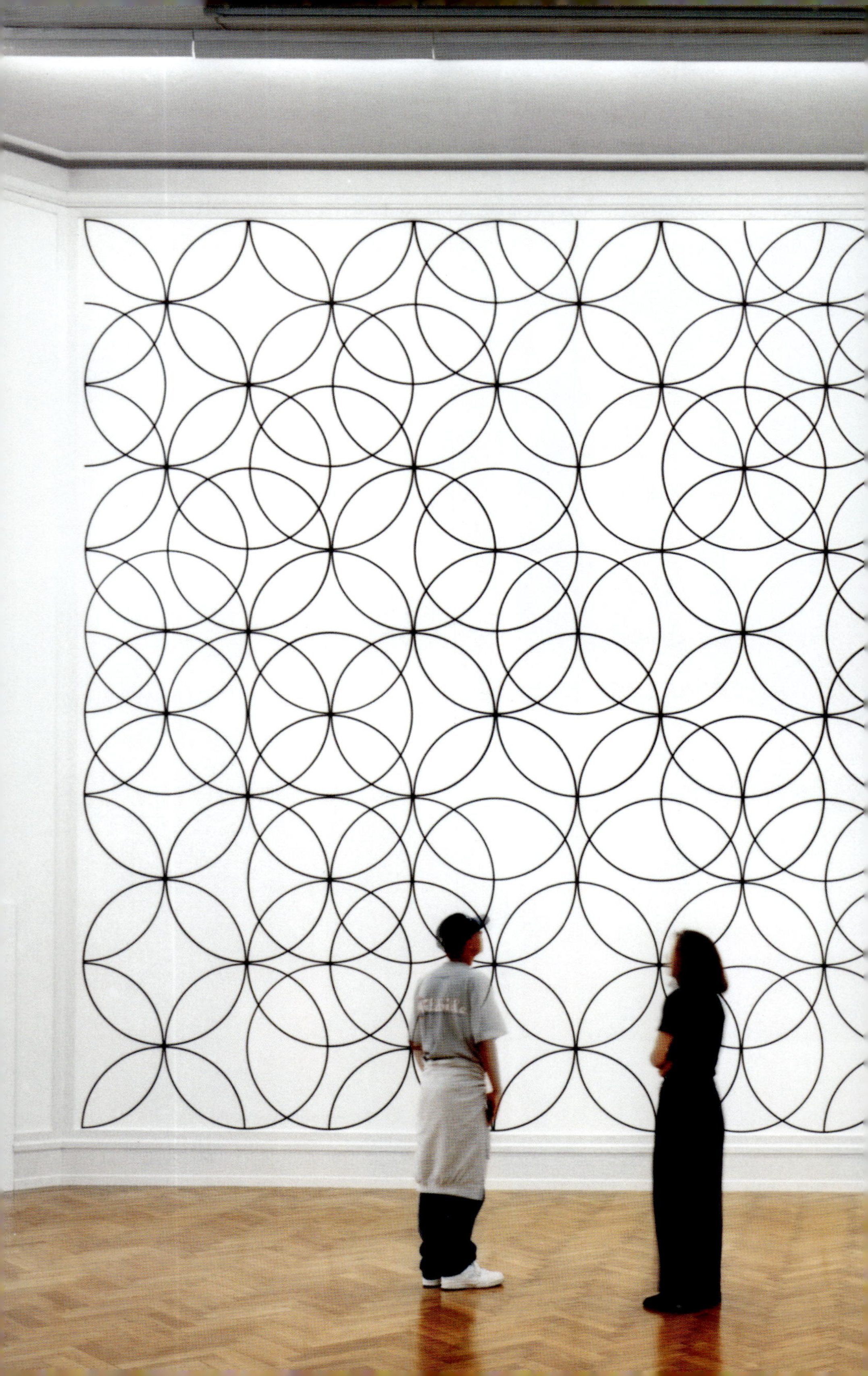

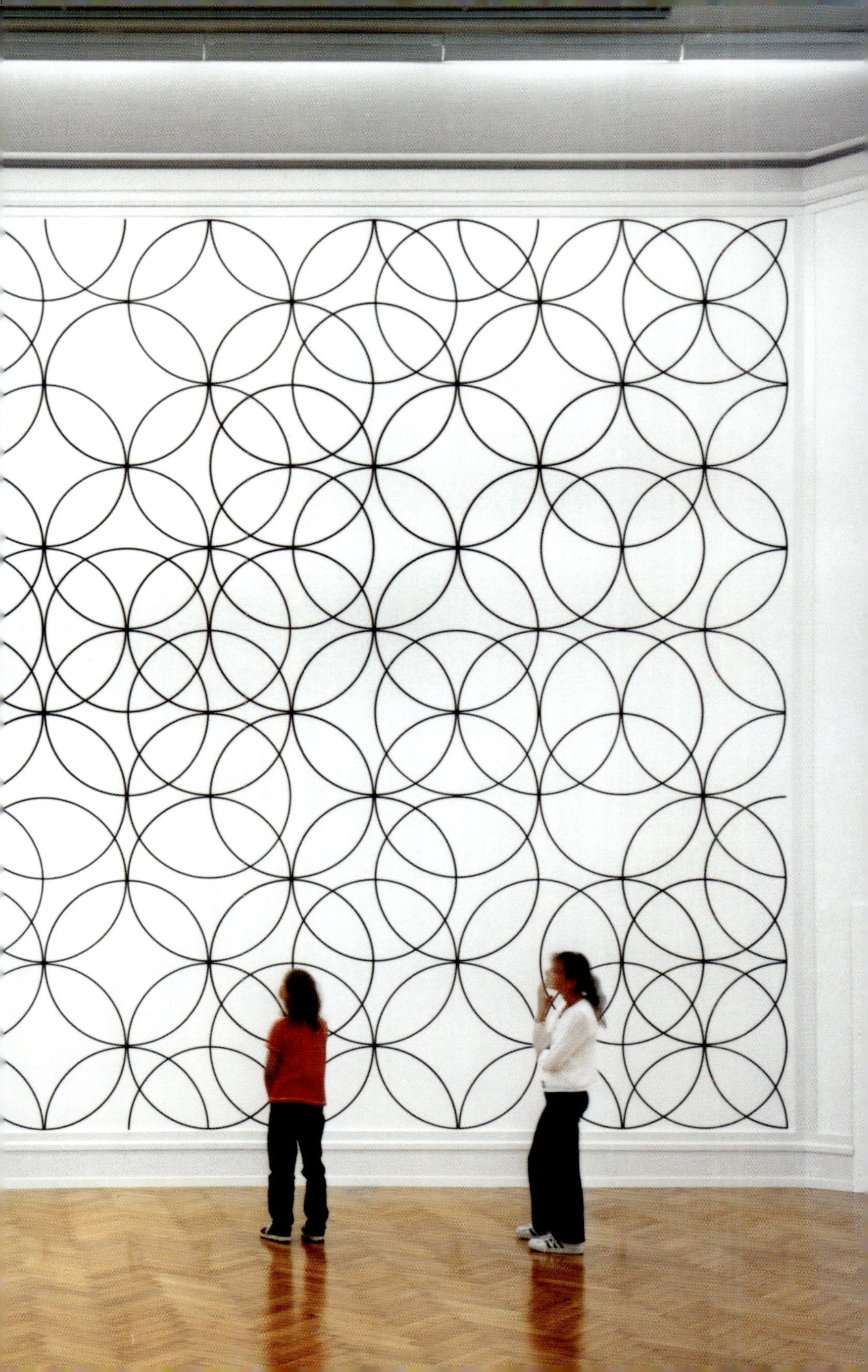

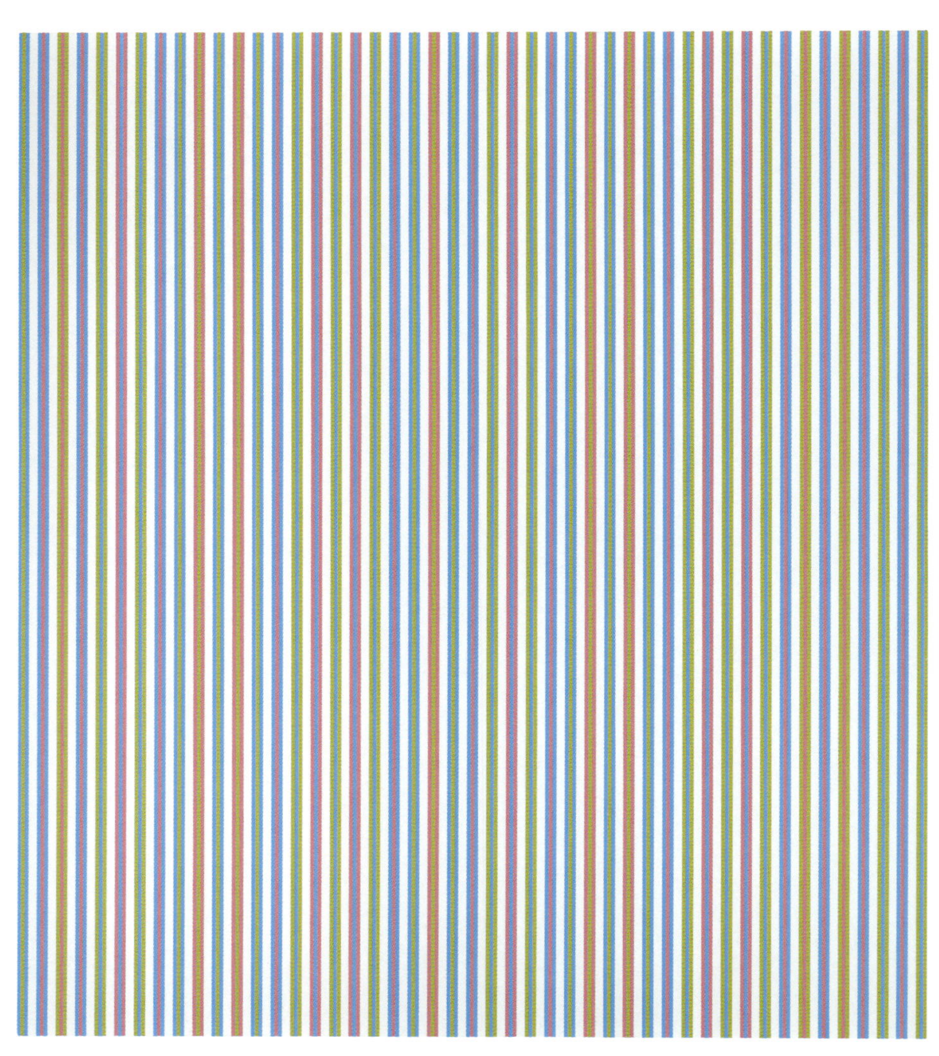

Elysium 2003/1973
Acrylic on canvas
261 × 236 cm | 102¾ × 92⅞ in
Metropolitan Museum of Art, New York

224

Bridget Riley: The Edge of Animation
Richard Shiff

> I want [people] to feel as I do, or can sometimes, to have
> this particular joy… My aim is to make people feel alive…
> An artist feels a need 'to do something' about the very
> fact of being alive.
>
> — Bridget Riley, 'Personal Interview by Nikki Henriques', 1988

A memory

During wartime, between the ages of eight and 14, Bridget Riley lived
with her mother and sister in a primitive cottage near the sea in
Cornwall. There was no electricity, no running water, few neighbours, no
regular schooling. For entertainment two choices were available: reading
and looking. This childhood, Riley says, 'should have been a miserable
time, but it wasn't'.[1] The relative isolation of wartime in Cornwall instilled
in her 'the confidence that one can make something out of very little'.[2]
  Among her many writings, Riley's best known may be 'The Pleasures
of Sight', which recounts her Cornwall experience. It first appeared in
1984 in an abbreviated form, titled 'On Swimming Through a Diamond'.[3]
Riley's diamond metaphor is set within paragraphs flowing with other
verbal jewels: 'All was bespattered with the glitter of bright sunlight and
its tiny pinpoints of virtually black shadow – it was as though one was
swimming through a diamond.' The quoted sentence closes a description
of the dynamic light and colour effects Riley observed while swimming in
the vicinity of the family cottage. The same paragraph begins: 'Swimming
through the oval, saucer-like reflections, dipping and flashing on the sea
surface, one traced the colours back to the origins of those reflections.'
And later: 'The entire elusive, unstable, flicking complex [was] subject to
the changing qualities of the light itself.'[4] Her description recalls the
watery events that Claude Monet had struggled to paint, sometimes
finding it, as he admitted, 'impossible to do'.[5] After practising painting for

many years, Riley had the greatest respect for Monet's views of his lily pond, 'in which unexpected colours appear in the depths, or elusively in reflections'.[6] In Cornwall, however, Riley was not yet a painter; she was a looker.

Riley's account of swimming among the reflections – 'and all between, the actual hues of the water' – is only the first of 11 childhood 'pleasures of sight' she chooses to recall. Her experiences in viewing are complex, yet elemental. Some conjure up the extreme contrasts of Riley's early work in black and white. Others relate to the brilliant chromatic range of her paintings of the 1970s and 80s. Aside from the first memory, the other ten involve walking or standing in the open air, as she passes through a changing environment or is transfixed by a visual spectacle. It doesn't surprise me that the swimming memory heads her remarkable list, because, uniquely, it derives its character from the nature of an indeterminate medium, rich with the fluidity and openness she would later bring to her art. Sea level, the zone of the swimmer, is neither air nor water. Always in motion, the surface of the sea tends neither towards the heights nor towards the depths. Traversing that level, 'dipping and flashing' in mimetic harmony with the surface reflections, you easily lose sense of up and down, heaviness and lightness, all direction. This medium, where air and water make contact, is a liminal edge between two environments, yet it envelops. The visual sensation is intense and intimately linked with other aspects of physicality. Looking at sea level, all perception flows into that one sensation of the very special place where you are.[7] It involves even non-lookers in looking.

'Pain'

A condensed exchange between Bridget Riley and interviewer David Sylvester, 1967:

BRIDGET RILEY I remember being very surprised when people first complained that [my painting] hurt their eyes, because it has never hurt mine…

BR No – no pain! It gives me pleasure…

DS *The painting [of yours that I own], I've had it for years, but it still hurts my eyes…*

BR Yes, but surely you get involved with the painting?[8]

During the mid-1960s, critics who objected to the American manifestations of Op art (including Riley's showings in New York) attributed both optical pain and pictorial illusionism to Op's optical illusions. Thomas Hess, editor of *ARTnews*, mentioned vertigo, migraine and a general queasiness as common responses to the disorienting sensory tensions. He suggested that the 'decorous violence' of Op would 'drive the illusion like a needle through the brain'.[9] This was a verbal image of pain consistent with the visual neatness and precision typical of Op technique.

Writing only slightly later, Rosalind Krauss felt none of the pain to which Hess confessed; yet she also took none of Riley's pleasure. Instead she intellectualised her perceptions, applying interpretive categories of optical and tactile experience. Like Hess, she noted Op art's tendency to exaggerate perspective techniques and indulge in other devices of *trompe l'oeil*. The perceptual results were to be distinguished from those of true 'optical painting', such as that of Barnett Newman or Larry Poons (Krauss's examples). The practice of Op addressed its illusions to touch as well as vision, generating tactile sensations of volumetric objects in an imaginary space; in contrast, 'optical painting' retained its pictorial honesty, returning vision to the 'actual flatness' of the canvas. Krauss invoked Riley's *Current* (1964) as a picture 'unified and organied by illusionistic projection' and which, like other Op paintings, lent itself to being, 'characterised as textural and as aimed at achieving the coherent illusion of a tactile object, or surface.'[10] She chose to view Riley's undulating wave form as if it were *in* the surface, warping it: this is illusionism. The alternative would be to see the undulation as an effect *of* the surface, that is, a sensation felt in the immediate presence of the painting, an illusion. Both responses can be articulated verbally, becoming subject to verbal confusion. Had Krauss seen the difference sufficiently clearly as she made her verbal choice?

Illusionism may be a misleading term in this context. Because illusion and illusionism are lexical cousins, they hint deceptively at a correspondence. Yet one need not lead to the other. Illusion is a natural condition of vision, a physiological fact suited to study in *Scientific American* as much as to use in painting. In 1965 curator William C Seitz organised the *Responsive Eye* exhibition for the Museum of Modern Art, New York; this was the event that sparked Hess's and Krauss's reflections on Op art. Seitz's favoured umbrella term was not 'optical' but 'perceptual abstraction', and this was Riley's preference also.[11] For his catalogue introduction Seitz turned to a recent issue of *Scientific American*, appropriating a definition from psychologist Paul Kolers's account of 'The Illusion of Movement': '[Visual illusions] are genuine perceptions that do not stand up when their implications are tested… The principal property of an illusion is that it is convincing [and] a vivid perception.'[12] With regard to logical implications, illusions do not pan out. Yet such perceptions are 'genuine', 'convincing', 'vivid'. They are neither dreams nor fantasies, nor do they take second place in a contest for human attention. Illusions are strong sensations that cannot be coordinated with what a viewer knows by other means, perhaps with equal certainty. Might they not cause mental confusion and the kind of disturbance a person would be tempted to call 'pain'? Illusionism can be a match for illusion. It too 'stands up' – but not necessarily for everyone. Its effects have been constructed for the pictorially indoctrinated.

Whereas illusion has no history, illusionism does and is a fit subject for interpretive scholarship. EH Gombrich's *Art and Illusion: A Study in the Psychology of Pictorial Representation*, published in 1960, is a historical study of the pragmatic exploitation of natural effects of illusion by successive generations of artists who refined a conventional illusionism.[13] Although illusionism often profits from illusion, these two referential fields are hardly one. Illusion is real, what we experience at the very moment of looking; it does not substitute for another visual sensation. Illusionism removes us from reality; it refers to a type of real experience, now absent, that the viewer may or may not have had at some other time. The devices of illusionism change through history and from one culture to another. But illusion, where the link between perception and reason seems to snap, is built into the body, the human physiological medium. You do not need to be taught how to experience illusion; you already know. Yet familiarity is not likely to reduce its surprise. Illusionism depends on a certain conditioning, strongly instilled by European cultural forms. Its ingrained conventions determine not so much that we sense dimensional difference within flat patterns (a factor of illusion), but something far more specific. Illusionistically, we're conditioned to perceive any rectangular painting surface as if viewed through a window, encompassing a distant perspectival space, with juxtaposed colours regarded as if situated on different representational planes of the imagined scene.[14] The tradition of representational easel painting is so strong in the West that even when two colours are juxtaposed within a composition intended as an abstraction, the perceived shift or difference in spatial dimension – a physiologically normal optical illusion – may seem to allude to an absent natural condition. A painting intended as an abstraction can connote representation to a degree alarming to its maker. It may fail to present itself and instead represent something other. 'The perceptualism of the present', Seitz wrote, 'is more concentrated than that of impressionism because the establishment of abstract painting has made it permissible for colour, tone, line and shape to operate autonomously.'[15] As Riley herself has stated, abstraction has 'only its own reality to contend with'.[16] Such autonomy may have become permissible, yet not always possible, in fact impossible to achieve without interference. Interpretive metaphors are not easily suppressed. The trick is to get as close to the impossibility of autonomy as is possible.

Op art escaped the perception of illusionistic representation far more effectively than most other abstraction. Nor was the autonomy of these paintings particularly subject to being compromised by referential allusion. Autonomy was their strength even if it could not be absolute. According to Riley, by 1960 it seemed to younger English artists that 'forms such as triangles, squares, circles, rhomboids, etc. were no longer burdened by the heavy load of associations and symbolic overtones [of] constructivist motifs'.[17] Such elements could be arranged into relatively repetitive structures with highly charged effects of simultaneous contrast,

after-image, implied movement and the like. Op artists exaggerated
these effects, ensuring that they would not mesh with the relatively
restrained illusionistic effects analogous to them. An eighteenth-century
landscapist might have set a penumbra of pale lavender around a
golden-toned figure to cause it to project forward, but an Op artist would
push that simultaneous contrast all the way to saturated hues of blue or
violet and orange or yellow. Such aggressive chromatic force is hardly
something to remain subservient in a scenic background. For this reason
Riley's contemporary Donald Judd called optical illusions, such as
chromatic after-images, 'absolutely objective'; no one would fail to see
them for what they were.[18] The stronger the illusion in Op painting, the
weaker the play of illusionism and its arbitrary interpretive allusions.

Consider Riley's *Movement in Squares* (1961). In terms of any
potential for illusionism, it has a very odd, disruptive feature. Within its
approximately square external shape, its black-and-white rectilinear
elements change or 'move' in only one dimension, across the horizontal.
This creates a very specific spatial illusion but violates illusionistic
perspective, in which forms must vary across two dimensions in order to
evoke the third, becoming shorter as they become narrower, taller as
they become wider – not necessarily systematically, but at least
suggestively. If the perspective of *Movement in Squares* represents an
object or a situation, it is one no one has ever encountered. Krauss had
assumed that Riley's art 'aimed at achieving the coherent illusion of a
tactile object'.[19] What perspective, what coherent point of view (which is
what a 'perspective' is), was Riley's work supposedly representing?
Consistent with Kolers's definition, we perceive the illusion Riley creates;
yet that experience alludes to nothing, not even to its own predictable
termination, because Riley, applying her visual judgment, shifts the axis
of recession to the right, bringing asymmetry to the symmetrical square
format and denying any obvious compositional resolution. Perhaps
nothing can be safely said about *Movement in Squares* except that with
each viewing, its animation appears as convincing and as novel as ever
before. It compels looking.

Some critics implied a difference between illusion and illusionism,
but not necessarily to the advantage of the painter of optical effects. Late

in 1963, when Larry Poons first exhibited irregular patterns of relatively
small dots of bright colour set against fields of equally bright, often
complementary hues, Michael Fried responded that 'one begins to fear
for one's retinas if not for one's mind'. Fried recognised that the
potentially irritating illusion of 'optical flicker' would be experienced
identically by 'all normal persons'. (Here we encounter a normative effect
having no cultural tradition or convention – no history – behind it.)
Poons's painting, Fried reasoned, was 'coercive': its effect was so
removed from the volitional vagaries of individual judgment that it
converted viewers into 'subjects', not 'spectators'. It subjected all people
in its vicinity to a sensation they could not ignore (like a blinding sun:
one of Riley's Cornish memories is 'looking directly into the sun [at
rocks]… all reduced to a violent black-and-white contrast').[20] 'Coercion',
Fried argued, is 'counter to art.'[21] His modest review of Poons established
an evaluative standard that would be implicit in the critical writing of
many who faced Op, Minimalism, Land art, process art, performance art
and other innovative modes of the 1960s: if the physiological effect of an
artwork becomes too insistently real, the work no longer inhabits the
realm of art. No doubt, the underlying distinction is valid. There are
effects that lend themselves to normative critical practices and which
exercise hard-won evaluative principles, and there are effects that are
'normal' only in the relative uniformity of the physiological responses
they elicit. Applied to the new art of the 1960s, however, this rational
distinction became unreasonable: it ruthlessly narrowed the range of
expressive practices that might be regarded as significant contributions to
contemporary culture. Intelligently constructed, this conceptual framework
blindly limited what could be understood through visual experience.

I have asked whether Krauss, who tended to follow Fried's lead
during this period, made the right choice in deciding that Riley's *Current*
was more illusionistic than illusion, its ultimate effect more fictive than
real. Krauss gave Riley's work a metaphoric meaning and a cultural-
historical context at odds with the painter's own attitude. Riley believed
that her practice did have a history, but it was not the kind Krauss or
Fried would consider (an account will follow). Faced with the optical and
tactile categories invoked by the young American critics, in 1965 Riley was

positioned to lose either way: if *Current* was received as no more than a
bold optical illusion, it would be 'coercive' in Fried's sense; if its illusion
stimulated a tactile imagination, it would be regressively illusionistic in
Krauss's sense. The distinction would hinge on the relative *strength* of
the effect on the viewer. Illusionism leads into familiar patterns of
criticism; strong illusion shocks the viewer out of enjoining such
interpretive modes. This is why younger artists, interested in extricating
modernist art from some of its most ingrained but unilluminating
practices, were becoming enthusiastic about illusion. They were trying to
return aesthetic experience to immediate reality.[22]

A corollary of strength is pain. 'It still hurts my eyes', David Sylvester,
a supportive critic, told the artist. Was it coercion that he experienced as
his 'pain' – a consequence of his having lived with the strength of Riley's
painting, which 'hurt' his eyes with the force of its illusion? The work in
question was *Horizontal Vibration* (1961). Its elongated horizontal bands
never quite fall into a coherent, generalisable sequence. The painting
twitches. Perhaps this is what had troubled Sylvester: the painting's
'vibration' distracted him enough to unsettle his thought. He may have
been interrupted every time he looked or merely glanced in that
direction. Psychologist Anton Ehrenzweig, another of Riley's early
admirers, commented with fascination that 'our eyes are attacked and
"devoured" by [her] paintings', which frustrate the 'need of the brain for
[a stable] gestalt'.[23] Recall that both Hess and Fried, perhaps frustrated,
regarded forceful optical effects as threats not only to the eyes but to the
mind. By stimulating visual perception, Riley's art was also challenging
cognition. Perception is alive. Wrestling with it, attempting to coordinate
thought and sensation, we have no guarantee of success, as either artist
or viewer: 'The medium is every bit as strong as any human psyche, or
will, or brain', Riley has said; 'one is well matched, if not sometimes
outmatched.'[24] Riley's respect for perception allows her to enter into
dialogue with her own artistic process. Her work is very precise, like that
of the Op artists with whom critics once associated her; but she never
experiences total control of her vision. Nor would she wish to. The effects
she seeks inhabit an elusive medium. With her friend the aesthetician
Robert Kudielka, the following (condensed) exchange occurred:

When light 'happens', you notice it – an interruption. It 'catches' you in a new dialogue you may never have imagined entering. 'Sometimes', Riley has said, 'I feel [my painting] right up against my face, the thing that refuses to be thought.'[26]

Kudielka relates a telling anecdote. He and Riley were dining outdoors in Munich on a bright early spring day in 1972. She suddenly interrupted their conversation exclaiming, 'Look at it! Just *look* at it!' But, Kudielka comments, 'there was nothing to look *at* in the proper sense of the word, no particular incident or object to be observed'. Riley's attention had been caught by a 'shine which filled the air… some permeable medium which crystallised momentarily, only to become fluid again.' Kudielka recalls that on such occasions, when a decentred perception of ambient light and colour would suddenly overwhelm the articulated perception of people and things – when sensation would force thought into momentary retreat – Riley would say, 'Don't look *at* it, just glance!' An oblique glance would be appropriate to the fundamental discordance of the sudden appearance of shine or crystallisation or veiling. A more focused view would conflict with the sensory uniqueness of the event; it would lock the intellect into structuring the sensation, boxing it into a category. Resuming the suspended conversation in Munich, Riley said: 'And some people complain that my paintings are too dazzling to look at – that they are positively unnatural!'[27] She realised, as she must have previously, that her art caused no more dazzling 'pain' than nature on a not uncommon spring day. As always, she took pleasure in these involuntary interruptions. Coercion was not an issue, because she had no cause to want to resist.

Riley has never intended to capture or recall natural effects through light, colour, a sense of movement or the spatiality of her paintings; this would be illusionism. The analogies she perceives between art and nature have more to do with the relative strength and character of their effects, whether or not one labels them illusions. There are illusions and confusions in nature, just as in art: 'You couldn't tell whether this shimmering shale was near or far, flat or round', Riley remembers, regarding a dangerous drive up Mont Ventoux, France. She was recounting how she arrived at a painting eventually titled *Static 1* (1966), with its 'mass of glittering units like a rain of arrows'.[28] Riley usually acknowledges such analogies only after the fact, becoming aware that the experience of a painting and the experience of a transient moment in nature may share an emotional resonance. A painting, like any moment's experience, can sometimes amount to 'an overall state of being'.[29] The painting spurs recognition, 'but of no specific instance… It's the recognition of the sensation *without* the actual incident which prompted it.'[30] Both painting and incident are sources and objects of perception. 'Perception', she writes, 'is the medium through which states of being are directly experienced.' In 1965 Riley addressed this thought to the misunderstandings evident in the reception to her participation in Seitz's *The Responsive Eye*. She also disclaimed any illusionism: 'The fact that some elements [in my paintings] can be interpreted in terms of perspective or *trompe l'oeil* is purely fortuitous and is no more relevant to my intentions than the blueness of the sky is relevant to a blue mark in an abstract expressionist painting.'[31]

'Don't look *at* it!' Riley would exclaim. She might have added, 'Look *with* it', that is, take the light in, move with it, let it show you what it is and how you see. Become aware. Let the internalisation of vision, its sensation, be seen: 'It seems that as sight is always in action – is working all the time – whatever one looks at one cannot help but look through one's own sight.'[32] Painting, guided by one's sight and itself a product of vision, makes sight and vision visible: 'I discovered that I was painting in order to "make visible"… in order to see one had to paint and through that activity found what could be seen.'[33] Painting is an extension of the animated visual apparatus. This is Riley's argument, related to Maurice Merleau-Ponty's. Riley has been inspired by Merleau-Ponty's phenomenological appreciation of painting, especially as expressed in the essay 'Eye and Mind', the last he published during his lifetime (1964).

There Merleau-Ponty referred to 'a "visible" of the second power', a way of letting the most intimate feelings about the world appear in visible form. The resultant image 'is not a faded copy, a *trompe l'oeil*, or another thing… I would be at great pains to say *where* is the painting I am looking at… it is more accurate to say that I see according to it, or *with* it, than that I see it.'[34] For Merleau-Ponty, the visible is a living sensation, not a point of reference: you do not look at it but with it, and its location is neither fixed outside your body nor within your mind. Merleau-Ponty wanted to counter interpretations that derived the meaning of an artist's life and work from fixed ideological and psychological conditions – from life regarded as if formed independent of one's moving sensory perception.

Riley has had some excellent commentators. One of the most sensitive descriptions of her art comes from Andrew Forge, a fellow painter. Implicitly, it evokes Merleau-Ponty's 'visible of the second power', while more directly it eliminates the metaphorical 'as if' that would link Riley's painting to illusionism:

> I might speak of the glowing colour in one of the recent paintings. I might have used the same word of the muted red centre of a Rothko, meaning that I could picture it as if glowing, or that that particular area acts out a 'glowing' part in relation to the cool umber that frames it. But when, after a period of looking at Riley's coloured stripes [in *Byzantium*, 1969], my eyes can no longer keep up with the struggle to separate and locate the blues and greens within their bounding of red, and the whole colour charge of the picture seems to detach itself from the canvas and come free in my eye, then glowing takes on a different meaning. Glowing is my word, my verb, for what is actually happening in my eye.[35]

Forge is looking-with rather than looking-at. To speak of Rothko's red 'glowing' would be metaphoric, but Riley's glowing, a sensation, actually happens. Forge's perception of Rothko leads to description, conceptualisation; his perception of Riley leads only to sensation. The glow in *Byzantium* requires no description. To choose 'glow' as a good metaphor is voluntary; to sense glowing in the act of looking is involuntary. The forceful shift from one type of experience to the other may well put stress on perception and 'painfully' disturb the mind. But such, Riley would say, are the 'pleasures of sight'.

'Don't look *at* it, just glance!' Riley told Kudielka. 'Sometimes in a mere glance one can see more than in the close scrutiny of a thousand details.'[36] In a painting, details can usually be counted. Riley's *Static 2* (1966), has precisely 625 of them, the number of little black ellipses distributed across a neutral field, which form the grid of this square painting. Focusing on one of the ellipses reveals little about the totality. To the contrary, a glance may not indicate the precise geometrical identity of the elements, but it registers how the painting as a whole feels, its sensation. *Static 2* moves, vibrates, hums, crackles – effects that seem to derive from its grid of small dark spots. Why would this happen? It cannot be because the painting suggests to Riley 'a field of static electricity', somehow like the 'rain of arrows' she imagined on her drive up Mont Ventoux, for Riley alone has lived this connection. The source of the disturbance must lie elsewhere. 'It is visual prickles,' she says, 'but I don't find that a painful physical thing.'[37] Perhaps the source of the 'prickles' is a painful *mental* thing.

Each of the 625 ellipses that together constitute the slightly irregular but symmetrical grid of *Static 2* is itself an asymmetrical form, at least in one respect; unlike a circle or a square, an ellipse is longer along one axis than along the other. In *Static 2*, each of the rows of little ellipsoidal dots rotates; scanning across or down a row indicates that the longer axis of each successive ellipse shifts from vertical to horizontal. This no doubt accounts for much of the optical vibration or prickle of the painting. Because the overall format is a square, and because the number of ellipses in each horizontal row, 25, is equal to the number in each vertical row, it seems – logically, at least – that the image ought to be quite stable. But Riley has done something subversively cunning: she has rotated the vertical rows at a faster rate than the horizontal rows. This, in fact, is one of her characteristic interventions: to create the illusion of movement at abruptly contrasting 'speeds'. Confusion results as to whether the painting contains one compound movement or two contrasting movements.

Each horizontal row contains two full rotations. Beginning with an upright ellipse in the upper-left corner, with its longer axis precisely vertical, the top horizontal row of the canvas has a second precisely vertical form halfway across and a third at the upper-right corner. The situation in the vertical rows is different. There the same type of rotation occurs two-and-a-half times. This means that at the bottom of a vertical row, the axis of the ellipse will be turned opposite from the position at the top of the same row. So Riley has generated asymmetry within a deceptively symmetrical format. *Static 2* has a curiously animated movement with a double rhythm, built into a situation that might otherwise appear stable and static. But *Static 2*, like an electrical charge, is unstable, moving and abrupt. Even an inattentive observer will have to notice this, although perhaps 'painfully'.

Describing Riley's paintings can be laborious. Summation and generalisation do not come easily, if at all. The title *Static 2* fortuitously offers a play between static as an adjective for still and static as a noun for crackle or vibration. Riley's art itself plays areas of relative stability and 'repose' against others of intense optical activity, what she calls a 'disturbance'.[38] But her art has little to do with manipulating concepts, and her best critics have tended to find their own application of conceptual terminology inadequate. Forge remarked that even his looking, let alone his writing, could 'no longer keep up' with the pace of Riley's visual movement.[39] Describing her art with words becomes a demonstration of how the structuring potential of ordinary language fails to correspond to the visual perception. It is as if a work like *Static 2* is moving in at least two dimensions at once, and linear description moves only in one. When paronymy (partial resemblance or punning) makes language multidimensional, its 'higher' dimensions do not necessarily correspond to those of vision. I myself feel a 'painful' inadequacy in attempting to describe Riley's art.

Our usual categories and systems of analytical opposition, our distinctions between front and back, up and down, vertical and horizontal, dark and light, hardly begin to capture what happens in perceiving Riley. Perhaps this would be true of the verbal description of any painting. But such an observation misses the point, just as early

commentators on Riley and Op – Hess and Krauss, for example –
missed the cultural significance of the unusual strength of certain
structured illusions. Riley's work stimulates an intensified visual
perception and therefore cannot be approached effectively with critical
language appropriate to perception of a different order. This is not to
deny that excellent accounts of Riley's individual paintings and their
evolution already exist: for example, the detailed descriptions by Robert
Kudielka, John Elderfield and Lynne Cooke, not to mention Bridget Riley's
own, in which she might invoke 'point movement' (*Shift*, 1963), the
'twist' (*Zing 1*, 1971), the 'roll-over' (*Cataract 3*, 1967; *Gamelan*, 1970), and
other devices for accelerating, retarding or otherwise developing a sense
of movement or enhancing the effects of colour.[40] Yet Riley's painting
remains disjoined from words and thoughts to a greater degree or in a
more overt manner than we're used to encountering. Art is diacritical:
degrees of difference matter as well as absolute, categorical differences.
The relative strength of its effects is much of what makes Riley's art
significant. Is that strength coercive? I leave coerciveness aside for the
moment to ask a different question: Is it pleasurable?

Despite Riley's fond memories of life in Cornwall, Elderfield has
made a provocative suggestion: 'Looking for unusual visual sensations
was a distraction from the anxieties of [Riley's] childhood – in particular,
from the [wartime] absence of her father. And that interpretation of the
sudden visual pleasure – as a distraction – is one that remains.' For Riley,
then, visual distraction would always be 'beneficent' (Elderfield's word)
and pleasurable, never painful or unproductive.[41] Productivity and
distraction converge in her practice. Asked whether she works every day,
she answers, 'I would love to.' In fact, Riley uses much of her studio
activity as a kind of mental distraction to withdraw her mind from her
eyes: 'I occupy my conscious mind with things to do' – organising lines
and curves, mixing and testing colours for studies (these eventually
develop into the finished paintings that she directs her assistants to
execute).[42] Riley controls the process of investigation and production
with extraordinary rigour. In turn, that circumscribed control leaves a part
of her attention open to the glancing events of the eye.[43] She learns
from unforeseen incidents as much as from what is already planned,

working to preserve and enhance the source of stimulation until it attains an intensity that satisfies her artistic standards. The standards themselves change along with her continuing experience.

Whether felt as pleasure or pain, the visual interruption perceived in nature and pursued in painting is involuntary, or, as Riley often says (putting a more sanguine spin on it), a 'surprise': 'the pleasures of sight have one characteristic in common – they take you by surprise… in order to see one had to paint and through that activity found what could be seen.'[44] I quote the latter part of this remarkable statement a second time, for it bears expanded consideration. Riley is using her painting the way once, as a child, she used looking – not so much to draw sensation from the world, but to fill a world with sensation. To draw sensation from the world is to abstract it, as a reduced essence. Nevertheless, to fill a world with sensation is equally an act of abstraction.

Abstraction in reverse

'The literary type expresses himself with abstractions,' said Paul Cézanne, 'whereas the painter, with drawing and colour, makes his sensations, his perceptions concrete.'[45] What is abstraction? In the nineteenth century it was mental: thinking extended to impractical limits, to its quintessence (invoking a term with connotations of alchemy, the abstraction of matter into essence). To certain art critics, intellectual abstraction represented an academicism of the mind, a match for the polished detail of the French Salon painters' most enervated renderings. In 1846 Charles Baudelaire referred to the concept of absolute beauty as a rarefied 'abstraction'; those who pursued its austere linearity were 'philosophical types who abstract the quintessence'.[46] Abstraction did not enhance or intensify sensory experience but reduced it, eliminating the passionate, animating pulse of life. Even today, we identify a mentally distracted, confused or absorbed person by his 'abstract' look.[47] Around 1900, to speak of a painter's 'tendency toward abstraction' was more likely to suggest involvement with philosophical notions than with the material 'abstraction' of a simplified palette or an accented linearity (although it could be both).[48] Some of the early champions of Paul Cézanne defended his art against charges of abstraction by shifting attention from the mental to the material; they stressed the insistently physical nature of his brushmark, interpreting it as a material, not a conceptual, abstraction of the painting process.[49] Yet he himself understood the word in an older sense, as conceptualisation taken to excess.

Sometime during the late 1950s Riley became interested in Cézanne's *Trees at the Jas de Bouffan* (c.1883), one example among many of a screen of brushmarks that exerts 'a directional pull' (her description). Riley's understanding of Cézannean effects could well apply to her own works of the 1990s, such as *High Sky 2* (1992): Cézanne 'knew that the diagonal thrust helps to activate the slow backward and forward pulse of colour… Through a multiplicity of diagonals Cézanne [or Riley herself] builds up a highly sensitive visual field which allows [the painter] to accumulate and disperse tensions, to shift changing rhythms through the painting.'[50] In *Trees at the Jas de Bouffan*, elements of dense foliage appear to move in from the upper left, while other elements cascade down from upper right towards bottom left: 'The [compositional] diagonals… carry blocks of colour whose brushmarks run counter to the diagonals.'[51] When Riley looks at Cézanne, she sees 'abstraction' in its material-physiological sense, not its intellectual sense. In *High Sky 2* parallelograms linked by associated hues and values drift down from left to right while the diagonal linear structure counteracts that rhythm, right to left, and the regularly spaced vertical divisions slow both movements. Riley's wall drawing *Composition with Circles 1* (1998) operates similarly but without colour and at a grand scale. An irregular arrangement of initially static circles begins to move in depth and generates diagonal chains of almond-shaped forms as well as phantom verticals. Like the skewed, asymmetrical illusion in *Movement in Squares*, such contrary patterns of virtual motion do not resolve into a system of symmetries and balances. They simply keep moving: vibrating, flickering and otherwise provoking sight.

Riley was not the first to have responded to Cézanne in terms of instability and movement. Many early viewers found his manner of representation awkward and even ugly, but others were intrigued by the

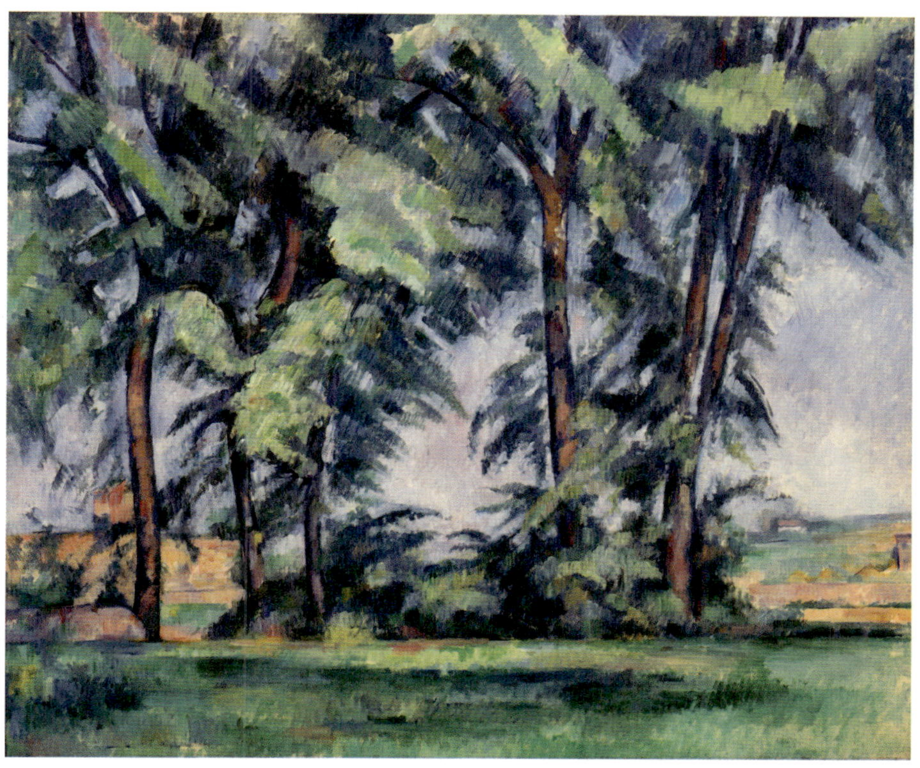

Paul Cézanne
Trees at the Jas de Bouffan c.1883
Oil on canvas
65 × 81 cm | 25⅝ × 31⅞ in
The Courtauld Gallery, London

degree to which they were stimulated, as if led to see something not quite visible. In 1904 the German critic Julius Meier-Graefe acknowledged that perceiving Cézanne was a deeply physical experience: 'There is no movement; it's a matter of a simple still life. Still lifes don't have legs. Yet it feels as if something in the pupil of my eye is quivering with life, set in motion by some movement located in a higher dimension.'[52] Meier-Graefe realised that his experience could only be described phenomenologically. Viewing Cézanne's painting deflected his process of thought from any existing concept of 'still life', turning it to a concept of 'life' – 'something in the pupil of my eye is quivering with life'. To read Meier-Graefe's paragraph is to sense his elation. Mentally, his reorientation may also have caused 'pain'.

To the attentive viewer, Cézanne's effect was not of apples, cut flowers or crockery but of 'movement located in a higher dimension'. Analogously, Riley's colours are not of the dawn, the sunset or like 'swimming through a diamond'. Her colours do not represent light, the light of something. Instead she paints an experience of illumination: 'I don't paint light. I present a colour situation which releases light as you look at it… [My painting] comes to life when looked at from a certain distance… What you focus upon is not what you see.'[53] Real illusion, unlike fictive illusionism, is critically affected by the viewer's distance and focus. At a certain distance the sensations of colour and light that derive from the twisting curves of *Song of Orpheus 5* (1978), or the parallel bands of *Bali* (1983), produce a quivering, an animation. It will be hard to know whether the colour is moving or the eye is moving. This is what Meier-Graefe, quite involuntarily, perceived in Cézanne, an experience that induced him to record his troubled thoughts in writing: 'How can such effects be produced in a picture?'[54] Meier-Graefe describes the effects but cannot explain them. Like a Cézanne still life, Riley's vertical bands (as in *Bali*) surely 'don't have legs'. Why do they appear to move? Sometimes, in part, because of a punctuating use of black and white; sometimes, in part, because of the varied distribution of a dominant hue; sometimes, in part, because of a shift in the quality of the fugitive, virtual colours that arise from the presence of the actual colours. Such answers, however, seem more precise and circumscribed than actual sensation.

                                                  RICHARD SHIFF

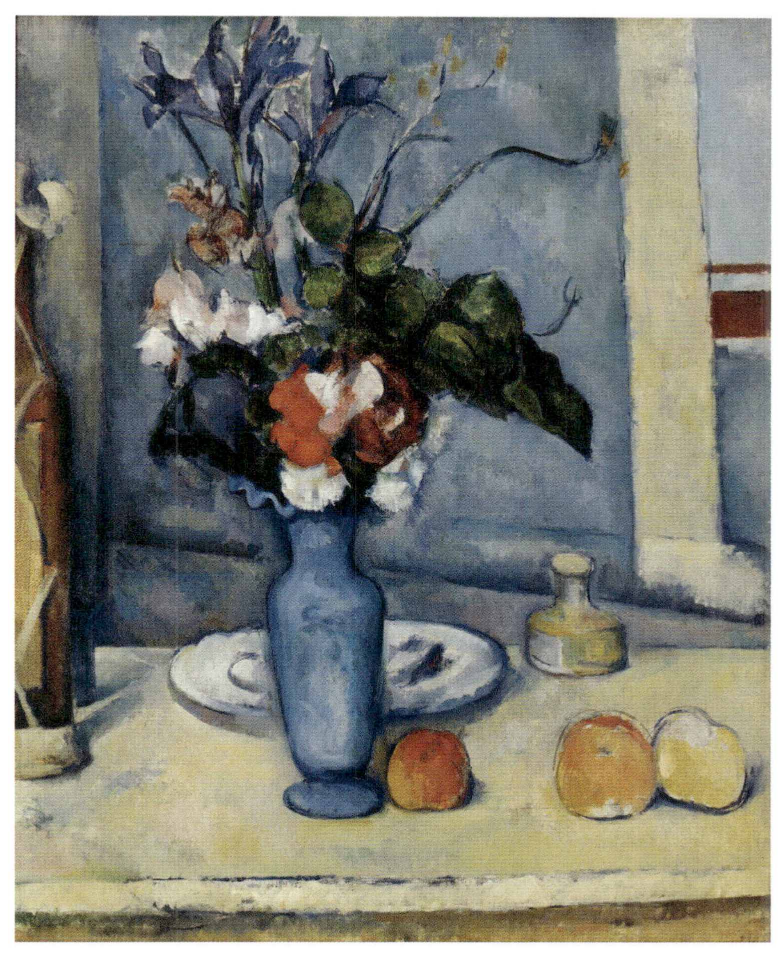

Paul Cézanne
The Blue Vase 1889–90
Oil on canvas
61 × 50 cm | 24⅛ × 19¾ in
Musée d'Orsay, Paris

We do not know how Riley's colours move, but looking proves that they do.

Obliquely, Merleau-Ponty explains Meier-Graefe's experience: 'The picture makes movement visible by its internal discordance… [its] mutual confrontation of incompossibles.' Merleau-Ponty argues that painting's illusion is not illusionistic; it follows neither conventional laws of perspective nor other proven devices for realism. Traditional realism in painting generates a still picture, like an instantaneous photograph. Painting that moves with life, on the contrary,

> portrays the body in an attitude which it never at any instant really held[,] when, for example, a walking man is taken at the moment when both his feet are touching the ground… Each [bodily] member's position, precisely by virtue of its incompatibility with the [other members] is not 'in time' with the others; and since all of them remain visibly within the unity of a body [either the depicted figure or the picture itself], it is the body which comes to bestride time… Painting has made itself a movement without displacement.[55]

'Movement without displacement' is another term for the quivering Meier-Graefe felt and also Sylvester's 'pain'.

The exterior symmetry of the human body implies a structural stability that any specific movement, carefully observed, may appear to violate. Riley does not represent symmetrical bodies, but her formal patterns start with strong elements of symmetry while, as they develop, they undermine that general impression with numerous slight irregularities and the occasional reversal or incompatibility. She creates what Merleau-Ponty in one instance called the 'confrontation of incompossibles', and at another point in his argument, the decentred, displaced effect of 'internal animation'.[56] In *Arrest 2* (1965), Riley set one sequence of wavy bands against another. Discerning which is which is difficult: considered in terms of their implied directional movement, a group of six on the left faces a group of nine on the right; considered in terms of their tonal gradation, a group of nine on the left faces a group of six on the right. One wants to see all of those waves as a single, coherent pattern; but no way of doing it emerges, and the effort only leads to the familiar intellectual distress. The waves keep moving, oblivious.

The effect of *Entice 2* (1974) is similar. Its general linear pattern appears to repeat; but there are areas where red and green conjoin to a greater degree than elsewhere, giving those areas a phantom yellowish cast, violating the implied symmetry. Symmetry and asymmetry at once: incompossible. 'The basis of colour is its instability,' Riley writes:

> Instead of searching for a firm foundation, I realised that I had one in the very opposite… By accepting this paradox I could begin to work with the fleeting, the elusive, with those things which disappear when you actually apply your attention hard and fast… One looks here and colour is there.[57]

Riley locates the origin of her kind of abstraction in the late impressionism of Cézanne and Monet and the pointillism of Georges Seurat, but more explicitly in Paul Klee and Henri Matisse.[58] From Klee she understood a distinction parallel to the one Cézanne's early supporters articulated, 'between schematic or theoretical abstraction [which is mental] and Abstract painting [which is material and physical]'. 'Abstract painting' acknowledges the abstract character of the means, of the process of painting, perhaps of vision itself, as opposed to an abstraction of the represented model or scene. According to Riley, Klee established that:

> the meaning of abstraction lay in the opposite direction to the intellectual effort of abstracting: it is not an end, but the beginning. Every painter starts with elements – lines, colours, forms – which are essentially abstract in relation to the pictorial experience that can be created with them.[59]

Like Klee, Matisse 'reversed' the Impressionist practice of abstracting a particular sensation of colour from the flow of nature's sensations. He intuited that 'pictorial colour [as opposed to observed colour] could become the vehicle of sensation'.[60] Matisse's abstraction expanded sensation, building it up rather than distilling it down.

We may not realise how radical it is to set abstraction in reverse.[61] Cézanne, Klee and Matisse – whether or not consciously intending it – turned what we see, our perception, back on itself so that vision would encounter an enriched sensation rather than a limiting concept. With abstraction in reverse, sensation is not momentary. Just as Merleau-Ponty described it, sensation 'bestrides' time as a 'confrontation of incompossibles'. The still picture (no legs) moves.

Riley argues that the purpose of abstraction is to 'rebuild' painting, 'starting from the elements – the realities of the actual thing [painting] – and finding out what could be done'.[62] Sensation is yet to be known in its fullness. Riley opens sensation up, explores it. Her colour is not something extracted from a nature already known, but something at painting's disposal. When she uses a colour that creates 'shine', it is not the limited shine of some particular substance, but the 'abstract' quality of shine, with which a comprehensive vision can be built.[63] The pattern of *Burn* (1964) lies flat while it also lifts like a vapour. *Orient 4* (1970) shines. *Aurulum* (1978) glows. *Reflection 1* (1994) sparkles. *Apricot and Pink* (2001) – with its interrupted vertical waves, interrupted diagonal bands and curiously compounded colour-shapes – moves with 'internal animation'.

Nothing

'Examination… only examines that which can be examined. For an artist those fleeting sensations which pass unrecognised by the intellect are just as important as those which become conscious.'[64] In 1992 Riley reviewed the Seurat retrospective organised for the centenary of his death. Seurat had always been important to her: in 1959 she learned by doing Seurat, copying a reproduction of his *Bridge at Courbevoie* (1886–87); she also created pointillist works of her own (*Blue Landscape*, 1959–60; *Pink Landscape*, 1960).[65] Riley was struck by Seurat's having conjoined 'uninflected and non-referential' paint application with colour that was 'abstract' – it set sensation ahead of description. In her view,

RICHARD SHIFF

Seurat had understood perception as the 'medium': 'Perception itself had to be examined, methodically objectified and built up into a technique… Monet goes *with* perception, looking along its sightlines as it were, whereas Seurat looks *into* perception and shows it to be the activity which produces what it sees.'[66]

To look *into* perception (that is, reversing its normal direction) is to look *at* nothing in particular. Identifiable things appear only on the far side of perception in the form of conceptualised information; within perception lies sensation. Seurat, according to Riley, worked with 'the technicalities of nothing'; he 'turned a searchlight on nothing, and exposed it – not as a fraud but as a fact'.[67] Certainly, others had commented on Seurat's capacity to peer into nothing, bringing concrete sensation back. It was often Seurat's summer paintings of expanses of sand, water and sky that elicited this response: a 'sensation of the visual void', commented one early critic.[68] 'Who before Seurat ever conceived exactly the pictorial possibilities of empty space?' Roger Fry asked later; 'His pictures are alive, but not with the life of nature'.[69] In Riley's view this 'life' was the animation proper to abstraction, and it might be found anywhere in Seurat, not only in his sand, his air or his blank walls. It was in the mark of his colour. The 'nothing' is what we see, or what we see *with* (recall Merleau-Ponty). Painting returns to that level of perception at which vision sees itself: in Seurat's art, Riley concludes, 'what we see is ourselves looking'.[70]

Riley finds the words, but the thought still fails the experience. Knowledge will never be adequate to perception's movement. She speaks of the artist's need to seek out and exploit 'the vital tension between knowledge and sensation'. This is the edge of animation, the liminal state of nowhere that corresponds to the swimmer's sea level, with its 'dipping and flashing'. Seurat shows what 'we cannot *quite* see[,] an experience just beyond our visual grasp'. Using perception as the medium, he faces us with 'the *im-perceptible*'.[71] The painter's perception lets us see how we see but undermines vision by recording too faithfully – the presence of perceptual failure. Yet, so long as we move with our vision, taking in the pleasures of sight, we avoid the mental pain of trying to match a general concept to an experience of nothing.

Despite the division between Monet (looking 'with perception') and Seurat (looking 'into perception'), Riley includes both among the 'great painters of "nothing"'. Monet, she argues, paints, 'what we actually experience in looking, the drifting and gathering of sight itself… [His views of the lily pond are,] with their multiple reflections (transparencies, water surface and depths)… about virtually nothing'.[72] Here, Riley's sensations at sea level seem to lie just below the surface of her words; she saw what Monet saw before she knew Monet's paintings. Painting brings such experiences to mind, but is unique to itself.

On at least two occasions, Riley linked Monet's perceptual 'nothing' to Western culture's loss of certainty:

> Focusing isn't just an optical activity, it is also a mental one. [Our] lack of a centre has something to do with the loss of certainties that Christianity had to offer… Monet's late water lily paintings [are] without a single focal point… If one does not deceive oneself and accepts this lack of certainty, other things come into play[,] like colour, whose instability can become another form of certainty.[73]

Monet painted visions that could not be stilled – so many unfinished views. His accumulated knowledge produced neither full control nor full understanding. Riley's abstractions move as Monet's colours do, without focus: 'One looks *here* and colour is *there*.'[74] Their animating illusions define the viewer's presence as much as the painting's. From the aesthetic side of uncertainty, Riley's art demonstrates that sensation and thought are incompossible: neither finds congruence with the other. Her art nevertheless provokes thought as much as sight. To the extent that we reflect on what we see, any compelling sensation constrains us to 'think otherwise than we have been thinking'.[75] Our attempt to match existing thought to immediate sensation inevitably fails yet stimulates the mind to expand. Incompossibility is a background fact of living. Attending to that unsettling fact is a risk but not necessarily painful. It makes a person all the more alive.

We have lost our certainties, Riley says. An alternative 'form of certainty' comes from trusting in the pleasures of sensation, despite all the instability. In her painting, Riley wants nothing more than 'to let things happen.'[76] Such openness may seem passive yet is an exemplary constructive act: 'An artist feels a need "to do something" about the very fact of being alive.'[77]

Paul Moorhouse (ed), *Bridget Riley*, exhibition catalogue, Tate Publishing, London, 2003, pp.81–92.

Note: I thank James Lawrence, Alexander Dumbadze, Mette Gieskes and especially Bridget Riley for essential aid in researching this essay.

1   Bridget Riley, 'Personal Interview by Nikki Henriques' (1988), in Robert Kudielka (ed), *The Eye's Mind: Bridget Riley, Collected Writings 1965–1999*, Thames & Hudson, London, 1999, p.21.

2   Bridget Riley interviewed by John Tusa, BBC Radio 3, 5 January 2003.

3   Bridget Riley, 'On Swimming Through a Diamond', *Vogue*, vol.141, March 1984, pp.292–93, 350.

4   Bridget Riley, 'The Pleasures of Sight' (1984), in Kudielka (ed), *The Eye's Mind*, *op.cit.*, 1999, p.30.

5   Claude Monet, letter to Gustave Geffroy, 22 June 1890, in Gustave Geffroy (ed), *Claude Monet, sa vie, son oeuvre*, vol.2, Grès, Paris, 1924, p.47.

6   Bridget Riley, 'Practising Abstraction: Talking to Michael Craig-Martin' (1992), in Robert Kudielka (ed), *Bridget Riley: Dialogues on Art*, Zwemmer, London, 1995, p.63.

7   Swimming in the ocean, of course, evokes what Freudian psychologists call 'oceanic' feeling. According to Anton Ehrenzweig, who often referred to Riley's work, 'Oceanic dedifferentiation usually occurs only in deeply unconscious levels and so escapes attention; if made conscious, or rather, if the results of unconscious undifferentiated scanning rise into consciousness, we may experience feelings of manic ecstasy.' Anton Ehrenzweig, *The Hidden Order of Art: A Study on the Psychology of Artistic Imagination*, Weidenfeld & Nicolson, London, 1967, p.295. Is it 'oceanic' to be 'swimming through a diamond'? In January 2003 I asked Riley whether she had learned more from Ehrenzweig or he had learned more from her; she replied that it was about even. To my mind, swimming also evokes another of Riley's intellectual mentors, Maurice Merleau-Ponty: 'Immersed in the visible by his body, itself visible, the see-er does not appropriate what he sees; he merely approaches it by looking, he opens himself to the world.' Maurice Merleau-Ponty, 'Eye and Mind' (1961), in James M Edie (ed), *The Primacy of Perception*, Carleton Dallery (trans), Northwestern University Press, Evanston, IL, 1964, p.162.

8   Bridget Riley, 'Interview with David Sylvester' (1967), in Kudielka (ed), *The Eye's Mind*, *op.cit.*, pp.73–75.

9   Thomas B Hess, 'You can hang it in the hall', *ARTnews*, vol.64, no.2, April 1965, pp.42, 50.

10 Rosalind Krauss, 'Afterthoughts on "Op"', *Art International*, vol.9, no.5, June 1965, p.75. Contemporary opposition to the spirit of Krauss's interpretive analysis might have come from Susan Sontag, 'Against Interpretation', *Evergreen Review*, vol.8, December 1964, p.93: 'In place of hermeneutics we need an erotics of art.'

11 William C Seitz, *The Responsive Eye*, exhibition catalogue, Museum of Modern Art, New York, NY, 1965, p.7; Bridget Riley, 'In Conversation with Maurice de Sausmarez' (1967), in Kudielka (ed), *The Eye's Mind*, *op.cit.*, p.61. Riley refers to her classification as an Op artist during the later 1960s as a 'mantle' that 'descended' on her about five years after she had begun working in what could be called her perceptual abstraction mode; Tusa, *op.cit.*

12 Paul A Kolers, 'The Illusion of Movement', *Scientific American*, vol.211, October 1964, p.98; Seitz, *op.cit.*, p.5.

13 EH Gombrich, *Art and Illusion: A Study in the Psychology of Representation*, Princeton University Press, Princeton, NJ, 1960.

14 With traditional sculpture, a similar illusionism results from the fact that any three-dimensional object set on a base evokes a figure in space.

15 Seitz, *op.cit.*, p.7.

16 Riley, 'In Conversation with Isabel Carlisle', *op.cit.*, p.8.

17 Bridget Riley, 'In Conversation with Robert Kudielka' (1972), in Kudielka (ed), *The Eye's Mind*, *op.cit.*, p.82.

18 Donald Judd, 'Some Aspects of Color in General and Red and Black in Particular', *Artforum*, vol.32, summer 1994, p.77.

                                                                    RICHARD SHIFF

19 Krauss, *op.cit.*, p.75 (emphasis added).

20 Riley, 'The Pleasures of Sight', in Kudielka (ed), *The Eye's Mind*, *op.cit.*, p.30.

21 Michael Fried, 'New York Letter', *Art International*, vol.7, 16 January 1964, pp.55–56. Fried links his early response to Poons with his later, essentially moral, objections to the 'heightened perceptual experience' of Minimalist (or 'literalist') art; see Michael Fried, 'An Introduction to My Art Criticism', *Art and Objecthood*, University of Chicago Press, Chicago, IL, 1998, pp.40, 67, 53. On illusion in Minimalist art, see Richard Shiff, 'Donald Judd: Fast Thinking', in *Donald Judd: Late Work*, exhibition catalogue, PaceWildenstein, New York, NY, 2000, pp.8–13.

22 Both Fried and Krauss derived their early criticism from the example of Clement Greenberg, who was equally unimpressed by perceptualist art; Clement Greenberg, 'Recentness of Sculpture' (1967), in John O'Brian (ed), *Clement Greenberg: The Collected Essays and Criticism*, vol.4, University of Chicago, Chicago, IL, 1993, p.252. Today, all the more, we tend to question references to 'immediate reality' and situations of unconditional perceptual openness. During the 1960s such notions were complexly motivated and should hardly be dismissed as either naive or disingenuous (then or now).

23 Anton Ehrenzweig, 'The Pictorial Space of Bridget Riley', *Art International*, vol.9, no.1, February 1965, p.21.

24 Bridget Riley, 'In Conversation with Maurice de Sausmarez' (1967), in Kudielka (ed), *The Eye's Mind*, *op.cit.*, p.59.

25 Riley, 'In Conversation with Robert Kudielka', *ibid.*, pp.85–86.

26 Bridget Riley, quoted in Robert Kudielka, 'Nothing but Appearance', in *Bridget Riley: Works 1959–78*, exhibition catalogue, British Council, London, 1978, p.13.

27 Riley, quoted in Robert Kudielka, 'Bridget Riley', in *Bridget Riley: Paintings 1982–1992*, exhibition catalogue, Hayward Publishing, London, 1992, pp.8–9 (original emphasis).

28 Riley, 'Interview with David Sylvester', in Kudielka (ed), *The Eye's Mind*, *op.cit.*, pp.76, 78.

29 *Ibid.*, p.78.

30 Bridget Riley. 'A Reputation Reviewed: Talking to Andrew Graham-Dixon', in Kudielka (ed), *Dialogues on Art*, *op.cit.*, p.72 (original emphasis).

31 Bridget Riley, 'Perception Is the Medium' (1965), in Kudielka (ed), *The Eye's Mind*, *op.cit.*, pp.66, 68.

32 Bridget Riley, 'Perception and the Use of Colour: Talking to EH Gombrich', in Kudielka (ed), *Dialogues on Art*, *op.cit.*, p.44.

33 Riley, 'The Pleasures of Sight' (1984), in Kudielka (ed), *The Eye's Mind*, *op.cit.*, p.33. I had assumed that Riley's phrase 'make visible', which she sets within quotation marks, derived from Paul Klee: 'Art does not reproduce the visible but makes visible'; Jürg Spiller (ed), *Paul Klee: The Thinking Eye*, Ralph Manheim (trans), Lund Humphries, London, 1961, p.76; quoted by Riley in 'Making Visible', in Robert Kudielka (ed), *Paul Klee: The Nature of Creation*, exhibition catalogue, Hayward Publishing, London, 2002, p.18. When I inquired about this, Riley replied that it would have been 'an unconscious reference… Sometimes one can absorb something so completely and find it so profoundly in sync with one's own as yet unidentified feelings that it eventually becomes truly integrated'; statement to author, 17 February 2003.

34 Merleau-Ponty, *op.cit.*, p.164 (emphasis altered).

35 Andrew Forge, 'On Looking at Paintings by Bridget Riley', *Art International*, vol.15, no.3, 20 March 1971, p.16 (original emphasis).

36 Riley, 'The Pleasures of Sight', in Kudielka (ed), *The Eye's Mind*, *op.cit.*, p.30.

37 Riley, 'Interview with David Sylvester' (1967), *ibid.*, p.76.

38   Bridget Riley, 'Statement' (1970), *ibid..*, p.79.

39   Forge, *op.cit.*, p.16.

40   Robert Kudielka, 'Building Sensations: The Early Work of Bridget Riley', in Lisa G Corrin (ed), *Bridget Riley: Paintings from the 1960s and 70s*, exhibition catalogue, Serpentine Gallery and Koenig Books, London, 1999, pp.23–33; John Elderfield, 'The Change of Aspect', in Lynne Cooke and Karen Kelly (eds), *Bridget Riley: Reconnaissance*, exhibition catalogue, Dia Center for the Arts, New York, NY, 2001, pp.11–43; Lynne Cooke, 'Around and About: *Composition with Circles 2*', *ibid.*, pp.45–65. By 'roll-over' Riley refers to her practice of 'slowing' the progression from one end of a scale of hues or values to the other. For example, if a sequence of three bands in a composition has the values four, five and six, then the following three might have the values five, six and seven, instead of seven, eight and nine. Roll-over creates an odd tension between the general advancement of a progression and its local reversal.

41   Elderfield, *ibid.*, pp.30–31.

42   Riley, interview by Tusa, *op.cit.* Significant segments of Riley's studio time are occupied in mixing subtly different hues from a great variety of pigments; after Riley does the mixing, an assistant labels and preserves the unique colour in a tube (interview by author, 26 March 2002). A distinction seems to be made between inventing colour and classifying and cataloguing it. Consistent with her role as inventor of the conditions of visual perception, Riley has removed herself from the final execution of her paintings, regarding any 'expression' of authorial identity or 'exercise [of] taste' as a distracting element in the viewer's perceptual experience (interview by author, 15 October 1002). She initiated the use of assistants around 1961, when 'this aspect of my work passed virtually without comment... I wanted the actual (visual) content of the paintings to come through unchecked by any kind of touch... It's part of the meaning of the work that I don't want to interfere with the experience of what can be *seen*'; Riley, 'Practising Abstraction: Talking to Michael Craig-Martin', in Kudielka (ed), *Dialogues on Art, op.cit.*, p.60 (original emphasis). Riley makes the unusual observation that 'with his tin and the splatter stick [Jackson Pollock] most explicitly avoids any direct physical "touch"'; Riley, 'In Conversation with Isabel Carlisle', *op.cit.*

43   According to Riley's precise instructions, studio assistants execute revisions of existing studies within a continuing process of refinement, providing the artist with 'a body of work I can explore'; Riley, interview by Tusa, *op.cit.*

44   Riley, 'The Pleasures of Sight', in Kudielka (ed), *The Eye's Mind, op.cit.*, pp.32–33.

45   Paul Cézanne, letter to Emile Bernard, 26 May 1904, in John Rewald (ed), *Paul Cézanne, correspondence*, Grasset, Paris, 1978, p.303 (author's translation).

46   Charles Baudelaire, 'Salon de 1846', in Claude Pichois (ed), *Oeuvres complètes*, vol.2, Gallimard, Paris, 1976, pp.426, 493 (author's translation).

47   Expressing his disdain for theories of abstraction, Willem de Kooning referred to a confused acquaintance known by the 'very abstract look on his face'; Willem de Kooning; 'What Abstract Art Means to Me', *Museum of Modern Art Bulletin*, vol.18, spring 1951, p.5.

48   André Fontainas, 'Art moderne', *Mercure de France*, vol.29, January 1899, p.238.

49   See Richard Shiff, 'Apples and Abstraction', in Eliza E Rathbone and George TM Shackleford (ed), *Impressionist Still Life*, Abrams, New York, NY, 2001, pp.42–47.

50   Bridget Riley, 'The Experience of Painting: Talking to Mel Gooding' (1988) and Bridget Riley, 'The Colour Connection: In Conversation with Robert Kudielka' (1989), in Kudielka (ed), *The Eye's Mind, op.cit.*, pp.123, 170. One of Riley's specific references was Cézanne's *The Bathers* (c.1906). On Riley and Cézanne, see also Cooke, *ibid.*, p.46.

51   Riley, statement to author, 31 January 2003.

                                                    RICHARD SHIFF

52 Julius Meier-Graefe, *Entwicklungsgeschichte der modernen Kunst*, vol.1, J Hoffman, Stuttgart, 1904, p.166 (author's translation). Allusion to experience of a 'higher dimension' was a common trope at least from the 1880s on; see Linda Dalrymple Henderson, *The Fourth Dimension and Non-Euclidean Geometry in Modern Art*, Princeton University Press, Princeton, NJ, 1983, pp.3–43.

53 Riley, 'In Conversation with Robert Kudielka', in Kudielka (ed), *The Eye's Mind, op.cit.*, p.85; Bridget Riley, 'Practising Abstraction', in Kudielka (ed), *Dialogues on Art, op.cit.*, p.56 (original emphasis).

54 Meier-Graefe, *op.cit.*, p.166.

55 Merleau-Ponty, *op.cit.*, pp.184–85 (sentence order reversed). Merleau-Ponty was inspired by the explanation of movement in sculpture in Auguste Rodin, *L'art: entretiens réunis par Paul Gsell*, Grasset, Paris, 1911, pp.77, 85–88.

56 Merleau-Ponty, *op.cit.*, pp.182, 185. On Riley and Merleau-Ponty, see also Cooke, *op.cit.*, pp.62–63.

57 Riley, 'Practising Abstraction', in Kudielka (ed), *Dialogues on Art, op.cit.*, p.56 (emphasis partly eliminated).

58 Klee and Matisse, along with Cézanne, were major sources for Merleau-Ponty as well; see Merleau-Ponty, *op.cit.*, pp.164, 183–84.

59 Riley, 'Making Visible', *op.cit.*, p.15. Riley presents a similar account of the significance of Mondrian: 'From Mondrian [I learned] that for a painting what happens on the canvas is "real": the relationship between the lines and colours that he creates there constitutes his reality… This "realism", in turn, becomes the point of departure for the abstract artist.' Bridget Riley, 'Reading Between the Lines', *The Art Newspaper*, no.72, July – August 1997, p.11.

60 Bridget Riley, 'Colour for the Painter', in Trevor Lamb and Janine Bourriau (eds), *Colour: Art and Science*, Cambridge University Press, Cambridge, 1995, p.58. On Riley and Matisse, see also Cooke, *op.cit.*, p.52.

61 Compare Richard Shiff, 'Mark, Motif, Materiality: The Cézanne Effect in the Twentieth Century', in Felix Baumann *et al.*, *Cézanne: Finished Unfinished*, Hatje Cantz Verlag, Ostfildern, 2000, pp.99–123.

62 Riley, interview by Tusa, *op.cit.* Robert Kudielka states Riley's position succinctly: 'For Riley, "literal abstraction" – the process of abstracting from experience – is the essence of everything abstraction in art is *not* about.' Robert Kudielka, 'Bridget Riley', in *Bridget Riley: Paintings 1982–1992*, exhibition catalogue, Hayward Publishing, London, 1992, p.9 (original emphasis).

63 'Modern painting is about building a way of looking – it has less to do with *what* exactly you are seeing than with *how* you are made to look at it': Bridget Riley, 'Painting Now' (1996), in Kudielka (ed), *The Eye's Mind, op.cit.*, p.204 (original emphasis). See also Bridget Riley, 'Something to Look At: In Conversation with Alex Farquharson' (1995), *ibid.*, pp.118, 130. Compare Merleau-Ponty, *op.cit.*, p.161: 'Only the painter is entitled to look at everything without being obliged to appraise what he [or she] sees.'

64 Bridget Riley, 'The Artist's Eye: Seurat' (1992), in Kudielka (ed), *The Eye's Mind, op.cit.*, p.180 (emphasis eliminated).

65 Compare Bridget Riley, 'The Experience of Painting' (1988), *ibid.*, p.125.

66 Bridget Riley, 'The Artist's Eye: Seurat' (1992), *ibid.*, pp.178, 180–81 (original emphasis).

67 *Ibid.*, p.180.

68 Paul Adam, 'Peintres impressionnistes' (April 1886), in Ruth Berson (ed), *The New Painting: Impressionism 1874–1886, Documentation*, vol.1, Fine Arts Museums of San Francisco, San Francisco, CA, 1996, p.430.

69 Roger Fry, 'Seurat' (1916), *Transformations*, Garden City, New York, NY, 1956, pp.250–51.

70 Riley, 'The Artist's Eye', in Kudielka (ed), *The Eye's Mind*, *op.cit.*, p.181.

71 *Ibid.*, pp.175, 181–82 (original emphasis).

72 Riley, statement to author, 18 February 2003; Riley, 'The Experience of Painting', in Kudielka (ed), *The Eye's Mind*, *op.cit.*, p.121; Riley, 'Practising Abstraction', in Kudielka (ed), *Dialogues on Art*, *op.cit.*, p.63.

73 Riley, 'The Experience of Painting' in in Kudielka (ed), *The Eye's Mind*, *op.cit.*, p.122; Riley, 'Practising Abstraction', in Kudielka (ed), *Dialogues on Art*, *op.cit.*, p.63.

74 Riley, 'Practising Abstraction', *ibid.*, p.56 (original emphasis).

75 Such involuntary mental reorientation defines meaningful 'experience': Charles Sanders Peirce, 'Phaneroscopy or the Natural History of Concepts' (c.1905), Charles Hartshorne and Paul Weiss (eds), *Collected Papers*, vol.1, University of Cambridge Press, Cambridge, 1960, p.170.

76 Riley, interview by Tusa, *op.cit.*

77 Riley, 'Interview with Isabel Carlisle', *op.cit.*, p.8.

 RICHARD SHIFF

Abstract Figuration: On Bridget Riley's Recent Curve Paintings
Robert Kudielka

> The court ladies wore the so-called *jūni-hitoé* meaning
> 'twelve-layer' garment. It consisted of an outer robe of
> gorgeous brocade and embroidery and 12 or even more
> silk undergarments of different colours and shades which
> were arranged in such a way that each robe was slightly
> smaller and shorter than the one below it, so that a
> beautiful colour stratification might be visible at the neck
> and the outer edges of the sleeves.
>
> — Toshihiko Izutsu, 'The Elimination of Color in
> Far Eastern Art and Philosophy', 1974

In June 2000, when Bridget Riley showed her new curvilinear paintings for the first time at Waddington Galleries, London, she was surprised to find that they seemed to be immediately accepted. At the opening the late Bryan Robertson, who had organised her first retrospective at the Hayward Gallery, in 1971, said to her: 'This is the easiest work you have ever done.' Indeed the appearance of the paintings seems to be much less demanding than that of the preceding rhomboid images, or of any earlier group. The number of colours in *Rêve* (1999), *Parade 2* (2002) and *Evoë 3* (2003) is limited to four and the structure is characterised by broad, curved shapes moving at an even pace across the canvas. Only after a while does one become aware that this ease is not the result of a simplification or mere enlargement of the formal elements, but a triumph of Riley's structural ingenuity. The works' apparent boldness and simplicity completely conceal the fact that they embody distinctly different layers of *ordering*. In fact, these paintings could be said to be the outcome of the most complex conjunction of pictorial factors Riley has ever attempted.

It would be futile to deconstruct these layers in an attempt to lay bare the essence of the work. No reality lies 'behind' or 'underneath' these paintings. The final compound *is* the body of experience, as has been said of the famous robes of the Heian period: 'The garment *was* the person; it was the direct symbol of his or her personality.'[2] However, the different strata of composition in Riley's recent work are not merely superimposed to form a cumulative image. They are interlaced in such a way that each new level of ordering opposes the preceding one. This interplay between assertion and dissolution, composition and decomposition, generates the inner dynamism of these paintings and encourages an analytical approach as a preliminary to a more rewarding way of looking.

Combining opposing layers of construction has been a device fundamental to Riley's paintings, ever since she introduced tonal progressions into her black-and-white work. In *Pause* (1964), for instance, the transformation of circles into ovals carries the super-imposition of light to dark grey sequences diverging both in tempo and in structural registration. As a result the two movements hold each other in suspension, they form – a pause. This approach culminates in *Deny 2* (1967) in which a regular grid is 'denied' by the revolving movements of the oval elements, upon which in turn tonal progressions of different paces are imposed, and the whole structural complex is set in a cool, bluish grey that contrasts with the warm grey of the ground. Obviously such an intricate fabric could not be extended, but by breaking down her formal vocabulary into thin stripes of colour, as in *Late Morning* (1967–68) for example, Riley began to build up a similar counterbalance with the perceptual interaction of colours. The stripe paintings of the late 1960s and early 1970s, as well as a considerable number of the subsequent curve paintings, are based on the opposition between the vertical organisation of the actual surface hues and the horizontal spread of luminous, disembodied colours. Instead of simply extending limitations, or overthrowing compositional devices, Riley confronts different forms of ordering aimed at a tension between stability and instability. It is her way of establishing the vital contradiction that she admires in Mondrian's 'dynamic equilibrium'[3] and in Paul Klee's concept of 'unstable balance'.[4]

The particular development evinced by the paintings created since 1997 lies in the range covered by such contradictory structures. There is still that vertical register that underlies most of Riley's abstract work.

ROBERT KUDIELKA

However much her themes may vary, the top to bottom relationship underpins the general layout and formal extension. But the new curvilinear movements also incorporate the biggest destabilisation of this vertical bias. In 1986 Riley crossed the vertical register with a field of parallel diagonals rising from bottom left to top right. For the next ten years she worked with this dynamic opposition until she began to connect the regular vertical pulse with the diagonal subdivisions through circular segments. The reintroduction of a curved element in 1997 eventually resulted in the recent group of paintings.

At first glance the vertical foundation of the movements is hard to discern in the paintings. In fact *Rêve* is one of the few paintings in which an actual vertical can be found in the bottom left of the work. But if one traces this line imaginatively upwards, one realises that the perpendicular swing of the first fully reversed curve is twisted around the same invisible vertical. Moreover, once alerted to the presence of such a metre, the spectator begins to sense the regular pulsation and, consequently, visual perception itself becomes more acute. For instance in *Rêve*, and indeed in all subsequent paintings, one notices a recurring free-floating element, which looks like a lancet. Scattered across the canvas in numbers, these shapes loosely resemble a fall of petals. But how is it, then, that these tilted elements seem so firmly integrated into the structure? Closer inspection provides the clue. The two formative curves are slightly trimmed along the top left and bottom right, and if a connecting line were to be drawn between these two trims it would reveal the vertical register that forms the spine of the new work.

If the vertical grid is a fairly subliminal device, the parallel diagonals severing the pictorial field play a more prominent role in the formation of the paintings. On one hand they seem to drive the movement, giving rise to a number of distinctive shapes. There are the big, blade-like cuts and giant commas that seem to simply press forward. But there are also the more ambiguous shapes that ride the crest of the movement. In *Rêve* one finds the slender, waisted shapes created by two diagonally displaced undulating curves and the tilted squares with two curved sides that punctuate and accelerate the flow. These latter two forms have become indispensable to Riley in drawing out a rhythm horizontally, because the diagonal fissions not only act as driving agents, but also provide an essential opposition against which the power of the curves can rise and gather momentum.

Although this opposition is a new function of the diagonal structure, it could be said to fulfil part of Riley's original intention in introducing this one-sided thrust in the late 1980s. 'I wanted more,' she has said in explanation of her move, 'a way of working which allowed me to get to grips with plastic issues, to get closer to the real problems of painting.'[5] The key word here is 'plastic'. By upsetting the balance of the vertical band structure she created a tension that demanded drastic compositional operations such as the displacement and re-allocation of whole units in the pictorial fabric in order to counter this imbalance. As a result, the strong block-like formations of *New Day* (1988) appeared and, by establishing an open interplay of weights, stabilised the underlying dynamism and the disturbance of the field. In 1989, when a group of these early rhomboid paintings was shown at Galerie Schlégl in Zurich, Franz Meyer, the celebrated ex-director of the Kunstmuseum Basel, said to the artist: 'If one might associate the space of your earlier colour paintings with landscape, then one could say that you are now beginning to work with a kind of figure space.' His diagnosis of Riley's shift of interest was remarkably perceptive. That summer the National Gallery, London, presented Riley's *The Artist's Eye* exhibition for which she had selected seven great colour paintings from the collection, all characterised by dense, figurative compositions and animated by a diagonal dynamism.[6]

Reading the catalogue interview accompanying this exhibition, it becomes clear that some of Riley's descriptions of the selected paintings foreshadow aspects of her own subsequent work. The motif of the 'entry figure' leading into the painting from the left-hand side, for example, that she observed in Rubens's *Peace and War* (1629–30) clearly has an abstract equivalent in her recent paintings.[7] In the same way her term 'collective figuration', coined for Titian's *Bacchus and Ariadne* (1521–23) and Poussin's *Triumph of Pan* (1636), could be applied to her new compositional approach.[8] Nevertheless her aim of an increased plasticity could not be achieved solely through the means employed in *New Day*.

   ROBERT KUDIELKA

The almost hieratic firmness of this work's pictorial formation conflicted with Riley's other reason for introducing the diagonal emphasis: 'I wanted to be able to go around a painting, to take your eye upwards, downwards and diagonally across in all sorts of ways and rhythms that I could not manage with just the vertical bands.'[9] What was needed was a more fluid and flexible space than the one provided by the block-like constellations. Consequently the paintings of the early 1990s seem to move in virtually the very opposite direction to a constructive consolidation. The big compounds of rhomboids are broken up, giving way to glittering passages of smaller shapes that act almost like brushmarks, and the number of colours increases accordingly until each painting may resonate with up to 20 or more specific hues.

With hindsight one can see that this renewed dissolution of the pictorial fabric prepared Riley for an unprecedented mode of circular composition. In practically all of her later rhomboid paintings the colour movement is introduced by a strong accent in the top left corner and descends with and against the formal diagonal until it reaches a point – usually just off centre right – from which it is reversed. In the area on the right-hand side of *High Sky 2* (1992) this circular return is clearly visible, and its revolving tendency is enhanced by a new structural device: the amplification, and occasional reduction, of the blue, violet and green rhomboids by one third of their width.

The employment of a tripartite proportion in addition to the straightforward repetition and multiplication of the basic rhomboid unit was of seminal importance. It allowed for a 2:3 ratio in the rhythmic structure, which was a device frequently employed by composers of vocal music in the Middle Ages, as a means of both enhancing and deflating dynamic tension. This shift of metre can also be found in Baroque dance music of the seventeenth century, for instance in the *Courante*, and again in the nineteenth century, when it was favoured particularly by Frédéric Chopin, Johannes Brahms and Franz Liszt.[10] In *Reflection 1* (1994) one can see how Riley developed this device in her later rhomboid paintings. The extended one third and two thirds divisions intermittently suspend the regular vertical register creating a temporary rhythmic dislocation. The resulting disturbance acts in two ways: slowing down or accelerating the tempo, before the regular pulse resolves these frictions again.

Apart from adding to the rhythmic complexity of the rhomboid paintings, the tripartite proportion eventually offered a way of reintroducing a curve element. Having worked for quite a while with virtually circular movements, in the mid-1990s Riley began to search for the structural means that would allow her to include actual curvilinear shapes in her compositions. *Lagoon 1* (1997) shows an early step in this direction. In the centre of the painting a blue rhomboid form encompassing six basic units is joined by a curved fragment, a green crescent of an equal length. But the apex of this curve extends to only two thirds of the regular width of the rhomboid. Riley had found that a fuller curvature could not be contained by the underlying vertical and diagonal frameworks. Moreover, the reduced curve initially did not allow for a swing in both directions. All curvilinear elements in *Lagoon 1* are directed towards the left side, pressing against the diagonal thrust.

It was nearly two years before a satisfactory solution emerged. This lengthy interval was due not only to the extensive preparatory work on *Composition with Circles 1* (1998), a temporary wall painting measuring 5 by 9 metres commissioned by the Kunsthalle Bern, but also to the rigorous decisions required to fully integrate the new curve element. First of all Riley had to reduce the number of colours – *Lagoon 1* still comprises eight hues – in order to cope with the structural complexities. She had always known that complex colour relationships and dense formal structures do not sit well together,[11] and just as she had reduced her formal vocabulary to the repetition of stripes in 1968, she now had to restrict her range of colours to accommodate the added formal complexity. All paintings made after *Rêve* are based on a palette of four or at the most five colours. At the same time it seemed to be necessary to increase the scale of the imagery, and consequently the size of the canvases, to allow for the kind of spatial resonance demanded by a curve that could swing both ways. However musical the rhythmic structuring of the new paintings may be, the decisive change brought about by the curvilinear element was the introduction of a virtually physical sensation of weight into Riley's pictorial world.

For a long time the most puzzling aspect of this development was the balance of the colour relationships. Although Riley had intuitively arrived at a working colour bracket with the four colours of *Rêve* – blue, green, yellow and yellow ochre – she did not immediately understand its implications. Having worked for almost ten years with a broad orchestration of harmonies and contrasts it took her a while to find the new rationale intrinsic to the plastic problems which her work now presented her with. Certainly colour opposition was of primary importance because 'opposing' is a basic proposition of her pictorial logic. But what about the third position, the mediating and modifying factor that had become essential ever since she introduced grey into the black-and-white work? In her early colour paintings such as *Orient 4* (1970), for instance, the three colours – cerise, turquoise and olive – encompass an opposition of red and green, and, through an emphasis on the blue tendency present in both cerise and turquoise, destabilise the contrast. The new work however was no longer so concerned with overt colour interaction. In reviewing the group of paintings executed between 1999 and 2001, it is fascinating to follow the step-by-step establishment of an approach that is inherent in *Rêve*: two neighbouring colours (blue and green) form, with two opposite relations (yellow and yellow ochre), a paired contrast mediated by an implied harmony (green and yellow ochre).[12]

Very often in Riley's work blue and green, in a carefully attuned balance, form a kind of tenor against which a lighter pair of colours is pitched – magenta and pink in *Evoë 3*, or orange and pink in *Paired Colours* (2001). Occasionally two greens, one fully saturated and the other yellowish, are opposed by an unexpected contrast of blue violet and pale blue in *Parade 2*, or of apricot and pink in the painting named after these colours, *Apricot and Pink* (2001). This paired relationship, rhythmically disposed throughout the paintings, chromatically complements the formal structure, or rather the structural topography. For there are, strictly speaking, *no forms and intervals* in these new paintings. Each shape is an area delineated by the interplay of the diagonal and curvilinear orders and defined in its characteristics by colour. This is not unlike Mondrian's replacement of form by rectilinear compartments of weight and colour, except that Riley's complex layering of vertical, diagonal and curvilinear divisions enabled her to extract shapes that are surprisingly particular, although they do not attain an individual status. There is room for invention, but the range is nevertheless limited, constituting Riley's abstract cast of a 'collective figuration'.

The particular character of this working basis becomes clearer when one compares it with certain qualities Riley admires in earlier paintings. In 1997 she wrote a short piece describing the composition of Matisse's *Dance 2* (1909–10). In pointing out the different characteristics of the painting's five central figures, she drew particular attention to their collective nature and to the equal status of figure and interval:

> The group, subject to the overall organisation of colour and rhythm and entranced by the act of dancing, lose their separate identities and become one pictorial form, one organic unit. And yet, figure by figure, interval by interval, how brilliantly Matisse shows the change of pace, mood and character. Each state, fast or slow, tense or relaxed, demonic or gentle is only an aspect of dance as a whole. One feels that they are interchangeable, that any one dancer could the next moment assume the role and gesture of another.[13]

This fluid, protean quality can be found in Riley's new abstract figurations, too, with one important difference. The five red figures in Matisse's painting are set against a background of blue and green, and although this background is flattened it is still a distinctly separate spatial plane from that of the figures. In Riley's curvilinear paintings, however, the spatial planes have become interchangeable to the degree that the figure–ground ambiguity is completely dissolved.

The elimination of this ambiguity marks an essential difference between Riley's new work and the hard-edge, colour-field painting of the 1960s, which relied heavily on the figure–ground relationship. Thanks to the complex compositional stratification of her recent paintings there is no longer a stable ground plane carrying the painting, nor do isolated forms exist against some kind of background. Instead, the colour shapes shift, contrast and alternate in space according to a structural rhythm that is specific to each particular painting. In *Rêve*, for instance, the firmness of the composition almost conceals the surprising opposition between the two sides of the painting. Only after a while does one discern a virtually hallucinatory reversal: the very same blue that advances on the left side of the painting recedes on the right – and in its wake all the related colour planes reassemble in an unexpected way. In contrast to *Rêve*, *Evoë 3* is an overtly turbulent painting in which the spatial planes are continually shifting. The seemingly steady tenor of blue and green is kicked off dynamically, backwards and forwards, through the contrasting pink and magenta in each new constellation.

Such vivid changes in spatial positioning are of course facilitated by the absence of figurative recognition in abstract painting. But making use of spatial mobility has a telling history in representational work as well. Riley herself regards the two horsemen in the Panathenaic procession depicted in the West Frieze of the Parthenon as an informative example of plastic understanding both for sculpture and for painting. There again a collective figuration is created by rendering the limbs of the horsemen, and the heads and the legs of the horses, as 'interchangeable' angular shapes, in order to articulate an animated forward movement. However, this rhythmic device also permits an evocation of depth within the strict confines of relief technique. The second horseman, riding alongside and to the rear of the first, is perceived by the viewer as being in front, although both horsemen actually exist on the same physical plane in the relief. It is the sensation of movement, as opposed to the mere superimposition of images, which opens up a totally convincing plastic space.

There are other aspects of the Parthenon relief that demonstrate to what great extent the principles of building a visual rhythm remain objective despite historical distances and cultural differences. For instance, the bodies of the two horses are joined in a rising diagonal supporting the forward thrust, while a steep falling diagonal formed by the undulating shapes of the back of the first horse and the front of the second asserts the weight and power carried by this movement. One can even find a clear indication of the vertical balance, the plastic check as it were, in the virtual plumb lines connecting the head of the first rider with the hoof of the left back leg of his horse, and the hand of the second rider with the same point in his horse. But perhaps the most stunning device is the turning back of the first rider towards his companion. It is a clear, truly classic example of the perceptual fact that in order to make a directional movement visually plausible in the plastic arts, it is necessary to include or to suggest the opposite direction.

Riley has repeatedly emphasised the importance of this principle to her own work and has remarked on its presence in other works from the past.[14] In conversation with Neil MacGregor she analysed Mantegna's *Introduction of the Cult of Cybele at Rome* (1505–06) in these terms:

> The subject is the carrying of a statue into Rome. I was amazed to see that Mantegna holds together the narrow horizontal format of his frieze in one long, all embracing rhythm. The verve with which the first figure steps in, is stopped, cut short by the straight line of the statue, as though by an enormous comma; then this movement, introduced by the first figure, is picked up by the next two, turned round in the supplicating figure and continues in reverse until the very last figure where it changes back to echo the first.[15]

This description seems to anticipate the developments in her recent work. But, again, there is a decisive difference. Mantegna structures his frieze by extending the 'turning both ways' motif, so beautifully employed in the Parthenon relief, through groups and pairs of figures. The curve in Riley's paintings, however, seems to enable her to fuse these opposite directions into an almost simultaneous sensation. Instead of a steady epic flow, a dynamic concurrence of opposing movements is established, and the slender waisted shape made up of two diagonally displaced curves in the centre of *Rêve* is its emblem.

Riley did not dwell overly on this poised resolution. On the whole she has tended to avoid finite constellations, preferring an open and contradictory rhythm. Progressions, reversals and the interplay between successive reading and instantaneous sensation have been staple devices in her work since *Movement in Squares* (1961). So it is not

   ROBERT KUDIELKA

surprising that with her new, layered method of composing she attempted the squaring of the circle, so to speak: a rhythmic movement based on the simultaneity of a progressive sequence and its reversal. This prompted an unexpected and initially rather awkward consequence because in order to carry the weight and draw out the dynamism of the new curvilinear structures she had to drastically increase the scale of her work. *Evoë 3* measures 193.3 by 581.4 centimetres, *Parade 2* measures 226.7 by 527.4 centimetres. To manage these enormous formats she split each painting into two canvases.

The simultaneity of the movements is, of course, not literal. Both works engender the sensation of concurrent, opposing developments by starting with a rhythmic cadence on the left side. In *Evoë 3* the large pink comma acts as an entry figure, pushing forward a dense muscular movement that seems to relax towards the centre. There it is momentarily delayed by two magenta lancets, accompanied by a pair of green, waisted shapes. These waisted shapes are then repeated, taking on weight, and, under the pressure of a pink hammer-like shape, initiate a second, more delicate sequence which is received by two big shapes, a magenta form resembling a bell clapper and a pink buffer, which swing the whole sequence back. If the initial movement had a falling momentum, the reversal rises upwards. It is carried by the step-wise ascension of the green shapes and helped by the apostrophes, which support the upward drift like little sails until this surging current meets the resistance of the passage initiated by the entry figure.

The same circular structure, which is perceived as a series of simultaneous events, can be found in *Parade 2*. But this painting is experienced in a remarkably different way, the character of the composition being almost opposite to that of *Evoë 3*. In the upper left of the canvas, at the point of entry, two related shapes in violet and yellow-green start the movement swiftly. It continues along a steep diagonal towards the centre where the impetus seems to vanish. But in that open green passage a curiously inert, violet shape, defined by two curves – one plain, the other undulating – picks up the momentum, setting the pace for a steady horizontal flow towards an area dominated by a pale blue configuration. This large sliced and interlaced shape echoes the cloud-like spread of the same pale colour on the left side and acts as a rebound of the entire movement. As *Parade 2* is clearly a two-sided painting, the reversal happens in two stages: firstly a broad phalanx advances towards the centre, and secondly, an elegant rise returns to the beginning.

In describing these two paintings one is unavoidably reminded of human gestures and movements. Riley herself admitted this: 'When I had finished *Evoë* and was thinking about its title I toyed with the idea of calling it "Bacchanal without Nymphs" and another painting, still untitled, "Bacchanal without Satyrs". But then I remembered, just in time, that I am after all supposed to be an abstract artist.'[16] There is indeed a painting by Poussin called *A Bacchanalian Revel before a Herm of Pan* (c.1633) in the collection of the National Gallery, London, which has a somewhat related lateral rhythm. It begins with the entry figure of a nymph, who is turning back to hold out a bunch of grapes to two children while the forward thrust of her body partakes in a revel with two male dancers. Engaged in a complicated figure of dance this group is linked by three legs lifted in a parallel upward swing. This rising movement is countered by the falling diagonal of a tree behind which continues down to a group of four figures tumbling in the opposite direction to the dancers. All are linked by their gestures: the two running women and the satyr through the downward thrust of their arms, and the third woman, in the satyr's embrace, through reaching in the opposite direction. This hopeless resistance is not enough to reverse the whole chain of events, and in terms of content, is clearly not meant to do so.

Despite the obvious divergences there are sufficient similarities to beg a crucial question. If Riley in her recent work is so clearly involved with the spirit of exultant collective figurations, why does she not turn directly to the human figure? One answer is simply historical. The individual human figure has never been a vehicle for the expression of such states of being. It was the Bacchic and Arcadian mythology that lent itself to the celebration of an ecstatic reconciliation with nature in the arts even after the cultural validity of these pagan visions had long expired. When Poussin painted his bacchanals for Cardinal Richelieu

　　　　　　　　　　　　　　　　　　　　　ROBERT KUDIELKA

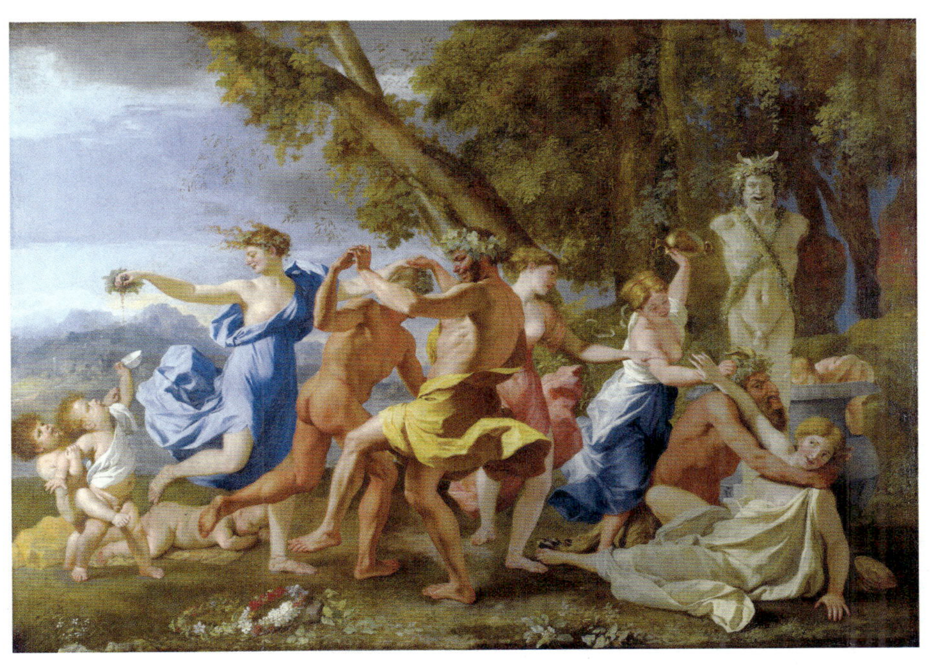

Nicolas Poussin
A Bacchanalian Revel Before a Term 1632–33
Oil on canvas
98 × 142.8 cm | 38⅝ × 56¼ in
National Gallery, London

and other humanist clients, they were anachronisms, replete with obsolete forms of imagery; and this is even truer of Picasso's recreation of the same mythical themes in the twentieth century. But what other pictorial language could be appropriate for the portrayal of these feelings?

The second answer touches upon the *raison d'être* of abstraction in modern art. Although Abstract art has many different and often contradictory meanings, one of its great possibilities, as Riley sees it, is its ability to give form to certain spiritual states that cannot be expressed by straightforward realism.

> Figurative painting without the relevant context of religion or mythology won't do – it's no longer a language. I think that an artist today has to totally accept this lack, has to start from a 'placelessness', virtually as a point of departure. I can see no real alternative to abstract painting if, in fact, the painter wants to address those particular issues.[17]

In this regard her understanding seems to be very close to that of Mark Rothko, who saw his paintings as dramas, with the shapes and colours in the role of performers: 'They have been created from the need for a group of actors who are able to move dramatically without embarrassment and execute gestures without shame.'[18] Although Rothko's drama tends towards the tragic while Riley's seems to be coloured by almost the opposite spirit, the same could still be said of her abstract collective figurations. The complex rhythmic structure of her new curvilinear paintings allows her to express states of joy and elation without provoking the inference of self-reflection unavoidably connected with the human image.

The critical link between figurative art and this understanding of abstraction seems to be Matisse's work on the *Dance* decoration for Dr Alfred Barnes's Pennsylvania-based Foundation in the early 1930s.[19] The so-called *Paris Dance Mural* (1931–33) in particular marks an important step in his development of this theme. While the earlier *Dance* painting of 1909–10 retains a connection with the physical

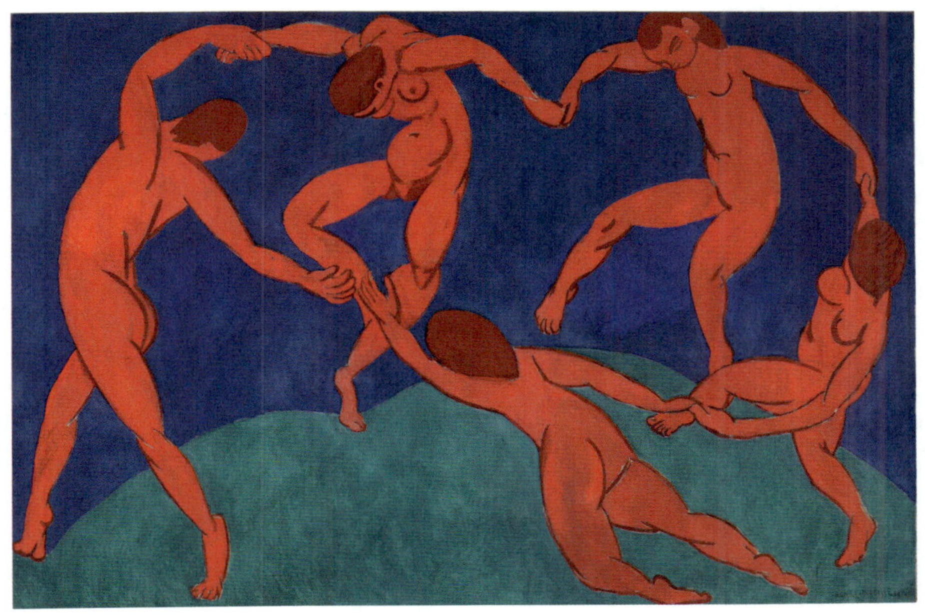

Henri Matisse
The Dance 1909–10
Oil on canvas
260 × 391 cm | 102³⁄₈ × 154 in
The State Hermitage Museum, St Petersburg
© Succession H. Matisse/DACS 2016

presence of the figures through the red colouring of their bodies and their mask-like faces, the recapitulation of the self-same cast of figures severs both these associations. The dancers of the *Paris Dance Mural* have no physiognomy and are a light, neutral grey that anticipates the final departure from any resemblance to flesh colour in the Blue Nudes of 1952. In accordance with this radical withdrawal from individual representation Matisse treats the human figure in an unprecedented way. Using the arcs of the three areas predetermined by the site of the commission, he fragments and dismembers the six dancing poses in order to re-assemble their parts in autonomous dynamic configurations. Each fragmented figure is 'cut in' from the edges and stretched to full tension within a sequence of rising and descending diagonals running through the three areas. The powerful dancer in the centre is even accompanied by formalised limbs, which are not fully accounted for by any of the figures in the neighbouring fields.

Looking at this rigorous figurative abstraction affords a clearer perspective on Riley's approach. Far from trespassing the confines of pure abstraction – whatever this may be – her recent work aspires to a similar collective sensation, though from primarily structural considerations. The shapes she extracts from the matrix of her layered orders can loosely be classified according to figurative attributes and associations. There are the waisted shapes of variable vivacity and volume; they are related to the cross-over spreading gestures, poses of maximum exultation, which are directly opposed to the softly curling, almost passive shapes; while the rhythmic beat is kept up by the big diagonal blades. These main characters are accompanied by a flurry of smaller, lighter accents: the lancets, commas, apostrophes and buoyant squares with two curved sides, which drive and punctuate the rhythm, riding the current or acting like little chinks of light. But being non-figurative derivatives, these elements can also adopt guises not necessarily related to the human figure. This becomes particularly clear in the most recent, scaled-down paintings Riley has made. The moment the almost physical sensation of weight recedes other areas of resonance open up, notably those of nature and of lively exchanges, such as conversations, competitions and conflicts, in general.

                                                    ROBERT KUDIELKA

The colours in *Blues and Greens* (2001) are in themselves
suggestive. But it is in fact the subtle balance of tones and hues that
creates the sensation of deep and glittering vegetation. Three greens –
a dark yellow-green, a turquoise and a lighter, slightly yellowish turquoise –
are paired with two blues, a light and dark one, in such a way that the
dark green and blue are of the same tone while the pale turquoise
equals the light blue. However, this apparent harmony of tones and
colours implies latent contrasts, which are released and intensified
through the structural organisation of the painting. Despite the apparent
tonal closeness there is a friction between the yellow-green and the
blue, and provoked by the dominance of the greens the light blue takes
on a reddish tinge and turns towards violet – an unexpected reminder of
the perceptual activity that characterised much of Riley's colour work of
the 1970s. The pervasive pulse of this low-key animation seems to be
strong enough to turn our attention away from the connotations of
dramatic action and to shift the associative character of these same
shapes towards moving blades, leaves, bells, reflected lights, all rippling
like new growth in a fresh breeze.

Subtle differentiation within a narrow bracket is, however, not the
only direction in which Riley has extended her new range. *Two Reds*
(2000) shows the opposite approach in terms of colour. Here the paired
opposition consists of orange-red and magenta-red set against a dark
and a light yellow-green, with a pale blue of virtually the same tone as
the mediating light green. The high colour contrast results in sudden
shifts of pace and emphasis. But the rising turbulence is firmly checked
by a clear distinction of plastic functions between the two sides of the
painting. While on the left side the greens are carried into action by the
other colours as it were, on the right they, by an ingenious shift of
structure, themselves become the carriers of the movement. This
dynamic two-sidedness within the coherence of one painting anchors
and enhances the sensation of a rhythm advancing into two opposite
directions simultaneously.

Given the fundamental difference that Riley's recent paintings do not
unfold in one progressive direction of time only, looking at *Two Reds* is
not unlike listening into an intense musical dialogue of the sort that

Nikolaus Harnoncourt has observed in Johann Sebastian Bach's *Brandenburg Concertos* (1721). In describing the final allegro of the sixth concerto he writes:

> Here, already with the first entry of the whole orchestra… rhythm and metre are very firmly marked and at the same time called into question. Even though the movement begins with an up-beat involving a skip, it is already attached through syncopation to the third measure, so that one gets the impression that the violas begin the measure on the last eighth. The chords played by all other instruments decisively against this, but still on the beat, lead as in the first movement to a struggle for the 'right' measure.[20]

It is a struggle that probably will never be resolved definitively in any work of art, let alone in life. On the contrary, to have kept this struggle alive, and to have deepened and strengthened it, as Riley has done over 40 years of work, is an achievement to be celebrated.

Paul Moorhouse (ed), *Bridget Riley*, exhibition catalogue, Tate Publishing, London, 2003, pp.151–57.

1 Toshihiko Izutsu, 'The Elimination of Color in Far Eastern Art and Philosophy', in Adolf
  Portmann and Rudolf Ritsema (ed), *The Realms of Colour/Die Welt der Farben/Le
  Monde des Couleurs,* Leiden, Brill, 1974, p.432.

2 See Bridget Riley, 'Mondrian: The "Universal" and the "Particular"' (1995), in Robert
  Kudielka (ed), *The Eye's Mind: Bridget Riley, Collected Writings 1965–1999,* Thames &
  Hudson, London, 1999, p.196.

3 This basic concept of Klee's teaching and its relationship to Mondrian is discussed in the
  author's contribution to *Paul Klee: The Nature of Creation*, exhibition catalogue, Hayward
  Gallery, London, 2002, pp.82–83.

4 Bridget Riley, 'According to Sensation: In Conversation with Robert Kudielka' (1990), in
  Kudielka (ed), *op.cit.*, p.161.

5 *The Artist's Eye: Bridget Riley*, exhibition catalogue, National Gallery, London 1989. The
  conversation 'The Colour Connection: In Conversation with Robert Kudielka' included in
  this catalogue has been reprinted in a reduced form in Kudielka (ed), *op.cit.*, pp.142–73.

6 Riley, 'The Colour Connection', in Kudielka (ed), *ibid.*, p.161.

7 *Ibid.*, pp.148, 166.

8 Bridget Riley, 'Something to Look At: In Conversation with Alex Farquharson' (1995), in
  Kudielka (ed), *op.cit.*, p.131.

9 It is interesting to note that in the 1980s the composer György Ligeti experimented with a
  superimposition of rhythmic strata related to this ratio in his *Études pour piano* (György
  Ligeti – Erika Haase [piano and harpsichord], *Premier Livre* [1985], collegno Musik-
  produktion, AU–031 815 CD. In the leaflet accompanying this disc the composer describes
  the structural principle of his pieces: 'The pianist plays coordinated, even pulsations in
  both hands. Superimposed onto these pulsations is a gridwork of irregular accents which
  at times, however, progresses synchronously in both hands, thereby temporarily
  producing the impression of order. This impression slowly disintegrates as the accents in
  one hand begin to lag behind those in the other. In doing so the metric relationship is
  gradually blurred until we reach a point where we are unable to discern which hand
  leads and which lags behind. A state of order is in due course restored as the two
  successions of accents shift closer and closer to one another, eventually falling
  simultaneously in the two hands, at which point the cycle begins anew.') Riley refers to
  one of these *Études* in a conversation with the author, published under the title
  'Supposed to Be Abstract', *Parkett*, no.61, May 2001, pp.25–26.

10 In 1972 she explained the transition from her complex black-and-white structures to her
   early colour paintings in the following way: 'Form and colour seem to be fundamentally
   incompatible – they destroy each other. In my earlier work, when I was developing
   complex forms, the energies of the medium could only be fully released by simplifying
   colour to a black-and-white constant (with occasional grey sequences). Conversely colour
   energies need a virtually neutral vehicle if they are to develop uninhibitedly. The
   repeated stripe seems to meet these conditions. Bridget Riley, 'In Conversation with
   Robert Kudielka' (1972), in Kudielka (ed), *The Eye's Mind, op.cit.*, p.82.

11 This colour balance has a remote precedent in the palette of the tiled Safavid wall
   paintings of the seventeenth century. Called *haft-rangi* (seven colours) technique, this
   palette consists of black and white, cobalt blue, turquoise and three warm hues, yellow,
   yellow-green and ochre. In her colour-mixing studio Riley treasures a North African tile
   which is related to this Persian scheme.

12 The piece was commissioned by the *Daily Telegraph* and published in an abbreviated
   version under the title 'Pick of the Hermitage', 27 October 1990, p.55.

13 In 'The Experience of Painting' (1988), for instance, she recalls another example of this

contradictory logic of plastic representation: 'I discovered a well-known principle (it's always exciting when you find things for yourself): that you cannot have movement without its opposite – stasis. There is no change without a constant.' Kudielka (ed), *The Eye's Mind*, *op.cit.*, p.123.

14 Robert Kudielka (ed), *Bridget Riley: Dialogues on Art*, Zwemmer, London, 1995, p.23. Neil MacGregor commented: 'That's a very musical way of analysing a painting.'

15 'Supposed to Be Abstract', *op.cit.*, p.26.

16 Kudielka (ed), *Bridget Riley: Dialogues on Art*, *op.cit.*, p.28. This concept of abstraction seems to be the reason why Riley, when speaking about her work, generally prefers to relate to the figurative art of the past. When in 1995 Alex Farquharson pointed out this tendency to her, she replied: 'I think abstract art should try to be as resourceful and as expressive as the great figurative art of the past [...] I would like to show that my abstract chromatic and formal means make as good and practical a basis to start from as figurative subject matter did in the past.' Riley, 'Something to Look At', in Kudielka (ed), *The Eye's Mind*, *op.cit.*, p.132.

17 Mark Rothko, 'The Romantics were prompted...', *Possibilities 1*, winter 1947–48. p.84.

18 See Jack Flam, *Matisse: The Dance*, exhibition catalogue, National Gallery of Art, Washington, DC, 1993. This publication traces the evolution of the dance theme in Matisse's work from *The Joy of Life* (1905–06) to the late paper cut-outs, focusing on the three major mural decorations of 1931–33: *Unfinished Dance Mural* (1931), *Merion Dance Mural* (1932–33) and *Paris Dance Mural* (1931–33).

19 Nikolaus Harnoncourt, *The Musical Dialogue. Thoughts on Monteverdi, Bach and Mozart*, Amadeus Press, Portland, OR, 1997, p.164. (The translation of this dense passage has been checked with the German original and slightly revised.)

Rasters in Paradise
Richard Shiff

> All impressions are 'first impressions'… The minute it
> ceases to be 'first', the impression tumbles from paradise
> into history… The more acute historical consciousness
> becomes, the more it tends to stimulate its subconscious
> opposite. Paradise is the historical unconscious.
>
> – Pierre Schneider, *Matisse*, 1984

> For an artist those fleeting sensations which pass
> unrecognised by the intellect are just as important as
> those which become conscious.
>
> – Bridget Riley, 'The Artist's Eye: Seurat', 1992

Bridget Riley is perceptive: observant, sensitive, discerning. She concerns
herself with what goes 'unrecognised' – or, as she also identifies it, 'the
im-perceptible'.[1] Whether or not she can answer the philosophical
question of what painting is or ought to be, her experience in the studio
has shown her what painting does. It opens a 'small gap of pure
perception'. Art preserves this opening, a temporal clearing that allows a
world of sight to appear 'before conceptualisation takes over'. Entering
such a rarefied yet commodious realm gives Riley emotional
'satisfaction', an uncompromised feeling of 'happiness'.[2] For her, painting
is pure perception, awareness, a light on 'the im-perceptible', prolonged
happiness, paradise.

What kind of paradise? Pierre Schneider's monograph on Henri
Matisse opposes 'paradise' to 'history'. This distinction emerges as
Schneider explores Matisse's lasting involvement with Impressionism in a
chapter Riley particularly admires.[3] Her enthusiasm may reflect the fact
that Schneider kept not only Matisse in mind as he wrote, but also
Marcel Proust, another longstanding Riley favourite ('I love Proust').[4] She
would no doubt be comfortable in contrasting the analytical order that
constructs 'history' to the blissful, enraptured sensation associated with

paradise. Like both Schneider and his subject Matisse, Riley separates the speculative evaluation that we apply to art (its criticism, theory and philosophy, all of which cast art into history) from the sensory experience of an actual painting, experience which lets art into an individual life. 'I am acquainted with all the known theories,' Matisse stated in 1941, 'but, as far as I am concerned, I have no theory when I am working.'[5] Matisse's 'as far as I am concerned' is an astute proviso, which acknowledges the likelihood that the painter's critics will invent theories of their own to attribute to him. 'When I am working' is his additional proviso, for there are times when even Matisse has theories. Theories allow him to engage a programme in advance of his art or to explain it after the fact. Yet – this is the paradisal element – the actual production of art occurs in an enduring state of immediacy. Just as sensory and emotional immediacy generates art, the same human condition is required for its paradisal appreciation.

We need no heaven to enter paradise. An artistic paradise is an earthly, enclosed garden (from old Persian, *pairi*, passing around, circumscribing, enclosing, and *da za*, wall, a thing that moulds or forms what lies within; or from Greek, *peri*, around, and *teichos*, wall).[6] This type of enclosure does not restrict access, nor does its external perimeter limit the capacity for internal fullness. Instead, the enclosure protects against contamination. Cultural, intellectual constructions are contaminants. Life cannot eliminate them: in fact, social life depends on them, and paradise itself – with its pagan, Hebrew, Christian and Muslim variants – is a pervasive cultural construction. Yet, for the sake of experience, there is value in holding in check as many cultural contaminants as possible, since they often diminish the character and quality of sensation. In Oceania, a mythic paradise for Europeans, Matisse recognised that the 'tranquil desert island, the solitary paradise doesn't exist. One would be quickly bored there.'[7] Despite the capacity of nature to seduce and inspire, an artist finds paradise not by the remote lagoon, but isolated at work in the studio.

 RICHARD SHIFF

The im-perceptible

'You can't experience [my early] black-and-white paintings,' Riley recently
remarked, 'if you only count and measure their elements instead of
seeing what they do.'[8] Her reduction to black-and-white in 1960–61
allowed her to eliminate from her painting its vestiges of naturalism and
generative external reference. Riley used the blunt opposition of black
and white emotively, subtly manipulating patterns of contrast and their
potential for creating virtual movement. Transferring her art from
residually naturalistic colour to achromatic abstraction, she lost little if
anything of its evocative force. In *Movement in Squares* (1961), she
activated a raster of orthogonals by introducing dramatic asymmetry, all
without violating the rectilinear parallelism of the vertical-horizontal grid.[9]
A normative, static order became an eccentric, moving image. In
Exposure (1966), she created a virtual flow of waves, setting its diagonal
orientation in tension with the horizontal format containing it.

Having limited her painting to black and white, Riley caused it to
move as much as it ever had in her preceding work in full colour. It now
moved all the more emotionally – 'from seeing to feeling'. This phrase is
not taken from Riley (although it might have been) but from Schneider,
who used it to explain Matisse's lasting commitment to the
accomplishments of his Impressionist predecessors, painters factoring
their emotions into attempts to capture by colour the brilliance of natural
light. 'The transition from seeing to feeling is achieved by colour,'
Schneider writes, 'which has the power to invade, to make qualitative
leaps over distances that are quantitatively not bridgeable.' Here he
draws Riley's line between quantitative counting and measuring and the
qualitative experience of seeing. Or perhaps Riley drew Matisse and
Schneider's line. We easily grasp the logic of a connection from Riley
back to Matisse. It is far more obvious now that Riley has been working
not only in full colour, but also (at least from the time of *Lagoon 1*, 1997)
with subtly curving forms derived from the arc of a circle sliced into
vertical sixths – forms at first crystalline, and later, having more of a
vegetal organicism.[10] In a way reminiscent of Matisse, Riley has been
developing the final version of her recent paintings through studies

made with cut paper – for her, a longstanding practice. 'I didn't come
from Matisse,' she stated in 2000, 'I arrived at Matisse, which was very
surprising for me… One drew courage from the fact of Matisse, after the
event, as it were.'[11]

In the same context, Riley announced a kind of pragmatist credo:
'You must be prepared to go wrong – [every work] is the beginning of a
dialogue [within the work]. It means that there is a right, even if you can't
find it… Nothing is set. It just emerges, from the looking.'[12] The looking is
hers: an effort informed by a life of experience. When she uses her sixths
of a circle, the determining radius is itself determined by the size of the
particular canvas, but intuitively, not by any formula or mathematical
ratio.[13] 'If I explore something and keep an open mind I may stumble
across something which can be developed – and that's enough.'[14]
Openness is the key: openness of mind; openness of process;
openness, even, of composition, traditionally the most fixed feature of a
painting (along with the foundational, but often invisible, raster).

Matisse's late works in cut paper have Riley's sense of openness.
With *The Wave* (1952), Matisse constructed a white, wavy, oceanic
horizontal – or rather, a sequence of waves, white and blue – by making
a continuous, rolling cut through a single sheet of blue painted paper. He
separated the two halves and set them against a white backing, with the
bottom half slightly askew, left to right, as if to imply a shift along a
diagonal axis. Matisse allowed a reserve of white at the left and bottom
margins to frame or contain the internal 'wave' of the same whiteness.
This reserve acts as a contrasting, stabilising element, appearing to
confirm a lesson Riley learned from independent experience early in her
career: 'I discovered a well-known principle (it's always exciting when
you find things for yourself): that you cannot have movement without its
opposite – stasis.'[15] In *The Wave* the reserve of white at left and bottom
is stasis: a neutral, rectilinear, raster-like element against which all else
becomes movement. Here the raster does not preexist the image, except
perhaps to the extent that the given format, quite conventional, is itself
rectilinear. The diagonal shift that Matisse established in positioning the
two halves of his cut paper determined both the figural wave and the
raster grounding it. The ground, the passive raster, became actively

                                                        RICHARD SHIFF

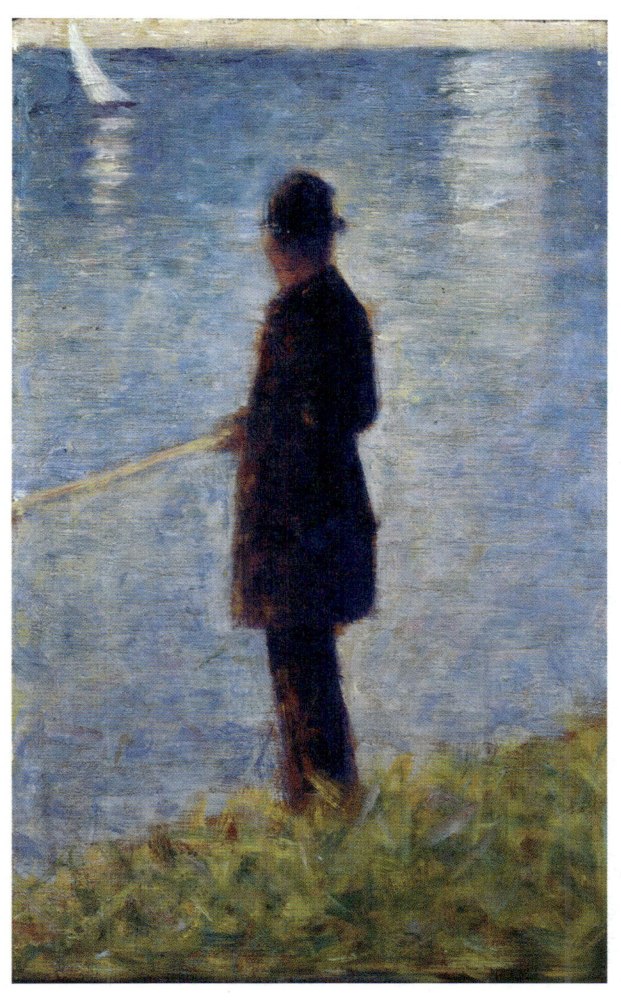

Georges Seurat
Angler c.1884
Oil on panel
24 × 15.2 cm | 9½ × 6 in
Private Collection, on loan to The Courtauld Gallery, London

visible only as the wave appeared. The two effects are interdependent, with the geometric raster as open to vision as the oceanic image. Matisse's efficient, intuitive engagement of raster and image is a paradisal act. Unconscious of history, he anticipated Riley's way of putting image or 'figure' and raster or 'ground' into such intimate linkage that the two conceptual elements move as one perceptual wave, neither figure nor ground. 'I arrived at Matisse… after the event.' As 'unconscious' as Matisse but intensely aware, Riley could enter Matissean paradise.

Yet her aesthetic position needs no concept of paradise, which here as elsewhere is merely a fruitful metaphor, alluding to a way of painting and its effect. Any manner of explanation – whether by counting and measuring or by a concept of paradise – becomes 'historical' (in Schneider's sense). Explanation converts art into history, coming after the fact and firstness of experience.[16] It limits experience. By practicing historical analysis, a critic risks losing the paradise of painting, the quality of fulness intended to be explained. This dilemma may have led Schneider to Proust's manner of writing *around* his object, enclosing but not containing it.[17]

To the extent that they become caught up in concepts – who among us escapes? – artists risk still more than their critics whenever they reflect on art. Like Matisse, Riley has nevertheless articulated in writing what it may have meant for exceptional artists to have worked as they did. Having identified Proust as 'a writer without a single focal point', she becomes Proustian in her understanding of Georges Seurat, who shows what 'we cannot *quite* see… an experience just beyond our visual grasp' (*The Angler*, c.1884).[18] While her statement captures the fineness of Seurat's vision, it also indicates that analytical description, although it may contain the painter's subject matter and its social context, will never coordinate fully with the movement of line, colour and light. Nor will analysis catch up to life. With a Proustian sense of spiralling, introspective time, Riley adds: 'Seurat looks *into* perception and shows it to be the activity which produces what it sees.'[19] If such perceptual production were calculated and self-conscious, a closed strategy rather than an open experience, its own repetitiveness would bring it to a halt. A good part of looking 'into perception' must be unconscious – for Seurat, just as for

Matisse. Or perhaps this kind of perception is 'sacred', like time spent in paradise. According to Schneider, whenever Matisse set his conscious attention on thematic issues associated with religion, this focused his intellect, 'allowing the unconscious to wander [elsewhere] in search of the sacred'.[20]

It was in assessing the quality of experience she perceived in Seurat – 'beyond our visual grasp' – that Riley invoked 'the im-perceptible'.[21] Although the term *imperceptible* (not ordinarily hyphenated) designates that which cannot be sensed, it refers more exclusively to whatever cannot be perceived, discerned or categorised by the intellect, particularly in situations where the very qualities perceptible to sense are too fine and subtle to be anything but felt. Feeling is paradise, the sacred, 'the im-perceptible'. Riley's word *im-perceptible* contains within it the divide between conceptualisation and perception, history and paradise. Perhaps her instinctive use of the hyphen is the sign of an essential split in meaning, as this graphic insertion divides intellectual perception from the sensory perception that may yet remain when intellectual concepts fail. Musing over the strange logic of a case of misinterpreted handwriting – the graphic decoding having been guided by mistaken expectations (that is, by history) – Proust concludes: 'We guess as we read, we create; everything starts from an initial error.'[22] This is to say, conception distorts perception. Here, Riley's affinity to Schneider's Proustian Matisse becomes especially evident. We think, as Schneider does, of the Matisse who at the end of his career advised students to 'retain only what cannot be seen'.[23]

In our everyday conversation, seeing is often a metaphor for understanding ('Do you see my point?'). 'What cannot be seen' must be those things we cannot know. In what sense of knowing? Robert Kudielka identifies the fundamental issue that Riley's art addresses as 'the difference between the way we normally "see" things' – our metaphorical, conceptualised view – 'and their actual visual appearance'.[24] This is the difference between what we already know and what we might experience freshly, whether new to us or not. For Matisse, then, 'what cannot be seen' would correspond to 'actual visual appearance'. Although this reality cannot be 'seen' (we cannot regard it with intellectual comprehension), it can be painted. By painting, artists become imperceptibly conscious of the unconscious. Painters, according to Riley, 'have always needed a sort of veil upon which they can focus their direct attention. It's as though the more fully the consciousness is absorbed, the greater the freedom of the spirit behind.'[25] Riley's 'veil' would cause an artist to fall into what Schneider calls the sacred. Behind, beyond, or at the edge of conscious visuality lies unconscious vision, the perceptual paradise. 'You must be prepared to go wrong,' Riley says. 'Nothing is set. It just emerges, from the looking.'[26] She also states: 'In order to see [I] had to paint and through that activity found what could be seen. The black-and-white paintings which I did in the sixties laid bare this circular process.'[27] Her circle has as yet no closure.

Sacred perception

Certain images are so direct that nearly everyone readily perceives them without consciously applying a concept or demanding critical explanation. At least initially, these images seem open to the most ordinary vision, having nothing mysterious or exceptional about them. *Kiss* (1961), the earliest and simplest of Riley's black-and-whites, is of this type. But it has a biographical complication. At least in part, it was motivated by an event in the artist's personal life, the breakup of a significant relationship; and it marks her psychological state at the time.[28] Riley wanted to approach absoluteness in sensation, and through sensation, to express an intensified, 'absolute' emotion – a quality of feeling that another person, a specific person, would have had to acknowledge.[29] Do we need to know this novelistic fact? Probably not. Sensation, according to Schneider, is at the core of what we call an impression, and 'the impression inevitably kindles feeling… One could say that emotion is the inner face of the impression [which] gives access not only to history [the outside world of ordered facts] but also… to the sacred, which escapes history and negates it.' Emotion – every felt emotion – has a sacred potential.

We can feel the emotion of a painting without knowing the personal history or mood that connects to it. Similarly, in order to feel the nature in a painting such as Riley's *Dark Light* (1991), a work with a title suggestive of specific environmental effects, we need not know whether any particular location, situation, or condition inspired the artist. The sacred realm of feeling is paradise, where pure emotion as well as pure sensation is to be experienced in a thoroughly personal way – each viewer's own way. This is what Schneider might call a 'first' impression, nevertheless admitting the redundancy of that designation ('All impressions are "first impressions"').[30] Perhaps personal experience is the only locus of the sacred for those who find no value other than the contingent and historical in organised religious faith, mass cult, mass education and cultural fashion. In the chapter that Riley so appreciates, Schneider appears to support this notion, defining Matisse's art as evidence of, 'the belief that paradise can [now] exist only in painting and that the role of painting is to depict paradise exclusively'. But then Schneider adds: 'This paradise has no justification, no meaning, except in history.'[31]

Why does Schneider append this qualification ('except in history'), which seems to undermine the distinction he establishes? Does his commentary take the side of history or the side of paradise? He suggests that paradise will be sought and appreciated only in an era when – because of the collective course of history itself, and through nobody's individual design – paradise has become a dream and a memory, something belonging to the mythological past, subsumed in the dominant sociocultural history that constitutes not only the past (including the distant time of myth), but also the present and even the future. History nevertheless admits the possibility of a certain sanguine reversal or reinitiation. 'Since anything that comes first is sacred, is it not possible,' Schneider asks, 'to draw from the personal source the indispensable energy that has vanished with the collective source?'[32] Matisse's involvement with paradisal space reflected a sense of the sacred that was entirely personal, even when he was decorating the Chapel of the Rosary at Vence. 'Do I believe in God? – Yes, when I work', the painter declared shortly before his involvement in this nominally religious undertaking. Schneider glosses Matisse's statement, advising readers to understand that God appears in the work, 'when [it] goes beyond what was originally intended, escapes comprehension and control'.[33] The source of Matisse's religious feeling was neither doctrinal faith nor some heavenly perfection, but the earthly paradise, 'his own private cult of happiness'.[34] This 'cult of happiness', his font of private faith, may be analogous to what Riley calls a 'small gap of pure perception'. She suggests that, for those born into our era, inspired perceptions replace 'the certainties that Christianity [once] had to offer.'[35]

The happiness that accompanies perception derives from creativity in work. 'Work cures everything', Matisse advised an old friend in 1953.[36] Riley, an enthusiastic traveller, has remarked in a related spirit: 'The sort of holidays I take are part and parcel of my work as a painter… The closest companion of artists is their work.'[37] Unfamiliar environments stimulate sensation, granting the painter a level of experience against which to measure the open potential of creation in the studio. 'Isn't it curious,' Riley muses, 'that nature immediately looks so much better once I've got a painting together.'[38] Experience in the studio fulfils, but does not imitate, her experience of nature. Between the two, and sparked by their coexistence, lies the 'small gap of pure perception' and also happiness and a very human kind of faith.

Is Riley's *Kiss* a work of personal experience, an ahistorical, paradisal figure? Perhaps its title refers to a human kiss; perhaps (more likely) it refers to a certain generalisable type of physical contact, exemplified not only by lips that kiss but by billiard balls that kiss or even graphic marks that kiss. Typically, Riley's titles come after the fact, evoked by effects emerging from the work. She recently named an unusually large painting *Day and Night* (2003) not because she intended it as a landscape but in response to the two yellows within its palette of only four colours: a deep yellow, suggesting sunlight; a pale yellow, suggesting moonlight. It might be fair to say that each of Riley's paintings has a subject, even many subjects; but the subject matter, which can be conceptualised as either actual or potential, hardly determines the experience. Whatever the case with *Kiss*, whatever its links to specific events and feelings, its form establishes a presence without requiring prior explanation. *Kiss* makes a definite impression, stimulating both sensation and emotion. We have no need to be advised of a telling detail or of Riley's

psychological condition at the creative moment. As for a history specific
to art, although it might be hard to imagine *Kiss* having been produced
before the twentieth century, nothing suggests that it must date to 1961.
If there were some reasoning that would situate its specific moment, this
would hardly affect how the work would be perceived – at least by those
having sufficient faith in their senses to be willing to enter the paradise
of painting.

Kiss has only three elements: a large bowed or curved form in black,
weighted asymmetrically downward toward the left; a horizontal bar,
equally black, upon which the curved form seems to descend; and
between them, a passage of white, reduced to a sliver where the upper
black form would otherwise meet the lower.[39] Upper and lower create
the sense of a 'kiss', either just barely or just barely not, depending on
how one judges the effect of the sliver of white, brought to a perceptual
and material minimum. Riley made the white narrow enough for a
viewer to sense it as the narrowest it can be. She created a perceptual
absolute, while expressing no concern for a corresponding absolute in
conception, except to suggest that here the perceptual overrules the
conceptual (as it must in aesthetic paradise). Viewing *Kiss*, we feel that
contact is about to be made, has just been made, or is being held in
potential as a kind of tension. The starkness of this painting connotes
precision; yet there is ambiguity, because we cannot know whether the
two black forms have actually 'kissed' or ever will. Nor can we be certain
whether this image signifies movement or stasis. These, however, are
interpretive concerns. Our perception of the image, of the play in its
three component shapes, we feel immediately. Our judgment after the
fact is what wavers.

'We guess… we create'

When I visited Riley's studio in winter 2004, there to view *Day and Night*
as well as studies for other 'curve' paintings in progress, the artist
casually mentioned that *Kiss* was the unplanned prototype – a kind of
empirical inspiration for her involvement with curved and straight forms

in interaction. I suppose that *Kiss* might be described as consisting of one curved form, the upper black, set against one straight form, the lower black. Its third form, in white and at once curved and straight, simultaneously mediates and intervenes. If the position of the white renders *Kiss* ambiguous with regard to a sense of contact, its black forms may still have the virtue for the analytically minded of illustrating how the curved and the straight must differ in concept. In this respect (not in others), the forms of *Kiss* are sufficiently distinct to keep perception and conception in sync.

Riley's subsequent paintings do not offer this analytical comfort. Her characteristic new forms – not to mention many of her old ones, as in *Descending* (1965–66) – so intimately link the curved and the straight that the conventional intellectual categories are proven inadequate by any direct experience of the work. Viewers predisposed toward Euclidean distinctions and cultural dualisms encounter frustration. Take Riley's own description of *Descending*, recorded in 1988, as a hint of the 'small gap of pure perception' that would accompany her curve paintings a decade later, forcing the abandonment of conceptual expectations: 'Every other vertical is straight and evenly disposed across the canvas. So that the movement goes in a zigzag progress through alternating straight and curving verticals, from a narrow closing at the top left descending to the narrow strip of diagonals at the bottom right. It is one thing against another.'[40]

'One thing against another': in the terms of Riley's early art, movement against stasis. Where, however, are the verticals located, whether straight or curving, rigid or moving? What moves and what does not is itself not obvious. Preliminary studies for *Descending* would presumably have verticals drawn as explicit lines (compare the pencilled diagonals of *Twisted Curves*, 1977); but in the completed painting such lines exist only virtually, perceived as phantoms created by the zigzag pattern of black and white, which also generates an optical illusion of peaks and valleys. Although 'every other [phantom] vertical is straight and evenly disposed', these neutral guides become part of a single perceptual movement. They are neither foundation nor superstructure. Theoretically, the evenly spaced verticals ought to have constituted a

RICHARD SHIFF

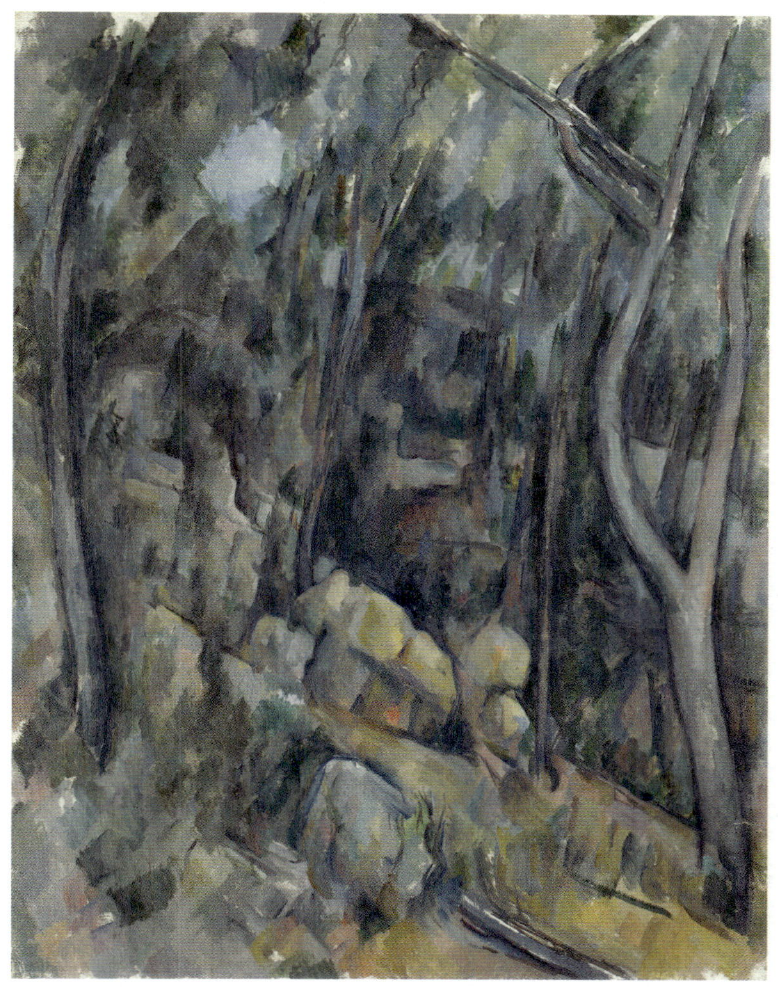

Paul Cézanne
The Grounds of the Château Noir c.1900–04
Oil on canvas
90.7 × 71.4 cm | 35¾ × 28⅛ in
National Gallery, London

measured raster, a passive regulator for the active image, which would include the deviant set of verticals spaced between the regular ones. Here, a distinction between deviant and regular, figure and raster, seems to slip away into perceptual paradise. The raster, the static element, moves along with everything else and just as actively, contributing to the sensation rather than grounding it.

Aptly, Riley places Paul Cézanne into this context, for he 'knew that the diagonal thrust helps to activate the slow backward and forward pulse of colour… Even the brushmarks have a directional pull.'[41] Few would deny that Cézanne's landscapes project emotion as well as sensation. Often the imagined orthogonal raster of a densely coloured Cézanne landscape is skewed, as if an assistant had failed to coordinate the composition with the plumb-line of its stretcher bars (*The Grounds of the Château Noir*, c.1904). If Cézanne's repetitive stroke seems to follow the vertical axis of a grid, it also falls into a diagonal pattern at odds with an expected rectilinearity. Many of Riley's works of the 1980s reveal a similar tension between rectilinear and diagonal rasters (*Ease*, 1987). Her diagonals are set at an angle of 45 degrees, which maximizes the separation. Referring to paintings that followed in the early 1990s, Kudielka evoked the Cézanne effect in Riley's 'glittering passages of smaller shapes that act almost like brushmarks' (*By Way of Yellow*, 1993).[42] The sensation seems all the more complicated in curve paintings of the late 1990s and beyond, where an off-axis 'curvilinear swing' develops diagonal movement, the same kind of motion we might discern in *Kiss*, given the asymmetrical 'swing' of its single black arc.[43]

Has Riley's attitude toward perception been constant over the years? Matisse believed that an artist's core is unlikely to change: 'You know, you have one idea, you are born with it, and all your life you develop your fixed idea, you make it breathe.'[44] Is it possible that Riley's recent work – such as *Four Colours with Orange* (2002), or *Turquoise and Others* (2004) 'breathes' with the naturalness of *Kiss*, its remote prototype, produced so directly and simply with a few forms limited to black and white? Seen in reproduction, the characteristic shapes of the new paintings leave an impression of greatly increased complexity, difficult to describe. Would detailed description be of any use? The actual

                                                   RICHARD SHIFF

paintings are spacious; their colour and light immerse the viewer in intense sensation. *Day and Night* extends to nearly 21 feet in width.[45] Even with the relatively modest width of nine feet in *Turquoise and Others*, what may appear merely decorative in reproduction comes as a challenge to living, embodied perception when seen at actual scale. Viewing the separate shapes in the fullness of their size and colour, we need feel no analytical compulsion to trace out the complex forms. We are free to perceive their collective effect with immediacy (a 'first impression') rather than ponder variations on a pattern or reinvent a compositional procedure. This is so, despite the fact that Riley may require months to complete a painting to her satisfaction. Both the artist and her viewers must wrest their impressions from the traps set by conceptualisation.

Each of the recent curve paintings manifests a set of parallel diagonals. A submerged array of vertical divisions may also be discerned: imagine Riley's shallow arcs as sometimes spanning, sometimes curving around or pivoting on, the hidden verticals. We would be hard-pressed, nevertheless, to use a resultant grid of parallelograms to establish a plan for the 'figures' that Riley disposes upon or across this 'ground'. It may seem that her fragmented diagonals constitute elements of an inviolable foundational raster. Yet they also operate as active figures against the still more grounded set of verticals. Do the curving colour-shapes become by default the only candidates for a true foreground? Possibly, the contour curves, generatively interrelated, function instead as a third raster. It proves impossible to identify one curving shape as the nearest, another as the most distant, still another as the dominant one, or to determine that a given pair relate as active and passive elements within a complex motif. Relationships of this sort – figure to ground, shaped colour to reiterative line, active to passive – assume no stability in Riley's paintings.

Destabilised, the contour of a single shape (a shape defined by a single colour) may shift from curved to straight or concave to convex. Typically, a given curve will seem to rise or descend, passing virtually seamlessly into a straight segment of one of the underlying diagonals. When this happens, the diagonal no longer underlies the image, but becomes itself the image in an act of perceptual reorientation. Near the lower left corner of *Paired Colours* (2001), what may at first appear as a lozenge or flattened ellipse, as it were, constructed entirely of curves, proves to be just as much of a warped rhomboid with two straight edges completing the movement of its two arcs (see as well the many instances of this effect in *Enchant*, 2004). How does Riley make this distinctive ambiguity happen? Her use of a curve based on a sixth of a circle produces an arc sufficiently gentle to shift into straightness with more grace than drama. Yet the difference between a straight edge and a curve ought to have remained obvious – it is our concepts that tell us that, not our looking.

Riley causes conceptual differences to come and go, fade in and out, in perception. What she says of Seurat applies as well to her: she creates perceptual phenomena 'we cannot quite see'. There are no names, no readymade categories for Riley's shapes, even though they are utterly geometric and as graphically precise as printed words. These shapes also have no predictable limits. A yellow-green form spans the entire distance between top and bottom margins of *Apricot and Pink* (2001); as it does, it incorporates segments of four different parallels belonging to the diagonal raster. This form weaves figure into ground, ground into figure. Somewhat to the right of it, in the lower right corner of the painting, a complex orange shape appears to have been cut into segments by the force of an implied diagonal, a part of the raster. Swinging, curved contours conflict with downward sliding, straight contours, all belonging to this one orange form. As a result, the shape 'moves' in at least two, and probably several, directions.[46] These are not directions we can identify with assurance, and yet the perception of movement surely occurs. It is as if the shapes that Riley has been discovering through her open 'dialogue' with painting were indecipherable symbols, unreadable words, configurations of 'the im-perceptible'.

Although Riley's recent works contain many unique shapes, they typically have only four or five different colours. When there are four, as in *Paired Colours*, two hues that are chromatically similar (an apricot-orange and a pale flesh-orange) may differ in value, while the other two may be similar in value but chromatically more distinct (medium blue, medium green). Riley's way of distributing her colours allows neither hue

　　　　　　　　　　　　　　　　　　　　　　RICHARD SHIFF

nor value to dominate as an organising concept. *Two Reds* (2000) has five colours: its rose-red and orange-red form a pair similar in both hue and value; its green and yellow-green are similar in hue and chromatic saturation, yet different in value; and its light blue appears as an estranged chromatic partner of the greens, somewhat closer to them than it is to the reds. By definition, light blue ought to be a cool, recessive colour; but Riley's way of shaping it undermines formulaic notions of the behaviour of cool in opposition to warm and of light in opposition to dark. I wonder, within the chromatic context that Riley creates, whether the blue might ally more with the reds than with the greens, for rose-red can assume the chromatic personality of a blue. If Riley's titles are something of a retrospective guide, then she experiences in families of colour a kind of growth beyond the limits set by names. The three 'blues' in *Blues and Greens* (2001) range from bluish green to bluish violet. Perhaps we perceive a quality of 'blueness' throughout this painting, a blue 'gap' opening unexpectedly in our perception.

Along with its diagonals, *Two Reds* contains a single vertical: a large green shape and a small orange-red shape share a common vertical edge near the bottom margin at the right of centre. This linear element is anomalous; it exposes the ubiquitous, but otherwise suppressed, vertical raster. In *Painting with Two Verticals* (2004), however, the raster returns – up to a point. Two vertical segments appear, symmetrically disposed left to right. But they are asymmetrical in that the left-hand vertical reaches to the top margin, whereas the right-hand vertical extends to neither margin. We can regard these verticals as contributing to the shaping of certain areas of colour, or as the intrusions of a raster that could just as well have remained imperceptible. The vertical raster now seems openly to compete with the diagonal raster in configuring the perceptual image.

Forms of art that are unusually moving – perceptually, emotionally – cause a critic to rethink conventional definitions. *Painting with Two Verticals*, *Two Reds*, *Blues and Greens*, *Enchant* and Riley's other curve paintings have altered my sense of how a pictorial grid might operate. Although a grid of parallelograms ought to result from crossing verticals with diagonals – although this ought to be true in concept – it is not

what I feel I perceive. Instead, I see the moving traces of a double raster:
an array of verticals, largely implicit; an array of diagonals, largely explicit.
Riley's double raster creates mutual interference as force and
counterforce. Her two rasters energise each other as if in affirmation of
her early discovery: 'You cannot have movement without its opposite –
stasis.' Now, however, the perceptual effect of her art passes beyond the
reach of this traditional principle.

To function, Riley's rasters need not 'map' anything 'onto' or in
relation to anything else, as the common analytical metaphor would
have us imagine. By 'mapping', acts of painting and picturing become
algorithmic and even linguistic, with one structure translating, figuring, or
being 'mapped onto' another.[47] Rather than insisting on a measured,
map-like order, a kind of standard projection, Riley feels free to set
individual elements of a raster at varying intervals and in fragmentary
form, so that the raster becomes both highly visible and ultimately
indeterminate. The regularity that it connotes and actually contains does
not necessarily appear. Such a raster assumes a unique sensory quality
like that of a colour, and its action 'colours' its associated image
emotionally. In Riley's art, the grid-like fundament acquires a sense of
movement or emotivity to be perceived with no more analytical
comprehension than we might bring to our understanding of the
greenness of a certain green. With Riley's recent art, line becomes
colour, but 'colour' of a very strange sort – a dissolution of both
categories.[48]

Riley's new direction has Proustian intuition built into it, as ever
before: 'We guess as we read, we create; everything starts from an initial
error.' If we view her painting as a conventional pictorial composition, it is
unreadable. We would have to guess where each of her forms should be
located within the compositional space: near, far, heading up, heading
down, twisting this way or that. There are too many possibilities to
control, and we are left to keep guessing. To put perception in order, we
would have to coordinate our guesses, seeking evidence of a definitive
plan or system, ideally with no violations; we would need reasons for the
anomalous vertical in *Two Reds* and for the disruptive emergence of the
raster in *Painting with Two Verticals*. In the immediacy of perception,

　　　　　　　　　　　　　　　　　　　　　　RICHARD SHIFF

however, nothing is anomalous; and nothing disrupts any more than anything else. The raster can be the figure. The lines can be the colour.

Rather than translating a known effect, Riley's rasters, curves and colours produce an effect, which may or may not be 'known'. Her paintings sometimes recall a certain quality of light, a certain movement, a certain sense of change. And sometimes, just as likely, we feel light itself in and through the shaped colours, or we feel movement, or we feel the perceptual change we recognise as the sign of life – all without any pressure to understand why.

Riley's art must take leave of Proust, at least to some extent, for in reading or misreading each of her paintings, we have no 'initial error' to commit. The paradise of perception is error-free. When perception is 'pure', it moves, but as if suspended in time. Nothing exists behind it or ahead of it to be misinterpreted. This does not mean that anything goes. Nor is a countercultural avant garde or simple novelty the issue: these are stances encouraged by a historical mentality. Originality is also not at stake; it, too, is a matter of history, to be judged in relation to an artist's advancement of a particular discipline. The emotive immediacy of perceptual paradise may actually be discovered in a place already entered by someone else (Cézanne? Seurat? Matisse?). Revisiting the site of paradise does not lessen the impact of its discovery. A 'small gap of pure perception' conveys meaning, wherever and whenever the experience occurs.

Bridget Riley: Recent Paintings, exhibition catalogue, PaceWildenstein, New York, NY, 2004, pp.5–19.

Note: I thank Charlotte Cousins for essential aid in researching this essay; and, of course, Bridget Riley.

1   Bridget Riley, 'The Artist's Eye: Seurat' (1992), in Robert Kudielka (ed), *The Eye's Mind: Bridget Riley, Collected Writings 1965–1999*, Thames & Hudson, London, 1999, p.175.

2   Bridget Riley, in conversation with the author, London, 3 March 2004.

3   Pierre Schneider, *Matisse*, Michael Taylor and Bridget Romer Strevens (trans), Rizzoli, New York, NY, 1984, pp.73–93.

4   Bridget Riley, 'Personal Interview by Nikki Henriques' (1988), in Kudielka (ed), *op.cit.*, p.28. On Riley and Proust, see also Robert Kudielka, *Bridget Riley: Paintings 1982–1992*, exhibition catalogue, Kunsthalle Nürnberg, Nuremberg, 1992, pp.21–22.

5   Henri Matisse, statement written for the exhibition *Henri Matisse – Dessins à l'encre de Chine, fusains (oeuvres récentes)*, Galerie Louis Carre, Paris, 1941; quoted in Schneider, *op.cit.*, pp.12–13. Compare Henri Matisse, 'Notes of a Painter on His Drawing' (1939), in Jack Flam (ed and trans), *Matisse on Art*, University of California Press, Berkeley, CA, 1995, p.132: 'I work *without theory* [emphasis original]. I am conscious only of the forces I use, and I am driven by an idea that I really only grasp as it grows with the picture.' See also Flam's commentary on this passage, p.19.

6   On the relationship between painting, gardens (often framed or enclosed by windows), the sacred and Matisse's studio practice, see Schneider, *op.cit.*, pp.22, 685, 692. The English word *peri* can be linked with paradise, both conceptually and etymologically. It signifies an elf or fairy formed of fire, descended from fallen angels and excluded from paradise until penance is achieved; by extension, a male or female concubine; or simply, a beautiful, graceful girl (a common subject in Matisse's art). Proust played on the connections in his narrator's evocative description of Albertine: 'that little peri [*petite péri*], more seductive to me than she of the Persian paradise [*paradis persan*]'; Marcel Proust, *À la recherche du temps perdu* (In Search of Lost Time), CK Scott Moncrieff and Terence Kilmartin (trans), vol.1, Random House, New York, NY, 1981, p.852. On Matisse's involvement with gardens and use of decorative motifs and formats in relation to Persian or Islamic evocations of paradise, see also Pierre Schneider, 'The Moroccan Hinge', in Jack Cowart (ed), *Matisse in Morocco: The Paintings and Drawings, 1912–1913*, exhibition catalogue, National Gallery of Art, Washington, DC, 1990, pp.17–56; Deepak Ananth, 'Frames within Frames: On Matisse and The Orient', in Paul Duro (ed), *The Rhetoric of the Frame*, Cambridge University Press, Cambridge, 1996, pp.153–77; Roger Benjamin, *Orientalist Aesthetics: Art, Colonialism, and French North Africa*, 1880–1930, University of California Press, Berkeley, 2003, pp.186–90.

7   Matisse, 'Interview with Andre Verdet' (1952), in Flam, *op.cit.*, p.214.

8   Bridget Riley, 'Supposed to Be Abstract: Bridget Riley in Conversation with Robert Kudielka', *Parkett*, no.61, May 2001, p.23 (emphasis eliminated).

9   Raster is a term that can be substituted for grid, with somewhat different connotations. A raster operates as an organisational and distribution system, with implication of a time dimension as well as spatial dimensions; accordingly, a raster affords movement. Neither horizontals nor verticals are required; the raster grid can be structured by any geometry. For example, the raster of a conventional, cathode-ray television screen consists only of horizontals, which actually slant at a slight downward angle, left to right. The lack of a vertical component in such a grid does not prevent the projected image from appearing to move along that axis. The nature of the raster affects the character of the image, but every raster accommodates every image.

10   On the nature of Riley's characteristic shapes in works of 1997 and later, compare Robert Kudielka, 'Abstract Figuration: On Bridget Riley's Recent Curve Paintings', in Paul Moorhouse (ed), *Bridget Riley*, exhibition catalogue, Tate Publishing, London, 2003, pp.151–52.

11   Bridget Riley, quoted from a conversation with Lynn MacRitchie, 'The Intelligence of the

                                                    RICHARD SHIFF

Eye' (2000), in Martin Hentschel (ed), *Bridget Riley: New Work*, exhibition catalogue, Kunstmuseen Krefeld, Krefeld and Hatje Cantz Verlag, Ostfildern, 2002, p.19.

12   *Ibid.*

13   Riley, in conversation with the author, *op.cit.*

14   Riley, quoted in MacRitchie, *op.cit.*, p.19.

15   Bridget Riley, 'The Experience of Painting: Talking to Mel Gooding' (1988), in Kudielka (ed), *The Eye's Mind*, *op.cit.*, p.123.

16   I use the somewhat awkward term *firstness* as an allusion to the existential categories proposed by Charles Sanders Peirce, for whom 'Firstness' (alternatively, 'Originality') distinguishes a realm of sensory qualities devoid of referential ties to objects or contexts: 'a quality of unanalysed feeling… something which is what it is without reference to anything else within it or without it, regardless of all force and of all reason'; Charles Hartshorne and Paul Weiss (eds), *Collected Papers of Charles Sanders Peirce*, vol.2, Harvard University Press, Cambridge, MA, 1960, p.46 (emphasis eliminated).

17   In several independent communications with the author during 2003 and 2004, both Riley and Schneider warned of the danger of explaining works of art too thoroughly. Yet both are accomplished critical writers. Their respect for the inviolability of works of art makes it all the more difficult for them to achieve a proper tenor in their writing and all the more impressive that they do.

18   Riley, 'The Experience of Painting', in Kudielka (ed), *The Eye's Mind*, *op.cit.*, p.122.

19   Riley, 'The Artist's Eye', *ibid.*, p.181 (original emphasis). One of the features that Riley has appreciated in Seurat is his elimination of flourishes of the brush that would deflect the concentrated work of vision; Riley, 'The Experience of Painting', *ibid.*, p.125. Accordingly, since the early 1960s, she has used assistants to produce the final painted surface of her canvases, avoiding the temptations of her own touch while instructing her assistants to exercise restraint as well.

20   Schneider, *op.cit.*, p.676.

21   Riley, 'The Artist's Eye', in Kudielka (ed), *The Eye's Mind*, *op.cit.*, p.175 (emphasis eliminated).

22   Proust, vol.3, *op.cit.*, p.671.

23   Introducing his own critical method, Schneider quotes this line from a notebook Matisse began in 1946; Schneider, *op.cit.*, p.10.

24   Kudielka, *Bridget Riley: Paintings 1982–1992*, *op.cit.*, p.10.

25   Bridget Riley, 'The Colour Connection: In Conversation with Robert Kudielka' (1989), in Kudielka (ed), *The Eye's Mind*, *op.cit.*, p173.

26   Bridget Riley, quoted in MacRitchie, 'The Intelligence of the Eye', *ibid.*, p.19.

27   Bridget Riley, 'The Pleasures of Sight' (1984), *ibid.*, p.33.

28   See Riley, 'Personal Interview by Nikki Henriques,' *ibid.*, p.25. Riley explains that an affair with an older, more sophisticated man had recently ended; she expressed her dismay and anger by 'paint[ing] a message so loud and clear [that he would] know exactly how I feel.'

29   Compare Paul Moorhouse, 'A Dialogue with Sensation: The Art of Bridget Riley', in Moorhouse (ed), *op.cit.*, p.14; Riley, 'The Experience of Painting', in Kudielka (ed), *The Eye's Mind*, *op.cit.*, p.125.

30   The notion is Proustian. Compare Proust's claim that the memory of a particular sensation is vivid only when the recollection remains embedded in an indeterminate context and the source of the sensation (and therefore its historical meaning) is yet to be conceptualised; Proust, vol.3, *op.cit.*, pp. 902–03. Such memory, thoroughly personalised, is experienced as a first impression belonging to paradise, not history.

31 Schneider, *op.cit.*, p.88.

32 *Ibid.*, p.90. Schneider continues: 'This transference [from collective history to personal
    paradise], or rather its revelation, is the great theme of [Proust's] *Remembrance of
    Things Past.'*

33 *Ibid.*, p.673. Matisse's words are from an imaginary conversation inscribed in his
    illustrated book *Jazz*, published in 1947; see Flam, *op.cit.*, p.173. Father Marie-Alain
    Couturier, who equated artistic genius with godliness and supported Matisse's plans for
    Vence, made a note of these remarks in 1949; see Marcel Billot (ed), *Henri Matisse, M.-A.
    Couturier, L.-B. Rayssiguier, La Chapelle de Vence, Journal d'une création*, Editions du
    Cerf, Paris, 1993, p.140.

34 Schneider, *op.cit.*, p.692.

35 Riley, 'The Experience of Painting', in Kudielka (ed), *The Eye's Mind, op.cit.*, p.122.

36 Quoted in Schneider, *op.cit.*, p.740. See Matisse, letter to André Rouveyre, 2 September
    1953, in Hanne Finsen (ed), *Matisse Rouveyre Correspondence*, Flammarion, Paris, 2001,
    p.642.

37 Bridget Riley, 'Holidays: Talking to Vanya Kewley' (1996), in Kudielka (ed), *The Eye's
    Mind, op.cit.*, pp.44, 46.

38 Riley, statement to Robert Kudielka, 1991, as reported in Kudielka, *Bridget Riley: Paintings
    1982–1992, op.cit.*, p.12.

39 In the process of fabricating works in black and white, although a layer of white might be
    applied as an initial ground, Riley's white shapes do not act as a neutral or recessive field
    for her black shapes; rather, in most instances, white and black become equally active
    optically.

40 Riley, 'The Experience of Painting', *op.cit.*, p.123.

41 Riley, 'The Colour Connection', *ibid.*, p.170.

42 Kudielka, 'Abstract Figuration', in Moorhouse (ed), *op.cit.*, p.152.

43 Riley refers to 'curvilinear swing' in 'Supposed to Be Abstract', in Kudielka (ed), *op.cit.*,
    p.25.

44 Henri Matisse, 'Interview with Andre Marchand: The Eye' (1947), in Flam, *op.cit.*, p.175;
    quoted in Schneider, *op.cit.*, p.13.

45 Because Riley's shapes are irregular products of at least two orderly rasters (vertical and
    diagonal), they relate to the rectilinear margins of her canvases in arbitrary that is, precise
    but unruly, unpredictable – ways, as if transcending their own measurable, physical limits.
    This may cause the painting to feel even larger and more expansive than its dimensions
    would indicate. Matisse referred to a similar effect in his mural painting: 'I use a fragment
    [an oddly truncated form] and I lead the spectator by the rhythm, I lead him to follow the
    movement from the fragment he sees, so that he has a feeling of the totality… to give
    the idea of immensity within a very limited surface'; Matisse, 'Interview with Georges
    Charbonnier' (1950), in Flam, *op.cit.*, p.191.

46 This detail of Riley's painting exemplifies what is characteristic of the whole of this and
    other works of its type: an implied downward, leftward movement of the diagonal raster
    offsets an implied downward, rightward swing of the curved 'figures'.

47 Algorithmic mapping has been the dominant concept for understanding the operation of
    grids as well as for deploying them – from Albrecht Dürer's use of ruled screens for
    tracing objects, to the modernist and postmodernist notion of the picture surface as an
    implicit grid that maps itself reiteratively. Riley seems to be reaching for something else,
    as if to enter a paradise of perception beyond the conceptual apparatus of the mapping
    metaphor. For the critic, always at a loss in addressing an artist who herself is addressing
    perception, it helps to shift from discussing grids to discussing rasters. Grids generate

                                                                    RICHARD SHIFF

readable, syntactical maps; rasters generate unreadable, moving images ('the imperceptible'), even when activated in the stilled format of painting. Compare the discussion of 'incompossibility' and related notions in Richard Shiff, 'Bridget Riley: The Edge of Animation', in Moorhouse (ed), *op.cit.*, pp.81–91.

48 Compare Riley's thinking with regard to her 'Egyptian' series of the early 1980s: 'I chose long thin vertical stripes, because they have very little body and are mostly 'edges'. The interaction between colours is most intense when one colour borders on another. The long edges of the stripes maximize this relationship. When placed vertically the colour event is seen as a horizontal spread of coloured light'; Riley, 'The Experience of Painting', *op.cit.*, p.127.

The Architecture of Perception: Bridget Riley's Art

Paul Moorhouse

For over 45 years two imperatives have guided the course of Bridget Riley's art. The first is a sensibility which delights in order, relation and the creation of structure. Echoing but not imitating nature, her paintings proceed from simple elements. Shape, space and colour are her basic materials which are then drawn into complex and subtle pictorial arrangements. This abiding will to bestow order generates her work's internal momentum, and over the years it has become a source material in itself. Structures evolve, change, are subjected to permutation and variation, and are then put aside – only to resurface in a different context at a later date. In this way her art feeds upon itself.

Given this degree of self-containment, it is perhaps surprising that the second imperative manifests itself as an urge to reach out towards the observed world. Since 1960 her art has eschewed literal depiction. Indeed, it is central to Riley's thinking that the imitation of appearance is just that: a kind cf shadow play, replicating the outlines of nature without conveying anything of the unique relation that exists between the individual and the thing observed. It would however be a profound error to take her rejection of verisimilitude as indifference to her surroundings. Riley's earliest memories are bound up with what she has described as 'the pleasures of sight' – experiences rooted in the observation of nature. Her art celebrates and recreates such pleasures. But it does so informed by the knowledge that the past is a faraway place and memory a pale reflection of the original experience. For that reason, her paintings depict no specific previous experiences. The visual pleasures yielded by her art exist in the immediate present and in terms of its own simple elements and invented structures. That said, her work creates a kind of poetry for the eye that arises from a syntax shared with nature. Light, form, space and movement are common to both. In that sense her art – though self-possessed – inflects continuously towards nature.

The six paintings in the present exhibition are all based on studies that Riley made n the summer of 2005. In these works, issues of pictorial structure and equivalence to nature are engaged in ways that build upon her previous treatment of these themes and then take those ideas into unexplored territory. *Painting with Verticals 2* (2006) announces these developments. Using four colours only – lilac, green, yellow and orange-red – the surface of the painting is fractured into numerous interlocking irregular shapes. The curved forms appear to cut across a succession of vertical divisions. This interpretation of the painting then collapses as the same arabesque shapes cease to read as solid planes, suggesting instead apertures and deep, recessional space. The eye is drawn into the visual argument as it seeks a constant, a fixed point – and finds none. An apparently firm structure dissolves, opening up an ambiguous inner space occupied by strange, flickering organic forms: an endless, elusive movement in depth. This is a world like no other, yet tantalisingly familiar.

The enigma is compounded when it is realised that the same world, or one very like it, is explored in *Painting with Verticals 1* (2006). A similar horizontal expanse falls into a series of vertical divisions and, as before, a succession of cascading shapes move across and through these stages. The protagonists seem related to those in the earlier painting. The eye recognises the floating leaf motif at centre left and the lithe, hourglass form in the middle of the argument. Elsewhere, however, the context has changed. Larger forms have fragmented into smaller shapes and, overall, the complexion and dynamic of the painting is different. Cast in a different visual key – yellow, magenta, turquoise and red – the phrasing has moved on, assuming an alternative expressive character. Form and space interact in fresh ways. As in the experience of nature, there is that sense of a familiar place being revisited but never appearing the same on successive occasions. The light, the mood, the internal world of the viewer – all inflect the experience in myriad ways. Yet common to both paintings is a restless, formal ambiguity and an enticement to the viewer to structure visual experiences that hover at the edge of recognition.

Although in formal terms the new paintings appear very different from Riley's earlier work, they continue concerns that were apparent from the outset. The black-and-white paintings that she commenced in

1960 had, by the mid-1960s, defined her position as a distinctive artist of
international stature. In common with the present works, early paintings
such as *Movement in Squares* (1961) were structured according to
principles which sought to provide a containing fabric for units of
sensation. During the 1960s, the individual quanta were discrete shapes:
circles, squares, ovals and lines disposed in a variety of different ways. In
1967 she introduced colour, organised subsequently as stripes, twists and
curves. The interaction of this range of elements provided a build-up of
optical excitement. When subjected to destabilising forces within the
pictorial argument, the resulting sensations give rise to intense,
sometimes entrancing perceptual experiences connected with the
appearance of movement and light. These experiences arise from the
viewer's engagement with interpreting what they are seeing. The action
of looking, and of absorbing the visual information being presented,
activates the perceptual process. Unlike their black-and-white and colour-
stripe predecessors, the new paintings do not yield overt perceptual
experiences. Even so, in all these works the viewer is drawn into a
dynamic visual dialogue with individual paintings through seeking to
interpret and structure what they are seeing.

After 1980, the relation between pictorial structure and equivalence to
nature in Riley's art took a new direction. Progressively her paintings
moved away from a build-up of sensation leading inexorably to a
perceptual response. Instead, their formal organisation took on a more
intuitive character. Beginning with a return to vertical stripes, individual
units of colour were arranged according to principles of relation and
chromatic interaction, but increasingly were connected to the implication
of space, rhythm and depth. From the mid-1980s, these developments
were animated further by the incorporation of a diagonal element which
cuts across the verticals, rising from left to right. The effect was to shatter
the picture plane. In these fascinating paintings, the viewer is confronted
with a matrix of individual, lozenge-shaped units of sensation, advancing
and receding within a constantly shifting arena. The individual colours
both create and occupy space. Individually, their capacity to suggest
plane or aperture remains contingent, dependent entirely on the viewer's
perception of their context and relation to the whole. By these means

Riley opened up a new visual domain: a plastic fabric of pure sensation, preceding and inviting recognition.

In terms of their structure, the rhomboid paintings are the immediate source for the present paintings. They defined certain rules of engagement which still inform her thinking. They established her use of a grid formed by a repeated vertical traversed by diagonals. Overt in the rhomboid paintings, this is the hidden, underlying foundation of the new paintings. The third element in her formal argument – the sinuous arabesque – came in 1997. *Lagoon 1* (1997), in which it is first seen, commences a phase which Riley continues to develop and explore. Somewhat fragmented and discontinuous in *Lagoon*, Riley subsequently found in the curve an ideal counterpart to the geometric structure she had evolved previously. *Evoë 3* (2003), is a bravura performance. Utilising this new language, colour, shape, space and movement are brought into a new, startling synthesis. In this magisterial painting Riley succeeded in sustaining a remarkable tension between plane and void across an imposing horizontal expanse. Quoting Aristotle, the philosopher Schopenhauer defined space as, 'that in which bodies can be'. This seems the very essence of this most recent phase in which space and form have become inseparable and indistinguishable: a perfect synthesis.

Even so, Riley – alert to the finest nuances of internal balance – speculated about the implied relation of space and body. When *Evoë 3* was shown in her retrospective exhibition at Tate Britain in 2003, some commentators alluded to echoes of Henri Matisse in the painting's use of luxuriant arabesque. Others suggested a growing tendency towards connotation, the long curves being linked with a range of anthropomorphic and organic implications. Such references were unintended. The movement implied in *Evoë 3* is disembodied; abstract form and structure alone carry the essence of dynamism. Nevertheless, an issue had emerged: how to develop the potential of the new formal language without incurring further unintended figurative resonances?

In the last two years, Riley has addressed this question and her most recent paintings are the extraordinary outcome. The remarkable work *Painting with Verticals 3* (2006) exemplifies these developments. There

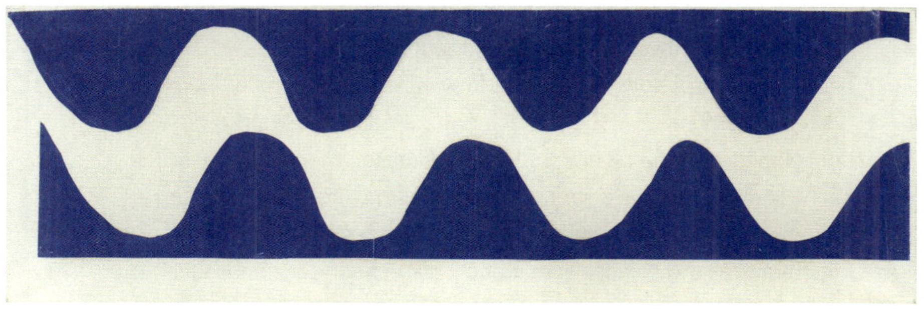

Henri Matisse
The Wave c.1952
Gouache on paper, cut and pasted
51.1 × 158.4 cm | 20⅛ × 62⅜ in
Musée Matisse, Nice
© Succession H. Matisse/DACS 2016

are two key advances. The first is an expanded range of rich, resonant colour. The painting employs turquoise-green, a very pale blue, warm yellow, light violet and the orange-red encountered previously. The resulting intense primary colour relationships – yellow against blue, orange against green – strike a strident, majestic note. Previously a more restricted range of colours entailed fewer chromatic jumps. In *Painting with Verticals 3*, such transitions are bold, investing the edges where colours meet with vibrant energy. The second development is a fresh approach to deploying the curve. No longer long and discursive, arabesques enclose and define individual shapes more succinctly. A curve traces a short movement and then disappears.

The result of both these steps forward is the creation of a highly differentiated surface. The character of individual shapes is more developed, and the relation of forms articulated more assertively. Riley's achievement is to have strengthened this structure and, at the same time, rendered it more ambiguous. The apparent surface quickly fragments as the eye seeks to identify plane and space. Individual colour-shapes advance, dissolve to void and then reassert themselves as solid forms. Collectively, the internal space of the painting is animated by a constantly changing structure in which movement and depth are united. The eye roams within that space, pausing, alighting, skipping from point to point. It tests each shape in turn and finds endless variety – an unceasing dynamic of opposition and harmony, geometry and curve, abstract form and metaphor.

Riley's earliest works create a world of pure perception. Eye and mind are caught up in pictorial structures that act as a kind of score for the paintings' unexpected visual performances. These evocative optical experiences – dazzling, dissolving and softly fading – resonate with the seductive power of nature, yet return the viewer inexorably to the context of art. The paintings that followed in the 1980s touch the world in different ways. The viewer feasts on a spectacle of pure visual excitement, returned to the condition of the infant with its insatiable yet unknowing eye. The paintings that Riley is now making occupy a new place, poised somewhere between these extremes. Their source is sensation and their mysterious architecture provides a rich, delightful context for looking, exploring and imagining. Leading to the threshold of recognition, they echo those formative, structuring processes by which the child begins to perceive the world he occupies. Schopenhauer tells us, 'Perception is not only the source of all knowledge, but is itself knowledge'. As such, these new paintings refine and deepen the relation of Riley's art to the world. They also illuminate a vital aspect of human experience.

Bridget Riley: New Paintings and Gouaches, exhibition catalogue, Ridinghouse and Timothy Taylor Gallery, London, 2005, pp.5–11.

Encore

Lynne Cooke

> A young artist must be aware that he does not have
> to invent everything anew: his job is to sort out in his
> mind the compatibility of the different approaches in the
> works of art that impress him and at the same time
> question nature.
>
> — Henri Matisse, 1945

> It is important to look at the best — and it is not
> immodest or lacking in respect to do so. The great
> paintings are the clearest; they have been made by those
> who made the greatest effort to overcome confusion and
> to arrive at clarity… [I]t is understanding this sorting out —
> and what it is that has been sorted out — that is so
> valuable to other painters.
>
> — Bridget Riley, 'Painting Now', 1996

I

Pink Landscape (1960), the best known because most reproduced, of
Bridget Riley's formative works, is rarely shown. Implicitly relegated to the
realm of immaturity since it is based on studies made *sur le motif*, this
small yet scintillating oil pays homage to a great neo-Impressionist
precursor as it expands his 'method' in new directions. Well versed in
Georges Seurat's practice from her close copy, made the previous year,
of one of his smaller landscapes, *The Bridge at Courbevoie* (1886–87),
Riley based *Pink Landscape* on a view over an expansive plain outside
Siena, a view even more austere than the vistas Seurat customarily
favoured. A lowering haze, foreshadowing the approaching storm, and
rendered by means of a patchwork of small strokes ranging from
succulent pinkish yellow through bluish lemon, suffuses the plain. In

conjunction with the high horizon, the square format creates an all-over field whose vertical axis is bisected by a faint zigzag which demarcates transitions in elevation from one hillock to the next. In this glowering light Riley's nominal subject is virtually dematerialised. Emblematic of the way that perception itself would become her medium, *Pink Landscape* stands on the threshold of an abstract optical art.

Executed some six years later and almost double the size of *Pink Landscape*, *Static 3* (1966), is comprised of an uninflected monochrome ground laced with an irregular grid of small black ovals, variously oriented. The title was consciously chosen with reference to, 'a field of static electricity'. Yet the origin of this lattice of 'visual prickles', and hence of the sensation of 'arrows… being discharged in front of your face as you look at it', lies in an experience Riley had when ascending a mountaintop covered with shale one summer, in the mid-1960s, in France. 'It was an extremely hot day', she recalled:

> I was getting anxious because we were going in a car up a steep narrow road. Visually it was total confusion; I felt there was no possibility of understanding the space of this situation. You couldn't tell whether this shimmering shale was near or far, flat or round. One of us said it was like the desert. We found it so alarming that we got out of the car, which of course intensified the sensation. But it was much cooler at the top, and into my mind came the beginnings of *Static*, a mass of tiny glittering units like a rain of arrows.[1]

When closely scrutinised, the (grid of) tiny ovals begin to sway and turn, destabilising the ordered regularity so that space opens in a subtly elusive flow which picks up speed, then subsides and fades away, only to resume its evasive trajectory shortly after. Few commentators have been inclined to link the dots connecting these two works, for soon after painting *Pink Landscape* Riley's style changed dramatically. She adopted a sharply contrasting black-and-white palette, focused on a vocabulary of simple, repeating geometric units, and began employing assistants to execute her works to ensure an anonymous, impersonal handling. Heralded in *Movement in Squares* (1961), the painting that has most often inaugurated retrospective overviews of her work, this style was quickly identified as her signature mode. While reference to works by both Piet Mondrian and Jackson Pollock is critical to this shift in direction, there is, however, no fundamental hiatus in her evolution: their impact on her thinking did not detach her from her roots but, rather, grounded her more fully.[2] Analysing Seurat's drawings in a review of a centennial exhibition of his work many years later, Riley offered the following incisive commentary:

> There is an almost overpowering sense of the mysterious. Curiously enough, although its treatment may differ from subject to subject or from manifestation to manifestation, one has an unmistakable sense of the mystery being singular and constant. Superficially it can be explained to some extent by what is depicted… But the heart of this mystery, it seems to me, lies more in its employment of our powers of perception. We cannot quite see. Within the myriad subtle distinctions of close tones, or through the magic weaving of conté marks, we cannot sometimes be sure of the identity or even of the actual forms we are looking at. To put it another way, by confronting us with an experience just beyond our visual grasp, with something unfathomable, the imperceptible in short, Seurat asks: What is it that we are looking at?[3]

Though the terms in which she realised *Pink Landscape* and *Static 3* are substantially different, their effects are not so far removed – and her analysis of Seurat's effect applies with equal validity to both of her own paintings. For once, 'the basis of vision rather than its appearance' became her point of departure, she continued to explore perceptual sensation. Thus irrespective of how systematic any single line of enquiry might prove – as seen in the close variants that comprise the four works titled 'Static' – her practice has never become programmatic or predetermined but remains, as Anton Ehrenzweig argued, always, 'aware of its ultimate mystery, [of] that transformation which will give her work its independent life and secret "presence".'[4]

II

In the early 1960s Riley gained widespread recognition as a key figure in the emerging British scene. Her meteoric rise to critical and popular acclaim coincided with, as it was shaped by, a remarkable sea change in British culture. As the postwar economic recovery generated a widespread cultural efflorescence, 'Swinging London' became the most dynamic city in the world. The explosion of artistic activity across numerous fields from music through fashion, film, photography, theatre and the visual arts shared certain features, generating a collective image based in youth, vitality, creativity, originality, irreverence, excitement; 'clean, crisp and straightforward', 'pure, high-octane nervous energy' and 'cool' were typical epithets applied across the various spheres, from politics to culture, to capture the new ethos.[5] Among the leading artists of her generation, which included David Hockney, Peter Blake, Allen Jones, Bernard and Harold Cohen, Richard Smith and Anthony Caro, Riley stood apart on account of her formation as much as her mode of radical abstraction. Yet her decision to join the Robert Fraser Gallery in 1965 placed her firmly at the centre of that cresting wave, as did participation in certain key shows that had launched the New Generation, as this loose coterie came to be known.[6] Committed to the new cr, better, opposed to the Establishment in all its manifold guises, their work was enthusiastically championed for its assertive newness. In many cases, in the visual arts as elsewhere, novelty if not originality was achieved by means of rupture and rejection. Yet too often desperation usurped the role of inspiration as a radical hiatus with both the artist's formative or student years and with the art of the past became the prerequisite for the mandatory 'breakthrough' (as such reorientations were then termed). In Riley's case, however, her passage to such iconic works of the mid-1960s as *Pause* (1964), *Current* (1964), *Fall* (1965), or *Descending* (1965), evolved by way of a deep absorption in and engagement with a uniquely determined set of mentors. That is, far from becoming unmoored from the past, it was premised on the option of drawing from any and all sources within the modernist canon as they seemed relevant and appropriate: thus, for her, Seurat could be as

pertinent an examplar as Pollock, or Giacomo Balla as relevant as
Mondrian.

When Riley's work debuted in New York in 1965, it became a cause
célèbre, enthusiastically embraced by the popular press and plagiarised
by the fashion industry.[7] A solo show of 16 paintings at the Richard
Feigen Gallery was timed to coincide with *The Responsive Eye*, a high-
profile exhibition curated by William C Seitz for the Museum of Modern
Art, which featured two of her most recent paintings. Taking their cues
from the strong representation of Josef Albers and Victor Vasarely, who
were the senior artists highlighted in the exhibition, the inner circles of
the New York art world perceived this heterogeneous show as a
promotion of a *retardataire* European-based art, an art whose roots lay
in early twentieth-century abstraction. Typical in his response was painter
and *Artforum* denizen Sidney Tillim, who traced a lineage from the
Bauhaus through Constructivism to the generation of mostly younger
European avatars of the latest manifestation, dubbed Op art, among
whom he included Riley.[8] For his colleague Barbara Rose, a more
impassioned proponent of so-called advanced art, only the works of a
few Americans, namely Ellsworth Kelly, Morris Louis, Kenneth Noland,
Larry Poons and Frank Stella, warranted attention, even though she
found their inclusion anomalous, ancillary to Seitz's governing premises.
Albeit from a more rigorously articulated position, her fellow contributor
Rosalind Krauss reached almost identical conclusions.[9] Based in high-key
colour, a holistic composition, a disembodied optical space and a
de-personalised handling, the work of this loose-knit cluster of New York
artists was vigorously championed by Michael Fried, Rose and others
identified with *Artforum*, a highly influential if internally fractious cabal at
the very centre of the centre. Ironically, their contestatory theoretical
rhetoric rendered them impervious to almost all work created outside
their immediate backyard.[10]

The inclusion of numerous drawings and working studies in Riley's
second Feigen show the following year revealed the painstakingly
wrought basis of her practice, and its foundations in traditional methods
and preparatory techniques. Whether consciously or not, their presence

countered the false accusations levelled the year before that she
adopted or borrowed wholesale scientific diagrams, optical experiments
and the like. In her perceptive review of these works, Rosalind Krauss
incisively analysed a final study for *Arrest* (1965). Yet she concluded by
categorising Riley's whole endeavour as 'timidly pleasant', as mired in
safe taste, a judgement wildly at variance with the responses accorded
Riley's art in her homeland from both the professional and the popular
sectors of the art world.[11] Whereas to her London-based apologists her
work bore the strong imprint of postwar American art in its ambition,
radical abstraction, flatness and all-over composition, their Yankee
counterparts generally dismissed it as outside the bounds of the
permissible, the (narrowly) viable.

In 1968, in her third exhibition with Feigen, Riley presented four
paintings plus sundry drawings and prints. This particular selection
included one older work, alongside three new ones, all on a more
monumental scale than those she had previously shown in Manhattan:
two paintings from the Static series, *Exposure* (1966) and *Ascending and
Descending Hero* (1963–65). The bold but relatively straightforward
compositions of these latter two paintings contrast with the expansive
but elusive, subdued and subtle compositions of *Static 1* (1966) and
Static 2 (1966). Compared, however, with the powerful, pulsating
vortices that characterise the modestly sized works of 1963–64, the four
canvases taken together signal a growing tendency to a fugitive, rippling
shallow optical space, proximate to the picture surface. Destabilised in
ways that almost elide perception, that verge on the imperceptible, they
(together with two works titled *Deny*, which immediately followed)
mark the culmination of a highly fertile period in Riley's career. In
addition, they reveal telling correspondences with certain works painted
in the United States of America at that moment: a related concern with
issues of perception – with seeing as an embodied act in time, that is,
involving time – informs the current work of Ad Reinhardt, Agnes Martin
and Robert Irwin (all of whom were included in *The Responsive Eye*).
Their works too employ a process of de-differentiation in a highly
conscious way as part of the act of looking. Recourse to dedifferentiation –
to a broad unfocused scanning as a component within the act of

Agnes Martin
Garden 1964
Synthetic polymer and coloured pencil on linen
183.2 × 183.2 cm | 72⅛ × 72⅛ in
Hirshhorn Museum and Sculpture Garden, Washington, DC

perceiving – in order to construct a holistic, all-over field contrasts fundamentally with the compositional strategy generally preferred by Louis, Noland and their cohorts; the use of a *gestalt* which coheres almost instantaneously.

The reasons that affinities between Riley's, Martin's, Irwin's and Reinhardt's work escaped contemporary notice may lie as much in the presumption that all these artists occupied positions on the periphery of the dominant discourse on painting at that moment – that is, on sectarianism – as in the insularity of local critics' perspectives.[12] At the heart of this indifference lay Riley's contravention of certain key tenets – notably the privileging of a disembodied viewer, the commitment to high-key colour as the principal means to structure and construct a shallow optical space, and an ineffable content apprehended as, 'a state of grace' – that characterised the abstract painting then heavily promoted in New York. Riley, as Thomas Crow perceived with the benefit of hindsight,

> had the temerity to exercise a certain control over the viewer's mental state, to trigger palpable physical experiences of heightened mental alertness: she meant the viewer's involuntary cognitive responses to recall sensations, in her words, of 'running… early morning… cold water… fresh things, slightly astringent'. For taking that reasonable measure of the powers of abstract painting, as well as for recognising the inherently physical, bodily character of optical perception, the[se] modernists could never forgive her.[13]

III

In a conversation published in 1965, British critics Andrew Forge and David Sylvester, recently returned from visits to the reigning art capital, sought to characterise the salient differences between the Manhattan and London scenes. 'The over-riding impression' Forge had gained from his trip 'was of the enormous variety and also the enormous compactness of the American [actually, New York] situation – the feeling one has that everybody knows about everybody else's painting and that there is a kind of running commentary going on within each work'.[14]

> This creates a very concentrated and electric ambience: the least inflection that an individual artist puts into it counts and has repercussions and echoes, which other people can pick up and use. There is a kind of critical activity which is going on hand in hand with the creative activity, a kind of questioning, a kind of standing aside from the involvement of art in order to criticise, to take up fresh attitudes and then to find a way of incorporating them in the work itself. So far from being an inhibition, as one can be sure many painters here would regard it, the criticism actually becomes creative material to be built in to the production of the artist.[15]

This seemed to him radically different from the situation facing the stereotypical English artist: 'a solitary man of conscience working simply with what God gave him in his studio'. Agreeing that British artists' work usually evolved as a response to internal arguments in the absence of important external ones, Sylvester speculated that the malady was endemic to a provincial situation. In support of this claim he invoked an observation offered by Max Kozloff, an American contributor to *Artforum* who was also familiar with the contemporary British context, that the centre was never outward – but always inward-looking, that 'an inspired hermeticism… is a contingency of advanced art'.[16]

Optimistically, all three commentators anticipated a significant change in the British situation. For, unlike their predecessors, Patrick Heron, William Scott, Francis Bacon *et al.*, (who had initially looked to Paris), the newly emerging sixties generation had encountered the groundbreaking work of the Abstract Expressionists at a formative moment: consequently they were, 'able to assess its quality not as a novelty, but simply as part of their experience of learning what painting consisted of': unlike the previous generation, they had 'a much more integrated attitude towards the great stylistic changes that American painting brought about'.[17] Yet, in contrast to their American counterparts, for whom those titanic father figures were still unavoidably present, these young British artists had a broader pool to draw from: they needed to consider not only the immediate past; they could adopt a longer, historical perspective. Thus the trio of critics concluded that this promising context would produce artists who were acquisitive and canny, learned yet open, where their predecessors had too often been restrained, amateurish, fastidious, timorous and well-bred – in short, bland.

Like many of this generation, Riley had attended the Royal College of Art, London, in the early 1950s though, compared with the rigorous training in draughtsmanship she had received as an undergraduate at Goldsmiths, she found the experience disappointing.[18] In the late fifties she too responded strongly to the onslaught of abstract-expressionist painting, and in particular to the work of Pollock then being shown for the first time in Britain.[19] Her US debut also coincided with that of others of her immediate circle. Following the equivocal (mis)reading of her work in the mid-1960s, however, she adopted a path that distanced her further from contemporary American developments whereas they generally did not. At the same time, the London art world in the later sixties failed to realise the creative potential that Sylvester, Forge and Kozloff had envisaged: in place of the vital, generative, critical environment they anticipated, it remained eclectic, conciliatory and dispersed: a provincial New York outpost. Largely self-fashioned, Riley's hard-won aesthetic not only increasingly divorced her from the American vanguard establishment, it also isolated her in London. Her abiding conviction, stemming back to her early training, of the necessity of always focusing on 'the best' meant that she remained as engaged with the great pioneers of modernism as with any of its subsequent avatars.[20] Estranging her inevitably from her immediate fellows and from topical and local issues, this belief also alienated her from the whole Greenbergian derived mindset concentrated on so-called 'advanced art'. In pursuit of what she called, 'the real problems of paintings' embodied in a long and continuous pictorial tradition stemming from the Renaissance, she did not, however, repudiate her self-consciously modernist position.[21] That this relative and largely self-imposed isolation has not mired her in her studio, working simply with what God gave her, to adopt Forge's formulation, is evident from the enthusiasm with which

she travels to see exhibitions of her mentors, and the closeness with
which she has scrutinised the art of, first, Jasper Johns, and more
recently, Bruce Nauman and Richard Serra among her contemporaries.[22]

IV

In 1960, Riley felt the necessity of renouncing colour in favour of black
and white as she tried to absorb the lessons of the new American art,
and of Pollock's work in particular. Colour seemed inherently wayward,
impossible to discipline, and hence, like the trace of the author's hand,
an impediment to clarity and simplification, to the principal means for
conveying visual sensations. She did not, however, give up on colour
altogether but in the following years made a number of attempts – albeit
futile – to incorporate it into her practice. Unable to create colour-form
as distinct from what she regarded as merely coloured forms,[23] she only
gradually integrated it in the later sixties through the vehicle of tonal
greys, that is, of greys ranging from the warmer and cooler ends of the
spectrum as found in *Deny 1* (1966) and *Deny 2* (1967). Beginning with
Late Morning (1967–68) and culminating in *Pæan* (1973), she finally
resolved the problem by restricting her palette mostly to intense, highly
saturated reds, blues and greens. Weaving this triad together in narrow
bands, interspersed with white, created a vivid light, a flickering surface
play equivalent to what she had formerly achieved in her signature black-
and-white works, such as *Blaze 1* (1962). As Riley confronted the problem
of creating an optical space with high-keyed colour she had recourse
once again to Seurat, a choice that further removed her from her
American peers for whom the art of Matisse was the prerequisite point of
departure for any engagement with colour. Luminous breathing colour –
the sensation of light suffused from within – that was a hallmark of
Matisse's work for artists in the sixties depended on the sensitivity of his
touch, on his nuanced handling. These were means that Riley had long
renounced. If Matisse therefore seemed to offer her few options at that
time, this impression may have been enhanced by the almost dogmatic
fervour with which his art was then embraced by American painters.[24]

Several factors therefore must have predisposed Riley to revisit her former mentor whom she considers an abstractionist *avant la lettre*: working with pure colour in carefully controlled and studied relations Seurat had created an extraordinary range of luminous effects. Moreover, while he explored a scientific basis in his study of chromatic relations, this was never at the expense of an intuitive study of its emotional and expressive qualities. In this, he also drew on lore long known to the greatest colourists from Titian and Veronese through to Delacroix. While curious about the quasi-scientific analyses pursued by Seurat and others in the late nineteenth century, Riley, too, quickly recognised that colour ultimately has no systematic, knowable foundation but can only be handled by means of experience, intensive analysis and patient research.[25] By deliberately constraining and scrupulously controlling her chromatic options, restricting her composition to slender vertical stripes and adopting a larger format, Riley created in *Pæan* (and its siblings) a painting that initially was encountered as a single holistic entity: a horizontal movement of light in counterpoint to a vertical field of brilliant stripes in pure hues. Since its parts would only reveal themselves on extended viewing, the pleasures of sight could be exercised in the extraordinarily fresh, luminous diffusion parsed across a monumental surface that was as grand as any in postwar painting. Nonetheless, a straight line can still be drawn connecting *Pink Landscape*, *Static* 2 and *Pæan*, a line whose fundament is the work of Seurat.

During the mid-1970s, as witnessed by *Song of Orpheus 1* (1975) and *Andante 1* (1978), Riley interwove into complex skeins serpentine ribbons drawn from a nuanced palette ranging from pinks and yellows to lavenders. Colour-form, as she had now come to understand it, had dual roots in modernism: one strand, originating in Impressionism and Claude Monet above all, then developed by Seurat, created an optical space from scintillating hues; the second, stemming from Paul Cézanne, produced a more plastic space. To this latter she turned in the early 1980s in what was to become known as her Egyptian series.

As colour continued to occupy the forefront of her formal concerns, drawing, her first love, was relegated to a subordinate position. In pursuit of the maximum chromatic luminosity, Riley had turned to stripes, which, having very little body (in that they are mostly 'edges'), intensify the interaction between colours that share their extended borders.[26] Only in the later eighties, when she began producing the series of rhomboid paintings, also known in studio parlance as zigs, did drawing take on a more active role. In the guise of a tightly knit armature, it permitted the introduction of an unprecedented range of hues, structured and combined in highly complex ways which draw the eye around and through the picture space. Composed from up to 20 different hues these works bear affinities structurally to Divisionism (and Futurism) filtered through Mondrian. Her quest for an intense chromatic interplay that draws the eye around, across, back and forth along multiple divergent axes in a dynamic vivacious sparkle, was not, however, resolved by a study of neo-Impressionism any more than it resided fully in probing Cézanne's methods. As intimated in Dave Hickey's moniker for these works, 'Bridget's Veroneses', its roots lie much deeper in traditions that form the core of Western painting.[27] Fostered by her seven-year stint as a trustee at the National Gallery in London from 1981 through 1988, Riley examined these traditions closely. In 1989 when planning her contribution to *The Artist's Eye* series (in which an artist, serving as curator, chose works from the National Gallery's collection), she initially proposed to focus her exhibition on the theme of perception in relation to nature: this would have involved a selection of mostly landscape paintings by Cézanne, Monet, Seurat and their peers. Ultimately, she opted to examine the colourists' lineage in figure painting: her final constellation stretched from Titian, through Veronese, El Greco, Rubens and Poussin, and ended with Cézanne, represented by an image of bathers conjured in his imagination rather than by studies made after nature, *sur le motif*.[28]

In pursuing this line in her own work as well as in her exhibition, Riley did not in fact depart from the model offered by Cézanne and his generation of modernists, who argued that their home was in the museums as much as in nature. Yet in her persistently 'long' vision across the spectrum of modernist endeavour and into the deeper reaches of the past, she again parts company with her American peers, Johns, Marden, Martin and Ryman, among others, who appear to have a

shorter memory span in that they are inescapably burdened with the
challenge of digesting the ever-present legacy of Pollock, Newman and
their associates. Even those American painters, ranging from Milton Avery
through Ellsworth Kelly, who sought salvation directly from Matisse,
found few avenues which permitted them to shake off the constraining
commitment to a declaratively 'advanced' form of art.[29]

V

Since her course had been determined primarily by internal imperatives,
reinforced by a particular set of circumstances (and possibly also by an
instinctive recoiling from the long shadow cast by Matisse on those of
her New York-based peers who counted themselves his heirs), Riley
entered her fourth decade, in 1990, as a painter having never addressed
in any significant way the legacy of the twentieth century's greatest
colourist. By the end of that decade she found to her surprise that while
she had not deliberately sought him out, she had 'arrived at Matisse.'[30]
This belated and most singular of Riley's dialogues with one of the
founding figures of modernism is still in a highly active state, so it is too
early to draw clear conclusions from the encounter. But on the evidence
to date, it may prove to have generated one of the most thoroughgoing
transformations in her oeuvre.

As would have been evident to Riley, who is her own best critic, as to
anyone else closely following her evolution over the past four decades,
her characteristic tendency is always to move forward by looking back.
Given an overriding commitment to clarity and simplicity, which she
shares with Matisse, whenever her work appears to be threatened by
refinement, by an intricate complexity, she has pulled up short and
sought a new direction: 'As Matisse knew', she commented in 1990, 'to
preserve a freshness in working one sometimes has to go back to first
principles'.[31] Thus, for example, in the late seventies the Song of Orpheus
paintings were followed by the grander and graver Egyptian series. By
the mid-1990s she had reached a related impasse with the lozenge
paintings. Resolution came unexpectedly through a commission for a

large wall drawing for a group show in Berne in 1998. Wrestling with lessons learnt there she eventually introduced series of interlocking arabesques into the zigs. Coupled with a radical pruning of her palette in the interest of clarity and simplicity, these rhythmic arabesques brought her (back) to Matisse. Completed in 1999, *Rêve* is the first painting in this, her latest body of work. Evoking the dream-like arcadian world beloved of Matisse, its apt title also recalls, perhaps fortuitously, the villa in Vence, 'La Rêve', where Matisse spent the years 1941–48, the years in which his last great phase, the *papiers découpés*, emerged along with that remarkable *gesamtkunstwerk*, the chapel of the Rosary.[32]

The ground for this encounter had been well prepared: Riley was no stranger to Matisse's art. In 1959–60 she visited the chapel in Vence for the first of many times. Today she still vividly recalls the impact that the row of narrow windows with their symmetrically composed leaves in blue, yellow and green made on her. As they cast pools of brilliant colour on the white floor they simultaneously created an ambience of magenta light – an effect that the delighted Matisse also had not anticipated. In 1977 she made a special trip to Detroit to see the landmark exhibition of *papiers découpés* presented at the Detroit Institute for the Arts. And in the winter of 1993–94 she travelled to Paris to see the newly (re-)discovered third of the three cartoons Matisse executed for the Barnes Mural, when it was shown together with the other two versions. Earlier that year she had spent an extended period in New York in order to study closely the Matisse retrospective at the Museum of Modern Art. Most recently, in 2000, enthralled by the prospect of comparing the twin colossi of the twentieth century, she saw the Matisse/Picasso exhibition in two of its three incarnations: in London and New York. Contrary to current wisdom, she concluded that Picasso was the artist with more charm, that Matisse was the 'tougher' of the two.[33]

While Riley had obviously encountered a vast number of Matisse's works elsewhere, on other occasions, it is telling that this singular history of concentrated interactions begins with his late works, with the Vence chapel and the great decorative schemes. In such works as *The Swimming Pool* (1952), *The Snail* (1953) and *Mimosa* (1949–51), with their layered fields of limpid warm and cool hues, Matisse carved directly into pure unmodulated colour in order to synthesise line and colour, and to find a new potential for structural decoration. To date Riley has commented only briefly on Matisse's work, in a short text devoted to *Dance 2* (1909–10), now, with its companion *Music* (1910), in the Hermitage in St Petersburg. In the rare level of abstraction – thematic as much as formal – that is a hallmark of this pair of exceptional works, lie the seeds of his final phase. While drawn to their brilliant effects of luminous colour, Riley emphasises the crucial role played by the rhythmic linear armature in conjuring the subject:

> [H]e settles the colour on a bold contrast and harmony principle… and concentrates his efforts on pulling out the huge curves and diagonals which play with and against each other around the canvas. Arms and legs, whole bodies even, are lengthened and shortened as the development of the rhythm demands… The group, subject to the overall organisation of colour and rhythm and entranced by the act of dancing, lose their separate identities and become one pictorial form, one organic unit… In literal terms the subject may be one man and four women dancing, but the content as it emerges is the plastic expression of the spirit of the dance, movement represented as a visual rhythm in which interchange acts as a constant.[34]

It is this aspect, above all, that links these works most closely to two of the most ambitious works in the recent series: *Parade* (1999) and *Evoë* (2000). Imbued with intimations of a resonant figural scale, they evoked 'bacchanals without the revellers'.[35] Yet it is elsewhere, in works such as *June 12 Bassacs* (1998) and *Apricot and Pink* (2001), that something even more unexpected begins to emerge: a way of synthesising drawing with colour to more decorative, expressive ends. For they foretell a novel way of structuring in which radiant irregular shapes, unmoored from the taut rectilinear scaffolding still implicitly undergirding the field, appear almost to float. Gently tethered by their contours to elements in a second dominant hue, these liberated shapes of limpid colour generate an ebullient radiant energy and sensuous

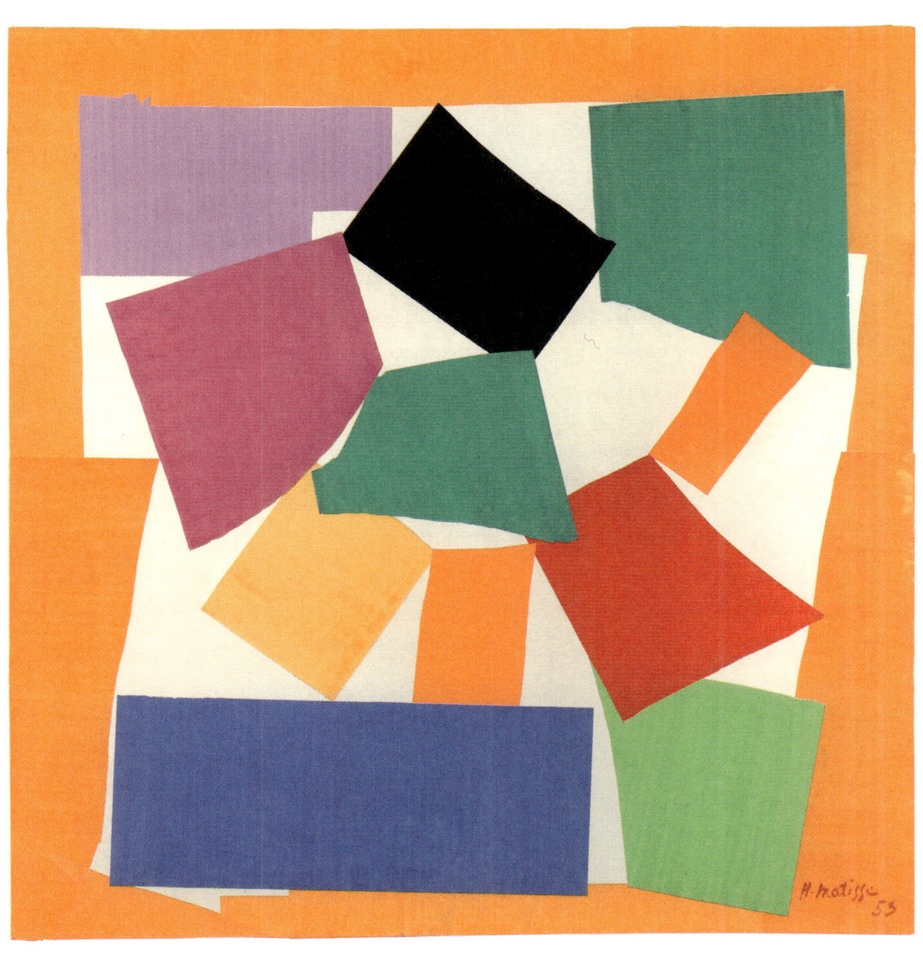

Henri Matisse
The Snail 1953
Gouache on paper, cut and pasted on paper mounted on canvas
286.4 × 287 cm | 112¾ × 113 in
Tate, London
© Succession H. Matisse/DACS 2016

immediacy. In subsequent works such as *Two Reds* (2000) and *Enchant* (2004), no single colour-form reads as figure to another seen as ground, that is, none becomes fixed as a positive in relation to its neighbour read as negative. Rather, they fluctuate in a reciprocal movement that keeps both active at once, a contrapuntal movement that recalls the equivalency binding black and white in many early works, such as *Descending* (1965). More pertinently, it also recalls certain ways of drawing a motif that Matisse developed in later life. Maurice Merleau-Ponty, whose writing on the embodied viewer was a seminal influence on Riley's thinking from her earliest days, eloquently conjures this effect: 'It is Matisse who taught us to see their contours not in a "physical-optical way" but rather as structural filaments, as the axes of a corporeal system of activity and passivity.'[36]

Nonetheless, the biggest shifts to date – an engagement with a Matissean sense of the decorative – originate in some of Riley's more modestly scaled works on paper. In several of her most adventurous recent studies with a more vertical orientation, such as *July 9, Bassacs* (1998), or *November 1, Magenta and Green* (1998), singular, almost idiosyncratic shapes – flame-like forms in two contrasting hues of equal value – flicker over the surface in dynamic play, a flux of rivalrous solicitations. Despite the restriction to two or three basic colours, their expansive mood opens new options, reminiscent of the decorative as Matisse employed this multivalent concept.[37] Over the course of his life, albeit with shifting inflections, he employed it to encompass a nexus of interrelated notions: the investing of pattern with spatial properties, a fealty to the totality of the painted surface, and later, an all-over chromatic field that radiated light. In their repetition of related but slightly different elements, and their playful effervescent delight in reversals and ambiguities, these works bear affinities in their disjunctive patterned interlaying of close valued colour with, say, *Mimosa*, while in their corporeal interchange they echo the reversals in *Swimming Pool* where some of the swimmers' bodies are rendered in white and others in blue. As seen in *Painting with Two Verticals* (2004), Riley is just starting to venture into this arena with large-scale oils. A monumental tripartite composition, *Painting with Two Verticals* imbricates shape with armature

LYNNE COOKE

so that the blue forms are momentarily identified as ground, then
chameleon-like, and almost simultaneously, they assume the guise of an
active integer, a figure – or vice versa. In this finely calibrated flux, a
fugitive stability, anchoring and ordering, temporarily supervenes within a
larger dialectic, a lateral weighing and balancing poised on the central
section, a 'panel' whose borders are determined by the eponymous two
verticals. Earlier this year, Riley made a trip to the Alhambra, the acme of
Islamic ornamental sophistication. It is surely not irrelevant that Islamic
art was for Matisse a lifelong and primary source of inspiration, above all
for its colouristic richness and strong decorative appeal.[38] Taken in
conjunction with certain of her subsequent works notably *Painting with
Two Verticals*, this visit attests to a deepening fascination with questions
of how colour-form not only creates space but how painting and
decoration may interact in architectonic terms.

VI

In an illuminating recent study, Richard Shiff links Riley to Matisse
through what he sees as a shared preoccupation with paradise, with an
arcadian world enclosed and set apart temporally as well as spatially.[39]
For both artists, he argues, this Edenic milieu is conjured through
sensation, that is, it is generated by the very means of painting itself as
much as by any particular subject or thematic. While throwing much new
light on Riley's vision and conception of what a painting could and
should be, his essay does not situate Matisse relative to the other key
figures within Riley's pantheon: Seurat, Cézanne, Klee, Mondrian and
Pollock. Nor, given the fundamental accord he believes has aligned their
visions from her earliest days, does he indicate why Riley might formally
have arrived at Matisse's art so late in her career. It may not be irrelevant
to her formation that Seurat and Cézanne, who first occupied her so
deeply, should be well represented in public collections in London
whereas Matisse is not. Prior to any sustained engagement with art were
the transforming experiences she had as a child in Cornwall during the
Second World War, where, stimulated by the natural world around her,

she developed an avid and acute taste for visual perceptions. She honed an acute responsiveness to natural phenomena and sensory impressions. Thus she did not come to art through art: only through pleasure in perception was she eventually drawn to Impressionism, and from there to the idea of becoming an artist herself. Given this background, Riley was almost inevitably predisposed towards the art of Seurat and Cézanne, a bias that the cultural context itself reinforced.

Although Riley has returned periodically to Cornwall where she has a studio, this is not her sole escape from her London home and the daily business of her practice, which involves working with various assistants. If she continues to find in Cornwall a rich vein of nourishment, at least as important to her in recent years is the residence she acquired in the south of France in the early sixties. In 1962 Riley purchased a property in Vaucluse where she could live and, later, work in seclusion. Although it was not until the seventies that she actually set up a studio there where she can work undisturbed for long stretches of time, her allegiance to this Mediterranean milieu is deep and profound. Long an unparalleled fount of European culture, its memorable terrain is thoroughly imbued with the spirit of not only Cézanne but Matisse (and Van Gogh – but that is another story). Although to her an adopted world, this seedbed of modernist painting has become the repository for her deepest cultural roots. Occupying a seminal role in her imaginary, it is symptomatic of the profound difference that still separates her from American peers for whom (Cy Twombly apart) Europe is ultimately the old (world) rather than a site of continuous cultural renewal. In Matisse's case the past remained an active force in his experience rather than an attenuating one, Pierre Schneider argues in his great monographic study, a book Riley admires.[40] One of the key insights informing Schneider's analysis, this notion can be applied with equal validity to Riley's practice: for her too, the past is vigorously alive, an ever-present point of departure.

Bridget Riley: Paintings and Drawings 1961–2004, exhibition catalogue, Ridinghouse, London, 2005, pp.101–12.

LYNNE COOKE

1   Bridget Riley, 'Interview with David Sylvester' (1967), in Robert Kudielka (ed), *The Eye's Mind: Bridget Riley, Collected Writings 1965–1999*, Thames & Hudson, London, 1999, p.76.

2   For a close account of the impact of these two artists on her work and thought, see John Elderfield, 'The Change of Aspect' and Lynne Cooke, 'Around and About *Composition with Circles 2*', in Lynne Cooke and Karen Kelly (eds), *Bridget Riley: Reconnaissance*, exhibition catalogue, Dia Center for the Arts, New York, NY, 2001. Riley has referred repeatedly to this connection, i.e. 'In Conversation with Maurice de Sausmarez (1967), 'According to Sensation: In Conversation with Robert Kudielka' (1990) and 'Mondrian: The "Universal" and the "Particular"' (1995), all of these were reproduced in Kudielka (ed), *ibid.* In several other paintings from 1961 containing what she refers to as 'buried forms', such as *Tremor*, or *Hidden Squares*, where images are imbedded in a larger field. Critical to the maturation of Riley's work in 1960–61 was her close association with Harry Thubron, Maurice de Sausmarez and others who were then devising a foundation course based in a Bauhaus return to first principles, and in the practice of Paul Klee, as set forth in his seminal texts, 'The Thinking Eye' and 'Pedagogical Sketchbook'. Solidly grounded in the rudiments of drawing from her earliest days as a student at Goldsmiths, 1949–52, Riley seems to have imbibed from that much valued training a conviction that she should know her means, as both a craft and a tradition to be embraced. Tradition in this sense was understood not as a predetermined or fixed canon but something to be constructed by each individual artist as needed from a study of the best. At this time she also became convinced, via the writings of Igor Stravinsky, that constraint and self-imposed limits were an essential part of the learning process.

3   Bridget Riley, 'The Artist's Eye: Seurat' (1992), in Kudielka (ed), *op.cit.*, p.175.

4   Anton Ehrenzweig, 'The Pictorial Space of Bridget Riley', *Art International*, February 1965, p.21.

5   For a study of these sweeping historical, social and cultural changes see Christopher Booker, *The Neophiliacs*, Gambit, Boston, MA, 1970, especially chapters 1 and 2: 'Portrait of an Image', 'Awakening toward a Dream'.

6   The principal show defining this group was *The New Generation*, held at the Whitechapel Art Gallery, London, in 1964, under the directorship of Bryan Robertson. Note also *Painting and Sculpture of a Decade, 1954–64*, Tate Gallery, London, 1964; and *Contemporary British Painting and Sculpture*, Albright-Knox Art Gallery, Buffalo, NY, 1964–65, which then toured through the United States of America.

7   For a fuller analysis see Lisa G Corrin, 'Continuum: Bridget Riley's 60s and 70s: A View from the 90s', in Lisa G corrin (ed), *Bridget Riley: Paintings from the 1960s and 70s*, Serpentine Gallery and Koenig Books, London, 1999, pp.35–43.

8   Though a frequent contributor to *Artforum*, Tillim published this review in *Arts Magazine*, a more eclectic forum: 'Optical Art: Pending or Ending?', *Arts Magazine*, January 1965, pp.16–23. It was not only American commentators who made this link. See, for example, Norbert Lynton, 'Optical Art', *New Statesman*, 29 May 1964, pp.853–54.

9   Barbara Rose, 'Beyond Vertigo: Optical Art at the Modern', *Artforum*, April 1965, pp.30–33. Rosalind Krauss's review of the exhibition was in fact published in *Art International*; 'Afterthoughts on "Op"', *Art International*, June 1965, pp.75–76. Very different in tone, spirit and evaluation were the encomia, more journalistic than academic: John Canaday, 'The Responsive Eye. Three Cheers and High Hopes', *New York Times*, 28 February 1965; 'That's Right It's Wrong', *New York Times*, 14 March 1965.

10   The exception was British sculptor Anthony Caro whose work was championed by Michael Fried and others in the early sixties. While he, together with several British

sculptors such as Philip King, was featured in the landmark *Primary Structures* exhibition held at the Jewish Museum in New York in 1966, he was soon eclipsed by the rising Minimalists, who quickly dominated critical discourse.

11   Rosalind Krauss, 'Bridget Riley', *Artforum*, June 1966, p.50. See also Kermit Champa, 'Recent British Painting at the Tate', *Artforum*, March 1968, pp.33–37, for a similar assessment.

12   A study of the relations between these and other abstract painters then closely engaged with issues of perception, and the fertile conceptual ground on which this was premised remains to be undertaken. Relevant to all these artists' work is *The Hidden Order of Art* (published posthumously in 1967) and other writings by Anton Ehrenzweig, Riley's friend and early supporter.

13   Thomas Crow, *The Rise of the Sixties: American and European Art in the Era of Dissent*, Abrams, New York, NY, 1996, p.113. A British art historian now living and working in the US, Crow's study of the decade offers a fresh, independent account, at odds with more canonical texts written from a New York perspective.

14   'A Kind of Anarchy: A Conversation between Andrew Forge and David Sylvester', *Encounter*, vol.23, 1964, pp.44–48. Forge and Sylvester were, arguably, the most incisive and best-informed British critics of the day.

15   *Ibid.*

16   *Ibid.*

17   Max Kozloff, 'British Painting Today', *Encounter*, January 1964, pp.39–42.

18   Bridget Riley, 'Student at the Royal College of Art' (1988), in Kudielka (ed), *op.cit.*, p.35.

19   Two shows in particular were critical in bringing Pollock's work to her attention *Modern Art in the United States*, Tate Gallery, London, 1956, followed by a retrospective of his painting at the Whitechapel Art Gallery, London, in 1958.

20   See Riley 'Personal Interview by Nikki Henriques' (1988), in Kudielka (ed), *op.cit.*, p.28.

21   Quoted in Riley, 'According to Sensation: In Conversation with Robert Kudielka', *ibid.*, p.116.

22   See, for example, her essay, 'Nauman's Formalism' (1999), *ibid.*, pp.212–16.

23   Bridget Riley, 'Bridget Riley in Conversation with Robert Kudielka' (1972), *ibid.*, p.82.

24   See, for example, Clement Greenberg, 'Influence of Matisse', exhibition catalogue, Acquavella Galleries, New York, NY, 1973, n.p.; Stephanie Barron, 'Matisse and Contemporary Art', *Arts Magazine*, May 1975, pp.67–68; Gunda Luyken, '"Painting alone remains full of adventure": Matisse's Cut-Outs as an Inspiration for Nicholas de Stael, Ellsworth Kelly and Andy Warhol', in *Henri Matisse: Drawing with Scissors. Masterpieces from the Late Years*, Prestel, New York, NY, 2002, pp.151–59; for a more in-depth study see John O'Brian, *Ruthless Hedonism: The American Reception of Matisse*, University of Chicago Press, Chicago, IL, 1999.

25   Bridget Riley, 'Perception and the Use of Colour: Talking to EH Gombrich' (1992), in Robert Kudielka (ed), *Bridget Riley: Dialogues on Art*, Zwemmer, London, pp.33–49.

26   Bridget Riley, 'Into Colour: In Conversation with Robert Kudielka' (1978), in Kudielka (ed), *The Eye's Mind, op.cit.*, p.92.

27   Dave Hickey, 'Bridget Riley for Americans', in *Bridget Riley: Paintings 1982–2000 and Early Works on Paper*, exhibition catalogue, PaceWildenstein, New York, NY, 2000, p.7.

28   *The Artist's Eye: Bridget Riley*, exhibition catalogue, National Gallery, London, 1989. See also Bridget Riley, 'The Art of the Past: Interview with Neil MacGregor' (1992), in Kudielka (ed), *Bridget Riley: Dialogues on Art, op.cit.*, 1995, pp.16–32.

29   Conversely, through the Museum of Modern Art, New York and Alfred Barr, American artists had unrivalled access to Matisse's art in the 1950s, 60s and 70s. In conjunction

with a retrospective in 1951 Barr published a book, *Matisse, His Art and His Public*, that is among the finest monographs on any twentieth-century artist; and the holdings of Matisse's work in MoMA's collection are also exceptionally rich.

30 Quoted in Lynn MacRitchie, 'The Intelligence of the Eye', in Martin Hentschel (ed) *Bridget Riley: New Work*, exhibition catalogue, Kunstmuseen Krefeld, Krefeld and Hatje Cantz Verlag, Ostfildern, 2002, p.19.

31 Bridget Riley, 'According to Sensation: In Conversation with Robert Kudielka' (1990), in Kudielka (ed), *The Eye's Mind, op.cit.*

32 Numerous other parallels can be drawn, such as the fact that each has a black-and-white drawing style quite different from their concurrent work in colour; compare Vence Chapel, with Riley's wall drawings and oils.

33 Personal communication with the author, 6 September 2004.

34 Bridget Riley, 'Henri Matisse: The Dance', unpublished text, September 1990. An abbreviated version of this text was published in *The Telegraph Magazine*, 27 October 1990. Yet her interest in composing for such a frieze-like format goes back some years, see, for instance, her comments to Neil McGregor on Mantegna's frieze, *The Introduction of the Cult of Cybele at Rome* (1504–05), in the collection of the National Gallery, London. Bridget Riley, 'The Art of the Past: Interview with Neil McGregor', in Kudielka (ed), *The Eye's Mind, op.cit.*, p.23.

35 *Bacchanal without Nymphs* was a first proposal for *Evöe*, and *Bacchanal without Satyrs* for another untitled painting. Quoted in Robert Kudielka, 'Abstract Figuration: On Bridget Riley's Recent Curve Paintings', in Paul Moorehouse (ed), *Bridget Riley*, exhibition catalogue, Tate Publishing, London, 2003, p.155.

36 Maurice Merleau-Ponty, 'Eye and Mind', in *The Primacy of Perception*, James M Edie (ed), Northwestern University Press, Evanston, IL,1964, p.184.

37 Some measure of the distance her thinking has moved in recent years may be gauged by comparison with these comments from an interview in 1978: 'Form and colour seem to be fundamentally incompatible – they destroy each other', Riley argued. 'In my earlier work when I was developing complex forms, the energies of the medium could only be fully realised by simplifying colour to a black-and-white constant (with occasional grey sequences). Conversely, colour energies need a virtually neutral vehicle if they are to develop uninhibitedly. The repeated stripe seems to meet these conditions'. (Quoted in Lynne Cooke and Karen Kelly (eds), *Bridget Riley: Reconnaissance*, Dia Center for the Arts, New York, 1999, n.p.) For Matisse's relation to Islamic art, see John Golding, 'Introduction', *Matisse Picasso*, exhibition catalogue, Tate Publishing, London, 2002, pp.15–16.

38 For Riley, travelling, even for pleasure, is ultimately connected to her practice: 'The sort of holidays I take are part and parcel of my work as a painter', she stated in an interview in 1996. See Bridget Riley, 'Holidays: Talking to Vanya Kewley' (1994), in Kudielka (ed), *The Eye's Mind, op.cit.*, p.44.

39 Richard Shiff, 'Rasters in Paradise', in *Bridget Riley: Recent Paintings*, exhibition catalogue, PaceWildenstein, New York, NY, 2004, pp.5–19.

40 Pierre Schneider, *Henri Matisse*, Rizzoli, New York, NY, 1984.

New Cadences: Paintings by Bridget Riley, 2004–07
Marla Prather

In his 1960 essay, 'On the Humanity of Abstract Painting', Meyer Schapiro
cogently argued in favour of a contemporary non-figurative art,
underscoring its vital relevance to modern life, its continuity with the
representational art that preceded it, and its capacity to elucidate older
art in new and significant ways. 'Looking back to the past,' he wrote, 'one
may regret that painting now is not broader and fails to touch enough in
our lives. The same may be said of representation, which, on the whole,
lags behind abstract art in inventiveness and conviction; today it is
abstract painting that stimulates artists to a freer approach to visible
nature and man. It has enlarged the means of the artist who represents
and has opened to him regions of feeling and perception unknown
before. Abstraction by its audacities also confirms and makes more
evident to us the most daring and still unassimilated discoveries of older
art.'[1] In the postwar era, abstraction has had no more ardent exponent or
dedicated practitioner than Bridget Riley. Schapiro's essay dates to the
beginning of Riley's career, just as she was creating the electrifying works
that, within half a decade, would establish her as a major figure of
international contemporary art. Through the example of her painting, a
significant body of writings and her occasional roles as teacher, curator,
museum trustee and, not insignificantly, inveterate traveller, Riley has
arguably spent nearly half a century endorsing Schapiro's conviction,
though she has championed painting of many genres and art across
many centuries. She advocates active, ongoing dialogues with the past as
a naturally sustaining practice for a modern artist. On the occasion of a
recent retrospective in Sydney, she observed: 'To give your work more
than a personal validity you need the support of a more objective
framework. Where can one find this if not in the past? I believe that it is
possible to rediscover principles and laws in older work quite
independently of the styles in which they initially appeared.'[2] For *The
Artist's Eye*, a 1989 exhibition she organised for London's National
Gallery, Riley assembled a group of seven large figure compositions from

the collection by Titian, Veronese, El Greco, Rubens, Poussin and Paul Cézanne. In a fascinating conversation about the project with scholar Robert Kudielka, a longtime friend and travelling companion who has written extensively on her work, the artist thoughtfully outlined the shared characteristics, ones based on building pictures in plastic terms, that drew her to the selected works.[3] Her lively descriptive language pulls the imagery of the past into our world while providing telling indications about formal elements in her own paintings. Whether highlighting the bold thrust of Titian's diagonals or the armature of Veronese's colour structure, one is struck by how her comments reverberate with concerns in her own work.

In addition to her eloquent commentaries on the Old Masters through numerous essays, lectures and interviews, or on the modern painters she considers pivotal to her formation as an artist – Claude Monet, Georges Seurat, Paul Klee, Piet Mondrian, Jackson Pollock – Riley is lucid and forthright as a spokesperson for her own enterprise: 'My work has grown out of my own experiences of looking, and also out of the work that I have seen in the museums and in galleries, so I have seen other artists seeing, and that has been an enormous help to me and a kind of pattern maker, in that it has shown me how a formal structure of looking is shaped and can shape in turn the way that one proceeds with one's own work.'[4] In 2006 Riley travelled to Washington, DC, specifically to see an exhibition at the National Gallery of Art, *Cézanne in Provence*, organised to mark the centenary of the artist's death. Riley does not look, learn and internalise exclusively for her own purposes, but often records and shares her insights. In her review of the show for *The Burlington Magazine*, she wrote with her customary erudition and a painter's inimitable sensibility. Her close reading of Cézanne's *House on a Hill, Provence* (1904–06) is noteworthy both for its acute powers of observation and for the ways in which it inevitably reveals her own artistic preoccupations:

> In *House on a Hill, Provence*, great movements in colour sweep
> across the canvas, generating intervals and incidents only as needed
> according to the integral rhythm of the whole. The speed at which

MARLA PRATHER

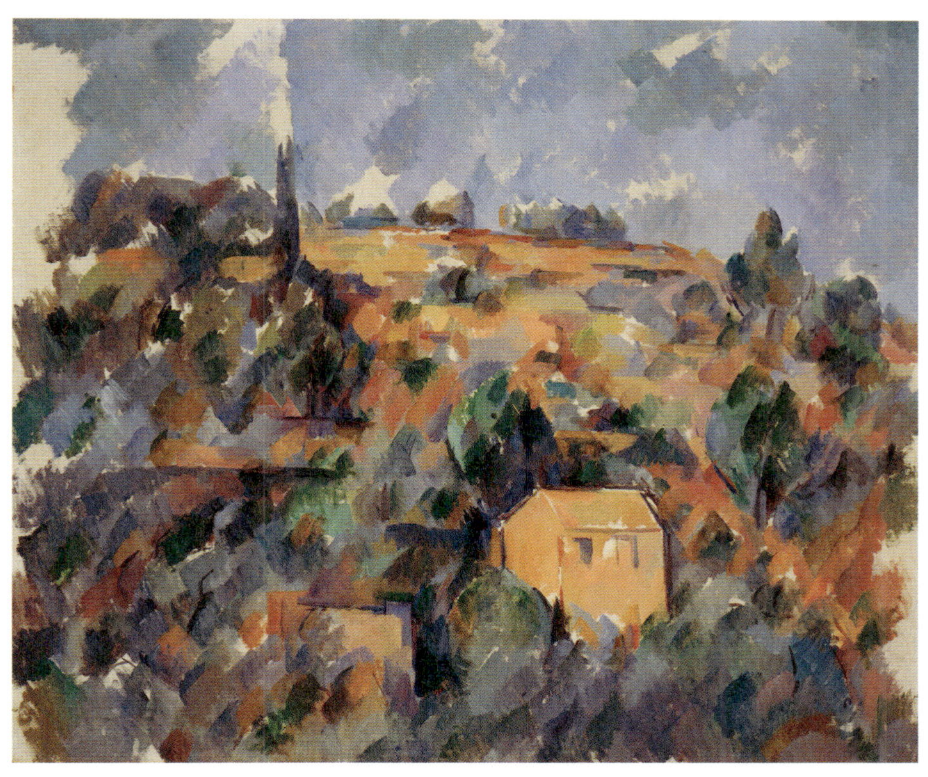

Paul Cézanne
House on a Hill, Provence 1904–06
Oil on canvas
65.7 × 81 cm | 25⅞ × 31⅞ in
White House Collection, Washington, DC

one's eye is taken through the repetitions, mirrorings and contrasts is
breathtaking. That very speed is then reversed, the eye drifts, falls in
slow arcs, settles and pauses. This musical sense of movement is
conducted by the planes of colour. Dull violets, brown-magenta, grey-
blues, dark reds, olives, spiked with turquoises and brighter reds, rise
and fall in successive formations. Sudden interjections of blocks of
ochre gather momentum and turn in a great arc toward the blues
of the sky.[5]

In *House on a Hill, Provence*, Cézanne vividly conveyed the foliage
rising up through the landscape by assembling his brushstrokes into
overlapping, semitransparent patches of colour that he aligned into
powerfully diagonal rhythms. The abstract patterns that result reduce
distinctions between solid and void, figure and ground, and set up
luminous colour vibrations across the surface. The issues Riley singles
out seem especially pertinent to her current work, with its emphasis on
rhythmically dispersed colour shapes, musical overtones and the
complex interplay of directional forces. It comes as little surprise that
Riley would feel a particular affinity for Cézanne's magisterial late
landscape. Not only has she spent considerable time in the south of
France, where she has maintained a studio for years, but, despite her
unwavering commitment to abstraction, she has searched like the
Frenchman to express in painterly terms deeply felt visual sensations in
the natural world.

Riley aims not for consistency but change, progress and renewal. In a
spirit of persistent enquiry, she develops work in phases, reconsidering
pictorial issues arising from previous work and proceeding intuitively to
address the inherent demands of the work under consideration.
Compositions are generated one from another in steadily evolving
investigations. 'Paintings breed',[6] she has said, and their genetic links are
provided by the elaborate preparatory works she undertakes for each
new painting. In this, her first show in New York since 2004, Riley
presents 12 paintings, most of which belong to a body of work she has
produced over the last decade. In these so-called curve paintings, her
largest works on canvas to date, Riley has gradually established a

                                                    MARLA PRATHER

personal repertoire of colours, shapes and compositional structures that
have become as closely identified with her unique aesthetic as the black-
and-white squares, lines and ovals of her paintings of the 1960s.

Devices recur; motifs are cast in new contexts. Curves in many guises
have intermittently appeared from the beginning of Riley's career,
whether boldly stated in her first black-and-white-painting, *Kiss* (1961),
implicitly suggested in geometric works such as *Straight Curve* (1963), as
vehicles for colour in the earliest colour paintings such as *Cataract*
(1967), or as the gently lyrical undulations of the curve series, with works
such as *Song of Orpheus 5* (1978).[7] But the curve wholly disappeared
from 1980 to the mid-1990s, when Riley made a series of paintings
based on vertical stripes followed by a large group of lozenge or so-
called zig paintings. The latter, begun in 1985, contain brilliantly coloured,
tilted rhomboids stacked vertically (zigs with no zags). When aligned, the
angled units create a forceful diagonal momentum that begins in the
lower left of the canvas and travels to the upper right, a compositional
mainstay of Riley's work ever since. The rhomboids are either identical in
size or enlarged and made to shift across the adjacent vertical register.
The multifaceted, interlocking shapes form sparkling, irregular lattices of
colour (of up to 20 hues) with multiple points of focus. The dizzying
kineticism of these works can unsettle the terrain beneath our feet in
ways that are reminiscent of the intense perceptual interactions
mandated by the work of the 1960s. Thrilling staccato rhythms build up,
as colour shapes ricochet off one another, causing the eye to dart about,
searching out the patterns that circulate through the composition. The zig
paintings developed from Riley's desire to elaborate her painting
structure after the restrained stripe paintings and provoke a more varied
visual encounter. 'I wanted to be able to go around a painting,' she has
explained, 'to take your eye upwards, downwards and diagonally across,
in all sorts of ways and rhythms that I could not manage with just the
vertical bands.'[8]

The artist locates a significant period of transition in her work in the
mid-1990s, after a decade of refining the zig paintings. 'I tried to give
fuller reign to the curves and arcs that had been filtering through the
colour organisation of my diagonal paintings.'[9] After many studies and

experiments, she reintroduced the curve in works such as *Lagoon 1*,
Lagoon 2 and *21st September, Bassacs, Study after Cartoon* (all from
1997). The curve does not recur as a continuous wave, but in the form of
segmented circles that are aligned vertically with elongated rhomboids.
In the study *21st September, Bassacs* (named for the French village
where Riley sometimes works), the convex sides of the sliced circles face
exclusively left, countering the force of the diagonal thrust. Although the
circles are occasionally truncated, they stand as themselves, only once
merging with neighbouring quadrilaterals to create new unclassifiable
forms (the white form on top to the left of centre). As the eye scans the
surface, the distinctive diagonal and vertical registers take turns
dominating our field of vision, fluctuating back and forth through the
space-creating capacities of Riley's colour. Shapes can suddenly appear
to pop forward, perpendicular to the picture plane, then flatten out again.
Riley eliminated black from the high-keyed palette of *21st September,
Bassacs*, where the bright candy-coloured pastels call to mind the soft,
opalescent palette of *Song of Orpheus 5* and other related paintings of
the late 1970s, though to obviously different effect.

As she endeavoured to integrate curvilinear forms into her new
paintings, Riley received a fortuitous invitation from the Kunsthalle Bern
to participate in its group show, *White Noise* (1998). Her contribution
was *Composition with Circles 1* (1998), a 30-foot-wide wall drawing
consisting of overlapping black circles, each a metre in diameter,
executed on a white wall with a compass. These elemental, transparent
forms intersect in controlled but not identical ways, projecting and
receding, rising and falling, producing visual oscillations across the entire
surface. The delightful effervescent sensation recalls similar effects in
early black-and-white paintings such as *Static 1* (1966). At the same time,
clearly established horizontal and vertical registers, however obscured,
ensure the stability and proportional integrity of the whole. The wall
drawing was a kind of lynchpin composition that continues to intrigue
the artist – to date she has composed four additional variations on the
original work in Bern.[10] New avenues opened in the wake of its
completion as Riley set about revising the organisation of the entire
picture plane to accommodate the newly reformulated curve.

                                                                                   MARLA PRATHER

In *Rêve* (1999), the artist's first fully realised curve painting, the palette has been narrowed to four colours (she habitually uses four or five hues in these works, preferring to compose with pairs or triads of colour). The multicoloured, segmented circles that populated *21st September, Bassacs* recur in *Rêve* only as a single green blade at the bottom left and the blue inward-facing circles sliced by each side of the canvas edge. The distinctive vertical divisions in the 1997 picture could not accommodate the larger, swelling forms and dynamic spatial flow of *Rêve*, where curving shapes gracefully segue into one another, creating new, amalgamated forms through the interplay of the diagonal and curvilinear orders.

Despite the shared palette that relates *Rêve* to *Painting with Two Verticals 3* (2005), much changed in the six years that separate the two canvases. The sinuous shapes that swing upward through *Rêve* are held in greater check by the slanting divisions that dramatically traverse the 2005 picture, whether they are explicitly set forth or merely sensed through the pervasive structural matrix. A new compositional device emerged in the vertical elements Riley began to introduce in 2004, present in *Painting with Two Verticals 3* as straight edges that, although they do not extend the full height of the canvas, suggest a tripartite division in the composition and run counter to the diagonal 'drive', as the artist has described the forces at play in her work. The shifting roles of figure and ground, positive and negative invite alternative readings. Shapes advance and recede. Do they interpenetrate or overlap? The yellow areas with one straight side may form a background that pushes forward the blue and green pointed ovals in the centre of the canvas, or they may function as three idiosyncratic shapes that come forward and dovetail with the curving, pointed forms they abut. Forms echo and respond to one another – the orange curving quadrilateral at the lower left is answered by its yellow counterpoint at the upper right. Such formal reciprocity lends the work a sense of proportion and balanced asymmetry.

The subjective possibilities of a gestural technique have never appealed to Riley, who does not paint the final canvases herself, but rather oversees a highly experienced studio staff. The surfaces of her paintings are immaculate, not to say mechanical or inert, and their internal contours are indicated with gratifying precision. This superlative execution and the absolute clarity of the imagery are among the many rewards for the viewer. These qualities depend on Riley's skill as an exacting technician who prepares each work with numerous drawings, often with copious notations, colour studies, collages, small gouaches and full-scale cartoons. It is during this stage, according to the artist, when the crucial decisions are made: 'I have to build up a bank of visual information, first – about colours, forms, proportions, directions, etc. This is the essential basis to my work.'[11] A single drawing may be the progenitor of several final works, though it inevitably mutates through many, carefully considered sequential changes. 'I never jump to conclusions,' she insists, 'I never presume to know.'[12] For the curve paintings, Riley developed curvilinear pencil grids on graph paper. As the curves multiply, and gouache is introduced in the so-called ground studies, the underlying scaffolding is partially submerged. The vertical divisions of the early studies give way to an overlay of curving colour forms and to the pronounced diagonal registers that lend the final curve paintings their unique structure and rhythm.[13]

For over 20 years Riley has also has used pieces of pre-cut and painted paper as an expedient and highly flexible approach to the compositional process. As she arranges the coloured shapes she can easily edit, efface and revise, with a kind of spontaneity that traditional draughtsmanship does not allow. Some ideas, she explains, 'go by the board, and when this happens I simply lose that particular instance and opportunity – yet others will arise in their stead. If this "placing" goes well the actual sensation becomes part of the formative fabric of the painting. But until the whole is brought together, everything is uncertain and subject to change.'[14] Although Riley does not regard the studies as definitive works of art, they are far more than supportive documents, with much visual interest of their own. She has often agreed to exhibit and illustrate them, allowing us to watch her mind at work and broadening our own appreciation for the intricate backstory of the final paintings. 'The studies aid accessibility,' she has said, 'I don't want there to be anything mysterious about the way that I work.'[15]

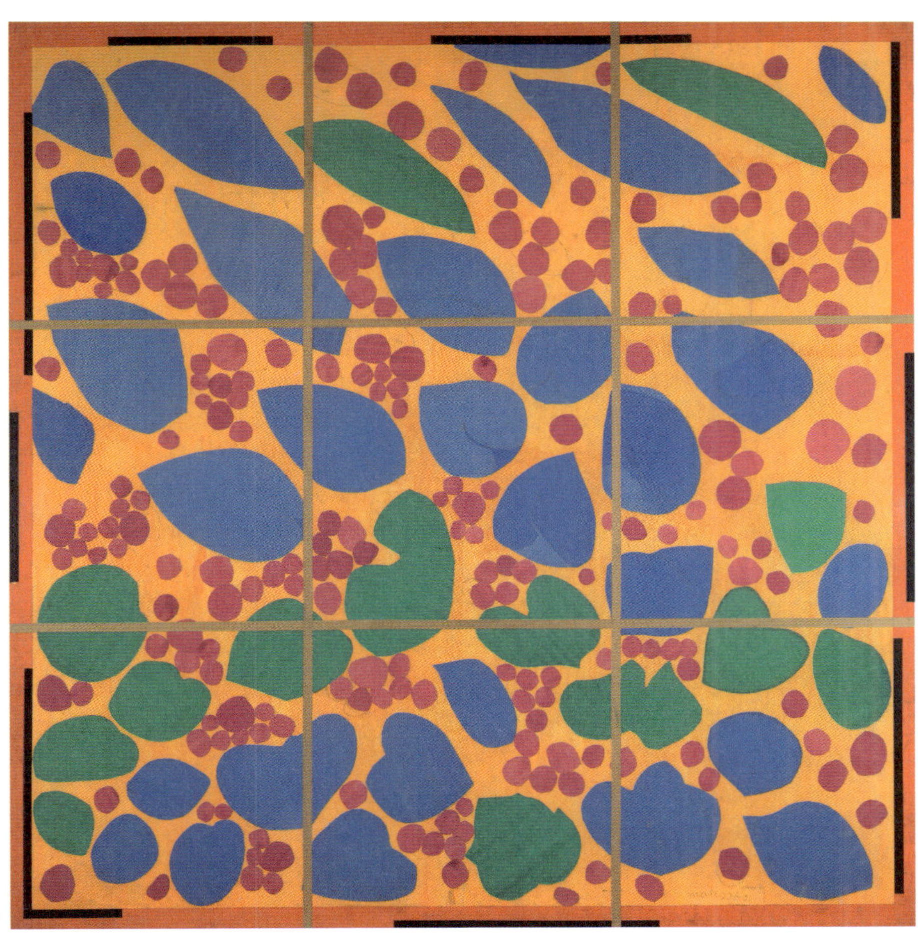

Henri Matisse
Ivy in Flower 1953
Coloured paper, watercolour, pencil and brown paper
284.5 × 284.5 cm | 112 × 112 in
Dallas Museum of Art
© Succession H. Matisse/DACS 2016

When Riley's friend the critic David Sylvester saw *Rêve*, he was
reminded of Henri Matisse. 'It isn't a bit like Matisse,' he told the artist,
'but I think it's an avenue that you would not pursue were it not for Matisse.
There seems to be more than one way out of Matisse.'[16] The artists'
mutual reliance upon the practice of composing with painted pieces of
paper is one of the many tempting reasons to think of their work
together. Although she has looked at Matisse's work seriously for years,
Riley has only recently developed for him the kind of deep admiration
she has held for other key modernists. She concurred with Sylvester but
has since clarified the nature of the connection: 'I didn't come from
Matisse, I arrived at Matisse, which was very surprising for me.'[17]

Like Riley, Matisse had used *gouache découpée* as a preparatory
technique; it was only in the last decade of his life, when infirmities kept
him mostly sedentary and indoors, that it became an end in itself.
Obviously Riley ultimately translates the paper forms into another
medium. Matisse, on the other hand, gave up the very substance of his
art to date – conventional drawing, gestural brushwork, the very *matière*
of his easel paintings in oil – for the radical new technique he called his
'ultimate method'. The cut-out technique required less concentration on
the physical fabrication of paintings and greater focus on the intellectual
activity of creating colour shapes and determining their organisation.

Riley's *Painting with Two Verticals 3* is comparable in scale to *Ivy in
Flower* (1953), a maquette for a stained glass window composed near
the end of Matisse's life. Each has four colours, some quite similar, that
describe curving, stylised forms. Though hardly a literal interpretation of
visual fact, Matisse's ivy is a generalised replication of things
remembered, pared to their plastic essence. However simplified, his
forms remain rooted in the variable, irregular contours of nature, legible
signs for leaves, heart-shaped petals and clusters of red berries that
vividly communicate his memories of the natural world, once keenly
observed. 'With my eyes wide open,' Matisse recalled, 'I absorbed
everything as a sponge absorbs liquid.'[18] The delicate leaves are evenly
dispersed but appear to drift freely across the yellow background,
beneath the divides of the rectilinear grid, and seem to cascade gently
downward from the upper left to the lower right. For Matisse, this

                                                    MARLA PRATHER

implied motion originated in the tremulous vibrations of nature, a light breeze under a brilliant Mediterranean light.

Riley's art is inextricably linked to the world of natural phenomena, from the landscapes of her native Cornwall, to the Provençal environment of Cézanne and Matisse, to the many lands she has visited. She has found that colour, unlike her early restrictions to black and white, inevitably brings the experience of art closer to nature. But as she has explained, 'I deliberately avoid carrying any sort of image or combination of local colours back into the studio – that simply does not work… If I am outside in nature I do not look *for* something or *at* things, I try to absorb sensations without censoring them, without identifying them.' In a circuitous way, the paintings lead back to nature, as she goes on to say: 'I start from my materials, from the colours and forms, and eventually I may recognise in them particular relationships, sensations somehow familiar from nature.'[19]

Riley's autonomous forms, evolved through countless pictorial experiments, are the records of the endless perceptual transactions, 'the sensations', that uncannily reside in her prodigious visual memory. Despite their chromatic buoyancy, the shapes that inhabit *Painting with Two Verticals 3* do not float freely but are firmly integrated with one another and within the overall diagonal structure. Movement is internally motivated by the fluid, repeating rhythms of the curved forms that both surge toward the upper right and, as in the Matisse, descend toward the lower right. While both artists reach for formal equivalents for visual experience, it is clear how Matisse's vision retains its origins in organic reality and how resolutely abstract Riley's example remains. More recently, in *Arcadia 1 (Wall Painting 1)* (2007), Riley perhaps approaches Matisse's model in yet another way, creating an environmental work where forms have opened up to move beyond the frame, allowing the ambient white of the wall, so central to Matisse's concept, to become integrated into the colour composition.

Two paintings from 2006, *Painting with Verticals, Cadence 3* and *Painting with Verticals, Cadence 6*, indicate the heightened complexity of Riley's more recent curvilinear paintings. An expansive horizontal format and increased scale were adopted to accommodate the proliferating

forms that are rhythmically deployed across the compositions, now like
vast panoramas. As the shapes have multiplied, they have become more
pliant and cursive. They bend and arch, compress and expand, nestle
into one another or make tantalising contact at a single point, weaving
their way in looping fashion across the vertical divides that serve to
articulate the curving imagery and to counter the overall momentum
with a slower rhythm of their own. Riley's distinctive vocabulary of colour
forms is by now familiar. Still, despite their precise delineation, they
elude easy apprehension, for there is always potential for mutability.
There is the segmented circle; the attenuated, pointed ellipse,
sometimes given flame-like tips; the sliced crescent that resembles a
scimitar; and the beautifully tapered and lithesome hourglass shapes
that, when cinched at the waist (as in the white forms at either side of
Painting with Verticals, Cadence 3), seem to twist in space. Most
recently, Riley has reintroduced small rhomboid shapes that punctuate
the curves and accentuate the diagonal course of the composition. The
forms are not accidental; their subtle permutations evolve through Riley's
careful manipulation of the curves. But in the process, discrete forms
may be cut off by the edge of the canvas, become incorporated into
contiguous forms, sometimes of the same colour, and new hybrid
configurations are born. Despite the idiosyncratic shapes that may result,
there is a consistent logic to their contours and coherence to the overall
spatial effect.

These manifold encounters of shapes and colours that animate the
pictorial space invest the whole with an irrepressible sense of internal
locomotion. Our eyes travel up and across, pause, scan back and move
generally from left to right through the virtual diagonal pathways. 'When
played through a series of arabesques,' Riley has said, 'the curve is
wonderfully fluid, supple and strong. It can twist and bend, flow and
sway, sometimes with the diagonal, sometimes against, so that the
tempo is either accelerated or held back, delayed.'[20] The vertical
elements are clearly indicated as stabilising foils for the whiplash curves
and diagonal trajectories, whereas in earlier paintings, such as *Out There*
(2004) the vertical register is insinuated as a latent aspect of the overall
rhythmic structure. Riley's use of the vertical brings to mind Matisse's

                                    MARLA PRATHER

well-known text in his *Jazz* folio about his constant awareness of the
vertical as he establishes his own arabesques.

> Around this fictive line the arabesque develops. I have derived
> constant benefit from use of the plumb line. The vertical is in my
> mind. It helps me make precise the direction of my lines, and in my
> rapid drawings I never indicate a curve, for example that of a branch
> in a landscape, without being conscious of its relationship to the
> vertical. My curves are not mad.[21]

Like Matisse, Riley has regularly turned to musical analogies to
describe the appearance and 'indefinable content' of her non-
representational work.[22] The language and expressive capacity of music
seem especially pertinent to any understanding of the curve paintings,
which are composed around recurrent themes and variations, subtly
manipulated rhythms and the orchestration of complex colour
relationships. These broad compositions contain internal divisions like
measures, and melodic phrases unfold as forms move up and down,
assuming different tonalities and volumes. Their particular timbre and
modulation may range from the deep sonorous chords of *Painting with
Verticals, Cadence 6* to the lightly syncopated, lyrical tones of *Painting
with Verticals, Cadence 3*. The brilliant chromatic progressions of five
colours in *Painting with Verticals 3* (2006), for example, are amplified
through repetition and surge in dramatic crescendo with the trio of
intensely hued forms – green and orange-red – in the centre of the
canvas. Subsequently, petal-like forms descend along the right side of
the painting in a kind of visual diminuendo. Riley's persistent cadences,
the unifying rhythmic organisation of her paintings, infuse her effulgent
colour with invigorating, pulsating energies. The pictorial harmonies that
result induce in us a sense of not only visual but physical exaltation, and
one is grateful to embrace abstract painting, as Meyer Schapiro advised,
'as an obvious and necessary enrichment of our lives.'[23]

Bridget Riley: Recent Paintings and Gouaches, exhibition catalogue, PaceWildenstein,
New York, NY, 2008, pp.5–13.

1   Meyer Schapiro, 'On the Humanity of Abstract Painting', in *Mondrian: On the Humanity of Abstract Painting,* George Braziller, New York, NY, 1995, p.17.

2   Bridget Riley, 'Bridget Riley in Conversation with Jenny Harper', in *Bridget Riley: Paintings and Drawings 1961–2004,* exhibition catalogue, Ridinghouse, London, 2004, p.95.

3   Bridget Riley, 'The Colour Connection: In Conversation with Robert Kudielka' (1989), in Robert Kudielka (ed), *The Eye's Mind: Bridget Riley, Collected Writings 1965–1999,* Thames & Hudson, London, 1999, pp.142–73. See also Bridget Riley, 'The Art of the Past: Talking to Neil MacGregor', in Robert Kudielka (ed), *Bridget Riley: Dialogues on Art,* Zwemmer, London, 1995, pp.16–32.

4   Bridget Riley, 'Perception and the Use of Colour: Talking to EH Gombrich', in Kudielka (ed), *Dialogues on Art, op.cit.,* p.33.

5   Bridget Riley, 'Cézanne in Provence', in *The Burlington Magazine,* no.148, September 2006, p.628.

6   Bridget Riley, 'Interview with David Sylvester' (1967), in Kudielka (ed), *The Eye's Mind, op.cit.,* p.73.

7   Robert Kudielka has pointed out that a relationship between *Kiss* and *Rêve* was made in the exhibition *Bridget Riley: Selected Paintings 1961–1999* at the Künstverein für die Rheinlande und Westfalen in Dusseldorf. See Robert Kudielka, 'Biographical Notes', in Robert Kudielka (ed), *Robert Kudielka on Bridget Riley: Essays and Interviews 1972–2003,* Ridinghouse, London, 2005, p.242. In 2004 the artist told Richard Shiff that *Kiss* was an 'unplanned prototype' for her recent curve paintings. See Richard Shiff, 'Rasters in Paradise', in *Bridget Riley: Recent Paintings,* exhibition catalogue, PaceWildenstein, New York, NY, 2004, p.11.

8   Bridget Riley, 'Something to Look At: In Conversation with Alex Farquharson' (1995), in Kudielka (ed), *The Eye's Mind, op.cit.,* p.131.

9   Bridget Riley, 'Supposed to be Abstract: Conversation' (2001), in Kudielka (ed) *Robert Kudielka on Bridget Riley, op.cit.,* p.206.

10 For a full discussion of the *Composition with Circles 2* (2000), installed at the Dia Center for the Arts, see Lynne Cooke, 'Around and About *Composition with Circles 2*', in Lynne Cooke and Karen Kelly (eds), *Bridget Riley: Reconnaissance,* exhibition catalogue, Dia Center for the Arts, New York, NY, 2001, pp.45–65. In 2003 a third version of the original Bern drawing was created for the artist's 2003 retrospective at Tate Britain in London. In addition, Dia's *Composition with Circles 2* was installed again for a 2005 retrospective of Riley's work at the Aargauer Kunsthaus in Aarau, Switzerland. That same year, *Composition with Circles 5* was created for the Akademie der Künste, Berlin.

11 Bridget Riley, 'Conversation' (1972), in Kudielka (ed), *Robert Kudielka on Bridget Riley, op.cit.,* p.19.

12 Bridget Riley, 'In Conversation with Maurice de Sausmarez' (1967), in Kudielka (ed), *The Eye's Mind, op.cit.,* p.54.

13 For an illustrated examination of this process, see Martin Hentschel, 'Bridget Riley and the Performance of Colour', in Martin Hentschel (ed), *Bridget Riley: New Work,* exhibition catalogue, Kunstmuseen Krefeld, Krefeld and Hatje Cantz Verlag, Ostfildern, 2002, pp.49–59.

14 Riley, 'Something to Look At', in Kudielka (ed), *The Eye's Mind, op.cit.,* p.130.

15 Bridget Riley, 'Bridget Riley in Conversation with Jenny Harper', in *Bridget Riley: Paintings and Drawings 1961–2004, op.cit.,* p.98.

16 *Ibid.* For discussions of Riley's relationship to the art of Matisse, see Lynne Cooke, 'Encore', in *Bridget Riley: Paintings and Drawings 1961–2004, op.cit.,* pp.108–12. Cooke points out that the villa in Vence where Matisse lived in the 1940s and made many of his

greatest cut-outs was named *Le Rêve*, and that Riley, beginning in 1959, has been a frequent visitor to his Chapel of the Rosary in Vence. On Matisse and Riley, see also Shiff, 'Rasters in Paradise', in *Bridget Riley: Recent Paintings*, *op.cit.*, pp.5–19.

17   Bridget Riley, quoted in Lynn MacRitchie, 'The Intelligence of the Eye', in *Bridget Riley: New Work*, *op.cit.*, p.19.

18   Henri Matisse, 'Oceania' (1946), in Jack Flam (ed), *Matisse on Art*, University of California Press, Berkeley, CA, 1995, p.69.

19   Bridget Riley, 'Things to Enjoy: Talking to Bryan Robertson (1992)', in Kudielka (ed), *Dialogues on Art*, *op.cit.*, pp.79–80.

20   Riley, 'Supposed to be Abstract', in Kudielka (ed), *Robert Kudielka on Bridget Riley*, *op.cit.*, p.208.

21   Henri Matisse, 'Jazz' (1947), in *Matisse on Art*, p.173.

22   Bridget Riley 'Perception and the Use of Colour: Talking to EH Gombrich' (1992), in Kudielka (ed), *Dialogues on Art*, *op.cit.*, p.42. Riley has explained how in a group of stripe paintings from the early 1980s she 'deliberately used a classic music structure.' See Riley, 'Something to Look At', in Kudielka (ed), *The Eye's Mind*, *op.cit.*, pp.130–31.

23   Schapiro, *op.cit.*, p.17.

Making Visible

Anne Montfort

Writing about Bridget Riley's work today inevitably involves mentioning Op art – a phenomenon that was recently brought back into focus by three consecutive exhibitions in Strasbourg, Columbus and Frankfurt.[1] However, it is still important to question this identification of the artist with what could be considered a movement, by recalling Jean-Claude Lebensztejn's warning to us in 'Sol' (1967): 'A name is launched; the historian's unconscious job will be to take this name and make it into a concept, and then to make this concept into a tangible thing: quite a remarkable type of realistic illusion.'[2] Firstly, the artist herself never claimed to be part of any group. As early as 1965, when Op art was particularly popular, she emphasised the originality of her process by insisting on the absence of a direct link with science.[3] Secondly, it is important to take a closer look at the characterisations of this trend: 'The provocation of the eye as a mere sense organ, the extreme activation of vision in the sense of physiological events…'.[4] Or, in a more nuanced contemporary interpretation, 'the largest common denominator is surely an art of perception that is based on the deliberate confusion of vision indicating that the most important feature of Op art lies in its effects on certain physiological processes of the eye and brain of which we are not normally conscious…'.[5] These descriptions imply that a work of art can be defined entirely by how it is perceived. Nevertheless, phenomenology has often proved that perception is not an unchanging fact but is instead the condition of both a context and an individual. Furthermore, by ascribing only a minor importance to the form of a work of art, these definitions do not sufficiently explain the importance of painting for Riley, in terms of craft as well as tradition. Finally, they reduce the apprehension of a work of art to a merely physiological phenomenon. Incidentally, let us note that even the purest abstraction cannot escape one's cultural projections or, as TJ Clark ironically put it: 'The band will always pick up the tune. "Let's sit down I see a figure".'[6]

After all, how can one fail to observe that in most of her writings and interviews, Riley likes the word 'sensation' better than she does 'perception'. Sensation conveys a more ambiguous notion meaning both sensing and feeling. Could this difficulty with fitting into a movement be the manifestation of the renowned insularity of British art? Upon closer examination, there is no filiation between Riley and the British exponents of geometric abstraction from Ben Nicholson to Riley's immediate predecessors, such as Victor Pasmore and Kenneth Martin.[7] By the longevity of its national and international recognition, Riley's work is also atypical in the history of British art. To fully grasp its originality, it is important to return to an examination of her paintings and drawings, with the help of the artist's comprehensive writings. A constantly evolving theoretical reflection and the condition of the creative process and its sources are outlined throughout these texts. Although literature has no direct impact on Riley's painting, her careful reading of Marcel Proust and Samuel Beckett sheds light on the relations between her work and reality, tradition and abstraction.

Ever since Riley's first solo exhibition at Gallery One in London in 1963, there was a tendency to treat her paintings as 'perceptual experimentations'.[8] Obviously abstract, they are not only described in terms that have been borrowed from science but they also appeared to some critics as transpositions of scientific imagery – for example, the repetitive structures were interpreted as moiré patterns, 'as the mathematical solution to the interference of two periodic functions'.[9] Seen from this point of view, the artist was substituting an objective mode of representation or analysis of the real for traditional realism (understood in the sense of an exact figuration of appearances). The context of the 1960s, a time when the technological utopia prevailed, partly explains this first reading. The development of the Op art phenomenon during the exhibition *The Responsive Eye*, organised by William C Seitz in 1965 at the Museum of Modern Art in New York, arose from the belief that the works being presented drew their actuality from a successful marriage between art and science. Riley made her own position clear: 'To begin with, I have never studied "optics" and my use of mathematics is rudimentary and confined to such things as equalising, halving, quartering and simple progressions. My work has developed on the basis of empirical analyses and syntheses, and I have always believed that perception is the medium through which states of being are directly experienced.'[10] In practice, the artist first chooses a module through which she can visually explore the behaviour of interacting shapes and/or colours. The repetition or declinations of this module, the switch in scale, then allow her, in her own words, 'to clarify' the effect she is after. Although there is no clearly defined protocol, as exists in scientific experimentation, this method implies the possibility of mistake, adjustment and synthesis. It also assumes the existence of criteria on which to base a judgement.

One has to go back to the roots of this abstraction in order to fully understand its specific character. Riley insists that her painting is born from – and feeds on – her own visual experience, developed in close contact with nature and works of art seen in museums. In her autobiographical writings, she never mentions the picturesque aspect of a landscape but instead notes the events that animate it: the movement of grasses in the wind, the reflection of sparkling light on water, etc. In the same way, the titles of her works, though given after completion, refer to movement (*Fall*, 1964; *Tremor*, 1961) or to transitory states (*Black to White Discs*, 1962; *Ease*, 1987), and when actually mentioning a place, an object or a subject by name (*Cataract 3*, 1967; *Saraband*, 1985), they evoke a visual impression or, even, an acoustic one. Not only do they specify the sensation, they can also give indications as to Riley's artistic reflections at the time. The title *Shih-Li* (1975) is a reminder of the artist's interest in Chinese painting, which she became acquainted with through the exhibition *Chinese Painting from the Collection of Mr and Mrs Earl Morse* (1972) and George Rowley's book *Principles of Chinese Painting* (1970). According to Rowley's explanation, *Shih* means both the structural relations that give an ensemble coherence and the interaction of forces (of elements) endowing the work with life – a notion Riley sums up by the term 'alive-ness'.[11] As for *Li*, it is a dynamic equivalent of the Greek *eidos* (idea) and implies concentration on the essential. By connecting these words, Riley emphasises their complementarity and also their inextricability, as she states in her interview with Lynne Cooke:

'No matter how facile and vivid the brushmarks might be, unless they were imbued with a basic truth, *Li*, the scroll painting was worthless. I liked the way in which the criteria were to do with state of being, and that painting conveyed frames of mind.'[12]

This last comment offers a hint as to how Riley regards aesthetic judgement. Significantly the artist is not particularly interested in paintings she finds purely illustrative. In talking to Neil MacGregor, she gave the following explanation of her indifference towards Caspar David Friedrich's work: 'I can see it could be meaningful for people, but it seems to me that this whole sphere of feelings, of sensibilities, is not quite at home in painting.'[13] For Riley, there is no difference between the nature of figurative and abstract painting, because she conceives both as 'invented realities'.[14] In her opinion, painting lost its narrative role when the mythological and religious iconographies, which once formed a universal language, became obsolete. When talking about Nicolas Poussin's *Landscape with a Man Killed by a Snake* (1648), she confines herself to describing the serpentine loops that lead back into the depth of the painting, and when Neil MacGregor points to the frightening aspect of the scene, she replies: 'what I find thrilling about it is that it shows an aspect of nature which one feels is always there just under the surface. Poussin has placed it at the base of his canvas, below the people, below the city, below the sky, below everything which rises from it. By this positioning it's turned into something fundamental.'[15] According to Riley works of art are not contextual documents; on the contrary, they remain contemporary in the true sense of the word by offering solutions to problems that are endemic to painting (space, colour and tone, the distribution of lines and shapes, and so on).

Riley's response to the training available at art school forecasts an important aspect of her working method. Although she has been critical of the lack of academic instruction in the art of painting, she greatly appreciated the classical training she received in Sam Rabin's drawing class at Goldsmiths, London. In several texts, she refers to Rabin's pedagogy, his way of progressively helping his students analyse the pose of a model in order to find a way of representing it. It is these teachings, completed by the study of Old Master drawings at the British Museum,

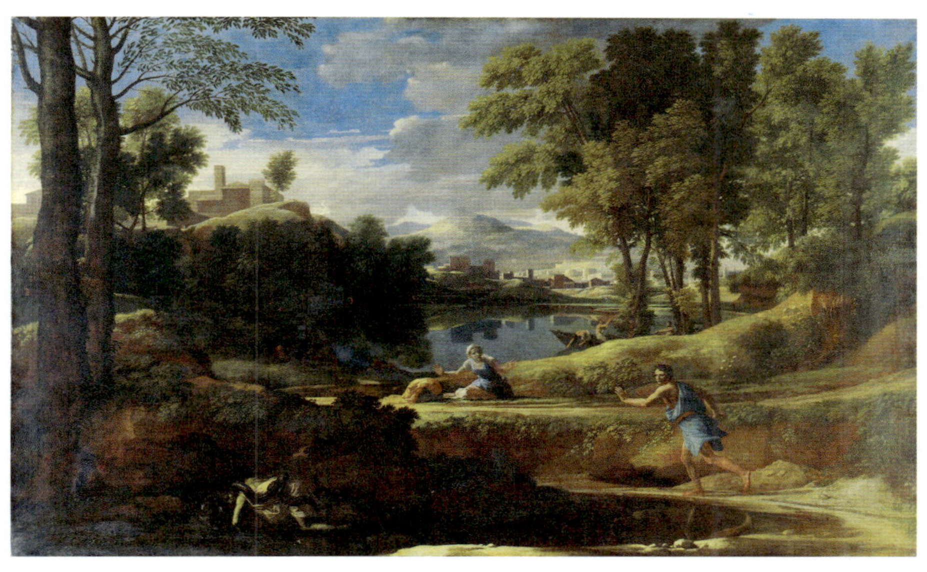

Nicolas Poussin
Landscape with a Man Killed by a Snake c.1648
Oil on canvas
118.2 × 197.8 cm | 46½ × 77⅞ in
National Gallery, London

London, which Riley credits with her ability to organise her work methodically, to include a figure in a visual field, to structure her images (distribute lines of strength, balance masses, etc.), in short, her ability to, '[strip] away the pictorial image to see what's beneath'.[16]

When faced with the problems of colour, the young artist concurrently turned to Georges Seurat making a copy of his painting *The Bridge at Courbevoie* (1886–87). Instead of working from the original, Riley used a smaller-sized reproduction. While she was interested in the neo-Impressionist painter's 'way of thinking',[17] she did not wish to imitate his precise pointillist touch. She chose a larger stroke to discover the divisionist principle of colour. By deliberately limiting her copy to this purpose, Riley focused exclusively on the method. In this craftsman-like approach she found herself corroborated by Beckett's interpretation of Proust's view of the artist: '"The task and duty of a writer (not an artist, a writer) are those of a translator". This could also be said of a composer, a painter or anyone practising an artistic *métier*. An artist is someone with a text which he or she wants to decipher.'[18] Therefore, the task of the artist would consist in adapting, interpreting or even transposing a generic content into the specific language of a given artistic discipline. In this way Riley gradually developed her own 'text'. She did not aim to attain an art based on 'quintessence'. Referring to Piet Mondrian, she notes: 'He was certainly striving for a universal principle, but at the same time he realised that this could not be imposed as an absolute. There seemed to be no alternative to expressing precisely this insight, and expressing it solely through the bare and simple means of the painting itself.'[19] Riley seems to accept Beckett's interpretation of Proust, according to which only habit makes one believe in permanence and the world exists only in each individual's conscious projection. By emphasising in her writings and interviews that the object of painting is now sensation, she implicitly places herself back within the context of her own work.

However, the technique of her paintings suggests a deliberate self-effacement. Right from the beginning of her black-and-white work in 1961, Riley delegated the final execution of her paintings to assistants. This was in strong opposition to a prevailing amateurism much in favour with the English art establishment. The personal 'touch' had become synonymous with spontaneity and originality not only in academic quarters but also among those painters who followed American Abstract Expressionism. In this climate Riley's approach was provocative, as for instance when she admitted that she sometimes cleaned the surface of her paintings with detergent. Yet unlike Minimalist artists such as Donald Judd she had no ambition to integrate industrial techniques and models into her practice. Scorning the use of masking tape, she trains her assistants to apply paint in a precise and neutral manner with the brush, thus deliberately retaining a fine handmade finish to the work. Her decision to leave the final execution of a painting to assistants can be explained by her intention to concentrate entirely on the exercise of critical judgement. Adopting the role of the first spectator of her own work also seems to be linked to Riley's belief in the radical isolation of the modern artist, which she sees as both a token of social alienation and the instrument of freedom. She gave the following explanation to Neil MacGregor: 'An artist today has to make his entire context, his own criteria, has to explain, has to account for his procedure as it evolves. It's almost as though he has to take on the role of being his public, his own critic, his own everything.'[20] Somehow, it seems that the artist has to come up with a value system on his own, while at the same time paradoxically admitting the impossibility of objective criteria. This statement is reminiscent of Beckett, in his taste for Pedro Calderón de la Barca's work, and his use of the baroque scheme of *mise en abyme*. In his novels, written in the first person, Beckett allows his characters to freely wander away from the course of the plot, thus becoming the delegates of the author, who then turns into his own first reader.

By exerting this control over both the work's conception and its reception, Riley succeeds in assimilating the subject of painting with its object – sensation. The word bears a double meaning, since it is relevant within the field of psychology – sensation being, above all, everything that touches – as within that of physiology (perception). Furthermore, it supposes the notion of feeling. According to the artist, the series of paintings Static can thus be linked to a specific experience. The first impulse came to her during a journey up Mont Ventoux in the south of France: 'a mass of tiny glittering units like a rain of arrows'.[21] However,

Riley carefully specifies that the idea for her paintings is only born from visual experience 'from time to time' and in an 'indirect way': 'in that visual experience, all experience of reality adds up to a whole thing, an overall state of being.'[22] Moreover, the title *Static* – the first painting was originally entitled *Discharge* – refers only to the eponymous energy. This refusal to lock visual experience within a precise context could be explained by an English formalist tradition, such as defined by Roger Fry: 'It demands the most complete detachment from any of the meanings and implications of appearances… in such a creative vision the objects as such tend to disappear, to lose their separate unities, and to take their place as so many bits in the whole mosaic of vision.'[23]

This refusal to identify particular instances of perception is in keeping with a personal logic in which visual experience becomes incarnate in, and feeds off, the remembered image. In an autobiographical text, 'The Pleasures of Sight' (1984), the artist indicates the essence of her work through her childhood impressions. She does not give any geographical indications as to exactly where in Cornwall the place she refers to is, it is characterised only by its deep valleys, ragged coastline and ever-changing landscape. It also seems strangely timeless and its peaceful appearance is in contrast with the context of the Second World War.[24] By evoking natural phenomena, she actually initiates another approach to remembrance, the same as that outlined by Walter Benjamin in his *Berlin Chronicle* when he was trying to analyse Proust's *À la recherche du temps perdu* (In Search of Lost Time, 1913–27):

He who has once begun to open the fan of memory never comes to the end of its segments; no image satisfies him, for he has seen that it can be unfolded, and only in its folds does the truth reside; that image, that taste, that touch for whose sake all this has been unfurled and dissected; and now remembrance advances from small to smallest details, from the smallest to the infinitesimal, while that which it encounters in these microcosms grows ever mightier.[25]

It is precisely because Riley's paintings conjure up these micro-events that they prompt this impression of familiarity in the spectator, this feeling

ANNE MONTFORT

of déjà vu. Benjamin also described the mechanics of this evocation: 'One ought to speak of events that reach us like an echo awakened by a call, a sound that seems to have been heard somewhere in the darkness of past life.'[26] Like memory, Riley's images are of a durable yet fugitive nature. Their large scale calls upon the spectator's physical presence, while their visual saturation stimulates an involuntary eye movement. Both elude total and definitive comprehension. For example, *Cataract 3* is based on an identical curve descending diagonally at regular intervals. This formal structure carries a paired modulation of two contrasting colours. Their contrast almost disappears where the colours are degraded in a common grey – along the top and the bottom of the canvas. Conversely, where the grey tones recede the contrast of pure hues is fully exposed. This occurs across a wide passage in the lower part of the painting, giving rise to a pinky red tint. The perception of the painting operates in this to and fro between its stable factual structure and the surprising sensation of a flush of disembodied colour.

Since Riley's works act as a place of recall and projection, they can appear devoid of meanings of their own. Yet they display – in the sense that they show and account for – an internal organisation. In fact, they exhibit a state of mind that the artist alludes to, once again, by quoting Beckett: 'when Beckett says "the expression that there is nothing to express, nothing with which to express… together with the obligation to express" it is a consolation – and an encouragement to know that he felt this.'[27] In *Molloy* (1951), the writer goes as far as stating that: 'For to know nothing is nothing, not to want to know anything likewise, but to be beyond knowing anything, that is when peace enters in, to the soul of the incurious seeker. It is then the true division begins, of twenty-two by seven for example, and the pages fill with the true ciphers at last.'[28] It is worth emphasising that this statement leads Beckett directly to mathematics as if, when reduced to mere operations, they made up the first basic system of organisation. While insisting on the rudimentary nature of the mathematical operations she uses, in her paintings Riley offers compositions based on repetition, geometrically shaped forms and progressive partition of space. The neutral precision of the composition helps evidence the logic of the work. The artist likes to include her preparatory drawings in her exhibitions and catalogues, because they elucidate her working method: studies of a module in pencil on graph paper, often with handwritten notes on them (according to Riley, the form has to be 'deliberate'), and gouaches, many of which use coloured cut-out papers in collage technique.[29] Her preparatory studies clearly show the geometrical structures that underpin the surface of the finished works. In *Sheet 2 Analysis of Study 11 for Composition with Circles 2* (2000) the centres of the circles are lined up on a grid that makes it possible, as Robert Kudielka puts it, to 'draw and disperse attention'.[30] Riley works by setting specific rules for herself in a manner she found confirmed in Igor Stravinsky's *Poetics of Music* (1959): 'My freedom thus consists in my moving about within a narrow frame that I have assigned myself for each one of my undertakings. I shall go even further: my freedom will be so much the greater and more meaningful, the more narrowly I limit my field of action and the more I surround myself with obstacles.'[31]

The first *Wall Painting (Arcadia)*, created for Galerie Max Hetzler, Berlin, in autumn 2007 is delineated by horizontals and verticals that suggest a virtual plane. Some shapes escape and expand beyond this plane, while the white of the wall enters into and opens up the painting. *Wall Painting* picks up the curvilinear forms and vertical rhythm of Riley's recent paintings, but she pushes them further in order to tap into new possibilities. On various occasions, the artist has said that her work progresses organically in the sense that one stage yields the next. Each phase of her evolution is defined by the development of one or several principles until their possibilities seem to be exhausted. The stripe paintings of the early 1980s, employing a limited range of bright, saturated colours, led in time to the introduction of the diagonal, thus imparting the group of succeeding works with a new spatial complexity. By diffracting the surface into lozenges, colourful effects were achieved that induced a circular eye movement. These eventually affected the organisation of the paintings, giving way to a new use of curved forms. In fact, Riley's painting seems to proceed by aporia. It is worth noting her response to the image of Beckett's Molloy, with 16 pebbles in his pocket, coming up with various ingenious calculations never to suck on the same

ANNE MONTFORT

pebble before transferring it into another pocket: 'This image of a man sitting on a beach building up this kind of structure has always seemed to me to be a most beautiful abstract work.'[32]

Riley has based her conception of abstraction on a double premise: on the one hand, the end of an artistic system that justified painting by the accuracy of representation, on the other hand, the failure of a utopia that sought to deduce at drawing an abstract universal language from appearances. This new state of things not only had consequences for the painter's craft (by what criteria could one in future methodically develop a body of work?) but also for the reception of painting (to what extent can the work remain a vector of communication or, in other words, what interaction is there left between the painting and its spectator?). For the artist, the answers to these questions lie in the very nature of painting: an invented reality, guided by criteria discovered in the process of making the work. Formalist as they are, Riley's paintings retain the ability to create illusion as described by EH Gombrich: 'a magical power of metamorphosis, which words cannot express'.[33] They make up for their limitations by inducing an impression of space, movement or duration. Unlike traditional painting, however, these illusions are trapped within the work, the spectator is invited to become aware of them: the achieved effect vanishes under scrutiny, only to return in a transformed state. This continuous stimulation turns Riley's works into receptive agents that develop and open up vision. Referring to Paul Klee's statement, 'Art does not reproduce the visible; rather, it makes visible', the artist wrote:

This is not meant as a revelation in the sense of rendering visible something that was previously unseen, but as the opening up of our vision to the greater and fuller span of the generative force of life. In painting the thing seen is, at best, a factor that gives rise to both the actual perception and to the sensation that places it within our experience.[34]

Bridget Riley: Retrospective, exhibition catalogue, Ridinghouse, London and Arc/Musée d'Art Moderne de la Ville de Paris, Paris, 2008, pp.22–29.

1   *L'œil moteur. Art optique et cinétique, 1950–1975*, Musée d'Art Moderne et Contemporain, Strasbourg, 13 May – 25 September 2005; *Optic Nerve: Perceptual Art of the 1960s*, Columbus Museum of Art, Columbus, OH, 16 February – 17 June 2007; *Op Art*, Schirn Kunsthalle Frankfurt, Frankfurt, 17 February – 20 May 2007.

2   Jean-Claude Lebensztejn, 'Sol', in *Annexes – de l'oeuvre d'art*, Éditions La Part de l'Œil, Paris, 1999, p.17.

3   Bridget Riley, 'Perception Is the Medium' (1965), in Robert Kudielka (ed), *The Eye's Mind: Bridget Riley: Collected Writings, 1965–1999*, Thames & Hudson, London, 1999, pp.66–68.

4   Max Imdahl, 'Probleme der Optical Art: Delaunay, Mondrian, Vasarely' (1966), cited by Martina Weinhart in 'In the eye of the beholder, a brief history of Op art', *Op Art*, exhibition catalogue, Schirn Kunsthalle Frankfurt, Frankfurt, 2007, p.29.

5   Weinhart, in Imdahl, *ibid*.

6   TJ Clark, *Farewell to an Idea: An Episode from a History of Modernism*, Yale University Press, New Haven, CT and London, 1999, p.365.

7   Although she did attend the classes of basic design conceived by Victor Pasmore with Harry Thubron, and despite the fact that Kenneth Martin had been one of her teachers at Goldsmiths, she never makes any reference to their teaching and, instead, seems to favour life-drawing classes of Sam Rabin.

8   Anon., 'Gallery Guide', *The Observer*, 27 May 1962, p.27.

9   Gerald Oster and Yasunori Nishijima, 'Moiré patterns', *Scientific American*, May 1963, pp.54–63. For a more in-depth analysis of the critical reception of Op art, I refer you to Frances Follin, *Embodied Visions: Bridget Riley, Op Art and the Sixties*, Thames & Hudson, London, 2004.

10 Riley, 'Perception is the Medium', in Kudielka (ed), *op.cit.*, p.66.

11 Bridget Riley, 'Bridget Riley in Conversation with Lynne Cooke', in *Bridget Riley: Retrospective*, exhibition catalogue, Ridinghouse, London and Arc/Musée d'Art Moderne de la Ville de Paris, Paris, 2008, p.145.

12 *Ibid.*

13 Bridget Riley, 'The Art of the Past: Talking to Neil MacGregor' (1992), in Robert Kudielka (ed), *Bridget Riley: Dialogues on Art*, Zwemmer, London, 1995, p.27.

14 Bridget Riley, 'Practising Abstraction: Talking to Michael Craig-Martin' (1992), in Kudielka (ed), *ibid.*, p.53.

15 Riley, 'The Art of the Past', in Kudielka (ed), *ibid.*, p.23.

16 Bridget Riley, 'Personal Interview by Nikki Henriques' (1988), in Kudielka (ed), *The Eye's Mind, op.cit.*, p.24.

17 Bridget Riley, 'Seurat as Mentor', in Jodi Hauptman (ed), *Georges Seurat: The Drawings*, exhibition catalogue, Museum of Modern Art, New York, NY, 2007, p.187.

18 Bridget Riley, 'Painting Now' (1996), in Kudielka (ed), *The Eye's Mind, op.cit.*, p.199.

19 Bridget Riley, 'In Conversation with Isabel Carlisle', *Bridget Riley: Works 1961–1998*, exhibition catalogue, Abbot Hall Art Gallery, Kendal, 1998, p.7.

20 Riley, 'The Art of the Past', in Kudielka (ed), *Dialogues on Art, op.cit.*, p.30.

21 Bridget Riley, 'Conversation with David Sylvester' (1967), in Kudielka (ed), *The Eye's Mind, op.cit.*, p.78.

22 *Ibid.*

23 Roger Fry, 'The Artist's Vision' (1919), *Vision & Design*, Oxford University Press, Oxford, 1981, pp.35–36.

24 During the Second World War, Bridget Riley lived in Padstow with her mother, younger sister and aunt, since her father had joined the army and had been taken prisoner in Asia. Of those days, the artist especially remembers isolation and the return to a rural lifestyle.

                                                    ANNE MONTFORT

25 Walter Benjamin, 'A Berlin Chronicle', in Peter Demetz (ed), *Reflections: Essays, Aphorisms, Autobiographical Writings*, Schocken, New York, NY, 1986, p.6.

26 *Ibid.*, p.59.

27 Riley, 'Bridget Riley in Conversation with Isabel Carlisle', *op.cit.*, p.7. Excerpt from Samuel Beckett, *Trois dialogues* (1949), Les Éditions de Minuit, Paris, 1998.

28 Samuel Beckett, *Molloy* (1951), Patrick Bowles (trans), Alfred A Knopf Publishing, New York, NY, 1997, p.69. I am very grateful to Pierre Schneider for enticing me to draw a parallel between Beckett's understanding of mathematics and Riley's use of them.

29 See Riley, 'Bridget Riley in Conversation with Lynne Cooke', *op.cit.*, p.147.

30 Robert Kudielka, interview with Bridget Riley, tapescript, 13 March 2007.

31 Riley, 'Perception and the Use of Colour', in Kudielka (ed), *Dialogues on Art*, *op.cit.*, p.36.

32 Riley, 'Bridget Riley in Conversation with Lynne Cooke', *op.cit.*, p.142.

33 EH Gombrich, *Art & Illusion*, Phaidon, London, 1960.

34 Bridget Riley, 'Making Visible', in *Paul Klee: The Nature of Creation, Works 1914–1940*, exhibition catalogue, Hayward Gallery, London, 2002, p.18.

Attention and Event in the Work of Bridget Riley

Jonathan Crary

Over the past two decades, criticism and commentary on Bridget Riley has frequently claimed for her work an impressive position within a mainstream genealogy of twentieth-century painting. The affinities of her work with crucial features of Henri Matisse, Jackson Pollock, Paul Klee, late Piet Mondrian and numerous others has been variously and often convincingly demonstrated. Certainly there is no question that Riley is one of a small number of truly original painters in the second half of the twentieth century. However, many of the affiliations (such as the School of Paris) that have been posed as interpretive entryways into her work have had the tendency to bypass or domesticate some of the most important or defining features of her painting.[1] Numerous critical accounts are based on the assumption that Riley's extraordinary work of the 1960s was widely misunderstood and misconstrued amid the popular response to her innovations and through the cultural milieu with which she was uncritically associated. But perhaps by so fully relocating Riley, in the interests of distancing her from the extravagance and wrong-headedness of what was written about her initial aesthetic and cultural impact, some crucial and enduring elements of her work and some of its singular challenge have been lost to view. In this brief essay I propose a few suggestions for engaging Riley's work along less-discussed lines of affiliation and association in the interest of recovering some sense of its intrinsic alterity.

First, let's consider a straightforward given about the artist: her nationality. I mention this not in any way as a determining factor for her art or her practice but rather as a speculative framework, historically and conceptually, for reflecting on some of the ideas at stake in her work. English visual art certainly has had a deeply mixed status within the persistent clichés and platitudes that persist within twentieth-century critical traditions. Of course English writers themselves often have shared in such broad generalisations, with doses of either resignation or defensiveness. Nonetheless, I deem Riley to be a groundbreaking artist, an unmatched creator of perceptual experience, in part because of her

alignment with the axis defined by the figures of William Blake and
JMW Turner. The discipline of art history, born in Continental Europe, has
never quite known what to do with these immense and idiosyncratic
figures from the British Isles. Of course their importance and originality is
acknowledged but they have been effectively excluded from any of the
most influential explanatory schemas of nineteenth- and twentieth-
century art. Different as they are from each other, Blake and Turner can
stand for certain understandings or assumptions about vision and
perception to which Riley is linked as much as she is to any continental
ideas and practices. At stake, of course, are the familiar truisms about
English insularity, the ambivalence toward the burdens of academic
traditions and hierarchies, and the related Protestant wariness about the
accumulated pictorial achievements on the walls of European ecclesiastical
and dynastic monuments. But while there is an exemption from the
demands of tradition, there is a simultaneous immersion in the claims
and exigencies of deeply personal canons or pantheons, both pictorial
and textual: for Blake it was the twin stars of Michelangelo and John
Milton; for Turner, at least early on, it was a patchwork of Claude, Virgil,
Titian, the Dutch and many others. More important, however, is the way
in which a visionary autonomy is derived from an intense engagement
with the physical world, from an apprehension of forces and relations at
work in nature. In unique but parallel ways, Blake and Turner shared the
conviction that the intuitions of an unmediated, subjective vision will
provide the truest or most authentic accounts of lived reality, and the more
thoroughly existing pictorial codes and conventions are abandoned for
new ones, the more readily this visionary translation of nature will occur.

Most relevant for considering Riley's work in this context is the
decisive renunciation by both Blake and Turner (after 1835) of the
fundamental place of chiaroscuro in painting. Over several centuries, the
conceptualisation of a pictorial tableau in terms of an organised
distribution of lights and darks had established some of the dominant
models for the exercise of intellectual control over the inherent disorder
of perception. It was also a system through which the conventions of an
implied pictorial syntax could operate and which postulated a spectator
competent to 'read' it. Of course Blake and Turner were not in any sense

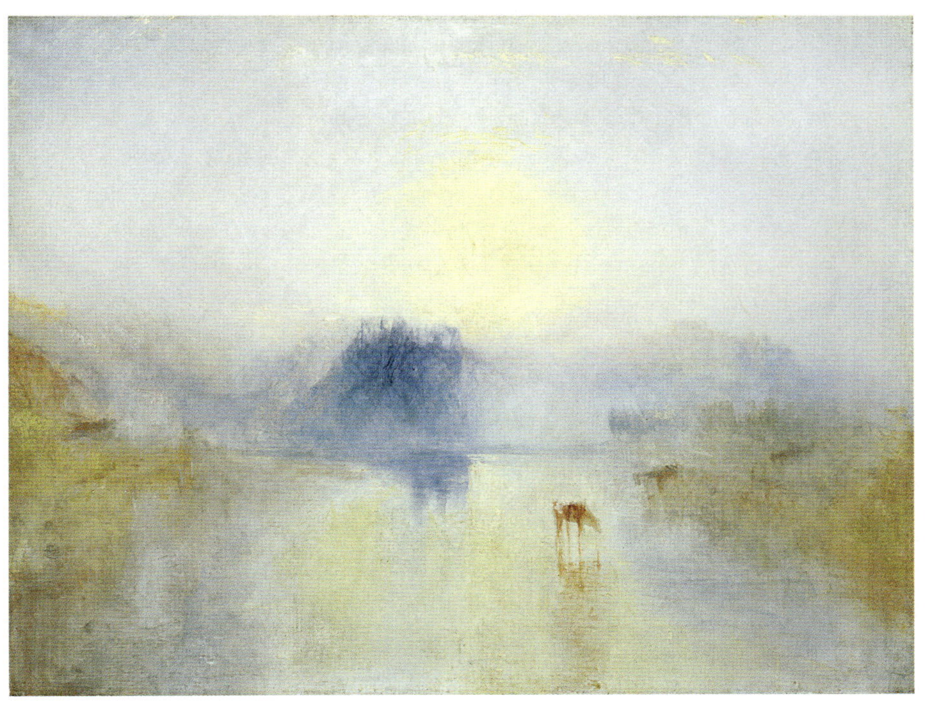

JMW Turner
Norham Castle, Sunrise c.1845
Oil on canvas
90.8 × 121.9 cm | 35¾ × 48 in
Tate, London

attempting to replicate the evidence of the eye. Rather, their respective practices extrapolated from experience that one perceives (contra Reynolds) not a world structured around binary oppositions, but a single continuous field of illumination, however variegated it might be. In Blake's terminology, it is the superiority of the indivisible light of one's 'emanation' over the divisions and falseness of one's 'spectre', the superiority of his translucent colours over the gravity and opacity of Venetian and Dutch canvases impacted with pigment. With Turner, it is his rejection of René Descartes's prohibition of perceptual dazzlement, most evident in numerous later paintings in the figuration of unmediated encounters with solar radiance. These encounters lead not to madness, as Descartes and others insisted, but to revelatory insights into nature and history. The overturning of the presuppositions of chiaroscuro obviously is part of a larger history in which the phenomenon of luminosity begins to be privileged as an autonomous term, extracted from its *relational* position in an older set of codes, from its *reciprocal* pairing with shadow or darkness. In this history, additional elements of English art play a significant role as well, including some of the pre-Raphaelites, James Abbott McNeill Whistler and the broad emergence of watercolour practitioners in the late eighteenth century.

To reiterate, I am simply proposing a tentative way of considering Riley's work in relation to historical precedents that have generally not been central to evaluations of her work. It's tempting to elaborate her own biographical accounts of her youth and rural upbringing in terms of existing English archetypes and narratives: the childhood in a natural, often austere, environment, uncluttered by the distracting products and reified images of urban culture, where there is born a heightened sensitivity to the subtleties and refined modulations occurring within an infinitely rich and living milieu. But regardless of what contexts with which it is affiliated, her painting, in all its major phases, affirms the pictorial surface as a continuous network of luminous events that are irreducible to an underlying dualistic structure. It implies that the conceptual equivalent of shadow does not effectively exist for her. Rather, in Michael Baxandall's terms, there are only variations or discontinuities in brightness.[2] To what extent this predilection is a

JONATHAN CRARY

conceptual choice or is actually derived from lived intuitions accumulated from childhood or a mixture of both, is something finally not demonstrable. Even in her work of the 1960s, which might seem superficially compatible with binary models of various kinds, Riley generates optical fields in which black and white, light and dark are bereft of any intrinsic values and are subservient to the larger dynamic forces at play in the work. As has often been noted, there is no opposition of black and white for Riley; instead she works with them as extremes of the single indivisible phenomenon of colour. It is her particular distributions of colour that produce, not the drama of internal relations which defined much mid-twentieth-century abstract painting, but a range of events that occur in the transactions between painted surface and embodied spectator. The specific character of these transactions has modulated along with shifts in her style and formats but some core ambitions of her project have remained relatively constant.

Riley's work solicits from its viewer a particular mode of engagement, which she herself has referred to as 'receptive attentiveness'. As Ludwig Wittgenstein and other modern philosophers have demonstrated, attention is not necessarily synonymous with either consciousness or perception: one can choose to attend to various aspects of individual experience but never all at the same time. And Riley seems highly aware of the many ways in which it can be deployed or directed. Attention is not only concentration, in terms of a kind of willed effort, but it is perhaps more importantly an act of selection. Most often it functions involuntarily and unconsciously: one selects a limited range of potentially relevant stimuli in order to avoid being overwhelmed by too much information or sensation. But as both artists and scientists have discovered in different ways, human attention is an imperfect and volatile capability with internal limits. Paul Cézanne, perhaps more than any single artist, learned of and explored these limits. His work is marked by the creative discovery that looking at any one thing intently did not lead to a fuller and secure grasp on its presence or immediacy. Rather it led to perceptual instability, to the breakdown of fixed form or positions. And his experience of that breakdown was one of the conditions for his invention and discovery of previously unseen relations and forces.

We all know from our own experience what happens when we look
at some unchanging object or form for too long: our visual hold on it
begins to dissolve in a series of perceptual modulations. As the eye
fatigues, the constancy of colours and shapes undergoes various
transformations. As Riley clearly understands, attention is never some
timeless exchange between a rapt spectator and an inert object. Rather,
she creates conditions within which viewers become aware of their own
attentiveness as part of a dynamic continuum, in which the identity or
even the physiognomy of the individual work is always in the midst of a
process of self-differentiation. Early on Riley must have realised the
impossibility of assuming the unmediated givenness of sensorial data
and at the same time realised that she could not make visual art
predicated on notions of perceptual constancy.

Let's consider her work from the mid to late 1970s, in which she
developed a stunning series of ribbon- or wave-like fields. Clearly Riley
tapped into an enormously potent vocabulary of dynamic form, drawing
on a variety of specific interactions of light and matter. One can look
back to the notebooks of Leonardo for a related kind of exploration, to
his studies of streams of water in which he attempted to identify some
fundamental regularities within ceaseless movement and activity. Thus, in
a painting like *Song of Orpheus 5* (1978), Riley produces a unique field
of autonomous optical events that are nonetheless parallel to the effects
generated in the natural world, such as the reflections of sunlight off a
moderately calm ocean surface or the undulations of a large expanse of
tall grass moving in a steady wind. One's attention to *Song of Orpheus 5*
then begins amid a very real sense of perceptual volatility, but one of
Riley's remarkable achievements is to provide the conditions for an
attenuated and continually reactivated engagement.

The specific texture of one's encounter with the work depends to
some degree on one's physical distance from it. Unless one is quite
close to the painting, the experience of looking both fixedly and panning
across its width involves unusual interactions between the central and
peripheral parts of the eye. Whatever we see with the fovea (or the small
central area of the retina, which registers the clearest detail or the
sharpest colour discriminations) can simultaneously be in competition

                                                    JONATHAN CRARY

with our retinal periphery (which is highly sensitive to the least sensation of movement, whether real or illusory). Thus any sustained regard of Riley's iridescent and torquing ribbons of colour is unsettled by the subdued intrusion of perturbations and flickerings at the edges of our visual field. Any significant change in distance, either closer or further away, from the work allows a noticeably different but related network of effects to occur: the pulsating routes through which we are led at some point suggest the question of where these events are taking place.

One can also observe Riley's painted surface up quite close and plainly examine the patterned sequence of marks out of which *Song of Orpheus 5* is made. However, none of the previously mentioned shimmerings and undulations will be detectable. Similarly, a very near view of a Georges Seurat discloses the systematic and molecular structure of painted touches out of which his images are constructed. For example, one can observe an area made up exclusively of dots of orange, blue and yellow-orange. Yet when seen from a distance of approximately 15 feet, that same area is perceived as a hazy glimmering violet. Of course as is well known, Seurat was working with considerable knowledge about the physiological capacities of the human eye, specifically the way in which the retina could synthesise the appearance of several adjacent colour sensations into the optical impression of a new colour that existed only subjectively. In this sense much of what is fundamental to our experience of a Riley painting has a related *atopic* or placeless character. The stunning perceptual events, which in various ways define her work, provoke us to ask not only *what* exactly we are seeing but *where* in fact it is 'taking place'. And Riley makes clear that the answer to latter question will never be clear cut or categorical. There is always an indissoluble and active play between eye, mind and the artwork itself.

Riley has had an abiding interest in many aspects of Seurat's painting and drawing, but her own work could never be said to have any programmatic ambitions. Despite her rich awareness of the science, psychology and philosophy of both mind and vision, such knowledge is never allowed to intrude on the beauty and mysterious life of the work and how we encounter it. The ideas of various philosophers have been productively enlisted to elucidate Riley's art. My own sense is that there are valuable affinities between Riley's own evident rejection of a subject/object bifurcation and the vitalism and anti-dualism in Alfred North Whitehead's 1929 book *Process and Reality*.[3] Criticising the belief in the possibility of 'simple location' or in the notion of inert, enduring entities, Whitehead defined our relation to the world as a 'structure of activity' in which we are always a constitutive part of continually developing occurrences. The vibratory interweaving of vision, consciousness and art object that Riley brings into being with work after work, privileges the reality of process and flow over the idea of independently existing minds or matter. This is something she probably did not learn from books but more likely from those initiatory and youthful immersions in natural environments.

Riley's concerns, though, are hardly just philosophical. What seems to matter to her in the end is the vocation of the artist and its accompanying responsibilities. In this connection I want to conclude by again positioning Riley in an English context by invoking the name of John Ruskin, perhaps the most extraordinary thinker on the relation between vision, art, nature and the responsibility of the artist. For this still-misunderstood writer, vision was always an open-ended process without a final goal or object. If there was a 'truth' of vision for Ruskin it was to be grasped in terms of its inexhaustible capacity for refining and extending its own limits and sensitivity. But it was also in understanding the inexhaustibility of visible reality, which for Ruskin meant great art or the natural world. To look at nature, for Ruskin, whether a leaf, a rock formation or even a cloud, was to inhabit a process of formation that had no closure, no finality. And for Ruskin the artworks of the greatest value were those which were similarly indeterminate and unfinalisable. Riley, in her own fashion, has transferred her intuitions about nature into a conviction that the artwork too, as it interacts with the human sensorium, can be a cascade of novelty, of unprecedented occurrences that challenge any habituation or standardisation of perception.

Bridget Riley: Retrospective, exhibition catalogue, Ridinghouse, London and Arc/Musée d'Art Moderne de la Ville de Paris, Paris, 2008, pp.38–43.

JONATHAN CRARY

1   The term School of Paris refers to post-Impressionism and movements thereunder.
2   Michael Baxandall, *Ombres et lumières*, Pierre-Emmanuel Dauzat (trans), Gallimard, Paris, 1999.
3   Alfred North Whitehead, Process and Reality: An *Essay in Cosmology. Gifford Lectures Delivered in the University of Edinburgh During the Session 1927–1928*, Cambridge University Press, Cambridge, 1929.

In Search of a Direction: Bridget Riley's Work in the 1950s
Robert Kudielka

The exhibition *Renoir: Landscapes 1865–1883* that Bridget Riley saw at
London's National Gallery in the spring of 2007 revived her long-held
admiration for an artist whose work does not comply with the aesthetic
predilections and intellectual aspirations of twentieth-century art. Riley
was particularly impressed by the courage and vigour with which Pierre-
Auguste Renoir tackled the unconventional colour schemes he
discovered through working *en plein air* and, although many of the
rather small early paintings didn't seem to be fully resolved or finished
she liked the immediate sense of recognising 'what he must have seen'.
But the exhibition also clarified for her why landscape did not continue
to be Renoir's main subject: 'I think he concentrated on the human
figure after the mid-1880s because landscape didn't offer a structure.'

This may seem like a surprising comment from an artist who has
been working in an abstract manner for almost half a century. Why
should a figurative motif be more suited to structuring a painting than,
say, meadows, shrubs, trees, hills and clouds? Isn't structure something
that a painter imposes on the sensations inspired by the respective
subject? And with regard to abstract art, how else could one conceive of
structure if not as the artist's autonomous fabrication? Riley, however, has
consistently refused this notion. 'I never feel that I confer any energy on
anything, it's all there to be unlocked and articulated', she said in 1967 in
reference to the dynamism of her early black-and-white work.[1] This
insistence on the inherent structural potential of the forms and colours
she uses reveals how profoundly her approach to painting has been
affected by her figurative training. Her later remark 'life drawing was
about the only thing I learned in art school' should be seen not only as a
criticism of the teaching standards of her student days but also as an
appreciation of a skill she actually *learned* at art school.

In 1949, at the age of 18, Riley was accepted to Goldsmiths, London,
where she was introduced by an inspired teacher, Sam Rabin, a Russian
Jew who had emigrated to England, to the classical discipline of 'drawing

from the nude', once regarded as the core of academic instruction. Even
after she had entered the Royal College of Art, London, in 1952 she
continued to attend his private classes for a while. This strangely
conservative attraction to a seemingly outdated exercise had one clear
motivation: under Rabin's tuition Riley learned that in order to render the
perceived object satisfactorily, it was essential to penetrate its intelligible
structure. This required more effort than the mere application of
anatomical knowledge. In a recent essay Riley recalled Rabin's relentless
questioning:

> He taught that it was only by the patient study of appearance and by
> making the effort to understand what one saw that one could
> discover the particular kind of information needed for drawing. He
> would say 'What is the model doing?' and repeat this question until
> he received the reply 'She is standing', he would then ask, 'And is
> your drawing standing?' And, indeed, was it?[2]

To make a figure 'stand' in the picture plane one had to find a structural
equivalent to the posture perceived in space.

No aspect of landscape lends itself to such inquiry. Not even a tree —
the nearest equivalent to erect human posture — offers a similar
challenge, particularly when covered in foliage.[3] The human body, being
the only entity we can simultaneously view from the outside and
somehow experience from within, seems to hold the clue to any
structural penetration in rendering appearance. Paul Valéry accordingly
feared that the Impressionists' predilection for landscape might signal a
slackening of this effort. In *Degas Danse Dessin* (1938) he proposed the
term *informe* (formless) to qualify that compound of visual incidents we
call landscape. 'There are things, patches, masses, contours and volumes
which have only a factual existence, as it were: we simply perceive them,
but know nothing about them; we cannot reduce them to a single law,
deduce their wholeness from an analysis of their parts, reconstruct them
through rational operations.'[4] This is not to say that these 'unformed'
phenomena are *without* form, but rather that their forms deny any clear
reproduction by the human mind, be it through drawing or just in the

                                                      ROBERT KUDIELKA

imagination. 'They have no property other than occupying an area in space.'[5]

Valéry's critical observations clearly support Riley's insight as to Renoir's choice of the figure as subject, but she herself in no way felt predisposed by her figurative training against tackling *l'informe*. Although many of her early black-and-white paintings, such as *Fall* and *Pause* (both 1964), show how deeply engrained the contrapposto stance – the opposition of a contracted side with an expanding one – is in her pictorial thinking, she found her own form of expression via an intensive study of landscape. After graduating from the Royal College in 1955 she embarked on a 'rational operation' of defining those seemingly vague 'areas in space' that Valéry, despite being a respectable draughtsman himself, curiously omitted in his critique. If there is one overt, indisputable link between Riley's abstract colour work over the last 25 years and French impressionist painting, it is her concern with organising the spatial planes of colour perception – *les plans*, as Paul Cézanne termed them. This interest also originated in Rabin's life class when, at the end of a day's work, he would set five-minute poses to be treated as tonal studies. 'He taught these in the same way that he taught figure drawing: by question, answer and demonstration,' Riley remembers. 'He would say:

'What is the lightest area you can see?' This was followed by 'And what is the lightest area in your study?' At first one had difficulty in establishing this 'lightest area' because the paper itself was the lightest thing. This, however, was precisely the point. It wasn't a question of depicting light but of discovering it within the means. If this paper white was to be reserved for the form or shape of the lightest area, it followed that everything else had to go down one tone of diagonal hatching. From this palest grey field a further stage of elimination defined the next lightest part, the rest of the study being uniformly lowered by further hatching.[6]

Tamarisk Tree (*Cornwall*) (1956) is a bold early example of the application of this method to a landscape motif. The sky, being the most luminous area, is represented by the colour of the paper, or 'paper white', followed by the darker tone of the immediate foreground and of the beach visible behind the hedge that diagonally crosses the field of vision. A third level of tonal gradation distinguishes the sea in the far distance as well as the hazy transparent outlines of the tamarisk tree in the centre, and its companion on the far left. The first really dark level equates the traversing hedge and the shadow of the tree growing next to it. Only the cross-hatching in the foliage of this tree attains deeper tones, resulting in actual black. A small white spot denoting a patch of sky visible through the dark volume of the tree's crown creates the strongest black-and-white contrast and makes one aware that one is reading the drawing in the opposite direction to how it has been composed: the intense black of the tree seems to provide the contrast that illuminates all other components.

The practical limits of this procedure add to the pictorial abstraction rooted in identifying maximum lightness with the white of the paper. The infinite variety of shades in natural light is reduced to a limited range of five, six at the most, properly manageable gradations. Moreover, the exercise of studying tonal relationships favours an approach that encompasses the whole field of vision rather than focused observation. Instead of concentrating on isolated objects and their particularities, tonal differentiation relates all areas within the visual field solely according to their relative lightness of darkness. An early untitled drawing (1956) by Riley made in the life class at Goldsmiths reveals the extent of this visual abstraction. The profile of the model, the upper part of her body and the front of her crossed legs are all accorded the same level of lightness, as are parts of the elevated platform and the vertical passage behind her chair; whereas the darkest end of the scale is indiscriminately assigned to her hair, to parts of a cupboard in the background, the shadow under her chair and the mop of hair of the female student in the bottom left corner. This may be the result of a rather conventional exercise, but in the years 1957–58 Riley's preoccupation with the potential of tonal structuring became an important step in her search for direction.

In *Self-Portrait at the Drawing Table* (1956), which also dates from this period, Riley pushed the autonomy of the *clair obscur* calculation far beyond its academic purpose. Pure white occupies the top left of the drawing, defining the opening of a window that is supported by three darker horizontal areas below. On the right the same stark tone marks the bordering passage that seals off a sequence of narrow vertical divisions, which taper off in irregular succession. These two areas act as a rectangular scaffold supporting the figure in the centre. The silhouette of the head and the body are merged with that of the drawing table forming a homogenous compound of the deepest, mostly black, tones. But this firmly centralised disposition of weight and mass is upset by a group of initially puzzling shapes. On the right side of the drawing three oblong forms hover in space, their tone barely distinguishable from the paper white; and under the drawing table two almost quadrangular intervals of the same tonal weight disrupt the delineation of the figure's legs. Whereas the floating vertical shapes can be attributed to reflections of light in the interior, it may rightly be deduced that the artist was wearing white socks when drawing this self-portrait.

However charming this discovery might be, it should not detract from the rigorous pursuit Riley had embarked on in the late 1950s. Pushing tonal structuring to an extreme was an attempt at forging an expressive formal language and the artist who inspired this quest was, perhaps surprisingly from today's viewpoint, Edvard Munch with his powerful figurative deformations. However, in following this direction Riley soon reached the limits of light and dark differentiation. In the study *Man Lying Down* (c.1957–58) the reclining figure is still clearly discernible, despite the drawing's extreme tonal contrast and the Munch-like positioning of the subject in the immediate foreground. Resting on the elbow of the right arm the huge head faces the spectator, one side brightly illuminated, the other cast in deep shadow. But one's attention is distracted from this almost monumental presence by a strange figuration in the background of the upper part of the drawing. Is it a stack, an edifice or a cart driven by a barely distinguishable figure? Tonal abstraction has rendered this secondary motif virtually unintelligible, with the result that it unduly distracts our cognitive faculties.

This dilemma could of course be avoided by choosing less distinct and complex motifs. The study *Trees in Blossom* (c.1958) may be seen as a step in this direction. The actual scene can be identified without difficulty: fringing a kind of clearing in the foreground, and largely following a horizontal path in the middle distance, a line of trees dominates the composition. The indistinct, *informe* character of the site lends itself to a totally convincing, loosely scattered structure of tones ranging from the bright white of the path to the deep, dark shadows of the foliage on the upper left of the drawing. One might even speculate that this study could have led to a painting in the manner of Pierre Bonnard whose colourism Riley admired at the time. However, both these options – tonal diffusion and Bonnard's intuitive approach – ultimately went against the grain of her creative temperament. However uncertain she felt about the direction of her work, avoiding difficulties and abandoning the analytical approach didn't seem to be the right solution.

On the other hand Riley clearly was approaching the limits of her solitary quest. Some sort of succour was needed. In the spring of 1959 she saw *The Developing Process: New Possibilities in Art Teaching*, an exhibition at the Institute of Contemporary Arts, London, which promoted a new concept of teaching art that seemed sympathetic to her interest in method and procedure. So she decided to take part in a summer school to be held the following year in Suffolk under the aegis of Harry Thubron, one of the initiators of the exhibition. There she met a group of practitioners and lecturers who were to become the first committed supporters of her art in the 1960s: the art historian and critic Norbert Lynton, the psychoanalyst and theoretician of iconoclasm Anton Ehrenzweig and, above all, Maurice de Sausmarez, a painter, scholar and distinguished educationalist, who recognised Riley's special creative gift and turned her attention to the work of Georges Seurat. In retrospect this connection seems almost too obvious considering the body of tonal drawings and preparatory studies Seurat had produced. But the master of neo-Impressionism was not a hero of the 1950s. Robert L Herbert's book *Seurat's Drawings* did not appear until 1962, and little was known about the artist's method apart from the relevant passages in John Rewald's classic *Post-Impressionism: From Van Gogh to Gauguin* (1956). This was not, however, entirely to Riley's disadvantage. To find out more

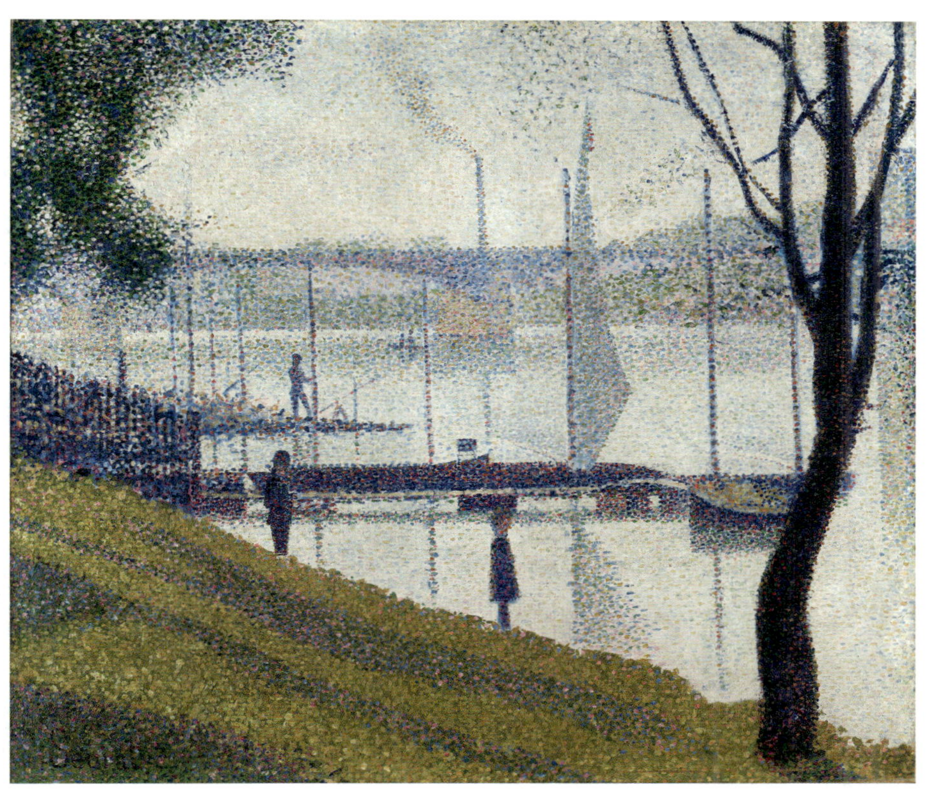

Georges Seurat
The Bridge at Courbevoie 1886–87
Oil on canvas
46.4 × 55.3 cm | 18¼ × 21¾ in
The Courtauld Gallery, London

about Seurat's approach to painting she had to revert to the oldest method by which the secrets of the *métier* were discovered and appropriated by artists.

In late autumn 1959 Riley copied what seemed to her a manageable painting, *The Bridge at Courbevoie* (1886–87). Her copy is larger and its grain coarser than that of the original, mainly because she was not interested in pointillist handling as much as in Seurat's way of thinking. Discovering his method had an explosive effect on her own working situation, as De Sausmarez observed when he visited her studio in early 1960: 'The walls were covered in fragments of colour theory, an enlarged commercially produced three-colour half-tone of some apples with the colour dots the size of cherries, and, in the kitchen, a big reproduction of Seurat's *A Sunday Afternoon on La Grande Jatte – 1884* (1884–86).'[7] The association with Seurat supported and strengthened the methodical streak of Riley's artistic temperament. Initially the pleasure that prompted her 'to dismember, to dissect the visual experience' almost seemed to surpass her interest in the pictorial result.[8] Three studies on the motif of a vineyard, *Vineyard in Italy* (1960) – the result of a visit to Italy with De Sausmarez in the summer of 1960 – are a fine example of this approach. A linear sketch establishing the main axes and the characteristic contours of the motif is fleshed out by a tonal drawing, which concentrates solely on the light-dark scale, and finally complemented by a colour study registering, in accordance with Seurat's method, the optical mixture of colours *en plein air*. The delicate cross-hatching of blues, blue-violets, reds, orange-reds, yellow-greens and blue-greens indicates in each instance the particular mélange of local hues, light reflections and inflections, shadows and fugitive complementary colours, deliberately avoiding the traditional hierarchy of local colour.

With hindsight this new, methodical treatment of colour may be seen as anticipating the disembodied colour sensations engendered by Riley's stripe paintings of the early 1970s. At the time the difference between the powerful tonal structure and the tender colour fabric must have felt almost irreconcilable: how could she combine the vigorous, assertive light and dark rhythm of the vines with the diffuse, evasive colour mixtures enshrouding them? Nevertheless *Pink Landscape* (1960), Riley's

   ROBERT KUDIELKA

last painting made in the neo-Impressionist manner, achieved this contradictory unity thanks to a unique coincidence of method and motif. It was painted after her return from Italy on the basis of studies (now lost or untraceable) similar to those in the Vineyard in Italy group from 1960. The exceptionally large colour patches may have been encouraged by the bold employment of colour divisionism in Giacomo Balla's painting *Girl Running on a Balcony* (1912), which Riley saw on her Italian sojourn in the Galleria d'Arte Moderna, Milan. But the feeling of energy and movement conveyed in her painting is quite different from that of the Futurist artist. David Thompson was the first to point out that *Pink Landscape* is 'already concerned with a kind of optical sensation which constantly recurs in her later work – that of a dominant formal pattern under the pressure of disintegration.'[9] This may have been helped by the motif: 'a stretch of landscape in the hills south of Siena, drenched in a blinding shimmering heat-haze, that ended in one of the fiercest storms of that summer'.[10] In recreating this dramatic situation Riley happened upon the structural configuration that was to become the hallmark of her work: the unstable balance between form and *l'informe*, stability and dissolution. Like all good ends in art this was the promise of a beginning that could only be fulfilled by sacrificing what had brought it about, the simple rewards of working from nature and, for a time at least, the magic of colour.

Bridget Riley: Retrospective, Ridinghouse, London and Arc/Musée d'Art Moderne de la Ville de Paris, Paris, 2008, pp.52–57.

1   Bridget Riley, 'In Conversation with Maurice de Sausmarez' (1967), in Robert Kudielka (ed), *The Eye's Mind: Bridget Riley, Collected Writings 1965–1999*, Thames & Hudson, London, 1999, p.58.

2   Bridget Riley, 'Seurat as Mentor', in Jodi Hauptman (ed), *Georges Seurat: The Drawings*, exhibition catalogue, Museum of Modern Art, New York, NY, 2007, p.186.

3   See the advice of Jean-Baptiste-Camille Corot, when Eugène Delacroix asked him how to paint trees: 'Il m'a dit d'aller un peu devant moi, et en me livrant à ce qui viendrait' (He told me to let myself go a little, and to entrust myself to what would happen), in Eugeune Delacroix, *Journal 1822–1863*, Pion, Paris, 1980, p.143.

4   Paul Valéry, Jean Hytier (ed), *Œuvres*, vol.2, Gallimard, Paris, 1960, p.1194.

5   *Ibid.*

6   Hauptman, *op.cit.*, p.186.

7   Maurice de Sausmarez, *Bridget Riley*, exhibition catalogue, Studio Vista, London, 1970, p.27.

8   Riley, 'In Conversation with Maurice de Sausmarez', in Kudielka, *op.cit.*, p.51.

9   David Thompson, 'British Artists at Venice 1: The Paintings of Bridget Riley', *Studio International*, vol.175, no.901, June 1968, p.296.

10 De Sausmarez, *op.cit.*, p.27.

   ROBERT KUDIELKA

The Persistence of Image

Éric de Chassey

Reviewing Bridget Riley's second solo exhibition in 1963, art critic Norbert Lynton made a distinction between 'two types' of works: the 'field paintings', which 'could spread in all directions', and the 'image paintings', in which a 'clear shape' is set within the boundaries of the surface'.[1] Very soon, however, most commentators would come to consider her oeuvre as being of the first type, if for no other reason than the common-sense idea that the notion of the image runs counter to the practice of abstract painting.

Initially the critical emphasis was put on chronology; the diffuse compositions being seen as following the focused ones, the latter supposedly having completely disappeared by 1965.[2] Subsequently the oeuvre as a whole was taken to be grounded in a rationale of dissemination, which made the pictures less paintings to be looked at than secondary vehicles for complex perceptions henceforth regarded as elementary. In 1965 William C Seitz, curator of the exhibition *The Responsive Eye* at the Museum of Modern Art in New York – and the man who did so much for Riley's international reputation by putting a detail of one of her pictures on the cover of the catalogue and on the invitation card – stated that, 'These works exist less as objects than as generators of perceptual responses.'[3]

The reception given to Riley's work since the 1960s has been masterfully analysed by Frances Follin, who has demonstrated that it led, rapidly and systematically, to an insistence on the works' effects on viewers – effects often perceived as particularly aggressive.[4] It should be noted too that the recent rehabilitation of Op art, with Bridget Riley in the forefront – there have been no less than three major exhibitions on the subject: in Strasbourg (2005), Columbus, Ohio (2007) and Frankfurt (2007) – has very largely come about because the movement can be seen as anticipating a form of current art that is less concerned with objects than with dematerialised sensory experiences. From this perspective the multisensory spectacles of Carsten Höller, Olafur Eliasson and Ann Veronica Janssens are direct descendants of Riley Op, despite the obvious differences between these artists.

Two recent experiences have convinced me, however, that the image aspect of Riley's paintings deserves fresh consideration. This interpretation should not necessarily eclipse one whose validity is substantiated by widespread acceptance, but its existence is too often ignored, even though it plays its part in ensuring that the artist's already venerable early works still seem up to date, while at the same time her most recent pictures indicate that she is a contemporary artist in the fullest sense of the term. In the 2005 exhibition *Stroll On! Aspects de l'art abstrait britannique des années soixante (1959–1967)* at the Musée d'art moderne et contemporain (MAMCO) in Geneva, I placed works by Riley from 1963–68 in the same room as a sculpture by Phillip King. My reason for bringing these two artists together was, prosaically, to recreate the pairing from the English pavilion at the 1968 Venice Biennale, at which Riley won the International Painting Prize. But an unforeseen outcome of that pairing was to highlight the merits of Riley's works as images: not in the sense that they gave you the urge to go hunting for some hidden iconography, but in the sense (just as when looking at King's sculpture) that you were induced to find in them individually identifiable images or a kind of formal repertoire.

However it was mainly the second experience – a solo exhibition by the artist at the PaceWildenstein in New York in winter 2007–08 – that acted as a revelation. In two big galleries, paintings and gouaches on paper made me realise that, while there certainly was a continuity of the picture field, the coloured forms making up this field could be identified, and formed a vocabulary that was not readily nameable but which the title curve series attempted to encapsulate. Of course I had already seen pictures from this series begun in 1998, notably at the major Tate Britain retrospective in 2003, and at PaceWildenstein a year later, but for reasons not easy to explain – doubtless as much to do with a shift in my sensibility or the zeitgeist as with the fact that they had been given the logical, chronological sequence of a retrospective – they had not had this effect on me at the time. When the effect did come, however, it was inevitable that it should modify my way of seeing the oeuvre as a whole;

not because a teleological point of view compels the opinion that the truth of the beginnings is also to be found in the beauty of the conclusion, but simply because a great artist is often, implicitly, a sound commentator on his or her own work.

It would be pointless and tedious here to begin looking into the way Riley's works become images, especially since detailed analyses of this kind, covering her work period by period, have already been published by one of the leading authorities on the artist, the professor of aesthetics Robert Kudielka. I should simply like to state, without having to provide proof, that the image logic is present only to a limited and very secondary extent in the works made between 1967 (with the return of colour) and 1996 (with the end of the series using rhomboidal motifs), except in so far as each series is founded on a recurring motif. I have no intention whatever of setting out to reinterpret the oeuvre in terms of this effect; I merely wish to highlight an aspect of it that I believe has been unjustly neglected. At the very least this will enable a reconsideration of the idea that Riley's paintings, in addition to a general tendency to make identification of figures impossible, actually reject images; for it seems to me that this idea prevents us from correctly situating the works historically and, more annoyingly, from understanding why they remain so artistically efficient.

For most commentators, Riley's paintings, since they made their public appearance in the early 1960s, are to be understood as part of a vast current of so-to-speak de-Americanised or de-Greenbergised late modernism in which formalism stripped of the modernist ethic, tends towards dematerialisation of the work of art or, at least, towards a transition from object of contemplation to vehicle for experiences that then become the main aspect of the art. In this context it is hardly surprising that a work like *Continuum* (1963/2005) should be seen as important enough to justify its recreation for the *L'Œil moteur* exhibition at the Musée d'Art Moderne et Contemporain in Strasbourg in 2005. The critical success of this work doubtless has to do with the numerous photographs it generated, including various portraits of the artist in the mid-1960s which played quite a part in presenting her – to some extent in spite of herself – as an iconic 'swinging London' figure in cigarette

trousers or pencil skirt. But this success also hinged on the way
Continuum seems to suggest a transcending of easel painting by some
overall sensory experience in which it is less a matter of seeing images
than of feeling sensations, less a matter of exteroception (perception of
the object) than of proprioception (perception of oneself). Thus to enter
into *Continuum* would be to undergo, 'a total breakdown of one's
physical orientation and capacity for estimating both distance and space,
an hallucinatory experience'.[5] However the artist has recently expressed
severe strictures regarding the work: 'This experience pointed in a
direction I didn't want to take. It was too literal, since the viewer found
himself actually 'in' the work, whereas all I wanted was visual
absorption.'[6] Most notably of all, she very soon destroyed the work,
thereby indicating that this tendency towards dematerialisation left her
dissatisfied and this at the very time when – if we are to believe Robert
Kudielka – her work was supposed to have abandoned the image
dimension in favour of a focus on 'field paintings'. It may have been the
case that the artist had strayed – with no loss of talent – onto ground
that was and would remain more that of Op art's practitioners in the
United States of America and in Continental Europe. As it happened, one
of the rare English figures of this movement, Peter Sedgley, a close
friend of Riley offered a literal dematerialisation of colour and the
generation of pure light effects with his fluorescent-paint *Vidéo-Disques*
(1968–69), spinning in a darkness alleviated only by a stroboscopic
ultraviolet spotlight.

In the catalogue for Riley's first retrospective in 1971, Bryan Robertson
makes the striking suggestion that, 'colour and light, or light as colour…
do not exist in themselves on the actual surface of her paintings. They
come into being… at a precise stage in their journey toward you.' This
leads him to conclude that the artist 'has freed [them]… from "matter"
or substance and dematerialised them as clouds of coloured light
floating in the space between an already depersonalised surface and the
spectator.'[7] I repeat that my intention is not to challenge this conclusion,
but to transpose Robertson's intuitive insight to the domain of images.
Many of Riley's pictures of 40 years ago, as well as of recent years, only
succeed in creating an environment, an inhabited space between viewer

　　　　　　　　　　　　　　　　　　　　　　ÉRIC DE CHASSEY

and work, because they combine an insistence on complex sensory effects – some of them perhaps hallucinatory – with a grounding in and on the image. Far from inducing the kind of radical disembodiment provoked by psychotropic drugs – to use a common comparison certainly not applicable to all her different types of works – these paintings have their roots in the here and now of a bodily perception that can only function in the presence of a stable object. The viewer perceives an image on the surface of the work – canvas, paper, sometimes Plexiglas – and identifies it at the very moment when the image's complex perceptual effects make themselves felt, whether or not he or she is conscious of them, concentrating on them or simply looking while paying no particular attention. In her notes and studies on paper and her essays the artist herself accurately explored these effects on various scales. The image actually present on the surface, whose elements remain identifiable as separate figures, is amplified by these effects into a new image within the viewer's perception.

In the case of the field paintings, the initial effect is certainly a hallucination and scrambling of visual perception. This stimulation of the senses has been closely analysed by Anton Ehrenzweig in an article dating from 1965: 'The first phase can be called cold, hard, aggressive, "devouring".'[8] In the 'image paintings' the first step is that of the recognition of a stable form. In this respect Riley is also, to quote a 1962 article by David Sylvester (for this reason often accused of a lack of discernment) a 'hard-edge abstractionist' – even if she was not only and simply that when she painted *Kiss* in 1961, using a compositional approach similar to that of certain paintings of the time by Ellsworth Kelly, such as *Rebound* of 1959.[9]

In the first case what is involved is the prelude to a form of perceptual repose described by Ehrenzweig as follows: 'At a certain point in our experience this relentless attack on our normal viewing habits can peel our eyes into a new crystal-clear sensibility which has none of the cold aggressiveness of the first phase.'[10] In the second case the moment of identification is soon joined by another, in which the senses put together a new, more complex image. But the viewer confronting the 'image paintings' never achieves definitive repose; rather he or she experiences a state of oscillation between the two moments, according to his or her physical distance from the work and the level of perceptual attention. I identify one or more figures/images, I combine them with their complex effects to create a new image, then I come and go between the first images and the second in a kind of embodied contemplation.

It can be said that in a way Riley starts out from images – identifiable figures – and then comes back to them. This is the movement suggested by certain specific works and also by the oeuvre in its entirety, that great bridge spanning the period from the 1960s to the 1990s and 2000s. In both cases the image/figure that takes shape at the end of the process is not exactly the same as the one seen at the beginning. To put it briefly, in the 1960s there was an image, generally comprising a number of similar images (themselves often including tiny, increasingly similar variations) isolated and identifiable on a plain white ground; in recent years this ground has disappeared and the figures, much more clearly differentiated and each identified by an area of colour different from those around it, are juxtaposed to form an overall rectangular image that is more or less stable depending on the contrasts, the complexity of the composition, and so on.

Many of the paintings from the 1960s explicitly abide to the logic of images: they present a centred motif surrounded with white. While this white is marked by optical effects, it remains identifiable as a ground, except in those pictures in which the field effect dominates: as in the two versions of *White Discs* of 1964, in which the only painted images are black discs. These are arranged, however, in the certain knowledge that they will count for less in the overall effect than the figures conjured up and designated by the title. It is possible that at the time all her pictures could have been taken as resulting from a meticulous balance 'between her geometrical, or near-geometrical units, so as to make them destroy each other', to quote Ehrenzweig's text for the 1963 exhibition at Gallery One.[11] Today this balance seems less striking, perhaps because, 40 years on, video games, music videos and 3D animation have inured us to visual assaults markedly more violent than those in these pictures. Thus the four versions of Blaze (1962–63), which Riley herself described as the locus of, 'the most extreme point of optical intensity', are also, first

ÉRIC DE CHASSEY

and last, images of a striped disc, surrounded by white and with a white disc inside.[12] There is absolutely no scope here for inversion of ground and figure, the first being irrevocably linked to the plain white areas and the second to the concentric black lines. We have only to compare this picture to Marina Apollonio's near-contemporary and apparently similar *Dinamica Circolare* (1968) – even in its static form, before a motor sets it in motion – to realise how optically clear it is; doubtless because, unlike the Italian, the British artist chose to put the white disc inside the striped one, like a reciprocal deductive structure, rather than push it off to one side.

Moreover, it suffices that the quantity of repeated and varied elements be relatively limited, or at least not too large – thus preventing the identification of each unit within a whole – for the eye to seize one or more images. Thus the operation described by the artist in 1965 – 'The basis of my paintings is this: in each of them a particular situation is stated. Certain elements within that situation remain constant, others precipitate the destruction of themselves by themselves. Recurrently, as a result of the cyclic movement of repose, disturbance and repose, the original situation is restated'[13] – functions without destroying the images. In *Shift* (1963) identification of the basic motif, a triangle stretched horizontally in one direction or another, is immediate and never lost from view, except that the variations in this context of repetition are barely perceptible in themselves – by which I mean in their comparative specificities – and form an overall image that ultimately incorporates what the eye has also identified as a white ground and a repeated black 'form'.[14] This overall image is made up of a host of small images, of the 'units' the artist has made 'visible' in the course of her work.[15] This can also be the case when a work makes play with tonal gradations from grey to white, as in *Black to White Discs* of 1962, in which one readily identifies the formal unit represented by a disc of unvarying size, and an overall image in the form of a tilted square set against the white square of the support.

A marginal series from the 1960s is the clearest evidence that the artist was not allergic to the image issue – far from it, in fact. The series in question is Fragments, ten silkscreen prints on Plexiglas. These are irregular pieces of what could have been finished paintings: as Kudielka has put it, 'Images thrown up in making a painting which were not fully integrated into the final work, and yet were specific enough to stand on their own.'[16] Their fragmentary character does not explain everything, however. This series is proof that Riley had no qualms about leaving forms hanging before they become field compositions and more or less amorphous – all-over, in other words. Many of her drawings show the same thing, but rarely with such intensity. *Untitled [Fragment No.2]* (1965) nicknamed 'Chinese Curves' by the artist and *Untitled [Fragment No 7]* (1965) are perhaps the ones that go the furthest in this direction, making particularly manifest the uneven curves of a predominantly dark image on a translucent white ground. Their elements are black shapes and white interstices, and the outcome is an all-over dark grey image set, as Robertson puts it, in the space between the Plexiglas and the viewer. The image in *Fragment No.2* is born of the superimposition in ten rows of crescents of different widths, resulting in a highly rococo shape with a sort of implicit white disc towards the bottom. *Fragment No.7* offers a kind of arrow made up of more or less flattened black ovals, as if we were looking at an impossible fragment of the median area of the painting *Where* of 1964. The main effect of their character as image is to endow them with great visual efficacy and to draw the attention of a viewer goaded to anatomise their elements so as to better understand their functioning. Some of them – *Untitled [Fragment No.5]* (1965), for example – almost take on the force of an advertising logo, which is hardly surprising when we know that just before she began her mature work the artist was exposed to 'basic design' by two of its founders, Harry Thubron and Maurice de Sausmarez. At the same period, and until 1964, she worked for the advertising agency J Walter Thompson and in 1965 she designed the logo for the Stage Sixty programme at the Theatre Royal in Stratford East, in London.

The recycling of some of her compositions as illustrations also points up this aspect of her work. Thus a variation on the 1963 painting *Disfigured Circle*, whose character as image comes largely from its being based on eight regular foldings of a drawing of 17 concentric circles, appeared on the cover of a science-fiction book in 1965.[17] More

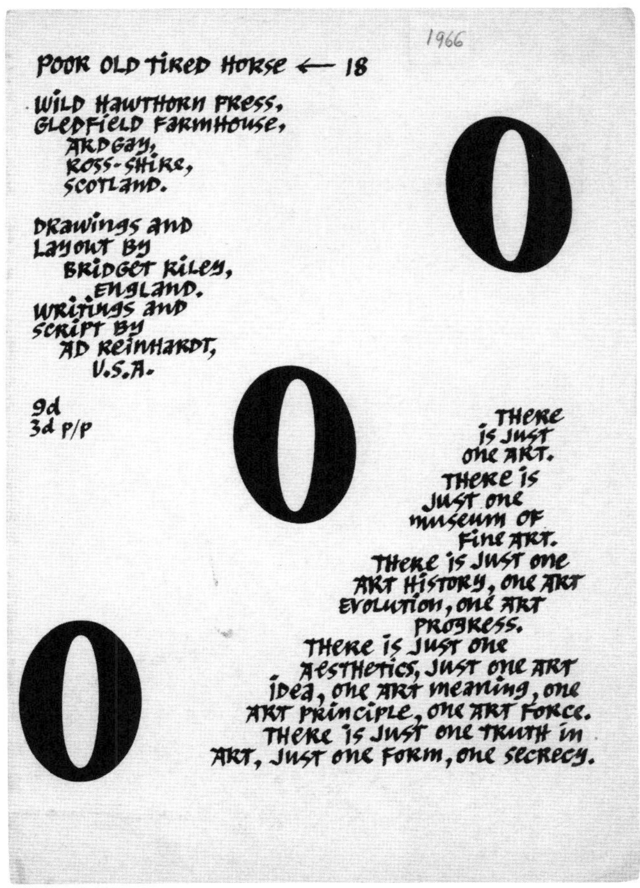

Cover of *Poor Old Tired Horse*, no.18, 1966
Drawings and layout by Bridget Riley; writings and script by Ad Reinhardt

importantly, and much more inventively, in 1965 the basic structure of *Disturbance* (1964) – a superposition of ovals tilting in slightly different directions – recurred on a reduced scale both in *Untitled [Fragment No 4]* (1965), creating a square of which each component, used in a limited number, is specifically identifiable and free of all interference, and on the cover of and inside the little magazine *Poor Old Tired Horse*, no.18, accompanying texts and calligraphy by Ad Reinhardt. Here the oval interacts with the typefaces, setting them, so to speak, in motion, and so turning them into images as singular as they are seemingly prosaic.

The fact that after 1965 Riley, infuriated – or rather fed up – with the way fashion had lifted the images in her pictures to make fabrics and dresses, had abandoned the image issue in most of her work, does not mean it was not there prior to that time, and in a way that certainly contributed to its survival in people's visual memories well after the Op art mode was past. In my opinion this is demonstrated, although with no great subtlety, by the early 1980s reuse of some of these images by New York painters like Philip Taaffe and Ross Bleckner: fin de siècle appropriationism was running hot, and there was a return to an idea briefly outlined in certain critical texts of the 1960s. Without pushing reductiveness as far as these artists did – together with critic Lil Picard, who wrote in 1965 that, 'The new mathematical art equation reads POP-P=OP. That means simply: drop the letter P and op we go'[18] – we can at least conclude that opticality does not necessarily exclude image effectiveness.

It was not until 1997–98 that images returned in force in Riley's painting, with the curve painting series. Here ten or so basic forms make up a vocabulary that engenders figures through combination, which the eye can make out and identify from one picture or drawing to another, and which the mind is even tempted to name as 'almonds', 'commas', 'flames' or 'sails'. The figures are accompanied by others too irregular to be named but which, because of this, are particularly evident, although always remaining abstract. There is no real rupture here, however: all these figures have been obtained by cutting up the rhomboids that served as the base motifs for the previous series with its zig paintings. In the run-up to the definitive creation of a work the artist takes these base images, in the form of paper cut-outs painted different colours, and assembles them at will, sometimes superposing them to create more incongruous figures. Moving to the scale studies, she continues to use cut-out motifs, but bigger ones. Organised as a structure of verticals and diagonals punctuating the long surface with horizontal rectangles, these shapes become the elements of a moving, all-over dynamic image, without their character as specific, separate images being absorbed by this movement – somewhat in the manner of a frieze or, rather, of a scanner sweeping across some mysterious surface – for all these works show a markedly lateral, generally ascending, movement.

The combinations of ellipses and often very steep diagonals produce particularly lively unexpected images referring to no object existing in the outside world, nor to any basic mathematical shape – in any case not to any of those which the mind grasps immediately and the eye takes in without prolonged observation. One is very much aware that there is nothing natural or principal about these shapes. They are simultaneously singular images – a singularity in no way diminished by their appearance in several pictures in the series; on the contrary, repetition renders it more visible – and manifest traces of the process of construction and assemblage that has given birth to them. They are sometimes complete images, sometimes fragmentary ones, in a combination whose possibilities seem never to stop increasing if we compare the first pictures in the series such as *Lagoon 1* (1997) and *Rêve* (1999), with the works of 2007.

The complexity of the vocabulary used, which stems from the very broad possibilities of the combinatorial rules of a limited number of forms, means that in certain cases forms that in the preceding series could in no way be perceived as identifiable figures here become images. Thus the little right-facing rhomboid, a simple, repeated motif bereft of all character, like a brick in a wall in the zig pictures of 1987–97, becomes a figure in its own right in *Painting with Verticals, Cadence 8* (2007), repeated five times in white (at the bottom and the top of the picture only) and twice in pink.

In *Red with Red 1* (2007), restriction of the palette to three colours and, even more so, the close proximity of two of them (a pink-red and

an orange-red) could have made the images disappear, given that they
were hardly visible in the red figures because of the colour temperature.
Paradoxically, however, this limitation suddenly gives rise, to a bright blue
'flame' in the very centre of the picture, isolated against large areas of
flat red whose cutting-up, despite its regularity, seems no less assured.
Here the suddenness is a source of pleasure, as the artist had stressed
previously when speaking about the spectacle of nature and in a way
anticipating the effect her pictures would produce two decades later:
'The pleasures of sight have one characteristic in common – they take
you by surprise. They are sudden, swift and unexpected.'[19] The cutting-up
is vital here, bringing a 'sensation of burning ice', as Georges Duthuit said
of Henri Matisse's cut-outs.[20] Here the image is what stands out against
a continuous field, the particularity of Riley's most recent works being
that this field is itself formed solely by the juxtaposition of these cut-up
shapes. We isolate each figure in relation to the others, and each leads
us, because our attention is drawn to its edges, to isolate the figures
around it. Thus we gradually scan the entire composition, in a movement
which the size of the picture imposes on the whole body, and not just
on the eyes. While such movement is usually instigated by works of art
that tend towards dematerialisation (to the benefit of the immediate
environment) or at least display a mistrust of isolated images (to the
benefit of the all-over effect), the works that cause it here are, on the
contrary, saturated with images.

In truth I know only one other artist who has succeeded in
combining this expansively dynamogenic effect with a singularity of
images that the viewer can cling hard to so as not to lose his footing and
be overwhelmed by the spectacle: I mean Matisse, and the elements I
have just listed are pretty much the constituents of what he saw as the
principles of the *decorative*. Commentators on Riley's recent work have
often insisted on this kinship, but it would be mistaken to think that the
similarities are restricted to the recent works.[21] As early as 1964 the artist
said, 'I wish somebody would give me a big wall to destroy. I mean, to
make it no longer seem a wall',[22] which was doubtless an unconscious
echoing of Matisse's urge to make 'the walls pull back'. This indicates
that her pictures of that period already embodied questions that are

                                              ÉRIC DE CHASSEY

reactivated by the recent paintings and mural works. In its different incarnations so far, at Galerie Max Hetzler in Berlin and PaceWildenstein in New York, *Wall Painting 1* (2007) makes notable play with the wall to the extent that some of its figures are made of the white of the support and are continued on in it (unless it is the case that the support is entering the motifs) in a way also found in Matisse's cut-outs, at least in the photographs showing them in his hotel room in Nice.

Recently Riley admitted that without having sought to do so, she had 'arrived at Matisse'.[23] As a rule her catalogues and exhibitions have put the emphasis on a movement in her oeuvre that has its roots in Georges Seurat and began with the symbolic gesture of the 1959 copy of *The Bridge at Courbevoie* (1886–87) and the first step towards the pulverisation of solid forms and then towards 'field painting'. In fact, the character as image of her abstract paintings in the 1960s and over the past ten years makes it clear that the movement with its origin in Matisse is at least just as relevant. The French artist was a touchstone in the lead-up to the oeuvre. Maurice de Sausmarez has recounted that 'My first visit to Bridget Riley's studio… was in the summer of 1959… Around the walls stood some largish canvases much influenced by late Matisse.'[24] Thus her recent pictures 'rediscover' Matisse and so we await with great impatience the showing of Bridget Riley's paintings with the two versions of *The Dance* (1931–33) from the permanent collection of the Musée d'Art Moderne de la Ville de Paris.

Bridget Riley: Rètrospective, exhibition catalogue, Ridinghouse, London and Arc/Musée d'Art Moderne de la Ville de Paris, Paris, 2008, pp.70–79.

1   Norbert Lynton, 'London Letter', *Art International*, vol.7, no.8, October 1963, p.84.

2   Robert Kudielka has written that, 'The concern with images gave way to a more open field organisation which she attributed at the time to the example of American painting.' Robert Kudielka, 'Building Sensations: The Early Work of Bridget Riley', in Lisa G Corrin (ed), *Bridget Riley: Paintings from the 1960s and 70s*, exhibition catalogue, Serpentine Gallery and Koenig Books, London, 1999, p.27.

3   William C Seitz, quoted in 'Op Art: Pictures That Attack the Eye', *Time*, 23 October 1964, p.42, reprinted in Frances Follin, *Embodied Visions: Bridget Riley, Op Art and the Sixties*, Thames & Hudson and Ridinghouse, London, 2004, p.54.

4   See my review of the book by Frances Follin in *Cahiers du Musée National d'Art Moderne*, no 93, autumn 2005, pp.114–15.

5   Maurice de Sausmarez, *Bridget Riley*, exhibition catalogue, *Studio Vista*, London, 1970, p.29.

6   Bridget Riley, 'Note de Bridget Riley à l'occasion de la presentation de son oeuvre', in Arnauld Pierre (ed), *L'Œil moteur. Art optique et cinétique, 1950–1975*, exhibition catalogue, Musée d'Art Moderne et Contemporain, Musées de Strasbourg, Strasbourg, 2005, p.50. In a way that is certainly not fortuitous, the artist uses the same terms as Michael Fried in his 1967 condemnation of Minimalist art and, in his later work as a historian of the art of the eighteenth and nineteenth centuries, his advocating of a certain kind of art seen as heralding modernism; see notably Michael Fried, *Art and Objecthood*, University of Chicago Press, Chicago, IL, 1998. So instead of 'literality', another term for 'theatricality', we should prefer, in the case of Bridget Riley as of Michael Fried, works conducive to 'absorption'.

7   Bryan Robertson, 'Introduction and Biographical Note', in Bryan Robertson (ed), *Bridget Riley: Paintings and Drawings 1951–71*, exhibition catalogue, Hayward Gallery, London, 1971, p.7.

8   Anton Ehrenzweig, 'The Pictorial Space of Bridget Riley', *Art International*, vol.9, no.1, February 1965, pp.20–21.

9   David Sylvester, 'Bridget Riley', *The New Statesman*, 25 May 1962. To put it briefly, the optical discharge produced by the encounter between the two forms would lead Ellsworth Kelly to avoid this kind of composition and, initially to emphasise the calm presence of a clearly defined form against a ground, then the autonomous presence of a single coloured form. Riley, by contrast, would set out to create and accentuate these optical effects.

10   Ehrenzweig, *op.cit.*

11   Anton Ehrenzweig, 'Introduction', in *Bridget Riley*, exhibition catalogue, Gallery One, London, 1963. reprinted in De Sausmarez, *op.cit.*, p.50.

12   Bridget Riley, 'A Repetition Reviewed: Talking to Andrew Graham-Dixon (1992), in Robert Kudielka (ed), *Dialogues on Art*, Zwemmer, London, 1995, p.70.

13   Bridget Riley, 'Perception Is the Medium' (1965), in Robert Kudielka (ed), *The Eye's Mind: Bridget Riley, Collected Writings 1965–1999*, Thames & Hudson, London, 1999, p.66.

14   Robert Kudielka's reading of this picture is substantially different from the one I suggest here. For him, 'a purely additive structure of triangles… is in practice not analytically grasped, as a sum of discrete single units, but synthetically conceived a priori: as a totality of one and the same mathematical concept, the idea of "triangle", represented by an indefinite number of manifestations.' In Robert Kudielka, 'Nothing but Appearance', in *Bridget Riley: Works 1959–78*, exhibition catalogue, British Council, London, 1978, p.16.

15   'When I've selected a unit which I'm thinking of using in a painting, I make this unit visible, so that I can see its attendant problems and its potential'; in 'Bridget Riley Interviewed by David Sylvester', *Studio International*, vol.173, no.887, March 1967, p.132.

   ÉRIC DE CHASSEY

16   Robert Kudielka, 'Introduction', in *Working Methods 4: Bridget Riley Silkscreen Prints 1965–78*, exhibition catalogue, Arts Council of Great Britain, London 1978, n.p.

17   The book in question is Brian W Aldiss, *Best Science Fiction Stories*, Faber & Faber, London, 1965. Although the credit states that 'the image on the jacket is by Bridget Riley' it does not seem to be her work. The folding of *Disfigured Circle* is reproduced in De Sausmarez, *op.cit.*, p.48.

18   Lil Picard, 'Op-report', *Kunstwerk*, July 1965, quoted by Follin, *op.cit.*, p.10. The works by Riley were shown in the same venues as those of the main representatives of British abstract Pop: like her, Derek Boshier took part in the *New Generation* exhibition at the Whitechapel Art Gallery in London in 1964; and Gerald Laing's first solo exhibition took place at the Richard Feigen Gallery in New York in November 1965, between Riley's first and second solo shows.

19   Bridget Riley, 'The Pleasures of Sight' (1984), in Kudielka (ed), *The Eye's Mind*, *op.cit.*, p.32.

20   Georges Duthuit, 'Le tailleur de lumiere', *Verve*, no.35–36, summer 1958, reprinted in Rémi Labrusse (ed), *Écrits sur Matisse*, ENSBA, Paris, 1992, p.181.

21   The connection between Matisse and the works in the series in progress has notably been analysed in Robert Kudielka, 'Abstract Figuration: On Bridget Riley's Recent Curve Paintings', in Paul Moorhouse (ed), *Bridget Riley*, exhibition catalogue, Tate Publishing, London, 2003, pp.153–57; Lynne Cooke, 'Encore', in *Bridget Riley: Paintings and Drawings 1961–2004*, exhibition catalogue, Ridinghouse, London, 2004, pp.108–11; and Marla Prather, 'New Cadences: Paintings by Bridget Riley, 2004–2007', in *Bridget Riley: Recent Paintings and Gouaches*, exhibition catalogue, PaceWildenstein, New York, NY, 2007, pp.10–12.

22   Bridget Riley, 'Something to Blink At', *Time*, May 1964, p.45, quoted by Follin, *op.cit.*, p.84. Henri Matisse, quoted by Georges Duthuit (1949), reprinted in Dominique Fourcade (ed), *Henri Matisse*: *Écrits et propos sur l'art*, Hermann, Paris, 1972, p.154.

23   Bridget Riley, quoted in Lynn McRitchie, 'The Intelligence of the Eye', in Martin Henschel (ed), *Bridget Riley: New Work*, exhibition catalogue, Kunstmuseen Krefeld, Krefeld and Hatje Cantz, Ostfildern, 2002, p.19.

24   De Sausmarez, *op.cit.*, p.26.

Bridget Riley and the Art of the Brain

Semir Zeki

I have always considered art within the broader context of one of the main functions of the brain, namely, the acquisition of knowledge.[1] I do not mean that when embarking upon a work the artist necessarily consciously seeks to acquire or impart knowledge. Rather, that he or she uses an apparatus – the brain – whose function is to acquire knowledge. Through its use the artist not only acquires knowledge and transposes it into his or her chosen medium, but introduces a dialogue between the work and the viewer, through which the latter also acquires knowledge, usually without even realising it, just as we acquire knowledge about daily events without realising that we are doing so. Bridget Riley's work exemplifies this perfectly and, for the neurobiologist, also raises explicit and critical questions about how the seeing apparatus – consisting of eye and brain – functions. These are questions that promise to lead to a deeper knowledge about visual perception. In this, Riley's work is part of a line that includes several past masters, among them Pablo Picasso, Paul Cézanne, Kazimir Malevich and Piet Mondrian, whose work likewise constitutes an explicit exploration of vision and thus of the visual apparatus. Visual research may seem an odd way to describe works of art, traditionally thought to belong in a world divorced from and remote from science. Yet the questions raised by her work are not only specific but also scientifically compelling and of huge neurobiological interest. Her work is a perfect illustration of Paul Klee's statement that, 'Art does not reproduce the visible; rather it makes visible.'[2]

In writing this essay, I have chosen to discuss aspects of Riley's work that seem to me to be especially interesting in raising important questions about how the visual brain functions. They illustrate perfectly the notion, which I have tried to emphasise in the past and which is gaining acceptance among other neurobiologists,[3] that the artist, besides being an artist, is also a neurobiologist who explores the visual brain, though through a medium that is unique and distinct from the scientific techniques used by the neurobiologist.[4] Art, in other words, is another means of acquiring knowledge about ourselves. Many, perhaps even most, people might be tempted into thinking that the works exhibited here acquire their magic because of some kind of trick created by the artist. We see in these works motion where there is none, or forms that do not objectively exist. We have even invented a term for the apparent discrepancy between the objective reality and what we perceive. We call them 'illusions' or 'illusory figures' because we believe that what we perceive departs from the physical reality. This is to misunderstand or be unaware of a cardinal fact, namely that there is, perceptually at any rate, no reality but brain reality and no knowledge but brain knowledge. If one actually perceives motion in some of the static works displayed here, it is because the realities of how the brain is organised and functions impose a perceptual motion – which is in every sense perceptually real. This perceptual reality cannot be overridden by a higher intellectual cognitive component, which is why I like so much the essential distinction made by Riley between the cognitive and the perceptual reading of a work of art.[5] The two really are separate. The perceptual reality induced by the works reproduced here, as well as the reality of the separation between the perceptual and cognitive, both of which contribute to knowledge of the visual world, can be easily tested by trying *not* to see motion, in the (intellectually but not perceptually derived) knowledge that there is objectively none in the works depicted here. It just will not work. Riley is not using any tricks, illusory or otherwise. She is merely using the capacities of the visual brain to make us perceive the realities that it creates, thus opening the doors to a better understanding of how the brain creates these realities.

Colour, form and motion

In neurobiological terms, Riley's work addresses three critical issues: colour, form and motion. Not only is each of these attributes interesting in itself, but the interplay and interaction between them is of fundamental importance, both for understanding her work and for understanding how the visual brain and, by extension the brain at large,

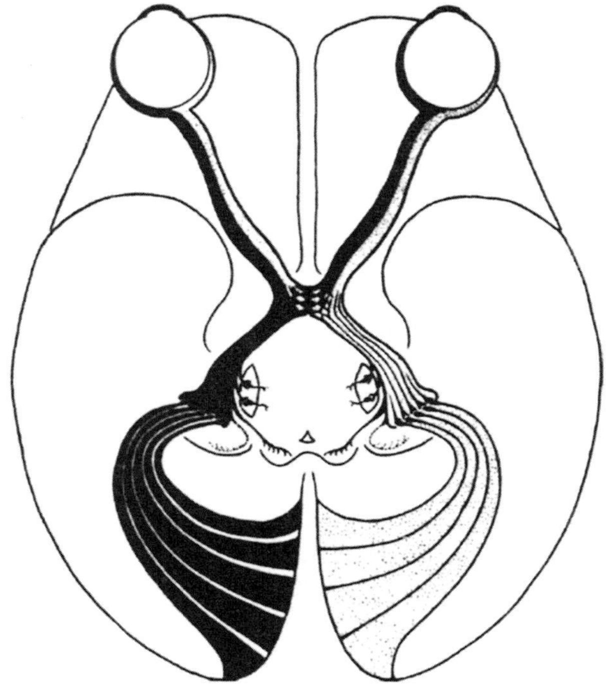

Diagram showing the trajectory from the retina to the visual
cortex receptors located in the posterior part of the brain.

functions. Indeed, at a certain level, one could say that the interest in these works is the light they throw upon the process of interaction in the brain between these different visual attributes.

For over a century, following the discovery of the (primary) visual centre in the brain in the 1860s, neurobiologists were inclined to account for all vision in terms of a single visual area, area V1.[6] In the 1970s,[7] it was found that there are many other visual areas outside the primary visual receiving centre in the brain, and that these different visual areas are specialised to process different visual attributes.[8] Chief among these are the attributes so prominently explored in the work of Riley, namely, colour, form and motion. An important question, though not the only one, raised by this neurobiological demonstration is the interplay between the three, the very question addressed artistically in her works. That we become aware of different attributes of the visual world because of activity in geographically distinct visual areas in the brain and, moreover, that we become aware of different attributes at different times – the perception of colour preceding that of form by 40 milliseconds and of motion by 80 milliseconds[9] – implies that visual consciousness is distributed in space and in time and that there is no single visual consciousness at the phenomenal level. Instead there are many. This naturally raises the question of how the separate perceptions of these attributes (the visual consciousnesses) are brought together or integrated in the brain to give us our unitary perception of the visual world, whereby all attributes are apparently seen simultaneously? Or are they? For the different attributes in the compositions of Riley and other artists can be perceptually teased apart, even if they belong to the same work. And yet there is no doubting the interplay between them, which is what gives these works their power. And therein lie important questions about the organisation of the brain.

Motion and depth from form

In some of Riley's compositions, motion is either strongly implied or actually perceived. In this her abstract compositions go far beyond the cognitively implied motion of earlier static compositions, such as Marcel Duchamp's *Nude Descending a Staircase* (1912) or Henri Matisse's *Dance II* (1910) or, indeed, in her own *Paired Colours* (2001). The compositions also depart from examples found in kinetic art, where motion is perceived because objective motion is actually a part of the work of art, as in the work of Jean Tinguely and Alexander Calder.[10] An excellent example is to be found in the work entitled *Blaze 3* (1963), where the arrangement of diagonal lines into spirals induces a perception of rapid motion. It is not the lines themselves, individually, that produce a motion percept, but rather their arrangement in relation to each other, their juxtaposition. There is good reason to believe that the perceived motion is the result of neural activity in a specific area of the visual brain, area V5 (the visual motion centre), activity which is then projected onto the work of art.[11] Nor is just any arrangement effective;[12] it must have specific features, arrived at through perceptual experimentation by the artist. In that specificity, which is being studied,[13] lies the secret of how the cells in the specialised visual motion centre of the brain become activated to generate motion from form, a topic of profound neurobiological interest. The cells of area V5 are most potently driven by spots of light actually moving in a specific direction, and are hence referred to as 'directionally selective cells'. The actual form of the moving object seems to be of minor interest to them, which is why Calder's mobiles would be such an effective stimulus for activating V5.

However, the activation of V5 by *Blaze 3* is not direct in the sense that it is not produced by objective motion. Rather, it is derived from a specific arrangement, of which *Blaze 3* is just one example. Thus, these works raise the question of what the neural mechanism is by which a juxtaposition of specific forms – rather than spots of objectively moving light – generates a motion percept. The perception of motion in these (objectively) static compositions leads to another point, which is obvious enough but nevertheless worth repeating and emphasising, that the motion is not physically there; it is entirely produced by and in the brain and projected onto the work of art. It constitutes an excellent example of a more general fact: that in viewing any work of art, the brain projects its own concepts onto the work and, hence, viewing the work is not a passive enterprise but an active one in which the brain, through dialogue with the work, actually creates what it perceives. Matisse was right when he wrote that, 'Seeing is already a creative operation, one that demands an effort.'[14]

The interaction of elements which, collectively, produce a reality that individually they are incapable of producing is also illustrated by *Cataract 3* (1967), one of several compositions in which wavy lines induce a perception of depth as well as motion. Here again it is not the individual wavy lines that produce the effect but their specific juxtaposition. Note that the perceptual effect produced is much more real and arresting than the effect produced in, for example, Katsushika Hokusai's *The Great Wave* (1829–32), where any depth imparted to the painting is more cognitive than perceptual. Cézanne strongly believed that seeing is a creative process occurring in the brain; it is activity in the brain that relates one part of a composition to other parts, thus giving the whole a pictorial unity. This process was summarised in his favourite word, *réalisation*. He wrote, 'Only from their sum, their relation and interaction, do the objects they define reveal themselves to the viewer'.[15] But where does this interaction occur? In the brain of the perceiver, of course. The interesting question for the neurobiologist thus becomes, 'Where in the brain, and how?' It is the use of compositions such as these that will eventually give us the answer to the question, for these compositions are of course the product of the brain and obey the laws of the brain, which is why they are compelling to so many viewers and constitute such interesting material for the neurobiologist.

Colour interactions

The above examples constitute interactions across visual attributes, or rather the generation of one attribute from another, for example, motion from form. The generation of one attribute from another depends upon our neural machinery and constitutes a compelling example of the creative capacities of the brain, in this instance produced by the interaction of subdivisions of the visual brain dealing with different attributes of the visual world. Perhaps one of the most remarkable examples of this creative capacity of the brain in its knowledge-seeking role is to be found in colour, another attribute strongly emphasised in Riley's work. The cardinal rule in colour vision can be summarised in one word – comparison, which is of course undertaken by the brain.

For many years, scientific theorising about colour was restricted to the great laws of colour mixing, derived from the work of Thomas Young and Hermann von Helmholtz, and the subsequent discovery that there are only three colour receptors in the retina, each responding to an extensive region of the visible spectrum but having a peak sensitivity at a particular point. The general supposition was that the brain somehow mixed the wavelength signals coming from a surface and determined its colour, just as is done in colour-mixing experiments. This supposition neatly sidestepped the vexed question of colour constancy – of why it is that a green leaf, for example, which reflects more red light (as indeed most do when viewed at dawn or dusk) is still perceived as green – by supposing that the colour is imposed through memory, judgement and past experience of knowing what colour a leaf should have or, in Riley's words, by reading colour cognitively rather than perceptually. Helmholtz thus supposed that 'colour is not due to an act of sensation, but to an act of judgement',[16] while another German psychophysicist, Ewald Hering, thought that, 'All the colours which we know or think that we know, we see through the spectacles of our memory colours and therefore quite differently from the way which we would see them without these, always providing that we are not thinking about the colour', implying that it is our memory that imposes the colour, not the wavelength composition of the light reflected from an object.[17] In summary, it was believed that a higher cognitive factor was brought to bear upon what is perceived, thus forcing the interpretation in a certain direction, a formulation which, if one thinks about it, neatly separates perception from knowledge.

The discovery that there is a colour centre in the brain, area V4, changed all that.[18] Cells in the colour centre respond not only to spectral light (e.g. red, green or blue) but to extra-spectral combinations, such as purple (a combination of red and blue), as well. Many seem to behave as if they are concerned with the colour of a surface rather than with the wavelength composition of the light reflected from it (since the wavelength composition can change significantly without modifying the colour category). A V4 cell responding to green, for example, will respond to a green surface even if it reflects more red light but still looks green,[19] through the operation of the principle of colour constancy, by which the colours of surfaces do not change when the illuminant in which they are viewed changes dramatically[20] (for example between tungsten light and sunlight).[21] Such cells acquire their unique behaviour by virtue of the fact that they are able to compare the wavelength composition of light reflected from a given surface with the wavelength composition of the light reflected from surrounding surfaces. Through such comparisons, the brain is able to disengage itself from the continually changing lighting conditions in which a surface is viewed. What the brain seems to do is record the ratio of light of all wavebands reflected from a surface and from those surfaces that surround it. This ratio never changes, because the reflectance of a surface (the percentage of light of any given waveband reflected from it as a function of light of the same waveband incident on it) never changes. It is the brain that determines these ratios and it is their comparison, in the brain, that determines the colour of a surface. Colour therefore is a creation of the brain.[22] It does not exist in the world outside. It is a creation that gives knowledge about a physical property of a surface, namely its reflectance or capacity to reflect light of all visible wavebands in relation to the capacity of the surrounds to reflect the same wavebands. Moreover, it is a creation that is critically dependent, not upon activation of the higher centres of the brain that are traditionally associated with cognitive functions, but upon the healthy activity of a visual perceptual area, area V4, without which the human subject is not able to construct colours, even when the retina and the optic pathways leading to the brain are intact. Subjects with a wholly damaged V4 describe the world in terms of 'dirty shades of grey'.[23] Here, then, is knowledge gained by a simple perceptual operation conducted by the brain, without the mandatory involvement of higher cognitive factors. Here, too, is a good demonstration that knowledge cannot be separated from simple perception, a formulation of which Riley's work is a forceful artistic demonstration.

The behaviour of V4 cells is critically dependent upon the surrounds of the area whose colour is being judged; in fact it is the presence of surrounds that enables the brain to construct and assign a constant colour to a surface. Surrounds thus acquire a critical importance, which artists know about much more than scientists, since they have been experimenting with them for centuries. Surrounds change the perceived colour of a given surface in both subtle and not-so-subtle ways, and hence I imagine that the term colour constancy must seem an anomaly to artists. The term 'constancy' implies a stability, whereas Riley has emphasised that 'the basis of colour is its instability' because 'one never sees a colour isolated, and so you never know exactly *what a particular colour is in itself*' (original emphasis).[24] In the change that one colour imposes upon a surrounding or even remotely located colour, we are confronted once again with the problem of interaction, but this time not between attributes but within an attribute. What are the laws that dictate that surrounds should change in the way they do? There are obviously the well-worked laws of simultaneous colour contrast, but an examination of Riley's work suggests that there is much else besides which has remained unexplored. To the innocent eye, the piece interestingly entitled *Conversation* (1992) stands in sharp contrast to *In Attendance* (1994). The colours seem to interact or converse much more intimately in the former, giving it greater power and immediacy. The physiologist may want to classify the colours in the two works into a gamut, yet the observer will perceive the same colours to differ significantly in the two contexts. If colours are generated by the brain, then so are the interactions between them. It is hard to believe that these associations do not obey some kind of law. What kind of law remains to be determined but the works displayed here provide a good pointer. André Malraux was right when he drew attention to Cézanne's maxim that, 'There is a logic to colour; the artist should obey only that, never the logic of the brain', describing it as *cette phrase maladroite* in his book *Les Voix du silence* (The Voices of Silence, 1951).[25] It is indeed clumsy for there is no logic to colour but brain logic, and the brain applies its well-defined logic to generating colour. I do not wish to imply that these laws of colour interaction can be derived directly from viewing the works displayed here, but these works give us a hint of the kind of laws that must govern the appearance of juxtaposed patches; they constitute the beginnings of an enquiry by the observer no less than the scientist into brain laws that govern the perception of one of the leading perceptual products of the brain, namely colour. Of course, the modulation of one colour by a juxtaposed colour or a remotely located one is also a feature in paintings by the Old Masters – Giorgione, Titian, El Greco and Rubens, among others. But the immediate reading of such works is more cognitive than perceptual, whereas with Riley's work the dominant perceptual element makes the determination of the nature of the relationships easier to study.

The liberation of colour

The presence of surrounds also means that colour cannot be divorced from form, for the border separating a given surface from its surround always has a form or shape. Yet provided there is a surround, the exact shape or form between the surface and its surround does not matter; it could be straight or curved or diagonal and the surrounding surfaces could be rectangular or oblong or circular. This indifference to the exact form gives the artist considerable freedom in playing with colours and giving them supremacy, without worrying too much about the exact configuration. The Fauves tried to 'liberate' colour in order to give it greater emotional intensity. Not being able to divorce it from form, they settled on another approach, that of investing familiar objects with unusual colours (unusual in terms of our experience). In emphasising colour in her abstract compositions, Riley has commonly de-emphasised form or rendered it meaningless. Instead, form is used as a vehicle to generate colour interactions. It is the colours, and their interaction, according to rules which have yet to be documented, that give the compositions their perceptual and aesthetic vitality. Riley has recorded her admiration for Monet's late works, which are, 'about virtually nothing;

about looking into a huge expanse of water set with a few lilies in which unexpected colours appear in the depths, or elusively in the reflections. It is a most mysterious, extraordinary subject in which he invests all his experience and power. In the end there seems to be hardly any subject matter left – only content.'[26] This interesting statement is equally applicable to some of her own work. *New Day* (1988), *Reflection 1* (1994) and *August* (1995) each consist of a seemingly arbitrary assembly of diagonally oriented lines and rectangles; yet each has a distinctive personality derived from its colours and their juxtaposition. It is all content.

The use of colour interactions to give unity to a painting is of course nothing new. It was used by the great masters of the past. Cézanne and Mondrian also understood this critical feature of colour, which is that it derives its power largely from how it is assembled together on canvas in relation to other colours. 'Nothing is beautiful without unity', wrote Denis Diderot in his essay 'Pensées détachées sur la peinture, la sculpture, l'architecture et la poésie' (Isolated Thoughts on Painting, Sculpture, Architecture and Poetry, 1776). To him, the details were not important. Objects could be distorted if they served the higher purpose, that of unity. To achieve that unity, the entire canvas had to be painted and to advance at once, advice given to Cézanne by Pissarro and enthusiastically accepted. Cézanne wrote, 'I advance… all of my canvas at once, together. In the same movement, the same conviction, I bring into relation everything that is scattered'.[27] Mondrian, too, experimented with the colour of the rectangles in his abstract compositions until he achieved what he believed to be a unity that was serene and free from tension. But where is that unity achieved? Not on canvas, but in the brain of the perceiver.

Cézanne experimented with how colour modulates form, but the forms in Cézanne's work are never constant. In contrast, in the paintings alluded to above, Riley imposes a constancy on the forms by restricting them severely and modulates them with colour. In the process, the form becomes subordinate to the colour. Here colour is given a phenomenal or perceptual primacy that is vastly different to the cognitive primacy it acquires in fauvist works. It is perhaps worth emphasising that cells in the brain that are specialised for registering wavelengths or generating colour are largely indifferent to the form of the stimulus. Their preoccupation is with colour alone. Perhaps the real way to liberate colour from form is not to dress well-known forms in unusual colours but to de-emphasise the forms and make them indifferent, as does Riley, whose works impart a perceptual knowledge that is immediate and not dependent upon higher cognitive factors.

The pursuit of form

One of the most intractable problems in visual neurobiology has proved to be the problem of form. Different artists have explicitly pursued the problem in different ways. The Cubists, at least in the early analytical phase of Cubism, wanted to represent form on a two-dimensional surface in such a way that the lighting conditions, viewing distance and angle all ceased to matter. For Mondrian, who considered that the Cubists had failed to pursue the logical consequences of their discoveries, the critical question was: what are the essential constituents of all forms? He believed that art 'shows that there are also constant truths concerning forms' and saw as the aim of art to reduce all complex forms to one or a few universal forms,[28] 'to discover consciously or unconsciously the fundamental laws hidden in reality', seemingly oblivious to the concept that it is the brain that creates the reality.[29] He settled for the vertical and horizontal straight line, defining form as the 'plurality of straight lines in rectangular opposition'. The straight line also became a critical feature of the work of the suprematist Kazimir Malevich, and his successors. Malevich wrote, 'Art wants nothing further to do with the object as such', and exhorted artists to produce what was in their mind.[30]

The discovery, in the 1960s, that many cells in both the primary visual receiving centre and some other areas of the brain are selectively responsive to lines of a given orientation led many physiologists to a supposition that was remarkably similar to the earlier theorising of Mondrian: that these so-called 'orientation selective cells' are the 'physiological building blocks' of form.[31] Yet almost 50 years of intensive visual research has failed to uncover how complex forms are constituted from simple oriented lines or, to phrase it neurobiologically, how orientation selective cells interact to generate cells that are capable of responding to more complex forms. I am increasingly inclined to believe that neurobiologists have been mistaken in their supposition that the orientation selective cells are the building blocks of form perception. Rather, the construction of form by the brain uses different mechanisms in parallel and does not necessarily elaborate complex forms from simple lines.[32] This naturally leaves unanswered the question of what the real role of the orientation selective cells may be. A glance at some of Riley's work, for example *Big Blue* (1982), shows how effective perceptually the oriented straight line is. Such compositions would act as powerful stimulants of the orientation selective cells in the brain. Yet orientation selective cells are indifferent to colour, in the sense that a cell that responds selectively to the vertical orientation will do so irrespective of the colour of the oriented line. The perceptual power of these compositions derives more from the use of oriented lines to provoke colour interactions, keeping the form constant as before, but even more so. How the interactions can occur, and across how many oriented lines, is an unsolved problem. But it is equally important for us to recognise that the entire work acquires a unity that is independent of the lines themselves or, rather, is more than the sum of its parts. It is not at all clear that the manner by which the brain processes such figures consists of a piecemeal registration of the oriented lines, to which colour is then added and the whole subsequently assembled together. Rather, all the evidence suggests that the work would be processed in parallel by different visual subsystems of the brain. The orientated lines will naturally stimulate the orientation selective cells, and the activity of cells in V4 will correlate with the colours. But beyond that, it is more than likely that the entire composition will stimulate a further area in the lateral occipital complex of the brain, which has been found to be critical for the perception of forms.[33] The point I am trying to emphasise here is that, by all means concentrate on the elements if you choose to, but do not lose sight that perceptually as well as neurobiologically, the composition has a unity to it and is registered as a unity by the brain.

The same is true in the composition entitled *Entice 2* (1974). Here, the wavy lines generate diagonally slanted oriented lines, which are not physically there but are generated by the interaction of the wavy lines. The lines so generated would also be very effective stimuli for the orientation selective cells of the visual brain, since these respond even to virtual lines.[34] But of course they are only part of the compositions, produced by an interaction within the composition. It is very likely that the brain will treat the entire composition in a separate system from the one that it uses to register oriented lines, although the oriented lines will retain their power to stimulate the orientation selective cells. All this is to emphasise, neurobiologically, what Riley has said – that the elements are lost but retain their identity.

There are other compositions in which the form is totally dominant, the compositions themselves being achromatic. A favourite of mine, both aesthetically and neurobiologically, is *Composition with Circles 1* (1998). Here we have a seemingly simple form that is actually quite complex. The interaction of the elements gives an exhilarating impression of space, but one that is somewhat mysterious, thus provoking a more intense dialogue with the viewer. Note that here one is beginning to shift from a purely perceptual reading to a cognitive one as well. The recognition of the interlacing circles constitutes a perceptual reading. The impression of space straddles the boundary between the perceptual and the cognitive, but its inaccessibility constitutes, to me at least, a strongly cognitive reading, for there is nothing in the work itself to suggest that it is accessible or inaccessible. The work, moreover, is ambiguous in the sense that I can project multiple concepts onto it and different viewers can project their own concepts that may be different from mine. It thus also induces a dialogue with the viewer. Such a cognitive reading is a prominent feature of other works. The title *Kiss* (1961) implies, and even forces, a certain interpretation. But the composition is ambiguous enough to allow other interpretations. *Tonal Study Nude* (c.1951), though perhaps constrained by the title, nevertheless allows multiple interpretations. Ambiguity, I have argued elsewhere, is a prized characteristic in art as long as one defines it in the neurobiological sense – not uncertainty, but exactly the opposite – certainty, but the certainty of many different concepts projected onto the work, each one of which is sovereign at any given moment, and none of which is correct, since they are all correct.[35] It is notable that a straightforward perceptual reading of for example, *Cataract 3* does not allow multiple, and even contradictory interpretations. The viewer is not at liberty to not see the depth or the motion. Any projection of concepts onto such a work – for example to interpret it as the waves of the Mediterranean at sunset on a Greek beach, would be strictly cognitive. And this makes it interesting to consider briefly the differences and similarities between perceptual and cognitive knowledge.

Perceptual knowledge and cognitive knowledge

In this article I have emphasised a distinction made by Riley herself, between perceptual and cognitive elements. Her work illustrates perfectly what I believe to be a critical feature of the visual system, namely that through the operation of its perceptual system, it is able to endow us with knowledge that is distinct from the cognitive element, which is not to say that there is no cognitive element in her work, quite the contrary. It seems useful to summarise here that distinction in neurobiological terms, sketching out the similarities and the differences between the two.

To obtain knowledge, the brain uses two systems that are distinct though intimately related. In a sense, they both require the use of concepts. The first set of concepts are inherited ones, through which the brain organises the (often chaotic) visual signals in such a way that they become meaningful. One could as well call these brain programmes, but there are various reasons why I prefer not to do so.[36] The generation of colour is one example of the operation of an inherited brain concept, which organises the signals according to an inherited brain rule. In this case, it does so by comparing the ratios of light of different wavebands reflected from one surface and from its surrounding surfaces. Inherited brain concepts have a critical characteristic, in that they are immutable, and there is no (cognitive) appeal against them. For example, one cannot decide that a green leaf (or surface in a natural surround) that is reflecting more long-wave (red) light should look red, even though one knows that the surface is reflecting more red light. Much the same is true of the apparent oriented lines in *Entice 2*. Perhaps this can be nicely summarised in the lines of that old English nursery rhyme:

> As I was going up the stair,
> I saw a man who wasn't there.
> He wasn't there again today,
> I do so wish he'd go away!

Riley's work is rich in displaying other kinds of concepts, almost certainly inherited, that organise certain configurations in ways against which there is no appeal, and hence tell us something important about the way in which the brain manages these signals. The patches of colour that we perceive in her works acquire their hue because of interactive laws in the brain. One cannot isolate a coloured patch in a work such as *August* and determine its hue when viewed alone, and then hope to perceive the same hue when it is re-embedded in the composition. Equally, one cannot pretend that, because the composition entitled *Cataract 3* is on a flat two-dimensional surface, the dimension of depth or of motion should not be perceived. There cannot, in short, be a cognitive override that modifies the way that we experience these works. This perceptual stability gives these works enormous interest from a neurobiological perspective, for they give us hints to be exploited experimentally as to the rules that the brain uses to organise the sensory visual input. This of course amounts to obtaining invaluable knowledge about the operations of the brain.

To be able to obtain knowledge about the world, the brain also constructs another concept – the acquired concept. These are active throughout life and are continually modified in the light of experience. They are synthetic in the sense that the concept at any given moment is a synthesis of all the concepts of a particular object that one has acquired up until that point. I can illustrate this by saying that my concept of a plane today is different from the one I had as a child, when there were no jet engines and jumbo jets, and when a trip to Japan entailed several stopovers. No doubt it will be different in years to come, when we are promised pilotless jets that can travel from London to New York in 30 minutes. Equally, my (cognitive) reading of many of Riley's works might be different if I had visited Egypt, which has inspired some of her work. Here, as opposed to the inherited concept, I can decide to interpret works in different ways at different times, and differently from others as well. The very satisfying element in Riley's work is that the two kinds of brain concepts can be readily isolated and yet also allowed to interact.

I am not oblivious, of course, to the fact that this is an artistic exhibition, not a scientific one, should one choose to emphasise such a difference. But science is about curiosity, and the scientist should be prepared to draw his inspiration from any source, including the artistic. It seems, through reading some of Riley's writings, that she herself has reached conclusions from her artistic work that are remarkably insightful scientifically. But what about the aesthetic side? That of course must remain a matter of individual taste, based to a significant degree on acquired concepts of what constitutes the beautiful. Yet even here, we can determine with fair certainty what individuals consider to be beautiful. Recent experiments show that the experience of beauty correlates with activity in a given part of the brain, the orbito-frontal cortex, which is part of the reward system of the brain. The intensity of activity in it relates directly to the declared intensity of beauty experienced by an individual.[37] If the day comes when we are able to get an objective measure of the beauty experienced by individuals when viewing works of art, I would be surprised if we did not find that it is those works in which artists have used perceptual rules and brain laws about which science yet knows nothing that will be pronounced to be rewarding. This exhibition has plenty of them.

Bridget Riley: Retrospective, exhibition catalogue, Ridinghouse, London and Arc/Musée d'Art Moderne de la Ville de Paris, Paris, 2008, pp.114–25.

1   Semir Zeki, *Inner Vision: An Exploration of Art and the Brain*, Oxford University Press, Oxford, 1999.

2   Paul Klee (1948), quoted in HB Chipp (ed), *Theories of Modern Art*, University of California Press, Berkeley, CA, 1968, p.182. His actual words were 'Kunst gibt nicht das Sichtbare wieder, sondem macht sichtbar'.

3   Patrick Cavanagh, 'The Artist as Neuroscientist', *Nature*, no.434, 2005, pp.301–07.

4   Semir Zeki, *A Vision of the Brain*, Blackwell Publishing, Oxford, 1978, and Zeki, *Inner Vision*, op.cit.

5   Bridget Riley, 'The Colour Connection: In Conversation with Robert Kudielka' (1989), in Robert Kudielka (ed), *The Eye's Mind: Bridget Riley, Collected Writings 1965–1999*, Thames & Hudson, London, 1999.

6   See Semir Zeki, 'Bridget Riley and the Art of the Brain', in *Bridget Riley: Retrospective*, exhibition catalogue, Ridinghouse, London and Arc/Musée d'Art Moderne de la Ville de Paris, Paris, 2008, p.100, ill.01: Diagram to show the projection of the visual pathway from the retina to the primary visual receiving cortex, located at the back of the brain.

7   Semir Zeki, 'Functional Specialisation in the Visual Cortex of the Rhesus Monkey', *Nature*, no.274, 1978, pp.423–8; Semir Zeki *et al.*, 'A Direct Demonstration of Functional Specialization in the Human Visual Cortex', *Journal of Neuroscience*, no.11, 1991, pp.641–49.

8   See Zeki, 'Bridget Riley and the Art of the Brain', *op.cit.*, p.101, ill.02: Reconstruction of a brain imaging experiment during which human subjects viewed a colour abstract pattern (left) and a pattern of dots in motion (right). Areas of activity are shown in white, red and yellow in these horizontal sections through the brain. Area V1, the primary visual receiving centre, which constitutes the entrance to the rest of the visual brain is active with both kinds of stimulation. On the other hand, colour activates area V4 (left) while motion activates V5 (right), thus showing the function specialisation in the visual brain. V4 and V5 are two among many other visual areas in the brain.

9   Konstantinos Moutoussis and Semir Zeki, 'A Direct Demonstration of Perceptual Asynchrony in Vision', *Proceedings of the Royal Society London B*, vol.265, 1997, pp.393–99; Konstantinos Moutoussis and Semir Zeki, 'Temporal Hierarchy of the Visual Perceptive Systems in the Mondrian World', *Proceedings of the Royal Society London B*, vol 264, 1997, pp.1415–19.

10 For a review of this subject see Semir Zeki and Michael Lamb, 'The Neurology of Kinetic Art', *Brain*, no.117, 1994, p.607–36.

11 Semir Zeki *et al.*, 'Going Beyond the Information Given: The Relation of Illusory Visual Motion to Brain Activity', *Proceedings of the Royal Society London B*, vol.252, 1993, pp.215–22.

12 Isia Leviant, 'Does Brain Power Make Enigma Spin?', *Proceedings of the Royal Society London B*, vol.263, 1997, pp.997–1001.

13 Tribhawan Kumar and Donald A Glaser, 'Illusory Motion in Enigma', *Proceedings of the National Academy of Sciences of the USA*, vol.103, 2006, pp.1947–52; Kai Hamburger, 'Apparent Rotation and Jazzing in Leviant's Enigma Illusion', *Perception*, vol.36, 2007, pp.797–807.

14 Henri Matisse, *Écrits et propos sur l'art*, Hermann, Paris, 1972.

15 Joachim Gasquet, 'Ce qu'il m'a dit…' (1921), in PM Doran (ed), *Conversations avec Cézanne*, Macula, Paris, 1978.

16 Herman von Helmholtz, *Handbuch der physiologischen optik*, vol.2, Voss, Hamburg and Leipzig, 1911.

17 Ewald Hering, *Outlines of a Theory of the Light Sense*, Leo Hurvich and Dorothea Jameson (trans), Harvard University Press, Cambridge, MA, 1964.

                                                                    SEMIR ZEKI

18 Semir Zeki, 'Colour Coding in Rhesus Monkey Prestriate Cortex', *Brain Research*, no.53, 1973, pp.422–27; Semir Zeki, 'The Representation of Colours in the Cerebral Cortex', *Nature*, vol.284, 1980, pp.412–18. See also Zeki *et al.*, 'A Direct Demonstration of Functional Specialization in the Human Visual Cortex', *op.cit.*

19 Semir Zeki, 'Colour Coding in the Cerebral Cortex: The Responses of Wavelength-Selective and Colour-Coded Cells in Monkey Visual Cortex to Changes in Wavelength Composition', *Neuroscience*, vol.9, 1983, pp.767–81; Bevil Conway *et al.*, 'Specialized Color Modules in Monkey Extrastriate Cortex', *Neuron*, no.56, 2007, pp.560–73.

20 Edwin H Land, 'The Retinex Theory of Colour Vision', *Proceedings of the Royal Institute of Great Britain*, no.47, 1974, pp.23–58.

21 See Zeki, 'Bridget Riley and the Art of the Brain', *op.cit.*, p.104, ill.03: The reaction of a colour-coded cell in area V4 to different patches of a multicoloured display. When tested with lights of different wavelength (above), the cells responded to long-wave (red) light alone. When tested with the different patches in such a way that each patch reflected the identical amount of red, green and blue light, though each maintained its colon (because of colour constancy), the cell responded to the red patch alone, thus showing that it was registering the colour and not the wavelength composition.

22 Semir Zeki, 'The Construction of Colours by the Cerebral Cortex', *Proceedings of the Royal Institute of Great Britain*, no.56, 1984, pp.231–57.

23 Semir Zeki, 'A Century of Cerebral Achromatopsia', *Brain*, no.113, 1990, pp.1721–77.

24 Kudielka, *op.cit.*

25 André Malraux, *Les Voix du silence*, Editions La Pléiade, Paris, 1951.

26 Bridget Riley, 'Practising Abstraction' (1992), in Robert Kudielka (ed), *Bridget Riley: Dialogues on Art*, Thames & Hudson, London, 2003, p.65.

27 Gasquet, *op.cit.*

28 Piet Mondrian, 'Toward the True Vision of Reality' (1941), in Harry Holtzman and Martin S James (eds and trans), *The New Art – The New Life: The Collected Writings of Piet Mondrian*, GK Hall & Co, Boston, MA, 1986, pp.338–41.

29 Piet Mondrian, 'Plastic Art and Pure Plastic Art' (1937), in *Mondrian, from Figuration to Abstraction*, exhibition catalogue, National Museum of Modern Art, Tokyo, and Thames & Hudson, London, 1987.

30 Kazimir Malevich, *The Non-Objective World*, Howard Dearstyne (trans), Theobold, Chicago, IL, 1957.

31 David H Hubel and Torsten Wiesel, 'The Ferrier Lecture: Functional Architecture of Macaque Monkey Visual Cortex', *Proceedings of the Royal Society London B*, vol.198, 1977, pp.1–59.

32 Velia Cardin and Semir Zeki, 'Form Construction in the Human Visual Brain', in *Program*, vol.46, no.20, 2005.

33 Joakin Vinberg and Kalat Grill-Spector, 'Representation of Shapes, Edges and Surfaces Across Multiple Cues in Human Visual Cortex', *Journal of Neurophysiology*, Epub 2, January 2008..

34 Rüdiger von der Heydt *et al.*, 'Illusory Contours and Cortical Neuron Responses', *Science*, no.224, 1984, pp.1260–62.

35 Zeki, *Inner Vision*, *op.cit.*

36 Semir Zeki, *Splendours and Miseries of the Brain*, Blackwell Publishing, Oxford, 2008.

37 Hideaki Kawabata and Semir Zeki, 'The Neural Correlates of Beauty', *Journal of Neurophysiology*, no.91, 2004, pp.1699–1705.

A New Experience of Space: Wall Compositions 1998–2008
Nadia Chalbi

The practice of wall painting first appeared in Bridget Riley's work in 1998, on the occasion of *White Noise*, a group exhibition at the Kunsthalle Bern. Since then, it has continued and expanded, leading to more complex *Compositions with Circles 4* (2004) and, more recently, to *Arcadia 1 (Wall Painting 1)* (2007), a colourful painting that the artist initially made for her solo show at Galerie Max Hetzler, Berlin, in 2007.

The different works created so far – six black-and-white wall drawings, making up the Composition with Circles series, and one Arcadia work, forming a continuity with the artist's most recent curve paintings – are each unique, varying both in composition and size. Abiding neither by any preconceived system that would apply equally to each painting, nor to a random method, these works are the result of compositions determined by the spaces for which they were specifically created.[1]

Although the artist had already spoken of the possibility of transforming a wall as early as the 1960s, the opportunity for her to actually create a temporary wall piece only presented itself in 1998.[2] Its elaboration was closely related to a proposal she received at the same time for the creation of a 46-metre-high work in situ, for the atrium of the headquarters of Citibank in London, designed by Norman Foster. For this she planned at first to use circles, but then realised that they would need a mural support and decided to create a semi-transparent suspended structure, made up of a great number of colourful lozenges in keeping with the diagonal paintings she had been working on since the mid-1980s. Since the sheer monumentality of the atrium space would only allow a partial view of the work from any of its 18 floors, Riley drew on her experience of Tiepolo's huge composition for the ceiling fresco covering Balthasar Neumann's staircase in the Würzburg Residence, which offers a succession of varying views.[3] The solution she found in order to master the scale of the site, combined with her initial idea of uniting circles with an architectural element brought about her first wall piece, *Composition with Circles 1* (1998).

Made for the Kunsthalle Bern, this very large drawing (5.5 by 10 metres) uses 150 circles, 1 metre in diameter, drawn directly onto a white wall. Their outline is made up of two parallel pencil lines, 9 millimetres apart, and painted black. When the director of the Kunsthalle, Bernhard Fibicher, invited Riley to contribute a wall work, he had assumed that the piece would follow from the diagonal paintings on which she was working at the time. Instead, the artist devised this new, more pared-back composition, using the circle as the only formal element. It set the basis common to all her wall drawings: black circles on a white background, laid out according to an overlapping organisation comprising multiple equidistant centres. The number of circles and their distribution depend on the size and proportion of the wall surface.

Marking Riley's return to black and white after over 30 years of meticulous and methodical exploration of the properties of colour, this composition is not unlike her earlier black-and-white paintings associated with Op art. The circular element is among the main themes of her 1960s repertoire and can be found in her most famous works, in the form of discs (*Black to White Discs*, 1962; *White Discs 2*, 1964), of discs progressively becoming ovals (*Fission*, 1963; *Loss*, *Pause* and *Where*, all 1964) or of ellipses (*Disturbance*, 1964; the group of Static paintings, 1966).

The opening up of space, which is common to all her wall compositions, also borrows some pictorial principles from her earlier black-and-white works, such as the concept of a shallow, multifocal open space, inspired by Jackson Pollock's all-over paintings.[4] Nevertheless, while these early works engaged the viewer in an interaction between the spectator and the picture plane, the artist increasingly focused on opening an interior space in the work itself, thus creating a sense of depth made up of successive planes.[5] She worked with this pictorial depth for the first time in her diagonal paintings, whose planes of colour she compares to a 'relief space', thus evoking a sculptural dimension.[6]

This new spatial concept was developed with great precision in her wall compositions. Although the work is perceived as a whole whose various components equally solicit the spectator's attention, the overall sense of a multifocal space remains. The spectator feels encouraged to explore a new sense of depth through the succession of planes no longer built up by complex colour relationships but solely by the transparency of the black-and-white drawing.[7] The relation to the spectator, which is central to Riley who considers that 'the spectator is part of the work itself',[8] becomes all the more crucial now that he or she is faced with a duality of spatial experience: the space opening up towards the viewer and simultaneously receding in the picture plane.

The network of interwoven circles in the wall compositions forms an ensemble of planes that successively and continuously move from the back to the foreground of the work, thus bringing about a spatial experience that has both depth and dynamism. This is not the classic illusionist, perspectival space inherited from the Renaissance and built on a single vanishing point, nor is it a structure based on the figure–ground relationship; instead it is a space conceived as an entity constructed through the mobility of planes.

The circles intersect, juxtapose and superimpose not only in the depth of the pictorial space, according to an oscillatory motion back and forth but also on the surface of the work according to ascending, descending and lateral movements, thereby creating a multiplicity of rhythms. By avoiding all symmetry, centralisation and systematic repetition, Riley disperses the circular elements to the periphery of the pictorial field. This irregular, though mastered, distribution of shapes, which defines zones of various intensities, allows the drawing to be active across its whole surface and to effectively capture the spectator's attention by successively holding and releasing it. By alternating active and passive sections, dense and fluid areas, zones of focus and dispersion, the artist creates a balance between stability and dynamism, according to a formal logic that is inherent to the work. The intersection of the circles also gives rise to a multitude of arcs and arabesques that inject even more dynamism into the composition and make its surface appear intensely vibratory thanks to a web of horizontal, vertical and diagonal movements.

All these wall compositions, developed through many preparatory studies – some of them full-scale – are built on 'an infinitely subtle grid',[9] whose linear, geometric organisation of verticals and horizontals, although not apparent in the fluidity of the forms ensures their stability and cohesion.

Oppositions, tensions and contrasts are essential to the sensation of movement sought by Riley,[10] they are the driving principle behind her work.[11] Beyond the immediate visual experience, her wall drawings offer a spatial and temporal sensory experience.[12] Whether slow or fast, the varying rhythmic sequences, which accent and structure the compositions, seem to be indivisible from a temporal dimension.[13] They call to mind the rhythmic organisation of musical compositions, because of the sensual, yet abstract experience they give rise to, exemplifying the connections between painting and music often mentioned by the artist.[14]

Riley's second wall drawing, *Composition with Circles 2* (2000), initially presented on the occasion of the exhibition *Reconnaissance* at the Dia Center for the Arts in New York, and then recreated identically in 2001 for the Lyon Biennale and again in 2005 for the artist's retrospective in Aarau, Switzerland, demonstrates her increased interest in rhythms. Unlike the Bern drawing, the spatial constraints of the New York institution favoured an extremely elongated, horizontal format (4 by 13.7 metres), which meant that the organisation of the composition would have to be more 'sequential', as Lynne Cooke emphasises in her detailed study of the piece.[15] Despite the obvious differences in construction and colour, the drawing shares the frieze-like format of the 'curve paintings' of the same period, rich in rhythmic sequences punctuated by intervals.[16] Its elongated structure led Riley – yet again – to study the distribution of rhythms in Pollock's works of a similar format.[17]

This work was followed by a new series of wall compositions: *Composition with Circles 3* (4.8 by 17.6 metres), created in 2003 for Riley's retrospective at Tate Britain in London; *Composition with Circles 4* (3.9 by 16.7 metres), created in 2004 for a travelling retrospective at the Museum of Contemporary Art in Sydney; *Composition with Circles 5* (6 by 7.5 metres), created in 2005 for the inaugural exhibition *Prolog* in the new building at the Akademie der Künste in Berlin and shown again there in 2007 for the international survey *Raum. Orte der Kunst*; and now *Composition with Circles 6* (c.4.7 by 26 metres), created for the artist's retrospective at the Musée d'Art Moderne de la Ville de Paris in 2008.

These different compositions show Riley's particular interest in relating her work to architecture, constructing fluctuating pictorial spaces

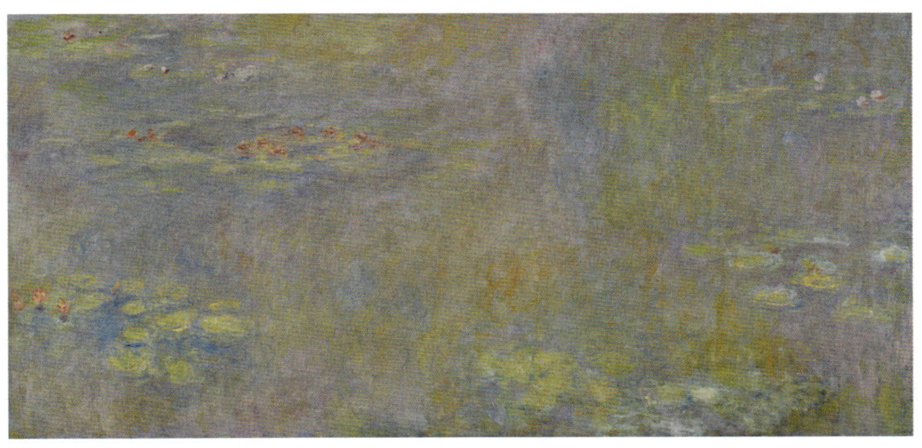

Claude Monet
Water Lilies after 1916
Oil on canvas
200.7 × 426.7 cm | 79⅛ × 168 in
National Gallery, London

animated by transparent circles. At the same time they reveal a progressive evolution towards airier, more open structures. Thus, in *Composition with Circles 5*, an overall sensation of calm and balance prevails, in contrast to the density and tensions inherent in the pictorial field of her earlier works. The artist focuses her attention on what interests her most: a depth made up of moving planes. The opening up of the composition towards the spectator allows the energy of the moving circles – gliding through the pictorial space – to be felt, and confers the same sensation of rhythm and pulsation on the work itself. Robert Kudielka observed the similarity with the pattern of circles generated by raindrops falling on the flat surface of water.[18]

Comprising over 200 circles, *Composition with Circles 6* is by far the largest wall painting by Bridget Riley. Its singularity lies in the fact that it is drawn on the huge curved wall of the Musée d'Art Moderne, in close proximity to the artist's recent 'curve paintings'. Once inside the gallery, the configuration of the space with its curved wall leads the spectator to pass alongside the work, literally following the revelation of its composition, over more than 25 metres. The resulting unfurling of a multitude of viewpoints gives rise to a completely new sensory experience, reminiscent of Claude Monet's *Water Lilies* in the oval room of Musée de l'Orangerie in Paris, a work of art the artist admires.[19]

Alongside the development of her Compositions with Circles series, Riley recently exhibited a new form of wall composition with *Arcadia 1 (Wall Painting 1)* (2.6 by 4.9 metres), which she showed at Galerie Max Hetzler in Berlin in autumn 2007, and subsequently recreated for the PaceWildenstein in New York in the winter of 2007–08 and for the Musée d'Art Moderne de la Ville de Paris the following summer. This work has developed in conjunction with the new curve paintings, begun with *Rêve* (1999), which signalled the introduction of curvilinear elements within the diagonal structures. Despite repeated attempts since the mid-1990s, as seen in *Lagoon 1* (1997), it was only after her first big wall drawing that Riley succeeded in integrating the curve into her paintings. Fluidity, a simplification of colours, as well as an enlargement of the formal elements and the size of the canvas have ensued.[20]

Unlike the wall drawings, the limits of which are clearly defined,

Arcadia 1 turns the supporting wall, expanding beyond the borders of the painted surface, into an integral part of the pictorial field. The origin of this evolution can be traced back a year earlier, when Riley, during a session in her studio in the south of France, first experimented with coloured paper cut-outs extending beyond the picture plane. From acting as mere support, the wall henceforth became one with the work, offering the possibility of exploring a new relationship between inside and outside.[21]

Arcadia 1 appears as the dissolution into space of *Painting with Verticals, Cadence 7* (2007), which anticipated it both in structure and colour. As Robert Kudielka has noted, the intrusion of white, especially in the upper part of the work, conveys the impression that the wall invades the space of the painting.[22] The sensation of dissolution, which also derives from the green diagonals that progressively ascend the wall in a vertical movement and disrupt the outlines of the work, is nevertheless tempered by the horizontality and stability of the large blue plane. Kudielka has pointed out the connection between the spatial development of these dynamic, arabesque shapes and Arabic, and more precisely Kufic calligraphy.[23]

Being closely linked, both forms of treating the wall as a pictorial element occupy a prominent place in Riley's art. *Composition with Circles 1* brought about profound changes that gave rise to a new sense of scale, pictorial space, line and colour. The fluidity of the curve and the reduction of colours have altered her compositional approach, infusing her recent work with singular vitality and energy. Playing with perception and the senses, by their sheer complexity and originality these paintings reveal an ever-evolving creative process, open to new variations.

Through the interaction they create between the pictorial field and the wall surface, as well as the dynamism of their composition, these works echo other wall paintings, such as *The Dance* (1932–33) created by Henri Matisse for the Barnes Foundation in the United States, and the studio walls that Piet Mondrian treated as extensions of his paintings in Paris and New York.[24]

Bridget Riley: Retrospective, exhibition catalogue, Ridinghouse, London and Arc/Musée d'Art Moderne de la Ville de Paris, Paris, 2008, pp.158–63.

1   Bridget Riley, transcript of a public discussion with Robert Kudielka on the occasion of the exhibition *Raum. Orte der Kunst*, Akademie der Künste, Berlin, 13 March 2007, n.p.

2   Bridget Riley, 'Something to Blink At', *Time*, 1 May 1964, p.45.

3   Riley and Kudielka, transcript, *op.cit.*

4   Bridget Riley, 'In Conversation with Maurice de Sausmarez' (1967), in Robert Kudielka (ed), *The Eye's Mind: Bridget Riley, Collected Writings 1965–1999*, Thames & Hudson, London, 1999, p.62.

5   Bridget Riley, 'The Experience of Painting. Talking to Mel Gooding' (1988), in Kudielka (ed), *The Eye's Mind*, *op.cit.*, p.122.

6   Riley and Kudielka, transcript, *op.cit.*

7   Bridget Riley, 'Bridget Riley in Conversation with Isabel Carlisle', in *Bridget Riley: Works 1961–1998*, exhibition catalogue, Abbott Hall Art Gallery, Kendal, 1998, p.10

8   Bridget Riley, 'Bridget Riley in conversation with Lynne Cooke', in *Bridget Riley: Recent Paintings and Gouaches*, exhibition catalogue, PaceWildenstein, New York, NY, 2007, p.17.

9   Bryan Robertson, 'Introduction and Biographical Note', *Bridget Riley: Paintings and Drawings 1951–71*, exhibition catalogue, Hayward Gallery, London, 1971, p.14.

10   Bridget Riley, 'The Experience of Painting: Talking to Mel Gooding' (1988), in Kudielka (ed), *The Eye's Mind*, *op.cit.*, p.123.

11   Bridget Riley, 'According to Sensation (1990)', in Kudielka (ed), *ibid.*, p.116.

12   Bridget Riley, 'Something to Look At: In Conversation with Alex Farquharson' (1995), in Kudielka (ed), *ibid.*, p.134.

13   Bridget Riley, 'Painting Now' (1996), in Kudielka (ed), *ibid.*, p.206.

14   Bridget Riley, 'Perception and the Use of Colour: Talking to EH Gombrich' (1992), in Robert Kudielka (ed), *Bridget Riley: Dialogues on Art*, Thames & Hudson, London, 2003, p.43.

15   Lynne Cooke, 'Around and Cbout *Composition with Circles 2*', in Lynne Cooke and Karen Kelly (eds), *Bridget Riley: Reconnaissance*, exhibition catalogue, Dia Center for the Arts, New York, NY, 2000, p.56.

16   *Ibid.*, pp.51–52.

17   *Ibid.*, p.56.

18   Robert Kudielka, 'Bridget Riley', in *Raum. Orte der Kunst*, exhibition catalogue, Akademie der Künste, Berlin., 2007, p.337.

19   See Bridget Riley, 'Practising Abstraction: Talking to Michael Craig-Martin' (1992), in Kudielka (ed), *Dialogues on Art*, *op.cit.*, p.65.

20   Bridget Riley, 'Supposed to Be Abstract: Bridget Riley in Conversation with Robert Kudielka' (2001), in Robert Kudielka (ed), *Robert Kudielka on Bridget Riley: Essays and Interviews 1972–2003*, Ridinghouse, London, 2005, p.201.

21   Robert Kudielka, 'Sound, Unrest, Dance and a Flourish on the Wall: Bridget Riley's Departures', *Bridget Riley*, exhibition catalogue, Galerie Max Hetzler and Holzwarth Publications, Berlin, 2007, p.19.

22   *Ibid.*

23   *Ibid.*, p.20.

24   Riley and Kudielka, transcript, *op.cit.*

Introducing the Art of Bridget Riley: An Act of Translation

Michael Bracewell

Attending Bridget Riley's exhibition at the Hayward Gallery, London, in 1971, it was revealing to witness the dramatically involving effect that her work had on its viewers. These were paintings that rewarded the gaze directly, coming to vibrant, motion-filled life, at once immediate visceral and deeply meditational. 'No painter, dead or alive,' began Robert Melville's review for the *New Statesman*, 'has ever made us more aware of our eyes than Bridget Riley.'

The truth of Melville's pronouncement would be self-evident to anyone who has stood in front of a painting by Riley – from any period in her career – and accepted its invitation to look and to see. Each painting comprises its own closed circuitry of movement and form, refining our perception to pure sensation, beyond intellect.

As the viewer begins to look, so they are swiftly drawn into a series of interrelated optical negotiations and visual surprises. There is no single place on the work where the eye might attempt to find rest and to focus – no apparent 'magnetic north' by which it might take its bearings. Rather, as the eye explores, so the painting reveals its own individual life, at its own pace and on its own terms. Movement, agitation, interruptions, reversals, disappearances and new 'actions' all occur within the work, often faster than the eye can keep up with them, and drawing the viewer into what might be called the consciousness of the painting, with all of the engulfing power of a strong current. And thus, at the Hayward Gallery and at all of Riley's exhibitions, each painting appears to attract its own audience of viewers – each one of whom, through the act of looking and seeing, also become participants in its visual and emotional world.

The aesthetic and emotional power of Riley's art is the product of continuous artistic enquiry on the part of the artist, the findings of which liberate the wholly autonomous sense of movement and independent 'life' within each work. This process of enquiry derives from both the heightened nature of Riley's sensory engagement with the world around her, and from a deeply felt engagement with the work of earlier artists.

The nature of this dialogue with the past, with specific reference to
the sense of 'life' within a painting, was well summarised by the artist in
a conversation with Michael Craig-Martin:

> It's amazing that some paintings from the past are so extraordinarily
> modern while others, even some contemporary paintings, appear
> quite stale. It seems that painting presents certain problems with
> which artists inevitably have to come to terms no matter what period
> they are living in… To treat them [paintings from the past] as
> historical documents or evidence of past concepts is wrong – they
> are particular solutions to continuing artistic problems, and it's that
> which makes them real, or as you say, 'living'.[1]

What might be the nature of this 'aliveness' in the art of Bridget
Riley? Clearly, as can be seen from the connections made in this current
exhibition, it is an analysis of sentience that derives on one level from
Riley's career-long absorption in the problems posed by the history of
art, and by painting in particular. In her pioneering development of
abstract painting, Riley has accepted the challenges and questions posed
by modernism – Kazimir Malevich, Igor Stravinsky and Marcel Proust are
all key figures in her dialogues and writings – and re-phrased through the
artistic innovations of the early and middle years of the last century. In
her lecture 'Painting Now', delivered at the Slade School of Art, London,
in the autumn of 1996, for example, Riley looked to Samuel Beckett to
define the task of the artist:

> When Samuel Beckett was a young man in the early 1930s, and trying
> to find a basis from which he could develop, he wrote an essay in
> which he examined Proust's views on creative work and he quotes
> Proust's artistic credo as declared in *Time Regained* – 'the task and
> duty of a writer (not an artist, a writer) are those of a translator'. This
> could also be said of a composer, a painter or anyone practising an
> artistic *métier*. An artist is someone with a text that he or she wants
> to decipher.[2]

                                                    MICHAEL BRACEWELL

As interpreted by Riley by way of Beckett, the artist's 'text' 'cannot be created or invented but only discovered within the artist by him or herself, and that it is, as it were, almost a law of his own nature. It is his most precious possession, and, as Proust explains, the source of his innermost happiness.'[3] For Riley, in order for the artist to achieve real progress – and more, emotional acuity – within their work, they must ceaselessly study and test their own progress, learning particularly the necessity for sacrifice within the creative process. In this, Riley has identified a lineage of enquiry; and the development of her own work – her translation of her own text – stems in part from her continuing participation within this art historical relay of self-questioning.

Black to White Discs (1962) is an early example of Riley's translation of idea and enquiry into autonomous sensation and emotion. A square comprised of small, uniformly sized and evenly spaced circular discs, appears to be balanced on one of its corners, thus assuming a diamond-like shape. The discs comprising the left hand side of the balanced square appear to emerge from a mist – the disc furthest to the left seeming the palest (nearest to white) and those towards the right acquiring a gradually deepening shade of grey, line by line, until we reach the axis of the vertical line of near black discs which runs down the square's centre. But the true black runs just to its right.

The gradual 'fade' from black through shades of grey appears to have the twofold effect of softening and 'slowing down' the energy contained within the finished painting's scale and visual impact. The square acquires the sensations of new properties: it becomes both weighted and weightless; it seems to drift, or rotate through space. Above all, it is possessed of a sense of deceleration.

In a conversation with Maurice de Sausmarez, conducted in 1967, Riley said of *Black to White Discs*: '…when I had *Black to White Discs* on a small scale it was a slow painting, and when it became larger it became slower still. When its character was revealed in this slowness I realised that by increasing the scale a more positive statement of slowness would be made.'[4]

A further refinement of the relationship between movement and scale discovered within *Black to White Discs* can be seen in *Study for*

White Discs, made in 1964. This smaller work comprises black discs of varying size on a white background; as the viewer shifts their gaze these discs leave the fleeting optical effect of a white after-image, hovering just above the surface of the work. *Study for White Discs* is a slightly 'faster' work than its predecessor, yet still it remains tranquil; in its abbreviated diagonal groupings of varying sized discs, it seems also to introduce the impression of twisting DNA-like columns of downward movement, caught in a dead slow horizontal drift. The somewhat elegiac feel of *Black to White Discs* seems therefore replaced by both a lightening and tightening of mood.

In one sense, *Study for White Discs* depicts another square, and yet the demarcation of the sides of this square – porous to the white of the background – propose its solidity and aesthetic purpose to be a consequence of its very effervescence. In this, Riley's art achieves a further liberation: to create deft reversals of pictorial effect – solidity becomes space; black becomes white; that which is still begins to move.

For the newcomer to her work, the art of Bridget Riley can appear simultaneously inviting – spectacular, even – and possessed of a sensory power that can be epic to the point of overwhelming. There is no lack of grandeur in her art – as her recent Composition with Circles series of wall drawings prove with such force and grace; but likewise, as can also be seen in Composition with Circles, the emotional power of each work, and its internal animation, derives from a translation of perception into form that is so refined and meticulous as to resemble a formula of aesthetic calculus, in which the values of simplicity and discipline are attained from the algebraic resolution of sense and emotion.

With this in mind, one can see how the sheer drama of Riley's earliest 'black-and-white' (or Op) paintings of the early 1960s are gradually advanced in their complexity ('paced' is Riley's own term for her cumulative enquiry into the capacities of a form) until they reach what might be called the critical mass of their aesthetic. Then, greys were introduced by the artist and paced, to be followed by colour; linear and geometric forms could subsequently give way to twists and undulations; later still, diagonals and zigs appeared; and so on to curves and curvilinear forms. And the journey is far from over.

   MICHAEL BRACEWELL

In an illuminating statement, Riley has observed of her early black-and-white paintings how, 'People at the time thought, and some people still seem to think, that they were paintings having to do with optical experiment… really they were an attempt to say something about stabilities and instabilities, certainties and uncertainties.'[5] The development of this intention can be seen in Riley's earliest enquiries into colour, of which *Arrest 3* (1965) is an example. Here Riley appears to first acknowledge, and then embrace, a fresh spirit of harmony and centrality. Her later colour paintings – such as the warm and vivacious *Saraband* (1985) – are by then possessed of exuberant assurance, as though they can barely contain their lifted spirits. (One might compare them, in literary terms, to Walt Whitman's 'Song of Myself', 1855, or André Gide's prose hymn to nature, *Fruits of the Earth,* 1924.)

Arrest 3, by contrast, is a cooler and more measured work. Its power lies in its fluidity, rhythm and sudden pause, as conveyed by the undulation of its horizontal, ribbon-like lines. The dialogue between 'certainty' and 'uncertainty' remains, but now it seems that there are shades of 'assurance' in between. In the uppermost third of the painting, the curved bands change colour from near black, through warm and cold greys. They have a gentle swell, the motion of which appears reanimated by the reprise of black, halfway down the painting, which is followed by a repetition of the upper colour sequence, but comprised of narrower ribbons of colour. The swell intensifies. Marking the start of the painting's lower third, a fine undulation of light grey is followed by an abrupt 'stop' – and a change in the direction of the flow (from right to left) and by a gradual lightening of colour to mist-like whiteness – somewhat reminiscent of the softness and gentle movement conveyed in the left hand side of *Black to White Discs*.

In *Arrest 3*, the gradual deepening of colour from near translucent whiteness, to a shining hue (a hue which seems to have the texture of satin) and then on to near black, appears more temperate – warmed to sea temperature, so to speak, from the chill of sepulchre or deep space. When, in the lower section of the painting, the curved bands change direction and the visual authority of black falls away, there is a feeling that the dominance of this dark shade must now accept its place within the parity and process declared by the work as a whole. The era of confrontation is over. In the lower third of the picture the paler colours appear to take command: strength begets strength and confidence begets confidence. That which was 'stopped' seems to resume, as though in a minor key, serene.

The painstaking precision with which Riley works towards new statements within her finished paintings can be seen from the meticulous studies by which they are preceded. Often made on finely ruled graph paper, these studies are both the 'working out' of Riley's paintings and, in an important sense, the declaration and template of the 'narrow frame that I have assigned myself for each one of my undertakings' – as the artist has quoted from Stravinsky's *Poetics of Music* (1959), to describe a 'guiding principle' of her working methods. The quotation from Stravinsky concludes: 'I shall go even further: my freedom will be so much the greater and more meaningful, the more narrowly I limit my field of action and the more I surround myself with obstacles. Whatever diminishes constraint diminishes strength.'[6]

With this in mind, *Arrest 3* and its study possess a rhythm and musicality that Riley has also identified in the Mantegna frieze in the National Gallery, *The Introduction of the Cult of Cybele at Rome* (1505–06). It is as though Mantegna, too, had understood in advance of Stravinsky the artistic strengths to be gained from constraint. Speaking about that work with Neil MacGregor she observed:

> I was amazed to see that Mantegna holds together the narrow horizontal format of his frieze in one long, all-embracing rhythm. The verve with which the first figure steps forward is stopped cut short by the straight tine of the statue, as though by an enormous comma; then this movement, introduced by the first figure, is picked up by the next two, turned around in the supplicating figure and continues in reverse until the very last figure where it changes back to echo the first.[7]

Riley's description of the frieze is thus particularly insightful, revealing the precision with which she deconstructs works by earlier artists in

MICHAEL BRACEWELL

terms of their composition, and, more specifically, how that composition is in its turn descriptive of the artist's mind at work – the deduction and decision-making which comprise the Beckettian 'act of translation'.

Towards the end of the 1990s, Riley commenced making new paintings and gouaches that explored the relationships between diagonals, verticals and curves. In fresh, vivid shades (orange, violet, blue, cerise, yellow, for example) solidity and fluidity coexist within these bold and muscular paintings, seeming to push to its limit the confluence of directions of visual momentum. Vertical sections appear to underlay diagonals, in turn traversed by sinuous fragments of curve and arc. One might think of a plant on a riverbed, its frond-like leaves caught in the current, drifting yet tethered, fixed yet always in motion.

Red with Red 1 (2007) comprises areas of dark blue, magenta red and orange red. The painting is traversed by nine diagonal sections, with a vertical plane running down its centre. The straight edges that form the boundaries of these sections are under constant interruption and intervention by curved and curvilinear areas of colour.

To decipher what system of repetitions and overlays might govern the finished painting appears impossible – and, in one sense, a nugatory exercise. Rather, the viewer becomes aware that within this complex matching of curved and straight-edged areas of colour, of etiolated tears and blade-like curves, there is both horizontal and vertical movement marked by fragments of what appears to be twisting or rotating motion. Everything moves to the right, as though in procession, curved edges leading. Crucially, all movement within the painting feels to move towards a sensory-visual event: a 'breaking through' into opened new territories.

In her essay 'Cézanne in Provence' (2006), Bridget Riley sheds further light on both her profound relationship with the work of earlier artists (Paul Cézanne himself being one of her greatest ancestors within the history of art, along with Georges Seurat, Claude Monet and Piet Mondrian) and, tangentially, on the Proustian impulse of recognising those 'triggering' sensory events that serve to open memory and recreate perception. Describing Cézanne's *House with Red Roof* (1887–90), Riley identifies the use of a 'tilting' effect in the work that she declares as 'essential to the dynamics of the painting'. She observes, 'This is our first encounter with *ma petite sensation*' – referring to Cézanne's term for those fugitive moments of perception which seemed suddenly to reveal the world anew to him.[8] (Proust's *mot juste* and Virginia Woolf's 'moments of being' have a similar, although not identical function.) Riley's career-long study of Cézanne, and her direct engagement with the relationship between looking, seeing and painting which he pioneered, has been a vital informant of her work. Cézanne's *Still Life with Plaster Cast* (c.1894) is a work to which she has made reference, noting the occurrence of the *petite sensation* in a further instance of 'tilting' within the painting – in this case the sudden, logic-defying but sight-pleasing upward turn of the plane behind the plaster cast of the putto.

We might see a connection between Riley's identification with Cézanne, and her extensive reading of Proust. Both Proust and Cézanne, like Riley herself, are foremost pioneers of perception: in literary and visual terms respectively, they seek to understand first how we see the world around us, and then how that experience of witness can be 'translated' into art. As a young man, Proust, like Riley, undertook copying from earlier masters – seeking to both master their iconic styles and, by doing so, free himself from devotional imitation of their achievements. Only in this manner could he hope to discover his own style, and, in Riley's astute phrase, advance the solution to 'continuing artistic problems'.

Proust's (not uncritical) veneration of the writings and art criticism of John Ruskin led him to write an essay which both engaged with Ruskin's own literary style (his very temper, one could say) and allowed him to make a response. One passage touches closely on an artistic phenomenon very similar to Cézanne's *petite sensation*, and seems also to rehearse the case for pure abstraction in art. Proust seems to step forward from behind the technical brilliance of his pastiche to address Ruskin directly: 'No, I shall not find a picture more beautiful because the artist has painted a hawthorn in the foreground, although I know of nothing more beautiful than the hawthorn, because I want to remain sincere and I know that a picture's beauty does not depend on the things portrayed in it.'[9]

                                                        MICHAEL BRACEWELL

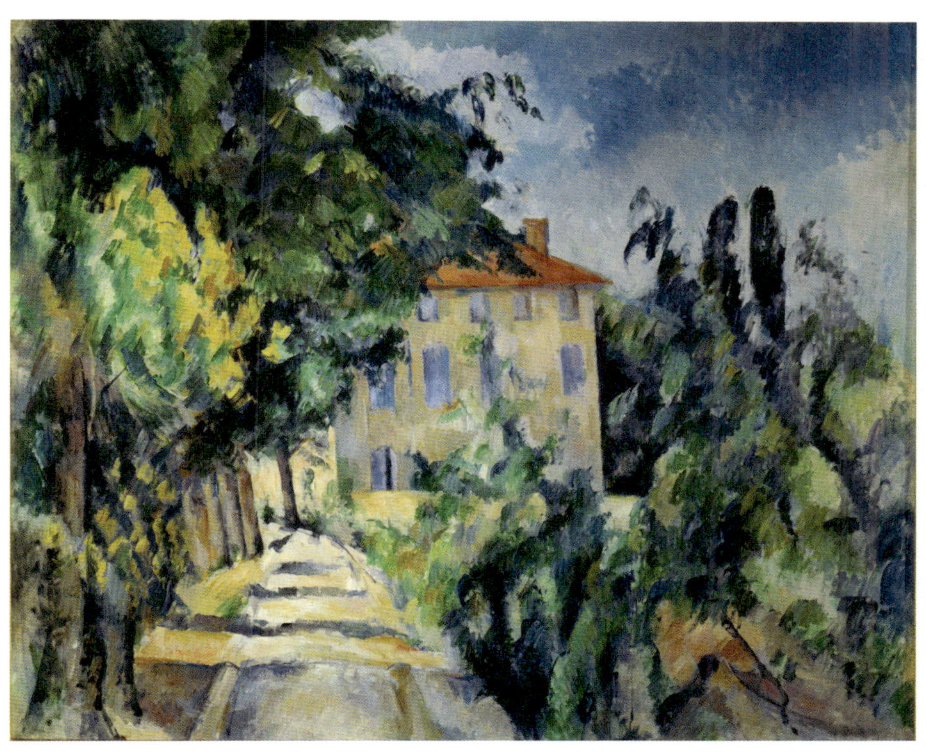

Paul Cézanne
House with Red Roof 1887–90
Oil on canvas
73 × 92 cm | 28¾ × 36¼ in
Private Collection

Proust's phrasing is subtle, containing a question within its statement: upon what does a picture's beauty depend, if not on the things portrayed in it? Riley's analysis of Cézanne's *House with Red Roof* seems to answer this question: the beauty depends on the working out of the problems each painting inherits or brings to light. Time and again, in her dialogues and essays, Riley returns not to discussions of subject matter, inspiration, theory or even philosophy; but to the precise sensory and technical means by which a painting may be freed from the hand of the artist and achieve its own life – born clean of its maker's fingerprints, or the imprint of their personality.

Equally clear – as the acuity of her deconstruction of the Mantegna frieze exemplifies – are the lessons and insights that Riley has gained looking at the work of other artists, always in terms of problems posed and problems solved. This, on the part of Riley, is an almost supernatural act of art critical empathy: in her close study of paintings by earlier artists, Riley enables herself to see as those artists saw – pursuing on their canvases the train of thought, insight and intuition which connected their eyes to their hand. In turn, through her finished paintings, Riley passes on this empathetic understanding of perception. She reveals to the viewer, as translated into living, freed and autonomous works of art, her own moments of being, and her own incidents of *petite sensation* – as surely as those by Cézanne or Mantegna or Raphael have revealed theirs to her.

Lise Connellan (ed), *Bridget Riley: Paintings and Related Work*, exhibition catalogue, National Gallery, London, 2010, pp.19–25.

 MICHAEL BRACEWELL

1   Bridget Riley, 'Practising Abstraction: Talking to Michael Craig-Martin' (1992), in Robert Kudielka (ed), *Bridget Riley: Dialogues on Art*, Zwemmer, London, 1995, p.51.
2   Bridget Riley, 'Painting Now', 23rd William Townsend Memorial Lecture, Slade School of Fine Art, London, 26 November 1996.
3   *Ibid.*
4   Bridget Riley, 'In Conversation with Maurice de Sausmarez' (1967), in Robert Kudielka (ed), *The Eye's Mind: Bridget Riley, Collected Writings 1965–2009*, Thames & Hudson and Ridinghouse, London, 2009, p.78.
5   Bridget Riley, 'The Experience of Painting: Talking to Mel Gooding' (1988), in Kudielka (ed), *ibid.*, p.147.
6   Bridget Riley, 'Perception and the Use of Colour: Talking to EH Gombrich' (1992), in Kudielka (ed), *Dialogues on Art*, *op.cit.*, pp.34–37.
7   Bridget Riley, 'The Art of the Past: Talking to Neil MacGregor' (1992), in Kudielka (ed), *ibid.*, p.23.
8   Bridget Riley, 'Cézanne in Provence' (2006), in Kudielka (ed), *The Eye's Mind*, *op.cit.*, p.25.
9   Marcel Proust, 'John Ruskin' (1904), in *Against Sainte-Beuve and Other Essays*, Penguin Books, London, 1988, p.190.

'Let the eye be agile': The Past as Present in the Work of Bridget Riley

Marla Prather

> Artists cannot help, it seems, but project some of their
> own preoccupations onto the art of the past, and this is
> more or less true of everybody, even art historians.
> However, as a painter you see reflections of common
> practical problems in the art of the past, and although the
> solutions obviously cannot be the same, it is still
> reassuring to see that one's own problems are not simply
> delusional but real, by witness of the fact that other
> painters have encountered them.
>
> – Bridget Riley, *The Eye's Mind*, 2009

In 1947, as Bridget Riley sought admission to London's Goldsmiths, where entry was highly competitive in the years after the war, someone suggested that she copy a painting for her portfolio. She chose as her model Jan van Eyck's *Portrait of a Man in a Red Turban* (1433), in the National Gallery's collection. Although access to the original was readily available, she painted the work from a postcard. It was not the elaborately complex folds of the sitter's extraordinary red headdress that drew Riley to Van Eyck's portrait, but rather the regular features of his 'beautifully constructed head', with its very distinct planes.[1] In retrospect it may surprise us that an artist who would become one of the most committed abstractionists of the last 50 years not only undertook an ancient academic practice, that of copying, but also turned to a masterpiece of meticulous realism. And her choice – a rare work by one of the greatest artists of the first half of the fifteenth century and among the most celebrated paintings in a British public collection – was hardly a timid one for a young student. It suggests even a concerted personal declaration, to select what may be Van Eyck's portrait of himself. But rather than an act of immodesty, it was Riley's first lesson in what she has called 'the old way of learning'. Copying is the greatest possible tribute to the continuing relevance of the past, particularly for an artist who believes that painting's central issues do not fundamentally change from century to century, that an artist can advance in her own work by embracing the past, and that figurative art can offer solutions to the abstract artist through the common ground of a shared medium. 'Doing the same' she claims, 'is a way of getting closer than you ever can by simply observing.'[2] Although the full implications of copying came later, Riley's choice of the Van Eyck in 1947 is an early manifestation of her conviction that the best artists in history (she dislikes the term Old Masters) offer the clearest models to students of painting: 'Look at the great painters; don't be frightened of them, they've seen more clearly, experienced more deeply and are more explicit. Weaker artists are confused. Read the best, look at the best. Don't rely on your contemporaries, look at the past.'[3]

Once she entered Goldsmiths, Riley devoted herself to the study of life drawing, a declining practice in art schools by that time, and she still remembers with great affection her teacher Sam Rabin and consistently credits the importance to her work of this early academic training. She does not personally execute her final paintings but she precedes them with studies, precisely rendered, notated drawings, gouache collages and cartoons. Rabin taught by example, and Riley learned in part by observing his actions as he drew. Like so much of her work, drawing is a form of enquiry, a means of gathering information through close examination of the visible world. In her essay, 'From Life' (2010), for a recent exhibition of some of these early figure studies at the National Portrait Gallery, London, Riley wrote, 'Drawing is an exercise in looking: one finds out what can be seen and at the same time one finds oneself having to organise the visual and emotional information extracted.'[4] Rabin also encouraged Riley to study drawings and prints in the collection of the British Museum, London – by Raphael, Rembrandt, Ingres – and she valued the intimate experience of examining works of superlative quality at close range. In May 2010 she delivered a lecture at the British Museum that coincided with an exhibition of Italian Renaissance drawings from its own collection and that of the Uffizi Gallery, Florence. Riley framed her discussion of these works in a manner that placed them within the context of her own artistic concerns and illustrated the broad historic

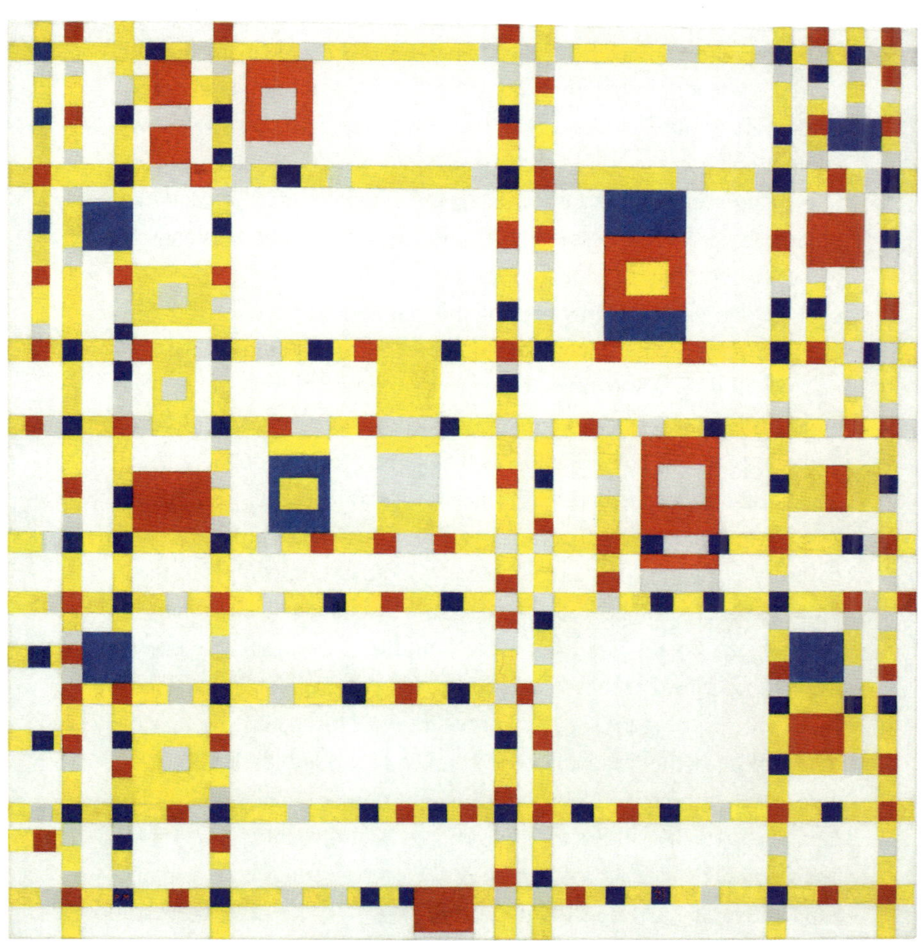

Piet Mondrian
Broadway Boogie Woogie 1942–43
Oil on canvas
127 × 127 cm | 50 × 50 in
Museum of Modern Art, New York

sweep of her sensibility. She began on a personal note with her own early figure drawings, followed by remarks about the Italian master drawings. She moved on to the drawings of three modern artists whose work she values so highly: Georges Seurat, Vincent van Gogh and Paul Cézanne. After a discussion of her early abstract work, she ended her commentary with Piet Mondrian's *Broadway Boogie Woogie* (1942–43), another painting she has long admired, written about and tried to copy. She abandoned the effort once it became apparent that she could not unravel the artist's process and therefore could not profit from copying his work. Appropriately, her talk was titled, 'Learning to Look'.[5]

Riley has explained that copying the Van Eyck was an isolated experience, not one she could build upon.[6] But it was a formative instance of Riley's work being nurtured by the extraordinary art at hand in her native London. Later, through her extensive travels, she became a dedicated student of European painting in museums throughout the world and has likened visiting museums to 'a journey in time, through which one discovers partners in imagination and whole areas of creative adventure'.[7] By 1959, her student training more or less complete, she turned to another artist for guidance in a very deliberate way, when searching for a path into colour after a protracted period of life drawing and various other pursuits, including teaching art to children and working in an advertising agency. It was *Bathers at Asnières* (1884), Seurat's early masterpiece in the National Gallery, that first provided the initial revelatory example, and Riley has included in the exhibition three of his luminous *plein-air* studies for the painting. But for copying she turned to The Courtauld Gallery's *The Bridge at Courbevoie* (1886–87), a small work in Seurat's fully developed pointillist manner. The exercise yielded a critical point of contact between a young painter at the brink of a mature career and a master of the past, one who was trained in the French classical tradition, who drew from the live model and the antique, and made many drawings after great artists, from Raphael to Poussin to Ingres. As with the Van Eyck, Riley based her Seurat copy on a reproduction (facing the original was 'too intimidating'), though her version is roughly 30 percent larger than Seurat's small canvas. Riley had tested other approaches as she searched for her own pictorial language:

MARLA PRATHER

I looked at paintings, read about artists I admired and tried many
avenues, in particular those opened up by Edvard Munch, Henri
Matisse and Pierre Bonnard – painters whose handling of colour was
a major factor in their art and all of whom had started out from an
academic background. I attempted to copy a Bonnard but
abandoned it because it seemed impossible to follow his train of
thought. I realised his work, beautiful as it is, relied on an impromptu,
almost ad hoc continuum of intuitive responses that left one at a loss
as to the order in which they had occurred.[8]

Seurat's painting, on the other hand, provided an exacting model, a
wholly legible surface that Riley could follow, feeling her way through his
process, discovering his train of thought. She realised, for example, that
the artist prepared his canvas with a traditional ground of diluted yellow
ochre and that beneath his tiny dots lay a network of larger hatch marks
used to initiate his forms. Though faithful to his composition, Riley took
liberties with Seurat's palette and touch, using a larger brush with the
aim to analyse rather than mimic his optical mixtures of colour: 'I was
trying to find out where he put what colour and why.'[9] Critically important
for her later work, in Seurat's pointillist technique Riley could explore
both the appeal and the limits of an objective, methodical approach,
where colour theory meets the workings of the human eye and heart.
Throughout her career, Riley has charted her own course, usually
operating outside prevailing artistic trends. As Robert Kudielka, Riley's
longtime friend and fellow traveller, as well as a leading scholar of her
work, has noted, Seurat was 'not a hero of the 1950s', and, apart from
John Rewald's seminal contribution, there was at the time a dearth of
current literature on his work.[10] But just before Riley's crucial encounter
with Seurat, Meyer Schapiro had taken issue with the notion that the
Frenchman's *méthode* derived from a purely programmatic or scientific
approach. 'Seurat's hand has what all virtuosity claims: certitude,
rightness with least effort… I cannot believe that an observer who finds
Seurat's touch mechanic has looked closely at the pictures.'[11] Similar
arguments were once waged against Riley's early black-and-white
abstractions, though the artist has long made it clear that she has never

relied on scientific theory. As Riley saw it, '[Seurat] wanted certainty, and what is so amazing is that he actually achieved it, though not in a scientific sense but in a painterly one… In the end the evidence was visual rather than cognitive.'[12]

The full impact of Riley's student apprenticeship to Seurat evolved over time. Her early enquiries clearly helped set her on the path to abstraction, but she has continued to draw sustenance from Seurat's work at various points throughout her career. Her tribute to him has extended well beyond her explorations in the studio, for she has spoken and written at length about the artist on several occasions. She reviewed the 1991 centennial retrospective at the Grand Palais in Paris and subsequently included remarks on Seurat in her 1993 lecture, 'Colour for the Painter'.[13] Most recently, she contributed an aptly titled essay, 'Seurat as Mentor', to the retrospective of his drawings held at the Museum of Modern Art, New York, in 2007. Her personal recollections of copying Seurat are thoughtfully integrated with her close reading of his tonal drawings, one of which she had also copied in 1984, and with insights into the evolution of her own work. On this occasion she quoted for the second time the marvellous exclamation of Seurat's great champion, Félix Fénéon, as he described *A Sunday on La Grande Jatte – 1884* (1884–86) at the last Impressionist exhibition in 1886: 'here in truth the accidents of the brush are futile, trickery is impossible; there is no place for bits of bravura – let the hand be numb, but let the eye be agile, perspicacious, cunning.'[14]

Building on her Seurat tutorial, Riley originated her own compositions in a pointillist technique culminating in *Pink Landscape* (1960). Though executed in her London studio, the work was based on studies made *sur le motif* during her summer travels in Italy in 1959 and is a vivid recollection of a sunny day on the plains around Siena. The heat was so intense, recalls the artist, and the experience so powerful, 'It shattered any possibility of a topographical rendering of it… the facts of local colour were quite unimportant. The important thing was to get an equivalent sensation on the canvas.'[15] Here Seurat's dots are so large and regularised that they nearly overcome the individual forms they

  MARLA PRATHER

depict and convey a pulsating, brilliant luminosity and chromatic punch
that would become a hallmark of Riley's later colour abstractions (see
Set Fair, 1989).

It is a testament to the power of Seurat's model that his work, on the
one hand, helped at first to launch Riley into colour and, then, in a
relatively short amount of time, led her away from colour to black and
white. The year after she completed *Pink Landscape*, she made *Hidden
Squares* (1961), a fully abstract composition in which tiny squares are
embedded in an overall grid of black discs. Although she built this radical
composition, as always with a new phase of work, through a
concentrated period of drawing ('there are no shortcuts'),[16] it seems an
astonishing leap.[17] To arrive at this point, Riley elected to temporarily
forfeit colour and all the pleasure of Seurat's exhilarating lesson. She did
not restore colour to the work until 1967, and then only after gradually
introducing varying shades of grey, as in *Arrest 3* (1965).

Recently, black on its own has returned in the form of a monumental
wall drawing, *Composition with Circles 7* (2010). Riley has found this
fundamental element – a simple, transparent circle so resilient that she
has composed seven variations on the wall drawing, and countless
studies along the way, beginning in 1997. Not since the 1960s, with works
such as *Study for White Discs* (1964), has Riley coaxed from a single
colour such complex optical effects. But she now has accomplished that
feat on an enormous scale and with a new spatial oscillation created as
the effervescent circles bubble up and across the surface but also
advance and recede in depth. When studying the wall drawing, as with
Study for White Discs, just as we think we have seized upon the
organisational system, it eludes us, for, despite the barely perceptible
underlying grid Riley's investigational and intuitive 'method' is only partly
apprehended through geometric means. Beneath the artist's shifting
circular planes, the wall itself is visually dematerialised, and Riley has
masterfully fulfilled a youthful ambition. 'I wish', she boldly told a reporter
in 1964, 'someone would give me a big wall to destroy. I mean to make
it no longer seem a wall.'[18] There were other premonitions of this move
to the wall in the artist's early work. In 1967, when the American abstract
painter Ad Reinhardt, who, Riley recalls, gave her much encouragement

and 'sterling advice', saw her 13-foot-wide painting, *Exposure* (1966), at a New York gallery, he foresaw that working directly on the wall was a temptation, and advised her to stay on the canvas. '*Exposure* is still an easel painting,' says Riley, 'but only just.' The positioning of the new wall drawing in the exhibition within sight of *Black to White Discs* (1962), her first painting comprised entirely of circular forms, allows visitors to discover connections in the artist's thought across nearly five decades. In 1971, when Riley's fellow painter and writer Andrew Forge attempted to describe what he called the 'optical barrage' produced by Riley's high voltage black-and-white canvases from the 1960s (and his comments could just as easily be applied to the present wall drawing), he resorted to the example of Seurat: 'To find anything like it one would have to look to the Seurat of *The Models* (1886–88). Here, in the fall of light on a curved surface, counted out in a determined notation of orange and blue dots, there is a similar miraculous meeting of physical sensation and thought-determined system.'[19]

In addition to her early application of Seurat's method, Riley is attentive to the underlying organisation of his compositions: 'Interval follows event: measure, rhythm and cadence all played their part in Seurat's impeccable structure.'[20] Even when considering a work from much later in Riley's career, such as her curve painting from 2005, *Painting with Two Verticals 3*, one can draw parallels, however unintentional, with the little *Bridge at Courbevoie*. In 2004 Riley had introduced straight edges into her curve paintings, forming vertical registers that partly hold in check the powerful diagonal momentum of her tapered, curving forms. Seurat established at regular intervals strong vertical elements – masts, smokestack, figures, tree – which are reinforced by their reflections in the water and crossed by the strict horizontals of the jetty and the distant bridge. The beautifully taut silhouette of Seurat's sail, which could be a template for Riley's scimitar-shaped curves, is countered by the bending tree at the far right, a tree that finds its abstract counterpart in the swayback curve of yellow in Riley's canvas. In each there is a strong diagonal component: the downward slope of Seurat's grassy river embankment and the diagonal sweep that rises from left to right in Riley's abstraction. There is as well a

similarity in mood in the two works, of reverie evoked by forms bathed
in soft light, and Riley's colour scheme of blue, green, yellow and orange
owes much to her love of Impressionist and post-Impressionist painting.
Even in her most recent curve paintings, the introduction of a new
element – horizontals that frame the perimeter – calls to mind Seurat's
startlingly modern painted borders. But in one significant way the
painters part company. The mysterious quality of stasis in Seurat's work
finds few parallels in the elusive, ever fluctuating forms of Riley's
paintings. Perhaps for the painterly antecedents of these qualities in her
work, one can turn to the example of two other French Modernists she
highly reveres, Cézanne and Matisse.

Riley's impassioned advocacy of the art of painting has taken many
forms. Well before the current fashion of artist-curated exhibitions, she
took time away from the studio to co-organise exhibitions devoted to
artists whose work she had a personal connection to, including surveys
of Piet Mondrian at Tate in 1997 and Paul Klee at the Hayward Gallery in
2002.[21] For *The Artist's Eye* in 1989, she brought together seven large
figure compositions from the National Gallery's collection by artists who
used colour in plastic terms, 'as an element of construction'.[22] Her
selection began with Titian and ended with *The Bathers* (c.1894–1905)
by Cézanne, the only modern work in the group, and the reasons behind
her choices are elucidated in an extensive interview in the catalogue.
Riley's work, it seems fair to say, has been nourished as much by
Cézanne as any artist she has studied in depth, a veneration reinforced
by the impressive Cézanne holdings in London museums, the artist's
pilgrimages to exhibitions of his work and, significantly, her own part-time
residency in the South of France. She never chose to copy Cézanne –
she found his manner less accessible than Seurat's – but her insights
into the work, based on close observation and recorded in her extensive
writings and interviews, illuminate the work from the inside with remarkable
painterly insight. The National Gallery's magisterial work *Bathers* is
Cézanne's grand, late manifesto of the timeless theme of harmony
between man and nature, all bathed in his beloved Mediterranean light.
One author has recently suggested that these idyllic bathers belong to
Cézanne's 'Arcadian repertory' of Provence that he struggled to establish

over a lifetime.[23] Perhaps it is in this spirit that Riley's 2007 wall painting
included here has acquired an additional title, *Arcadia I*.

Although Cézanne devoutly believed that artists must first train
themselves through the study of nature, he was of course a dedicated
student of art history. He made many copies in the Louvre, which he
called 'the book in which we learn to read', and he drew upon the work
of the painters he studied there – Veronese, Rubens and Delacroix – for
his early painting *The Feast*, about 1867–72 (a painting much admired by
Riley and, coincidentally, begun by Cézanne at the same age she took on
Seurat's *Bridge at Courbevoie*). When the enthusiastic critic Gustave
Geffroy saw the work in 1895, at Cézanne's first solo show at the Galerie
Vollard in Paris, he noted these artistic forebears but recognised the
painting not as passive transcription but as a work of individual
expression: 'This is not a servile admiration, it is a profession of faith, the
declaration of a new artist swearing allegiance to painting, to opulence,
to energy. It is respectful of past masters, but how ardently it wants to
speak in its own turn!'[24]

Riley's serious interest in Cézanne has developed over a lifetime. She
told Richard Shiff for example, that she was drawn to The Courtauld
Gallery's *Tall Trees at the Jas de Bouffan* (1883) by the late 1950s. In his
verdant depiction of the family estate through tall, foliated trees,
Cézanne painted the canvas with varying degrees of finish, but in the
most densely worked areas his parallel strokes form distinctive
sequences and patterns, vertical in the lower regions and diagonal in
upper leafy zones. These ordered strokes, however independent of the
forms they depict, persuasively convey the textures of nature and impart
a shimmering quality of coloured light, realising in paint what Cézanne
described as 'the vibration of the sensations reflected through the good
sun of Provence'.[25] Part of the painting's appeal for Riley lay in the larger
compositional diagonals and the palpable 'directional pull' that results
when Cézanne's constructive strokes run counter to them.[26]

Riley is especially mindful of diagonals, a compositional mainstay
throughout much of her work but particularly since 1985, when, in search
of a way to multiply the visual rhythms in her compositions, elaborate
the colour activity and encourage the eye to scan the painting in multiple

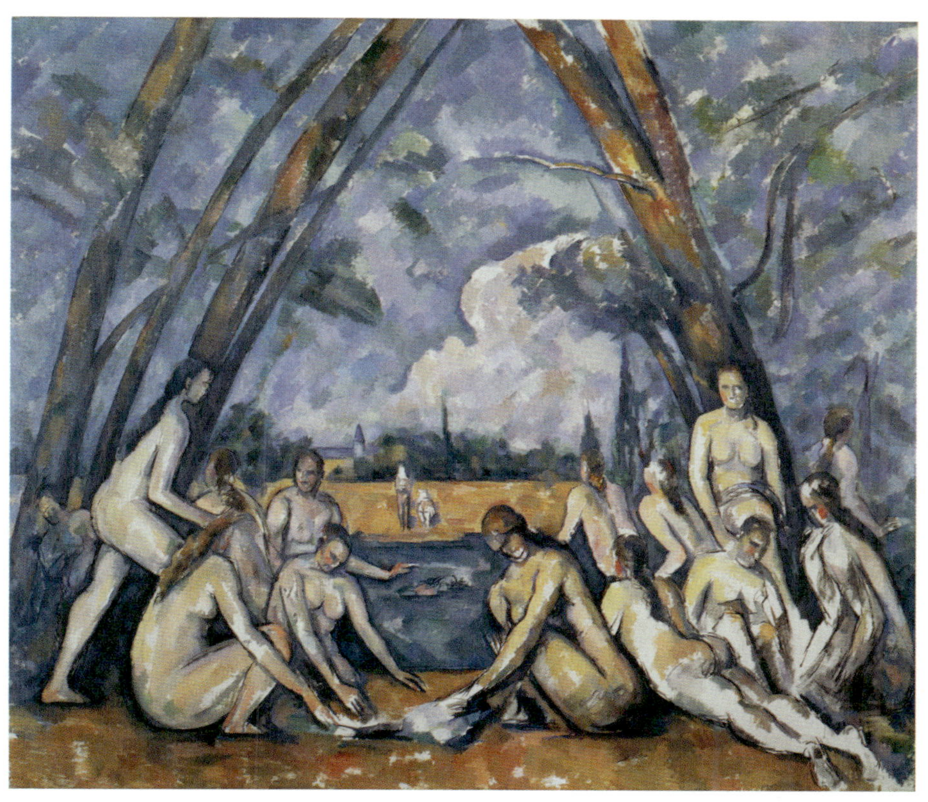

Paul Cézanne
The Large Bathers 1900–06
Oil on canvas
210.5 × 250.8 cm | 82⅞ × 98¾ in
Philadelphia Museum of Art

directions, she discontinued the compositions based on vertical bands of
colour and embarked on her rhomboid (or so-called zig) paintings,
including *Set Fair*. The vertical element remains but is here determined
by parallel stacks of multicoloured, interlocking lozenge shapes that travel
from the bottom left of the canvas to the top right in a dazzling,
ceaseless motion. Drawing, as in Cézanne, is achieved not by line, but by
colour. Creating their own 'directional pull', Riley's irregularly dispersed
colours, punctuated by brilliant white forms, course up and across the
surface, shifting in space depending on neighbouring hues to generate
optically vibrant patterns and a sparkling prismatic effect. Like Cézanne's
patches of colour, these chromatic vibrations convey through paint the
continuing flux of observed natural phenomena or what Riley has
described as 'the changing pulse of our experience'.[27] To come to terms
with the dizzying organisational complexity of Riley's zig paintings one
could invoke Roger Fry's description of Cézanne's celebrated *Portrait of
Gustave Geffroy* (1895–96) in the Musée d'Orsay: 'The mind of the
spectator is held in a kind of thrilled suspense by the unsuspected
correspondences of all these related elements. One is filled with wonder
at an imagination capable of holding in so firm a grasp all these
disparate objects, this criss-cross of plastic movements and directions.'[28]

In 2002, Riley observed to the artist and writer Lynn MacRitchie,
'I was still thinking about Cézanne when I became aware of the Matisse
connections.'[29] Given her involvement with colour, the graceful
arabesques of the new curve paintings she began in 1998, as well as the
collage methods she has employed to prepare her work since 1980, it is
no surprise that Riley's work invites comparisons with Matisse. When an
interviewer commented in 1995 that she seems to express greater affinity
for artists who work figuratively than for the leading abstract painters
(though notable exceptions include Mondrian and Jackson Pollock), Riley
replied that abstract art should be as 'resourceful and expressive as the
great figurative art of the past', and added that Matisse's use of colour in
his Fauve paintings and paper cut-outs was far more abstract than that of
the most innovative abstract artists. 'If Abstraction is going to win its case
and prove its viability,' she argued, 'it has to be more concerned with real
issues of painting than with concepts and theories.'[30]

In a short essay from 1990 on Matisse's *Dance II* (1909–10), Riley focused on the 'rhythmic organisation' and the 'huge curves and diagonals' as sources of the work's expressive power. Along with the intense red hues, boldly silhouetted against a blue background, these are formal characteristics the Matisse inevitably shares with a work such as Riley's *Red with Red I* (2007), which is not to say that *Dance II* was a starting point for the work any more than Cézanne's bathers. Nevertheless, when referring to her own painting, Riley returns to words like pace, movement, rhythm, cadence, speed – slow and fast – terms that apply to dance as well as to the compositional devices that govern her work. Suggesting a kind of abstracted *contrapposto*, the curves of Riley's paintings first move in one direction and then gracefully arch back in a counter curve, as one form seems to precipitate the movement of an adjacent form. Acceleration and syncopation are controlled by the size and frequency of the elements, the number of colours and the vertical intervals, which are subtly indicated but firmly perceived. These vertical divisions, as in *Painting with Two Verticals 3*, resonate with the abstract background Matisse introduced in the dance mural made for the Barnes Foundation, and like Matisse's dancers, Riley's tapered curves move across the straight-edged boundaries to keep the upward diagonal thrust in play.

A key difference with Matisse is the complex interplay of image and ground that animates Riley's curve paintings. This interest reflects her own recent preoccupation with opening the picture boundaries to the wall, a seemingly dramatic step that has gradually evolved through the intricate working process she has devised to compose her paintings, involving pre-cut pieces of painted paper, both for preparatory drawings as well as full-scale cartoons. Clearly demonstrated in her *Collage Study* (2005), as Riley wove and layered the cut paper, some shapes extend beyond the rectangular border. At the same time she introduced white into her colour abstractions and began to open these areas directly to the white support, dissolving the boundaries between inside and outside. From there it seemed a 'natural step' to dispense with the canvas altogether and incorporate the wall. Her challenge of late is to close off the edge again, corral her forms and, as she has said, 'to get it all

together as an easel painting, albeit a large one'. Hence, a new pictorial
solution arrived with *Blue (La Réserve)* (2010), in which the tips of the
curves lightly intersect or cross over and under the newly introduced
horizontal bands that run parallel to the canvas edge. For Matisse, what
began also as a preparatory method, the *papiers découpés*, became an
end in itself in the last decade.[31] The technique could lead to works of
astonishing simplicity and abstraction, particularly when used in a
decorative context. In his *The Tree of Life* (1950), the final maquette for
the nave windows he designed for the chapel at Vence, the stylised
leaves, set in a diagonal orientation seem to presage Riley's curved
shapes.

In 'Observations on Painting', his statement from 1945 written at the
age of 76, Matisse exhorts young artists to revere the past while finding
their own way, citing Cézanne's devotion to Delacroix and Poussin.[32] Like
Cézanne, Matisse had learned through copying in the Louvre as a
student, but he periodically continued the practice later in his career. In
1915 he famously reiterated and completely transformed, his own
rendition of Jan Davidsz. de Heem's *A Table of Desserts* (1640) – made
in the Louvre in 1893 – as unlikely a choice in retrospect as Riley's
selection of Van Eyck.[33] Also in 1915, Matisse made a lithograph, *Fruits
and Leaves (after Cézanne)*, diligently following a small oil by Cézanne
that he owned. Though he did not reproduce it, of inestimable
importance to him was another Cézanne in his collection, *Three Bathers*
(1879–82), which he acquired from Ambroise Vollard in 1899 and kept,
despite temptations to sell during moments of financial difficulty. When
he finally chose to donate it to a Paris museum 37 years later, his
account of its significance is a moving tribute paid by a mature artist to
his lifelong mentor: 'It has sustained me morally in the critical moments
of my venture as an artist. I have drawn from it my faith and my
perseverance.'[34] That Riley, in her words, 'drew courage' from Matisse
and came to him in part by way of Cézanne, is a fitting lineage within the
modern French tradition she so values.[36] In her lecture from 1996,
'Painting Now', much of it devoted to the extraordinary legacy of Matisse,
Riley concluded, 'From the viewpoint of the modern painter the true
tradition lies less in a succession of solutions than in recognising that the

MARLA PRATHER

problems of picture-making can never be solved as such. And it is just this that constitutes painting's continuing vitality.'[36] Viewing Riley's work within the rich context of the history of European painting in the National Gallery, not only enhances our understanding of her contribution, but will no doubt produce new, unforeseen connections with the painters who came before her. As Cézanne said, 'One doesn't replace the past, one only adds a new link to it.'[37]

Lise Connellan (ed), *Bridget Riley: Paintings and Related Work*, exhibition catalogue, National Gallery, London, 2010, pp.27–40.

1   Unless otherwise noted, quotations are from the author's conversations with the artist, June 2010.

2   Bridget Riley, 'The Experience of Painting: Talking to Mel Gooding' (1988), in Robert Kudielka (ed), *The Eye's Mind: Bridget Riley, Collected Writings 1965–2009*, Thames & Hudson and Ridinghouse, London, 2009, p.147.

3   Bridget Riley, 'Personal Interview by Nikki Henrique' (1998), in Kudielka (ed), *ibid.*, pp.30–31.

4   Bridget Riley, 'From Life', in Paul Moorhouse (ed), *Bridget Riley: From Life*, exhibition catalogue, National Portrait Gallery, London, 2010, p.9.

5   The exhibition, *Fra Angelico to Leonardo: Italian Renaissance Drawings*, was held at the British Museum, London, 22 April – 25 July 2010.

6   Riley, 'From Life', *op.cit.*, p.7.

7   Bridget Riley, 'Holidays: Talking to Vanya Kewley' (1996), in Kudielka (ed), *op.cit.*, p.45.

8   Bridget Riley, 'Seurat as Mentor', in Jodi Hauptman (ed), *Georges Seurat: The Drawings*, exhibition catalogue, Museum of Modern Art, New York, NY, 2007, p.188.

9   Bridget Riley, 'In Conversation with Lynne Cooke' (2005), in Kudielka (ed), *op.cit.*, p.314.

10 Robert Kudielka, 'In Search of a Direction: Bridget Riley's Work in the 1950s', in *Bridget Riley: Retrospective*, exhibition catalogue, Ridinghouse, London and Arc/Musée d'Art Moderne de la Ville de Paris, Paris, 2008, p.56.

11 Meyer Schapiro, 'Seurat' (1958), in *Modern Art 19th & 20th Centuries, Selected Papers*, George Braziller, New York, NY, 1982, p.103.

12 Bridget Riley, 'The Artist's Eye: Seurat' (1992), in Kudielka (ed), *op.cit.*, p.272n.

13 Riley revised and expanded this lecture, delivered at Darwin College, University of Cambridge, for her essay, 'Colour for the Painter' (1995), in Kudielka (ed), *ibid.*, pp.222–48.

14 Félix Fénéon quoted by Riley in 'Seurat as Mentor', *op.cit.*, p.185. Riley first recalled Fénéon's words in an interview, 'The Experience of Painting' in Kudielka, *op.cit.*, p.147.

15 Bridget Riley, 'Maurice de Sausmarez in Conversation with Bridget Riley', in *Bridget Riley*, New York Graphic Society, Greenwich, CT, 1970, p.57.

16 Bridget Riley, 'Work' (2009), in Kudielka, *op.cit.*, 2009, p.57.

17 Riley describes this process in 'Seurat as Mentor', *op.cit.*, pp.189–91.

18 Bridget Riley, quoted in 'Art: Something to Blink At', *Time*, 1 May 1964. The article was a review of a group show, *The New Generation*, at the Whitechapel Art Gallery, London in 1964.

19 Andrew Forge, 'On Looking at Paintings by Bridget Riley', *Art International*, vol.15, no.3, 1971, p.19.

20 Bridget Riley, 'The Artist's Eye: Seurat', in Kudielka (ed), *op.cit.*, p.273.

21 *Mondrian: Nature to Abstraction* was co-organised by Riley with Tate curator Sean Rainbird; *Paul Klee: The Nature of Creation* was selected by Robert Kudielka.

22 Bridget Riley, 'The Colour Connection: Bridget Riley in Conversation with Robert Kudielka', in *The Artist's Eye: Bridget Riley*, exhibition catalogue, National Gallery, London, 1989, p.7.

23 See Nina Maria Athanassoglou-Kallmyer, *Cézanne and Provence: The Painter in His Culture*, University of Chicago Press, Chicago, IL, 2003, pp.196–231.

24 Gustave Geffroy, quoted in Françoise Cachin *et al.*, *Cézanne*, exhibition catalogue, Tate Publishing, London, 1996, p.104.

25 Paul Cézanne, letter to Henri Gasquet, 3 June 1899, quoted in Benedict Leca, 'Sites of Forgetting: Cézanne and the Provençal Landscape Tradition', in Philip Conisbee and Denis Coutagne, *Cézanne in Provence*, exhibition catalogue, National Gallery of Art, Washington, DC, 2006, p.53. Riley's 2006 review of this exhibition for *The Burlington Magazine* is reprinted in Kudielka (ed), *op.cit.*, pp.249–65.

                                                                                 MARLA PRATHER

26 See Riley in Richard Shiff, 'Bridget Riley: The Edge of Animation' in Paul Moorhouse (ed), *Bridget Riley*, exhibition catalogue, Tate Publishing, London, 2003, p.87.

27 Bridget Riley, 'According to Sensation: In Conversation with Robert Kudielka' (1990), in Kudielka (ed), *op.cit.*, p.142.

28 Roger Fry, *Cézanne: A Study of His Development*, Macmillan, New York, NY, 1927, p.70; quoted in John Rewald, 'Catalog', in William Rubin (ed), *Cézanne: The Late Work*, exhibition catalogue, Museum of Modern Art, New York, NY, 1977, p.386.

29 Bridget Riley in Lynn MacRitchie, 'The Intelligence of the Eye', in Martin Hentschel (ed), *Bridget Riley: New Work*, exhibition catalogue, Kunstmuseen Krefeld, Krefeld and Hatje Cantz Verlag, Ostfildern, 2002, p.19.

30 Bridget Riley, 'Something to Look At: In Conversation with Alex Farquharson' (1995), in Kudielka (ed), *op.cit.*, p.156.

31 Riley discussed the importance to her of Matisse's *papiers découpé* in 'In Conversation with Lynne Cooke' (2005), in Kudielka (ed), *op.cit.*, p.315.

32 Henri Matisse, 'Observations on Painting' (1945), in Jack Flam, *Matisse on Art*, University of California Press, Berkeley, CA, 1995, pp.157–59.

33 The two works by Matisse are *La desserte (after Jan Davidsz. de Heem)* (1893), Musée Matisse, Nice, and *Still Life after Jan Davidsz. de Heem's 'La desserte'* (1915), Museum of Modern Art, New York.

34 Henri Matisse, in a letter to Raymond Escholier, 10 November 1936, quoted in Flam, *op.cit.*, p.124. The installation of the 2010 exhibition, *Matisse: Radical invention 1913–1917*, organised by the Art Institute of Chicago and the Museum of Modern Art, New York, began with this work by Cézanne.

35 Riley in MacRitchie, *op.cit.*, p.19.

36 Bridget Riley, 'Painting Now' (1996), in Kudielka (ed), *op.cit.*, p.302.

37 Paul Cézanne, letter to Roger Marx, 23 January 1905, in 'Cézanne on Art' in Cachin *et al.*, *op.cit.*, p.17.

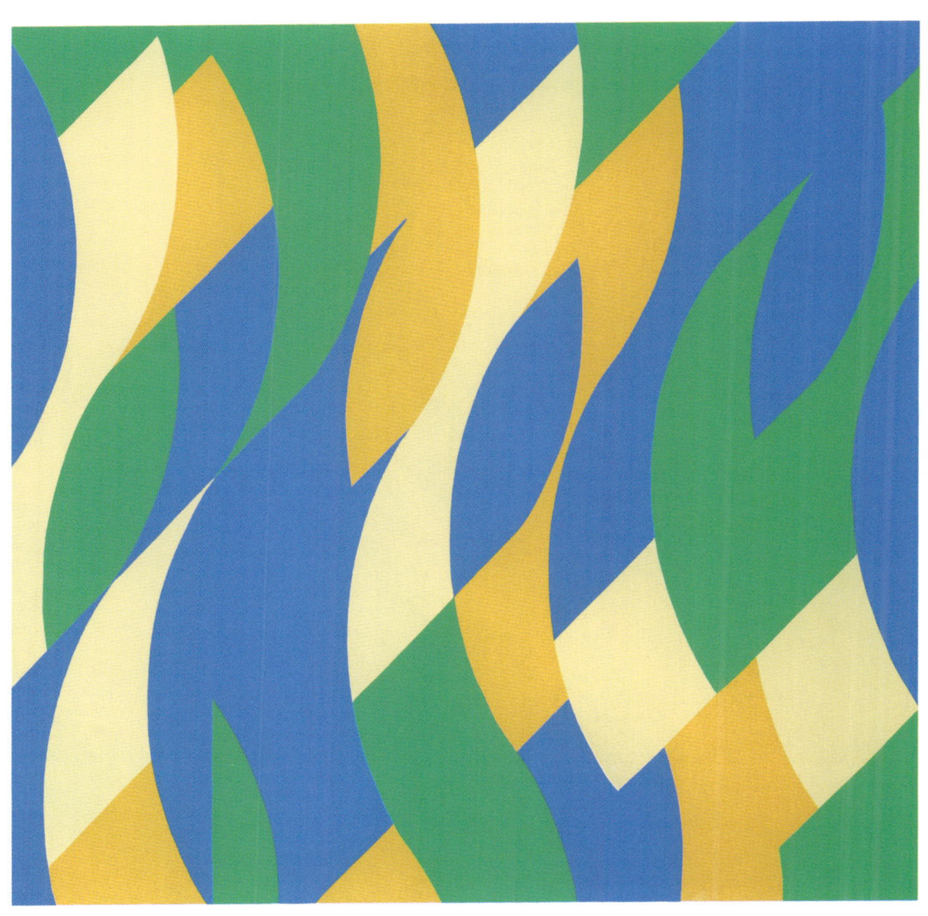

PLATE 26
Rêve 1999
Oil on linen
228.3 × 238.1 cm | 88⅞ × 93¾ in
Private Collection

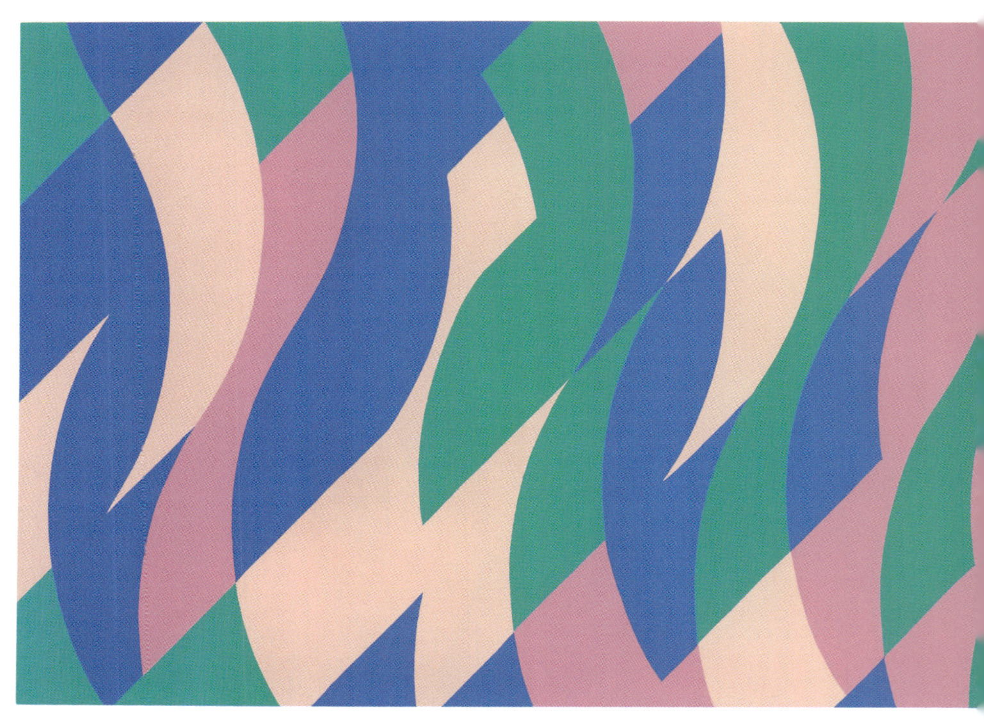

PLATE 27
Evoë 3 2003
Oil on linen
Two panels, overall: 193.4 × 579.8 cm | 76⅛ × 228¼ in
Tate, London

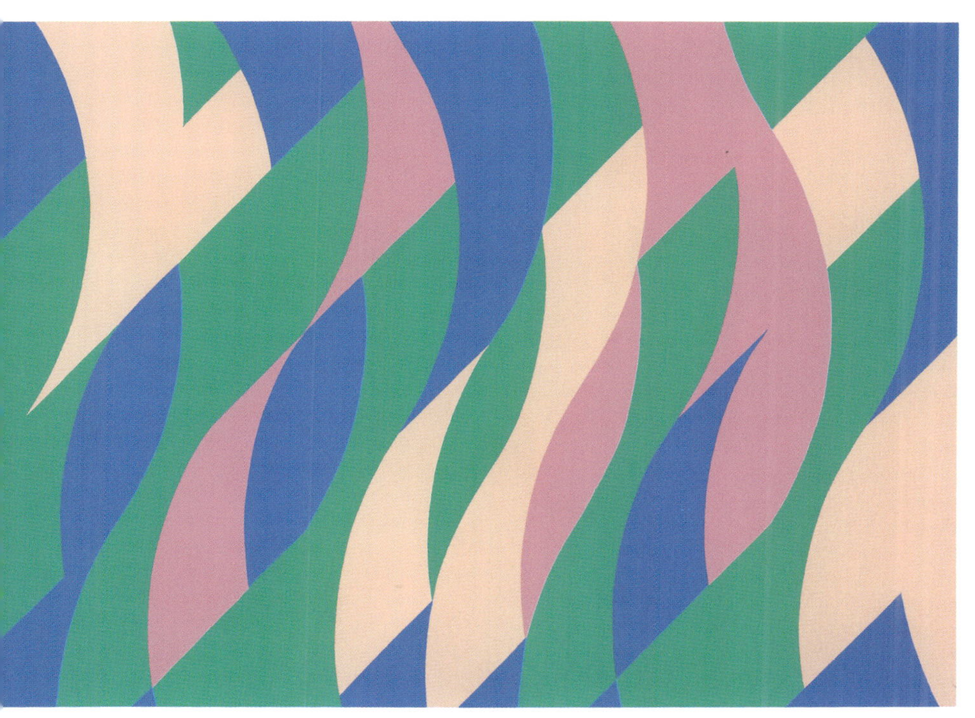

OVERLEAF | PLATE 28
Arcadia 1 (Wall Painting 1) 2007
Graphite and acrylic on plaster wall
2.7 × 5 m | 8¾ × 16½ ft
Private Collection

459

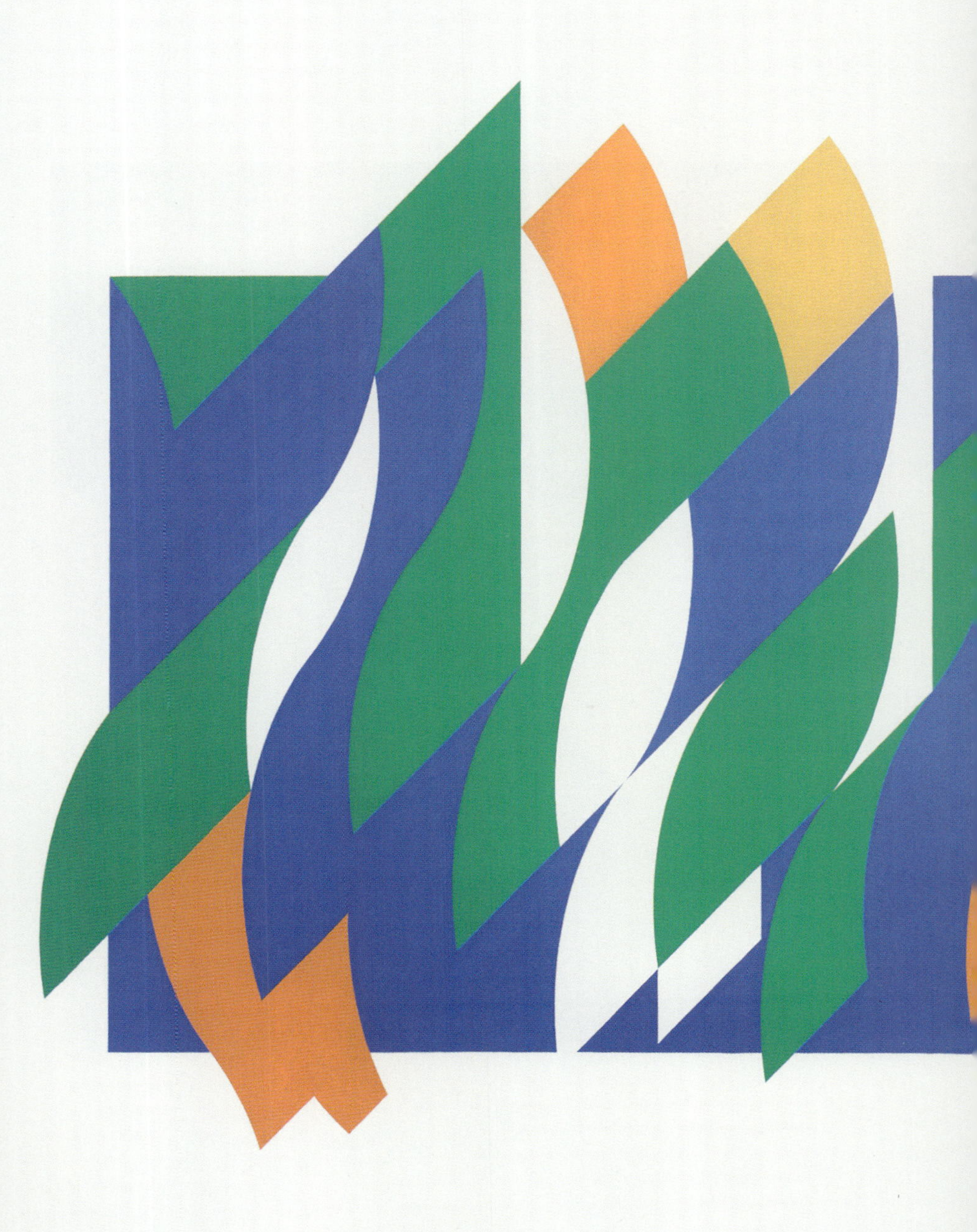

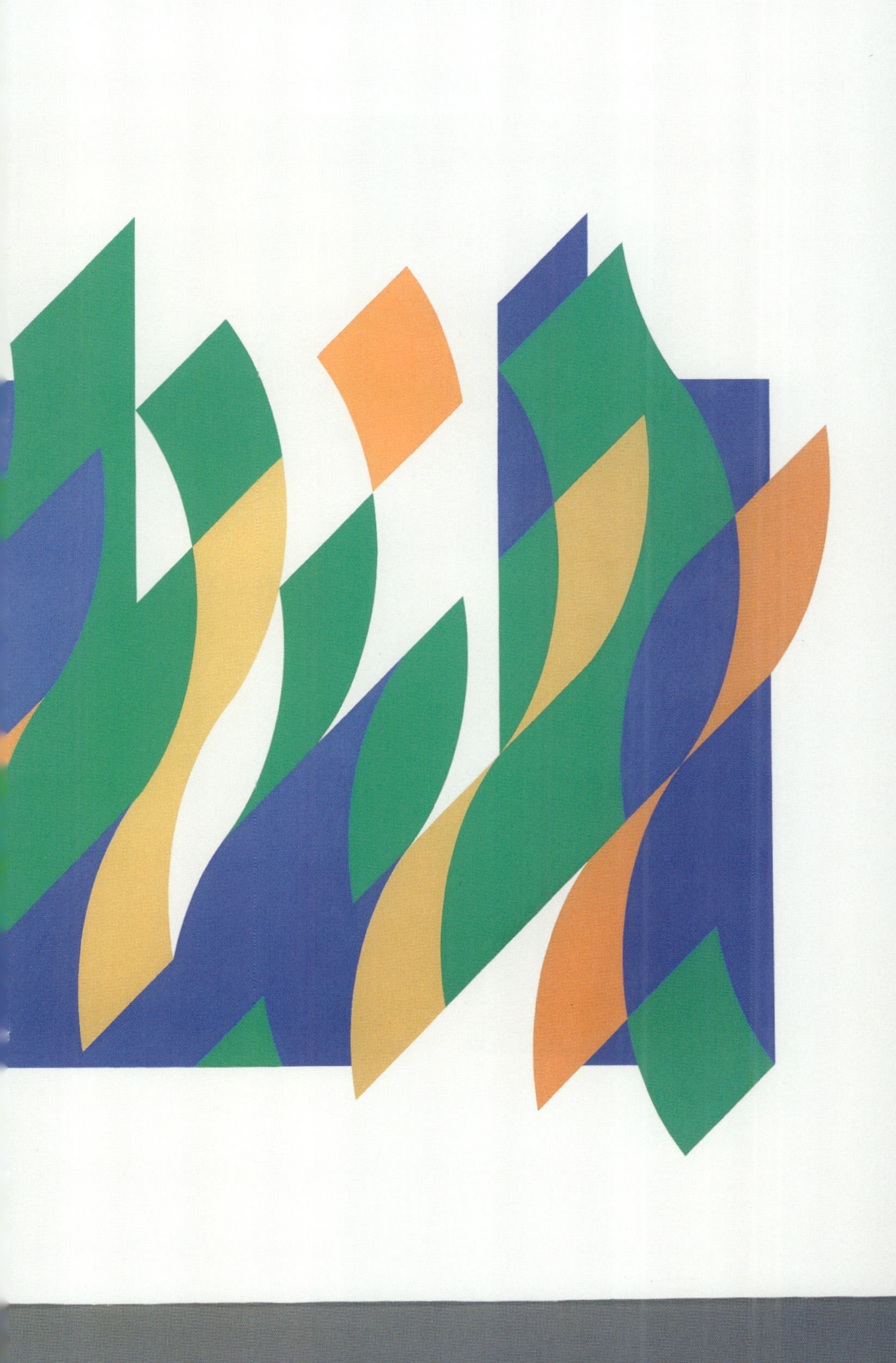

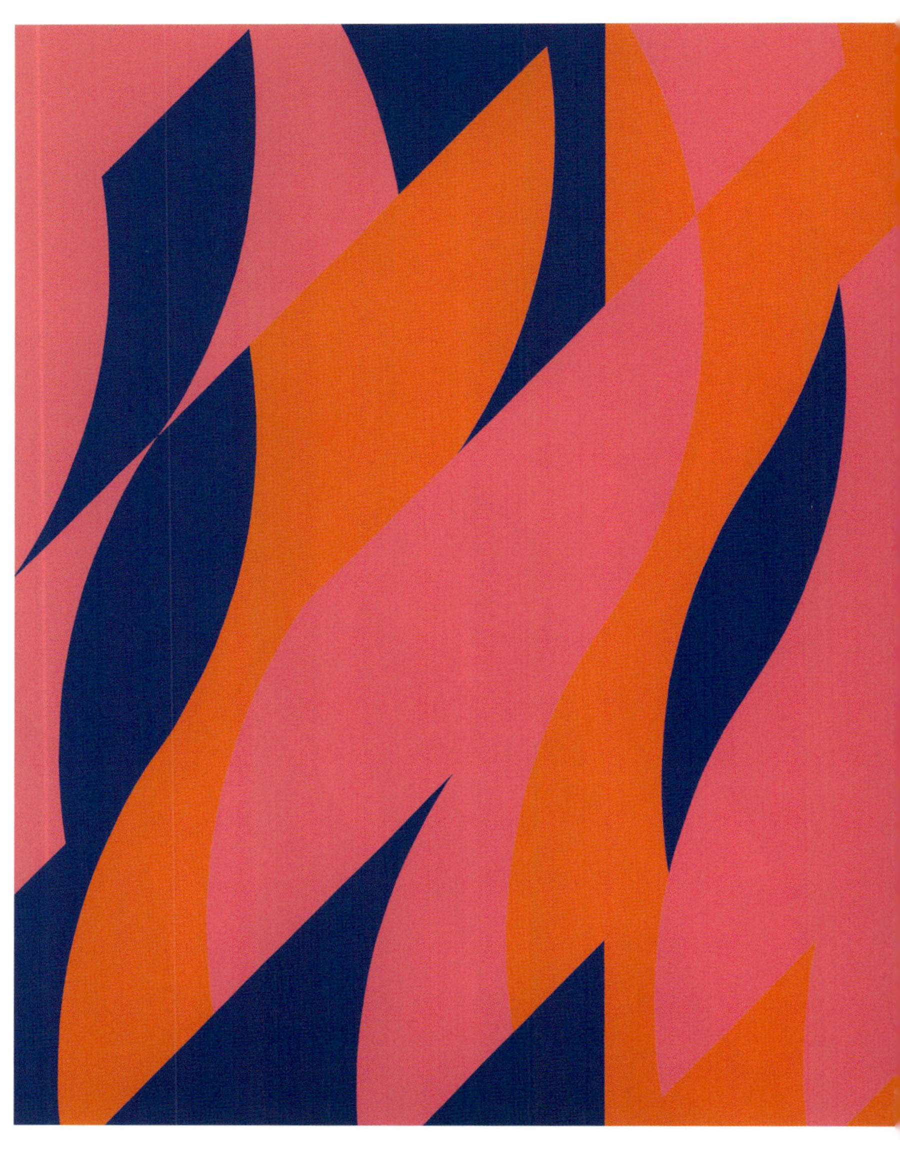

Red with Red 1 2007
Oil on linen
169 × 251 cm | 66⅝ × 98⅞ in
Private Collection

462

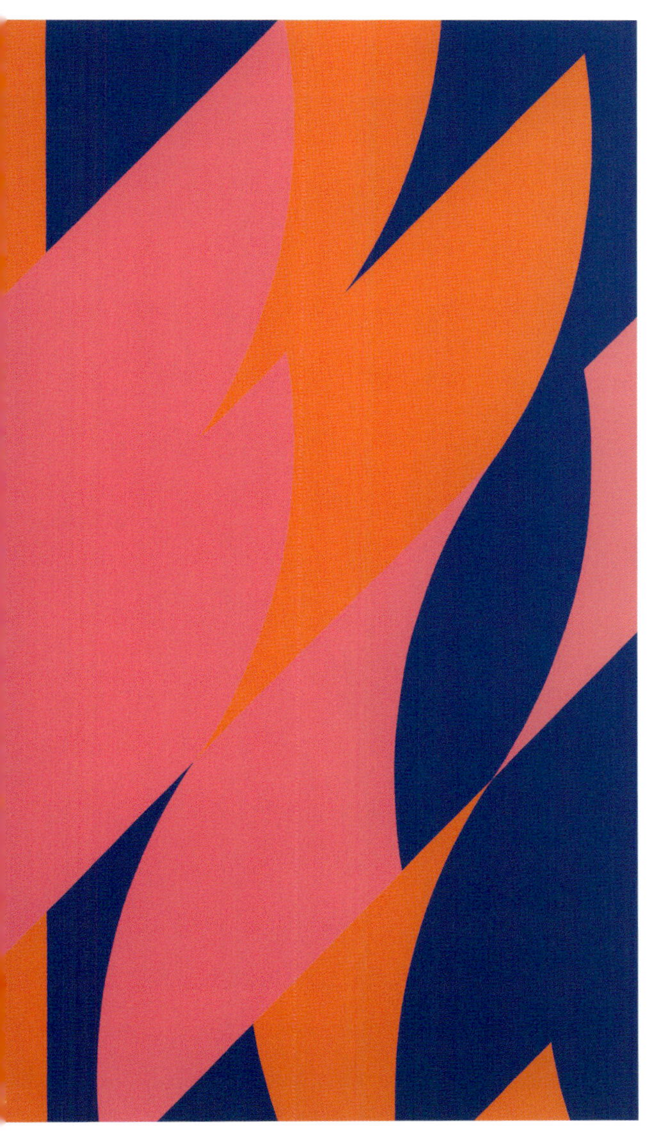

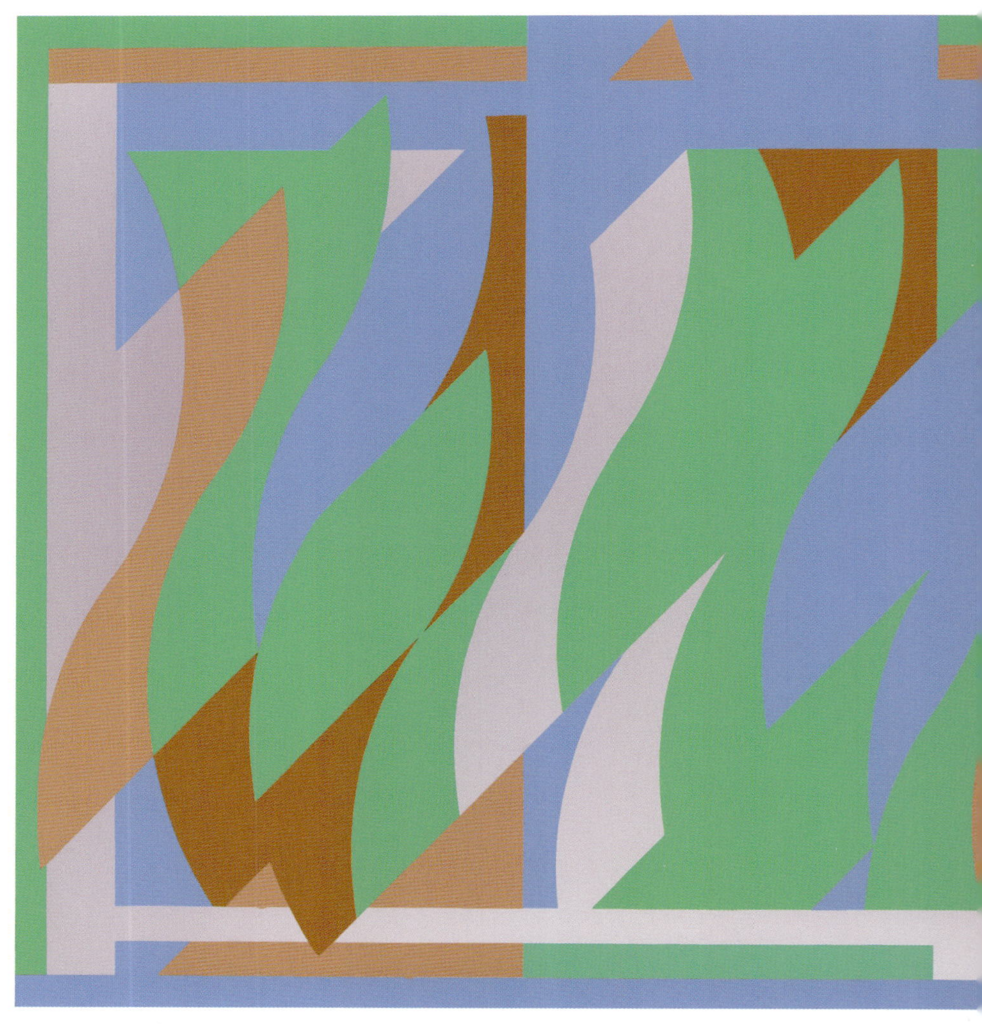

Blue (La Réserve) 2010
Oil on linen
183 × 381 cm | 72⅛ × 150 in
Private Collection

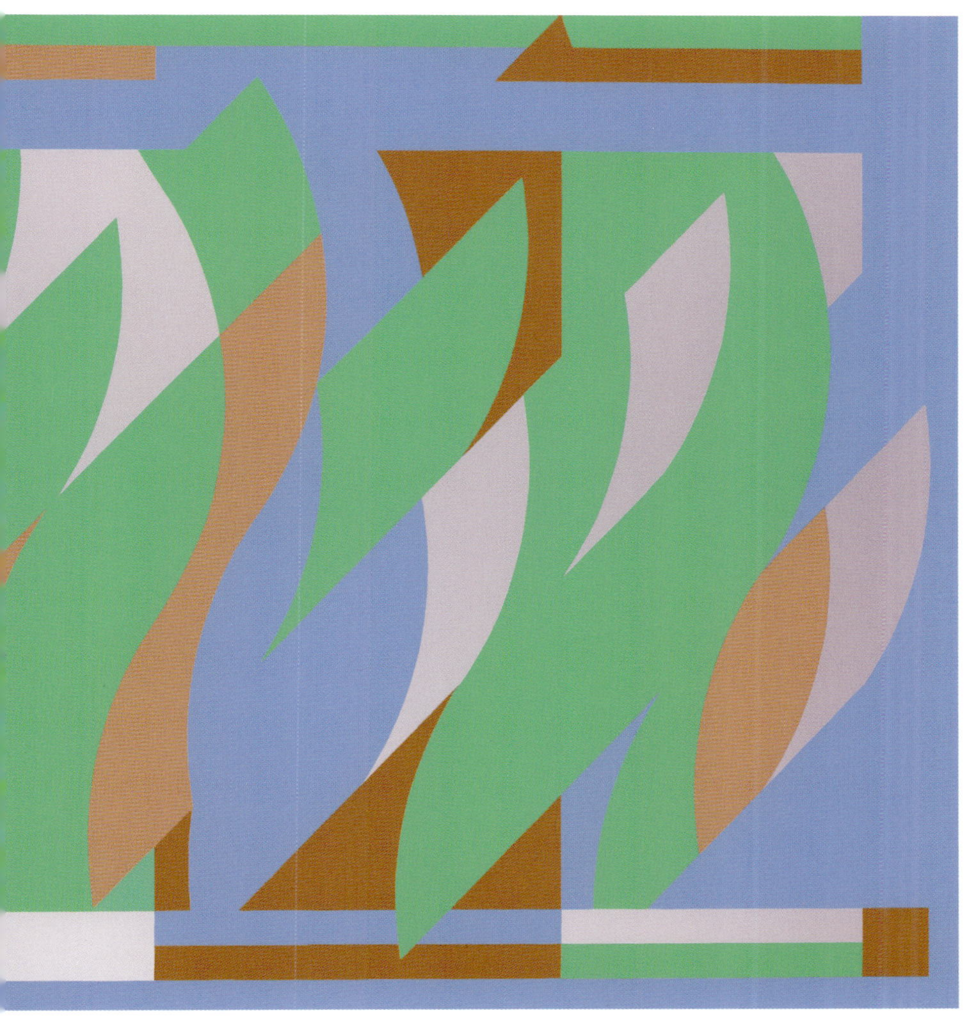

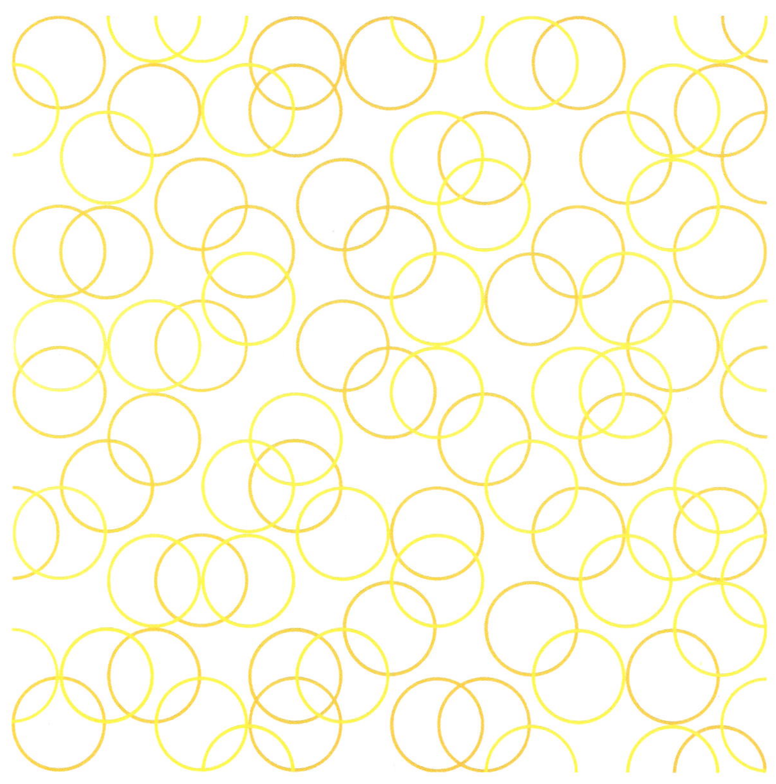

PLATE 31
Two Yellows, Composition with Circles 1 2011
Acrylic on canvas
112 × 112 cm | 44⅛ × 44⅛ in
Private Collection

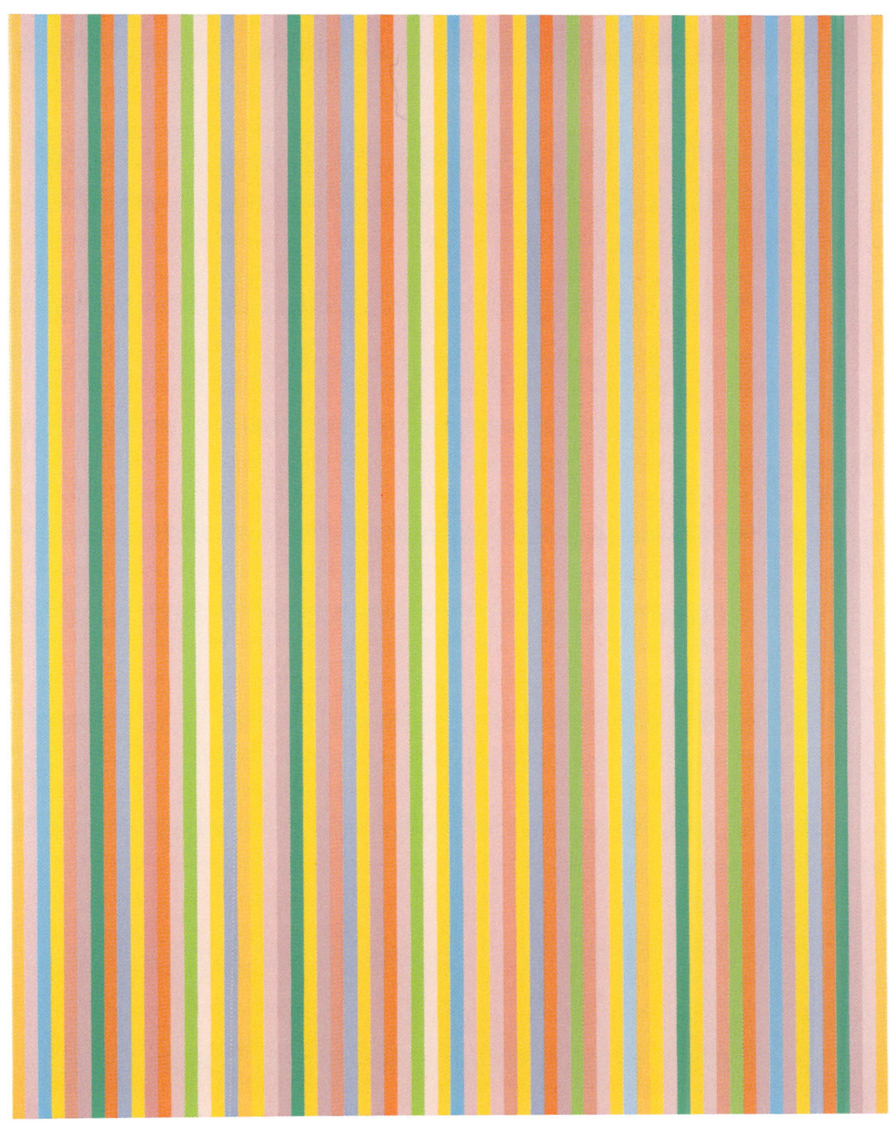

PLATE 32
Lux 2011
Oil on linen
211 × 167.5 | 83⅛ × 66 in
Private Collection

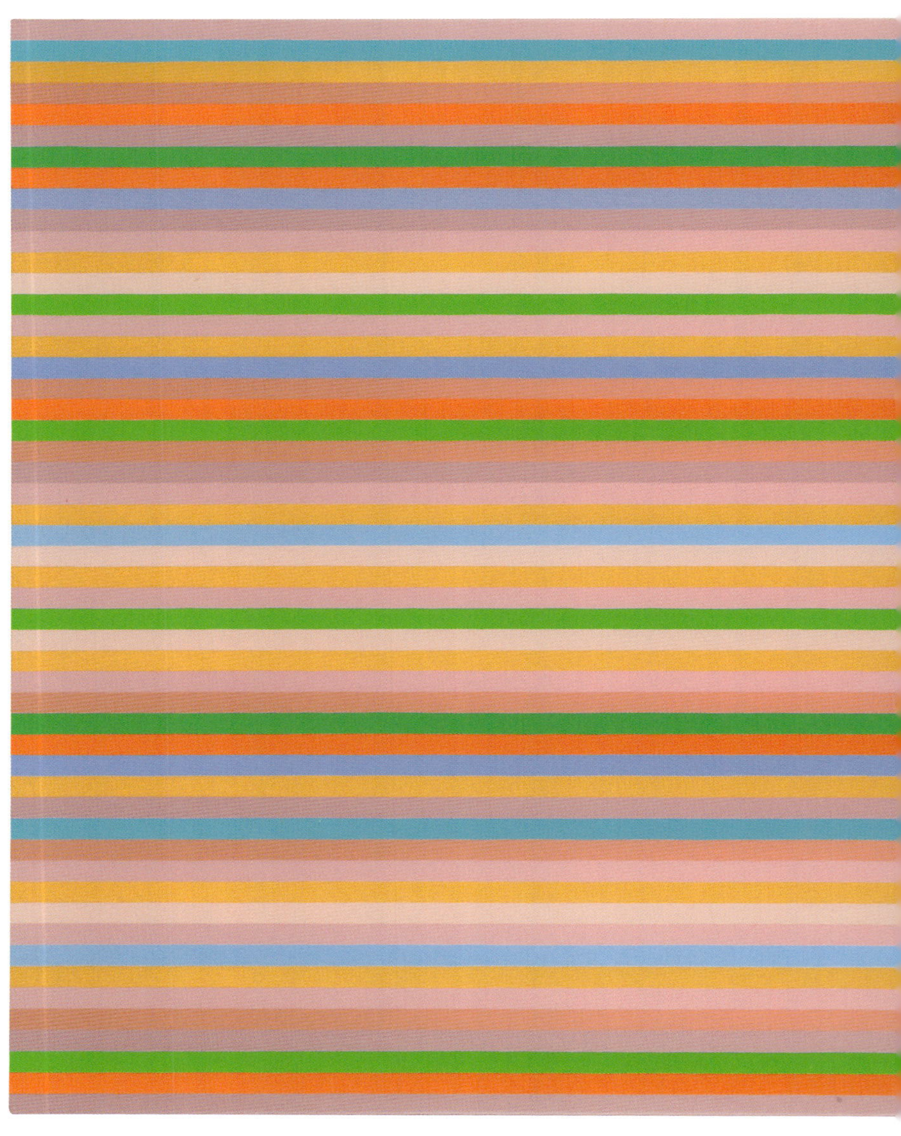

PLATE 33
Rose Red 2012
Oil on linen
132 × 238 cm | 52 × 93¾ in
Private Collection

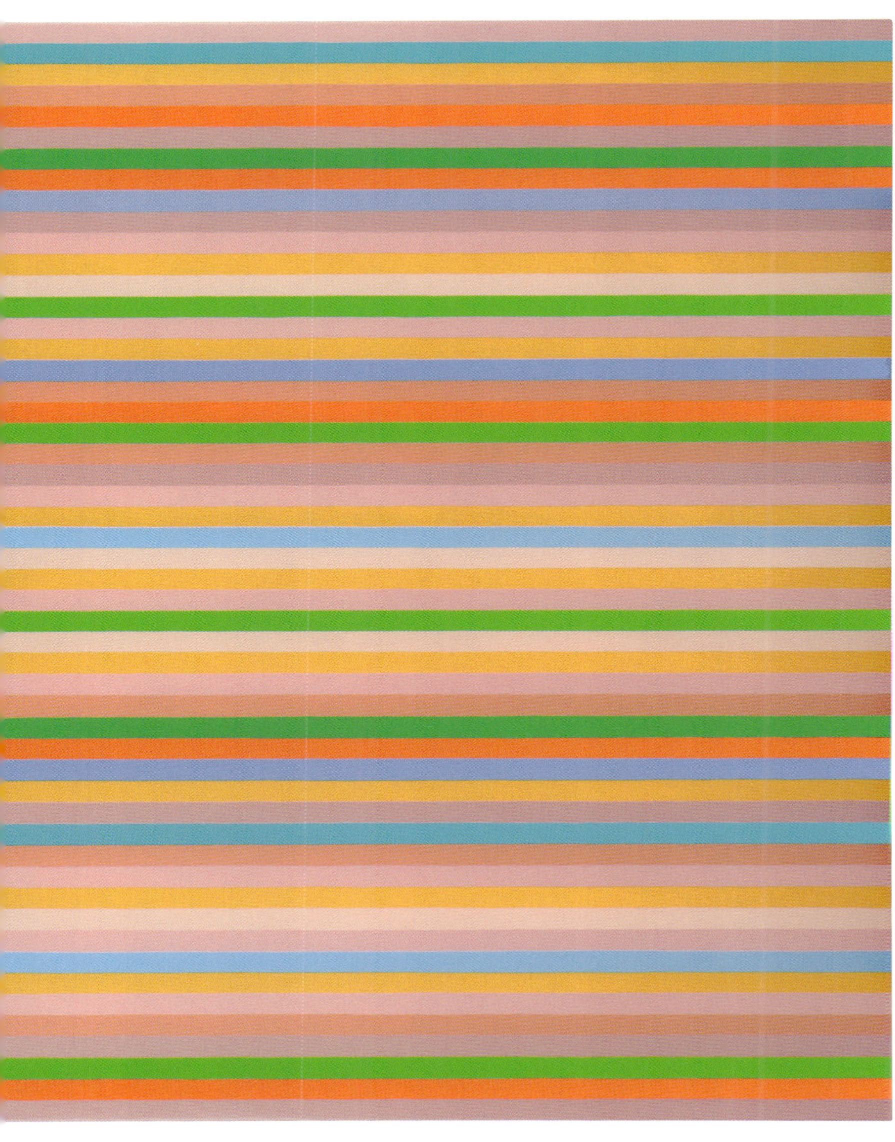

OVERLEAF | PLATE 34
Quiver 1 2013
Graphite and acrylic on plaster wall
4 × 10.4 m | 13 × 34 ft
Lambrecht-Schadeberg Collection, Museum für Gegenwartskunst Siegen

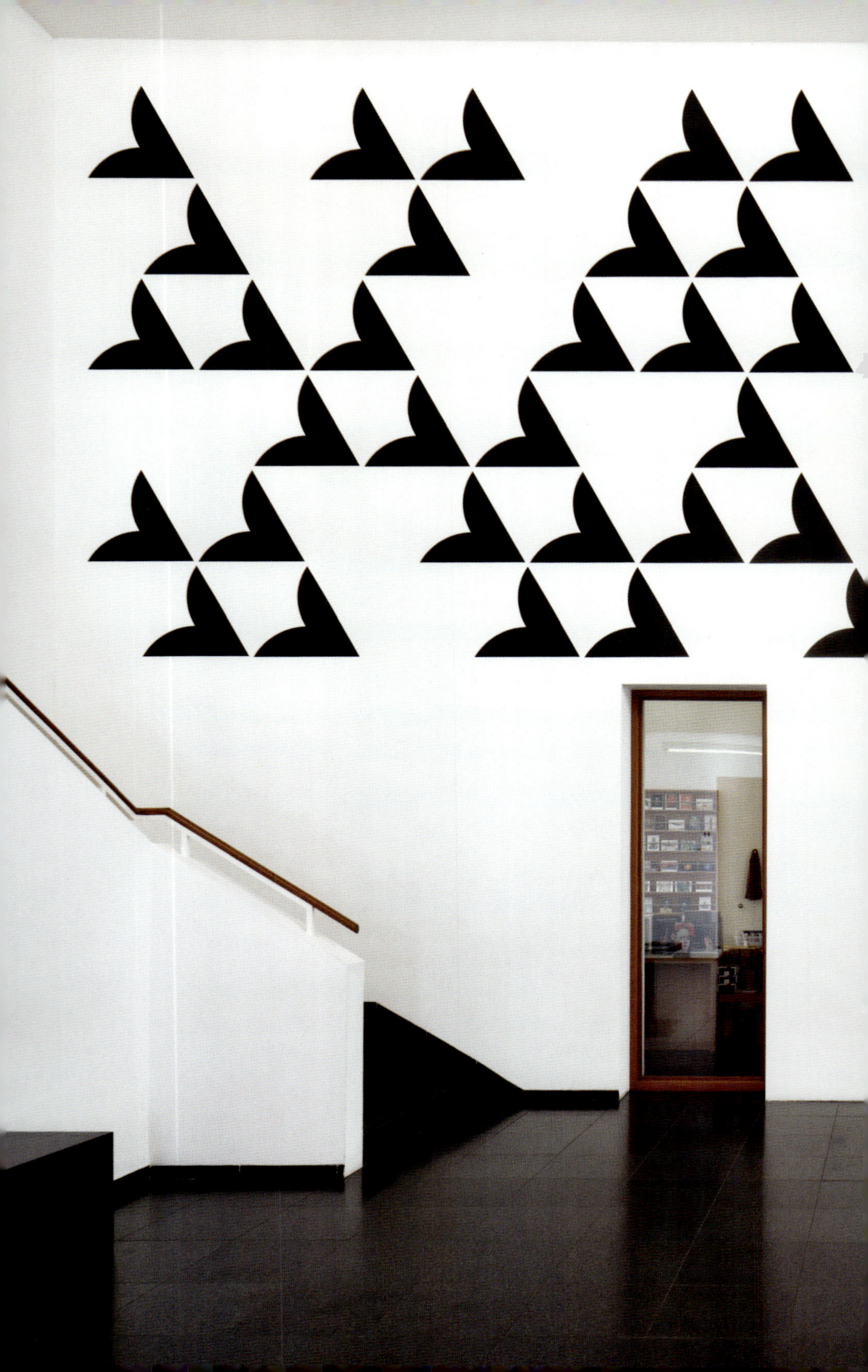

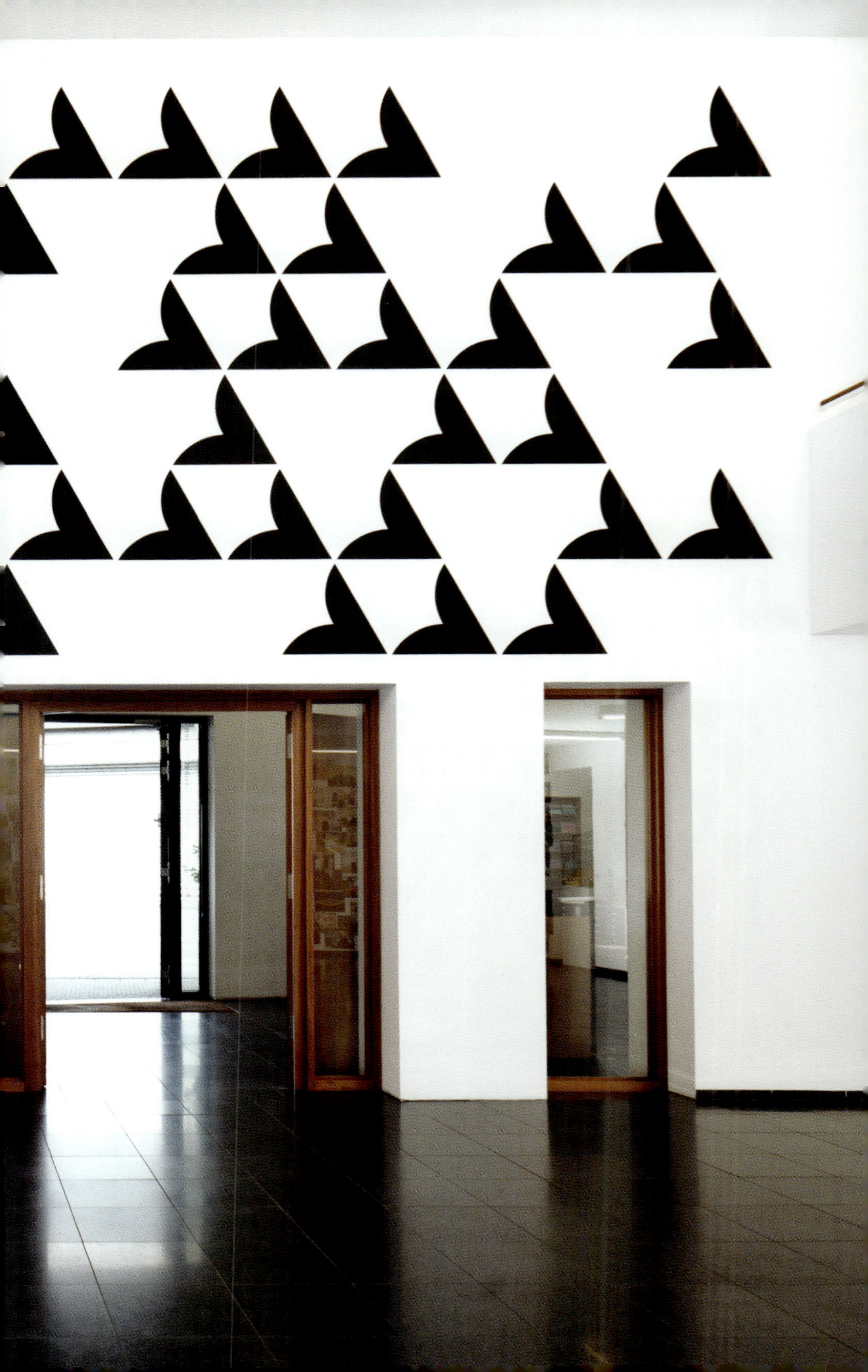

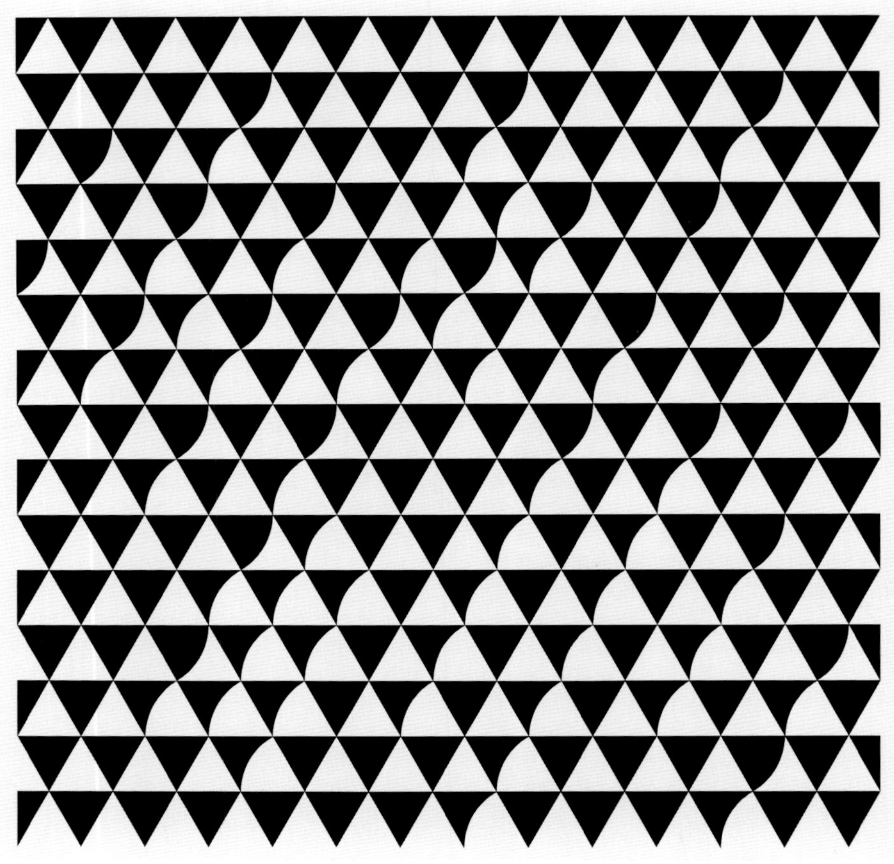

PLATE 35
Rustle 2015
Acrylic on APF polyester support
186.7 × 196.5 cm | 73½ × 77⅜ in
Private Collection

472

'In order to see one had to paint'
Lucius Grisebach

> My work has grown out of my own experience of looking,
> and also out of the work that I have seen in the museums
> and in galleries, so I have seen other artists seeing, and
> that has been an enormous help to me and a kind of
> pattern maker, in that it has shown me how a formal
> structure of looking is shaped and can shape in turn the
> way that one proceeds with one's own work.
>
> — Bridget Riley, 'Perception and the Use of Colour', 1992

What is a modern painting? One of the simplest definitions – invincible
in its simplicity – was formulated by the painter Maurice Denis: 'It should
not be forgotten that a painting – before it becomes a battle horse, a nude
woman or any kind of an anecdote – is fundamentally a plane covered
with colours in a particular arrangement.'[1] This statement was made in
1890, when modern art was still in its infancy, but it still makes one basic
fact clear: that a painting is neither a real nor an illusory window through
which another reality looms into view. It is a flat panel governed by its own
rules and laws, and all painting involves using brush and paint to create
something self-sufficient on the surface of just such a panel, something
that speaks credibly and convincingly in its own unique language. Even
after over 120 years this statement has lost nothing of its direct,
persuasive power. It explains in everyday terms what we mean when we
talk of the autonomy of a painting and of the thinking eye.

And, of course, this statement immediately comes to mind when we
contemplate the work of Bridget Riley, for it identifies precisely the crux
of her own approach to the tradition of modernist painting and the art-
historical starting point she chose for her own work. She has often
pointed to the fact that her work began in the very realms where this
statement was made – that is to say, in the colour paintings of the post-
Impressionists in Paris. Several of her exhibitions in recent years have
opened with paintings from 1959 and 1960 that use the pointillist

language of Georges Seurat; one of them is an exact copy of a Seurat painting from 1886–87.[2] It is rare that an artist so deliberately aligns him or herself with the pictorial traditions of modernist painting and speaks about it so openly. And when Riley so specifically explains that the highly developed, analytical pointillist painting of Seurat was the point of departure for her own artistic aspirations, she leaves the viewer and critic in no doubt as to her early and enduring interests and as to how she wishes her own development to be understood and evaluated. In her most recent comment on this subject, Riley expressly points out that Seurat was, 'an abstract painter before abstract painting emerged as a thing in its own right'.[3] Her interest has always been in creating a self-sufficient abstract painting. In this connection, the art-historically inclined viewer cannot help but be struck by the fact that Riley's *Pink Landscape* of 1960 in the style of Seurat is not in the horizontal format we typically associate with him but in a square format, which is much more closely related to the abstract paintings Piet Mondrian was producing in the 1920s and 30s.

The artistic development that we are considering here spans around 55 years from the late 1950s to the present day. It is that of an artist who evidently worked out with the greatest care exactly where, in the context of what we call 'modern', she could find the right place for her own interests, and who – ever since then – has pursued these interests with the utmost attention to detail and precision. We see her taking a path that is shaped by strictly analytical deliberations and a series of rigorous decisions that are always about reviewing what has been achieved to date and taking the next step that will open up new realms where her own painting can continue to develop on its own terms. At first sight this summary may appear too theoretical and non-artistic, bur Riley herself has described the process very clearly:

My paintings are not concerned with the Romantic legacy of expression nor with fantasies, concepts or symbols. I draw from nature, I work with nature, although in completely new terms. For me nature is not landscape but the dynamism of visual forces – an event rather than an appearance. These forces can only be tackled by

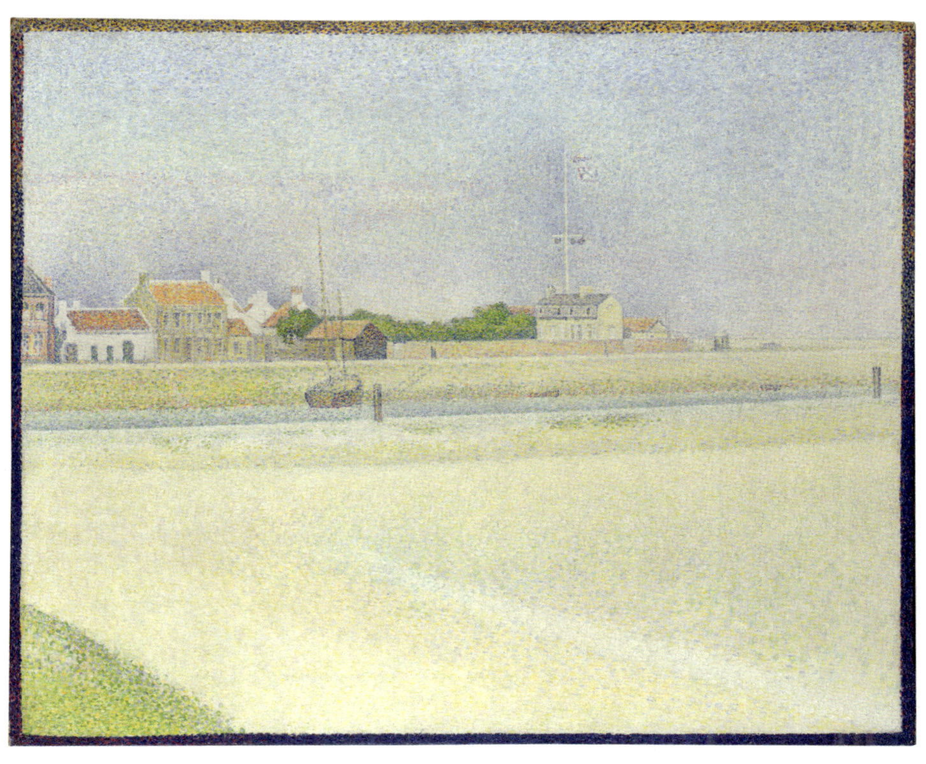

Georges Seurat
The Channel of Gravelines, Grand Fort-Philippe 1890
Oil on canvas
65 × 81 cm | 25⅝ × 31⅞ in
National Gallery, London

treating colour and form as ultimate identities, freeing them from all descriptive or functional roles.'[4]

This very 'theoretical' sounding analytical approach provides the key to new terrain, where colour and form can freely develop their identities – and this path into new worlds is only opened up by meticulous analysis. Over the decades we have seen how Riley's painting has in fact developed ever more complex forms. If there is anything that defines Riley as a truly modern artist, it is this resolutely conceptual manner in which she explains the basis of her painting.

Robert Kudielka, who has written so many illuminating texts on Riley's art, referred in his essay on her exhibition in Nuremberg in 1992 to a text in which Riley talks of 'the pleasures of sight',[5] thereby making it clear that we are looking here at a body of painting which is expressly not concerned primarily with inventing a new language of forms to contribute to the advance of modern painting, but purely with creating a self-contained, unique experience of seeing in the medium of painting. As Riley herself puts it: 'Long before I ever saw a major painting, felt the need to share an experience, knew the excitement of invention or painted my first watercolour, I had been fortunate enough to discover what "looking" can be – sometimes in a mere glance one can see more than in the close scrutiny of a thousand details.' She illustrates this with diverse experiences of 'looking' from her childhood in Cornwall:

But whatever the occasion might be, the pleasures of sight have one characteristic in common – they take you by surprise. They are sudden, swift and unexpected… They are essentially enigmatic and elusive. One can stare at a landscape, for example, which a moment ago seemed vibrant and find it inert and dull – so one cannot say that this lively quality of sight is simply 'out there in nature', or easily available to be commanded as wished. Nor is it a state of mind which, once acquired, can bend the most stubborn and unrewarding aspect of external reality to its own purposes. It is neither the one nor the other but a perfect balance between the two, between the inner and the outer. This balance is a sort of convergence which releases a

particular alchemy, momentarily turning the commonplace into the
ravishing… It seems to me that as an artist one's work lies here.
I realised partly through my own experience and partly through the
great masters of modern art that it was not the actual sea, the
individual rocks or valleys in themselves which constituted the
essence of vision but that they were agents of a greater reality…
I discovered that I was painting in order to 'make visible'. On one
hand I had to make something which had this essential quality of
precipitating itself as 'surprise' and, simultaneously, there was no way
of knowing with what one was dealing until it existed; so that in order
to see one had to paint and through that activity found what could
be seen … More than anything else I want my paintings to exist on
their own terms. That is to say they must stealthily engage and
disarm you. There the paintings hang, deceptively simple – telling no
tales as it were – resisting, in a well-behaved way, all attempts to be
questioned, probed or stared at and then, for those with open eyes,
serenely disclosing some intimations of the splendours to which pure
sight alone has the key.[6]

The aim here is therefore not the discovery of a new principle or the
invention of a new style for style's sake, but rather the instigation of new
experiences of seeing in the medium of painting on its own terms. The
repertoire of forms that was already available to Riley as she developed
her own specific language derived both from the wealth of forms in non-
representational compositions by painters ranging from Mondrian to
Jackson Pollock and from her own constant study – as she herself has
often pointed out – of great masters from Titian to Paul Cézanne and
Henri Matisse.

The beginning of this development was already remarkable. The
painting *Pink Landscape* in which Riley replayed and applied Seurat's
pointillism to such effect, was not followed by any more of its own kind.
On the contrary, she started working on compositions such as
Movement in Squares (1961) in a series of paintings in black and white
that were soon being described as 'Op art'. There could be no clearer
demonstration of the fact that these works were preceded by something

along the lines of positioning, which in turn led to what might be described as a new task:

> The marks on the canvas are the sole and essential agents in a series of relationships which form the structure of the painting. They should be so complete as to need, and allow of, no further elucidation. The basis of my paintings is this: that in each of them a particular situation is stated. Certain elements within that situation remain constant, others precipitate the destruction of themselves by themselves. Recurrently, as a result of the cyclic movement of repose, disturbance and repose, the original situation is restated.[7]

It is only in recent years that Riley – in a text with the telling title 'Work' (2009) – has talked of her own approach to painting and the stages in the development of her own oeuvre.[8] It is a remarkable text, for she repeatedly comes back to the fact that each step is entirely deliberate. An idea, on its own, is not admitted to her art: any new element has to arise from the existing paintings and has to prove its coherence and legitimacy in its painterly execution. First, there was the starting point for Riley's abstract paintings: 'Having discarded the figure and nature, what remained? Colour as colour itself, those simple shapes and forms that geometry and writing provided, and the material facts.' Then how her own generation should proceed: 'Everything that would constitute a viable art form had to be found, discovered, re-invented or recreated. It was an immense task but one that seemed essential if the implications and insights of modern art were to be pursued.' Riley follows this with a description of the making of *Movement in Squares*, the painting mentioned above, which she herself sees as the beginning of her own independent painterly work:

> I drew the first few squares. No discoveries there. Was there anything to be found in a square? But as I drew, things began to change. Quite suddenly something was happening down there on the paper that I had not anticipated. I continued, I went on drawing; I pushed ahead, both intuitively and consciously. The squares began to lose their

LUCIUS GRISEBACH

original form. They were taking on a new pictorial identity. I drew the whole of *Movement in Squares* without a pause and then, to see more clearly what was there, I painted each alternate space black. When I stepped back, I was surprised and elated by what I saw. The painting *Movement in Squares* came directly out of this study.

In this short description it is clear that Riley was not addressing an art-theoretical or conceptual problem, but rather working out a viable form to occupy the pictorial plane. And this continued as her art developed through the 1960s to the 1990s:

I had to work through the black-and-white paintings before I could even begin to think about possibilities of colour. There are no shortcuts. I had to go step by step, testing the ground before making a move. It would be a long time before I felt ready to leave the support of the greys for full colour… Although careful never to presume 'to know' what the pictorial elements would do in a particular situation, I began to feel that experience was fuelling my enquiry and that, whether I felt prepared to make some advance – or not – I had no choice but to do so. Having twisted my colour round the straight line, I looked again at the curve element and turned it into the supple twists of *Song of Orpheus* (1978). I drew these curves together into clustered fields by diagonals… The group of stripe paintings turned out to be a rich vein of colour thinking. In the end, that very richness precipitated a new approach. By making the effort to draw, I found my way. I had to lay aside the almost magical interactive power of colour that I had taken to a high level. The stripe itself went too; its limits had been reached. I needed to move the eye in different ways over the canvas. I searched for a new form that would be unlike any I had used before: a form that did not have the familiar identity of squares, triangles, ovals, etc. Eventually I found what I was looking for in the conjunction of the vertical and the diagonal. This conjunction was the new form. It could be seen as a patch of colour… acting almost like a brush mark. When enlarged, these formal patches became coloured planes that could take up different positions in space. They could serve several functions and being contained they were also movable: could change scale, harmonise or contrast with one another, repeat echo, 'create places', etc. A whole new field of relationships opened up.

Besides Riley's own comments, which make compelling and highly informative reading and underline her uniquely purposeful thinking,[9] the detailed essay written by art historian Paul Moorhouse for the catalogue for her retrospective at Tate Britain, London, in 2003 is also much to be recommended.[10] In depth and with the greatest possible precision, Moorhouse describes the path – sometimes painting by painting that the artist followed from one group of works to the next, from the purely black-and-white paintings from the period 1961–66 ('Visual dynamism') and the progressive introduction of variously tinted shades of grey starting in 1962 ('Transition') to the compositions with parallel, coloured stripes, starting in 1967 ('Colour and light') and the wave paintings, starring in 1974 ('A rhythmic vehicle for colour'), followed by the new approach to colour in 1980 ('From perception to sensation') and the subsequent development that is still ongoing. At all times, crucial importance is attached to the fact that the next stage develops out of the previous stage; that there is a constant expansion of painting's own innate potential and capacities; and that ever-new visual experiences arise from the work.

In 1980 there was a very particular change in Riley's work, which in retrospect looks like a qualitative leap. The stimulus was an encounter with art that produced a new sense of seeing for Riley when she was travelling in Egypt, in late 1979 and early 1980, and first saw with her own eyes the specific colours that feature in the art of ancient Egypt. She expounded on this in a lecture delivered in 1984: 'The Ancient Egyptians had a fixed palette. They used the same colours – turquoise, blue, red, yellow, green, black and white – for over 3,000 years.'[11] Riley's interest in this Egyptian palette led to a fundamentally new treatment of colour. Previously she had introduced colour into her planar compositions little by little, with the choice of colours being governed by the internal logic of the painting; now she turned her attention to colourism per se, to the interplay – in all its complexity – of colours in painting. Against the backdrop of her own artistic development up until that point, this new interest in colourist painting marked a radical new beginning in her work. Now, on her own terms and on the basis of her own reflective, describable approach to the medium of painting, she had to acquire and reformulate all the aspects of the colourism that had gradually formed over the centuries, ever since the Old Masters, in terms of practical skills and traditions.

Thus the predominantly structural wave paintings from the late 1970s, where lines and colours created a grid pattern of sorts, now gave way in 1980 to the new stripe paintings that Riley herself referred to in the passage cited above as a 'rich vein of colour thinking': compositions made up of vertical stripes where the colours suddenly emerge with a new freedom and individuality, paintings that resonate with tones and colours chords like a harp and that play whole melodies as the eye travels to and fro in a complex pattern of movements. The uniformly narrow, vertical stripes form the overall structure, but in a sense they are also the strings on a musical instrument designed to produce the sounds and resonances that are so important here. The paintings emerge from the interaction of colour chords, colour relationships, colour contrasts and colour movements. The colours generate a form of motion in which all the various parts communicate with each other, 'a context in which relatedness as such is of the first importance', as Riley herself once said with reference to the colour connections within a painting by Titian.'[12] The Egyptian palette that inspired this new phase was followed over the years by other colour constellations, including a very different Renoir-palette, with myriad oranges and pinkish reds shot through with blues and greens (see *Saraband*, 1985), inspired by the major retrospective of the work of Pierre-Auguste Renoir at the Hayward Gallery in London in 1985, and soon the shift from planar structures to colourism gave way to yet more developments. The structure of the vertical stripes was now overlaid with a diagonal counter-structure, which in turn led to the rhomboid paintings, where the entire picture plane is covered with diagonal building blocks in the form of upright parallelograms. Whereas the stripe paintings were exclusively restricted to horizontal connections and movements – hence the image of a harp – these new paintings now had access to all directions. The extent to which colour was at liberty to build up inter-connections within a clearly defined structure had now very significantly increased and the painting's associative potential, from the point of view of the beholder, had been correspondingly enriched; now, should the beholder want to describe what he or she saw in the painting, all sorts of natural phenomena might come to mind – landscapes with forests, waterfalls. Riley herself has described these paintings as coming from the 'interior of a tree'. This perfectly highlights the inexhaustible range of colour tones, sounds and chords, of colour contrasts, connections and movements that can arise in these paintings, and it indicates something of the wealth of emotions and associations that can flourish in each one of them.

These colourist paintings from the 1980s and 90s in turn became the point of departure for the pictorial form, the next pictorial stage, which is the focus of this exhibition. The new treatment of colour was followed by a new treatment of forms. A new type of curves and arcs has entered Riley's works, giving her ever-larger paintings a new, fluid buoyancy. As the artist herself has said, in a passage cited above:

> I searched for a new form that would be unlike any I had used before: a form that did not have the familiar identity of squares, triangles, ovals, etc. Eventually I found what I was looking for in the conjunction of the vertical and the diagonal. This conjunction was the new form. It could be seen as a patch of colour… acting almost like a brush mark. When enlarged, these formal patches became coloured planes that could take up different positions in space. They could serve several functions and being contained they were also movable: could change scale, harmonise or contrast with one another, repeat echo, 'create places', etc. A whole new field of relationships opened up.[13]

Eva Schmidt (ed), *Bridget Riley: Malerie/Painting 1980–2012*, exhibition catalogue, Hirmer, Munich and Museum für Gegenwartskunst Siegen, Siegen, 2012, pp.13–23.

                                        LUCIUS GRISEBACH

1   Maurice Denis, 'Definition du Neo-Traditionalisme', *Art et Critique*, Paris, no.65, 23 August 1890, pp.556–58.

2   *The Bridge at Courbevoie* (1886–87), The Courtauld Gallery, London. See also the artist conversation with Lynne Cooke in *Bridget Riley: Recent Paintings and Gouaches*, exhibition catalogue, PaceWildenstein, New York, NY, 2008, pp.16–23.

3   Bridget Riley, 'Bridget Riley in Conversation with Michael Harrison', in *Bridget Riley: Colour, Stripes, Planes and Curves*, exhibition catalogue, Kettle's Yard, Cambridge, and Ridinghouse, London, 2011, p.5.

4   Bridget Riley, 'Working with Nature' (1977), in Robert Kudielka (ed), *The Eye's Mind: Bridget Riley, Collected Writings 1965–2009*, Thames & Hudson and Ridinghouse, London, 2009, p.110.

5   Robert Kudielka in *Bridget Riley: Bilder 1982–1992*, exhibition catalogue, Kunsthalle Nürnberg, Nuremberg and Quadrat Bottrop Josef Albers Museum, Bottrop, 1992, pp.8–30, especially p.20.

6   Bridget Riley, 'The Pleasures of Sight' (1984), in Kudielka (ed), *The Eye's Mind, op.cit.*, pp.32–36.

7   Bridget Riley, 'Perception Is the Medium' (1965), in *ibid.*, pp.89–91.

8   Bridget Riley, 'Work', in *Flashback: Bridget Riley*, exhibition catalogue, Hayward Publishing, London, 2009, pp.15–18.

9   Bridget Riley throughout Kudielka (ed), *The Eye's Mind, op.cit.*

10 Paul Moorhouse, 'A Dialogue with Sensation: The Art of Bridget Riley', in Paul Moorhouse (ed), *Bridget Riley*, exhibition catalogue, Tate Publishing, London, 2003, p.11–27.

11 Bridget Riley, 'A Visit to Egypt and the Decoration for the Royal Liverpool Hospital' (1984), in Kudielka (ed), *The Eye's Mind, op.cit.*, pp.128–35, especially pp.130–33.

12 Bridget Riley, 'The Colour Connection: Bridget Riley in Conversation with Robert Kudielka', *ibid.*, p.19.

13 Riley, 'Work', *op.cit.*, p.11.

'If you can't go wrong, there's absolutely no way you can go right'
Éric de Chassey

From the Second World War to 1989, we lived in a bipolar world where choices were clear cut, between right and wrong, or at least between two mutually exclusive truths. There were 'third ways', but they were always seen somehow as compromises. The arts were concerned, too, by this bipolarisation. Abstraction, for instance, could only be of two kinds, the modernist and the expressionist: one that was based on pure form and medium specificity, and one that resulted from a confrontation with nature or with inner feelings. Artists could be claimed by the two sides at the same time, provided that their interpretations were contradictory – as was the case, for instance, with Jackson Pollock seen from the irreconcilable viewpoints of Clement Greenberg and Harold Rosenberg. The two positions remained strictly antagonistic, in a war less stylistic than ideological. Thus those few abstract artists who consciously trod a more complex path were excluded from the grand narratives that defined the mainstream and relegated them to a marginal situation. This applied especially to those who practised an abstraction that was both resolutely non-iconographical and strongly related to the world as we experience it. The advent of an appropriationist (or, more generally speaking, of a referential) abstraction, in the wake of postmodernism, did not really change anything: it was merely the return of iconography, with a vengeance. The singular experience of looking was displaced and replaced by a split experience of reading images as if they were texts and then submitting what you were looking at to what you had understood.

It is not surprising that, in the early 1980s, the art of Bridget Riley was subjected to such a displacement in the hands of some American postmodernist artists, who created long-winded variations on some of her most emblematic paintings. The advocated reason was that her art had heralded the provisional triumph of Op art in the 1960s, before the whole movement had been sidelined as out of fashion or not 'mainstream' enough. But a more unconscious reason was that she had long since forged a path of her own with her abstract work, a path that refused to fit into the grand narratives of post-Second World War histories of art because it failed to eschew a relationship with the world and nature (albeit not nature as a source but as a goal 'towards' which she worked), while at the same time consciously continuing the legacy of early modernism.[1] Indeed, Riley has been the epitome of the kind of modern artist who sees each artwork as an unforeseen adventure, in a manner that could be summed up by Édouard Manet's motto on a letter to Stéphane Mallarmé: 'Anything [or everything] happens [*Tout arrive*].' And, unbeknownst to her tongue-in-cheek imitators, she carried on, inaugurating a new series of stripe paintings in 1981, the so-called Egyptian paintings, which calmly signalled a new direction in her work. And she continues on her path as a modern artist in her most recent paintings. She has, in fact, always made use of an apparent sense of continuity. Riley's work since the 1960s is characterised by an enduring unfolding, in order to create groups of paintings which each yield specific experiences within a larger framework. Each painting, while 'limit[ing its] field of action' in the belief that it is a way to gain more 'freedom',[2] has been born of a thorough examination of what went before, a relaunching of questions raised previously, so that each can lead to a 'surprise' (to use a word Riley has associated with 'the pleasures of sight', which 'take you by surprise').[3] Her new work indeed stems partly from three different directions all initiated in the 1980s: the series of so-called zig paintings gave rise to the series of large curve paintings; the Egyptian paintings show a strong kinship with the present series of 'stripe paintings'; and her wall decoration for the Royal Liverpool Hospital in London can be linked to the wall drawings and 'wall paintings' (as well as to a new series, Two Yellows, Compositions with Circles, 2011).

The large curve paintings began at the very end of the 1990s: the painting titled *Lagoon 1* (1997) introduced some narrow curved forms into a succession of vertical bands fragmented in diagonal parallelograms, inherited from the zig paintings of the past ten years. It was a slight change, but one with consequences. Where the zig paintings created a shimmering surface, an all-over vibrancy with accents of light echoing throughout the few curved forms, although rhythmically spread,

　　　　　　　　　　　　　　　　　　　　　　　ÉRIC DE CHASSEY

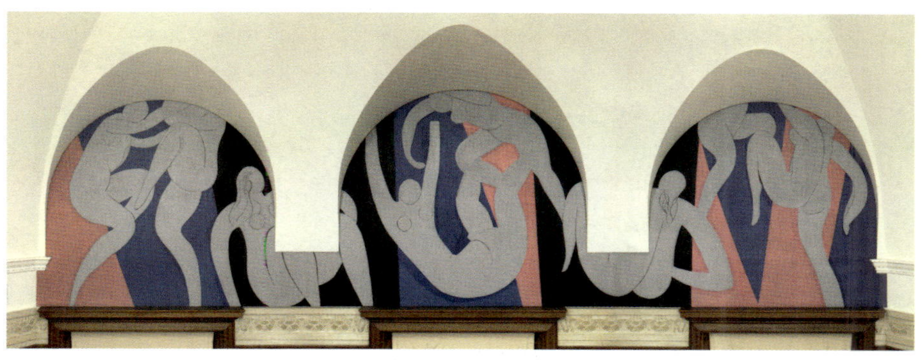

Henri Matisse
The Dance 1932–33
Oil on canvas
Left: 339.7 × 441.3 cm | 133¾ × 173¾ in
Centre: 355.9 × 503.2 cm | 140⅛ × 198⅛ in
Right: 338.8 × 439.4 cm | 133⅜ × 173 in
Installation view, Barnes Foundation, Philadelphia
© Succession H. Matisse/DACS 2016

suggested an intricate space, fragmented and broken down, without any safe ground or overall stability. For instance *Out There* (1987) gives the broad impression of a yellow cloud, rather like an 'appearance'. Vertical planes, apparent as such, dominated each painting of the past decade as a regularising structure, which sometimes, as in *Vespertino* (1988), supported a dynamic thrust of intricate rhomboids but without ever losing its poise. By doing away with this plainly visible structural support and taking into account her feeling that 'curves were coming – arcs' whilst working on paintings such as *November* (1990), Riley was prompted to clear the ground for a new move.

Starting with *Rêve* (1999), she made paintings that were completely rhythmic: grand symphonies of curves and counter-curves playing in and out of a subtle irregular grid of diagonals and verticals, never traced as such on the canvas but making their presence felt. I have compared their vocabulary and effect to that used by Henri Matisse in his first version of *The Dance*, conceived for the Barnes Foundation, Philadelphia, in 1932–33 and later reworked before being given to the City of Paris. It is now on permanent display at the Musée d'Art Moderne de la Ville de Paris, where Riley's largest retrospective to date was organised in 2008, an opportunity to experience in the flesh this kinship. These large curve paintings were not only based on full-size cartoons made with painted cut-out paper shapes – a method devised by Matisse and one that Riley has been using for over 20 years. They were indeed dances of their own, dances of flowing forms on the canvas that suggested similar movements in the eyes and bodies of their viewers. They reintroduced in Riley's work the question of the image, bringing forth flat areas of plain colours that acted as many points of focus, moments of stasis in an ongoing lateral rhythm.

But these images were not juxtaposed or loosely placed; they shape each other while contending with the underlying grid that intermittently straightens them. At first glance, they might have been taken for flame-like shapes, but where they tangentially meet the truncated diagonal and vertical lines of the implicit structure, their edges are straight. The combination of these shapes with a very diagonal structure and the rhythmically paced verticals – musical in its format – explains why their

                                                          ÉRIC DE CHASSEY

dance never becomes frenetic; why it has always seemed harmonious and controlled, like a well-mastered improvisation. The vertical partition of the surface is always to be felt, as the *fil à plomb* evoked by Matisse in *Jazz* (1947): 'I never indicate a curve… without being aware of its relationship to the vertical. My curves are not mad.'[4]

It created a series of poles around which shapes wrap themselves, visually pushing forth or receding backwards, depending not only where the viewer stands in front of the painting but also on the immediate context of each shape. In the first paintings of the series, these patterns were cut short by the edges of the canvas, as if they were but a portion of a larger universe, albeit self-contained by their inherent tension which avoids any hint of dislocation in favour of a breathing space. The centrifugal impetus of the compositions is thus checked by a counter centripetal cohesion. 'I would like to really break up the space', explains Riley. In *Red with Red 1* (2007), a place was established by a succession of three vertical planes that can most clearly be seen along the top and bottom of the canvas, where a central orange-red plane is braced on each side by two deep blue planes. This place is then broken up and energised by large curves of the same colours plus pink. The similarity in both tonal and chromatic values gives this painting a particular density and makes it a reference point in Riley's oeuvre.

Other canvases in this group pushed this formation of a stable place a step further, raising the possibility of a separation between the place and its animation by coloured shapes. Taking this development into account, Riley added two horizontal tiers along the top and bottom of the canvas in several of the most recent of the large curve paintings, such as *Two Reds with Violet* (2008), an explicit variation on *Red with Red 1*, or a painting aptly subtitled *La Réserve* (2010) – a French word that means, among other things, a storage for several paintings as well as the untouched part of a painting that is nevertheless read as a form or a line. Here, the rhythmic composition presents itself on a flat surface, as if the dance was taking place as a distant spectacle before a curtain or on a stage: that is to say, with a ground that can be experienced both as a background and as an active surface, as the colour takes part in the general interplay of forms. To reinforce stability in the series, Riley has also added several narrow horizontal bands at the bottom or top of the large curves of the compositions: their divisive presence creates a sort of polyptych within a single painting, a kind of container composed of several containers.

Sensing that she needed 'a shift of focus following the demands of the Red with Red group', Riley has recently taken up once more the format of the stripe paintings, first experienced in the Egyptian paintings from the 1980s. In fact, this represents less a return to a previous series than a new departure, made possible by the experience of colour and space of the large curve paintings. A palette of up to a dozen colours is used in these new 'stripe paintings', whereas most of the Egyptian paintings were done with only five colours, plus black and white. But it is true that the recent series and the one from the 1980s share a common principle, made clear by the fact that in 2008 Riley drew upon a preparatory study from 1983 to make *Lilac Painting 1* (2008/1983). Now the stripes are all of the same width and are painted evenly from one end of the canvas to the other, so that the question of the image does not apply.

The earliest of the Egyptian paintings, such as *Après Midi* (1981) or *Serenissima* (1982), made their rhythmic structure visible at first glance, as they were built upon an armature of black-and-white stripes. A working drawing from the previous year, *Black and White Rhythm* (1980), shows that the paintings evolved this structure from the idea of an irregular rhythm of blacks acting as visual beats, countered by whites that marked pauses in the progression. In the paintings, the blacks acted less as stripes than as lines and were quickly excluded. (In *Après Midi*, they can even appear as contours containing the coloured stripes that surround them.) In *Bali* (1983) for instance, the whites took on the function of the beat, without asserting themselves as solely heterogeneous means, as the blacks had done in the proceeding canvas, thus reflecting upon the traditional separation of drawing and colour. In the later paintings of the earlier series, such as *Saraband* (1985), Riley does away with both black and white, homogenising their vocabulary while unfurling an unforeseen richness not only in the colours themselves but also in the rhythmic and spatial effects achieved through colour alone.

　　　　　　　　　　　　　　　　　　　ÉRIC DE CHASSEY

The new stripe paintings use the means that had been laid aside
25 years before, and, in reproduction at least, they appear very similar,
although the feeling they actually give is rather different. Their palette
has been almost entirely carried over from the last Egyptian paintings:
close in value, their colours are sometimes bracketed in pairs or triads of
close hues. But where *Saraband* appears unambiguously structured by
the rhythm of the darkest stripes – a deep green – the new 'stripe
paintings' are more unified. The functions of structure and improvisations
within the composition become more interchangeable, a result, certainly,
of the way the curves were wrapped around implicit poles in the large
curve paintings. In *Lux* (2011), the main rhythmic structure seems initially
to depend upon five darker stripes; in fact it is composed of four green
stripes encompassing an additional stripe which is not green but blue.
This inclusion is the result of the blue stripe being close in tone and
value to the green stripes but also of its placement just off-centre. Colour
in these paintings is declaratively interactive; each hue, pitch and tone
appears to change according to its neighbours and to the instant in
which it is registered in the viewer's perception. In a very recent painting,
yet to be titled, this contextual use of colour is put to the test, as Riley
places two tones of pinky red next to one another. From afar they seem
to create a single stripe of a double width, but they regain their
distinctive character when seen up close. At the same time, depending
on these perceptual instances, the structural role is played alternatively
by the reds, the greens or the blues. An open visual field is created, one
that does not differentiate definitively between areas calling for a
focused vision and areas that stay on the periphery of attention. On the
contrary, this openness renders each stripe available to all functions and
modes of vision. Thus, in the series – including some new horizontal
stripe paintings, where this experience is further increased – the stability
and even the tenor of the surface brought about by the order of the
succession of equivalent forms and colours are provisional, while the
instability that viewers sometimes perceive is equally provisional. The
most regular of means – the juxtaposed coloured stripes of equal width
extending from the top to bottom – create both a flat surface and a
shallow space. It leaves open the existence of uncertainties, but, as Riley

herself specifies, these 'uncertainties are not doubts'; the stripe paintings
are utterly assertive and positive.

Before the dawn of the new millennium, Riley had worked directly on
the wall only in connection with hospital commissions; the first of these
was her decoration for the entrance corridor at the Royal Liverpool
Hospital in 1983.[5] The decoration was removed in 1990, but photographs
and studies make it possible to see that she applied to the wall surface
what was also happening in her paintings at the time. The vocabulary of
stripes and the palette were taken from the first Egyptian paintings, with
several changes that took into account the fact that 'a decoration should
not demand scrutiny, should have no details to attract attention… You
should become aware of a decoration almost bodily'.[6] The stripes
became horizontal instead of vertical, and of different widths, in order to
play with the architecture; the palette was reduced to four colours plus
black and white, so that the walls could 'give light'; print on vinyl was
used instead of oil on canvas, because 'it can be replaced'.[7] The
monumental wall drawings (started in 1998) and wall paintings (started
in 2007) are not exactly decorations, in the sense that they very definitely
ask 'to be looked at, like a painting'. But they partake in the decorative, in
the sense that they are one with the wall and are also meant to be
'taken in as a whole'.[8] They take stock of one of the major lessons of the
hospital decoration from the 1980s, namely the active and passive uses
of the white wall, around and inside the colour compositions.

The wall drawings make use of the wall in a rather discrete way: as a
foil for a linear structure. This leads the eye on a primary journey across
the surface and into a shallow space reminiscent of the paintings such as
November, whose spatial achievements in colour recur in the black-and-
white wall drawings. In the hospital decoration, the upper and lower
stripes also provided the substance for a visual journey, but it was much
more simple and directional. The purpose of this decoration was twofold:
firstly, it would accompany the visitors on their way; and secondly it
would identify the location within the hospital. By contrast, in the series
Composition with Circles, Riley puts the circle through its paces and
paints directly onto the wall. *Composition with Circles 1* (1998) included
four-leafed flower-like high focus forms; the subsequent wall drawings in

ÉRIC DE CHASSEY

this group, however, created concurrently with the large curve paintings, have in common the use of one basic element: the possibility of patterning as such has been avoided in favour of a purely rhythmic treatment of the surface. The eye is led up and down, in arcs that segue or are interrupted, by circular lines that are clustered or dispersed, their diverse densities providing a feeling of moving forward or backward in space. As Riley is always careful not to cluster the circles too densely – which could give the feeling of falling forward over the viewer – the wall is not destroyed as a surface but forms the background limit of the space created by the circular composition. This thus opens the way for a painterly use of the same device, albeit in colour, that the new series of Two Yellows, Compositions with Circles from 2011 starts to explore.

The vocabulary of the 'wall paintings' is strictly that of the 'large curve paintings', with curved and straight shapes flowing dynamically: *Arcadia 1 (Wall Painting 1)* (2007), for instance, is closely related to *Cadence 8* (2007) in terms of composition and palette. The inclusion of the white of the wall in the composition marks an important change. It makes each coloured shape a separate and discrete unit. It creates a centrifugal effect which is particularly dynamic, so that the composition opens itself up on its four sides and encompasses the whole surface of the wall (whatever the dimensions), while simultaneously retaining a strong lateral impulse. It imparts a pivotal role to the white surfaces, which take part in a dislocation of the composition's stability, as if mining it from within, as well as constituting both volume and plane in the shapes themselves. In a way that amplifies the role played by the large white median part in the 1983 hospital decoration, the wall is not only activated by the painting; it is also an actor in the painting. When looking at *Rajasthan* (2012), for instance, even as a full-scale cartoon, it becomes clear that 'the wall is embraced by the movements' of the coloured shapes. Furthermore, as it descends into the pictorial area – roughly rectangular, with fully realised figures that escape from its limitation – it also has to meet these movements. The ultimate green shape on the right, with its straight edge and subjection to the surge of red, is checked by the white of the wall that seems to push the general thrust of the composition back. On the left-hand side of the painting, on the other hand, there is a double-entry into the composition: a red curve swings in while the white of the wall pushes it forward.

The recent work of Bridget Riley is achieving something remarkable, in that it is simultaneously surprisingly adventurous and calmly masterful. Without emphasising the risks she takes in each painting or wall piece, as each positions itself in a long lineage of precedents without ever copying them, she is in fact continually exploring new questions and opening new perspectives. She has strictly limited her vocabulary to the non-gestural and the abstract, in the belief that 'figurative painting, without the relevant context of religion or mythology won't do… the *absence* of a shared vocabulary is, by virtue of absence, the only common basis that exists.'[9] This way of working and sharing experiences with the viewers as a sharing of surprises is not always immediately clear, but that is only because most of us have fallen into 'lazy viewing habits' and no longer heed Matisse's insistence upon looking as an active rather than a passive sensory experience.[10] If we agree to be active viewers, to enjoy looking, as Riley herself has always done, her work can indeed bring pleasures as well as thoughts. Abstraction in painting does not model itself on the world we know (although it does not necessarily abandon it either): it creates modes of vision and of thinking that can then be transferred to the world and subtly transform our attitudes and our ways of living. Riley's abstraction is an ongoing search, without any predefined goal: as she says, 'the search is for itself'. Each of her works teaches us, in its own specific way, to make one step at a time, with the knowledge that 'if you can't go wrong, there's absolutely no way you can go right'.

Eva Schmidt (ed), *Bridget Riley: Malerie/Painting 1980–2012*, exhibition catalogue, Hirmer, Munich and Museum für Gegenwartskunst Siegen, Siegen, 2012, pp.25–36.

ÉRIC DE CHASSEY

1   Bridget Riley and Bryan Robertson, 'Things to Enjoy' (1992), in Robert Kudielka (ed),
    Bridget Riley: Dialogues on Art, Zwemmer, London, 1995, p.80.
2   Riley has quoted Igor Stravinsky's *Poetics of Music in the Form of Six Lessons* (1942): 'My
    freedom will be so much the greater and more meaningful, the more narrowly I limit my
    field of action and the more I surround myself with obstacles.' See Bridget Riley,
    'Perception and the Use of Colour: In Conversation with EH Gombrich' (1992), *ibid.*, p.34.
3   Bridget Riley, 'The Pleasures of Sight' (1984), in Robert Kudielka (ed), *The Eye's Mind:
    Bridget Riley, Collected Writings 1965–2009*, Thames & Hudson and Ridinghouse,
    London, 2009, p.33.
4   Henri Matisse, *Jazz*, 1947, pp.75, 83–84, in Riva Castleman (ed), *Jazz*, Sophie Hawkes
    (trans), George Braziller, New York, NY, 1985, p.16.
5   Two other wall paintings were carried out in the corridors of St Mary's Hospital in
    Paddington, London.
6   Bridget Riley, 'A Visit to Egypt and the Decoration for the Royal Liverpool Hospital' (1984),
    in Kudielka (ed), *The Eye's Mind*, *op.cit.*, pp.134–35.
7   *Ibid.*, p.135.
8   *Ibid.*, p.134.
9   Bridget Riley, 'The Art of the Past: In Conversation with Neil MacGregor' (1992), in
    Kudielka (ed), *Dialogues on Art*, *op.cit.*, p.28.
10 Anton Ehrenzweig, *Bridget Riley*, exhibition catalogue, Gallery One, London, 1963 and
    Anton Ehrenzweig, 'The Pictorial Space of Bridget Riley', *Art International*, vol.9, no.1,
    February 1965, pp.20–24.

Creating a Way of Looking
John Elderfield

In the early 1960s, Bridget Riley created her first mature style by making black-and-white paintings, some of which induced the experience of prismatic colour as you looked at them. She continued by making multicoloured canvases that deliver chromatic experiences at times surprisingly altered, in our perception, from the actual pigment colours that compose these works. And, over the past decade, she has been making large, black-and-white murals that shape and articulate the environmental colour-space they occupy.

I don't mean to say, however, that her career is simply divisible into a development across these three kinds of works. Her development has been one of accumulation, of a carrying forward of common preoccupations in different, continually changing ways. And one common preoccupation is very readily noticed in all of her mature works: they are all rigorous as well as beautiful, disciplined as well as joyful, and they are meticulously but plainly made, with not a single touch of artiness about them.

The novelist Stendhal said that every morning, before working on *La Chartreuse de Parme* (The Charterhouse of Parma, 1839), he would read a few pages of the Civil Code. I don't know what Riley's mental preparation for work comprises, but it achieves a similar result. No pretention or bombast. No confectionary. None of what another writer – the poet Kenneth Koch – called '"kiss-me-I'm-poetical" junk'. Nothing extra. But everything you could possibly need – all the more intriguingly so because it reaches out to you even as it seems so intensely self-restrained as to be unconcerned about its own existence, like Pieter Saenredam's painting of the Old Town Hall of Amsterdam, or many of the works by Piet Mondrian at the Gemeentemuseum in The Hague.

The American artist Rackstraw Downes has written perceptively of such qualities in the depictive, realist paintings he admires, so they are not particular to abstract works like Riley's. Rather, qualities of restraint and understatement are (as Downes says) the means of a pictorial accuracy that speaks of probity and rectitude. This does not, of course, prevent paintings created in this way from being highly emotive works. To the contrary: it is precisely because they are purged of false sentiments that I, for one, find them so demanding of my affection.

That said, I shall continue, not to comment specifically on individual works by Riley, but rather, to speak generally about some of the characteristics and preoccupations that unify so apparently diverse an oeuvre as hers. And high among her preoccupations, I take it, is an equal concern with unification and diversification – a belief (shared by those who have followed her work closely) that what she has done comprises one single artistic practice, but also that diversification is critical to the maintaining of that singleness.

Another way of putting this is to say that any painting by Riley, and particularly, any group of her paintings, forces us to think about her identity as a painter: about her identity as revealed in her paintings. And this means, in turn, that we have to think about what identity means: the sense of self, of individuality, that provides continuity – but not necessarily sameness – in one's personality over time; the condition of being oneself and not another.

The fame of her black-and-white paintings of the 1960s – cemented by their prominent appearance in the 1965 exhibition *The Responsive Eye* at the Museum of Modern Art, New York – established her popular identity; and Riley-like images were regularly copied for all sort of commercial purposes. She concluded that it would take 20 years for anyone to look seriously at her paintings again. If she meant to refer to these paintings of the 1960s, then I think it is true: it did take a long time for many people to disassociate these works from their early, commercial employment.

As for her work after the 1960s, her refusal to repeat herself, even at the expense of surrendering the successes of that first decade, reminds me of Henri Matisse's celebrated statement in his illustrated book, *Jazz*, of 1947:

Success = Prison. And the artist must never be a *prisoner*. Prisoner? An artist must never be a prisoner of himself, prisoner of a style,

 JOHN ELDERFIELD

prisoner of a reputation, prisoner of a success, etc… Didn't the
Goncourt brothers write that Japanese artists of the great period
changed their names several times during their lives. I like that: they
wanted to protect their freedoms.

Change protects freedom. Not wilful change, but the kind of change
that – paradoxical though it may seem – is nurtured by repetitive
practice. As Richard Sennett wrote in his wonderful book *The Craftsman*
(2008), 'Going over an action again and again… enables self-criticism.'
This is one of the attributes of skill, and 'as a person develops skill the
contents of what he or she repeats change'. To follow very closely Riley's
work is to see that sameness is *courted* – because repetition is crucial to
an artistic practice – but sameness is also *avoided*, because it is in the
character of a true artistic practice to create change. So, to follow her
work is to see that the continuity of artistic identity is asserted, not
despite change, but *because* of change: because change is the very
means of achieving continuity.

In saying this, I am speaking not only of something technical. As I
observed earlier, to think about Riley's identity as a painter is to think
about what identity means: about the condition of being oneself and not
another. I have come to believe that the mark of a great artist is not only
his or her sensitivity to the boundaries of the self – to what actions are
and are not consistent with one's sense of one's own identity. Not only
that – for does not every thinking person have at least a dim perception
of what circumscribes his or her identity? More than this, however, the
great artist is willing to do something akin to what the Japanese artists
did who kept changing their names. The great literary critic Christopher
Ricks recognised this quality in the poet John Keats, saying that:

Keats was especially sensitive to anything which threatened or
discredited identity… and he was especially audacious in believing
that the healthy strength of a sense of identity depends paradoxically
upon the risk (of) openness and not upon self-protection; depends
upon risking the absence of identity rather than upon guarding the
circumscription of one's identity.

One important area in which such risk-taking will (or will not) occur is in an artist's relationship to his or her past. There is an all-too-common view of modern art – and, even more, of contemporary art – as representing a decisive break with the past. This basically apocalyptic idea, common in the writings of early twentieth-century critics, persists in the writings of twenty-first-century ones. In dull criticism, the old bellicose code word 'avant-garde' has been replaced by the sharp metaphor 'cutting edge', to an unintentionally ironical effect. Of course, we must believe in our own moment and the future it promises. 'If we cease to believe in the future', TS Eliot warned in 1944, 'the past would cease to be fully *our* past: it would become part of a dead civilisation'. He also insisted, however, that we must remain actively conscious of the past; otherwise, 'history is merely the chronicle of human devices which have served their turn and been scrapped, one for which the world is the property solely of the living, a property in which the dead hold no shares'.

The vital, living artist occupies a world that he or she shares with artists of the near and distant past. The great inventors have been revivalists, wanting to continue to learn from earlier examples. I think of Donatello and Brunelleschi measuring Roman antiquities. I now think of Riley, when I visited her in her studio last summer, reworking a Seurat-like landscape even as she was creating extraordinary, new stripe paintings.

The next time we were together was in Budapest in mid-October of 2012, for the opening of a great exhibition, *Cézanne and the Past*, devoted to Paul Cézanne's relationship to the art of the past. Cézanne famously wrote in 1905 that, 'The Louvre is the book in which we learn to read.' His terminology is interesting. It used to be common to think of the museum as paralleling a library; indeed, in the nineteenth century, many museums were located in the same building as libraries. But Cézanne thinks of the museum as paralleling not a library but a book, and a most unusual book in that it teaches you how to read.

This is very much Riley's view of the past and I urge those who are unfamiliar with her extremely perceptive critical writings on the art of the past to buy and read all 350 pages of the most recent edition of her

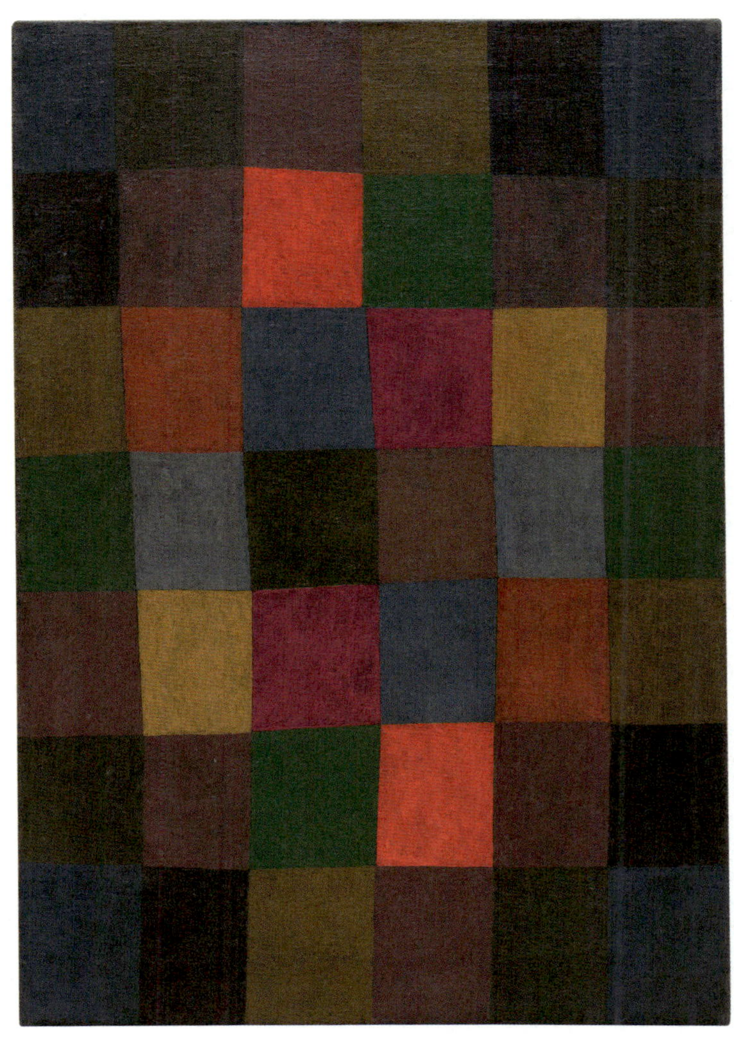

Paul Klee
New Harmony 1936
Oil on canvas
93.6 × 66.3 cm | 36⅞ × 26⅛ in
Solomon R Guggenheim Museum, New York

collected writings, published in 2009 under the Cézannean title, *The Eye's Mind*. It reminds us that there is a craft of seeing that we need to acquire in order to make sense of works of visual art and that the pleasures of sight we gain from older and newer art and from the world are not parcelled off from each other. But then, her paintings tell us that too; 'Perception Is the Medium' is the title of one of her essays of 1965. A somewhat later one, from 1977, is called 'Working with Nature'. It recalls for me a wonderful moment in an interview with the distinguished filmmaker Jean Renoir that Rackstraw Downes alerted me to.

CRITIC *I notice there is a lot of nature in your films.*
RENOIR Thank you very much.

Riley does not quite say that but she does say, 'I work from nature, although in completely different terms. For me nature is not landscape, but the dynamism of visual forces – an event rather than an appearance.' And later, 'it's the recognition of the sensation [of something observed and felt] *without* the actual incident which prompted it.'

In addition to Cézanne, among the modern artists she admires most is Mondrian. But her talk of nature as 'an event rather than an appearance' recalls more explicitly another artist in her pantheon, Paul Klee, who famously said that 'art does not reproduce the visible but makes visible'. He seems to have meant that art does (or should) not reproduce what we see, but rather, that it manufactures what we see. Under this interpretation, a painting is not a sort of mechanism that captures and displays existing visible data, but an engine to *create* a way of looking.

Furthermore, if a painting can be said to make visible, it may be said to do so for a beholder. Thus, although the artist makes the engine that makes visible, it is the beholder who turns it on, and keeps it running, by being a beholder. But Klee means something more than this. When he talks of the visible, he seems to be using it in its two senses of what is *commonly* seen and whatever *can* be seen. Thus art does not *reproduce* the visible – what is commonly seen; but *makes* visible what commonly is *not* seen but which the artist has intuited in his or her own uncommon

                                            JOHN ELDERFIELD

seeing and makes visible to us. That was Klee's gift to us, and it is Riley's, as well.

This gift requires our very attentive acceptance. Among the marginalia of the poet Samuel Taylor Coleridge is a note in which he recommended to himself:

> The overcoming [of] the habit of deriving your whole pleasure passively from the Book itself, which can only be effected by excitement of Curiosity or of some Passion. Force yourself to reflect on what you read paragraph by paragraph, and in a short time you will derive your pleasure, an ample portion at least, from the activity of your own mind. All else is Picture Sunshine.

That wonderful phrase, 'All else is Picture Sunshine'. 'Picture Sunshine' is what falls upon us without any will on our part. The radiating vivacity of Riley's paintings require our own active enjoyment in the pleasures of sight; call forth our own 'excitement of curiosity or of some passion', and usually both.

She has written that any and all pleasures of sight 'take you by surprise. They are sudden, swift and unexpected.' Her own paintings do that. The surprise of the first encounter with one of her paintings is owing to an astonishment that an inanimate object has apparently come to life and – more than that – is in communion with the viewer. The viewer's surprise is, we recognise, is a self-created surprise. Perception is the medium just as much as is the canvas and the paint – more so, in that a painting, the artist acknowledges, 'only comes to life when looked at from a certain distance'. In a way, it doesn't exist factually at all; only in the viewer's perception.

The precise form that the visual display takes is the painting's, hence the artist's, creation. But it is the viewer's approach to, and active looking at the painting that triggers it. To attend to a painting, then, is also to attend to our own attention, for the performance of the painting, we soon realise, evidently takes place not in the painting but in our eyes. And, from the very first attentive look, the painting changes. Thus, it may be said that the viewer will not in fact see the painting (the painting as a

single, literal thing), but will only see the painting *changing* – or, will not
see the painting *except* by the painting changing. Effectively, Riley makes
a pact with the viewer, through the medium of the painting, that they will
collaborate in eliciting from a particular painting a particular sort of
mobile visual array. And, when the viewer stops looking at the painting, it
will therefore be as if leaving something that continues to go on.

Bridget Riley: The Stripe Paintings 1961–2012, exhibition catalogue, Galerie Max Hetzler and
Holzwarth Publications, Berlin and Ridinghouse, London, 2014, pp.13–34.

Note: An earlier version of this text was presented as a laudation, on the occasion of the
artist's receipt of the Sikkens Prize for 2012 at the Gemeentemuseum Den Haag, The Hague,
on 28 October 2012.

JOHN ELDERFIELD

Bridget Riley: The Stripe Paintings 1961–2014

Paul Moorhouse

Bridget Riley's new stripe paintings mark the latest developments in a
career that now spans more than 50 years. Among squares, triangles,
discs, curves and the many other motifs that she has employed, one
formal element in particular has proved especially effective. Her use of
stripes has been a recurrent preoccupation and, as the present exhibition
demonstrates, the recent reappearance of this formal protagonist
suggests unfinished business.

From the outset Riley's work has actively engaged with instability.
Relinquishing a representational role, in 1961, her pictorial language turned
instead to the deployment of simple shapes, and, later, pure colours, to
appeal directly to the eye. This way of working, though it has undergone
complex changes, continues to the present. However, she has never
treated these basic elements as inert devices. The plastic relationships
that she creates trigger complex changing patterns of sensation and, on
occasion, elicit arresting perceptual experiences. As a result, diverse visual
events are experienced as absolute phenomena – as ends in themselves.
But this is not all. Nature is suggested in the way that light, colour and
apparent movement are revealed in a perpetual state of modulation.
Confronting her paintings, the viewer is cast as an active spectator in an
arena in which nothing is stable and everything contributes to an overall
impression of flux. Without resorting to depiction her art appears
animated and, in suggesting life, it draws closer to the outside world.

With *Movement in Squares* (1961), Riley first disclosed the rich
expressive potential of boldly contrasting abstract shapes. That seminal
painting was a persuasive exposition of her structuring principle of
repose, disturbance, returning to repose. Proceeding from left to right, a
regular tessellated sequence was progressively compressed and then,
reaching the opposite side of the painting, returned almost to its original
state. The effect was to provoke a crisis in the viewer's perceptual field.
In an unsettling departure from convention, the painting appeared both
irradiated and, structurally, to move unpredictably. Most disturbing was

the viewer's growing realisation that this display was entirely subjective,
a destabilisation in the chain of command connecting object, eye and,
ultimately, mind.

Within the same year Riley developed these radical insights, her use
of stripes now making a significant entrance. In *Horizontal Vibration*
(1961), the grammar, as it were, of *Movement in Squares* acquired a new
vocabulary. Still employing black and white only, in common with the
earlier painting, a formal progression is subjected to momentary duress,
creating a tension, and then released. Here, however, Riley employed a
horizontal format with long, traversing stripes replacing the squares. As
with its predecessor, variation in the width of the components creates a
zone of compression across the centre of the visual field. Taking the
argument further, the stripes are subjected to other, irregular inflexions
within the overall sequence. A similar instability ensues. As before, an
illuminated plane appears to buckle under the pressures generated. But
the stripes impart an entirely new and highly arresting experience. Like a
stringed instrument stroked by an unseen hand, the entire visual field
vibrates.

This spectacle was not, however, only visual. Riley saw that the
passage from stability to instability – from a state of certainty to
uncertainty – has a profound emotional resonance. The return to a state
of resolution deepens that experience further. As in life, we do not
respond to changes in our surroundings impassively. The world plays
upon our emotions as its events unfold and, at some deep level, we are
attuned to respond, seeking a relationship with our environment. Art that
engages with change – with destabilising and then restoring a situation –
has an equivalent affective disposition.

Such was the fertility of Riley's invention during that remarkable early
phase, she did not immediately pursue this particular line of enquiry.
Instead, an array of other formal elements was explored, each being
tested for its own unique characteristics. From 1961 to 1967, her attention
turned to triangles, zigzags, discs, dots, ovals and sinuous curves. These
elements supported her investigation of visual instability, some yielding
perceptual experiences that were powerfully visceral. The zigzags and
undulating lines seemed particularly suited to overt visual drama. *Blaze 1*

(1962) and *Current* (1964) are among Riley's most assertive paintings, being both immediate and intense in terms of implied light and movement.

Perhaps the artist sensed that, in comparison, the stripe seemed quieter, more anonymous and less confrontational. As *Horizontal Vibration* had intimated, in passing along a horizontal shape the eye encounters relatively less resistance. As that painting made clear, a progression of stripes contained enormous expressive potential. Even so, her involvement with that shape was suspended temporarily and it would not be until *Chant 2* (1967) that the stripe made a remarkable reappearance. In the meantime, Riley's involvement with simple black-and-white shapes yielded a diverse body of work in which certain themes were powerfully evident. Repetition, reversal, disruption and inversion were all implicated as dynamic forces. These freed her painting from stasis and positioned it in an active dialogue with the viewer. By the mid-1960s, a critical perspective on Riley's work was possible. Looking at her art entailed being responsive on several levels – visually, perceptually and emotionally. Having reached that position, the way was open to a new area of engagement. Colour now beckoned. But, as Riley was well aware, this involved penetrating a vast new terrain in which previous points of reference would need recalibrating. When working in black and white and, for a while, using greys of many kinds, her guiding principle had been that of creating and then destabilising an ordered situation. From instability she drew optical energy. However, the perception of colour operated in an entirely different way. Whether in nature or art, any chromatic relationship is a relative affair. Every colour is affected by its neighbours, and is perceived according to the way it interacts with its surroundings. The experience of red seen next to green is profoundly different from viewing the same red alongside pink. Seen together, the colours combine and destabilise each other. In advancing the role of colour, she would now be working with an agent that was *inherently* unstable. This was something that could be exploited, but harnessing it would require an appropriate formal vehicle.

In *Chant 2*, Riley found her compelling answer. Acknowledging the tendency of colours to interact with other, adjacent colours, in this magisterial painting she now worked with that phenomenon and, indeed, encouraged

it. A regular, directional shape, the stripe presented the longest possible
potential for contact and interaction between colours. In *Chant 2*, blue
and red are configured in an alternating sequence: two blues containing
a red, followed by two reds enclosing a blue. The width of these triads
expands as they progress towards the centre of the painting. The outcome
is a triumphant announcement of colour modulation. Moving beyond the
assertive contrasts presented in her black-and-white paintings, the colour
stripe enabled a subtle passage between chromatic events. In *Chant 2*,
this results in the appearance of a slowly diffusing light.

That achievement revealed a way forward. In the present exhibition
the important subsequent developments are represented by a group of
key early paintings: *Late* Morning 1 (1967), *Late Morning (Horizontal)*
(1967–68), *Rise 1* (1968), *Vapour* (1970) and *Prairie* (2003/1971). As these
works reveal, instability remained the foundation of Riley's approach. But
instead of precipitating a visual crisis, colour sensations and after-images
gradually interacted. The resulting perceptual response generates an
impression of tinted light inhabiting space. The basis of that experience is
the eye's passage from one colour event to another: gentle transitions
that are rooted in harmony, inflexion and gradation. Significantly, Riley
explored the orientation of the stripe sequence in relation to the particular
effect conveyed. *Late Morning 1* employs vertical stripes. Its successor
deploys colour relationships in a horizontal stripe arrangement. The later
work seems to expand sideways, creating a vista. This feeling was
developed further in *Rise 1* and also in the diagonally arranged *Prairie*,
both of which give rise to an enveloping, light-filled space. In this respect
they accord with our familiar, lateral view of the world. *Vapour* completes
the group, a wonderful evocation of atmosphere, as elusive as mist.

Between 1970 and 1973, Riley made other horizontal stripe paintings,
notably *Apprehend* (1970). She also continued to explore variations
within the stripe format using different orientations. *Veld* (1971) and
Rattle (1973) were notable additions to the diagonal approach, the latter
echoing her earlier black-and-white essays involving zigzags. In the main,
however, her preference appeared to be for vertical stripes, as if resisting
the intimation of landscape implied by a horizontal disposition of
elements. Vertical stripes countered the feeling of panorama. Also, an

PAUL MOORHOUSE

upright formation meant that as the viewer's gaze traversed the composition it encountered a resistant progression of colour events. This tended to maximise optical mixing. The eye became loaded with a succession of visual sensations, leading inexorably to a saturated and destabilised perceptual field.

Although organised intuitively, these works nevertheless follow certain logical principles. They are determined according to definite sequences involving repetition and variation. In *Gamelan* (1970), for example, the colours are situated according to a regular, pulsing rhythm. But *Pæan* (1973), one of Riley's major paintings from this time, stands out as an exception. The present exhibition includes the related work, *Elysium* (2003/1973). In *Pæan* and *Elysium*, colour was structured more freely, punctuating the space with irregular stresses. The effect is that of shifting, modulated light, shimmering through an organic structure. The eye seeks a rationale but is seduced by the constant movement of illuminated colour in space. Surprisingly, Riley did not immediately develop this more varied way of building a painting's plastic structure. Instead, she put the stripe format aside for seven years in order to pursue a separate trajectory. When it returned in 1980, the series that followed employed a new range of colours, the so-called Egyptian palette, derived from the artist's observation of ancient Egyptian art. These paintings also developed the principle of *free* chromatic distribution, thus picking up those ideas first advanced in *Pæan*.

Après Midi (1981) and *Serenissima* (1982) are prime examples of this new approach. In terms of the artist's development, they represent something of a watershed. Previously, her paintings had organised form and colour according to rational principles, the aim being to accumulate a build-up of visual sensation that then provoked a destabilised perceptual experience. From 1980, colour was arranged, instead, according to plastic considerations. The objective became that of building a pictorial structure whose primary purpose of generating purely visual sensations is an end in itself. *Après Midi*, for example, evinces a range of concerns related to amassing and distributing colour, density, weight, accent, rhythm and space. On one level, these are formal considerations linked to what Riley described as ' the real problems of painting: The way in which colours are modulated and distributed acquires a self-contained significance. There are also connections with music: interval, repetition and variation all underpin the complete experience. But, in an important anticipation of later developments, such paintings prepared the ground for a renewed relationship with nature. In their asymmetry there is an affecting sense of the external world's ambivalent order – forever in flux, always changing, endlessly becoming.

From 1980 to 1985, the stripe format dominated Riley's thinking. This focused body of formal activity was then supplanted by other considerations. It was not until 2009, almost 25 years later, that it once again resurfaced, signalling a renewed involvement with this motif. With *Rose Rose 5* (2009), certain developments were immediately clear. A new, warm and highly radiant palette was evident. Employing broad vertical stripes of regular width, the formal architecture was firm. Yet, as a successor painting *Lux* (2011) made apparent, this structure was anything bur rigid. Colour, light, space, depth and mass were still Riley's building blocks, but these components now provided an unexpected, transparent tissue of fleeting sensation. Previously supporting her visual argument, chromatic modulation now shifted to centre-stage, dissolving the picture plane. There was a sense that Riley's earlier concerns – with bold contrast, the interaction of colours, tonality, movement and the interplay of light and dark – were all being brought together in an astonishing synthesis.

Rose Red (2012) stands at the beginning of the resulting, first phase of new activity. With the stripe as the vehicle for this celebratory activity, in *Rose Red, Burnished Rose* (2012) and other paintings completed in 2012, the format switched to the horizontal. Having previously avoided a landscape connotation, such works accommodated it. That said, the sensuous warmth of Riley's palette, which includes rose red, purple, bright orange, yellow and magenta, seemed more redolent of human life than place. These colours intimate her long-standing admiration for Pierre-Auguste Renoir's palette. That particular chromatic range can also be understood in relation to studies made in 2012 connected with the corridor mural she was then contemplating for St Mary's Hospital in London. In the preparatory works for that architectural commission, Riley deliberately embraced uplifting colours linked with the human body.

PAUL MOORHOUSE

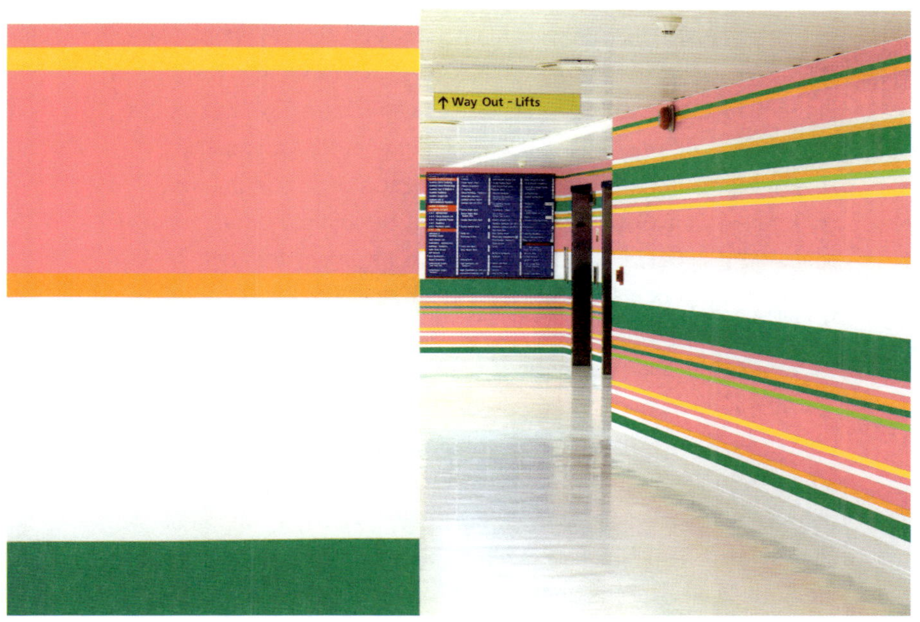

Mural, tenth floor, St Mary's Hospital, London, 2014

However, the expansive, lateral scale of those paintings seems
unmistakably connected with nature. This feeling was also engendered
by a further, surprising reprise of earlier preoccupations. The paintings'
structure embraced the purely plastic requirements of generating visual
sensations, but also moved beyond that imperative. Accentuating the
picture plane with its stresses and intervals, the organisation of different
colours gives rise to a perception of light and movement that animates
the entire visual field. The result is a constantly changing pageant – a
chromatic suffusion – that unfolds before the observer. Employing a
shared palette of warm colours, the first phase of stripe paintings
constitutes complex variations on a single, chromatic theme. Colour and
space are distributed in various ways, with weight, rhythm and density
moving around, dissolving and then re-forming. This dynamic is distinctly
musical and yet, conspicuously, it speaks to the eye, pressing and
caressing with subtle emphasis.

The present exhibition includes paintings completed since mid-2013.
Collectively, they constitute a second phase of the same series that
advances further into the new visual terrain. The 'pleasures of sight' a
principle that has guided Riley's work throughout its development, are as
surprising as ever. In *Tocatta (Green)* (2014–13) and *Arioso (Blue)* (2013)
for example, instability is linked with unpredictability so that, as in nature,
a sudden conjunction or intrusion of colours will catch us unawares. In
several paintings, notably *About Yellow* (2014–13), *Brioso (Orange)* (2013)
and *Red Modulation (Yellow and Orange)* (2014–13), the inflexion of
two different yellows is a connecting theme. In *About Yellow*, the
chromatic movement proceeds from the top edge through to the base line.
Proceeding via modulated passages of related pinks and reds, the eye
responds to the insistent, irregular thrusts of the two related colours. One
effect of distributing chromatic accents in this way is to open up the
space of the painting and then to inflect it. Apparently firm, the structure
is truly plastic. The stripes assemble into masses that undulate, shifting
their respective positions constantly. Few artists have used colour so
rhythmically. In harnessing visual sensations to the implication of depth
and space, each painting provokes an ever-changing cascade of visceral
responses.

                                                      PAUL MOORHOUSE

Throughout her development, Riley has drawn confirmation from
Eugène Delacroix's observation that 'the first merit of a painting is to be
a feast for the eyes'. Her most recent stripe paintings are a striking
reaffirmation of that principle, exciting and entrancing the eye in equal
measure. These expansive horizontal arrangements do not depict. But,
fed by memory and imagination, they are movingly redolent of things
seen and savoured – vast skies, the dying of the light, distant horizons
and new dawns. The latest works are none of these phenomena, and
yet – plastic and metaphorical – they recall the surrounding world.
Echoing nature, art provides a site for contemplation that seems invested
with the mysterious, affirmative quality of life.

But, beyond that, in the new work there is a sense of a something at
once profound and elusive which is occasionally glimpsed in nature. In
rare moments there is the intimation of a mysterious connectedness
between observed things that speaks of a deeper order. Alert to the
underlying unity that he believed was revealed in nature, the poet
William Wordsworth wrote the following memorable lines which capture
such experiences with subtle precision:

> While with an eye made quiet by the power
> Of harmony, and the deep power of joy,
> We see into the life of things.[1]

In a related way, Riley's most recent stripe paintings embrace
apparent disorder, and within seeming disparity they yield a surprising
logic that is at once reassuring and consoling. Their celebratory harmony
thus revealed, there is the suggestion that their source was indeed the
mind of a deeply penetrating eye.

Doro Globus (ed), *Bridget Riley: The Stripe Paintings 1961–2014*, exhibition catalogue, David
Zwirner Books, New York, NY and London, 2014, pp.7–18.

Note: An earlier version of this essay was published in *Bridget Riley: The Stripe Paintings
1961–2012*, exhibition catalogue, Galerie Max Hetzler and Holzwarth Publications, Berlin and
Ridinghouse, London, 2013.

1   William Wordsworth, 'Lines Composed a Few Miles above Tintern Abbey, on Revisiting
    the Banks of the Wye during a Tour. July 13 1798', in John O Hayden (ed), *William
    Wordsworth Selected Poems*, Penguin Books, London, 1994, p.67.

                                          PAUL MOORHOUSE

The Unaccountable

Richard Shiff

Ultimatum

'Painting has to be *made*; it doesn't just happen on its own.' The
statement is Bridget Riley's, in the context of a lecture delivered in 1996
at the Slade School of Fine Art, London. She spoke in support of painting
as a path to innovative art – a course that could no longer be assumed
as a natural one for students to take. During the 1990s, as perhaps now,
the medium of painting was in need of both advocacy and
reinvigoration. Riley expressed a sense of urgency, compelled to ask: 'Is
there any painting? And if there isn't, does it matter?'[1]

It wasn't solely the future of painting that was at stake, but the future
of all media of aesthetic enquiry. Riley lamented the fact that too many
prospective artists took their start from a readymade concept of what art
should be. They were choosing from a menu of concepts, as if each
student's fate as an artist could be decided before he or she had
explored any number of possibilities through the rigours of studio
practice – through 'work', as Riley would say. One can learn to refer to art
in far less time than it takes to acquire the wherewithal to make it. As an
example of such misdirection – art in name only, informed by its
theories in lieu of engaged practice – Riley invoked 'the ultimate
monochrome painting, requiring 30 coats of the same colour'. Her
typography indicated the pretentiousness she associated with the current
state of affairs: all too often, painting became 'Ultimate Painting'. Imagine
that the colour of theoretical choice were red, whether red as passion or
red as revolution. Art would then satisfy its conceptual demands by
producing ultimate redness, red for the sake of red and to end all red,
'a matter of quasi-religious obeisance rather than of aesthetic
judgement'.[2]

Riley's practice of colour requires neither theory nor religion as its
justification. Often, effects of nature inspire her; but her work is not their
illustration. She is pleased to use red, perhaps the red that some will see

in a flower and others will see in 'Ultimate Painting'. Her red relies on its sensory effect, not the intellectual or cultural context of its production. When I look at Riley's latest series of works, a group completed in May 2014, I perceive a decided redness in these canvases (as an example, *About Yellow*, 2014–13). Clearly, Riley has taken an interest in this chromatic range – neither 'ultimate' nor 'natural' redness, but red that is vibrant, resonant and deeply modulated. Various colours interact in these works, yet redness dominates, although hardly on the foundation of one and the same red. This redness is aesthetic. It didn't develop 'on its own.' Each individual red is a contingent hue, a product of experimentation in the studio. The colour arises as if it had never before been seen – first and last. Riley made this red happen.

Appearances are reality

For Riley, practice, not theory, is paramount: 'You do not know beforehand what you are going to need [for art]… *That* is what you have to find out. This finding out cannot be done intellectually; you can only find out by working.'[3] She led her recent series of paintings through many variations, not knowing what combinations of colours would be best, nor able to predict what result would represent success. She experiences unknowns at both extremes of her process, beginning and end. The paintings in question consist of horizontal elements, with individual stripes becoming areas of monochromatic linear expanse. In preparatory studies on paper generated at a reduced scale, Riley could quickly replace a single colour by superimposing a band of collage in an alternative hue. She noticed how great a difference in overall effect a single substitution might produce, as well as how in shifting the tone of one of the contrasting hues placed among the reds – for example, extending yellow towards either orange or olive – she might radically change the general atmosphere. With the two panels of *Red Modulation (Yellow and Orange)* (2014–13), the only physical difference from left to right is the substitution of two oranges for two yellows; this slight alteration generates distinct perceptual change.

In relation to the height of their horizontal format, Riley's stripes are narrow, one inch across: a canvas with a height of 59 inches contains 59 parallel stripes. Appearing more linear than rectilinear – with, as Riley puts it, 'a long edge exposure and very little body' these elements are too oblong to assume a familiar geometric shape or, for that matter, any shape.[4] Although the rectangle of the canvas actively establishes scale, its edges are only passive determinants of the two short sides of each stripe. Setting stripes of equal dimension beside one another maximises the interaction of their colours along the common edge, for no hierarchy of shape detracts from the chromatic concentration. 'I have always tried to avoid "colouring forms"'; Riley insisted at a relatively early moment in her career: 'I want to create a colour-form, not coloured forms.'[5] In perception, a stripe has more substance, more ontological status, than a line, yet less than an area. It has the curious distinction of occupying one and a half dimensions, transmitting both direction and colour yet without conveying form. A state of one and a half dimensions may be a rational impossibility – too confusing to be thought. Yet the reality of our senses is capable of denying the calculation of our reason. What will result from 59 stripes in parallel?[6] Apparently, it can be a general redness (see *Arioso (Blue)*, 2013). Where is the redness? It's hard to say. But we perceive it, so it must be in perception, if perception occupies a place.

The ratio of height to width for the majority of Riley's recent striped canvases is approximately 4:7 – more precisely, but less memorably, around 1:1.72. This is a relatively irrational proportion, neither a common mathematical measure nor a factor in cultural symbolism, neither science nor myth. It is no golden mean. Such numbers tell us something: Riley's rectangles are hers, solely hers; they acquire the judgement of her sense. The ratio is intuitive rather than theoretical: 'I judge by eye,' she states, 'and whatever that turns out to be can then be measured.'[7] For whatever reason, as she developed the scale of these paintings, a height somewhat under human size and a ratio hovering around 4:7 felt right, perhaps because such canvases become a bit too large to be encompassed by a glance (as opposed to a scan) and yet not so large that they lose a direct relation to the viewer who faces them, at ease in a position almost close enough to imagine touching them. Although the majority of the stripes in each painting elicit redness of some kind, they also represent variation in the values and hues that most of us would associate with this colour. Riley demonstrates that magenta is red, crimson is red, pink is red, rose is red, flame is red, *caput mortuum* is red, even purple is red (it has redness). These are among her colours. But how 'red' are her new paintings, really? They include stripes of green, blue, yellow and orange, in addition to the various tones of red and qualities of redness. Do the supplemental colours distract from an encompassing redness? Or do they enforce and even enhance a judgement of red?

Not long ago, Riley stated a paradox that her art confronts: '[Colour] is simultaneously one thing and several things – you can never see colour by itself, it is always affected by other colours.'[8] Because colour changes before our eyes, we hardly know with assurance what it is we see. While delighting the senses, colour frustrates language and its concepts. Its paradox is annoying, at least to the intellect. In reaction, common language ignores the paradox, while rarefied physical science circumvents it. Faced with Riley's recent paintings, we're likely to act as if we know what colour the designation 'red' signifies – at the least, it isn't green, blue or yellow. A physicist avoids the vagueness that plagues colloquial language by associating the name of a colour with the reflection of a segment of the visible spectrum: wavelengths of 620 to 740 nanometres constitute 'red'. Yet, within living vision, any definition so accurate belies experience: red veers toward violet when seen in proximity to a field of yellow and brightens when adjacent to green. Physical science lifts red out of these vagaries of sensory reality, isolating it within theoretical perfection, stabilising it, sterilising it. Unchanging, the wavelength assigned to a pure red follows conventions and adheres to rules and standards. A painter's red lacks this perfection but has the advantage of being as real as life: mutating, fugitive, forever unexpected. 'Unstable and incalculable' are words that Riley uses to characterise colour.[9] Her colour belongs to art – the art, not the science, that represents life – the art that is life because it lives in perception.

Colours change in perception. A red veers to violet only while seen, and only sometimes while seen. Accordingly, Riley concludes that

RICHARD SHIFF

'perception is the medium'.[10] The implication of her simple equation is less than obvious. Why would perception be the medium or pathway to something else, rather than the goal to be reached? By Riley's reasoning, the painter's medium is not colour itself (the chemistry of pigments), but how a person perceives colour (a matter of sensation). Early in her career, she realised the importance of stressing this distinction: 'My work has developed on the basis of empirical analyses and syntheses'– in other words, by experience. '[It] surprises me that some people should see my work as a celebration of the marriage of art and science. I have never made any use of scientific theory or scientific data.'[11]

Non-science

Science and art are alike in researching the unknown, but their parallel paths diverge. While the aim of science is to attain understanding, converting unknown to known, art satisfies its purpose even as its mechanisms and objectives remain, at best, vaguely comprehended. 'From the viewpoint of the modern painter', Riley argues, 'the true tradition lies less in a succession of solutions than in recognising that the problems of picture-making can never be solved as such.'[12] Each of the modern masters whom Riley admires has left the field open. The leaders of art are not those who create the 'Ultimate Painting', but those who admit to the ultimate insecurity of every aesthetic practice.

Given Riley's attitude, it may seem ironic that she sustains interest in the art of Georges Seurat, famous for applying a modern science of colour to picture-making (optical mixture, complementary contrast, irradiation). In Riley's view, Seurat's painting – like that of several other favoured predecessors, such as Pierre-Auguste Renoir, Paul Cézanne, Claude Monet and Henri Matisse – manifests a fundamental division within the human faculties: we see or sense more than we will ever understand by reason. The example of Seurat's art provokes Riley to conclude: 'Comprehension is not everything, the unaccountable has a place in our lives… Seurat, involuntarily perhaps, has presented us with the mysterious'.[13] Why did she phrase her sense of the mystery of

Seurat's art as she did – 'Seurat, involuntarily perhaps…'? I think she acknowledges here the involuntary nature of aesthetic intuition itself. To those who leave their intellects and emotions open to it, intuition arises. When an artist engages deeply but openly with a method, intuition steps in. Accordingly, Seurat's art became more than his method – this is what Riley appreciates. In fact, she distinguishes between the earlier Seurat and the later, despite the relative brevity of his career. Eventually, Seurat allowed method more control than was beneficial to his art: 'The more inflexible Seurat's method became, the less it could fulfil the role he had in mind for it.'[14]

The wonder of Seurat's art, Riley says, is its capacity to reveal what 'we cannot *quite* see'. Her succinct statement implies that we only barely see what true art shows, even after we've been shown it. The emphasis is Riley's: 'We cannot *quite* see… [We confront] an experience just beyond our visual grasp… the *im-perceptible*.'[15] In 1978, Robert Kudielka described this condition as Riley's own: 'Bridget Riley embarks on the near impossible endeavour to let things be seen which only *let* themselves be seen.'[16] This is a bit of a riddle. Riley drew a similar conclusion, expressed with the same intonation, but viewing the matter inversely: 'Examination… only examines that which *can* be examined.' The usual kind of examination focuses on what is already apparent – it takes a closer look, with the aim of scrutinising the known world. This investigation leaves everything else unexamined, including the multitudinous features of experience that have no existing cultural record, just barely available for inspection: 'For an artist those fleeting sensations which pass unrecognised by the intellect are just as important as those which become conscious… Seurat looks *into* perception and shows it to be the activity which produces what it sees.'[17] As Riley says, perception is the medium. Art like Seurat's, art like Riley's, assumes limited control, limited authority and is hardly 'Ultimate'. Aesthetic perception is a process suspended at the very edge of understanding, as if the viewer were resorting to a backward glance for guidance, while having already moved beyond.

To cast perception in a more forward-looking light: through art, vision stays at least one step ahead of the intellect. We perceive *that* we see,

                                    RICHARD SHIFF

but also realise that whatever we see must remain beyond our capacity to understand in full. As Riley tells Kudielka: 'I feel it right up almost against my face, the thing that refuses to be thought.'[18] The feeling of the aesthetic has become real – whether pleasurable, painful or stimulating in some other respect – while its equivalent or analogy in thought must remain in the realm of fantasy, a possibility as yet unrealised. We only guess at what the reality of sensation must mean and how it might fit within an order or science of knowledge. If this division of the faculties produces discomfort, work becomes its remedy. (In my various conversations with Riley, if there's one thing on which she has insisted, it's the human need to work and keep working.) With effort, an artist becomes knowledgeable concerning the methods associated with a medium, such as painting. Techniques can be mastered; skills can be acquired: 'While one has to accept that the role of art and its subjects do change, the practical problems do not.' Where the practice of each new generation leads is nevertheless unknown: 'Art assumes the role of enquiry. True modern painting', Riley states, 'should always be a beginning – its own re-invention, if you like.'[19] Artists master the known techniques, allowing sensation to lead elsewhere.

Riley's own inventiveness takes initial form as studies on paper, whether in black and white or full colour. She refers to her practice of drawing as 'a way of finding out – the first thing that I discover is that I do not know.' She adds: 'While drawing I am watching and simultaneously recording myself looking, discovering things that on the one hand are staring me in the face and yet on the other I have not yet really seen.'[20] She makes discoveries, things become visible to her, but only as optical or other sensory experience, not as formulations for the intellect. An artist's 'I see' doesn't entail 'I understand'. If an artist acts as if the goal of art is already known, then 'one begins to imitate the "look" of art.'[21] Mastering the 'look' leads neither to seeing nor to understanding.

In 1959, a crucial year for her development, Riley engaged in her own process of 'imitation'. Her aim wasn't to achieve 'the "look" of art', but to expose herself to the aesthetic principles, as well as the mystery, of a well-defined method. She set about learning from Seurat by producing a copy: 'Imitating a work is simply one of the best ways of internalising its

artistic logic.'[22] The work she copied – or rather, interpreted and
internalised – was *The Bridget at Courbevoie* (1886–87), which she
could see in London at the galleries of The Courtauld Institute. She
chose to work apart from the canvas itself, using a reproduction from a
popular monograph; with respect to the colour, this source was quite
reductive and somewhat blurred, as printed illustrations often were at
the time.[23] Seurat's painting has the modest dimensions of 46.4 by 55.3
centimetres (18¼ by 21¾ inches); its diminutive reproduction, Riley's
source, measures approximately 16.5 by 20.3 centimetres (6½ by 8 inches).
As the support for her copy, she chose a canvas considerably larger than
both, measuring 71.1 by 91.1 centimetres (28 by 35⅞ inches) (very close
to the proportions of the reproduction, slightly elongated in relation to
the original Seurat).

Because she was using a format of greater scale, we might imagine
that Riley magnified the divisionist marks of Seurat's canvas
proportionately. Instead, her marks are fewer and disproportionately large
(though still decidedly divisionist in character). Seurat himself tended not
to increase his scale of marking from a small canvas like *The Bridge at
Courbevoie* to the mural size of *A Sunday on La Grande Jatte – 1884*
(1884–86) and *The Models* (1886–88). This practice sometimes led even
ardent supporters to question his technical decisions. 'Too divided,' was
Paul Signac's judgement of *The Models*: 'The touch in it is too small. It
creates a mechanical and diminutive look… a greyish tonality.'[24] Riley's
copy of the Courtauld painting surely avoids this pitfall; its colours retain
their independent brightness and chromatic character at a viewing
distance suited to the scale of the canvas. Concentrating more on colour
than on light, she added several brilliant points of red in the left
foreground area of green grass, even though such colours were not
visible in the printed source. In fact, the source illustration has few areas
of visible redness (a later version of the same type of monograph with
the same illustration restores the substantial presence of red).[25] Riley
knew that spots of red existed in Seurat's actual painting, so they were a
fair topic of enquiry. And the crudeness of her printed source may have
worked to her advantage, affording leeway for the play of her aesthetic
imagination and exploration. Her reds seem to dance rhythmically across

RICHARD SHIFF

Plate 6

THE BRIDGE AT COURBEVOIE

(*Le Pont de Courbevoie*)

1885–1886

London: The late Samuel Courtauld's Collection

17⅞ in. by 21½ in.

Though built with material assembled for *Baignade* this picture was painted after *Baignade* was completed when Seurat was in full command of his Pointillist technique and the other procedures of his 'method'.

In some ways it is the most characteristic and faultless of all his pictures known to me. For here the elaborate mental calculations, the deliberate forethought and planning (that I have described in the Introduction) have produced a purely lyrical picture which imposes, like *Baignade*, its mood of peace upon us, unless, to our loss, we truculently refuse to surrender.

And here there is no false note like the profile portrait of the central boy in *Baignade*. The figures here are just figures, not particular people, and all three are themselves completely captured by the prevailing mood—the still quietness of the scene which keeps them also quiet and still; the fisherman has forgotten to draw in his fish and he will have nothing but bread and butter and a glass of Medoc for his supper; the little man in the bowler hat has missed his tram back to Paris and will be scolded by his wife; the child will be late for tea and spanked, maybe, by its mother. But all, I fancy, will reckon that this hour by the opal river has been worth it.

14

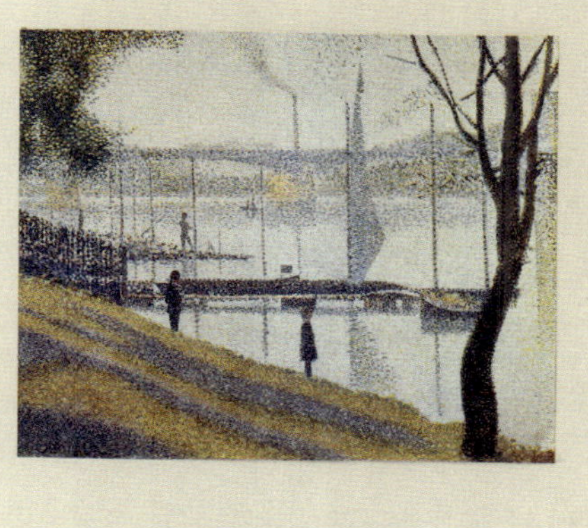

The artist's copy of RH Wilenski, *Seurat*, Faber & Faber, London, 1949

the surface, as Seurat's do in places; but this effect is much more
pronounced in Riley's version, especially in the area of the distant
shoreline and foliage.

Riley created an active imitation, a reinvention – an interpretive
gesture rather than a passive copy or replication. Where Seurat achieved
a desired *mélange optique* (optical mixture), with an attendant muting
or greying of the pictorial atmosphere, Riley attained an effect more akin
to that of her recent compositions of stripes. She counteracted Seurat
even as she learned from him, pulling bits of colour-play out of the
painting and exaggerating them as intensified optical experience. In her
copy, each hue exists in sufficient material quantity to retain its initial
purity even as it interacts with others within the perceptual process. This
is ironic, of course, because in 1959 Riley was far from reaching the
degree of radical abstraction that would enable her to exploit such direct
chromatic effects in full. She now regards her stripes as the parallel to
Seurat's dots, but with enhanced benefits.[26] Even as she conducted her
early study of Seurat, she was making a 'Riley' and becoming the
predecessor to herself. In 1959, just as in 2014, she was discovering the
paradox of colour, 'simultaneously one thing and several things.'[27] A
different way of saying this is: 'Change one thing and everything is
changed.'[28]

Movement

Late in 1960, Riley turned from her exploration of chromatic effects and
for the next five years restricted herself to studying visual perception in
terms of either starkly contrasting blacks and whites or a subtly modulated
range of greys. Between 1965 and 1967, she introduced coloured greys
and gradually brought her imagery back into full colour, taking advantage
of its potential for mysterious nuance, using stripes and other forms that
lacked recognisable shape (formless forms, so to speak, including wavy
lines and twisting bands). Before returning to colour, she developed
arrangements of geometrical figures with complexities of shape and
implied spatial projection, whether in or out, that could rival the effects

                                    RICHARD SHIFF

of chromatic interaction that she would eventually achieve. In 1972, reflecting on the two sides to her experience of the 1960s, Riley noted a pragmatic fact: 'Form and colour seem to be fundamentally incompatible – they destroy each other.'[29] She would convert this visual 'destruction' into something productive. 'Earlier I chose form, and later colour.'[30]

In 1961, as Riley sought to initiate an abstract art that she could regard as her own, she asked herself: 'Was there anything to be found in a square?' Everything about a square ought to have been as self-evident as the redness of red. If only from its definition as right-angled and equilateral, we think we already understand what this figure can be. But a square, like a colour, changes in perception. It was fair game for Riley's studio investigation. As she experimented with drawing squares, producing multiples of the actual shape, the geometric order of the world seemed to evolve: 'Quite suddenly something was happening down there on the paper that I had not anticipated… The squares began to lose their original form.'[31] From this experience, she inferred a principle: 'The motif is no longer *out there* in nature; the motif is *down there* on your piece of paper or canvas and so you are responding to what is happening between you and this newly sited motif.'[32] The motif of the square was moving as Riley drew it, just as Seurat's colour had moved as she freely copied it, becoming hers.

The painting that resulted from Riley's experimentation is aptly titled *Movement in Squares* (1961). By her rendering, the elemental geometric figure, the square, seems to exceed and violate its proper definition. Like a primary colour with a commonly accepted identity that nevertheless changes before our eyes, Riley's 'square' challenges the foundation of our understanding. It demonstrates a potential to transform itself, to abandon its presumed stability. Its essential symmetry grows asymmetrical, as it yields to pressure from the curiosity of human vision. In experience, in sensation, the most stable geometries prove alterable, gaining their freedom. Relatively few of Riley's gridded figures in *Movement in Squares* – only those in the vertical row at the extreme left – remain true to the equilateral nature of the geometry. The others are oblong rectangles of various widths. We have the impression of squares receding towards the right into a curving fold, optically narrowing, then projecting back outwards. This 'perspective' is Riley's invention, not her observation. In art, appearances become reality. Because the measure of the form changes only horizontally, while the vertical dimension remains constant, the effect that Riley creates finds no existing counterpart in everyday experience. Her art leaves it to our perception to confirm this effect, as if it were something seen 'down there' (as she would say), in the private optical realm that each of us possesses.

The departure from the ordinary that a painting like *Movement in Squares* indicates compels a viewer to share the experience. Do you see what I see? Is it *real*? The response is similar to the aftermath of observing what cannot quite be seen, cannot quite be believed (as in Seurat's revelations). Kudielka refers to a moment when he and Riley were eating lunch outdoors in Munich on an early spring day with extraordinarily bright light. She suddenly interrupted their conversation: 'Look at it! Just *look* at it!' Kudielka notes that 'there was nothing to look at in the proper sense of the word, no particular incident or object to be observed' other than a 'shine which filled the air'. Overwhelming sensations of this kind force thought to retreat. Riley would also say on such occasions: 'Don't look at it, just glance!'[33] A more focused view would conflict with the aesthetic singularity of the event, fixing the intellect into a structure or category inadequate to what was happening in perception, just then and there, in the shine of a glance.

The recession in *Movement in Squares* occurs in two dimensions, not three. We encounter a sufficiently convincing image of recession without the effect that we ordinarily associate with its illusion. In our convention-bound experience of recession, forms vary across two dimensions, not just one, in order to evoke the third. A figure becomes shorter as it becomes narrower, or taller as it becomes wider, with recession following a diagonal course, not a horizontal. The 'illusion' that *Movement in Squares* manifests is real in the sense that it refers to nothing other than its actual appearance. There's no allusion to landscape, no horizon, no vanishing point. If Riley's painting were destroyed, there would be no such movement anywhere else. The experience of her abstraction exists only in the presence of her art, not only for us but for her:

RICHARD SHIFF

I was not interested at all in questions of illusion and I was quite
sure that perspective was no longer a way of building pictorial space.
[I moved the square] closer and still closer until I felt the movement
had gone far enough. The only possible next movement was to
return to the original state of the square. [It] was only when I painted
each alternate space black that I could really see what I had done.[34]

This art has no model.

Some moments of reflection may be required to grasp what Riley
accomplished with *Movement in Squares* – it seems all too simple, yet it
is not. She didn't produce the illusion of movement but an actual
movement of a strange kind. Reality is in perception. We feel compelled
to perceive this movement, analogous to what occurs in the presence of
Riley's paintings of stripes, to come somewhat later in the decade: *Late
Morning 1* (1967), *Rise 1* (1968) and *Late Morning (Horizontal)* (1967–68)
are examples. *Horizontal Vibration*, a modestly scaled painting of 1961, is
their anticipation. Its elusive surface swells like an oceanic wave, a result
of the uneven distribution of black stripes of various widths, arranged in
varying densities. Bottom to top, a loosely organised segment passes
from thin lines to thick, followed by a group of tightly compressed lines
of medium width, then, moving upwards again, a loosely organised set
of lines passes from thin to thick. This description is rough; it fails to
indicate the minor irregularities within the greater irregularities. Anything
approaching absolute order in Riley's art is a rare occurrence. Here,
contrary to what we too often believe must be the case, looking, which is
specific, becomes more efficient than describing, which is general.

As an instance of Riley's return to full colour, *Late Morning
(Horizontal)* consists of compound chromatic bands, each a pair of hues,
one of which is red. The second colour can be blue, turquoise or green.
Although the sequencing of the banded colours is irregular, the presence
of green is strong in the middle of this horizontally oriented canvas, but
absent from its extremes of top and bottom. The uneven distribution of
colour generates perceptual movement to be associated with swelling
(as in *Horizontal Vibration*), a play of convexity and concavity – the
contrasting colours either advance or recede in interaction. Additionally,

a self-accelerating movement arises as a chromatic phantom, for the combination of red and green tends to induce an impression of yellow, and the combination of red and blue induces violet. Because yellow and violet are complementary, these subtle nuances are mutually accentuating. Uncertain as to the stability of Riley's colours, we discover what we 'cannot *quite* see'.

Forgoing recourse to traditional hierarchies of form (large and small, near and far) in both her monochromatic paintings of the early 1960s and her works in full colour later in the decade, Riley deployed sequencing and variation to induce virtual movement – movement that has a perceptual origin. If identifying her sense of pictorial composition with actual movement rather than with its illusion seems to be an irrational claim, perhaps a more agreeable statement would be this: Riley's art eliminates the gap between movement and its illusion; after all, this distinction is merely conceptual, not experiential. When the distinction between movement and the illusion of movement becomes imperceptible in perception, the status of the two phenomena must be the same.[35] Consider conventional film projection as a parallel. Its perceptual 'illusion' depends on the physiological reality of persistence of vision (the still images shift too quickly for the human eye to perceive them as still). We cannot say that the cinematic image isn't moving. In a similar way, Riley links movement to its source in human perception. Her art involves no tricks, just human invention, as intelligent as it is sensitive.

Subliming

Geometry is elemental; colour is elemental. Stressing the primacy of chromatic effects as well as the structural order of forms, Riley refers to her stripe paintings as the beginning of 'a very simple way to *draw with colour*. The [colour] movement is the form.'[36] She had asked herself, 'Was there anything to be found in a square?' She would ask the same of colour: 'What is yellow? Merely a name, an inert notion. But if you put a yellow with other colours, in different proportions and positions, it starts to show a certain potential… I just see what yellow can do.'[37]

   RICHARD SHIFF

Despite their elementary, foundational status, neither a square nor a yellow – and certainly not the blue-turquoise-green-red of *Late Morning* (*Horizontal*) – remains singular and fixed in experience. *This* square, in *this* context, assumes an un-square-like character; *this* red and green, juxtaposed in *this* manner, give rise to this sensation of yellow. The mutability as opposed to the permanence of elemental entities has been a point of paradox and an issue for philosophical speculation since the recorded beginnings of a human attempt to set experience in order. By definition, an element is elemental – if it substantially changes its character, it shouldn't be considered as one of the elements. But what should count as substantial change, change that registers a difference? We can consult the ancients for guidance:

> As the several elements [earth, water, fire, air] never present themselves in the same form, how can anyone have the assurance to assert positively that any of them, whatever it may be, is one thing rather than another?… Anything which we see to be continually changing, as, for example, fire, we must not call 'this' or 'that', but rather say that it is 'of such a nature.'

This acknowledgement of dynamic change is Plato's, or rather Timaeus's, in the dialogue known by his name.[38] On her part, Riley allows us to see that a particular colour is of such a nature; becoming now this, now that. Its potential is unlimited, the fullness of its nature unknown, so aesthetic discovery would only be compromised if we were to settle on defining what a particular colour is and how it must appear.

'Yellow', as Riley's art demonstrates, is merely a name. We would be short-changing our experience to assume that we know the entirety of yellow when we see its instance. Just as the material side of perception assumes a shifting nature, so does its intellectual side: 'You cannot deal with thought directly outside practice as a painter: "doing" is essential in order to find out what form your thought takes.'[39] When Riley told her London students, 'Painting has to be *made*; it doesn't just happen on its own', her statement had deeper implications than its colloquial manner might suggest. Concepts, including concepts of art, are like fire and colour: their nature is to evolve. For an artist, thinking develops through a practice. A concept needs a form.

Riley's involvement with the movement of colour pertains to every colour she chooses to use.[40] When two reds surround a green, the combination becomes yellowish-orange; when two greens surround a red, the combination becomes yellowish-green. Her *Pæan* (1973) – consisting of vertical stripes in a square format, 2.9 metres (9.5 feet) on each side – exhibits such effects on a grand scale. It mixes these evanescent chromatic phenomena (the composite yellows) with other, somewhat less volatile triads of pairs of colours: two blues surrounding a red, two greens surrounding a blue, two blues surrounding a green. The sequence of triads is irregular, as is their clustering into zones of repetition: for example, at the extreme left of the composition, a particular sequence – blue-red-blue, white, green-blue-green, white – repeats three times. With the irregularity, there is also regularity: every second vertical contains either one or two reds among its three separate elements. The resulting optical tensions are extreme, since the reds (as well as the bands of white that border the triadic stripes) establish a regular beat or rhythm, even as the chromatic variation weaves through it, in complex counterpoint or anomalous interference.

With so many factors of optical movement in play, the various colours of *Pæan* appear to rise from their material support, hovering in a space that vibrates as if it were filled with sound as much as light.[41] A pæan, of course, is a song of sorts; but this metaphor is hardly essential to the vision that Riley creates. She muses on the experience: '*Pæan* is like a powerful chant gathering momentum through assembling blocks of colour bands in an apparently random way. But there is an underpinning of order based on the different spatial sensations of these blocks. [I was] grouping blocks of colour solely according to their perceptual presence.'[42]

Given the paramount fact of 'perceptual presence', any number of additional metaphors might be invoked, along with Riley's allusion to song. She herself associates the combination of evanescent instability and inescapable presence that characterises her colour with the nature of a perfume.[43] To these aural and olfactory metaphors, we can add a tactile one – tactile because it evokes a thoroughly transformative physical process. I refer to this possibility: the various colours of Riley's *Pæan* are *subliming* as we see them. These colours *sublime*. Sublimation in this sense isn't a psychological mechanism but a physical phenomenon of phase change or change of elemental state.[44] As an example, consider the fact that under certain atmospheric conditions dihydrogen monoxide will pass from its solid state of ice to its gaseous state of vapour, without converting first to its liquid state of water. If we were to observe this direct transformation from solid to gas, we would say that the chemical compound known as H_2O was subliming. When stripes of red and green appear juxtaposed in Riley's paintings, I sense 'yellow' subliming. Like a solid passing to vapour without mediation, the rise of such a yellow from red and green is a fact without evident logic. A science of additive optical mixture can explain the effect but won't diminish its sensory wonder. 'The several elements never present themselves in the same form': what the ancients experienced with fire and water, Riley experiences with geometric figures and primary colours. Her colours change. They move. They sublime. It is no illusion.

In 1972, referring to her works in colour of the previous years, such as *Late Morning 1*, Riley stated: 'The colours painted on the canvas can be identified as certain hues – but as one looks at the painting one sees a luminous disembodied light, variously coloured… I don't paint light. I present a colour situation which releases light as you look at it… It only comes to life when looked at from a certain distance.' She proceeds to explain that if a viewer's position is too close, only the actual material hues will be seen – 'objective hues, say cerise, olive, turquoise'. If the position is too distant, the colour becomes 'a nebulous grey'. But at the preferred distance, a viewer perceives the 'area of activity – of light'.[45] This would be colour-light subliming as we see it, a change of state from the solid physical support and its pigmentation to the vaporous reality of perception.

Not all of Riley's paintings have metaphoric titles; but some, like *Pæan*, do. Another is *Vapour* (1970). Its colours are muted variants of the secondaries – a greyish violet, a greyish green, a greyish orange. Riley has arranged the three colours so that they appear to twist around each other in a sequence of vertical bands. The colours within the bands vary in the orientation of their twisted distribution, resulting in a complex of subtle effects of hue within a chromatic range already inherently unstable. Each twist is itself complicated by a kind of reversal in the course of its vertical extension; an analogy would be the braiding of three strands of colour. If, for example, we follow green upwards from the bottom of a twisting band and it appears to wrap around orange, towards the top the situation will change, and violet will appear to wrap around the same orange. It is as if a twist were being added to a twist. (I don't pretend to analyse this fully; but I can see it, or not *quite* see it.) Riley states that in making studies for *Vapour*, she sought to preserve 'the fugitive quality of something which is obscure or difficult to penetrate. A vapour or mist veils or hides something. It dematerialises the material and has a beauty all of its own.'[46] I would add that this type of vapour – this *Vapour* – sublimes.

Elysium (2003/1973) is a subsequent example of the cerise-olive-turquoise palette to which Riley happened to refer when she distinguished 'objective hues' from an induced or sublimed light. The effects of sublimation in *Elysium* are similar to those in *Pæan*. Another source of fugitive, vaporous colour-light is *Lilac Painting 5* (2008/1983). Its vertical stripes are white, yellow, green, turquoise and blue. A number of the stripes are double-wide: six of the blues have this dimension. The white stripes are slightly narrower than the coloured ones – an adjustment calculated to ensure that each of these neutral whites would acquire a faint complementary glow in acknowledgement of its neighbours. These variations suggest how intuitively Riley operates: she has no aversion to introducing anomalous elements into a rhythm or chromatic order. Within the context of *Lilac Painting 5*, the blues assume a violet or lilac cast, especially when coupled with turquoise. The violet sublimes. Riley did not use such a metaphor, but her description seems consistent with it: 'When I reworked the earlier studies in 2008, I was trying to intensify the violet hue (which is induced) and adjusted the widths of the stripes accordingly. In the earlier studies the violet was certainly there but it was less apparent.'[47] Whether less or more apparent, this violet exists in the medium of perception.

'The basis of colour is its instability,' Riley has said: 'What you focus upon is not what you see, at least not in terms of colour. I realised that what I was working with lay just outside the centre of attention. One looks *here* and colour is *there*. It's almost as though colour has no integral core or centre of its own.'[48] In other words, colour is an element that doesn't behave elementally. Sublimed colour is located wherever you wouldn't think to look for it. What you think and what you see are made to stand apart.

In ligature

Close to the beginning of this essay, regarding Riley's new set of stripe paintings and their dominant redness, I raised a rhetorical question: 'Where is the redness?' *Where* do we think it can be found? There are several red pigments, of course. But it also seems that redness sublimes from the material ground established by the stripes, not all of which are variants of red. For instance, in *Arioso (Blue)* the chromatic instability seems – to me, at least – sufficiently active to stimulate a perception of redness extending upwards along the surface as well as outwards. Movement occurs in both dimensions, planar and projective, movement within the picture but also towards the viewer. Riley has described this type of situation in a closely related way: 'Modulated reds create depth; [there's] increased rhythmic movement vertically; the spatial range reach[es] back behind the picture plane and quite a long way forward towards the viewer; the linear repetition expands the canvas along and across its breadth.'[49]

Each factor acquires equivalent status in perception: movement along the canvas surface, whether vertically or horizontally; movement away from the viewer; projection towards the viewer. Each makes a valid claim to reality. The situation presents a conundrum, a variant of the paradox that Riley noted in 2009 and no doubt earlier as well: '[Colour] is simultaneously one thing and several things.'[50] Yet, in a different respect, Riley's production of colour is singular. It isn't divided or conflicted over whether to serve a sensory end or a symbolic one. Its primary function is clearly aesthetic. We feel Riley's colour. We even think it. But we need not think *about* it, referring it to peripheral discourses that ultimately distract from its aesthetic singularity, or reconfiguring it as what our ideological frame indicates that it ought to mean. Riley's colour, along with the compositions that give rise to it, does not refer to art or concept or process, or even work. It adheres to its specific sensory effect. As insurance against inadvertently introducing any number of familiar distractions – cultural references to personal identity, creativity, social status, gender, political order and more – Riley renders the touch of her art anonymous by using studio assistants to paint the finished surface.

Despite the appearance of redness as the material grounding of a number of Riley's stripe paintings, her organisation of colour releases this redness, which moves elsewhere (see *Brioso (Orange)*, 2013; *Tocatta (Green)*, 2013–14; and other works in this series). By what mechanism does redness gain this freedom? The least 'red' colours are probably the cause of the agitation and physical escape of the red. Interspersed among the various magentas, roses, pinks, lakes, alizarins, vermilions and the like, are not only violets, oranges and yellows, but also luminous streaks of greens and blues, a chromatic range that might extend from deep emerald green to dense sky blue by way of apple green, acid green and turquoise. Because the stripes of colour are uniform in size and direction, nothing interferes with the bond established by the precisely defined edge shared by each juxtaposed pair. The interaction of colour is maximised at this edge, which acts as a tacit ligature, binding the two contrasting hues to their mutual effect. (A ligature converts two vowels to a diphthong, resulting in the look, sound and sense of each changing to the qualities of a third.)

At each side of the common edge, the colour remains as it is; yet it also becomes a third colour in sublimation. Subliming is one of the effects of ligature. Alternatively, because Riley's stripes are thin in relation to the overall height of the support, each can respond to its local triadic context as if it were itself an interactive edge – a contrasting element between two similar qualities. This virtual transformation of stripe into edge will occur if a green is bordered by two pinks, or a rose by two blues. In Riley's new series of works, chromatic situations of this type are

                                                            RICHARD SHIFF

more often asymmetrically assonant than symmetrically resonant: a turquoise stripe might be bordered by a flame red and a rose red, as opposed to being bordered by flame red on both sides. These irregular conditions nevertheless recall the regular structuring of triads in an A-B-A configuration, as seen in *Pæan* as well as in the diagonal bands of *Prairie* (2003/1971). In the latter painting, violet surrounds thin stripes of red-white-red, a ligature generating a phantom rose; and this situation alternates with violet surrounding thin stripes of green-white-green, which generates a phantom lime. *Prairie* is a diptych composed of identical panels that may appear dissimilar if scanned by eye horizontally, because each has variation within the spacing of the bands of white that separate one violet from the next. Standing before this expansive work, nearly 8 metres (26 feet) wide, a viewer has difficulty judging whether the right panel matches the left. But symmetry suddenly becomes evident along a diagonal axis – a surprise, both optical and intellectual. The stripe paintings of 2014 also create surprise, multiple surprises. Their rhythms lack a regular beat and are devoid of extensive zones of repetition. Their intriguing combinations of opposition and assonance – say, a strong blue adjacent to a strong orange, followed by a warm pink adjacent to a warm yellow – bear similarity to Riley's Egyptian paintings, such as *Après Midi* (1981) and *Serenissima* (1982).[51] The new works are an extreme outgrowth of qualities first intimated in the stripe paintings of the 1980s.

Riley would be able to list any number of precedents for her involvement with chromatic interaction that date before her own history. She devotes extensive looking, followed by thoughtful commentary, to many of the renowned masters of colour, from Titian and Veronese to Cézanne and Matisse.[52] With regard to developing a range of reds – including the versatile red-violet known as *caput mortuum* – Renoir proved especially instructive. Riley viewed his work at a Hayward Gallery exhibition in London, during the first months of 1985, an experience she remembers vividly.[53] Redness predominates in Renoir, even when a composition includes an array of greens, blues, violets and yellows, as in *Road at Wargemont* (1879), from the Hayward show. Renoir bonded red to the other colours by weaving it through them, as if his painting were a complex textile. In turn, Riley adopted the Renoir principle, only to develop it in its most abstract application. She eliminated her predecessor's commitment to naturalistic representation, picturesque composition and hierarchies of form, while retaining his sense of reds and non-reds in mutual response and enhancement, if not enchantment.

Among its several obsolete meanings, 'ligature' refers to a condition in which the intellectual faculties have been rendered passive, perhaps incapacitated by the force of sensation – a state in which thinking is bound to and restricted by feeling.[54] Recall Riley's interjection in Munich, her cognitive immobilisation in the face of atmospheric light: 'Just *look* at it!'[55] Ironically, in this context, ligature becomes a vehicle of liberation. This happens when the overwhelming emotion eventually releases its hold on the intellect. Thought is then free to pursue a new course, as if the sensory, emotional experience had shocked it into performing its calculations on a clean slate. Absorption in light and colour clears the mind. We can learn from sensation, and we can change accordingly. Although I've stressed the wisdom of Riley's acceptance of a fundamental division of the human faculties – 'Comprehension is not everything, the unaccountable has a place in our lives' – her reach into the substance of perception is also a move towards understanding.[56] We might say that perception is a channel or conduit for comprehension as well as for sensation. I would prefer a metaphor that establishes contact of a more intimate nature: perception itself is a ligature – it sets the faculties in ligature – linking sensation and emotion to intellect and reason.

Riley's studied observations and material explorations represent her contact with sensory perception – 'Sometimes… I feel it right up almost against my face', she says, at that moment speaking more literally than figuratively.[57] In turn, perception is the experience in which feeling and thought are likely to converge in mutual comprehension, if they ever do. Perception is a skill – the technique of the unaccountable. We would be mistaken to assume that its cultivation leads to ultimate clarity and certainty. It nevertheless brings acuity to both sensing and thinking. The various instances of sublimed colour – the greyish light of *Vapour*, the yellowness of *Pæan* and *Elysium*, the violet of *Lilac Painting 5*, the

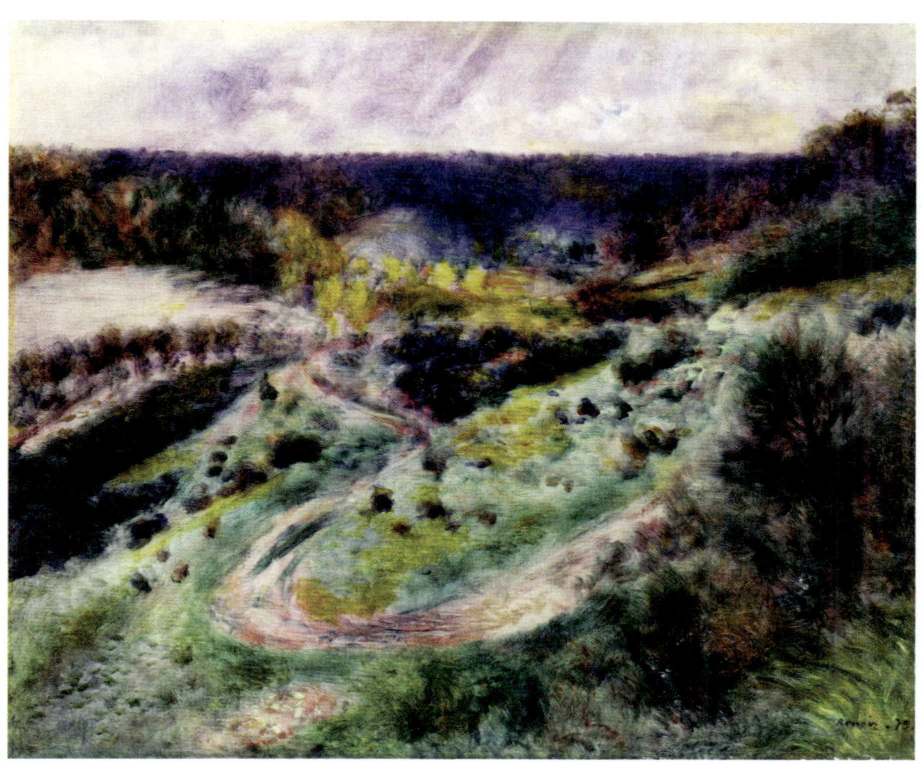

Pierre-Auguste Renoir
Road at Wargemont 1879
Oil on canvas
80.6 × 100 cm | 31¾ × 39⅜ in
Toledo Museum of Art

redness of the new stripe paintings – demonstrate the persistently dynamic nature of visual experience. Even elemental colours change. Perception, the human medium, registers the changes. We have only to pay attention.

'Is there any painting? And if there isn't, does it matter?'[58] It matters, for we can use painting and the other material arts as Riley does – to pursue our medium, our perception. As either producers or consumers of painting, we have a chance of catching up with the unaccountable. We become aware of 'the *im-perceptible*', an immense reserve of experience outside the present limits of conceptualisation and intellectual understanding.[59] We may already be tapping into this reserve, but without enough sensitivity for it to affect our emotional soul. We look, yet not always with discovery or edification. As Riley suggests, painting offers the opportunity to perceive colour and other qualities that, despite being unconcealed, remain unseen: 'In order to see, one had to paint and through that activity found what could be seen.'[60]

Doro Globus (ed), *Bridget Riley: The Stripe Paintings 1961–2014*, exhibition catalogue, David Zwirner Books, New York, NY and London, 2014, pp.19–42.

Note: I thank Bridget Riley for continuing conversations over a number of years and for her characteristically precise responses to numerous queries. For aid in research, I am grateful to Jessamine Batario, Karsten Schubert, the David Zwirner gallery and the Bridget Riley studio.

     RICHARD SHIFF

1   Bridget Riley, 'Painting Now' (1996), in Robert Kudielka (ed), *The Eye's Mind: Bridget Riley, Collected Writings 1965–2009*, Thames & Hudson and Ridinghouse, London, 2009, p.290 (original emphasis).

2   *Ibid.*, pp.293, 296.

3   *Ibid.*, p.295.

4   Bridget Riley, email to the author, 14 May 2014.

5   Bridget Riley, 'In Conversation with Robert Kudielka' (1972), in *The Eye's Mind*, *op.cit.*, p.104.

6   Bridget Riley determines the precise number of stripes according to the requirements of the movement of colour that she gradually develops for a particular canvas. She might see fit to increase 59 to 61. The composition would then be two inches greater in height, and its width would probably need to be increased proportionately (Riley, email to the author, 21 May 2014). In the case of *Brioso (Orange)*, Riley used 65 stripes, while deciding on a more elongated proportion of 1:1.90 – again, an intuitive judgement.

7   Riley, email to the author, 21 May 2014.

8   Bridget Riley, 'Work' (2009), in *The Eye's Mind*, *op.cit.*, p.58.

9   Bridget Riley, 'Into Colour: In Conversation with Robert Kudielka' (1978), in *The Eye's Mind*, *op.cit.*, p.111.

10 Bridget Riley, 'Perception Is the Medium' (1965), in *The Eye's Mind*, *op.cit.*, p.89.

11 *Ibid.*, pp.89–90.

12 Riley, 'Painting Now', *op.cit.*, p.302.

13 Bridget Riley, 'Seurat as Mentor', in Jodi Hauptman (ed), *Georges Seurat: The Drawings*, exhibition catalogue, Museum of Modern Art, New York, NY, 2007, p.95. In this instance, Riley was focusing on Seurat's drawings; but her remark pertains to the totality of his practice.

14 Bridget Riley, 'Colour for the Painter' (1995), in *The Eye's Mind*, *op.cit.*, p.242.

15 Bridget Riley, 'The Artist's Eye: Seurat' (1992), *ibid.*, p.267 (original emphasis).

16 Robert Kudielka, 'Nothing but Appearance' (1978), in Robert Kudielka (ed), *Robert Kudielka on Bridget Riley: Essays and Interviews 1972–2003*, Ridinghouse, London, 2005 p.37 (original emphasis).

17 Riley, 'The Artist's Eye: Seurat', *op.cit.*, pp.272–73 (original emphasis).

18 Kudielka, 'Nothing but Appearance', *op.cit.*, p.39.

19 Bridget Riley, 'The Spirit of Enquiry: In Conversation with Jenny Harper' (2004), in *The Eye's Mind*, *op.cit.*, p.173.

20 Riley, 'Work', *op.cit.*, p.55.

21 Riley, 'Painting Now', *op.cit.*, p.292.

22 Riley, 'The Spirit of Enquiry: In Conversation with Jenny Harper', *op.cit.*, p.74.

23 Riley's source was RH Wilenski, *Seurat*, Faber & Faber, London, 1949, p.15 (plate 6).

24 Paul Signac, journal entry for 28 December 1897, in John Rewald (ed), 'Extraits du journal inédit de Paul Signac, II: 1897–1898', *Gazette des beaux arts* 39 (April 1952), pp.270–71 (author's translation).

25 See Roger Fry, *Seurat*, Encyclopaedia Britannica, London, 1971, plate 29.

26 'I have again returned to the stripe for a closer, concentrated look at colour interaction … it is almost a return to Seurat's *mélange optique* but with the stripe as the agent rather than the dot. I have said somewhere that the stripe is the closest thing to Seurat's point but has a little more going for it, for instance length and direction'; Riley, email to the author, 14 May 2014.

27 Riley, 'Work', *op.cit.*, p.58.

28 Riley, 'Colour for the Painter', *op.cit.*, p.242.

29 Riley, 'In Conversation with Robert Kudielka', *op.cit.*, p.104.

30   Riley, 'Into Colour: In Conversation with Robert Kudielka', *op.cit.*, p.126.

31   Riley, 'Work', *op.cit.*, pp.56–57.

32   Bridget Riley, 'Bridget Riley in Conversation with Michael Harrison', in *Bridget Riley: Colour, Stripes, Planes and Curves*, exhibition catalogue, Kettle's Yard, Cambridge and Ridinghouse, London, 2011, pp.10–11.

33   Riley, quoted in Robert Kudielka, 'Bridget Riley' (1992), in *Robert Kudielka on Bridget Riley*, *op.cit.* p.130 (original emphasis).

34   Riley, email to the author, 13 May 2014.

35   Recall Riley's phrasing with regard to Seurat, who provides 'an experience just beyond our visual grasp … the *im-perceptible*'; Riley, 'The Artist's Eye: Seurat', *op.cit.*, p.267 (original emphasis).

36   Riley, 'Work', *op.cit.*, p.58 (original emphasis).

37   Riley, 'In Conversation with Robert Kudielka', *op.cit.*, p.104. Now, more than four decades later and as inventive with colour as ever, Riley comments on *About Yellow*: 'There the yellows have a very considerable spatial play; they tend to lie back in the light passages but move forward into the body of reds' (email to the author, 30 May 2014).

38   Plato, *Timaeus* 49, *The Dialogues of Plato*, 2 vols., Benjamin Jowett (trans), Random House, New York, NY, 1937, 2:30. A fifth element, the quintessence or aether, existed as a vehicle of containment for the others (see *Timaeus* 51).

39   Riley, 'Work', *op.cit.*, p.59.

40   Robert Kudielka provides an excellent sense of the 'form' that Riley's colour was assuming, beginning around 1968, with her introduction of stripes, both straight and waved: '[Riley discovered] that elongated forms such as stripes and curves, placed vertically or diagonally against the horizon of perception, were capable of setting off fleeting but clearly visible haloes and zones of immaterial colour… Two, three, four or five colours, alternating with each other, give rise to an event of such vivacity and chromatic abundance that the objective facts of the painting literally recede behind this effect'; Robert Kudielka, 'Bridget Riley's Pictorial Thinking' (1984), in *Robert Kudielka on Bridget Riley*, *op.cit.*, pp.82, 86.

41   On the place of *Pæan* in Riley's general development, see Paul Moorhouse, 'Bridget Riley: The Stripe Paintings 1961–2012', in *Bridget Riley: The Stripe Paintings 1961–2012*, exhibition catalogue, Galerie Max Hetzler and Holzwarth Publications, Berlin and Ridinghouse, London, 2013, pp.45–46.

42   Riley, 'Into Colour: In Conversation with Robert Kudielka', see p.47.

43   Riley, in conversation with the author, 7 March 2014.

44   Because phase change can be a source of wonder, physical sublimation relates loosely to the sense of the sublime in eighteenth-century aesthetics – but only loosely. I suppose that the analogy of phase change might also be a metaphorical way of comprehending psychological sublimation.

45   Riley, 'In Conversation with Robert Kudielka', *op.cit.*, p.107.

46   Riley, email to the author, 25 May 2014.

47   Riley, email to the author, 21 May 2014.

48   Bridget Riley, 'Practising Abstraction: Talking to Michael Craig-Martin' (1992), in Robert Kudielka (ed), *Bridget Riley: Dialogues on Art*, Zwemmer, London, 1995, p.56 (original emphasis).

49   Riley, email to the author, 14 October 2013.

50   Riley, 'Work', *op.cit.*, p.58.

51   On changes in Riley's colour effects associated with her adoption of the Egyptian palette, see Kudielka, 'Bridget Riley's Pictorial Thinking', *op.cit.*, pp.87–89.

52   See Riley, 'Colour for the Painter', in *The Eye's Mind*, *op.cit.*, pp.222–48.

53   Riley, in conversation with the author, 7 March 2014. The Hayward Gallery exhibition *Renoir* ran from 30 January to 21 April 1985. For its catalogue, see Anne Distel and John House, *Renoir*, Harry N Abrams, New York, NY, 1985.

54   'Ligature, among *Mystic Divines*, signifies a total suspension of the superior faculties, or intellectual powers of the soul [which] ceases to act, in order to be more ready and prepared to receive the impulse and communications of divine grace. This passive state of these contemplative people, they call their ligature'; Ephraim Chambers, *Cyclopaedia: or, an Universal Dictionary of Arts and Sciences*, 5 vols., JF and C Rivington *et al.* (eds), London, 1788, n.p. (original italics).

55   Riley, quoted in Kudielka, 'Bridget Riley', *op.cit.*, p.130 (original emphasis).

56   Riley, 'Seurat as Mentor', *op.cit.*, p.95.

57   Riley, quoted in Kudielka, 'Nothing but Appearance', *op.cit.*, p.39.

58   Riley, 'Painting Now', *op.cit.*, p.290.

59   Riley, 'The Artist's Eye: Seurat', *op.cit.*, p.267 (original emphasis).

60   Bridget Riley, 'The Pleasures of Sight' (1984), in *The Eye's Mind*, *op.cit.*, p.34.

Riley and Seurat: An Introduction

Karen Serres | Barnaby Wright

In the late autumn of 1959, Bridget Riley painted a copy of one of the highlights of The Courtauld Gallery's collection, *The Bridge at Courbevoie* (1886–87) by the French impressionist artist Georges Seurat. Riley had graduated four years earlier from the Royal College of Art, London and was trying to find her own voice as an artist. This experience represented a significant breakthrough, offering her a new understanding of colour and perception. The lessons Riley learned from Seurat emboldened her to strike out into the realm of pure abstraction and over the following years she produced the first major abstract paintings based upon repeated geometric shapes, stripes and curves that have brought her international renown.

This seminal moment of artistic discovery is the springboard for the exhibition *Bridget Riley: Learning from Seurat* (2015–16), which brings together – for the first time – Riley's copy of *The Bridge at Courbevoie* with its model. It follows Riley's evolution from the groundbreaking black-and-white canvases she produced in the 1960s to the development of the stripe paintings and return to colour at the end of the decade and in subsequent years. The exhibition celebrates how, at a time when examining the art of the past and copying from the Old Masters had lost their prominence in contemporary art education, Riley cultivated from her early formative years 'a habit of looking at the past because artists seem to face the same fundamental problems even though they are working in different styles'.[1] How had artists before her approached painting? How had they, at the most practical level, applied paint to canvas; in what order; to what aim?

Seurat's famed, methodical approach to painting – based on the building of forms through the tight juxtaposition of dots of pure colour – was the outcome of the artist's search for a formal framework with which to approach painting, and offered Riley an enticing model. There was never any question of copying Seurat slavishly or adopting his method as her own; rather, Riley was interested in discovering how the artist had answered the questions that troubled her. This exploration of Seurat's work went on to play a fundamental role in Riley's artistic development: not only did it provide revelatory insights into how 'light can be built from colour', but it also shaped her core beliefs on the very purpose and meaning of painting.[2]

Riley's first direct encounter with Seurat did not occur with *The Bridge at Courbevoie*; rather it took place a few years earlier in front of his early monumental canvas *Bathers at Asnières* (1883–84) at the National Gallery, London. The work was a revelation for Riley; she admired the way in which Seurat had managed to convey on canvas all the sensations of a clear, bright afternoon sun shining on a modest oasis of leisure, in the midst of the surrounding industrialisation. Riley's question was simple, but would ultimately prove far-reaching: 'where does the light come from?'[3]

The rendering of light had been a long-standing concern for Riley. As a pupil at Cheltenham Ladies' College in the years following the Second World War, she was introduced to tonal thinking by the head of the College's dynamic art department, Colin Hayes, who was a protégé of Kenneth Clark and later Reader at the Royal College of Art. With the use of black pencil or chalk – sometimes enhanced by white highlights – tonal drawing focuses on the rendering of variations of light and shadow falling on an object, shaping the face of a sitter or moving across a landscape. It requires the draughtsman to consider where light emanates, how it shifts and how it affects everything around it.

Riley noticed that in contrast to the Impressionists, who sought to capture the shifting luminosity and atmosphere of the landscape before them, Seurat's interest lay in creating light intrinsically. While Seurat certainly sketched outdoors – often painting with oils on small, portable boards – his large-scale works were carefully composed in the studio and grounded in three key principles: tone, line and colour. While tone aimed to capture variations in light and shadow, line focused on the structure of the composition and the forms within it. Finally, colour brought the motifs to life, with a particular attention to the way in which colour behaved and changed according to what surrounded it.

   KAREN SERRES | BARNABY WRIGHT

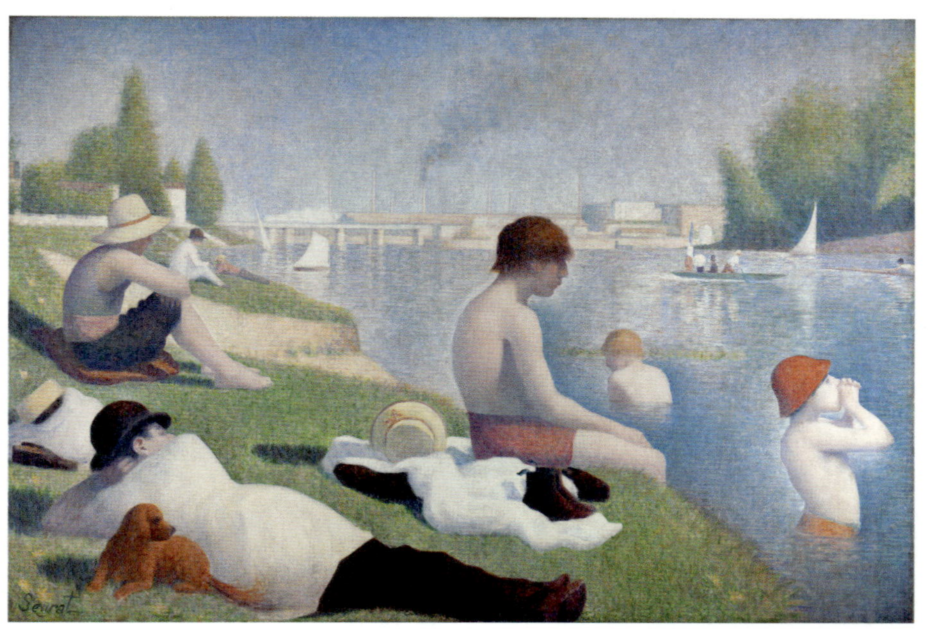

Georges Seurat
Bathers at Asnières 1884
Oil on canvas
201 × 300 cm | 79⅛ × 118⅛ in
National Gallery, London

The mutability of colour had been instinctively perceived for centuries by artists, who explored the harmonies and contrasts that could be created by juxtaposing different tones of the same hue or combining complementary colours (which is to say, colours that are opposite each other on the colour wheel, such as red and green or blue and orange). Seurat sought to rationalise these expressive values and was famously fascinated by contemporary developments in optical theory.[4] He sought a systematic way of approaching the rendering of light and colour, which he described as 'ma méthode'.[5] In addition, Seurat was keen to render the different effects that natural and artificial light had on colours in the composition. Finally, his application of paint in minute touches of pure colour, stemmed from contemporary experiments on the way colours were perceived by the human eye. Instead of blending the colours on the palette or on the canvas itself, the painter juxtaposed dots which – when viewed from a certain distance – mixed in the beholder's eye. This phenomenon, called 'optical mixture' or 'optical fusion', was believed to confer a greater vibrancy to the motif and the surface of the works.

Seurat's approach, however, remains highly theoretical and, while Riley had been able to examine *Bathers* very closely, she felt that she could only understand Seurat by experiencing his process for herself. The only way to become truly familiar with Seurat's work would be to retrace his steps, follow his struggles and replay his discoveries on the canvas itself. Historically, copying the works of Old Masters was a fixture in the training of young painters and a key didactic tool. Riley's mission, however, was much more ambitious: instead of slavishly reproducing the painting she sought to understand how Seurat thought and saw. As Riley has commented, 'if you copy something, you get inside somebody's mind in a way that you don't however carefully you look at it'.[6] Riley had tried to copy favourite paintings before, including works by Jan van Eyck, Pierre Bonnard and Henri Matisse, but the artists had either erased their process from the surface of their paintings (in the case of Van Eyck) or worked in such an instinctive and seemingly spontaneous way that there was little to detect and learn.[7]

Seurat, however, was different. Not only did Riley feel an intense personal connection with the work, but his methodical technique made

    KAREN SERRES | BARNABY WRIGHT

his process visib e on the very surface of his canvases. It remained to decide which work to choose; a close friend, Maurice de Sausmarez, suggested that she peruse RH Wilenski's publication, *Seurat*, from 1949. Together, they selected *The Bridge at Courbevoie*, most likely because they shared Wilenski's opinion that the painting was 'the most characteristic and faultless of all his pictures known to me'.[8]

In fact, this work represents a moment of transition in Seurat's oeuvre. The subject matter – stolen moments of leisure in the suburban landscape around Paris – recalls his earlier *Bathers at Asnières* and *A Sunday on La Grande Jatte – 1884* (1884–86), painted along the same stretch of riverbank. In *The Bridge at Courbevoie*, Seurat focused on a small port with sailboats; in the background, a few men appear to be fishing while the still and pensive doll-like figures on the banks look out onto the water. The composition is carefully structured, a new development in Seurat's work that was possibly influenced by his ties with the mathematician and aesthetician Charles Henry; the tall boat masts, echoing the factory chimney looming in the background, provide a rhythmic vertical emphasis, counterbalanced by the horizontal lines of the pontoons. The painting also represents a technical evolution for Seurat. Although the artist still began his composition by brushing on, in a cross-hatch pattern, broad planes of colour to define and block in its different sections, he then – in contrast to earlier work – added a 'skin' of smaller, tighter and more regular dots; an exactness that he developed before doing away with the underlying planes of colour altogether.[9]

Pointillism – founded upon Seurat's approach – was short-lived yet gained followers throughout Europe, even after Seurat's early death in 1891. His work also had a profound impact on later artists, well into the twentieth century. It fed into the experiments of the Fauves, the Cubists and the Futurists – in whom De Sausmarez was also keenly interested – and influenced artists like Matisse and Pablo Picasso over many years. The latter even adopted the pointillist technique after the First World War as part of a series of stylistic experiments after Older Masters. Seurat opened up radical questions on the subjectivity of perception and observation; he was thus embraced as a key precursor by the avant garde who sought to harness the instability of experience. As Gertrude

Stein noted, Seurat taught painters to question *what* and *how* they saw: '[in the late nineteenth century, painters] were all of them looking with their eyes and Seurat's eyes then began to tremble at what his eyes were seeing, he commenced to doubt if in looking he could see'.[10]

The critical revival of Seurat's reputation in France in the early twentieth century coincided with a rising interest in Impressionism and post-Impressionism in Britain. The key figure in this movement was the art critic, artist and curator Roger Fry, who organised a series of seminal exhibitions in the 1910s on 'modern French art'.[11] However, Seurat only came to the attention of the broader British public a decade later but in a spectacular way: the purchase for the National Gallery of the monumental *Bathers at Asnières*. This was made possible thanks to an acquisitions fund set up a year earlier by Samuel Courtauld, whose role as a collector of Impressionism and post-Impressionism helped to establish Seurat's reputation in Britain.[12] Courtauld became a dedicated collector of Seurat's works, acquiring in quick succession *The Bridge at Courbevoie, Young Woman Powdering Herself* (1888–90) and a number of oil sketches. As a result, The Courtauld Gallery held the largest collection of works by Seurat in Britain throughout most of the twentieth century.[13]

Seurat's reputation in Britain, however, experienced significant fluctuations. Fry himself was initially highly ambivalent about Seurat's work and included only two small and rather stiff landscapes in the earliest of his French exhibitions, Manet and the post-Impressionists at the Grafton Galleries, London in 1910–11.[14] He perceived Seurat as an artist devoted to precision and observation but who

> refused to see any implications other than the visual elements in a scheme of fixed and abstract perfection. Each figure seems to be so perfectly enclosed within its simplified contour, for, however, precise and detailed Seurat is, his passion for geometricising never deserts him… No other relation than a spatial and geometrical one is any longer possible.[15]

Fry here raises the key question of the divide between the stated aims of Seurat's method and its practical results. While Seurat searched

   KAREN SERRES | BARNABY WRIGHT

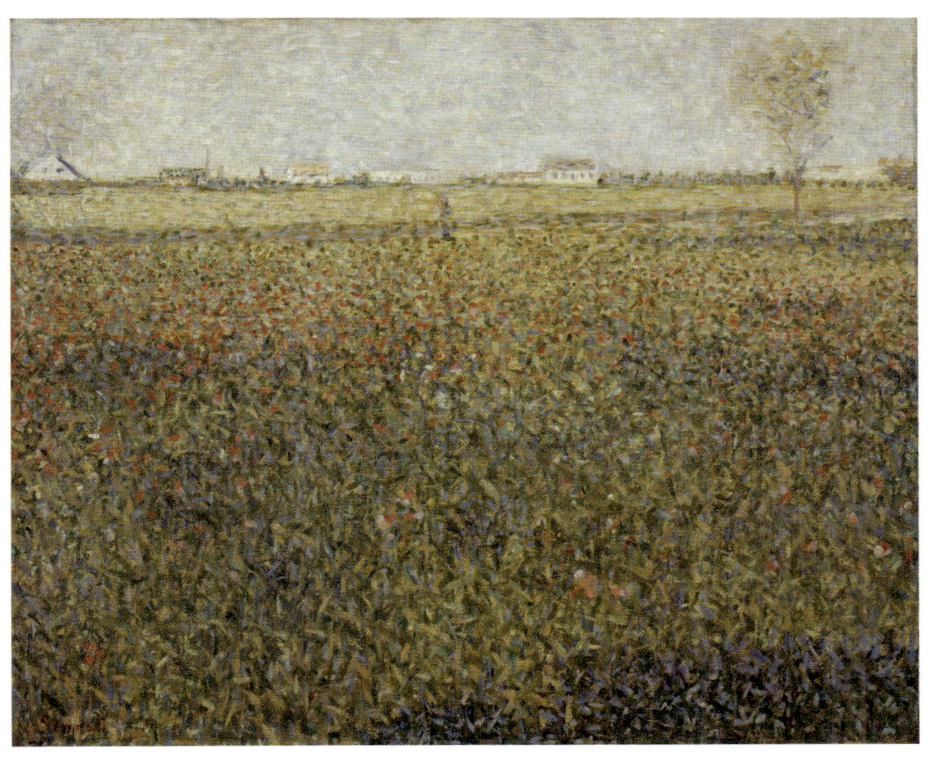

Georges Seurat
La Luzerne, Saint-Denis 1884–85
Oil on canvas
63.5 × 81.3 cm | 25 × 32⅛ in
Scottish National Gallery, Edinburgh

for a way to render reality as objectively and effectively as possible, Fry
felt that, in practice, this approach fell too easily into the trappings of
pattern and design at the expense of emotion and beauty. However,
perhaps spurred by Seurat's rediscovery by the French avant garde, Fry
slowly revised his judgement and came to see the artist's search for
harmony, the stress on the surface properties of his works and his
'passion for reducing the results of sensation to abstract statements' as a
model for the highest aesthetic experience.[16] By the 1920s, Fry heralded
Seurat as one of the two most important figures of post-Impressionism,
alongside Cézanne. He acquired one of Seurat's major early works, *La
Luzerne, Saint-Denis* (1884–85), and included it in another influential
exhibition of French modern art in 1922.[17]

Nevertheless, this clash between an avowed, absolute devotion to
method and the realities of painting is an issue that lies at the centre of
any exploration of Seurat's art. The artist's friend, Paul Signac, warned early
on that should he follow optical theory meticulously, the optical mixture
of dots would result not in a luminous vibrancy but in an overall grey
and dull effect: the smaller the dot, the duller the overall effect.[18] The
question of science versus aesthetic judgement, emotion and intuition
was already being raised in Seurat's time: the painter himself stated to a
friend that critics, 'see poetry in what I do. No! I apply my method and
that is it'.[19] In practice, however, Seurat had a much more empirical
approach and struggled with his method, which evolved in fits and starts.
In his introduction to *Seurat*, Wilenski remarked that 'like his science
which it inspired and his aesthetic which it served, [Seurat's] self-imposed
discipline was all the time subject to the poetry of his spirit'.[20] This was a
key lesson for Riley; from Seurat, she 'took the example of the method
rather than the method itself'.[21] In her own work, Riley would look to
create a discipline, a clear framework, but one that would then allow her
great creative freedom within it, in the same way that jazz musicians are
capable of virtuoso improvisations thanks to the understanding and
observance of the underlying structure and rules of music.[22]

Riley had seen *The Bridge at Courbevoie* in The Courtauld Gallery –
then located in Woburn Square in Bloomsbury – but crucially decided

                                          KAREN SERRES | BARNABY WRIGHT

not to paint directly in front of the original canvas. She felt that 'the privacy of learning' could only be achieved by working in her small studio on Warwick Road in London, day after day, removed from the aura and ascendancy of Seurat's canvas.[23] The colour plate from Seurat provided her with the detachment she needed, which was furthered by the choice of a larger canvas for her copy. This choice was due to less emotional than practical reasons: Riley scaled up and decided to adopt larger dots of colour because her objective was never to reproduce Seurat's exacting touch faithfully but to dissect his train of thought.[24] Her version of *The Bridge at Courbevoie* cannot, therefore, be labelled a copy but is more accurately described as a 'transcription'.

A final, notably unintentional, detachment from Seurat's original occurred with the rendering of colour. The quality of photographic reproduction in the 1940s was not without problems and the plate in the Faber & Faber publication distorts the colours of the original canvas; while the latter is relatively cool, the reproduction has an overall golden hue. Compounding this effect is the fact that some of Seurat's pigments have drastically shifted over the years. The zinc yellow Seurat purchased in the mid-1880s was especially unstable and, where applied pure, has turned from bright yellow to muddy ochre. It has also affected mixed pigments that contain yellow, such as greens and oranges.[25] The chromatic alterations undergone by Seurat's work, both through the chemical deterioration of pigments and through the distortion of photographic reproduction, further separate the two *Bridges*. Interestingly, these factors play a role in ensuring that each work exists on its own terms.

Riley's 'transcription' of Seurat constituted a significant step forward in her artistic practice; she extended the experience of looking at the world through Seurat's eyes by creating her own pointillist landscapes, which launched her independent work. In *Lincolnshire Landscape* (1959), Riley echoed Seurat's predilection for a high horizon line and flattened perspective. Through the use of short brushstrokes with varying tonal values, Riley rendered the sense of sunlight breaking through the clouds overhead and dappling the expansive meadow. Her work vividly echoes Seurat's *La Luzerne, Saint-Denis*, in which the myriad of coloured dots create a vast field of alfalfa peppered with poppies, which ultimately fuse together in the beholder's eye into a near-abstract pattern.

Riley pursued her direct exploration of Seurat's method from late 1959 into the summer of 1960, when she used his method to paint the rolling hills outside of Siena during a tour of Italy. Through a gradation of coloured spots of paint, ranging from light yellow at the bottom of the canvas to deep purple at the top, *Pink Landscape* (1960) captures the shimmer of the Italian countryside as the scorching heat dissolves the outlines of the landmarks. The painting represents both a culmination in Riley's journey of artistic exploration, and also an endpoint: it made her realise that she was more interested in capturing the sensations felt in front of the landscape than in the landscape itself. The following year, she moved away completely from figuration and the use of colour in her work, in an attempt to find out if what drew her to Seurat's landscapes could be harnessed in another way.

The leap from *Pink Landscape* to black-and-white abstraction may seem, at first, surprising, but in the canvases of the early 1960s, Riley managed to capture the very qualities she had been learning from Seurat: the generation of light emanating from within and a sense of vibration on the very surface of the canvas. Emulating Seurat's mark-making, Riley turned his small dots into repeated black-and-white geometric forms. It is important to note that nothing is mechanical in Riley's work; just like Seurat adjusted the size, direction and chromatic intensity of his brushstrokes to suit the motif, Riley created slight variations in a simple shape. In the case of *Tremor* (1962), the alternation of monochromatic triangles with different fluttering edges imbues the painting with a powerful visual tension. The shapes are laid out in a regular manner and with the same orientation (the black triangles all point downward); the difference lies solely in the lower-right edges of the triangles, which are either curved in, out or straight. These carefully arranged variations create a surface that seems to flicker and produce emerging forms – what Riley describes as 'buried images'.[26] Some viewers might perceive a mountainous landscape amidst the shapes, with large lozenges forming tall peaks that echo the rolling hills in *Pink Landscape* – but it remains an open and entirely subjective question.

The influence of Riley's earlier tonal studies is manifest in *Tremor* and even more so in *Burn* (1964). Alongside subtle variations in the outlines of her geometric shapes, Riley introduced an additional feature: a gradation in tonal value to create a range of greys. The effect is the illusion of two powerful diagonal beams of light cutting across the canvas and distorting the seeming uniformity of the triangular patterns. The viewer is thus prompted to ask the very question Riley posed in front of *Bathers at Asnières*: 'where does the light come from?' Looking closely at the surface of the work and observing the tonal gradation provides the answer to how this dazzling effect was created. These works, along with the other radical paintings created at that period, demonstrate that, with an approach both completely novel and deeply rooted in the study of the art of the past, Riley had found her artistic voice.

As a foil, however, to the leap made at the beginning of the decade from pointillist landscapes to black-and-white abstraction, Riley's interrogation on the meaning and function of painting led her, at the end of the 1960s, back to colour and to lessons learnt from Seurat. Her transcription of *The Bridge at Courbevoie* had not only revealed to Riley how colours behave when placed next to one another, but also 'how colour takes up positions in space'.[27] Riley decided to simplify her forms and rely solely on vertical or horizontal stripes, allowing colour to take over the length of the canvas. Her focus remained on the intense exploration into the instability of perception; however instead of generating disruption through the manipulation of shapes and tone – as had been the case in *Tremor* and *Burn* – Riley's main tool was now colour, 'unstable in its basic character'.[28]

Counteracting that instability – and allowing her to explore it fully – were two key features. The first was the use of the stripe, the most fundamental but retiring of forms, 'the edge par excellence'.[29] While echoing Seurat's method of juxtaposing pure colours to create chromatic harmonies and contrasts, the stripe provided a direction, length and volume that his dots lacked.[30] The second key element was the choice of a limited palette: one of Riley's earliest works in that vein, *Late Morning 1* (1967), is composed of an alternation of red/green and blue/red vertical stripes on a white background. One can only be struck by the dichotomy between the limited means employed (a repeated, simple stripe in a palette consisting of one colour [red] and the gradation between two others [blue to green]) and the powerful visual and emotional response provoked by the canvas.

Riley continued to explore these reactions and generated sensations. In *Vapour* (1970), the artist played on the imaginary distortion of the stripes through colour perception by creating thin diagonals of colour within each vertical band, so that they appeared to be twisting on themselves and thus distorting. Colour bounces off the white edges and against the surrounding hues, creating areas of colour that appear to spread horizontally across the canvas. In a sense, Riley managed to echo the structured composition of Seurat's paintings, based on strong verticals and horizontals, solely through the viewer's visual response to her work.

As Riley refined her method and extended her enquiries throughout the following decades, she constantly re-engaged with Seurat's work: learning new lessons, finding different solutions or strengthening core beliefs. *Ecclesia* (1985) is perhaps one of the most remarkable works from the 1980s, marking a return to regular vertical stripes after a period of exploration of curves, diagonals and lozenges. Compared to the earlier *Late Morning 1*, Riley extended her range of colours and broadened the bands, which allowed both the particular characteristics of each colour to come through and made their interaction all the more powerful when seen as a whole. It brings to mind the pleasure and paradox of looking at Seurat's dots, first in isolation – getting up close to identify their individual colour and shapes – and then stepping away to understand how they fit into the whole, how they interact with their neighbours and how that interaction affects our response to the painting. Painted 25 years after the beginning of her interest in Seurat and divisionism, *Ecclesia* is essentially – in Riley's words – '*Pink Landscape* in lines'.[31]

Despite Seurat's importance for avant-garde artists throughout the twentieth century, Riley has arguably engaged with his work more deeply than any other painter. As her friend and collaborator Robert Kudielka has noted, 'the association with Seurat supported and strengthened the methodical streak of Riley's artistic temperament'.[32] In Seurat, she found an artist driven by the same profound questions on the nature of perception and the role of painting that preoccupied her from the beginning of her career. She engaged with Seurat on both a visual and an intellectual level, as attested by two essays she has written on Seurat, included in this volume. Riley was able to be so influenced by Seurat – to learn so much from his example – thanks to her own investigative impulse and her early commitment to copying, which constitutes an unparalleled way of looking closely. Citing Matisse, Riley notes that, 'for my part, I have never avoided the influence of others. I would have considered that cowardice and a lack of sincerity toward myself'.[33]

The ability to look afresh remains a vital part of Riley's practice today. We were privileged to witness this first-hand during a recent visit to her studio. One of her large-scale canvases was due to leave the studio but Riley was not ready to see it go. There was a nagging problem with the band of dark Thulian pink in the centre of the canvas. Acting almost like a horizon line, it seemed to ground the composition but also, perhaps, weigh it down. Riley fashioned a full-size band in a lighter shade of salmon pink and taped it over the offending stripe. Instantly, the canvas transformed; the more luminous pink band changed the perception of the other colours around it, suddenly opening up a bold vortex at the centre of the painting. The incident encapsulated Riley's lifelong investigations and served as a reminder that, despite meticulous preparatory studies laying out the formal and chromatic relationships between the horizontal stripes lining the canvas, precise observation and aesthetic judgement remain the artist's guiding principles. Tellingly, the large canvas was leaned on a wall of the studio where Riley's transcription of *The Bridge at Courbevoie* usually hangs. This painting serves as a reminder of her continued exploration into the question of perception and contrast, and of the artist who played such an important role in setting her on her path.

Bridget Riley: Learning from Seurat, exhibition catalogue, The Courtauld Gallery and Ridinghouse, London, 2015, pp.9–23.

1   Bridget Riley, 'In Conversation with Lynne Cooke' (2005), in Robert Kudielka (ed), *The Eye's Mind: Bridget Riley, Collected Writings 1965–2009*, Thames & Hudson and Ridinghouse, London, 2009, p.315.

2   Bridget Riley, 'Interview with Julian Spalding', *The Third Ear*, BBC Radio 3, 25 January 1988.

3   Bridget Riley, conversation with the authors, April 2015.

4   On Seurat, see, among others, Félix Fénéon, *Œuvres plus que complètes*, Librairie Droz, Geneva, 1970; John Rewald, *Post-Impressionism: From Van Gogh to Gauguin*, Museum of Modern Art, New York, NY, 1956; César M de Hauke, *Seurat et son œuvre*, 2 vols., Grund, Paris, 1961; Françoise Cachin and Robert L Herbert (eds), *Georges Seurat 1859–1891*, Metropolitan Museum of Art, New York, NY, 1991; Paul Smith, *Seurat and the Avant-Garde*, Yale University Press, New Haven and London, 1997; and most recently, Michelle Foa, *Georges Seurat: The Art of Vision*, Yale University Press, New Haven, CT, and London, 2015.

5   See Françoise Cachin and Robert L Herbert (eds), *Georges Seurat: 1859–1891*, Metropolitan Museum of Art, New York, NY, 1991, pp.423–48, whose appendices helpfully include some of his sources as well as contemporary texts; and Bridget Riley, 'Colour for the Painter' (1995), in Robert Kudielka (ed), *op.cit.*, pp.240–42.

6   Riley, 'Interview with Julian Spalding', *op.cit.*

7   Riley, conversation, *op.cit.* See also Lise Connellan (ed), *Bridget Riley. Paintings and Related Work*, National Gallery, London, 2010.

8   RH Wilenski, *Seurat*, Faber & Faber, London, 1949, p.14.

9   This is most visible in works such as *Young Woman Powdering Herself* (1888–90). See Jo Kirby *et al.*, 'Seurat's Painting Practice: Theory, Development and Technology', *National Gallery Technical Bulletin*, vol.24, 2003, pp.4–37.

10 Gertrude Stein, *Picasso*, BT Bastford, London, 1938, p.1.

11 See Donald E Gordon, *Modern Art Exhibitions 1900–1916: Selected Catalogue Documentation*, 2 vols., Prestel, Munich, 1974; JB Bullen (ed), *Post-Impressionists in England: The Critical Reception*, Routledge, London, 1988; Anne-Pascale Bruneau, 'Aux sources du post-impressionisme. Les expositions de 1910 et 1912 aux Grafton Galleries de Londres', *Revue de l'Art*, no.113, 1996, pp.7–18; Anna Gruetzner Robins (ed), *Modern Art in Britain, 1910–1914*, Merrell and Barbican Art Gallery, London, 1997; Madeleine Korn, *Collecting Modern Foreign Art in Britain Before the Second World War*, 3 vols., PhD, University of Reading, 2001; Anna Gruetzner Robins, 'Marketing Post-Impressionism: Roger Fry's Commercial Exhibitions', in Pamela Fletcher and Anne Helmreich (eds), *The Rise of the Modern Art Market in London 1850–1939*, Manchester University Press, Manchester, 2011, pp.85–97.

12 In 1923, Courtauld established The Courtauld Fund, donating the substantial sum of £50,000 to the nation for the purchase of Impressionist and post-Impressionist paintings, which were hitherto largely absent from British public collections. See John House (ed), *Impressionism for England: Samuel Courtauld as Patron and Collector*, Courtauld Institute Galleries, London, 1994. Seurat's *Bathers at Asnières* was acquired for almost £4,000.

13 From 1932, when The Courtauld Institute of Art was established and became a public collection, until 1995, when the National Gallery received the Berggruen gift of seven oil sketches by the artist.

14 The paintings were *The Lighthouse at Honfleur* (1886) and *View of Crotoy from Upstream* (1889); see Anna Gruetzner Robins, 'Manet and the Post-Impressionists: A Checklist of Exhibits', *The Burlington Magazine*, vol.152, no.1293, December 2010, pp.790–91.

                                                    KAREN SERRES | BARNABY WRIGHT

15   Roger Fry, 'Seurat's La Parade', *The Burlington Magazine*, vol.55, no.321, December 1929,
     pp.289–93. See also Christopher Green (ed), *Art Made Modern: Roger Fry's Vision of Art*,
     The Courtauld Gallery and Merrell Holberton, London, 1999, pp.208–10.

16   Roger Fry stated that 'now that Cézanne's contribution has gradually been assimilated by
     the artistic consciousness of our day, it is evident that… the other outstanding figure of
     later nineteenth-century art is that of Seurat', in 'Georges Seurat', *The Dial*, vol.81, no.3,
     1926, p.224.

17   The painting is recorded as lent by Fry himself for an exhibition at the Burlington Fine
     Arts Club, London in *Catalogue of Pictures, Drawings and Sculptures of the French
     School of the Last 100 Years*, Burlington Fine Arts Club, London, 1922, p.13. It was the only
     work by Georges Seurat in the exhibition that, by contrast, featured seven paintings and a
     watercolour by Paul Cézanne.

18   See Kirby *et al.*, *op.cit.*, pp.29–30.

19   Recounted by Charles Angrand and quoted in Hélène Seyres (ed), *Seurat:
     correspondences, témoignages, notes inédites, critiques*, Acropole, Paris, 1991, p.130.

20   RH Wilenski, *op.cit.*, p.5.

21   Bridget Riley, 'Seurat as Mentor', in Jodi Hauptman (ed), *Georges Seurat: The Drawings*,
     exhibition catalogue, the Metropolitan Museum of Art, New York, NY, 2007, pp.185–95..

22   Riley, conversation, *op.cit.* Igor Stravinsky's *Poetics of Music* was famously also an
     important influence; see for example Bridget Riley, 'Work' (2009), in Robert Kudielka
     (ed), *The Eye's Mind*, *op.cit.*, p.56.

23   Riley, conversation, *op.cit.*

24   The proportions are also slightly different; Riley's copy is taller by 25 centimetres and
     wider by around 40 than the original.

25   See Kirby *et al.*, *op.cit.*, p.25.

26   Riley, 'Seurat as Mentor', *op.cit.*, p.68.

27   Riley, conversation, *op.cit.*

28   *Ibid.*

29   Riley, 'Interview with Julian Spalding', *op.cit.*; Riley added, 'It's very little bulk, there's very
     little weight to a stripe, but it's all edge, and it's along the edges that interaction happens.'
     See also Bridget Riley, 'At the End of My Pencil', *London Review of Books*, vol.31, no.19, 8
     October 2009, pp.20–21 and 'Conversation' (1972), in Robert Kudielka (ed), *op.cit.*,
     pp.29–35.

30   Riley, conversation, *op.cit.*

31   Riley, conversation, *ibid.*

32   Robert Kudielka, 'In Search of a Direction: Bridget Riley's Work in the 1950s', in *Bridget
     Riley: Rètrospective*, Arc/Musée d'Art Moderne de la Ville de Paris, Paris and Ridinghouse,
     London, 2008, p.57.

33   Jacques Guenne, 'Entretien avec Henri Matisse', *L'Art Vivant*, no.18, 15 September 1925.

Unbound Certainties

Éric de Chassey

Bridget Riley's latest body of works, easel and wall paintings, turns its back on what has been considered, since the mid-1960s, her main field of investigation: the exploration of the rich and unexpected properties of colour. By concentrating on black and white, she returns to her seminal work of the early 1960s, except that now the particulars of the paintings, as well as the current context, far removed from the teleological triumphalism of that period, are very different. There is no nostalgia in this going back to a long-gone past but rather a self-archaeology, in the sense of Giorgio Agamben rather than of Michel Foucault: a way of looking at the traces and orders left by the past not only to better understand the present but also to uncover some paths that were left aside or were developed in one direction only, when they could have been used differently – 'the self-revelation of the present as that which we had not been able to live or think'.[1]

While working on an ongoing series of horizontal stripe paintings that she had begun in 2012, Riley reverted to black and white and to a format that uses a combination of more or less triangular shapes. The new series was heralded by a wall painting commissioned for the lobby of the Museum für Gegenwartskunst Siegen, and completed in 2013, titled *Quiver 1* – this was promptly joined by *Quiver 2* (2013). As with a large number of Riley's wall works, they are in black and white, and yet they differ from the previous colourless wall works (1998–2008) – all of which were wall drawings rather than wall paintings – in which overlapping figures were drawn in black lines on a white ground, animated principally by their intersections. Instead, both *Quiver 1* and *Quiver 2* emphasise the interplay of active and passive shapes. In each of these wall paintings, a cloud of large white triangles is created optically by a succession of smaller black shapes made from the combination of two circular segments, which recall a pair of wings. The whole composition is dynamic and – although without colour – takes its lead from Riley's previous wall paintings including *Rajasthan* (2012), which since 2007 have adapted the principles of her large curve paintings to decorative projects.

In 2014, Riley followed the first black-and-white wall paintings with *Quiver 3*. Dispensing with the particular shape that constitutes the vocabulary of *Quiver 1* and *Quiver 2*, she now combined three triangular shapes – rectilinear (equilateral) or with a convex or concave curved side – flowing effortlessly one into the other. This effortlessness experienced by viewers is in fact the result of painstaking preparatory work, as has long been Riley's method, with studies and cartoons drawn and painted, as well as cut-outs she moves around freely on the surface until her composition reaches a state that seems – so to speak – natural. This vocabulary harks back to one of Riley's first mature paintings, *Tremor* (1962), and most specifically to a study for it. The whole surface of this work is covered by triangular variations, creating an all-over effect that elicits the appearing and disappearing of larger units. This effect was called Op art by many art historians and critics in the 1960s, and it led Anton Ehrenzweig to speak of the 'hallucination' created by Riley's work of the period.[2]

When returning to this vocabulary for *Quiver 3*, Riley treats the pictorial field in a new way with a more 'scattered' composition, now non-hallucinatory as each triangular unit remains a discrete part of the whole, and because – although uncentred – this whole is directional (or rather, multidirectional) and open on its sides. The small shapes are combined in order to form larger triangles that are unavoidably isolable and, at the same time, impossible to separate completely (one cannot establish their number), while leaving blank large portions of the wall which, as pointed out by the artist when talking about her earlier wall paintings, 'is coming down and entering into the composition, taking up different positions, with different identities'.[3] The white wall no longer functions as a neutral background but actively participates in the composition, which is primarily a composition of black figures on a white ground (because the ground that appears amidst the black shapes is the same as the surrounding surface), but also demands to be perceived as a composition of white figures on a black background, with smaller and larger units forming negatively. Black positive shapes and white negative

ÉRIC DE CHASSEY

shapes combine to create continuous and discontinuous fields and images. Reconciling these two modalities of painting has been Riley's particular achievement ever since she started the large curve paintings.

In 2014, Riley began to use the three triangular shapes of *Quiver 3* for paintings on canvas, thus addressing issues more closely related to what had happened in *Tremor*. Unlike her wall works, the paintings on canvas are closed up into themselves and demand a more stable attention, enabling the artist to release considerable energies without letting them destroy the unity of what is seen. In Riley's own words: 'I forego definition in order to let the movement really loose.'[4] Small departures from the 1960s format such as a white margin on all sides, or variation in the relative size of the constructive shapes, create considerable differences, as shown most clearly when comparing two square paintings like *Tremor* (1962) and *Rustle* (2015). If the works from the 1960s and from 2014–15 are both based on a modular grid, diagonal or orthogonal, this grid is much more assertive in the recent works. It even resists being dissolved by the alternative reversal of positive and negative shapes. In an unprecedented way in Riley's oeuvre, her shapes can be read positively (as black shapes on a white background) or negatively (as white shapes on a black background), creating, through the addition of the triangular units, larger triangular shapes that are conspicuous from the beginning of the viewer's experience rather than discovered only after a prolonged viewing. (If a 1961 painting was aptly titled *Hidden Squares*, there is nothing hidden here.) The artist acknowledges this fact when she makes this larger triangular shape the format for a series of small shaped-board paintings, titled Start Over (2015), where a different number of units radically transform the effects of a similar composition.

The 2014–15 paintings have much greater stability because they contain fewer contradictory events (or because their contradictions are balanced, as in the case of the diagonal directions) and are made up of proportionally larger shapes and less diverse combinations than 1960s paintings like *Shift* (1963) or *Shiver* (1964), yielding slower, self-possessed effects. In front of them, viewers never lose sight of the component units; they are never mesmerised or subjugated, but elated – invited on a peaceful journey of composing and recomposing images

(discrete images and cloud-like or shadow-like images). Whereas the
1960s black-and-white paintings created effects of rupture and agitation,
the accumulation of which opened up a conclusive state of pacification,
the recent paintings never depart from a clear structure – and the clear
perception of it.[5] Instead, they take one along a continuous view, slowly
and harmoniously changing, made up of a succession of black-and-white
shapes organised rhythmically in horizontal rows and diagonal fluxes,
which contradict themselves so as to create a certain poise. Where the
1960s paintings were like quick runs, going in many directions before
settling as an overall field of contrasts, the recent paintings are like
promenades or strolls – what the Italians call *passeggiate*, an activity that
involves the pleasure of being together – where viewers first take hold of
a harmonious whole before understanding that it is made up of several
different events. These never really contradict one another – unless for
balance – but lead into one another.

The black-and-white paintings not only enter into a dialogue with the
1960s works, but take stock of every painting experience Riley has
created during a long career. In 2009 she remarked: 'I had to work
through the black-and-white paintings before I could even begin to think
about possibilities of colour.'[6] The recent paintings stem from the
reverse: a working through the colour paintings has enabled her to come
to a new series of black-and-white works. Thus, when using an elongated
format, as in *Cascando* (2015), she particularly emphasises the spatial
effects of the horizontal structure, which elicit a swaying aspect, with
some lines moving forward and others backward, as in her recent stripe
paintings such as *Allegro Red* (2014), painted concurrently with the
black-and-white paintings. This is also an effect that Riley had discovered
early on, in a small group of divisionist paintings from 1959–60, in
particular *Pink Landscape* (1960). The composition of *Cascando* is
stabilised by the way in which the top and bottom of the picture are
mostly made up of identical equilateral triangles. This recalls how some
large curve paintings, such as *Blue (La Réserve)* (2010), anchored the
free movement of curves between a nearly continuous base and lintel.
The identical triangles in the bottom row of *Cascando* include – almost
unnoticeably – one concave curved triangular shape, while there are four

such shapes in the top row (a 1:1 scale cartoon shows that the slight
modulation of shapes in the bottom line was a late decision). The
animation of the horizontal structure by diagonals, which flow up and
down, harks back – albeit with a 180 degree rotation – to a device that
Riley first used in her zig paintings from the late 1980s/early 1990s,
where rhomboid shapes articulated diagonals across a vertical structure.
They seem to be doing to the horizontal stripe paintings – which are
their immediate predecessors – what the zig paintings did to the vertical
stripe paintings of the early 1980s.

In thus revisiting her own past, Riley does not forsake her allegiance
to the principles of modernism, which entails that each work of art is an
adventure with an unforeseeable result reached through a process of
trial and error, and not the illustration of a pre-existing idea or the mere
formalisation of a floating image. Riley simply leaves aside – as she has
long since done – the teleology that went with modernism up until the
1970s, in order to direct the viewers' attention to the particular effects
created by each painting.

The scale of the new paintings makes them not only a visual
experience, but a bodily experience too. Far from inducing the 'radical
disembodiment' associated with Riley's 1960s works, these paintings
have their roots in the here and now of a bodily perception that can only
function in the presence of a stable object. We identify an image on the
surface of the painting at the same time as the image's complex
perceptual effects make themselves felt, whether or not we are
conscious of them, concentrating on them or simply looking while paying
no particular attention. But unlike the large curve paintings, where 'one is
unavoidably reminded of human gestures and movements',[7] the new
black-and-white paintings are thoroughly non-figurative, without any
suggestion of bodies: they are to be experienced by an incarnated
eyesight, which is not replicated nor even hinted at in them. They are
more like landscapes, or rather, because they are reduced to a contrast
of black and white, they are like the movements of light and shadows
that you can experience on a stable surface or moving across a field.
Although this field is that of a picture or wall, it relates to experiences
made in nature: 'It did begin in Cornwall with walks on the cliffs,' Riley

has acknowledged. 'You walk one way and you walk back and the light is different.'[8] This is where the address of these paintings rests – not on the basis of a teleological notion of progress to which viewers would be led indiscriminately through excitation – but on that of a one-on-one relationship. What we experience first in these paintings are some harmonious certainties (and our uncertain world demands some certainties because we are lost enough in our everyday lives), which never lock themselves onto closed identities but, within a prolonged viewing, are at our disposal to be freely and pleasurably analysed, broken apart, recomposed, started anew – each time in a personal way.

Bridget Riley, exhibition catalogue, Galerie Max Hetzler, Paris and Holzwarth Publications, Berlin, 2015, pp.27–32.

ÉRIC DE CHASSEY

1   Giorgio Agamben, 'Philosophical Archaeology', *Law and Critique*, vol.20, no.3, 2009, p.223.

2   Anton Ehrenzweig, *The Hidden Order of Art: A Study in the Psychology of Artistic Imagination*, Weidenfeld & Nicolson, London, 1967, p.85. On Riley's Op paintings and their cultural context, see Frances Follin, *Embodied Visions: Bridget Riley, Op Art and the Sixties*, Thames & Hudson, London, 2004.

3   Bridget Riley, 'About Curves: Bridget Riley in Conversation with Paul Moorhouse', in *Bridget Riley: The Curve Paintings 1961–2014*, exhibition catalogue, Ridinghouse, London and De La Warr Pavilion, Bexhill on Sea, 2015, p.53.

4   Bridget Riley, conversation with the author, London, 23 March 2015.

5   In 1965, Riley wrote: 'The basis of my paintings is this: that in each of them a particular situation is stated. Certain elements within that situation remain constant, others precipitate the destruction of themselves by themselves. Recurrently, as a result of the cyclic movement of repose, disturbance and repose, the original situation is restated.' Bridget Riley, 'Perception Is the Medium' (1965), in Robert Kudielka (ed), *The Eye's Mind: Bridget Riley, Collected Writings 1965–2009*, Thames & Hudson and Ridinghouse, London, 2009, pp.89–90.

6   Bridget Riley, 'Work' (2009), *ibid.*, p.57.

7   See Robert Kudielka, 'Abstract Figuration: On Bridget Riley's Recent Curve Paintings', in Paul Moorhouse (ed), *Bridget Riley*, exhibition catalogue, Tate Publishing, London, 2003, p.155.

8   Riley, conversation with the author, *op.cit.*

How Seeing Feels

Richard Shiff

'Phenomenology? That's the study of how things feel.' I recall being amused by this thumbnail definition, offered long ago by a student more clued-in than I. It anchored an imposing six-syllable term to two words each so monosyllabically light that the concept threatened to drift into signifying anything or, just as likely, nothing. If 'how things feel' is the issue, what counts as a *thing*? It might be an object, event, action, emotion, condition or any number of other entities. When do we *feel* a thing? Are we not feeling things – or merely feeling – at every instant? Feeling might depend on a thing entering within range of our senses, yet we may also need to intend to feel a particular thing or be psychologically predisposed. Is distraction from things a thing? Do we feel *this* as well? Phenomenology, I thought, ought to answer such questions.

Phenomena are facts or occurrences that appear and are perceived in (or at) their appearance. One way or another, in a literal sense or metaphorically, such things are destined to be seen. We see an object, but we also 'see' the point of a discussion, which is a 'thing' too. Even extrasensory phenomena are regarded as perceptible, despite the paradox. Phenomenology involves the study, discourse or theory of perception – the study of appearance and our consciousness of, or feeling of, seeing a thing. We develop a philosophical form of phenomenology to lend words to appearances, giving speech to the eye: *phenomeno-*, the thing that happens or appears; *-logy*, ultimately from *legein*, to speak, to collect thoughts, to theorise. Phenomenology theorises appearance. As so often, pursuit of a definition becomes tautological: our terms for theory and theorising have an etymological sense of seeing or forming a view; the Greek and Latin variants of the term *theoria* refer to a thing looked at. So phenomenology looks at looking.

Despite the pitfalls of generalisation, here is a theory: vision or seeing not only provides sensory access to a thing but is itself a thing, a phenomenon as much as a faculty, method, or means. It seems that how seeing feels has long been Bridget Riley's central concern. 'Modern painting is about building a way of looking,' she states; 'it has less to do with *what* exactly you are seeing than with *how* you are made to look at it… We feel with our eyes more than we see.'[1] Inadvertently, she arrives at the 'how things feel' definition. When we see things as the targets of our sight, our vision renders them focused and precise. We can also feel what such seeing is, or how it is. 'Whatever one looks at,' Riley has said, 'one cannot help but look through one's own sight.'[2] Are we able to *focus* our seeing on seeing? This would be utterly distracting. So most of us, most of the time, do no more than glance at seeing.

Cause and effect in one

Riley the artist doubles as phenomenologist. With painting as the vehicle, a phenomenological probe of appearances proceeds more directly than by a theory of 'how things feel', even when the theory advances in monosyllables of plain language. 'The only way anyone can enter my painting is by looking,' Riley says; 'there's no theory in them'.[3] She nevertheless remains as much a thinking artist as a feeling artist. In her studio, the two converge: 'You cannot deal with thought directly outside practice as a painter: "doing" is essential in order to find out what form your thought takes.'[4] Just as Riley's vision informs her thought, her verbal accounts complement her visual pathways. As a skilled writer, she succeeds in evoking a factor of perception so elusive that it finds no satisfying discursive analogue. She acknowledges the fundamental phenomenological impasse: 'Sensations – visual sensations – defy attention. The moment they are focused upon they evaporate.'[5] But even if focusing loses its phenomenological object of attention, it may produce focus itself as a phantom presence. In this shadowy awareness, seeing becomes an object of seeing.

Riley reached this phenomenological intuition, which she attributed also to Georges Seurat. In the deep blacks of his drawings, he somehow conveyed what 'we cannot *quite* see'.[6] This was Riley's way of indicating Seurat's challenge to perception. He was her predecessor in the abstraction of visual phenomena, though he worked before the

   RICHARD SHIFF

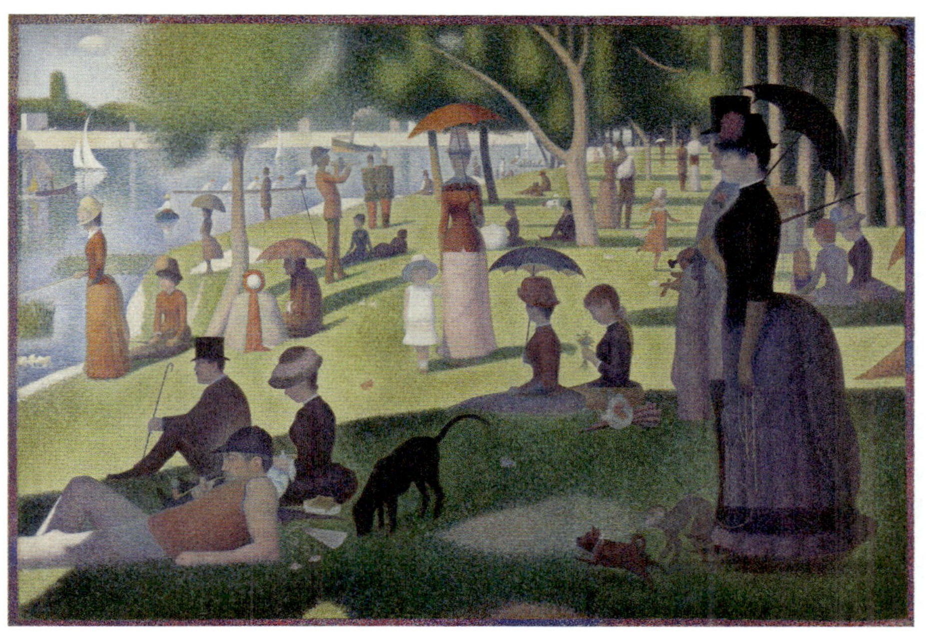

Georges Seurat
A Sunday on La Grande Jatte – 1884 1884–86
Oil on canvas
207.5 × 308.1 cm | 81¾ × 121¼ in
The Art Institute of Chicago

emergence of so-called abstract art (art that develops imagery devoid of manifest representational reference). Along with other works of Seurat's brief career, *A Sunday on La Grande Jatte – 1884* (1884–86) – however depictive and richly allusive – demonstrates that 'perception itself had to be examined, methodically objectified and built up into a technique'. Riley's analysis leads to a curious formulation: 'Seurat looks *into* perception and shows it to be the activity which produces what it sees.'[7] To look *into* perception is to look *at* nothing. Identifiable 'things' appear only on the far side of the perceptual process in the form of conceptualised information, available through cognitive association. Within perception itself lies only sensation. At the putative source of visual experience, we discover nothing fixed in the way that 'things' are; we find instead the mobile means of our seeing, which precedes the things. Our discovery is so intimate that it feels as if we created it. Perception remains the primary 'thing' we 'feel' – cause and effect in one.

Along such lines, Riley has more to say with respect to Seurat, who illuminated phantom experience:

> Seurat concentrates all his efforts on organising, in the full light of consciousness, a coherent perceptual structure, and as a consequence he extracts and focuses upon precisely that which normally escapes attention… He arouses the somnambulist element in perception. [His] intent scrutiny of phenomena, and the painting out of perception, step by step, as though it had been mapped, build up together a perfect hallucination.[8]

Riley's commentary not only interprets Seurat's art but assesses her own effort, for which Seurat had been an early model. She describes her experience in the studio: 'In order to see one had to paint and through that activity found what could be seen.'[9]

Why would Seurat's art, and perhaps Riley's as well, result in 'hallucination'? Novel perception – perception released from confirming what is already known – will seem hallucinatory unhinged from any base in fact other than its own reality.[10] In Seurat's case, the already known was Parisian behaviour, a common topic of illustration. He did not limit his art to its predetermined theme; his perception generated a dream-world existing in and for itself. Perception – 'pure perception', Riley might say – remains a dream until an edifice of reality is constructed to house it.[11] Parisian life was the reality before Seurat, and it remained after him. But his way of illuminating and colouring life at the Ile de la Grande Jatte became the dream. We know from our sleep that dreams are real when experienced. Immediate perception, like a dream, has no foundation, finds no corroboration beyond its sensory feel. This immediacy – a sensory and cognitive state – is not confined to the instant. It can continue through time. Even as perception remains spatially and temporally evasive, the perception *of* a thing secures it, inserting it into whatever reality the thing defines through its identity and attributes. Perception in isolation continues to present the feeling of 'how things feel' – but minus the things.

As I reach this introspective conclusion, Riley leads me along. She has arrived ahead of me, guided by her art of sensation. A painting spurs recognition, she says, 'but of no specific instance… It's the recognition of the sensation *without* the actual incident which prompted it.'[12] Colour is such a sensation: 'We usually see colour as the colour *of* something – it is not a natural thing to see colour simply as itself alone, unless, of course, we happen also to be painters.'[13] A painting like *Sentito (Blue)* (2013) prompts us to see 'colour simply as itself.' Horizontal bands of equal width, each bearing a distinct hue in relation to its neighbours, project an array of colour that lacks the complications that would stem from variant shapes and tonalities. We perceive the entirety of the uninflected field, which is sufficiently wide to generate flashes of peripheral chromatic activity from an agreeable viewing distance, scaled to the relationship of our body to the size of the painting. Tempted to draw closer, we focus on pairs or triples of colours, or compare one pair to another in its proximity, noticing how no particular colour appears always the same.

In *Sentito (Blue)* – as well as in *Aria* (2012), a vertically oriented counterpart – warm colours predominate (reds, oranges, yellows, violets), causing the relatively limited use of blues and greens to establish a high-pitched drama. In such works, Riley's geometry remains passively static while her colour tenses into active, even aggressive, movement. Individual colours jostle for a forward position, while none truly recedes. Our field of vision becomes saturated with after-images, and each band generates an arc of its own hue, in phantom interaction with surrounding hues. Collectively, the effect intensifies beyond what we might expect from the individual colours, which are neither aggressively strident nor recessively mellow. The ordinary becomes unusual. Many of Riley's hues are products of complex mixture, such as one featured in *Sentito (Blue)* that she calls 'dark yellow', an ochre or olive tone. In the context of her colour compositions, even the oddest of hues gives the impression of being central to the spectrum. Riley's art transforms impure hues into pure, projective perception.

Seurat set the precedent. His bits of colour, tonal value, light and contour live apart from the figures and environment they define; and his result is not just hallucinatory but, as Riley puts it, a 'perfect' hallucination. How could perfection characterise a configured dream or hallucination? She also designates Seurat's result as the perception of the 'im-perceptible'. I will retain her hyphen, which encourages reading the word as a positive even as it becomes a negative.[14] In principle, such unstable relations can hardly be perfected. Seurat's representational art, like Riley's abstraction, performs the near-impossible act of catching perception on the fly – making the im-perceptible perceptible and doing it perfectly, that is to say, incontrovertibly. To Seurat's impossibility, she adds her own. Seeing her colour is to dream a reality.

Commenting on Seurat, Riley introduces a consequential distinction. She suggests that her predecessor perfected his technique by *not* perfecting it. With a qualification that might itself escape notice, she refers to the painter's use of 'the dot' as an 'uninflected and non-referential mark [that] draws no attention to itself'.[15] Her language of negatives states what was so positive and productive about Seurat. Using an uninflected, non-referential mark, he developed neither a period style nor a personal style. With knowledge of art history in mind, we nevertheless associate his dot with the pointillist method of the neo-Impressionists who followed him. Riley grasps the irony: Seurat intended his technique to remain anonymous and ordinary within its cultural context. His mark presents colour and light but has no expressive personality. A dot in *La Grande Jatte* is not 'Seurat', just as a stripe of solid colour in *Sentito (Blue)* or *Aria* is not 'Riley'. Such an impersonal look leads into the im-perceptible – the perceptual experience you cannot foresee but can only discover, as if it were yours alone to experience yet independent of your existence. We perceive the im-perceptible as objective, removed from our subjective prejudices and desires. It insinuates itself; it imposes. We sense it whether seeking it or not.

In Seurat's representational art, Riley found objectivity—an impersonal abstraction. And in Egypt, she discovered an ancient version of the same: 'The Egyptians were not individual artists in the way we might think of artists today… There was no expression as we understand it but there was an all-embracing objectivity.'[16] Encounters with Egyptian art while travelling in winter 1979–80 inspired Riley's use of vertical bands of uniform colour. These are the antecedents of the horizontal bands in *Sentito (Blue)* and the vertical ones in *Aria*, energised in similar ways through their chromatic interaction. Riley limited the number of hues, though she extended them across a broad range: red, yellow, blue, turquoise, black and white (*Après Midi*, 1981, and *Serenissima*, 1982, are examples). Egyptian painting set these colours into a context of narrative figuration, which, as Riley realised, was straightforwardly 'processional'. The colours followed one after another as equals, as if marking out a beat or rhythm. The relatively narrow stripes of Riley's abstract version of Egyptian painting ensure that no figurative allusions emerge from this depersonalised element of drawing, a vehicle for colour and its multiple, light-generating interactions. Riley made her black-and-white stripes somewhat narrower than their chromatic neighbours because the two tonal extremes carry extra weight in the evolving order – 'the white airing the painting and black hammering out the rhythm'.[17] By the time she adapted the Egyptian palette to her abstract art, she had for two decades been using assistants to render the final versions of her works. This division of labour guaranteed that individualised expression would gain no hold over her viewer's aesthetic experience. She trained her assistants 'to apply the paint without emphasis and with no trace of handling' – skill without artifice.[18]

Nature is abstract

The principles to be derived from Riley's mature abstract art can be
traced to her early experience working from nature. She practiced life
drawing, where the usual aim is to deploy devices of representation
ingeniously yet as objectively as possible, to capture perceived features
of the human model. I say 'as objectively as possible', because mainline
teaching in modern art and aesthetics establishes subjectivity at the core
of observation. According to the common claim, our actual vision
presents neither an objective reality nor the permanent, ideal form
imagined by classically oriented minds of the past; instead, we see only
those features of the world consistent with our personal perspective,
both psychological and physiological. Modern truths, supposedly, are
relative, contingent, indeterminate. Theorists have often invoked
anecdotal evidence from landscape painters who realised that no two
artists, situated in the same place, would produce identical or even
nearly identical representations of the scene before them.[19]

We can understand the doctrine of 'truth is relative' if we accept that
it is itself relative. We can observe the transiency and instability of
appearances as the only reality we know, accepting this reality as
objective experience; in turn, pointless arguments over the dualistic
opposition of subjectivity to objectivity can be abandoned. Although
fleeting and dream-like, the experience of colour is our – everyone's –
'pure perception'. Any sensation of colour is objective because we
cannot deny it. It requires no proof. 'A perceptual judgment can only
refer to a single percept which can never re-exist,' CS Peirce wrote; 'and
if I judge that [an object] appears red when it did not appear red [either
to others or at a later moment], it must, at least, be acknowledged that it
appeared to appear red.'[20] Personal sensation that lacks corroboration
need not be regarded as subjective, as opposed to objective. Every
sensation is real; and if this conclusion seems absolutist, to claim that all
sensation is subjective is equally absolutist. Unmotivated acts of seeing –
'pure' seeing – undermine the subjective/objective distinction.

Riley's art dodges the ideological absolutism that our customary
separation of subjectivity from objectivity enforces. Starting from the

subjectivity of experience as an all-too-available given, she has long
sought 'the somnambulist element in perception', the factor of
experience she discovers in Seurat, recognised as objective – as real as
anything and unencumbered by arbitrary cultural associations.[21] She
often recalls the tonic effect of her experience of figure drawing in 1949,
under the tutelage of Sam Rabin at Goldsmiths, London:

> He taught that it was only by the patient study of appearance and by
> making the effort to understand what one saw that one could
> discover the particular kind of information needed for drawing. He
> would say, 'What is the model doing?' and repeat this question until
> he received the reply 'She is standing'. He would then ask, 'Is your
> drawing standing?'[22] Such a judgement ought to be, in Riley's terms,
> 'pure' – that is, objective.[23]

Life Drawing (Lying Figure, Back View) (1949) belongs to Riley's time
at Goldsmiths; this drawing succeeds at 'lying' or settling into its
environment, as if the effect of gravity as well as the body itself were
represented by the form. The figure projects a natural sense of weight,
captured within a complex play of diagonals and curves. We surmise that
human bodies are symmetrical, but we rarely perceive a body this way.
Its living animation, its continual movement, assures that an asymmetrical
rendering – classical contrapposto is an example – will be charged with
verisimilitude. Whether with empathy for the natural balance and rhythm
of the body or with deliberation on the means of drawing, Riley not only
animated but also stabilised the form of her model by tracing out its
contrapuntal elements: a calf inverts the curve of a buttock; a thigh rises
from a declining hip; an upper arm bends to become a strut-like forearm;
intervals between contours mark the proportions of limbs to torso. From
the start, Riley contained the figure within an implied orthogonal order,
indicated by the cruciform articulation of the upper back and shoulders.
When I retrace the lines and intervals of this drawing, when I mimic
Riley's gestures or her model's, I feel a rhythm, hers as much as that of
the model, and most of all the rhythm of the means. The feeling is real –
objective – and I perceive an 'abstract' form in the sense that Seurat's art

is abstract, achieving its figural ends by limited means, having recourse to a few elemental visual devices. *Lying Figure* relies primarily on the use of contour lines and tonal variation in the lines themselves; the latter induces a sense of illumination and volume wherever the anatomical features establish a turn in space. Riley's drawing is a study in observation, not style. It records her intimate optical and tactile experience, which does not deny perception its objectivity.

'What is of prime importance is that the hand responds to what is seen', Riley stated recently, concerning the discipline of drawing.[24] The play of echoing curves and reversing angles in *Lying Figure* anticipates what the artist would accomplish four to five decades later in paintings such as *High Sky* (1991), *Lagoon 2* (1997) and *Rêve* (1999). The arcing edges of various shapes in *Rêve* merge into diagonals, becoming straight; the effect recalls the understanding of form to be derived from the bend in the elbow of the supporting arm in *Lying Figure*.[25] In both, as Riley says, 'the hand [that draws] responds to what is seen'. The impetus to move from the likes of *Lying Figure* to the likes of *Rêve* came when Riley raised a new question: 'So, what is it that is seen? In earlier times I used to draw the thing seen, now I see the thing drawn.'[26] The phenomenologist in Riley might put it this way: 'I used to draw the thing (the figure), now I draw the seeing.'

When interviewed, Riley continues to muse over the centrality of the example of Seurat along with what Sam Rabin once taught her. Seurat had organised colours and tones 'onto a coherent formal basis [and this] is a kind of basis of abstract painting – the materials you have'.[27] An artist's materials (paint, graphite) and the forms they manipulate (lines, shapes, hues, values) are the elements of abstraction, whether or not the technique or method is applied to representational ends. Rabin's instructive question – 'What is the model doing?' – evolved through Riley's early practice as a general challenge to herself: What is the line, the colour, the form, *doing*? Like an experimental phenomenologist, she turned her attention from the model to the means:

> I had drawn from my experience of looking at other works of art
> [learning from Seurat], of being informed by a tradition that drew

                                                  RICHARD SHIFF

from nature, from external reality [Rabin's teaching]. I reversed this
and approached it from the opposite direction… starting to work
from the pictorial elements themselves.[28]

To determine what each graphic element might do became Riley's
concern. Whether the answers would arise out of subjectivity or
objectivity was irrelevant. The required judgment would be based in
sensation, not dualistic logic. Throughout the 1960s, Riley investigated the
basic forms of straight lines, curving lines, squares, circles, ovals, triangles
and the like. She would ask: 'What is the triangle doing?' This was
enough to generate a concerted effort: 'I looked around for something
that I felt needed doing… The urgent need was to find something that
had to be done… Just finding out was a necessary first step.'[29] She did
not ask what *she* could do to a triangle; rather, she asked what the
triangle might do to realise more of its potential, as if the effort were
collaborative. The triangle, as familiar as it was, needed aesthetic work,
phenomenological work.

Abstraction is natural

In 1962, Riley created *Tremor*, a diagonal grid of interlocking black-and-
white triangles that gradually reveals a dynamic structure with a certain
degree of symmetry. Because she painted the black triangles on a white
ground, the black forms can be regarded as positive and the white forms
as negative.[30] All of the triangles within *Tremor* are essentially equilateral.
If not strictly so, they leave this impression within the context of the
design. Some have one convex side, generated by using an edge of the
triangle as the radius of a curve arcing outward; if the same curve were
to continue to complete a circle, it would subtend six triangles. Other
forms have one concave side, generated by using the adjacent, 'negative'
triangle to supply the radius of a curve arcing inward. The convex edge of
a black triangle is shared as the concave edge of a white triangle, and
vice versa; correspondingly, adjacent black-and-white equilaterals share
their straight edges. I assume that Riley chose not to allow any triangle

to have more than one curving side because the form would cease to be sufficiently triangular.[31] Possessing two curved sides would be something that a triangle can *not* do. *Tremor* demonstrates that the anomaly of a triangle having one curved side exists within the potential of the geometrical form. Did this potential exist before Riley perceived it? A firm answer would require someone who is more of an idealist than I am.

For *Tremor*, Riley developed aggregate areas of uniform tonality by selectively distributing the different configurations of her three triangular forms. A black triangle with a convex edge contains the greatest amount of blackness; its corresponding white triangle with a concave edge contains the least amount of whiteness. These conjoined forms produce the darkest cumulative tonalities of *Tremor*. From dark to light, Riley developed a scale of values as she arranged combinations of her black triangular forms with each other and with their white triangular reserves: all convex (the darkest effect); convex alternating with equilateral; all equilateral; convex alternating with concave (equal in resultant tone to all equilateral, yet different in optical texture); equilateral alternating with concave; all concave (the lightest effect).

Gathering her six variations into distinct areas within *Tremor*, Riley created broad fields of uniform darkness and lightness, generating an optical composition of flat or superimposed planes, each distinguished by its particular tonality. By using an area composed of the basic equilateral triangle in two compositional locations, she brought the total number of planes to seven. I referred to a degree of symmetry in this work: each of the planar areas of tonality has an inverted counterpart at the opposite side of the panel. For example, the darkest area at the lower right, aggregating as a triangular shape pointing upward, corresponds to the lightest area at the upper left, aggregating as a triangular shape pointing downward. A central area, composed of alternating rows of convex and concave triangles, extends as a parallelogram from top to bottom and counterbalances itself with its tilt. This form at the centre of *Tremor*, however complex, seems to establish a neutral, middle position. The other areas become extremes or, to invoke a bodily metaphor, extremities. Virtually simultaneously, *Tremor* induces perceptions of symmetry and asymmetry, of the inorganic and the organic — a phenomenological wonder.

Forever seeking challenges, Riley recently asked once again: What might a triangle do? In her black-and-white paintings of the 1960s, she had established fields of optical vibration. She now recognised that her equilateral, convex and concave triangles could create perceptual wonders of a less definable kind, designs lacking the distinct areas of optical planarity that characterise *Tremor*. When distributed with greater irregularity (though not randomly), her three variations on the triangle tend to evoke transient illumination — a sense of atmospheric change or fleeting shadows. In *Clair Obscur* (2015), Seurat's moments of phantom perception have become Riley's abstraction — a pseudo-naturalistic case of abstract art. She reduced the orderly articulation of surface pattern that had been typical of her earlier work in black and white; this increased the subtlety of the effect across the whole while edging it closer to nature's chance.

Riley had been doing much the same when working with the motif of a linear circle, as in *Composition with Circles 2* (2000) — black acrylic applied to a plastered wall of 45 feet. Her irregular distribution of overlapping circles created local areas of endlessly altering density, perceived as fluctuation in light and acceleration or deceleration of movement. Struck by the shifting configuration of circles, our sensation becomes an organic pulse, changing as we feel our emotions change. Something more complex yet more elemental is happening: our perception is not a strict guide to our emotion, nor is our sensation the singular cause of how we feel. We cannot so easily graph the connections between self and image, which remain in formation, perpetually incipient. *Composition with Circles 2*, like *Clair Obscur*, represents a feeling, but not one that can bear a name or any other identity. This feeling lacks a definite thing to be felt. As Riley said of Seurat, here 'the unfathomable appears in the guise of total visibility'.[32] Translation: what cannot be perceived (the unfathomable, the im-perceptible) appears disguised as our objective perception. The statement amounts to a contradiction of a contradiction. Like a double negative, it results in a positive — our undeniable feeling.

For clarification, turn to nature, not geometry. In the horizontal expanse of *Clair Obscur*, the accumulation of small local changes, difficult to isolate or stabilise, threatens to collapse into nothingness. Despite the compound grid that results from the continuity of the diagonal edges of the triangles, no reliable patterns emerge. *Clair Obscur* may strike the viewer as all too close to chaos, yet what we dismiss as chaos approaches the reality of ordinary illumination. Another of Riley's recent compositions of triangles, *Rustle 2* (2015), seems to adopt a device of alternation: if we consider the diagonals that fall from top right to bottom left, every second linear row is perfectly straight, containing no curves. But a correction is necessary: the putative rule, if it ever was one, has an exception; one of the 'straight' diagonals contains a single concave curve.[33] Presumably, Riley felt that a bit less blackness or a bit more variation in tone was needed in this local area (close to the bottom left corner of the composition). She may have been reducing a sense of order that had become slightly too strong. Perhaps the perception of a minimal degree of order – *and no more* – amounts to 'pure' reality, an 'experience just beyond our visual grasp'.[34] Anything better understood becomes an ideological imposition on experience, a logical conclusion that nullifies forms of experience that would otherwise occur.

Riley seeks the very edge of perception, the moment of sensation at which our conscious awareness operates furthest from conceptual order, but not so far that we sense nothing memorable, nothing at all. Her art opens a path, a way into 'somnambulist' consciousness. By presenting art so close to 'pure perception', Riley brushes against the reality of chaos and the taut nerves of existence. Call the sensation immediacy, or just call it sensation. Her paintings project sensation – seeing in the raw. No previous experience required.

As seeing happens

'Pure perception – untrammeled perception – is very surprising', Riley remarks: '[It's] startling, exciting, powerful and beautiful. It's a kind of primary experience.'[35] She is adept at staging the conditions of 'pure

                                                                                       RICHARD SHIFF

perception'. She does it whenever she asks a version of the question,
'What can X do?' 'X' might be a geometrical form, a graphic configuration,
a format, a size or shape of support, a range of colour, a quality of scale.
It might be an 'X' I would never imagine existing, had it not become an
object of Riley's visual study – a novel 'thing' to be perceived. She is
both the observer and the creator of her 'X', engaged in phenomenological
reciprocity.

During the early 1980s, Riley explored the potential of the Egyptian
palette and the use of vertical stripes, eventually complicating the
chromatic interactions by eliminating black and white, which had
provided positions of optical stability and rest, and by injecting additional
colours. She then wondered what would happen if she introduced a set
of diagonals to intersect with the verticals. The aptly titled *Things of
Change* (1986) and *Out There* (1987) were among her results. Their
relative regularity is misleading, because every one of her putative rules
seems to develop an exception that becomes a salient feature of the
composition. Each exception signifies the play of perception – the artist's
response to seeing chromatic and other formal relations just as they
emerge, as phenomena that assume precedence over the fulfilment of
any preconceived order or structure. In *Out There*, unbroken areas of
colour, primarily yellows, expand and relax the general pattern, as if the
artist were reacting to a tension that needed to be relieved, generated by
sharp blues and greens woven into yellows, oranges and rose-reds. No
theory predicts that nominally cool blues and greens will threaten to
dominate nominally warm hues in any particular context; it simply
happens that this can happen. The reverse is equally possible. The
situation at hand must be observed as it occurs. Riley then takes action,
adjusting the configuration and balance of chromatic forces to intensify
the emergent qualities of the image, stopping short of reducing the
image to disorder. The pattern of *Out There* is an intellectual construct,
conceived as a project to realise. Its disruption marks the artist's
experience of immediate feeling.

Patterns involving vertical divisions, coupled with diagonals that slant
in only one direction – say, downward from top right to bottom left –
produce a jagged falling movement as the two directional vectors intersect

to create various parallelograms and rhomboids. If the tendency of Westerners is to scan a visual display from left to right, then a work such as Riley's *Vespertino* (1988) will give the impression of a gradual fall that circles back on itself in a compensatory movement. Just as the fall or downward tumble and bounce of elements proceeds from upper left to lower right, the strong effect of beams of colour and light from upper right to lower left draws the eye back toward an initial focus. Riley's works of this general type (with diagonals opposing verticals) vary according to the presence or absence of black and white, as well as the introduction of fractional units, such as vertical and diagonal divisions that might measure only a half or a third of the basic unit: see, for example, *High Sky* and *Reflection 2* (1994). All works of this type induce a tension between an evasive centre and a periphery that seems to impinge on it. Riley's distribution of colours converts her grid-like order of verticals and diagonals into such a dynamic play of forces that it is difficult to apply specific terms of analysis. One expects a rectangular composition to have a centre, a periphery and an external boundary; yet, in a work like *High Sky*, such a differentiation of areas and forces does not occur. Instead there is a constant relating and re-relating of formal elements. Such works live in immediate experience; they exist by themselves and in themselves. They are instances of seeing and are to be seen as such.

During the late 1990s, Riley introduced regulated curves (segments of circles), as if this type of curve were now her 'X'. The results extend from works such as *Lagoon 2*, where the curve is relatively restrained, to works such as *Rêve, Painting with Verticals 3* (2006), *Red with Red 1* (2007) and the wall painting *Rajasthan* (2012), where individual curves assert much greater presence in the composition. The irregular outside edges of *Rajasthan* developed from Riley's practice of using collage as a study technique in her studio. She could manipulate a composition in progress by creating a full-scale mock-up with painted papers fastened temporarily to the wall – quickly adjusting the positions of the forms, altering the shapes, or changing the colours. With collage as the medium, the study could proceed close to the pace of perception itself, or at least within range of the rapidity of the artist's changing impressions. To maintain the pace, she neglected trimming the edges of her various paper shapes as she happened to place them near the rectangular borders of her composition.

At some point, Riley took an interest in how the violation of the outside borders by oversized elements of collage enhanced the ambiguity of figure and ground in the entire composition, an effect she had encouraged in earlier work and which had intrigued her for many years. To recognise that a firm distinction of figure and ground is inessential to pictorial composition is to move closer to immediate sensation by eliminating a certain degree of conceptual artifice and perceptual delay. Perceptual psychologists accept the figure–ground relationship as fundamental, but an artist need not adhere to psychological theory. In painting, the figure–ground relationship is largely a holdover from representational practice that transfers into abstraction. Metaphorically, if the figure is alive, its ground is dead. Why not bring both figure and ground to life? As Riley increased the size of individual units of colour in works based on verticals, diagonals and curves, her shapes exerted physical pressure on the rectilinear format. In *Red with Red 1*, for instance, a single compound shape of orange-red extends from the top to the bottom limits of the canvas; its edges are part curved (both convex and concave), part diagonal and part vertical. This single shape, along with closely allied areas of the same hue that are easily imagined as its continuation, includes the sole vertical edges present within the composition. If only because these verticals echo the lateral limits of the rectangular support, analysis might conclude that the entirety of the orange-red area constitutes a ground for adjacent areas of rose-red and deep blue. Yet, if we glance just to the right or left of these vertical divisions, perception changes dramatically; we will imagine the blue as the ground, or the rose-red. As our act of seeing continues, no ground is ground, no figure is figure. Caught within seeing, no way out emerges.

Something similar happens in *Painting with Verticals 3*. If we accept contact at a single point as a point of continuity then three of the four constituent colours in this painting occupy complex shapes that extend from top to bottom of the composition. At moments, they seem to constitute figures; at other moments, grounds. The reality may be both at once, a logical contradiction. Figures that meet at a point of tangency are inherently ambiguous with regard to position and perspectival direction. The two shapes, usually comprised of both straight and curved edges, intersect in knife-like cuts while seeming also to bend as if hinged. Here again, perception, which is not a faculty of reason, has no obligation to be logical and non-contradictory. A complex shape may contain an area that seems overlapped by a more assertive form adjacent to it, while another area of the same shape projects forward. The green form at the upper left of *Painting with Verticals 3* appears to lie behind the self-contained forms of light blue and orange that it surrounds; yet the same green becomes an aggressive wedge (part diagonal and part curve) in relation to the blue to its right. Such relationships prevent perception from stabilising. The painting appears animated; and as we observe it, it changes.

Returning to *Rajasthan*, a composition designed to be painted on a white wall: its areas of interior white connect to the exterior and convey the spatial ambiguity that characterises *Red with Red 1* and *Painting with Verticals 3*. This ambiguity becomes especially evident when we notice that there are two diagonal slices of white in the shape of parallelograms, both surrounded by areas of fully chromatic colour and both positioned in what is more or less the lower register of the composition. At the extreme left edge of this lower register, an area of white in the shape of an incomplete parallelogram opens to the exterior of the painting (the wall or nominal ground); this form becomes both figure-like and ground-like as it exists both inside and outside the coloured shapes adjacent to it. And at the extreme right edge of the lower register, a parallelogram in red terminates an implied movement of what are now four similar forms, left to right, that establish an accentuated rhythm or beat.

To this observation, another must be added – not for the sake of analytical consistency, but to acknowledge the insistent plenitude of perception. The two white parallelograms may have the same measurements but are not visually the same 'thing'. One cuts just slightly into the adjacent green and orange shapes above it, which assert the same diagonal direction. The other continues the diagonal it shares with its adjacent shapes, in this case red and green. In other words, one of the white forms is slightly off-register, while the other accords with the implicit

RICHARD SHIFF

pattern in its locality, a tempered diagonal raster. Is the off-register element
an inexplicable anomaly? Perhaps inexplicable, but not an anomaly, for a
green parallelogram near the top left of the composition performs the
same overlapping or cutting action. It does the same 'thing'. How does
this 'thing' 'feel'? Is the green parallelogram affected by awareness of its
white counterpart and vice versa? We might as well ask the general
phenomenological question, 'How do things feel?' Both question and
answer are of the moment. Even the syntax conveys ambiguity. Do the
feelings belong to the perceiver or to the perceived? To grasp the nature
of perception, avoid dealing with such a question, for its either/or
structure denies the fluidity perception sustains. Whatever I myself
observe can only be of the moment and is changeable. My cumulative
experience of *Rajasthan* has led to no comprehension whatever, even
though each perception seems to touch on a number of intriguing
relationships that tempt me to describe them. When I do, my effort at
description distracts from my perception. A consolation: the engagement
with words has its own feeling for whatever the sensation may be worth.

If I were to elaborate further on the contradictory spatial relations that
Riley's forms suggest, my verbal account would become ever more
distanced from the immediacy of what happens in perception, when
perception encounters her painting. How things feel – how seeing feels –
is Riley's issue. Seeing answers questions of seeing; description answers
to description. Riley imagined Seurat asking, 'What is it that we are
looking at?'[36] He offered his reply not in words but in pictorial images.
So it is with Riley, despite the acuity of her statements and the thoughtful
responses they readily inspire. Ultimately, seeing is felt in the intense
silence of seeing.

Doro Globus and Lucas Zwirner (eds), *Bridget Riley: Works 1981–2015*, exhibition catalogue,
David Zwirner Books, New York, NY and London, 2016, pp.7–25.

Note: I thank Bridget Riley for numerous conversations over a period of years in which she
has generously detailed her thoughts about perception, art and technical procedure. For
facilitating access to Riley's works and archive, I am grateful to Karsten Schubert and Amanda
Sim, as well as to the David Zwirner gallery in New York and London. For essential aid in
research, I thank Jeannie McKetta.

1   Bridget Riley, 'Seurat as Mentor (2007), in Robert Kudielka (ed), *The Eye's Mind: Bridget Riley, Collected Writings 1965–2009*, Thames & Hudson and Ridinghouse, London, 2009, p.69, and Bridget Riley, 'Painting Now' (1996), *ibid.*, p.296 (original emphasis). Riley's position recalls the thinking of Maurice Merleau-Ponty, whose essay 'Eye and Mind' is a favourite (conversation with the author, January 2003). 'I would be at great pains to say *where* is the painting I am looking at. For I do not look at it as I do a thing… It is more accurate to say that I see according to it, or with it, than that I *see it*.' Maurice Merleau-Ponty, 'Eye and Mind' (1961), in James M Edie (ed), *The Primacy of Perception*, Carleton Dallery (trans), Northwestern University Press, Evanston, IL, 1964, p.164 (original emphasis).

2   Bridget Riley, 'Perception and the Use of Colour: Talking to EH Gombrich' (1992), in Robert Kudielka (ed), *Bridget Riley: Dialogues on Art*, Zwemmer, London, 1995, p.44.

3   Bridget Riley, quoted in Jackie Wullschlager, 'Bridget Riley: A London Retrospective', *Financial Times*, 6 June 2014, http://www.on.ft.com/1kGygvS, accessed 15 January 2016'

4   Bridget Riley, 'Work' (2009), in Kudielka (ed), *The Eye's Mind, op.cit.*, p.59.

5   Bridget Riley, 'A Reputation Reviewed: Talking to Andrew Graham-Dixon' (1992), in Kudielka (ed), *Bridget Riley: Dialogues on Art, op.cit.*, p.71.

6   Bridget Riley, 'The Artist's Eye: Seurat' (1992), in Kudielka (ed), *The Eye's Mind, op.cit.*, p.267 (original emphasis).

7   *Ibid.*, pp.272–73 (original emphasis).

8   *Ibid.*, p.273.

9   Bridget Riley, 'The Pleasures of Sight' (1984), in Kudielka (ed), *The Eye's Mind, op.cit.*, p.34.

10 Riley's reference to hallucination recalls the perceptual theory of Hippolyte Taine, an older contemporary of Seurat: 'Our external perception is an internal dream found in correspondence with external things; and instead of saying that hallucination is a false external perception, it should be said that external perception is a *true hallucination*.' Hippolyte Taine, *De l'intelligence*, 2 vols., Hachette, Paris, 1888, 2:12–13 (original emphasis; author's translation).

11 For Riley's use of phrasing such as 'pure perception', 'pure sensation' and 'pure judgment', see Bridget Riley, 'The Spirit of Enquiry: In Conversation with Jenny Harper' (2004), in Kudielka (ed), *The Eye's Mind, op.cit.*, p.179; and Bridget Riley, 'In Conversation with Lynne Cooke' (2005), *ibid.*, p.321. A state is 'pure' when no contingencies actively affect it: 'Like pure colour, [pure] judgment is distinguished by having no referential role outside the work itself.' Riley, 'The Spirit of Enquiry', in Kudielka (ed), *op.cit.*, p.179. On pure vision, pure painting and pure aesthetic experience as these notions have been applied within the discourse of modern art, see Richard Shiff, 'Dream of Abstraction', in Terence Maloon (ed), *Paths to Abstraction 1867–1917*, Prestel, Munich, 2010, pp.52–69.

12 Riley, 'A Reputation Reviewed: Talking to Andrew Graham-Dixon', in Kudielka (ed), *Dialogues on Art, op.cit.*, p.72 (original emphasis).

13 Bridget Riley, 'Colour for the Painter' (1995), in Kudielka (ed), *The Eye's Mind, op.cit.*, p.222 (original emphasis).

14 Riley, 'The Artist's Eye: Seurat', in Kudielka (ed), *The Eye's Mind, op.cit.*, p.267.

15 *Ibid.*, p.270.

16 Bridget Riley, 'Bridget Riley in Conversation with Michael Harrison', *Bridget Riley: Colour, Stripes, Planes and Curves*, exhibition catalogue, Ridinghouse, London and Kettle's Yard, Cambridge, 2011, p.10.

17 *Ibid.*, p.10.

18 Riley, 'In Conversation with Lynne Cooke', in Kudielka (ed), *The Eye's Mind, op.cit.*, p.310.

                                                                    RICHARD SHIFF

19 See, for example, Heinrich Wölfflin, *Principles of Art History*, MD Hottinger (trans), Dover, New York, NY, 1950, p.1; EH Gombrich, *Art and Illusion*, Princeton University Press, Princeton, NJ, 1960, pp.63–64.

20 Charles Sanders Peirce, 'Telepathy' (1903), in Charles Hartshorne, Paul Weiss and Arthur W. Burks (eds), *Collected Papers*, 8 vols., Harvard University Press, Cambridge, MA, 1958–60, 7:377, n.12 (original emphasis).

21 Riley, 'The Artist's Eye: Seurat', in Kudielka (ed), *The Eye's Mind*, p.273. Philosophical support for Riley's position might come from the writings of Merleau-Ponty as well as from the pragmatist tradition of Peirce and William James. Her art seems remarkably close to existing in a state of Peircean Firstness (feeling without reference of any kind, including consciousness of self); perhaps it settles into a condition of First-and-a-half-ness. 'As I go on working, there may come a point… that I am taken by surprise, startled into recognising a pure sensation.' Riley, 'In Conversation with Lynne Cooke', *ibid.*, p.321. One of Peirce's definitions of the condition of Firstness is as follows: 'something which is what it is without reference to anything else within it or without it, regardless of all force and of all reason.' Charles Sanders Peirce, 'Partial Synopsis of a Proposed Work in Logic: Originality, Obsistence, and Transuasion' (1902–1903), *Collected Papers, ibid.*, 2:46.

22 Riley, 'Seurat as Mentor', in Kudielka (ed), *The Eye's Mind, op.cit.*, p.61. See also Riley, 'Bridget Riley in Conversation with Michael Harrison', *Bridget Riley: Colour, Stripes, Planes and Curves, op.cit.*, p.6.

23 See note 11.

24 Bridget Riley, statement on drawing, January 2016, prepared for publication by the British Museum, London (courtesy Bridget Riley). One of Riley's screenprints from 2015, a composition featuring a single graphic form in six different orientations, has the title *Standing Up, Turning Round, Lying Down*, which may subtly allude to the artist's shift from figure drawing to non-representational abstraction – with the two practices capable of generating the same empathetic feelings.

25 Riley's work on paper, *Study for Rêve* (1999), provides a good indication of her compositional process. This study, one among a number, contains remnants of two verticals that recall the initial grid-like order of verticals, diagonals and curves. In the full-scale painting *Rêve*, a single vertical fragment remains. We might regard it as an anomalous intrusion since all other straight edges in the composition are diagonals. Yet this one bit of verticality is just as central to the conceptual order as any other feature. Only in perception does its singularity resound.

26 Riley, statement on drawing, January 2016.

27 Riley, 'Bridget Riley in Conversation with Michael Harrison', *Bridget Riley: Colour, Stripes, Planes and Curves, op.cit.*, p.5.

28 Bridget Riley, 'About Curves: Bridget Riley in Conversation with Paul Moorhouse', *Bridget Riley: The Curve Paintings 1961–2014*, exhibition catalogue, Ridinghouse, London and De La Warr Pavilion, Bexill on Sea, 2015, pp.43–44 (order of statements reversed). Compare Riley, 'Seurat as Mentor', in Kudielka (ed), *The Eye's Mind, op.cit.*, p.66. See also Bridget Riley, 'Encountering Seurat: Bridget Riley in Conversation with Éric de Chassey', *Bridget Riley: Learning from Seurat*, exhibition catalogue, Ridinghouse and The Courtauld Gallery, London, 2015, p.31: 'I have to find out what [the pictorial elements] can and cannot do: what characteristics they have, how far you can push them before losing an essential "squareness" or "linerality" [linearity] or a "particular quality" and how much manipulation can be tolerated… It seemed to me that these pictorial facts or elements were so strong that it is quite astonishing to realise to what an extent they have simply served [representational] purposes.'

29 Riley, 'Bridget Riley in Conversation with Michael Harrison', *Bridget Riley: Colour, Stripes, Planes and Curves*, *op.cit.*, pp.6–7 (original emphasis).

30 As in other instances, dualistic designations of this type are arbitrary and could be reversed; in perception, they remain fluid.

31 'A triangle is three angles and three sides. First of all I have to put that down, and then work with what can be done with three angles and three sides… If something is deliberate you can adjust or change it. But if it's woolly, just a grope, you don't have much chance when working with it.' Riley, 'In Conversation with Lynne Cooke', in Kudielka (ed), *The Eye's Mind*, *op.cit.*, p.309.

32 Riley, 'The Artist's Eye: Seurat', *ibid.*, p.273.

33 To be strict about the observation, there is a second anomaly: the last diagonal at the upper left of *Rustle 2* should contain a curve but does not. Yet, because it consists of only two units, it may not have counted in whatever reckoning Riley employed.

34 Riley, 'The Artist's Eye: Seurat', in Kudielka (ed) *The Eye's Mind*, *op.cit.*, p.267.

35 Riley, 'In Conversation with Lynne Cooke', *ibid.*, p.321.

36 Riley, 'The Artist's Eye: Seurat', *ibid.*, p.267.

Index of Names

Titian 66, 70, 132, 260, 320, 321, 334, 364,
    408, 447, 479, 537
Turner, JMW 364–66
Twombly, Cy 328

Uglow, Alan 153

Valéry, Paul 144, 374–75
Van Eyck, Jan 15, 172, 439–40, 442, 452, 548
Van Gogh, Vincent 21, 22, 172, 328, 442
Vasarely, Victor 22, 26, 313
Vermeer, Johannes 32–33
Veronese, Paolo 64, 67, 69, 70, 132, 320–21,
    334, 448, 537
Virgil 364
Vollard, Ambroise 452

Warhol, Andy 64
Whistler, James Abbott McNeill 366
Whitehead, Alfred North 370
Whitman, Walt 431
Wilenski, RH 549, 552
Wilson, Edmund 32
Wittgenstein, Ludwig 91–92, 367
Woolf, Virginia 434
Wordsworth, William 515

Young, Thomas 405

Credits

Image credits

All images of works by Bridget Riley: © Bridget Riley, all rights reserved.
p.19: Galleria d'Arte Moderna, Milan, Bridgeman Art Library, © DACS 2016; p.25: courtesy Gemeentemuseum Den Haag, The Hague; p.65: George Csema © The Museum of Modern Art/Licensed by SCALA/Art Resource, New York; p.99: © Tate Images, © DACS 2016; p.119: AKG Images, Francois Guenet; p.131: Ridinghouse; p.165: George Csema © The Museum of Modern Art/Licensed by SCALA/Art Resource, New York; p.175: Bridgeman Art Library, photo Studio Gonella 2012, su concessione della Fondazione Torino Musei, © DACS; p.243: courtesy The Courtauld Gallery, London; p.269: © National Gallery, London; p.271: © State Hermitage Museum, St Petersburg/Artothek/Bridgeman Art Library, © Succession H. Matisse/DACS 2016; p.281: courtesy The Courtauld Gallery, London; p.289: Ridinghouse; p.305: © Musée Matisse, Nice, photo © Francois Fernandez, Nice, © Succession H. Matisse/DACS 2016; p.315: courtesy Pace Gallery, New York, © The Estate of Agnes Martin; p.325: © Tate, © Succession H. Matisse/DACS 2016; p.335: photo John Webb/White House Collection, Washington, DC; p.341: Bridgeman Art Library, © Succession H. Matisse/DACS 2016; p.353: © National Gallery, London; p.365: © Tate; p.379: courtesy The Courtauld Gallery, London; p.391: courtesy David Zwirner, New York/London; p.401: © Semir Zeki; p.423: © National Gallery, London; p.435: AKG Images, Erich Lessing; p.441: Scala – V Bandelloni; p.449: AKG Images; p.477: © National Gallery, London; p.489: © Bridgeman Art Library, © Succession H. Matisse/DACS 2016; p.503: David Herald, © The Solomon R Guggenheim Museum, New York; p.513: Bridget Riley Studio, © Bridget Riley; p.525: Bridget Riley Studio; p.539: © Toledo Museum of Art, Toledo, OH; p.547: Ridinghouse; p.551: courtesy The Courtauld Gallery, London; p.571: © The Art Institute of Chicago, Helen Birch Bartlett Memorial Collection, 1926.224.

Text credits

All texts are reprinted with permission of their respective authors. The following additional credits and copyright notices apply: Dave Hickey (pp.63–70) and Marla Prather (pp.333–47): reprinted courtesy Pace Gallery, New York; Robert Kudielka (pp.257–76); Paul Moorhouse (pp.169–207) and Richard Shiff (pp.277–99): © 2003 Tate, reprinted by permission of the Board of Trustees of the Tate Gallery; John Elderfield (pp.499–506): reprinted courtesy Galerie Max Hetzler, Berlin, Holzwarth Publications, Berlin and Ridinghouse, London; Paul Moorhouse (pp.507–16), Richard Shiff (pp.517–40 and pp.569–90): reprinted courtesy David Zwirner, New York/London; Karen Serres and Barnaby Wright (pp.545–59): reprinted courtesy The Courtauld Gallery, London and Ridinghouse, London; Éric de Chassey (pp.561–66): reprinted courtesy Galerie Max Hetzler, Paris and Holzwarth Publications, Berlin.

Great care has been taken to identify copyright holders correctly. In case of errors or omissions please contact the publisher so that we can make corrections in future editions.

Published in 2017 by **Ridinghouse**

46 Lexington Street
London W1F 0LP
United Kingdom
ridinghouse.co.uk

Distributed in the UK and Europe by
Cornerhouse Publications
HOME
2 Tony Wilson Place
Manchester M15 4FN
United Kingdom
cornerhousepublications.org

Distributed in the US by
RAM Publications + Distribution, Inc.
2525 Michigan Avenue Building A2
Santa Monica, CA 90404
United States
rampub.com

Images © Bridget Riley 2017. All rights
reserved, unless noted on p.599
Texts © the authors, unless noted on p.599
For the book in this form © Ridinghouse

Edited by Doro Globus and
Karsten Schubert
Assistant Editor: Daniel Griffiths
Proofreaders: Sarah Auld and
Dorothy Feaver
Picture researcher: Jay Drinkall

Designed by Tim Harvey
Set in Formata
Printed in Italy by Opero srl

ISBN 978 1 909932 29 6

British Library Cataloguing-in-Publication
Data: A full catalogue record of this book is
available from the British Library

Front cover:
Lagoon 2 1997 (detail)

Ridinghouse